The Server

The Server
A Media History from the Present to the Baroque

Markus Krajewski

Translated and with an Introduction by
Ilinca Iurascu

Yale UNIVERSITY PRESS / NEW HAVEN & LONDON

Published with assistance from the foundation established in memory of Calvin Chapin of the Class of 1788, Yale College.

The translation of this work was funded by Geisteswissenschaften International— Translation Funding for Humanities and Social Sciences from Germany, a joint initiative of the Fritz Thyssen Foundation, the German Federal Foreign Office, the collecting society VG WORT and the German Publishers & Booksellers Association.

Yale University Press books may be purchased in quantity for educational, business, or promotional use. For information, please e-mail sales.press@yale.edu (U.S. office) or sales@yaleup.co.uk (U.K. office).

Set in type by Newgen North America, Austin, Texas.
Printed in the United States of America.

Library of Congress Control Number: 2017952552
ISBN 978-0-300-18081-7 (hardcover : alk. paper)

A catalogue record for this book is available from the British Library.

This paper meets the requirements of ANSI/NISO Z39.48-1992 (Permanence of Paper).

10 9 8 7 6 5 4 3 2 1

"Server" should be neither feminine nor masculine. Like "steer."

—Eduard Hahn, 1896

Contents

Part Three *Diener,* **Digital**

Introduction to the English Edition: Jeeves Transatlantic

The present translation of Markus Krajewski's *Der Diener* does not come unannounced: since the book's original release, several transatlantic envoys have set the scene for this publication, allowing its protagonists, human and digital figures of service, to increasingly gain media-theoretical attention.[1] Obviously, the author repeatedly reminds us, they have always already been there, precisely *as* media. To invoke Friedrich Kittler: "You never see them, and yet they're constantly doing something for you."[2] In other words, here we have the counterpart to the classic image of the Weimar-era salaried masses described by Siegfried Kracauer: not 'hidden in plain sight' but 'ever-present despite their apparent absence.'

The focus on the (invisible) 'operands of operations'[3] will be quite familiar to those who have been following the growing number of German new media theory studies translated in the wake of the English Kittler editions—monographs by Bernhard Siegert, Wolfgang Ernst, Sybille Krämer, Cornelia Vismann, and Markus Krajewski that have reshaped the disciplinary understanding of certain epistemic configurations and their media-technological networks of production. *The Server* fits directly into this tradition, particularly in its cultural techniques (*Kulturtechniken*) approach, which, to quote Siegert, implies a threefold undertaking: "Media are scrutinized with a view toward their technicity,

technology is scrutinized with a view toward its instrumental and anthropologi-
cal determination, and culture is scrutinized with a view toward its boundaries."[4]
To put it in terms more closely related to Krajewski's project, the book offers an
examination of *service as a cultural technique* and the *server as its central media-
technical figure,* in several intersecting configurations: the domestic transitioning
from the eighteenth-century court to the nineteenth-century bourgeois household; the "little helper[ ] of scientific work";[5] and finally (or rather, to begin
with), the electronic server as a prime mover of present-day information channels. Beyond these, Krajewski reintroduces the reader to a plethora of forgotten
or misremembered figures of subalternity, anchoring them firmly in the same
operational framework: Lessing's Waitwell and Goethe's Stadelmann, Maxwell's
demon and Gauss's Michelmann, dumbwaiters and Lazy Susan(s), library servants and internet bots. They all inhabit fictional, social, and architectural levels
of knowledge acquisition, storage, processing, and distribution—from the enfilades of the baroque courts via the upstairs–downstairs layout of turn-of-the-
century mansions through the distributed application structures and digitally
connected smart houses of today. The world beneath and above our visual horizon is teeming with the (invisible) hands and handles of service. In Krajewski's
interpretation, they are the ones producing, steering, guiding, channeling, *creating* the conditions of possibility of knowledge in the first place.

It is certainly tempting to get lost in the dazzling richness of material the
book has to offer and enjoy its playful use of arcane sources,[6] antihermeneutical
expositions of literary texts, blending of styles, discourses, theoretical models,
pop cultural and historical references—Jonathan Swift and Ludwig Boltzmann,
Jacques Tati and Aristotle, Thomas Aquinas and the Xerox PARC papers, Bismarck and The Smiths (the list could continue ad infinitum). But to stop here
would mean to miss the entire premise or to assume that the book proposes a
cultural history of subalternity, which traces the historical conditions underlying the transformation of the human subject of servitude into the digital media
of service. If cultural and social histories of servants are indeed part of the analytical arsenal of this volume, they rather serve a different end. Similarly, if the
(often) anonymous, silenced, effaced subjects of power are retrieved from their
dark disciplinary corners, it is not so as to offer "an inverted image of authorita-
tive knowledge."[7] The questions asked by Brecht's "worker who reads"—quoted
by Krajewski himself—remain as urgent as ever, and the subjects of service are
reestablished in the positions they rightfully inhabit as central agents and actors of history (of science, of literature, of culture, etc.). But the answers *The
Server* offers are no longer part of the same historical configuration. In fact,
they demand a radical rethinking of the concept of history. By proposing the

materiality of service and its operators as the basis of knowledge production, *The Server* shifts the entire question of temporality into the media-technical notion of *recursion.* To quote from the book:

> How does the server essentially function, and what does it do to the users under its command? In order to trace its operations one has to recur to the history of service, so as to reconstitute, via its specific iterations, the various functions and characteristics of subaltern spirits. With every iteration and each analytic description of a particular case study, the historiographic method comes a bit closer to the heart of the matter. . . . With each new iteration, the analyzed scenarios are further connected to the initial act of service—performed by the subalterns of the electronic domain. In other words, the figure of recursion invokes itself. (157)

In other words, rather than simply jumping back and forth between analog and digital formats or human and technical operators, the book proposes a *systematic historiographic effort* that exposes both sides of the media-theoretical coin at once, with an increasing degree of interpretive acuity. Methodologically speaking, the analysis can thus draw on both Bruno Latour's Actor-Network Theory and Hans Blumenberg's absolute metaphors to gradually reveal that the designation "server" is not just a case of linguistic contingency.[8] Rather, what the process enables is "apprehending the current electronic communication processes in cultural and media-theoretical terms by means of a conceptual-historical analysis of the servant as metaphor and of the far-reaching, cultural-historical tradition of servitude."[9] Each anecdote, each section and chapter, then, represents iterations that add new epistemic components, until the termination condition has been met at a certain level . . . and the process can start again. The end goal is obtaining sufficient information "about the initial state—in this case, about the question concerning the nature of electronic service and its historical genesis" (158). Not accidentally, the original subtitle of *Der Diener (Mediengeschichte einer Figur zwischen König und Klient)* insists on the *intermediacy* of the epistemic project: thus, the book does not promise to trace *a trajectory of service from* "king to client" but rather the transfer *between* them.

But what of it? Or rather, what of *us,* the kings of yore and clients of to-day, waited upon by armies of "little helpers" as we enter countless commands on our computer screens? If indeed, as Kittler reminds us, "through the use of keywords like user-interface, user-friendliness or even data protection" humanity is "damned . . . to remain human," the only hope of understanding our own condition lies in examining those keywords precisely via the iterations of the media history of service.[10]

Ilinca Iurascu

Introduction: Listen, James

Ich dien [I serve].
—motto on the heraldic shield of the Prince of Wales since 1346

"YOU'VE GOT MAIL": A PROLOGUE AT THE POST OFFICE

"You've got mail." The manager program sends a message and an audio alert. It's a familiar sound, the signal of a routine operation a computer performs a few dozen times a day. Someone has sent an email, which is instantly transferred to its recipient, ready to be opened and read. The postman only rings once;[1] meanwhile, behind the scenes, hidden underneath the software, a complex protocol has just concluded, and its only visible trace is that new mail alert. What are the steps that ensure the message has been promptly delivered? Which services and agents have allowed the virtual postman to ring the bell? With a click of a button, the sender first confirms the dispatch in the email client program, technically known as the mail user agent. In turn, the agent connects with the mail transfer agent, commonly known as the mail server. Its task is to ensure—after briefly communicating with yet another server, the domain mail server—that the message finally reaches its destination, with a little help from the mail delivery agent and the mail retrieval agent. Various agents quietly toil in the background; they come to the surface only in case of a communication error, like the infamous MAILER-DAEMON notification of transmission failure. On the one hand, they acquire anthropomorphic qualities. An email client, for instance, enters into an actual conversation with the mail server. After establishing contact, the mandatory greetings are succeeded by a more casual, friendly follow-up, like, Hello [uni-weimar.de], pleased to meet you. Beyond any protocol requirements, such programs continue to adhere to netiquette standards long after all human actors have left the scene. On the other hand, names are meaningful. We are therefore speaking of agents and demons. And even if they are not invisible, such creatures go largely unnoticed.

The mail server as well as the DNS, the FTP, and the web server remain inconspicuous. The internet seems to be populated by a dizzying multitude of servers, which, not unlike demons, perform their tasks fairly discreetly behind the scenes. Like Kafka's ghosts who drink up the lovers' written kisses, stealing them before they arrive at their destination, the demons that lurk in the channels of communication grow in information labs and secure the circulation and transmission of data by parasitically feeding off them. Unbeknownst to message recipients and senders, they regulate data streams, letting them through and simultaneously feasting on them; they act as guides, identify obstacles, and search for detours. In short, they share the attributes of a reliable and, under usual circumstances, inconspicuous communication server.

The function of such a server is immediately obvious: it consists of providing assistance or delivering various services, such as downloading documents, transferring messages, or transmitting data. The virtual agent supplies information to its clients but also provides them with things. Just think of amazon.com. Once an order has been placed, the postman actually rings twice: first, to confirm the online purchase and, second, when the package is delivered. The traffic with information on the net is firmly based in this client–server principle. Clearly, then, the server acts as a communication servant. What follows is an account of this very subject, of its functions and history as well as its complicated, entertaining, and occasionally unexpected aspects.

At this point, one may certainly ask, what is the meaning of the term "server" anyway? Is it an arbitrary notion, a vague formulation describing the current state of communication? Or are we dealing with a stock metaphor like "virtual desktop"? What does it actually mean when we refer to the basic mode of modern communication via the distinction between client and server and implicitly, the relation between master and servant? The present study, which examines the figure of the servant from several perspectives, ranging from architectural to literary and scientific contexts, will argue that the server metaphor involves much more than just a cursory formula or a decorative analogy. The term has a rich historical background. As a ministering spirit of communication, the server defies definitions, since the figure it invokes—the servant—fulfills a multitude of historical and media-specific functions. To speak with Hans Blumenberg, one might call it an "absolute metaphor." And it is precisely the long, multifaceted history of that figure that may provide assistance in unpacking the metaphor. Thus, the aim of the present book is to trace the intricate pathways of service in a broad arc that extends from the present day to the baroque.

Classic servant types, such as the butler or the governess, the footman or the cook-maid, are largely extinct nowadays, at least in human form. Historians treat domestics and factotums as more or less minor figures. In political science, valets or bodyguards are seen as the underrated custodians of power acting on the side stages of administration. In literature, the servant typically appears in comedies in the shape of a petty buffoon. And in the sciences, helpers and lab servants are almost entirely overlooked, and their productive contribution to research is deemed negligible. All disciplines, without exception, treat the servant as a figure of the past that has by now almost entirely lost its relevance. To sum up: until now, the servant has been relegated, by definition, to a subordinate, insignificant position. Its agency and functions have so far been researched only sporadically and tangentially. They have never been systematically examined across historical periods and disciplinary borders. Beyond the usual empirical data, we still lack an approach linking central aspects of cultural history to the key media practices of subalternity—an approach that may shed light on the foundational role servants play in processes of cultural development.

The present book seeks to fill this gap in a twofold manner. On the one hand, it traces the rich yet secret contribution of servants to processes of knowledge production, their complicity with power, and their epistemic status. The study aims to uncover their unique conceptual and media presence in order to provide a broad cultural-historical survey that incorporates epistemological and media-theoretical aspects. On the other hand, the goal is to determine the current impact of the server as media concept, especially in the digital domain. The classical functions of the subaltern have long been delegated to an inscrutable mass of machines, electronic networks, and standardized protocols which determine our mode of communication—for instance, via the global interaction of (electronic) mailboxes. A closer look at the metaphors used to describe communicative processes will uncover a vast spectrum of agents: demons continue to lurk in the channels of electronic communication; invisible 'ministering spirits' keep attending to the smooth operation and success of communication. After all, *Second Life* is no longer the only domain where avatars can act as proxies or assume an agency that goes far beyond the authority of their real-life masters. And, not accidentally, the name of the so-called client–server model, the central mediator of internet-based information traffic, points to the long tradition of the servant in the act of communication.

In conclusion, this study will examine the role played by seemingly minor helpers, servants, and assistants in the history of knowledge; it will identify their central functions and achievements as *media of knowledge production.* "Media" can mean things like instruments but also human beings, such as the lab servant who actively contributes to scientific discoveries. Even if some readers may expect a different, more specific and precise definition, the media concept applied here is intentionally broadly conceived. Consequently, the server / servant will not be treated as an exclusively human subject. Neither will the sole focus be on the development of objects and their increasing trend toward automatization. The present book aims to bring the two discourses together in order to broadly describe and analyze a gradual transformation from human to nonhuman service-media. First, in part 1, the focus will be on human beings, then on transitions in part 2, and, finally, on objects in part 3.

This study offers an account of the server from the present era to the baroque. It postulates that the servant does not function merely as a medium but increasingly also as a figure of exceptional importance in today's digital contexts, especially in the form of web servers. Organized into seven case studies that follow the gradual transition of agency from human to nonhuman actors, this study will provide a panoramic view of the birth of the digital *server* from the spirit of the classic *servant* represented by domestics and valets. Here, the focus will be on examining the roles assigned to the two media actors. Both, in fact, function as agents of communication, enabling not merely the execution of various operations but also the production of new knowledge: be it in the form of a metaphor or, more concretely, as the result of their human or technological activities. Despite occupying a seemingly peripheral position, the servant proves to be a figure of critical importance. Its relevance will be duly acknowledged at the end of this book, in the context of an epistemology of the marginal, in a brief theoretical account on the productive force of secondary figures.

This study draws on specific examples from historical or philosophical sources. But its aim is also propaedeutic: each of the seven chapters takes up a media concept in order to illustrate various methodological instruments at work: the use of recursion, of metaphor, the transfer of agency, or the productive instances of interference. Thereby, the chapters also reflect on the different strands within media historiography and, implicitly, on the contingent nature of historical writing. The analyses may thus ultimately provide the tools for a critical theory of the media. Only such a broad range of theoretical approaches can convincingly demonstrate how service carriers participate in the act of thinking. Therein lies the didactic aim of this book. Furthermore, a comparative discussion of media and cultural studies methodologies can also explicitly show that the figure of *the servant* is a complex phenomenon, requiring a broad analytical framework and multiple theoretical approaches in order to be adequately described.

The historical arc of this study stretches from the sovereign king of the baroque era, with his lowly subalterns and high-ranking subjects, to the contemporary clients, the internet users who are still bound to their *servers* via a service contract. What are the stages of this lengthy process of transformation? The history of service can be broken down—at first roughly—into four main periods, marked by three major moments of upheaval. The first and longest of them stretches from the abolition of serfdom to the French Revolution, when the official end of the estate-based society also marks the start of a new stage: the reduction of differences between rulers and servers in favor of the development of a modern subject. The second period is dominated by intense debates around the servant question, a subject taken up by the literature of the time as well— from Johann Nestroy to Theodor Fontane. That period broadly overlaps with the so-called long nineteenth century, when the formerly passive servants turn into serving subjects and slowly begin to gain their freedom. The third period, after the major rift caused by World War I, is marked by the oft-invoked disappearance of the servant class. But only the human carriers of service functions seem to vanish. Indeed, during the twentieth century, services begin to migrate into the world of things: servants are exchanged for telephones and the laundry day is replaced by the washing machine. The place of the subject comes to be occupied by a third other, an entity that could be defined as a quasi-object. As for the fourth period, that stage is currently unfolding under our very eyes: now, the services performed by 'inanimate' things reacquire subject-like features, either via a server or with the aid of electronic avatars, in the attempt to create an alternate world in the virtual domain.[2] Along with a selection of examples from the Enlightenment and the age of Weimar classicism, the initial focus in part I, entitled "Objects: Assistants, Analog," will be on the transition from the royal absolutist court to the bourgeois culture around 1800, when the servant function takes on a specific professional meaning. That transition also marks the ontic transformation of the object—the status held by the servant until the French Revolution—into a bourgeois subject who officially acquires the right to 'freely' submit to his duties. In the shift from feudal order to bourgeois culture, as late as the age of Enlightenment, the position of the servant leaves no room for interpretation: "a servant was an object."[3] Part I will therefore first provide a detailed analysis of the genesis of the modern servant during the eighteenth century, showing how that figure differs from other types of subalterns.

Chapter 1 begins with a discussion of the terminology employed. The brief history of service traced here will be accompanied by a systematic effort to find what distinguishes the servant from related figures like the slave, the bondsman, the apprentice, or the assistant, in order to then define, against this background, what a servant actually is. Based on various external markers of distinction like the livery, subalterns can be classified into (courtly) hierarchies whose logic and spatial organization will be discussed using the examples of baroque palaces and English manors. Last but not least, the chapter will analyze the figure of the *valet de chambre* as well as the relation of subalternity as a general structure that runs through all social ranks. A closer look at the royal court model will then circumscribe the spatial logic of the subaltern. More particularly, it will show how architectural standards correspond to the courtly ceremonial, and how the servants' paths across the secret corridors or their passage through the remote sections of palaces and manors give rise to a full-fledged service architecture. Thus the aim of the analysis is to literally locate its object of inquiry. In other words, it seeks to outline a topography of subalternity, both visibly and invisibly dominated by servants, and examine its representative spaces but also its hidden nooks and crannies. The chapter will conclude with a few comments on why service can be regarded as an exemplary cultural technique.

Besides offering brief insights into the common features of subalterns, such as their famed invisibility or their secret economic strategies, chapter 2 examines the figure of the servant as an information center, both in connection with and as opposed to modern search engines. The chapter proposes an analogy between the literary character Reginald Jeeves, the butler in P. G. Wodehouse's stories, and the search engine AskJeeves.com, which chose that literary figure as the prototype of its corporate identity. The idea is that the techniques of information retrieval, organization, and distribution which the classic butler or domestic employs already act as a search engine avant la lettre. The claim will be further illustrated with the example of the library servant and his transformation from a subservient carrier and sorter of books to the powerful electronic library catalogue OPAC of today. Here, the library servant appears as a medium of translation, linking the (signatures of) books, on the basis of identical topologies and logistics of address, with the (specific locations of) local users. Central to this discussion is the principle of mediation which the servant embodies—both in the electronic and the historical context.

Chapter 3 discusses the figure of the servant in literature. The focus here is on the eighteenth century, via a close reading of *Miss Sara Sampson*. Lessing's so-called domestic tragedy will be interpreted as less a bourgeois drama than a real tragedy concerning servants. The servant in literature will then be discussed in the context of Goethe's age and work relations during that time. The dramatic and fictional characters will also be linked to real-world subjects. Paying close attention to Goethe's long list of servants (and especially to his valet Carl Sta-delmann), the chapter will examine the articulation of power relations between master and subject and, further, the topos of the world upside down, which threatens to turn those power structures on their head. That topos will be con-sidered in more detail against the background of Ludwig Tieck's *The Land of Up-side Down* (1799). The chapter will conclude with a discussion of mimetic desire. Using examples from Goethe and Proust, the analysis will show not merely how servants mimic the behavior of their masters but also how the actions subalterns imitate come to affect, in turn, the models set by their superiors. Thus, the cen-tral focus of this chapter is on *recursion,* a notion discussed both in the literary examples offered here and in the historiographic context of the study itself.

Part 2, entitled "The Interregnum of the Subject," consists of three chapters. It examines the development and demise of the human servant as a bourgeois subject during the long nineteenth century, that is, during the time between the French Revolution and World War I. First it will offer a brief retrospective of the foundation of the English Royal Society at the end of the seventeenth century and the role of servants in the history of science. Central to this chapter is the figure of the lab servant and his contribution to knowledge acquisition.

The subsequent chapters focus on the rise and fall of the servant during the bourgeois era. In the wake of the political upheavals around 1800, the largely disenfranchised subaltern is suddenly declared a bourgeois subject. But not for long. A new process of transformation soon sets in, radically changing the sub-ject status servants had just acquired, discharging them from their role as hu-man actors. Central to this inquiry will be the gradual transition of the servant into a technological form. Over the course of the twentieth century, that form is increasingly defined by a profound media-technological shift from human to machine, be it in public, in the case of telecommunications companies, or in private, in the space of the electrified home.

Chapter 4 focuses on the history of sciences, more specifically, on the lab, as the operational headquarters of the marginalized helpers in the production of knowledge. Following a brief history of demons and their central role in thought experiments, the chapter draws parallels between the theoretical activity of the ministering spirits of science and the concrete, yet equally elusive work of lab servants. These figures evince negentropic qualities. Without their hidden yet constant (prep) work, any theoretical or experimental insight into the laws of nature would prove impossible. Starting from the precarious relation between the public scientist and his invisible aides, the chapter will further discuss the benefits of and issues with fictionality in the scientific domain. The analysis will address the role of metaphors in the process of cognition, and the productive difference between manual and mental work, which plays an essential role in the case of lab servants. The chapter will also consider the extent to which notions of fictionality and metaphoricity play an essential role in the exact sciences.

Chapter 5 turns to the servants of (tele)communication networks, particularly to their relation to the channel of information transmission. The central focus here is the transformation of the conditions of communication and the replacement of the classic server with technical media, in the introduction of electricity, the telegraph, and the telephone in the nineteenth century. With the aid of yet another scientific subaltern, namely Carl Friedrich Gauss's institute assistant, the chapter evokes a key moment in the development of modern telecommunications, an event that takes place in Göttingen in 1833. A threefold historiographical analysis will be undertaken here. The question framing the discussion is how the same event can lend itself to different views according to the various media-theoretical approaches employed. The aim is to reveal the contingent nature of historical discourse and weigh the different outcomes against one another. As the analysis shows, the servant figure is a full-fledged medium of historiography. These observations also point to yet another process of transformation and replacement of the subaltern. Looking at a marginal phenomenon, namely, the case of epistolary *curialia* [*Kurialien*], the chapter examines how long-established norms of conduct are altered under the impact of electrification. Taking as its point of departure the relation of both the classic and the electronic server to the channel of communication, the chapter closes with a commentary on the phenomenon of interference, a notion that plays a significant role in the modus operandi as well as in the historiography of the servant.

Chapter 6 shifts attention from the domain of telecommunications to the space of the home, particularly the areas of the kitchen and the dining room. Focusing mainly on the disappearance of the servant from the household, the chapter retraces the gradual replacement of human domestics with technical appliances in the process of automation, mechanization, and electrification. The shift of subaltern functions from humans to things uncovers a vast process of substitution, illustrated here with the history of the so-called dumbwaiters. Using the examples of Thomas Jefferson's *revolving serving door* and Gaston Menier's 'first cafeteria,' the chapter will discuss various kitchen and tableware utensils that contribute to the pervasive disappearance of human servants from the household. Michel Serres's concept of the quasi-object will help explain the central notion of *delegation* employed here.

Entitled "*Diener,* Digital," part 3 concludes the study with the turn of inanimate things into new types of agents that take their media functions into the virtual domain. Starting from the premise that the electronic context collapses the difference between human and nonhuman actors, as well as the classic dichotomy between subject and object, electronic subalterns may signal the return of the classic servant, precisely because in the digital domain things now become increasingly individualized. Indeed, there is a certain tendency to lend subjective values to electronic things and objects. In the case of internet servers or virtual worlds like *Second Life,* electronic avatars become both the witnesses and actors of this development. To put it more concretely: the different media functions traced and discussed in this history converge in the operations quietly performed by digital servants, both on and behind the screen. Thus, the main argument of this study is that, as human servants disappear, their prominent functions are transferred or assigned to things. Similarly, the services once performed by personal assistants, laboratory servants, or underlings are delegated to technical devices and electronic forms. Clearly, then, these new actors have long begun to quietly yet effectively run our daily lives as well as our modes of communication.

Chapter 7 examines the forms subalterns assume under the conditions of advanced technology. As servers, *demons,* or other virtual creatures, they work without being seen or ever taking a break. By means of a comparative analysis of early computing systems, the *mainframes,* and the first machines from the age of *personal computers,* the discussion will focus on the conceptual and historical transfer from *servant* to *server.* The analysis is based on fieldwork conducted in California in the 1970s, when researchers at the legendary *Xerox PARC* center take a closer look at the conditions of formation of electronic services. What defines the communicative structure of the internet is a specific informational architecture, the so-called client–server principle, developed in Silicon Valley after 1973. In the analysis of contemporary service structures, the chapter also raises the question of metaphors, which enable innovative communicative structures in the first place. In this context, Hans Blumenberg's theory of metaphorology will ultimately help determine the productive epistemological value of the ubiquitous servant metaphor in the digital domain. At the end of the media-historical journey proposed here we find not merely the client, but, yet again, the fundamental question about agency that traverses each and every service operation from the baroque era to today: who controls whom, especially when the operations of control appear to have long been superseded by machines? Once more, it is the concept of metaphor that will provide the answers. Its analytical labor will make it possible to locate, regulate, and define the discourses of digital service.

Finally, the epilogue will ask, what do machines actually do in their free time? What happens when computers are idle or in standby mode? Are they bored? Or are they working on an urgent problem not related to system maintenance? Can a machine ever not do anything? And what can we say about computers, when, not unlike their deserving human predecessors, they go idle or engage in acts of disinterested pleasure? The discussion will recapitulate the various elements identified as productive factors in the development of service from the baroque to the present. Last but not least, those elements will help outline a brief epistemological theory of the periphery.

The temporal trajectory this book proposes, and its various theoretical and conceptual perspectives, may seem excessive. Its gaps appear to greatly outnumber its case studies. And yet, as one of the theorists quoted here puts it: "Let us rejoice in this long chain of transformations, this potentially endless sequence of mediators, instead of begging for the poor pleasures of *adequatio* and for the rather dangerous *salto mortale* that James so nicely ridiculed."[4]

Methodologically, this study will draw on discussions of baroque- and bourgeois-era service regulations as well as contemporary manuals of conduct dedicated to both masters and servants. Apart from these, the analysis will centrally focus on literary treatments of the servant, especially in fictional and dramatic works as well as in epistolary correspondences from the early modern period onward. Working through close readings of literary texts, the study will explore the typologies corresponding to each of the epochs discussed and thereby find answers to an important question: what is a servant after all? The material presented over the course of the seven chapters is certainly diverse, ranging from archival documents, such as papers from Goethe's estate and the closely guarded Xerox PARC company archive, to diaries, literary sources, and manuals and instructions for kitchen appliances and computers, to (socio-)historical and canonical theoretical texts. Implicitly then, the theoretical approaches will also be diverse, yet not eclectic. Only by bringing together a range of different analytical models, by pairing discourse analysis and metaphorology with media studies and historiography does it become possible to engage with the historical, narrative, and theoretical complexity of such a vast topic as that of the servant. This book draws on a number of analytical approaches (by Michel Serres, Hans Blumenberg, Michel Foucault, and others), but also on the methods of the Actor-Network Theory (ANT) developed by Bruno Latour, Michel Callon, John Law, and Madeleine Akrich. ANT methodologies can shed light on questions concerning the 'life of things,' whether in the context of seventeenth-century labs, the electrified homes around 1900, or the operations performed by electronic servers. The interaction of operators within their respective networks can thus be represented in a way that allows for the study of service societies and the complexities of their emergence. And, last but not least, the account developed here follows an important ANT postulate according to which cognitive progress results from the detailed description of a particular process. "The explanation emerges as soon as the description is saturated."[5]

Over the past few decades a broad range of works have examined the role of women in the profession, not least since, historically speaking, female servants have almost always numerically exceeded their male counterparts.[6] In this regard,[7] we may even speak of the theoretical underexposure of the functions and activities associated with male subalterns. Thus, one might be tempted to emphasize the figure of the manservant instead and discuss not merely the figure of the butler but also the rather marginalized case of the male domestic worker in general. We may also recall that what we traditionally know of the servant as a participant in processes of knowledge production has so far been predominantly associated with masculine subjects. But that is not the direction taken here. The present study actually opts for a third approach: namely, it moves entirely away from questions concerning gender difference and any historical lines of inquiry that follow from that fundamental distinction. Instead, the figure of the servant is treated at a more abstract level, where that particular kind of difference is canceled out and other distinctions are foregrounded. Following a trajectory that leads from electronic servers and virtual clients to royal servants and back, the analyses are less concerned with questions of gender than with the distinction between subject and object, between human and nonhuman servants. The study of epistemological aspects associated with the figure of the servant requires a certain shift of perspective. " 'Server' should be neither feminine nor masculine," proclaimed the agrarian economist Eduard Hahn in 1896. The media practices and functions of service examined here call for excluding rather than privileging gender-related aspects.

The history of service is vast and complex. Since it is anchored in a fundamental social relation, the cultural technique of service traverses the entire course of history. For this very reason, the scope of the present study must necessarily remain very limited. But even within such a narrow framework, restricted as it is to the Western cultural-historical context, numerous aspects have to be left out, or must be reduced to the selective use of a vast catalogue of sources. This book draws primarily on sources and records from the Central European and North American cultural contexts. Sociohistorical phenomena from other regions such as Russia,[8] China, and India may play into the general theme of the work, but will not constitute its specific object of study.

The current phenomena of global migration of service employees and the illegal exploitation of work relations do not fall within the terms of this study.[9] A primarily media-historical line of analysis will also not investigate the broad range of specialized services available in the contemporary metropolis: a concierge position in Manhattan,[10] a pay-by-the-hour jogging partner or professional dog walker,[11] a bodyguard,[12] or even an old-school English butler.[13] Clearly, yesterday's services have not disappeared, even if the historical contexts have changed. The gesture of hiring a maid nowadays is not divorced from a rather questionable (hidden) agenda.[14] Each of these aspects promises to offer a fascinating analysis. But these lines of inquiry will not be followed here (if only for reasons of space).

Neither the discourse of robotics[15] nor the cinematic treatment of subalterns can be extensively discussed here, even if film obviously offers a rich media-theoretical platform and ample material for study. Some aspects will be tangentially discussed, but there is certainly room for a study specifically dedicated to servants as cinematic and televisual subjects. A list of titles could potentially include Joseph Losey's *The Servant* (1963); Robert Altman's *Gosford Park* (2001); James Ivory's adaptation of Kazuo Ishiguro's *The Remains of the Day* (1993); or Rodrigo Moreno's less familiar but no less exquisite *El Custodio* (2006), about an Argentinian politician who spares no effort to humiliate his bodyguard. Canonical motifs and aspects of service could also be examined in light of series like *Upstairs, Downstairs* (1971–75), the less successful German *Unter den Linden* (2006), or productions such as *Adventure 1900—Life at the Mansion* (2004) [*Abenteuer 1900—Leben im Gutshaus*]. And last but not least one could mention Alain Resnais's *L'année dernière à Marienbad* (1961), where subjects endlessly traverse the corridors of bourgeois interiors and where the servants' perspective overlaps with that of the camera. . . . But enough with the lists, with the 'ifs' and the 'buts.'

The scope of the present analysis is different. This book traces the classical figure of the servant through various epistemic constellations and thereby explores the historical imprints of our virtual reality. One of its main objectives is to offer, via a media archeology of the contemporary service society, a new perspective on our current relations of communication. The path to this goal is different from a traditional description of relations of service: the discussion is not organized along the lines of specific epochs, as social histories often are. Rather, it proposes multifaceted analyses of media practices associated with the figure of the servant, in a trajectory leading from the present to the early modern period and back. The following chapters thus predominantly examine the transformation of subalterns via media-technical operations and via the objects that symptomatically represent them. The focus will be on activities and processes that tend to be overlooked (waiting, attending, opening doors, and slipping out of sight) as well as on various architectural and systemic configurations (corridors, service stairs, liveries, stirrups, telegraphic wires, coatracks, and, finally, computers). All of the above are instrumental in the production of service, be it in traditional work processes or new technological interventions.

If the figure of the servant appears as the symptom of a profound transformation, then the task at hand is to identify its contribution to the increase of knowledge production. What role do subalterns play in modern scientific achievements? It may well be that the hidden niches, the shadows, and the marginal professional positions the servant occupies offer a specific advantage for knowledge production. While subalterns are by definition treated as peripheral actors, the thesis of this book is that they represent a unique force of production arising on the 'margins,' the periphery of canonical epistemic systems. Thus, their work leads to what will be defined here as an *epistemology of the marginal.* In fact, it is their (supposedly) insignificant actions, routine operations, and local, gestural, and silent knowledge that often give the decisive impulse, the solution to an epistemic impasse.

The goal of this analysis is twofold. One aim is to foreground the often-neglected, silenced, yet vital contribution of subalterns to processes of cognitive production and to emphasize their status as media figures of knowledge. At the same time, the study aims to locate the servant as a metaphor and (conceptual) figure of contemporary discourse and thereby show its impact on the digital domain and the language of informatics. The double focus on marginal historical figures and their transposition into the major automated structures of today may offer a point of entry into our perception of electronic information processes and, ultimately, even into the ways they perceive themselves. The multiple functions and effects of the contemporary figures of service call for a sound, historically informed analysis of the impact of metaphors and cultural practices at work in the virtual domain. Only in this manner can we begin to grasp the tremendous impact of a figure that may no longer assume a human form yet continues to quietly advance, deep into the smallest capillaries of contemporary communication structures.

Part One **Objects:**

Assistants, Analog

Chapter 1 Masters / Servants: Everyone Is a Subaltern

The master commands, the servant complies—what more is there to say?
—Richard M. Meyer, *The Audience with the Prince*, 1904

Early eighteenth-century London. A merchant is invited to dinner. In the foyer, the host bids him greet the ladies. Upon brief consideration, the merchant approaches the best-dressed woman in the room and gives her a kiss on the cheek. Hilarity ensues—to his utmost confusion. Following all standards of polite behavior, the guest has kissed not the mistress but the maid. The awkward mix-up keeps weighing on the merchant's mind. Barely containing his anger, he draws up a series of pamphlets, some quite extensive, against the common dress code of house and office servants: "The apparel of our women-servants should be next regulated, that we may know the mistress from the maid."[1] After a detailed description of how domestics manage to dress like their employers, the finger is pointed at the high wages the former receive. That is how they end up wearing fine silk and stylish frocks instead of plain clothes and hand-me-downs, often even outmatching, not merely copying, their masters' style. And so, the famous and eloquent merchant by the name of Daniel Defoe concludes, one must find a proper way to signal someone's subaltern status; servants, in other words, must be recognizable at all times: "Things of this nature would be easily avoided, if servant-maids were to wear liveries, as our footmen do; or obliged to go in a dress suitable to their station."[2] Still utterly embarrassed, Defoe cannot leave it at that single warning. A few pages down he gives a further account to illustrate the dangers that may befall lords and ladies unless the help are properly identified. A visitor calls while the servant is away. The master of the house opens the door to let a well-dressed woman in. She has come to see the master's sister. "Accordingly I handed madam in, who took it very cordially. After some apology, I left her alone for a minute or two; while I, stupid wretch! Ran up to my sister, and told her there was a gentlewoman below come to visit her."[3] The visitor doesn't mistake Defoe for his servant, but the confusion is still inevitable. She turns out to be a highly ambitious yet 'work-shy' maid applying for an open position in the household: "How great was my surprise when I found my fine lady a common servant-wench."[4] Defoe's firm demands remain unanswered. A century passes before his plea for distinctive markers for female staff members is heard: the classic maid uniform, with a white bonnet and apron over a black dress, is born.

When lavish clothes and confident manners fail to provide much certainty—regarding either women or men—alternatives must be found to create adequate distinctions; subtle differences among social ranks call for indisputable signs. But the clearest expression of who belongs where can be found in the dramatic lineups staged by the highborn heirs and self-made men wishing to leave a lasting impression on their visitors:

> Servants are without number. I have never dined out yet, even in a private untitled family, with less than three or four, and at several places eight or nine even, for a party hardly as numerous; but each knows his place; all are in full dress— the liveried servants in livery, and the upper servants in plain gentlemanly dress, but all with white cravats, which are likewise mostly worn by the gentlemen in dress. The servants not in livery are a higher rank than those in livery, never even associating with them. The livery is of such a description as the master chooses: the Duke of Richmond's were all in black, on account of mourning in the family; the others various, of the most grotesque description, sometimes with and sometimes without wigs, and always in shorts and white silk or white cotton stockings.[5]

Even when servants are in mourning attire, and their extravagant canary yellow and carmine red liveries are toned down for once, in come the lackeys. With their flashy coats, knee-high stockings, and full-bottomed wigs, they leave no doubt about their own lowly status and the great wealth of their masters.

Higher ranked subalterns are more difficult to distinguish from *gentlemen.* Their liveries alone do not suffice to tell positions apart, especially when they all come with matching white collars. Masters are therefore keen on subtle distinctions. A butler, for instance, is not expected to wear a uniform. He may dress à la mode or—as a cheaper alternative—wear his master's hand-me-downs. And yet certain changes in his getup confirm he is a servant. A pair of pants that doesn't quite fit or a wrong tie prevents the danger that so concerned Defoe: the risk of mistaking him for a master. Comical accessories and combinations may also contribute to that effect.[6] The higher the subaltern's rank, the greater the potential resemblance with the master. Since they want to maintain their positions, masters develop a quotidian semiotics that confers upon servants a broad array of signs of their subservience: both finely nuanced, subtle differences and grotesque markers, like brightly colored liveries.

But aside from festive parades and official reunions, the situation of the male staff is still not as clear as the ruling class would wish. All those colorful accessories that allow for immediate identifications are absent from everyday situations. Even if the master is rarely mistaken for a servant, the distinctive markers, especially those signaling higher ranks, are still difficult to ascertain. Writing in his journal *The World* in 1756, Adam Fitz-Adam addresses precisely this concern: "Our very footmen are adorned with gold and silver, with bags, toupees, and ruffles; the valet de chambre cannot be distinguished from his master, but by being better drest."[7] The situation in the professional domain is even more complicated, as Defoe warns yet again. In his *Complete English Tradesman* from 1725 he calls attention to a new risk of misidentification involving not merely maids but male servants as well. Things tend to become even less clear when the tradesman lets his assistant run his business and clients suddenly mistake the latter for the actual manager.

> 'Tis certain, a good servant, a faithful, industrious, obliging servant, is a blessing to a tradesman; but the master, by laying the stress of his business upon him, divests himself of all the advantages of such a servant, and turns the blessing into a blast; for by giving up the shop, as it were, to him, and indulging himself in being abroad, and absent from his business, the apprentice gets the mastery of the business, the fame of the shop depends upon him [. . .] Such a servant is well, when he is visibly an assistant to the master, but is ruinous when he is taken for the master.[8]

The master steps behind his servant, who is in turn taken for his master. The pitfalls of representation lie ahead. *Qui va à la chasse perd sa place* [Move your feet, lose your seat]. The act of substitution keeps on producing new masters.

Aside from proving Defoe's strong dislike of servants, these few episodes suggest the formation of a kind of desiring-machine that makes subalterns mimic their employers. By means of elaborate dress choices servants find ways to increasingly look like their superiors and even identify with them for an instant. The desired effect is to level out the otherwise obvious social differences. A further effect of this imitation strategy can be traced back to the critical moment that caused Defoe so much uncertainty. Time and again, the basic issue remains: who is the servant and who is the master? That is a key question running across all ranks, and it rarely yields easy answers.

We find the same question replicated in the most current contexts, for instance, in our interactions with the computer. But before looking more closely into the various constellations of domination and servitude at the onset of modernity, we must first establish what a servant actually is. Any answer to this question will likely be contingent upon observation. Its criteria will be discussed in detail in the following pages.

1.1. IDENTITY MARKERS: WHO'S WHO?

> In servitude dolor, in libertate labor [In servitude sorrow, in liberty labor].
> —motto at the Whitehall Palace, 1609

Servants can rarely be found in human form nowadays. To locate them, one must peer into cultural nooks and crannies. The classic type, instantly recognizable by the more or less fancifully colored uniform and headgear—a hat or a tricorne—can be encountered only on stage. But even so, servants are no longer easy to spot—the modern adaptations claim their due. Powdered wigs, velvet pants, impeccably white socks, and colorful, richly buttoned jackets: such details belong to the popular getup of the flute players or part-time Mozarts usually seen around the tourist attractions at Sanssouci or Schönbrunn. But they bear only a vague resemblance to the servants of the classic court. Defoe's game of mistaken identities belongs to the distant past. Aside from white-aproned and black-vested waiters or the common, passably dressed service personnel at information desks and hotels, servants seem to have vanished from everyday life. Their gradual disappearance is a phenomenon that defines the transition to the modern age. Not surprisingly, we find that issue amply discussed in Peter Laslett's major study on preindustrial England, *The World We Have Lost,* which features an entire chapter on domestic workers.[9]

Identifying servants presents a bigger challenge to Defoe's contemporaries, yet for the opposite reason. After all, servants are not hard to come by in the late seventeenth century. They are everywhere. Their ubiquity does not render the task any easier, especially when what is at stake is to clearly tell them apart from higher-ranked subjects. That is mainly because those subjects may also very well be servants, whether of the king or of God, the (ultimate) master. The reverse may also occur: namely, that servants may be masters and have subordinates of their own. Had Defoe been invited to court, he would have certainly been confused to see throngs of servants of various ranks everywhere. He would have felt frustrated trying to find his interlocutor and wondered how to single him out from among an army of underlings, all dressed in similar attire, in the endless hallways of the residence.

Servants are equally hard to identify and define. Unsurprisingly, therefore, they go by a remarkably long list of names. The term "servant" used to be exceedingly polysemous, encompassing a wide array of people.[10] It also served as an umbrella term for all sorts of folk [*Gesindel*] (in its original, nonpejorative sense of a "small following") made up of errand boys and porters, bailiffs and attendants, helpers and factotums, doorkeepers and chaplains, squires and assistants, farmhands and apprentices, clerks and amanuenses. Such terms are rather rare nowadays. Their representatives have long exchanged their positions for a minor spot in the museum of the history of everyday life.

Historians are reluctant to place servants from all periods in the same cultural category. Even if one goes against the historical grain and lumps them into a single economic class, as Thorstein Veblen does in his sociological study *The Theory of the Leisure Class*,[11] their professions are too diverse, their positions too uneven, the differences across the hierarchy too stark; some of their specific service functions may also drastically vary from one epoch to another. "The material for their history is scattered and difficult to assess; even the word 'servant' is not easy to define, and carried a wider meaning in the past than it does now."[12]

Even if the term strictly applies to eighteenth- and nineteenth-century servants, once their function becomes a profession, the concept still carries layers of meaning accumulated over time. If we dig a little deeper, the semantics of *servant* and *service* seem to have a very broad span and usually reach their target as fast as a hole in one in a round of golf. We must therefore consider multiple horizons of meaning, as we do when stumbling across the word "service" in Shakespeare, and have to keep in mind the different levels of the term in all its complexity. We don't just read "service," but also—depending on the situation—courtly love, sexual intercourse, banter, religious ritual, military command, or, obviously, the exchange of social courtesies.[13]

Before getting to that point, however, some further clarification is in order regarding the functions of servants. Two different strategies will be employed here. First, we will pin down the term by delimiting it from others or defining it *ex-negativo*. Then we will attempt to deduce it by trial and error rather than by heuristic methods, following the pattern of "a servant is someone who . . ." Many of these aspects may sound familiar. Still, it is the task of this book to synthesize and analyze them in a concise manner.

1.1.1. A Servant Is . . .

A servant is not a slave. Commonalities notwithstanding, the two sociotypes— the servant and the slave—are radically different from one another. They both perform activities to which higher-ranked subjects—openly or not—react with responses ranging from contempt to a mild 'I rather prefer not to.' Very rare are those who want to share their fate. They are charged with hard physical labor, toiling, and all kinds of lowly tasks. Their rights are drastically limited while their duties are overwhelming. They do not rule. They comply with the orders of their masters and their harsh tone, which they have long learned to heed.

But at least since the early modern age, the distinction between servants and slaves has been clear.[14] The main difference is that the servant freely enters a temporally restricted relationship of domination, whereas the slave's subjection to power is accidental and limitless. One may be born a slave or become one when captured in war. One may also turn into a slave by selling oneself or—if unlucky at play—by pawning oneself to pay off a debt. The philosophers of antiquity, Plato and Aristotle in particular, develop elaborate theories to justify slavery as a natural phenomenon. Against that tradition, starting with Saint Paul, Christianity launches a countermovement and a gradual reappraisal of bondage.[15] Ultimately, with the political displacement of the practice to the colonies, the notion of slavery is replaced by the idea of bondage.

The slave of antiquity is already someone who is denied property and rights (including those over one's own self), an identity, and a proper name.[16] Slaves usually acquire a new appellation each time they are sold at the market and their owner changes. As opposed to slaves, servants have in principle a documented given name, even if they are not often called by it, but rather by that of their predecessor.[17] This minimal form of individual rights of subjectivity is denied to slaves. Roman law does not grant them their own persona, and their legal status is not unlike that of animals and things. Aristotle describes slaves as "living instruments" that can be distinguished from things only by their use of language.[18] In passive terms, then, listening, understanding, and following commands are skills a (learned) slave may thoroughly possess in order to fulfill the task of sorting books or—if allowed to speak—act as a reader.[19] Personal initiatives, independent actions, even when framed by the tasks at hand, are not appreciated. Serious acts of insubordination are sometimes even punished by (face) branding.

Slaves are sometimes liberated from their formal state of captivity. But being bought or released into freedom by the master's mercy cannot lead to a less subservient life. A slave is often set free only in order to continue the same slavish activities, until he is able to pay off his own price. As opposed to this forced life of subjection, characterized by absolute submission and dependency, the servants' working conditions are legally grounded in a mutually binding work contract. What counts here, excluding crisis situations like poverty and other adverse circumstances, is that they enter service *by choice*.

A servant is not a bondsman. No other moment has had a greater impact on the development of the term in German than Luther's decision to replace the Greek δοῦλος with *Knecht* in his translation of the biblical urtext from 1522. Bondage, like slavery, knows no temporal bounds. The term *Knecht,* derived from the Middle High German root for *child* [*Kind*], designates a boy, a stepson, or an unmarried youth.[20] This etymology, however, takes the political edge off slavery. The bondsman is thus placed somewhere between the unconditionally unfree and, on the other hand, the higher social rank of the servant. What the reformer Luther may have aimed to achieve with his word choice was to construct a new theological concept that would allow the folk to visualize the end of their earthly dependence via the imminent promise of salvation. But the word rapidly found its way into everyday language. From that moment on, it started to designate those domestic subjects who—as opposed to the higher employment of the servants—were charged with the lowly jobs. As opposed to slavery, the political status of both bondsmen and servants theoretically implies freedom. Nevertheless, the continuous dependence on masters imposes limitations on this kind of freedom, whether in the form of the bondsman's labor services or the financial patronage received by servants from their masters. In legal terms, the service of servants and bondsmen is more clearly differentiated. The former is based on a contract of limited duration, whereas the latter has to make do with an indefinitely long work arrangement, one which nevertheless can be annulled by marriage.[21] Despite such temporal differences in the relations of employment, the general advice in the eighteenth century is toward a higher degree of trust in the interaction with servants, who not rarely have basic reading and writing skills. By contrast, one is instructed to exercise more caution vis-à-vis uneducated bondsmen and keep one's distance as much as possible.[22]

The servant holds the higher, more distinguished ranks among the staff of large royal courts and small estate households. As opposed to bondsmen, servants are allowed to marry. Being a servant therefore implies a higher degree of prestige and consequently also an upgrade of the position itself, occasionally even as the result of an act of self-attribution. For instance, a letter composed and written by a bondsman to his master, the merchant Anton Tucher of Nürenberg in 1515, is signed in a manner that actually does not befit its author: "Your honor's ever willing servant Heinrich Berreuther."[23] By this, he attests to his recently acquired literacy skills and, at the same time, lays claim to a higher rank and status. The strategic use of self-aggrandizement is blatant in this case. Its scope is to gain more prestige among the household personnel by joining the ranks of the servants. Up until the French Revolution, prior to the professionalization of servants in the nineteenth century and, implicitly, before their gradual fall from grace, the term holds only few negative connotations. First, as the servant category becomes more inclusive and the bondsman is increasingly pushed back to the lowest echelons of the hierarchy, the functions of the former expand to encompass almost all relations between rulers and subjects.[24] Since the Enlightenment, public officials have also been known as 'civil servants,' so as to highlight the nobler connotation of their activity. Second, even rulers are tempted to use the term. Not unlike the pope affecting humility with his *servus servorum dei*, the Prussian king Frederick William III performs a gesture of ceremonial self-abasement when he defines himself (albeit) in testamentary form as "the first servant of the State."[25] Thus at least since the age of enlightened absolutism one can claim: everyone is a servant. Just a few decades earlier, under the rule of the French Sun King, for example, the term would have hardly been conceivable as a title and an indicator of status.

As Reinhart Koselleck has shown in his analysis of the semantic transformation of the terms *Knecht* and *Knechtschaft* in German dictionaries and lexicons,[26] the meaning of the 'master'–'bondsman' pair is drastically reduced over the course of the eighteenth and nineteenth centuries. At the same time, the phenomenon increasingly becomes the object of historical reflection. In the second edition of the Brockhaus encyclopedia from 1817, for instance, in the wake of the transformations brought about by the French Revolution, the term can no longer be found. As the concept disappears, the practice itself seems to be relegated to historical memory. But one can still find entries for "slavery" and "bondage," indicating when those practices were abolished.[27]

For his part, Luther was keenly aware not merely of the distinctions between slaves and bondsmen,[28] but also those between bondsmen and servants (who had a more personal rapport with their masters). His relation to his own subalterns is proof of that, especially when compared to his rather critical position vis-à-vis underlings in general. Wolfgang Sieberger, Luther's half-literate servant, who interrupted his studies at the University of Wittenberg and served him for over thirty years, is treated kindly and indulgently, and his negligence is sometimes forgiven.[29] Nevertheless, Luther shows little mercy toward all the other lackeys and maids. His suspicion that underlings are not quite keen on work comes across in his sermons as well, along with doubts regarding their obedience. Consequently, he does not advise against treating them harshly from time to time: "Should a maid fail to be obedient, then strike her as you would a cow or a donkey," Luther counsels, for "the donkey would not carry the load gladly, and so does the serf not go about his work happily; [. . .] The stick should follow thereafter to strike with it."[30]

A servant is not an apprentice. The activities of servants and apprentices may occasionally overlap, especially in a more modest household, where the staff are in charge of a broader range of tasks. In principle, both can be seen as transitional stages in a professional career. However, an apprenticeship offers better development prospects and therefore seems more open-ended. It is typically the father who makes arrangements for the education of an apprentice. He is the one who signs a pedagogical contract with the master on behalf of the son. The contract usually stipulates that the novice is to be trained into a craft or trade for seven years—the learning years, not the earning years, as the saying goes. In exchange for free room and board, the apprentice vows to learn and to serve truly and faithfully, before finally receiving a certificate that allows him to gain autonomy (and the freedom to marry).[31] Upon performing their duties, younger servants are sometimes compensated with an apprenticeship, which may enable them to move out of their subaltern status and to make the career jump to urban life. But for the most part, subalterns must settle for lifelong employment as dependent servants.[32]

Not unlike the apprentice, the servant must also undergo a learning stage, but his training is never as structured as in the case of the apprentice of a guild, a merchant, or a craftsman. As far as underlings go, a brief period of introduction, usually conducted by a person of a higher rank within the servant hierarchy, is rapidly followed by the start of regular service, that is to say, of promptly following orders. Instead of long-term agreements like the training contract, the work contract between master and servant is renewed every year. Already in 1563 in England the length of employment for servants was set by law for the duration of one year. Neither party was allowed to unilaterally terminate the contract before its term without financial penalties.[33] Typically, service would begin and end on fixed dates, on Michaelmas (September 29) and Martinmas (November 11), in other parts also on Candlemas (February 2). At the end of his service year, the subaltern would then either be subject to the hazards of the free market or, if both parties were satisfied, his employment would be renewed for yet another year. Thus he would move from one job to the next, carried by the certainty that each new year might also be the last in the service of the same master.

While the apprentice could eventually become an independent merchant or craftsman, the underling would move up the household staff hierarchy, unless, of course, he turned out to be a murderer, like George Barnwell.[34] Finally, after serving faithfully for many years, he would often be compensated for his work after the death of his master with a life annuity or a larger sum of money. (In case of premature death, he would receive a dignified epitaph.)[35] As it turns out, the transitional status of the servant is rendered relative and becomes a long-term affair, unless the underling saves enough to make an independent life for himself with a small trade, for instance, by running an inn.

A servant is (and isn't) an aide or an assistant. Servants are rare in the late Middle Ages, with the exception of the royal court, where all—even the highest ranks—are placed in finely differentiated positions of subservience to the master. Occasionally, one can find servants in urban households, where merchants and larger manufactures have employees. Regular households are run with the help of women, children, and relatives. Things start to change only after the sixteenth century.[36] Once some individuals become more prosperous and a middle class begins to take shape, the demand for employment in the private sphere increases as well. In this sense, servants have always been a phenomenon of economic prosperity.

In the sixteenth and part of the seventeenth century young noblemen may be temporarily employed as "servants" of a large aristocratic household before coming into their inheritance or running their own domain. That is no longer the case in the eighteenth century, at the latest. Even the private servants in the highest positions are the offspring of workers, manufacturers, tradesmen, and farmers. The politician, author, and president of the Royal Society Samuel Pepys still treats his servants (especially the female staff) like friends. After 1800 that kind of behavior is hardly practiced anymore. If merchants, tradesmen, and even employees move up to the servant-owning class, the rift between *upstairs* and *downstairs* has visibly increased (and requires more steps and nerve to cross—starting from below).

Designations like "aide" or "assistant" do not belong to common, preestablished legal categories like that of the menial staff. Their position is not unambiguous like that of shop assistants. One has to look for specific signs in order to formulate their relation of subservience more specifically: for instance, to what extent does a subaltern remain subject to constant observation, irrespective of his formal belonging to a social group or financial relation of dependence? To what extent can he go about his (and other) business, without having to account for his actions? Based on such observations, one can make case-by-case distinctions between servants and aides.[37] The latter turn out to behave more independently and give their help freely, whereas the former act more devotedly and dutifully.

It should be clear by now that these amorphous categories are quite hard to delimit from each other, and one should treat each case on its own historical terms. To take the example of the so-called gentlemen scientists—and particularly that of Robert Boyle: as cofounders of the Royal Society and servant-owning noblemen, they use their large staff for domestic needs as well as scientific purposes.[38] It is, however, immaterial whether the servants excel at what they do and exchange scientific discoveries and observations with their masters like equals. It doesn't matter if they assist with scientific work by operating one instrument or another. Irrespective of all their achievements, whether they are employed as assistants with scientific ambitions or 'strictly' as domestics, they all fall under the same category: that of a servant who is compensated for his services.

A servant is a member of the household. Following a tradition that can be traced back to antiquity, the authority of the lord in the early modern period is that of a paterfamilias presiding over all his servants, that is, over the household in the classical understanding of the term. Apart from the materfamilias and the biological children, the household includes multiple other members, all those who live under the same roof, with their many duties and few rights. Relatives, apprentices, but especially domestics of all ranks and stations fall into this category. After all, the Latin term *familia* originally designated, in the Roman context, a group of servants (*famuli*).[39] Whoever he may be—a mere farmer, a manufacturer, a tradesman, a country squire, or rather a court aristocrat with a large retinue, a prince, a king, or even an emperor—the paterfamilias, broadly understood as the head of the "entire household," has the duty to take care of his people [*Gesinde*], to provide them with meals and lodging as well as compensate them for their services. The Old High German term *gasindi* designates the retinue of a prince at war or on a journey and implicitly suggests a specific kind of itinerant mobility. After the Thirty Years' War, at the latest, that freedom of movement is restricted by police and state decrees. During this time, the term *Gesinde* refers both to the royal court and to the staff outside the court.[40]

In the different forms of patriarchal organization, the royal court, the manufacturer's or the merchant's house, the farm or the estate, households vary by size. Accordingly, the number of service staff broadly varies: from the single servant of the parish priest to the household of the Earl of Lonsdale counting fifty people (forty-nine servants and the earl himself)[41] and up to the royal court that employs thousands of subjects of all social ranks. "During the 18th and 19th century, some members of the lower nobility made do with up to ten or twenty people; meanwhile, the staff count in influential aristocratic families was anywhere between fifty and hundred and twenty."[42] Until the nineteenth century the staff was typically made up of male servants. They were tasked with the hard manual labor but also with the display of conspicuous leisure, a far less demanding duty. Some areas of the household, like the kitchens of the English nobility, were associated with explicit gender bans. In 1670, for instance, women are not allowed, under any circumstance, to work in the kitchens of the Earl of Bedford's estate.[43]

Even if the notion of the household includes the masters' progeny as well as their staff, and despite the fact that both are in principle treated the same, the servants, as opposed to the children, have the option to break the family ties.[44] An early termination of service meant that the underlings were free to leave the familial community, without further demands. But as long as the servant lives under his lord's roof, he defers all authority over himself to the master, even if the latter mistreats him. For as long as the subaltern is in service, his person, his deeds, as well as his time entirely belong to his master. "All the servant's time, from the moment he was engaged, was supposed to belong to his master; he was expected to abandon all thought of maintaining a private life."[45]

A servant is subject to service regulations. Legal matters. Besides their master's authority, servants are subject to a number of agreements, which are typically part of a mutual employment contract or are stipulated in the service (or, court) bylaws of the household. The legal history is as complex as the typology of subalterns who are subject to those bylaws. We can therefore provide only a limited overview of the legal status of servants at this point.[46]

The relation between master and servant is grounded in inequality, not merely due to differences pertaining to real relations of power, bodily and intellectual capabilities. The asymmetry is much more an effect of the estate system. That system regulates class belonging and limits social mobility. As they occupy a lower level in the hierarchy, servants, as opposed to their masters, have few rights. The daily life of the household is therefore marked by the potential for unrest and latent conflict. That potential finds its juridical treatment in the laws concerning servants, which prevent the collapse of the system. The low status of servants is also evinced by the academic debate on the categorical distinctions between animals and human beings and whether servants should be included in one or the other category.[47]

None other than Leibniz takes a stand in this matter, when, in 1678, after some consideration, he ultimately declares the two to be slightly different. Despite being "born dumb" like beasts, servants still prove to be more useful than them. Nevertheless, the basic principle still stands: "Everything that a servant is, he is on account of his master."[48] Such ideas continue to be influential for decades, at least in literary contexts, as, for instance, in Friedrich Gustav Hagemann's 1792 comedy *The Prince and His Valet,* a piece not devoid of satirical intent, where the master still calls his servants beasts.[49] Many enter service by necessity or force.[50] But for the rest, there is a work contract in place, made on the basis of consensual agreement. According to the principle of medieval protection privilege [*Munt*], the custodian has the duty of care and the right to command; in turn, the ward has the obligation to obey the orders without objections. "Who seeks and takes protection, forgoes the right to refuse obedience."[51] In exchange for care, shelter, and usually modest wages, the servant agreed to a whole set of rules, which defined the contractual relationship. These included provisions concerning the commencement of service, its duration (usually set for a year, with the option of instant renewal, except for cases of unilateral termination), notice periods, wage ceilings, curfew times, interdictions against double employment, and the requirement to carry a register containing a brief list of previous positions held. All these sustain the master's mechanism of control. Should a servant oppose his duties or manifest any other form of "irreverence," he risks paying dearly for it. Even if the Prussian State Law cancels the special provisions of the servant laws and no longer allows for corporal punishment, some corrective practices, especially in the German Territories east of the Elbe, are still applied despite their general ban.[52]

As the roles and duties of subalterns multiply, the familial bonds within the household disappear, to make room for a depersonalized notion of service and implicitly an increasingly professionalized concept of wage labor. What used to fall under the purview of the paterfamilias, namely, a nearly uncontested authority and an unlimited jurisdiction over one's underlings, is now increasingly reformulated into the legal terms of servant law. The social standards that apply to the 'entire household' and are not juridically codified start to lose their importance. Consequently, there are increasingly detailed regulations that reach deep into servants' lives. Such rules no longer concern merely itinerants, as was the case in the sixteenth century, but the relation between master and servant as a whole, at all levels of the social hierarchy. "Legal norms are strictly or especially issued when other means of control fail. Norms are in this sense the expression of a political standstill."[53] Such moments of fixation of the social inequity that characterizes the relation between master and servant occur at increasingly shorter intervals between 1600 and 1800—an unmistakable sign of crisis and proof of profound structural changes taking place.

The relation of service between master and subaltern implies much more than a private agreement, since servant law amounts to a kind of social contract. The concerns of private and public authorities are intertwined. Their connection thus goes beyond the narrow confines of the family to ultimately generate a social form of organization in which binding, even if not necessarily effective, rules are invested with general, supraterritorial validity. That development culminated in the Prussian servant law of 1810. In effect until it was annulled in 1918, that law became the definitive authority in matters concerning relations between masters and servants, clearly in favor of the masters.

Passion(ate) Service: Definitions

> Everything that a servant is, he is on account of his master.
> —G. W. Leibniz, *The Natural Societies*, 1678

Our efforts to distinguish the term "servant" from various other professions and categories have hopefully shed some light into what servants are *not*. Let us now briefly look into the many historical definitions offered for the specific position they occupy. The question raised by Leibniz and others about whether servants should be classed as humans or as animals already signals the urgent need to assign (and general cluelessness about assigning) servants a viable place in the grand scheme of things. The servant is a figure of the in-between, an intermediary moving between different spheres and a medium that systematically slips through the mesh of fixed categories. The ambiguities of that position, which has preoccupied legal scholars and social theorists since the early modern age, have not yet been resolved; and the term is still possibly too vague to be captured in a single formulation. Everyone—including social historians—is unanimous: a servant cannot be easily defined.[54] Later studies, for instance, *The Theory of the Leisure Class*,[55] abandon any attempt at definition, the authors possibly assuming that readers may have a clear idea of what is implied by a servant or a domestic worker around 1900.

Since the early modern period, the employment of servants has had an economic basis. Property and wealth are unequally divided and allow the rich to have those less fortunate work for them. That is the premise of and drive for the phenomenon of service. "For as long as there have been rich and poor in society there have been domestic servants to minister to the wants of the well-to-do." The task of waiting on the wealthy is the job of the "underlings."[56] That job acquires a legal basis by means of a contract involving free mutual consent and mutual concessions. One party pledges to receive payment in exchange for following orders; the other commits to pay wages as well as feed, house, and protect his subject from all sorts of unpredictable situations. No matter what they are called—underlings, domestics, lackeys, subalterns, servers,[57] or simply servants—they all have the same task: that of waiting on their masters. To quote Adelung, that simply means "waiting for something, especially for someone else's order." Standing at attention, within his master's reach, the underling awaits new instructions. Waiting on someone therefore means "in its immediate and extended senses to serve someone, to carry out all sorts of lowly tasks for him."[58] The mention of lowly tasks already suggests that this can hardly be called a partnership of equals. But, as suggested by the topos of the world upside down, the authority of the master over the servant or their equal ranking are rarely predetermined and stable. Nevertheless, the weaker party in the often overdetermined master–servant relation has some degree of independence.[59] That ounce of freedom is implied in the English term "servant" as well as the French *serviteur,* which lack negative overtones.[60] These terms are rather neutral and can be applied to a minister—which is basically the same in Latin—and to the lowliest domestic worker. As opposed to them, the German *Diener* always evokes the subaltern status of the lower class, a specific form of servility and submission, which carries with it the fate of a restricted freedom. It is not surprising, then, that we find among the discourses of Prussian authority the requirement for the "most submissive subordination"[61] on the part of the subjects.

The broader the range of tasks performed by servants, the more diverse the attempts to classify their activity. One kind of approach, for instance, focuses on location as its distinctive criterion. Accordingly, all those in inferior positions serving within the home are called servants.[62] Here, the etymology of the term "domestic," derived via French from the Latin *domus,* has the connotation of being dominated.

A further definition proposes a system-based classification instead, by including some professional groups in the servant caste and excluding others. In 1752 a certain Giovanni Serantoni requests to be admitted into Bologna's professional association of servants of San Vitale. As soon as he gains admission, however, it turns out that he is employed as a litter bearer and therefore does not meet the criteria to join. According to the statute of the San Vitale Association, Serantoni is not "a real servant" since his activity is essentially carried out in public, meaning on the street, and involves serving multiple masters.

Litter bearers, kitchen maids, and other lowly servants are subject to strict exclusionary mechanisms based on the idea of prestige. Membership is granted only to commercial assistants, *cappenere* (domestics of higher rank, not wearing livery), *staffieri* (stable boys), lackeys, first coachmen, second coachmen, *cavalcanti* (outriders), head cooks, under-cooks employed on a regular basis and butlers; in short, all those who perform their service duties *outside of* the public gaze. Consequently, Serantoni loses his membership, only to finally regain it due to the vicar general's intervention—the very fact that the litter bearer turns out to be a troublemaker is sufficient proof that he is neither too servile nor insufficiently worthy as a servant.[63] In the background of this systemic definition, which follows strict mechanisms of inclusion and exclusion, already lies the suggestion of opacity, therefore of areas that remain for the most part hidden from the public eye. Domestics tend to perform their service in the shadows.[64]

Anchored in a sense of status but not entirely devoid of arbitrariness, the problematic attempt of the Bolognese association to find a proper definition clearly suggests that the question about what a servant is remains open to any epochal interpretation and threatens to become uncontainable, both in theory and in practice. That is especially the case when self-attributed labels overlap with competing formulations. Nevertheless, one can reach a simple, general conclusion: *A servant is someone who has a master.* (After all, it always takes two to tango.) Servant and master constitute an indivisible, yet uneven, couple, even if this book gives considerably less attention to the second member of that pair. The focus will instead be on the much more neglected figure of the servant, which tends to skillfully evade the attention of contemporaries (as well as historians)[65] because the practice of service presupposes operations that take place in the background.

Implicitly, the basic relationship between master and servant[66] may prove equally difficult to analyze, but one can easily augment the initial definition by adding further elements to it. One may consider, for instance, the length of their partnership, the type of services exchanged (labor and time versus protection against material deprivation), or their legal status. Such an expanded definition, containing many of the aforementioned elements, can be found in the writings of John Locke, who summarizes the emergence of servants in the following manner:

> Master and servant are names as old as history, but given to those of far different condition; for a free man makes himself a servant to another, by selling him, for a certain time, the service he undertakes to do, in exchange for wages he is to receive; and though this commonly puts him into the family of his master, and under the ordinary discipline thereof: yet it gives the master but a temporary power over him and no greater than what is contained in the contract between them.[67]

Writing in 1589, a century before Locke, Nicolò di Gozze provides an even broader classification, drawing upon notions of both affect and natural right. Di

Gozze distinguishes among various categories: "servants by nature," "servants by law," "servants by remuneration," and "servants by virtue or pleasure."[68] Here, the question about what makes a servant receives an additional formulation. Following Gozze's logic, one becomes a servant not merely out of plain economic necessity, which causes suffering, but also out of passion, which—at least in its baroque formulation—associates virtue with pleasure.

Regardless of carefully drafted work contracts and fervent aspirations for professional advancement, what unites master and servant is, first and foremost, the element of language. The mode of communication between the two parties revolves around commands. Giving orders has always been a defining feature of the master's identity. His status is practically built around that practice. In his treatise on domestic economy, Xenophon already points out that the paterfamilias "governs," in effect, controls the house by giving instructions.[69] A basic definition of the master–servant relation can therefore also be formulated in terms of the order of command: the former gives the orders, while the latter takes and follows them. That chain of activity already belongs to the grammar of dramatic techniques in ancient tragedy. Following it, the audience can also identify the servant roles, which, as opposed to eighteenth-century parts, do not involve a lot of talking. As soon as a (silent) domestic receives an order, he must carry it out without delay.[70] By performing the command, he not only fully submits to the master's authority but also enacts his thoughts in front of everybody's eyes. In return, the master takes responsibility for those actions. Retracing the steps from action back to possible motive, that configuration conveys the inner life of the character, who also happens to be the one giving the orders. The link between command and action, and the epistemic possibilities ensuing therefrom, hold the promise of uncovering the relation between humans and machines or, more concretely, between users and computers.[71]

Until the early twentieth century, when it was transposed into things and new operating agents, the master–servant relation remained the fundamental driving force of society. Not surprisingly, in his *Theory of the Leisure Class*, Thorstein Veblen calls relation between master and servant the decisive feature of a "quasi-peaceable" culture, distinct from a previous stage of "barbarism" grounded in warfare, religion, and sports.[72] Within a form of social organization based on private property, prestige, and the accumulation of wealth, as illustrated by Western societies from the late Middle Ages to the fall of the great monarchies, servants are assigned special symbolic value. Those with money employ servants. But that is not all. The wealthy strive to accumulate even more wealth in order to be able to surround themselves with even more servants. "Under this principle there arises a class of servants, the more numerous the better, whose sole office is fatuously to wait upon the person of their owner, and so to put in evidence his ability unproductively to consume a large amount of service."[73] Since capital is unevenly distributed, the numbers of servants also differ—a rising phenomenon after the seventeenth century.[74] Richard Neville, the wealthy and mighty Earl of Warwick, is supposed to have brought six hundred lackeys on his visit to the English Parliament in the mid-fifteenth century.[75] That number may seem of biblical proportions and should be taken with a grain of salt, or at least considered a striking exception in that era. But over the following decades the number of employees of landed aristocrats, in other words, of the typical representatives of the "leisure class," easily reaches the lower three-digit mark. The number of servants serves as an indicator of the master's social prestige and may help one roughly assess the latter's current rank on the social ladder. Those numbers may also be used to make seating arrangements for feasts.[76] Thus, from the perspective of economic theory, subalterns are nothing but signs of signs. "These specialized servants are useful more for show than for service actually performed."[77] They simply represent their master's wealth, by waiting on him— for instance, at dinner—and thereby (literally) *standing for* his capital, which, in monetary form, is also nothing but an arbitrary sign. This dance of representations would not be complete without a gender component that comes into play as well: as opposed to housemaids or chambermaids, male servants "are better fitted for this work, as showing a larger waste of time and of human energy."[78]

If we were to assess, at this point, our efforts to provide a more precise definition of the term "servant," the results would prove rather inconclusive. We started out with Daniel Defoe and his difficulties with identifying servants, which led to an effort of systematic distinction between the servant phenotype and its close relatives, like the slave and the bondsman, the apprentice, and the assistant. We then considered various competing (and partly conflicting) interpretive frameworks: speech-act theory and semiotics as well as system- and category-based approaches. John Locke's classic description helped circumscribe the idea of the genesis of the subaltern. Thus, servants are born out of a property division imbalance. That imbalance takes the form of an asymmetrical, legally fixated social relation—service and obedience in exchange for wages and protection—and manifests itself as an unequal, temporally limited power relation between two individuals. Finally, we reached a general, abstract formulation according to which the servant is the inseparable antonym of his master. Thereby, we brought a historically prominent (conceptual) pair down to its smallest common denominator and defined it as a fundamental social relation.

Apart from being invisible, ubiquitous, and indispensable, a servant is defined by having a master. That basic definition includes everyone, at least in societies that have not undergone a general process of secularization. Who does not have a master, if even the pope and the king are aware of a lord reigning above them? If everyone is a servant, then everyone *has* a master, and that relation of possession raises questions about the unstable threads of power and the deceptive signs of dominance. All hierarchical processes must be considered in this light.

1.1.2. Relations of Power

> Where I am, is always on top. And should I be on the bottom, then the bottom becomes the top.
> —René Weller, super featherweight ex–world champion, ca. 1996

> Princes must serve their servants.
> —Georg Henisch, *Of the German Tongue and Wisdom*, 1616

King Lear and his fool, Don Quixote and Sancho Panza, Louis XIV and Colbert, Frederick William III and Fredersdorf, Jacques the fatalist and his master, Goethe and Ecker-, I mean, Stadelmann,[79] Kara Ben Nemsi and Hadschi Halef Omar, Puntila and Matti, Pozzo and Lucky, Bush and Blair . . . the list of famous master–servant couples in (literary) history could go on and on. At first sight, the status assigned to each seems immediately clear. Judging by the names, at least, it seems fairly obvious who is who. The unequal distribution of wealth inevitably plays a major part here. But there is something else, much less quantifiable than monetary riches, allowing some to occupy a privileged position while forcing others into a submissive role. That quality rarely manifests itself directly but rather is mediated via various signs or exhibited by means of external cues. Its presence calls for a closer look at the master–servant relation, which instantly turns out to be a rather complicated construct.

Priest and layman, general and soldier, ruler and subject, patriarch and domestic, researcher and assistant, woman and man, all the "natural forms" of human coexistence are "eternal, even though with the passing of time the distance between master and servant, the intimacy of love, the authority of parents and the reputation of families vary and change."[80] While such dichotomies function as invariable cultural forms, they may still be subject to temporary or even extensive transformations. One may become a master on account of holding a prestigious position, by dint of noble birth, due to financial means, or simply via an inherited or hard-earned social status. But servants have always been subject to classification and subordination, toward either their masters or their fathers. They never appear as independent members of a society.[81] The crucial aspect about this basic dichotomy—beyond its eternal and dynamic character—is that it is defined by *a gradient of power.* In other words, to be a servant means nothing other than having someone on top whose orders one is supposed to follow.

Still, this relatively simple configuration of power is complicated by multiple superimposed elements. Thus the two-part relation quickly turns out to be a composite, dynamic network in which one cannot easily determine who controls whom. From a sociotechnical point of view, an invariable characteristic of Western forms of social organization is that no one is spared of this activity: all must serve. For the higher classes, the nobility and the clergy, there are at least three levels of submission: *deo, regi, patriae.* Even the ruler is bound to obey God or the pope, as his representative on earth. But beyond that, as far as the members of the middle or lower classes go, one serves not merely one's country, king, and God but also one's master. There can be several masters at once. After all, the paterfamilias, his wife, the employer, the manager, the teacher, and the ruler very rarely occupy the same position. In short, the various relations of dependence intersect and blend together. The relation is always more than what Carlo Goldoni was still able to deny in 1743: namely, that one always serves *several* masters at the same time.

As opposed to individuals born to privilege and wealth, servants are the product of sociotechnical relations. They represent the dynamic effect of careers and variable positions on a hierarchy where any subject (in the sense of anyone who is subservient) may rise or fall. "It is this very fact, that the position of servants has always depended more on human relations than on organizations or general conditions, that makes it so difficult to generalize."[82] Before the institutional establishment and professionalization of servants in the nineteenth century, acts of service in preindustrial Europe are not necessarily structured as specific, clearly defined tasks but rather exist in a constantly changing relation to other elements in the hierarchical order, and other subjects, ranging from stable boys to venerable court officials. Consequently, there is a particular kind of relationship,[83] a pure relation of power that turns a subject into a servant. "Domestic service is first and foremost a relationship."[84] And, as is the case with most relationships, such hierarchical connections are defined less by fixed categories than by constant change, occasional moments of stability, abrupt closure, persistent negotiation, and permanent readjustment.

If servants are primarily characterized by their relational quality, the structure that defines their rapport to the (Big) Other comprises three crucial aspects: (1) the recursive character of the master-and-servant pair; (2) the historical origin of the hierarchy of service and its divine, courtly, and domestic trajectories; and (3) the versatility of the hierarchical structure, which lends stability to the mechanisms of power but is also prone to turns and reversals at the same time.

Consequently, we must foreground the precarious instances, the watershed moments at the heart of each trajectory, when relations of power are renegotiated or even reconfigured from one moment to the next.

If we imagine a tree diagram and exclude the highest and the lowest node, then each position in the hierarchy has a double function. Seen "from below," the chain of control stretches endlessly upward; but from the same perspective, there is always someone lower in rank acting as a servant's servant. If all serve, then, implicitly, all rule as well. That concurrence between master and servant has a long-standing tradition going back to the medieval estate system. The thirteenth-century poet Reinmar von Zweter writes, "It man and woman doth astound, that a lord born free of bound become also unfree vassal, a knight, soldier and serf withal."[85]

To paraphrase F. W. Bernstein, all servants have servants of their own. So, for example, the Ulpia centurion from the Roman Legion has "a number of *Stratores* to serve him, and those have soldiers to help them."[86] Or in the case of the domestics criticized by Defoe: as household employees, they employ help in their turn, partly for their own purposes, and thus delegate their own tasks to other "menial servants."[87] In rural areas, servants cope with their workload by resorting to day laborers as "lower servants of servants."[88] Or in Carl Friedrich Moser's study *Master and Servant*—an aphoristic addition to his *German Court Law*—servants in a relatively low position at court act toward other servants with princely pomp.

Nothing is more laughable than a minor courtier putting on airs, letting hurried commoners and peasants knock at the gate for a long while before finally responding; the same courtier will act quite humbly in the anterooms of a higher official he wishes to see.[89]

Defoe and Moser both thus prove that the master-or-servant question is, to a large degree, a matter of perspective. By the same token, they also show that the hierarchical positions are organized recursively, generally in favor of those in power. In their turn, the latter constantly risk having their authority circumvented or thwarted by subalterns. Just a few years before Defoe's cautionary tale, a pamphlet released under the jocular pseudonym Traugott Warmund von Gleichzu [Godfaith Warm-Mouth of At-Once] left no one in doubt about the stance of its anonymous author: namely, that even those in higher positions turn out to be subalterns, since the power associated with their status is bound to erode. The basic premise is already formulated in the title: *The Lord a Slave of His Disloyal Servant, the Disloyal Servant and Slave a Master Ruling Over His Lord, or Brief yet Truthful Description of How Mighty Those Disloyal Servants Are at Many Great Courts Nowadays, How They Counsel the Lords in All Things in*

*Part through Their Followers and Devotees and Have Them Believe Whatever They
Desire. What Their Flaws Are and How They Lastly Come to a Grim End.*[90]

Hierarchies have long functioned as a proven platform and tool for stabiliz-
ing relations of power. Up until the early twentieth century their impact was
still noticeable, albeit in a subtle form, well beyond the realm of state(-like)
configurations. A case in point is the theatrical scripts which list the dramatis
personae not in order of appearance but according to their hierarchical rank:[91]
lords first, servants last. Unsurprisingly, therefore, during the early modern age
before the Reformation, in accordance with the sixth letter of St. Paul to the
Ephesians urging believers to also obey earthly lords (Eph. 6, 5–9), the relatively
rigid system made up of a sovereign and four arch-offices—treasurer, constable,
steward, and cup bearer[92]—develops into a minutely differentiated court and its
affiliated staff.[93] Each member of the devoted, increasingly numerous[94] crowd of
court servants is temporarily assigned a position that corresponds to that of the
lord and depends on the latter's favor. The many types of court servants—for instance, the court chief constable, the chief steward, the chief huntsman, or chief
falconer[95]—as well as "domestics, underlings, servants, valets, housekeepers,
maids, chamberlains, valets de chambre, etc."[96]—suggest a subtly differentiated
hierarchy of unimaginable proportions.

Given the staggering number of positions, especially at the two main royal
courts of Vienna and Versailles, listing all ranks and their respective duties
would have been a futile endeavor. That must have been just as difficult then as
it is now, and few would have been familiar with the specific designations. During the late seventeenth century, printed directories of service are introduced to
remedy the situation.[97] So, for instance, the *New Servant Book of Württemberg*
provides the names and functions of all (civil) servants in the history of the court
at Stuttgart, in a volume of impressive proportions even by today's standards.
The book lists the purveyors to the court, the hired service staff, and all salaried
clerks serving the prince. Only the purveyors of minor product categories—like
wood, lard, and saltpeter—are left off the list.[98]

Within each distinct section of the hierarchy, court servants are subject to a
certain (rather slow-paced) dynamic—some aspirants may wait decades to be
granted the cherished treasurer's key. Moreover, career jumps are fairly uncommon. But the middle and top sections of the hierarchy represent clearly distinct
categories—to the point that the differences between them seem literally cast
in stone. As Norbert Elias has shown in his pathbreaking study on the French
courtly society, the structure of the court hierarchy is also reflected at the level of
the urban residences of the nobility and their architectural forms.[99] The *Encyclopédie* points out the subtle terminological distinctions among various buildings

and their proportions, corresponding to the owner's respective rank at court: "Private dwellings take on distinct names, according to the various ranks of those who inhabit them. One speaks of the *house* of a bourgeois, the *hôtel* of a peer, the *palace* of a prince or a king."[100] Depending on the owner, the building itself, along with the suites of chambers and formal rooms, is a projection of or a replica of the royal palace in miniature. Similarly, the principles of court hierarchy are reflected on a smaller scale within each aristocratic household.

Besides the court, the other model that inspires the configuration of urban aristocratic residences is the country mansion with its large staff and specific, but less precise, hierarchical order. In turn, those residences and their respective forms of service organization become the model followed by wealthy bourgeois families. And when the latter advance to a certain social level and their houses grow, they must hire servants. For a long time, such models remain subject to subtle mechanisms of differentiation. Theodor Fontane, for instance, still distinguishes between "aristocratic" and "bourgeois" servants.[101] In any case, the cohabitation of large families and their help depends on a clear hierarchical system that is vital for establishing relations of power in the domain of domestic work. "No relations in society are so numerous and universal as those of Masters and Servants—as those of Household Duties and the performers of them."[102] Thus claims a guide to the organizational structure of large household staff from 1825. The book proceeds to list the whole gamut of positions, starting with the *bailiff* (administrator) as the highest-ranked servant, on to the butler and coachman to the lowest stable boy or undergardener, as well as their duties, grouped according to rank, income, and activity. Just as at court, keeping "luxury servants,"[103] that is, more staff than are actually needed, is a common practice. The abundance of servants who engage in "vicarious leisure"[104] and thus obviously lack work lead to new recursive relations. When a new servant, a secretary, for instance, arrives, the older staff have to attend to him:

> The marquis went up the steps of a little secret staircase two at a time and installed our hero in a pretty attic which looked out on the big garden of the hôtel. He asked him how many shirts he had got at the linen drapers. "Two," answered Julien, intimidated at seeing so great a lord condescend to such details. "Very good," replied the marquis quite seriously, and with a certain curt imperiousness, which gave Julien food for thought. "Very good, get twenty-two more shirts. Here are your first quarter's wages." As he went down from the attic the marquis called an old man. "Arsène," he said to him, "you will serve M. Sorel."[105]

At the onset of the modern era, aristocratic or high-bourgeois households were *ruled* not unlike a (royal) court or even a state, namely, with the aid of a complex hierarchy of ministers / stewards, officials / butlers, secretaries, and subalterns. Henceforth, the servant function could be derived from the art of governance and its treatises. (It should also be added that, in order to bolster the credibility of early modern state authority, treatises on the art of courtly governance reversed the relation between home and court once more, by drawing on the metaphors of the household and its economy in antiquity.)[106]

Apart from the secular hierarchical genealogy serving as an instrument of command over subalterns, there is yet another, divine, lineage. The historical origin of "hierarchy" is deliberately elevated, as in the works of the scholastics, or the Church Fathers, in Thomas of Aquinas's *Angelology* and via the reception of the early sixth-century apocryphal writings of Pseudo-Dionysius. And since order comes from above and is of sacred origin, transposing divine forms of organization onto the management of earthly affairs seems only natural. Giorgio Agamben has shown how this strategy works in Pseudo-Dionysius's *De coelesti hierarchia*: "It is a case, on the one hand, of placing the angels in a hierarchy, arranging their ranks according to a rigidly bureaucratic order and, on the other hand, of angelifying the ecclesiastical hierarchies, by distributing them according to an essentially sacred gradation. In other words, it is a case of transforming the *mysterium* into a *ministerium* and the *ministerium* into a *mysterium*."[107]

Importantly, however, not every angel receives a ministerial rank in this sacred–secular transfer. Angels were originally mere descendants of animal divinities or heirs to various figures, from messengers to representatives of sacred powers.[108] Following the Areopagite, Aquinas subsequently elevates (or rather, degrades) them to the level of agents who serve. The main distinction within the theological tradition is between the functions of praise and administration. Drawing on contemporary secular practices of command, Aquinas splits the divine hierarchy into a two-class society of *famuli* and *footmen*. That is to say, he decrees a difference between the distant administrators qualified to represent (*virtus administrandi*), on the one hand, and the servants constantly gazing upon (and praising) their ruler (*virtus assistendi Deo*), on the other hand.

"The angels are spoken of as assisting and administering, after the likeness of those who attend upon a king; some of whom ever wait upon him and hear his commands immediately; while there are others to whom the royal commands are conveyed by those who are in attendance—for instance, those who are placed at the head of the administration of various cities; these are said to administer, not to assist."[109]

God and his distant representatives communicate by angelic emissaries, acting like typical messengers (footmen). Only lower-ranked angels or servants are assigned such tasks.[110] Even if the scholastic classification is rather vague, it nevertheless greatly impacts the domestic hierarchy. Here, too, we find a basic difference between 'above' (steward, butler, valet, housekeeper, cook, who are all closer to the master) and 'below' (all the liveried staff and lower servants, who must keep their distance). Similarly, in the history of public administration, midranking positions are introduced, along with 'higher' and 'lower' offices, only during the nineteenth century.[111]

A further development comes to strengthen the divine lineage of secular domestic obedience. As a consequence of the Reformation, the Catholic Church develops a strong tendency toward hierarchical structures. A new interpretation of the fourth commandment becomes the premise for expanding the jurisdiction of the authorities subalterns need to obey. Apart from the biological father, there is the paterfamilias, the members of the clergy, lords, officials, educators, the elderly, and all other kinds of mentors.[112] Little wonder, then, that some Victorians still hold the servant status to be divinely ordained. To weaken or eradicate it would be sheer blasphemy.[113]

Even if courtly hierarchies ensure stable career paths—at least here on earth —guiding aspiring underlings toward the next step to be attained, advancement procedures may well be clearly delineated but under no imposition to be carried out. An 'arranged' career with a legal claim to promotion is out of the question. Everything depends on the sovereign's mercy and the master's whim. Apart from continuously seeking to place themselves and their qualities in the best light while waiting upon their masters, subalterns embrace the strategy of patiently *waiting things out.* So, for instance, an average courtier may spend years in the same position before a stroke of luck or a skillfully directed intrigue allows him to be advanced to stewardship.[114] For others, like the court actor, disabled harlequin, and famous "physics artist" Friedrich Joseph Müller (1768–1834), the long-awaited promotion to valet de chambre is bestowed only on their deathbed.[115] If everything else fails, all sorts of illicit career jumps allow courtiers to quickly improve their situation by stealth and cunning. Such practices are perfectly illustrated by the *mascarillo* figure,[116] a stereotypical character from the tradition of early Spanish comedy.

Nevertheless, for a large number of courtiers and domestic servants at aristocratic estates, a post, once obtained, becomes a lifetime position. Provided there is mutual satisfaction, each master–servant relation leads to a long-lasting bond of trust. At the same time, some subalterns use their position to achieve autonomy. For them, serving at the court or in aristocratic contexts is nothing more than a transitional stage in a process of moving up the social ladder without depending on a master. Such a move amounts to taking up a trade, switching to the hospitality sector, or managing a financial coup (not to say *scam*), a motif often employed in the late seventeenth-century French comedy of manners.[117]

Toward the end of the sixteenth century there is an increasing need to justify or defend aristocrats employed in higher positions—for instance, as valets de chambre.[118] One can clearly foresee what is already considered commonplace two centuries later in the contexts of gentry estates and princely courts. Starting with the lower levels of the hierarchy and moving upward, service positions are gradually assumed by nonaristocratic personnel. "The intimate personal tasks once performed by sulky young gentlemen were now carried out, more efficiently, by valets."[119] Toward the end of the ancien régime even higher service functions are, for the most part, filled by the sons of workers, craftsmen, merchants, and peasants.[120] Footmen have long ceased to be gentlemen. This marks the beginning of a shift that leads, as in England, for example, to a major process of restructuring that involves both the assigned positions and the class structure of the service staff. Consequently, the range of positions is reduced, and the pool from which servants are recruited for both wealthy households and the court becomes less heterogeneous.

"After the Civil War it was no longer customary to send young gentlemen into noble service for a short time, with the result that servants as a body became a more homogeneous collection. In the great houses the steward retained his original importance, though less likely now to be a man of gentle birth, but many offices disappeared."[121]

The development of the bourgeoisie brings about the end of the conventions of feudal domination.[122] Ultimately, in the nineteenth century the middle class emerges as the leading employer of servants. Servitude and its conditions drastically change between the baroque and the Biedermeier era. As a case in point, the aristocratic ladies who had been pushed out of the service ranks now return as impoverished noblewomen to serve in bourgeois households, starting at the lowest level. "As always, there was a large body of gentlewomen in reduced circumstances who were trained for no occupation. [. . .] The only field of labor left wide open was that which was now being rejected by a lower class: domestic service."[123] The relational structures of mastery and servitude prove once again to be highly dynamic. Not only are power relations at the microhistorical level prone to change at every turn, with masters becoming servants and vice versa. More important, a similar reversal effect can be detected at the macrohistorical level of the *longue durée,* unsettling the once-rigid laws of influence and authority, so that a noblewoman may become the subaltern of a bourgeois lady who has moved up the social ladder. Fixed hierarchical positions, too, can be shown to be grounded in an underlying dynamic, a principle of oscillation, or even a radical reversal of the relations of power. The philosophical authority behind this model is, above all, Georg Wilhelm Friedrich Hegel. In the famous section II.IV.A of the *Phenomenology of Spirit* (1807), Hegel reflects on the "Independence and Dependence of Self-Consciousness" and its implications for the relation of lordship and bondage. In the *Phenomenology*, the philosophical manual that, according to Friedrich Kittler, renders all other philosophy textbooks superfluous by omission,[124] Hegel develops over no more than six pages the entire history of a power dialectic between lord and bondsman, which his perceptive contemporaries most likely interpreted as raising the fundamental question of who controls whom.

The analysis of the relation of domination and submission belongs to a tradition which Hegel deliberately chooses not to mention. First and foremost in the genealogy of silenced influences stands Denis Diderot's novel *Jacques le Fataliste et son maître* from 1773, whose contents Hegel sums up in a different context: "The master does nothing but take snuff and see what time it is and lets the servant take care of everything else."[125] The servant puts his faith in absolute predetermination and emphasizes his belief with his fatalist motto that it is all "written up above,"[126] which, however, does not prevent him from acting on his own as he pleases. On the other hand, Jacques's master claims to be an adept of free will, yet for the most part resigns himself to doing nothing and lets his servant take over the action.

Silently echoing Diderot, Hegel develops the following argument: one of humanity's fundamental driving forces is the desire for recognition by others. Consequently, two equally ranked individuals (the term "individual" used here is a synonym for Hegel's notion of an 'autonomous consciousness') enter into an existential struggle against one another, seeking the recognition they long for from their opponent. Such a struggle, however, can have only one victor, and therefore one emerges as a master, the other as a bondsman. This is how the distinction between master and servant arises, even prior to the Middle Ages, as a power structure that endures for generations. Thus, despite its diverse manifestations, the existential conflict described here represents a cultural invariable that has hardly lost its relevance. "Whereas an English nobleman owed his lands to an ancestor who had pushed a rival off a horse, the wealthy American owed his brave new palace to a father who had broken a rival in the market."[127] The confrontation introduces a state of imbalance into what was once a symmetrical relation, but without resulting in a standstill. One individual is not ready to go as far as the other, who bravely risks his life and thereby becomes master. The vanquished freely accepts the distinction between lord and bondsman and recognizes the Other as his superior. But as Alexandre Kojève has shown in his brilliant reading of the passage, the reason the bondsman readily submits to the authority of the master is that he temporarily occupies, as a subaltern, a more advantageous position.

On the one hand, the lord is accepted by someone he himself does not acknowledge. The bondsman is ranked almost on the same level as animals and things, and what good is it to be acknowledged by things? The recognition is therefore highly unilateral and ambiguous, as it does not presuppose a meeting of equals. "The master's attitude, therefore, is an existential impasse."[128] On the other hand, the power structure is once again set in motion by the continuous lack of activity of the lord, who does nothing besides take pleasure in his achievements, and the steady work of the subordinate, who mediates and enables the master's enjoyment in the first place. As opposed to the lord, the bondsman is internally highly mobile and versatile. From his inferior position he is able to move and open up to change, as someone who has wisely surrendered and thus gained a deeper understanding of things. "Hence, he transcends himself by working—or, perhaps better, he educates himself, he 'cultivates' and 'sublimates' his instincts by repressing them."[129] As a result of his work of submission, the bondsman ultimately emerges from the process of recognition as the empowered one, since he alone succeeds in freeing himself from the situation, whereas the lord remains stuck in his existential aporia. Through the "supersession"[130] of the temporary rift between masters and subalterns, the bondsman becomes a bourgeois, an individualized subject. Switching from an individual to a collective perspective, that achievement continues to have an impact on nothing less than the course of historical development itself.

"The complete, absolutely free man, definitively and completely satisfied by what he is, the man who is perfected and completed by this satisfaction will be the Slave who has 'overcome' his Slavery. If idle Mastery is an impasse, laborious Slavery, in contrast, is the source of all human, social, historical progress."[131]

Consequently, historical progress is exclusively due to the activity of the subaltern. He is the driving force of history. The master is nothing but a 'catalyst' of an anthropogenic historical process, or even less than that, since masters also become subjects over the course of history by inactively serving the state, an ideology, or some other higher power.[132] It is at this moment, and no later, that one can speak, from a macrohistorical perspective, of a complete reversal of power. "But just as Lordship showed that its essential nature is the reverse of what it wants to be, so too servitude in its consummation will really turn into the opposite of what it immediately is; as a consciousness forced back into itself, it will withdraw into itself and be transformed into a truly independent consciousness."[133]

Clearly, then, the subaltern is assigned a position of unique privilege and importance. The process of mutual recognition also shows once more that there cannot be a master without a bondsman "because what is to happen can only be brought about by both."[134] Or, to put it more plainly: it takes two to tango. Without a servant, a master has no one to whom he can give orders. Nevertheless, soon after it is established, the basic power distinction between the two agents fails to remain stable but follows its course of development, with the subaltern being invested with full authority over his actions and the master being left with almost nothing. Instead of matching the outlook of those on top, historical progress is shown to come 'from below.' Ultimately, it is servants who drive things into motion from their inferior, marginal position. While they obligingly go about their tasks, they are able to follow a variety of courses of action. Equipped with an insider's perspective, subalterns take on a privileged position whose impact cannot be overestimated.

To be a servant is to find oneself in an asymmetrical relation to the power of official authority. That relation, however, may turn anytime—be it instantly or gradually—to the advantage of the subaltern. The question of whether the master controls the servant or vice versa can yield radically different answers, depending on each moment of observation. The connection between the two agents, the relation between the specific hierarchical positions they occupy at any given moment is constantly renegotiated, at every step of the way, with every new undertaking. The distribution of power is therefore in a constant state of oscillation. Nevertheless, only one side, namely, that of the subaltern, knows what the rules are and how to secretly dictate them:

> A servant is a man who makes it his calling to study another one's will in order to satisfy it. The profession has its virtuosos and artists, as all professions do. Brillat de Savarin used to gather kind, understanding dinner guests around his table in order to see how they would enjoy his masterfully conceived dishes. The talent of a servant is to look for a master who welcomes the fine pleasures of life and strives for a matching serving environment. He works and chisels away at that goal like an artist laboring over his masterpiece. He takes pleasure in the joys of fine living through his master, he rejoices over them like an art director over a successfully constructed stage design.[135]

One serves not out of need but out of curiosity, creative impulse, or a thirst for knowledge. The subaltern enjoys things by proxy, via his master, but without ending up like him, in a Hegelian existential impasse. The servant meets the standards of a director in that he controls all parameters and places all performers on stage and thereby precedes his master as an a priori function of planning and management. The would-be masters thus run around like puppets on stage, driven by the presumption of freedom and self-sufficiency. In reality, it is the servants who control them from nearby, from the margin. The subaltern determines the condition of the master.

The next section will continue to focus on the intricate imbalance at the heart of the master–servant relation. Who are the actors in this microphysics of power? Who maintains the upper hand in the interaction between humans and things? Who has more leeway for action and more authority within the temporary domain occupied by user and computer, client and server? The examination of these particular questions will once more help assess and test the validity of the Hegelian concept.

1.1.3. The Underling and the Signs of Service

> Providing one knew how to play the game, every individual could become for the other a terrible and lawless monarch: homo homini rex.
> —Michel Foucault, "Lives of Infamous Men," 1977

With their interplay of visible and invisible hierarchies, institutions demand a finely differentiated body of signs for various ranks and class distinctions. The function of uniforms and robes for the military, or the Church, must be channeled into other systems of signs in the civilian domain. Since language contains endless possibilities for *simulatio* and *dissimulatio,* for imitation and deception, the task of indicating each individual position must fall upon other external, unmistakable markers. One's clothes, one's look, the way one behaves become the telling signs of status and rank. One can thereby prevent mistakes when properly addressing others both at court and in private. But as Defoe's example indicates, identifying the right persons is easier said than done.

In the eighteenth century, with the proliferation of administrative hierarchies and the constant renewal of court regulations that assign a position even to the bread cutter or the chamber pot supervisor,[136] practically everyone is a servant. But the question is how to unmistakably distinguish underlings from higher servants like ministers. Precisely because the relation between master and servant is precarious, individuals may look for external signs of status. Sometimes, the depth of a bow and the angle of the body may indicate someone's rank.[137] And yet, such gestures ultimately prove to be just as arbitrary as language itself and therefore lend themselves to all sorts of strategies of deception. One consequently requires unmistakable signs. So, for instance, lower servants and domestics are banned from growing a beard.[138] The lack of that typical emblem of masculinity thus reduces them to the status of asexual beings.

As will be further shown, the attempt to transform servants into erotically ambiguous figures is doomed to fail. But the trend becomes quite apparent at the level of dress code impositions, for instance in the use of liveried uniforms for the lower personnel as an obvious step toward their feminization. Aristocratic servants are still a common sight during the Elizabethan era, even at smaller courts (and consequently numerous servants have many servants of their own). Then, during the mid-seventeenth century, especially the lower, nonaristocratic ranks of the staff begin wearing livery.[139] A court order from the early years of Louis XIV's reign puts an end to the gray uniforms previously used for the lower staff,[140] giving rise to a genuine competition among the members of the court for the most sumptuous attire worn by their respective underlings. Thereby servants not only become more immediately recognizable to their own masters and to others. More important, the possibility of linking them more directly to their respective employer holds the promise of added prestige at the court. Last but not least, the opulent look of one's own retinue may represent a contribution to the splendor of the court as a whole. "The embellishment of the social landscape through the separation of upper and lower ranks by means of clothing is a social necessity of higher civilization."[141]

Hardly any other signifying practice more eloquently captures the relation between master and servant than the livery. It represents the most visible form of power determining the relation between the two parties, as long as the ruler dictates the attire of his underlings as he pleases, up to the smallest details—like the color of the trimmings or the shape of the epaulettes. Derived from the term *liberata* in medieval Latin, meaning "what is delivered," the word traverses Spanish (*librea*) and French stations to enter the German states, where court ceremonials follow the models of Habsburg Spain and the court of the Sun King. From a historical point of view, the unique dress code is modeled after the striking attire of the heralds of arms at medieval courts. Not unlike the knitted shirts of knights, their clothes allow them to be identified from afar.[142] "The most immediate and infallible marker of the social rank of servants is their livery; it is the most adequate sign of distinction between those who impose it and those who wear it."[143] The livery perfectly illustrates the meaning of representation: as opposed to wearing the traditional, even unflattering colors of one's own familial coat of arms, the master has his servant wear livery and thus *represent* him.

The liveried underlings are the replica of their master's power and privilege. The latter's entourage exclusively (and literally) consists of free-floating signifiers dressed in foppish, color-coded clothes and serving no purpose other than constantly pointing to the signified, namely, their (idle) master: the larger and more

Figure 1. The livery and the invisible individual form a persona

ostentatious one's retinue, the higher the potential interest—and, consequently, prestige—at the court. Their sheer number and standardized, extravagant attire, but most of all their conspicuous display of idleness, allow liveried servants to stand in for their master's excess. The latter's abundance of riches (and leisure) exponentially grows with the number of servants in his employ.

"As the group whose good esteem is to be secured in this way grows larger, more patent means are required to indicate the imputation of merit for the leisure performed, and to this end uniforms, badges, and liveries come into vogue."[144] Finally, apart from attracting attention, the servant's attire serves yet another purpose, namely, to signal, circulate, or simply leave its mark on the often impenetrable social scene of the absolutist courts. Thus it stages a sumptuous play of shapes and colors and thereby acts as a powerful reminder of the master's presence. The livery and its (possibly) unique, sometimes all too "whimsical"[145] mix of cuts and colors displays to a certain extent the semiotic economy of a modern logos that points to its noble heritage via its constantly recognizable quality.

The epitome of the liveried servant is the lackey. His outfit consists of dark, buckled shoes, light, often white, silk stockings, and knickerbockers, not uncommonly fashioned out of velvet, paired with a richly ornamented jacket and matching vest and topped with a powdered, braided, beribboned wig under a bicorne or a tricorne. At least in the later nineteenth century that baroque look allows him to achieve the desired amount of attention. And quite recently, as, for instance, in the case of the House of Thurn and Taxis (in 1990), that uniform has found a truly outdated application.[146] During the eighteenth century, however—when the livery does not yet seem *démodé*—the master's prestige is secured by the growing crowds of dandies—augmented by luxury—and the highly groomed appearance of lackeys. Lackeys thus appear as their masters' doubles: multiplied, sometimes grotesque, yet always recognizable doubles.

The erotic allure of the livery, potentially enabled by its proximity to the military uniform, is also quite apparent in civilian contexts. Along with it, certain modi operandi such as posture, obedience, and hierarchical mechanisms are transferred on to the structure of service itself. If the master's authority is already signaled via lanyards, buttons, or other effigies, the lackey's good looks—an essential criterion when selecting liveried staff—also contribute to strengthening not one's own appeal but that of one's master. Beyond signaling the master's actual power of disposal, the lackeys' opulent clothing is not accidentally sometimes perceived as a pure fetish object mainly assigned symbolic rather than domestic attributes. So, for instance, in William Thackeray's 1848 novel *History of Pendennis,* the narrator is delighted to watch a charmingly idle and bored lackey waiting for his mistress in front of a London mansion.[147] The experienced eye of the narrator dissects the proxy into its different components: the silk stockings, the walking stick, his kid gloves and sumptuous livery, the shapely legs,[148] in short, an entire array of partial objects, dissected and thus fetishized by the other's gaze, whose actual object of desire is in fact the mistress herself. Thackeray's protagonist carries his examination so far that lackeys appear as fully feminized objects, to be treated with the same kind of attention as ladies of rank.[149]

Certain individuals can afford to arrive at court dressed in the simplest of habits, lacking all insignia of power and influence. Those very individuals are greeted with the greatest deference, with looks of awe and cascades of bows. That reaction, however, is reserved solely for an auratic presence and is triggered by the knowledge of the person behind the clothes.

The main function of the livery is to render servants instantly recognizable. But how effective is such a dress code in reality, particularly when compared to all the other regulations pertaining to the appearance of courtiers and guests? In antiquity, servants are certainly not permitted to choose their own clothing. Police ordinances dating back to the early modern period further attest to the effort of regulating dress.[150] In the sixteenth century that role is ascribed to the so-called costume books [*Trachtenbücher*]. Filled with copperplate engravings and accompanied by occasional rhymes, such books set in place dress norms based on gender, marital status, class, and location.[151] Their aim is to classify the population according to appearance, in order to establish (if rather unsuccessfully) an ideal ordering system with normative character. The dress code regulations of the baroque courts follow precisely that goal. Not unlike costume books, the rules are aimed at establishing an ordered, recognizable courtly dress structure— a system in which class differences may be readily identified, positions may be clearly delimited from one another, but where the court's distinctive character may be maintained via its external features. Such clear classifications, however, are constantly on the brink of being undermined. "Clothes have the irritating, unsettling, anxiety-provoking tendency not to achieve that which is demanded of them: instead of allowing us to clearly see the world as a well-ordered, stable system that gives survival chances to all and benefits to a few, clothing serves precisely as a means to efface borders."[152] Accordingly, critics at the time often denounce the external habitus of courtiers as the expression of constant insinuation, contrary to its main purpose of dissimulation. All too often an impeccable, tasteful set of clothes à la mode may belie the low rank of the person wearing it.

Such a form of *disguising* allows some courtiers to launch a game of deceitful signs in order to advance in rank (if only a little). In contrast, the livery appears as a steadfast countermodel. And while the normative imposition of a dress code may unwittingly offer the blueprint for an array of misuses,[153] wearing an unmistakable marker of difference like the livery solidifies the demarcation lines among various ranks, thus bringing an "extremely unstable universe in permanent motion"[154] to a provisional halt. Potential aspirations to higher positions are inevitably thwarted; also, there is no longer any doubt about which servants belong to a specific master. The livery fixes the rank and traces the limits of the person wearing it. Thus it effectively manages to prevent a bewildering array of subtle transitions, the play of pretense, and masquerade.

Well into the twentieth century servants do not dispose of their own time and rarely get to wear civilian clothes outside of their designated employment. One may therefore ask: How does the livery shape its wearer? How does the object affect the subject? Not unlike a military uniform or a liturgical vestment during Mass,[155] the livery depersonalizes the individual, strips him entirely of his intimate features, joining matter and subject into a new functional unit, a *persona*. From this moment on, the persona acts as an independent agent, dealing with new parameters and tasks.

The investiture of a servant amounts to no less than the birth of a new agent. "Donning the livery coincides with the transference of a different kind of comportment and hierarchical code onto the subject. One's posture, manner of expression, even mode of thinking are implicitly uniformed along with one's liveried body."[156] In other words, the professional dress code formats its users in a specific fashion; along with one's external position, which in this case is nothing but a material shell, it also transfers an internal system program consisting of a permanent standby mode and a firmly established position within a (domestic) hierarchy. Aside from a particular code of conduct in the form of service instructions, the servant is also assigned a clearly prescribed function within the structure of the system.

The moment the master presents the servant with his new work attire—an act that exceeds the significance of a purely symbolic gesture—concomitantly marks the instant the service format is established. The livery also provides the servers' operating system: by virtue of bodily media standards, the clothes enable the formation of a persona that is stripped of all individual properties and thus appears bare. Categorical service instructions as well as colorful accessories turn servants into masks. The liveried staff are thus transformed into pure signs. With their bodies they occupy a clearly defined domain of signification acts.[157] The semiotic power of the livery reflects back upon the master, while, on the contrary, the clothing veils the lackey, becoming—beyond the individual hidden underneath—no less than its own sign.

Ultimately, the semiotic character of liveried subjects always points to the masters, and therefore the activities servants perform are, first and foremost, symbolic acts. Nevertheless, despite their infamous lack of activity, servants do work, namely, to the extent to which they make use—again, as representatives of their masters—of (the latter's) money and things. "One portion of the servant class, chiefly those persons whose occupation is vicarious leisure, come to undertake a new, subsidiary range of duties—the vicarious consumption of goods. The most obvious form in which this consumption occurs is seen in the wearing of liveries and the occupation of spacious servants' quarters."[158]

Toward the end of the nineteenth century, as Veblen writes in his *Theory of the Leisure Class,* liveries gradually lose their heraldic connections and become less colorful. The servants' attire increasingly takes on a civilian character and can no longer be easily distinguished from the fashion of the day. Only the full gala livery largely preserves the old look; the liveries worn on semiformal occasions and on a daily basis are patterned after contemporary menswear and use muted colors such as black, navy blue, and shades of brown.[159] The symbolic value of clothes in particular has visibly decreased, if not turned into its very opposite. In other words, the semiotic structure of the livery has switched referents. "Vicarious consumption by dependents bearing the insignia of their patron or master narrows down to a corps of liveried menials. In a heightened degree, therefore, the livery comes to be a badge of servitude, or rather servility."[160] Instead of continuing to produce the same effect and contribute, by proxy, to the master's prestige, the livery points instead to the representamen itself, that is, to the servant, whose unique clothing can barely help him cut a fine figure any longer. Consequently, liveries can only occasionally be found around 1900, when they become clearly associated with a sign of servility. As per tradition, that sign ultimately reflects back upon the master, only now with the added negative connotation of a fossilized authoritarian mentality.

The gesture of holding on to the last remnants of traditional aristocratic dress codes cannot escape a certain tendency to slip into ridicule. That is not merely the case in those marginal areas of society where innovations are born and tested and the long arm of tradition does not often reach. After all, the fig leaf has long been viewed with high expectations.[161] At the first nudist beaches of the belle époque, servants are ordered to wear loincloths or aprons,[162] in an effort to maintain vanishing distinctions and clearly identify them as subalterns.

1.2. A SUBALTERN TOPOGRAPHY

Let us momentarily put our scientifically objective gaze to rest in order to embark, along with yet another protagonist who belongs more on the side of fiction than historical truth, on a small adventure: an audience with the prince. Let us therefore assume a different voice and briefly shift into an external, heterodiegetic narrative perspective.

Imagine you want to enter a castle. The year is 1713, and you are a righteous man, a horse dealer by trade, of good reputation, and you have two concerns, which were brought, to no avail, before various courts across the empire—from

Berlin to Dresden. For you have been wronged. Someone has seized two of your horses, two particularly handsome, well-fed, valuable animals, which you now seek to retrieve by every possible legal means. You have set that as your one and only mission. But your efforts have been thwarted by yet another misfortune, which greatly concerns you. In order to make headway with your business, you have already sent your wife to the court at Schwerin. Yet her attempt to bring the petition forward to be seen by the duke has failed; moreover, while the circumstances remain unclear—it appears that a guard wounded her with his spear as she was trying to reach the princely quarters—she tragically died.

In order to get justice within the limits of what is permissible, that is to say, in order to get your horses back, you have one last resort: you must seek an audience with the highest authority in the empire. Your *ultima ratio* is His Highness Charles VI, Holy Roman Emperor of the German Nation. So you set out for Vienna to seek the emperor and the highest jurisdiction in order to demand fair compensation for all the wrongs you have suffered: the stolen horses, the death of your wife, as well as the treatment of your groom, Herse, who has been hurt while taking care of the animals. Otherwise, you would . . . But wait, threats and menaces get you nowhere at the emperor's court.

As soon as you arrive in Vienna you are faced with an entirely different problem: how can you even get to see the emperor if you don't have ties to the court in a foreign city or a network of protectors and supporters to help? Things are not that complicated, in fact. You set out for the castle, like Kafka's K., announce your arrival, and seek an official audience. As opposed to K., you have two strategies available to reach your goal: the first is politeness, in other words, a precise knowledge of the etiquette which courtiers need to employ at all times; the second is the once highly popular custom of gifting [*Sportulieren*], involving small offerings to higher-ranking officials meant to appeal to their favor and thus allow you to make some progress. Let us now follow, in the company of our horse dealer, the specific stages one has to pass through at the imperial court of the Hofburg Palace. As is fitting for visitors who enjoy the pleasures of baroque spectacle, you will pay particular attention to the formal rooms, which—as we will show—are not built merely out of stone. In fact, such rooms hold a surprising secret, which, given your purpose, may turn out to be your saving grace.

You advance toward the Hofburg Palace from Michaeler Square and are stopped by the court guards in front of the first checkpoint at the outer gate. That is where your papers are checked first. According to Carl Friedrich von Moser's 1754 *German Court Law,* access to the imperial court is permitted only to members of the nobility.[163] But you were aware of that. You may not be an aristocrat, but you are well-dressed. So you pretend to be a foreigner, a second lieutenant in the Prussian army and valet de chambre of the prince elector, on a mission to seek an audience with the emperor concerning an urgent matter. You are allowed to pass and cross the old Swiss Court past the Inner Castle Court, where all sorts of lower officials go about their business. Finally, you reach the principal staircase, the passage to the imperial chambers via the so-called Leopold Wing, which has only recently (1666) been erected by the current emperor's father. There's quite a bit of commotion below; litter bearers are standing idly about while servants are busily carrying firewood across the inner courtyard on an unusually cold winter day.

As opposed to the court at Versailles, where any citizen, irrespective of nobility status or rank,[164] is theoretically able to see the king, at least from afar, in Vienna—to this very day, one might be tempted to say—everything depends on positions and titles. The French model is also based on the assumption that all hierarchies break down in the presence of the Sun King, since everyone seems equally insignificant when compared to him. In contrast, the Viennese imperial court uses a highly differentiated system of access to power. That system is reflected in the spatial configuration, in the sequence of rooms with their carefully defined rules of access, in other words, the architecture of power. If authority commonly takes the form of a subtle, highly specialized regime of significations, in this case it is also regulated at the architectural level. According to Carl Friedrich von Moser, what characterizes German courts in contrast to the French model is "the anterooms imposing the order of access according to one's title. These rules are strictly observed at all other great courts."[165] The so-called order of anteroom access takes the form of a minutely tiered gateway system based on presence and rank, ultimately leading to the very center of power, directly under the vigilant gaze of the doorkeepers. Going forward inevitably means going upward. With each step, the air gets thinner and information scarcer, yet no less significant. Given the lack of written documentation,[166] hardly anything is known about the state of affairs during Ferdinand II's reign. At a later stage, Leopold I eases the rigid set of rules imposed by Ferdinand III in 1637. But a new problem seems to have replaced the previous one: instead of locked doors, now there are overcrowded rooms. One thing is for sure: the situation presents a challenge, a seven-step "filter of the court"[167] made up of a sequence of guarded rooms, leading up to the emperor's living and sleeping quarters.

But enough of this; it is time to head to the imperial apartments and the sequence of rooms, anterooms, and ante-anterooms known as the enfilade.

1.2.1. *En Enfilade*

First, you walk up the principal staircase into the Guard Room. This is the military headquarters of the emperor's apartments, the location of the corps of imperial guards and the highest-ranking chamber guards. Their role is to defend the emperor, by force of arms if necessary. "The first anterooms are protected by guards; and so are all, up to the regents' chambers, where the last of the military guards can be found."[168] Upon arrival, visitors are registered into a logbook (or script) of access.[169] Twice a week the emperor also grants audiences to those who are not of rank, and on those occasions there is a heavy rush of people. But all is quiet now. The guards let you pass, and you arrive at the Knights' Hall.

You walk into a noisy room full of people, commoners from the higher echelons, and middle-ranking petty courtiers whom Moser calls the "courtly riff-raff."[170] That space serves as a good indicator of how efficient, or permeable the order of access actually is. The Knights' Hall is rich in informational content, a space where rumors, speculations, and news constantly circulate and where reputations are made and unmade. The place bears witness to all sorts of acts of impudence occurring in the anterooms. Contrary to the strict rules of courtly conduct, here one can casually walk around, speak in a loud voice, and run into various individuals who should not in fact be allowed to enter. Not accidentally, there have been complaints about some using the room to illicit ends, like warming oneself up by the fireplace and turning the whole place into a "tavern."[171]

Along with several other adjoining anterooms, the Knights' Hall hosts the most diverse group of professions and subjects from all classes and ranks. But here already there are filter mechanisms in place, preventing the majority from going any further. For instance, before entering the small antechamber beyond the Knights' Hall, all servants must be left behind. Permission to pass is granted only to emissaries, ambassadors, privy councillors, officers, and other members of the nobility but "never to their lackeys."[172] Even those holding such prestigious titles as the court jester's majordomo or the court dwarf's attendant have to stay behind.[173] To borrow a concept from communication technology: a high-pass (or low-frequency) filter is applied, quite literally allowing the higher ranks to pass and leaving the lower subalterns (like the court dwarf's servant) out.

Those unfamiliar with the courtly rituals who still hope to get in need to address the imperial high guards or the high court master to obtain permission to enter.[174] Apart from banquets, the emperor uses the Knights' Hall for official audiences. On festive occasions a throne is brought in, as shown in the accompanying copperplate engraving commemorating Joseph I's hereditary homage ceremony from 1705.

Figure 2. In the Knights' Room

Two significant elements should be mentioned here: the first is the door guarded by the high doorkeeper (marked with number 18) and his key, a strictly honorific object with no practical function. Two guards assist the doorkeeper. The second important element is the towering object in the foreground, to the left, to which we will return shortly. As an envoy of the Prussian elector, you have just received permission to proceed—"Go to Park Lane," as it were—and so you arrive at the Small (or First) Antechamber.

Here you have reached the next level of the filtering system. The space is populated by agents, secretaries (of envoys), and lower courtiers—like dance and fencing masters, squires and imperial officers. The space is internally divided into a first and second anteroom, a unique and—given the size of the interior—essential feature of the Viennese court. Up to twenty-two hundred people are employed in the service of the emperor,[175] requiring an even, hierarchical distribution across the suite of rooms. Second, the spatial division is imposed by the structure of the Leopold Wing itself: its length derives from its function as a building connecting two older sections of the palace.

The order of anteroom access and the enfilade make up a system of signs to be used by the emperor not unlike in a board game—Monopoly, for instance. The goal here is to take advantage of the unstable system of patronage and power and map it onto a particular spatial model with its specific logic of access. At the Viennese court, rank of office has precedence over rank of descent,[176] that is to say, over the fixed hierarchical position acquired at birth. The emperor is the only one who may confer honorary titles and grants his favorite courtiers elaborate arbitrary distinctions like Head Crown Meat Carver, Arbiter, and Shield Bearer[177] (all in one title!). Thereby, he may freely position his courtiers, at will, within the system of spatial coordinates, with all the possibilities of movement these entail. Everyone at court moves in the same direction: the course is set for the inner circle of power, which all the courtiers seek to access by various means. Their target is the imperial bedchamber, and each day brings the start of a new round of the game. The emperor, on the other hand, plays the part of the dice in the game: his decisions, governed to some extent by sheer arbitrariness, determine how far or near one can be to the finish line, which he himself represents. Honorary titles, that is to say, favorable positions on the game board of the enfilade, are highly desired. At the same time, the rules of the game are constantly disputed, subverted, and arbitrarily changed. All of this explains why, throughout the seventeenth century, the order of access is systematically renewed and is accompanied by endless complaints about its inefficacy.[178] At the threshold between one level and the next, the doorkeepers are constantly confronted with swarms of ambitious underlings. Thus, one can encounter a growing number of subjects from the lower ranks—for instance, imperial musicians and their progeny—in spaces that had been previously inaccessible to them. Even the court jester's majordomo has been sighted in the Privy Council Room, that is to say, right next to the emperor's private chambers.[179] But you can take great advantage of this new trend and slip through the holes of a system that has become permeable. Without great effort, you reach the second room, the Great Antechamber. Thus you get closer to the center of power. Following the official order of access, the Great Antechamber accommodates counts and barons, high officers and knights, high officials and prelates as well as other top-ranking courtiers like private physicians, barbers, and yeomen of the silver room.

The space is packed; a cacophony of voices signals the pressure under which the doorkeeper at the far end of the room must find himself. Being employed at court essentially means making yourself visible for as long as possible. The career-driven courtier who aspires to new privileges in order to move forward in the social game must seek constant exposure and presence in prominent spaces. At the same time, he must look busy at all times so as to be able to spend all hours, days, and even weeks waiting around in the anterooms of power. In other words, the court servant works toward perfecting the art of standing in wait, and some day when the opportune moment arises (that is to say, when the emperor arrives) to make himself available. The emperor's antechamber is not merely part of a huge information filter and a unique channel of communication. It also represents a stage, a platform for watching and being watched, divided by rank and consequently also by right of access. That stage offers its actors an increasingly more limited space for presenting themselves in the right light.

The flow of courtiers increases with every step of the way, with every imposition of status and restriction of space along the enfilade. The basic issue, therefore, is how to remove individuals from the overcrowded anterooms once they have received the right to pass. There is certainly no shortage of new orders of anteroom access. But, more important, the question of how to effectively enforce those rules remains. In any case, as the reforms of 1637 and the mid-1650s show, every time an order is released it threatens to be instantly undermined. That is precisely why, in the case of the new reform of 1666 under Leopold I, the official proclamation is abandoned in favor of an indirect strategy. Only the ushers in question are discreetly informed about the changes, in conformity with the new tactics of nondisclosure,[180] so that none of those who are rejected would feel snubbed or inclined to invoke their rights. No documentary proof, no warranted claim: that seems to be the logic in a nutshell. Even though the strategy ultimately proves to be just as ineffective as the rest, it nevertheless points to something crucial. It is not the normative order that regulates the access to power, but rather a very concrete media practice. It is the usher, the doorkeeper, a seemingly insignificant subject, who becomes fully empowered as soon as someone requests permission to enter. He is the one who decides on the privilege of access, following internal criteria that are outside the domain of accessible official orders and are based entirely on his judgment, whether requirements are met or not.

The usher stands on the threshold of power. Equipped with his symbolic key and often dressed in livery, he awaits potential intruders.[181] Additionally, he makes sure no one comes too close to the door, lest they become privy to the conversations taking place behind it. It is his responsibility to open one wing of the door upon request (only the emperor and his family are greeted by opening both wings)[182] to allow some to pass, or to stop others with a curt "Not you!" He does not merely *re-present* a higher order by indirectly controlling the access. He is in fact *the very site and embodiment of power*. He has the authority to keep some out and let others in by his sheer presence and words, just like Kafka's doorkeeper in "Before the Law": "But note that I am powerful. And I am only the lowest doorkeeper. From hall to hall, keepers stand at every door, one more powerful than the other."[183]

You approach the usher and ask permission to enter the Privy Council Room. He replies that it is not possible at the moment. Bribes notwithstanding, you are denied entry. The man at the threshold relentlessly dismisses you. Return to "Go." You briefly consider protesting. But if you did, the next move would be, "Go directly to jail. Do not pass Go." That would obviously not serve your cause. So you decide to wait for a better opportunity.

We will now bid farewell to the character of our half-fictional tale in order to add a few important observations. The question concerns the function of the anterooms beyond their role as a social filter or any board game analogies.

According to some classic theorists—like Max Weber, Elias Canetti, Nietzsche, and Foucault—power belongs to those who perform "the conduct of conducts."[184] At first, it appears as a neutral feature, independent of someone's designated rank. However, that definition is sometimes too rashly associated with the classic representatives of power, that is to say, with the sovereign, especially the absolutist ruler who has unlimited authority over his underlings. Drawing on Carl Schmitt, we will now examine the case of the subaltern. In his radio lecture "Conversations on Power and the Access to the Sovereign" from 1954, Schmitt associates the meta-perspective of "the conduct of conducts" with a concept from architecture. Even though, as Schmitt argues, power has its human roots, it manifests itself as "an objective, autonomous measure"[185] at the level of objects, be they representative symbols of royal authority or structural design elements such as the enfilade. "In front of each room of direct power there is an anteroom of indirect influence and authority, a passage to the ear and a corridor to the soul of the sovereign. There is no human power without such an anteroom and such a corridor."[186] At the Hofburg Palace, that type of corridor (or 'walkway,'[187] as it is known in sixteenth-century Spain) is made up of five staggered anterooms, where all the 'indirect' elements flock: servants of all ranks, from the highest ministers attending on their sovereign to the most insignificant underlings standing at the doors. "Those who speak to or inform the sovereign already partake of the power, irrespective of whether they are countersigning ministers, or those who get his attention by other means. [. . .] Every instance of direct power is instantly subjected to indirect influences."[188] Significantly, the manifestations of indirect authority and influence also appear to be spatially differentiated. On the one hand, the order of anteroom access provides—theoretically, at least[189]—a finely tiered corridor that not only traces the flow and impact of information and aspirations but also illustrates an exemplary model of spatial division of power.

On the other hand, the corridor represents, above all, a channel of communication that filters out more than just the low frequencies (that is, the lower ranks). It simultaneously functions as a noise filter that eliminates all other disturbing signals. The importance of the corridor and the relevance of access privileges increase with the concentration of power into small, well-defined spaces, like the emperor's private bedchambers, the cabinet, and the Privy Council Room. "The higher the concentration of power in a particular area and a single individual at the highest level, the more urgent becomes the issue of the corridor and the question about access to the top; and, by the same token, the more intense, relentless, and muted becomes the war among those who had occupied the anteroom and are in control of the corridor."[190] The head majordomo, who designs and maintains the order of access, or the ushers, who manage it by means of "infinitesimal touches"[191] like opening doors—those are the indirect forces endowed with the exclusive authority of keeping all the unpleasant, disturbing, or unwanted influences and incursions out. In this manner, they succeed in extracting profitable information from "the stormy, endless sea of truths and lies, realities and possibilities."[192] The closer one gets to the highest end of the course, the thinner the informational flow of the enfilade becomes. Not every piece of information reaches the emperor. Many insignificant aspects are filtered out due to the tireless work of indirect forces. Thus the enfilade enables the formation of a signal current. Filtered and narrowed down, only a mere fragment of what was supposed to arrive gets to its actual receiver. The channel of communication itself participates in the informational process that finally reaches the emperor. The enfilade, then, turns out to be an installation of power that does not merely secure the "conduct of conducts." More important, via the heightened influence of indirect forces, it activates a process of informational contraction. It functions not unlike an epistemic funnel with no opening.[193]

Simultaneously, the emperor's dependence upon his servants grows with every new anteroom they access. As Veblen points out in his *Theory of the Leisure Class,* not without an undertone of ironic satisfaction, absolute dependence only increases as an effect of delegating tasks to others. His example—quoted below—is meant as an allegorical warning to those who, in their hubris, deem themselves all too powerful: "In the absence of the functionary whose office it was to shift his master's seat, the king sat uncomplaining before the fire and suffered his royal person to be toasted beyond recovery. But in so doing he saved his Most Christian Majesty from menial contamination."[194]

Beyond the threshold where the horse dealer has been denied passage, despite the large sum he discreetly tried to pay, lies the council room, reserved for the most powerful courtiers or, to put it differently, the most direct of the court's indirect forces. Things are considerably quieter there. Apart from visiting archbishops, princes, and prince electors, the only other ranks one may encounter are privy councillors, chamberlains, and valets de chambre. They are in charge of the management of management, that is to say, of designing new orders of access. Therefore, they go about their work quietly, in the shadows, beyond the eyes and ears of the others, in the immediate vicinity of the emperor. The authority of indirect forces is accompanied by muffled sounds and indirect exposure. Up above (or rather, back), at the center of power, there is silence.

Right next to the council room are the emperor's private apartments, consisting of the *retirade,* that is to say, his living and sleeping quarters as well as his cabinet, where no one apart from the lord chamberlain has access. Not even a regular chamberlain, despite his much-coveted and much-disputed function, can gain entry, except after the emperor's return from Mass.[195] What a surprise, then, to peek into the emperor's private cabinet and see a stranger by his side, in fact, a stranger who looks quite familiar. Right now, he is fervently talking, and some of his words ("horse," "wife," "justice," "death") can be distinctly heard. How did he possibly get here? How did the horse dealer manage to reach the innermost and most private of chambers despite all interdictions and the long line of incorruptible doorkeepers?

For obvious reasons, the emperor's private apartments and all the areas visited so far are fitted with fireplaces. The 2008 visitor's guide to the Hofburg Palace mentions that the "interior layout, as shown in the case of the imperial quarters, goes back to the 18th century."[196] But a uniquely popular construction feature of the newer wings of the Hofburg as well as the Schönbrunn Palace is the *indirect* heating of the fireplaces. "Like all other rooms at the Hofburg, the Large Salon features ceramic stoves. Originally, the imperial and royal stokers would heat the fireplaces with wood, via an external heating duct behind the rooms, so as to prevent any dirt from entering. According to regulations, the room temperature during wintertime was not to exceed 14 degrees Celsius."[197] All fireplaces are therefore constructed so that they can be stoked from behind, since the masters do not wish to be inconvenienced in any way by the lower staff, whether by their stares or their sheer presence.

The official version stipulates that the measure is taken so as "not to disturb the imperial family and not to bring in any dirt in the stately halls."[198] But such a heating system presupposes a way of access from behind every fireplace. Indeed, both at the Hofburg and the Schönbrunn Palaces, there is an extended network of tunnels, shafts,[199] and narrow crosswalks over the entire course of the enfilade, where, indifferent to the courtly ceremonial, those on the bottom perform their work only steps away from those on the top. Additionally, the fireplaces in the stately halls are secretly connected to the shafts behind. Both the secret access routes and their users are inconspicuously hidden behind the walls. Besides the half-open doors of the enfilade there are also green baize doors, that is to say, half-doors disguised as part of the walls.

Clearly, then, Carl Schmitt's analysis of the passages of power failed in one particular regard. In his radio talk he states, "One cannot bypass antechambers."[200] The horse dealer proves him spectacularly wrong. Bypassing all the indirect forces still patiently waiting in the anterooms and at the threshold, the shafts and the green baize doors lead directly to the center of power. Curzio Malaparte might have added a brief chapter on "service architecture" to his 1931 *Coup d'etat: The Technique of Revolution.* After all, in the moment of revolution, it is not enough to take control of the channels of communication. More important, the access to power depends on finding shortcuts via secret passages or escape routes[201] that may successfully elude the structures of stately architecture. "Every art has its own technique."[202] And in this case, namely, the horse dealer's case, it is the cultural technique of service that takes advantage of the direct passages to make progress in the matter at hand. The practices used by the indirect forces—the minutely detailed regulations, the ingenious bypasses, the opening of doors, or the mere act of waiting for the opportune moment—all these techniques of service, broadly understood, represent modalities of direct access to and impact on the center of power. Taken as a whole, they amount to a genuine cultural technique.

1.2.2. Locating the Indirect Powers

> The words of the old man had opened a secret door [in him].
> —Novalis, *Heinrich of Ofterdingen,* 1802

By definition, underlings may not openly exercise power. After all, the relationship of servants to their masters presupposes servility, obedience, and self-restraint. Nevertheless, that pertains merely to what is on display, only the manifest form of a complex relation that inherently grounds historical processes. Indeed, there is a much more important aspect to the cultural technique of service: namely, not servility but its opposite, manifested as empowerment and high-handedness,[203] even when such traits cannot be easily detected or described. One of the main demands imposed on servants is to remain invisible despite their physical presence. Generally speaking, a servant's quality is to quietly exert control over the background. Such concrete power practices take on the form of minute actions: opening doors, keeping intruders away, finding one's own place and assigning places for others, engaging with the master's display of power by knowing where to stand and how to make oneself look small and insignificant with the aid of scrapes and bows. The secret practice of servility also includes the ability to find escape routes and manage arcane knowledge. The enfilades, the highways of power crowded with careerists and lined with doorkeepers and other indirect forces already have a double: the secret corridors of the underlings, the lowest of the servants, who become, in turn, direct agents via their unmediated access to the top. By reducing the number of indirect pathways and finding shortcuts to the fixed centers of power, servants are in control of knowledge and the stream of information, since those are the means whereby the upstairs and downstairs, the high and the low, come to interact in the first place.

So far, we have imagined the palace as a vast board game populated by direct and indirect forces, located both along and behind the walls of the enfilade. The same image can be applied to illustrate the direct authority subalterns exert inside the palace, by drawing on an argument from the field of architecture: if the enfilade functions like a yardstick of power, which courtiers use to advance step by step and square by square, the purported end goal of the game—the imperial enclosure—seems, on the contrary, abandoned and decentralized, precisely because power cannot not coalesce around one particular individual. Instead, power appears to be dispersed over a variety of unassuming locations: thresholds guarded by doorkeepers, green baize doors, and hidden corridors. Power is fragmented, its center taken apart, divided into stations, and delegated to underlings. Spread out over the entire suite of rooms, those underlings are all—each in their own manner—practicing power by means of various indirect techniques: opening and closing doors, stoking the fires, bribing, talking, and keeping their silence.

They are not indirect but direct forces since they alone have immediate access to power. Underlings exert power through their routine activities, to the extent to which their minimal gestures allow the continuous transition[204] of authority to the next stage in the chain. But the analysis of the microphysics of power traced above must go beyond the specific actions performed by subalterns; it must take into account the architecture of service as well, in other

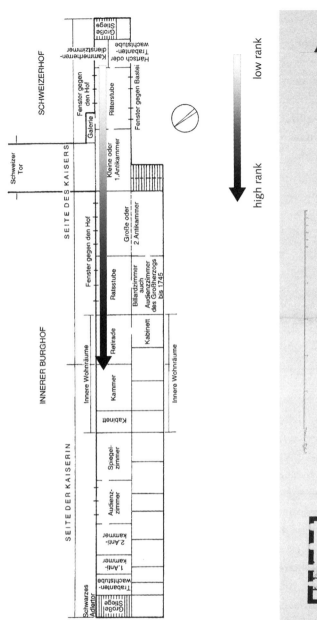

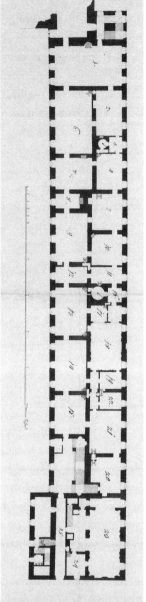

Figure 3. An "active" floor plan, including fireplaces and hidden corridors

words, the rigid structures that help regulate various positions of influence. The standard floor plans of the Hofburg and the Schönbrunn—from Joseph Bernhard Fischer von Erlach's first draft from 1688 to the modern-day Baedeker guides—must now be matched to the 'active' building plans. The distinction 'active' versus 'nonactive' corresponds to a terminology introduced by Maximilian II's Spanish court ceremonial from 1576.

The contrast here is between an official who is rarely seen at court—therefore, a chimera-like presence, an abstraction—and an 'active' public official. As opposed to the former, the latter has walked every inch of the palace, from the court gate to the guards' room and the area behind the emperor's retirade, although his service potentially involves a certain degree of boredom and long periods of waiting and standing around in antechambers.

Along with the concept of stately architecture we must therefore consider the notion of service architecture, which so far has been cast into the background. The term "master" would be meaningless without its counterpart, the "servant"; there cannot be a king without his court or a prince without his subjects, from the valet de chambre to the lowliest of boot cleaners. Similarly, one could argue, the significance of stately architecture would be drastically limited without its antonym, namely, service architecture. And yet, two hundred years after the fall of the Holy Roman Empire of the German Nation, that architectural structure, with all its nooks and crannies, its unexpected vents, green baize doors, and secret passages, still awaits thorough examination.[205]

What could we gain from studying subaltern architectural semiotics? A closer look could help us grasp the techniques whereby subjects appear and disappear; it would enable us to visualize the complicated pathways of power and its divided nature; finally, it would allow us to connect all the small gestures and movements of various servants and stokers into a counter-network that would match the structures of the court ceremonial. The emperor's portrait and the official suite of rooms would then no longer be the sole center of attention. The hidden passages behind the walls, the thresholds, and the secret stairways would also begin to come to the fore as distinctive elements of power, along with the staff entrances and separate service wings that are part of town houses and country manors. Only such arcane pathways allow for shortcuts, for alternate routes to the final destination despite the lack of full credentials.

The background is the location of choice for subalterns and indirect forces. Barring unforeseen accidents, servants waiting upon dinner guests remain invisible. With their attitude of professional reserve, they tend to be forgotten precisely as they pay the most attention, not least due to their perspective from above: "He who *stands* behind a fashionable table knows more of society than the guests who *sit* at the board."[206] Standing on the threshold, doorkeepers grant access to some, while rapidly and discreetly pushing unwelcome intruders away. Subalterns are only momentarily at the center of attention before they quickly retreat into their designated positions of (in)visibility. Those positions are tied to architectural forms that go hand in hand with the type of service performed. Our general—and inevitably[207] brief—overview will start with English country houses and their separate servants' wings, connected through long, dim underground corridors; it will then move on to town houses, where such spatial divisions are reproduced in miniature form; finally, via secret passages, it will reach the green baize doors concealed in the walls; beyond those doors, the usual spectacle of pomp and idleness runs its course on the aristocratic or bourgeois stages of representation.

Interior Passages

The royal palace is a space where the subaltern infrastructure, along with its hidden shafts and concealed doors, is always within reach, but also at the farthest remove from the center in terms of social hierarchy. Here, the service supply routes are in direct proximity to the masters' rooms. Aristocratic country houses, by contrast, are modeled after princely castles, thus there is a clear line of separation between the servants' wing and the manorial chambers. A common assumption among early Victorians was that there could never be a lack of servants—a notion that would be dramatically invalidated at the end of the nineteenth century. Prior to that moment, however, English architects like William Burn or Philip Webb designed their clients' vast residences based on their intended number of servants, not on spatial limitations or labor savings—as they would be compelled to do later. Consequently, this type of country house architecture imagines a division line between masters and servants that takes on a distinct structural form: namely, a section that is strictly reserved for the service staff. "The service wing as a whole covered a large amount of ground—more than the main block and private wing—and its corridors were immensely long."[208] Implicitly, the layout is designed to serve as a symbolic reflection of the gap between the privileged and their dependents. Apart from the steward, the butler, or the housekeeper, who occupy the highest positions, all the other staff members may not walk into those areas of the house they are not responsible for, let alone approach their masters with a request or speak without being spoken to.[209] At times, violations would result in humiliating sentences: "Housemaids in a country house in Suffolk had to flatten themselves face to the wall when they saw family or guests coming. In Wiltshire, an anonymous Lord M. as reported by his footman and valet 'never spoke to an indoor servant except to give an order and all the ten years I was with him he never, except on Christmas and New Year's Days, gave me any kind of greeting.' "[210]

The official rhetoric legitimates the need to keep the two social groups (or 'families') as far away from each other as possible, referring to the irritating noises coming from the kitchen and other neighboring areas (laundry room, heating room, water pump area, brewery, and butcher's station). Consequently, those areas can be reached only by crossing long distances inside the house: "Indoors it was almost impossible to avoid long dark passages and labor consuming journeys to the main house."[211] In order to ensure the utmost level of privacy for the owners, there is even an attempt to ban servants from looking outside into the garden. But whether it is their gaze or simply their place of work that is made to disappear, the effect is obviously the same: the daily activities of servants and even their very existence are to be completely removed from their masters' eyes and ears.

"It becomes the foremost of all maxims, therefore, however small the establishment, that the Servants' Department shall be separated from the Main House, so that what passes on either side of the boundary shall be both invisible and inaudible to the other."[212] The two distinct sections of the house are each bound to their own system of pathways, which function not unlike two disconnected electric circuits that can be reconnected when necessary. The order of traffic follows a general scheme whose central element—according to the Victorian country house architecture manuals—is represented by the servants' corridor.[213] That corridor determines the type of service performed. Moreover, according to the foremost Victorian architect, Robert Kerr, it also constitutes the basis for the subsequent room arrangement and disposition. The difference between a corridor and an enfilade is that the former is located within the building but outside the official suite of rooms. The corridor is thus exclusively used for accessing each room individually in the absence of an enfilade. The entrance to the masters' bedchambers is signaled by the notorious green baize door. Padded with noise-absorbing, soft woolen fabric, the green baize door operates like a sluice gate, separating two distinctly remote worlds and allowing only select individuals to pass: "It can still be a disconcerting experience to push through the baize doors, studded with brass nails, that divided the servants from the family, and pass from carpets, big rooms, light comfort and air to dark corridors, linoleum, poky rooms, and the ghostly smell of stale cabbage."[214] Behind the door, in the dimly lit underground area, are the service rooms of the higher-ranking staff, arranged according to their importance and, at a further remove, the kitchen, the servants' hall, the bedrooms of the lower staff as well

Figure 4. Corridors and staircases for masters and servants

as the laundry room. The corridor not only organizes the "routes of communication"[215] within and beyond the service wing. More important, it becomes a mirror of sorts, reflecting the division of power, both on a horizontal as well as a vertical level. Thus the butler's pantry is located at the nearest end of the corridor, right next to the staircase leading directly into the master's bedchamber: "An intricate system of backstairs and back corridors ensured that housemaids would get up to the bedrooms, [bring] the dinner to the dining room and the butler or footman to the front door with the least possible chance of meeting the family on the way."[216]

Back Stairs

During the Victorian era builders of representative urban residences—in London's stately Belgravia district, for instance—follow the sociotechnical coordinates of the country house style but reduce their scale in accordance to the new spatial conditions. The goal is to set in stone class distinctions between the high bourgeoisie and gentry versus their staff. If castles and palaces configure the access of servants via secret passages, green baize doors, and backrooms, the town mansion architecture, with its built-in class difference structures, confines the help to the basement level, where they can quietly go about their business far removed from their masters' sight. Even if the respective levels are connected via staircases—the main one for the masters and the back stairs for the help—there is a glass ceiling in-between ensuring that only those in charge of the higher tasks are allowed to pass.[217] In other words, there is an invisible barrier for those who are invisible, symbolically and materially represented by staircases and their strictly regulated instructions for use. In turn, that barrier becomes the organizing principle behind the imperceptible quality of servants, separating those that do not belong together. Any unexpected encounter with an underling seems to cause Victorians much unease, so that all unwanted situations are to be avoided, for instance, "that most unrefined arrangement whereby at one sole entrance-door the [noble] visitors rub shoulders with the tradespeople."[218] The strict distinction between the fashionable, bright salon and its subterranean operating system forms the basis of a construction model that is traversed by a rigid dichotomy and thus can be labeled *classed architecture.* That is particularly true from the perspective of the masters, who are never sighted in the basement area—apart from the occasional escapade, which is passed over in silence—let alone the attic rooms, which they know only from hearsay or books. "Pure undiluted gentility did not rise above the second floor. In the whole history of architecture there never was a more class-conscious house than this astounding product of Victorian democracy."[219] Officially, the segregation is justified by invoking the desire for privacy, which—so the claim goes—is shared by both sides:

> On the same principle of privacy, as we advance in scale and style of living, a separate Staircase becomes necessary for the servants' use; then the privacy of Corridors and Passages becomes a problem, and the lines of traffic of the servants and family respectively have to be kept clear of each other by recognized precautions; again, in the Mansions of the nobility and wealthy gentry, where personal attendants must be continually passing to and fro, it becomes desirable once more to dispose the routes of even this traffic so that privacy may be maintained under difficulties. In short, whether in a small house or a large one, let the family have free passage without encountering the servants unexpectedly; and let the servants have access to all their duties without coming unexpectedly upon the family or visitors. On both sides this privacy is highly valued.[220]

The mutual privacy imperative and the implicit need for separate means of access find their expression in two construction elements that are specific to classed architecture. On the one hand, there is a separate service door, in use since the mid-eighteenth century,[221] which can be found either tucked next to or under the main entrance or else to the side or at the back of the building. On the other hand, there are back stairs, which, despite their modest designation, are the main channel for vertical traffic inside the house. The back stairs are the actual backbone of the building. As opposed to the principal staircase, which connects the ground floor to the first floor, the back stairs tie all the levels together. Larger mansions sometimes offer a more finely differentiated backstairs system: a private family staircase, a servants' staircase for the help, and a bachelors' staircase for the young masters, so that they may enjoy their nocturnal escapades without running the risk of being seen. Finally, there is also the women's staircase, offering the prudish Victorians exclusively feminine access ways between maids and their ladies.

"The principal staircase, as a rule in any good house, is understood to be closed to the servants. Accordingly, a second Staircase is provided, called commonly the Back Stairs. They run generally from the bottom to the top of the house—from the Basement to the uppermost story; and, subject to further refinements in superior houses, they take, first, all the traffic of the servants to the Bedrooms; second, all the Nursery traffic; third, a great deal of family traffic which avoids the Principal Staircase for the sake of privacy, especially that of the young men; and, fourth, the traffic of the servants, in part at least, to their own Bedrooms."[222]

The nineteenth-century notion of privacy also implies other aspects apart from separate access ways, as Robert Kerr tentatively suggests in the following passage: "A Bachelors' Stair is one by which single men can reach their own rooms, from perhaps dirty weather outside, without using the chief thoroughfares."[223] The question remains whether the division itself is perceived by subalterns as a given, an act of discrimination, or rather as a sign of emancipation, as Kerr suggests in order to justify the masters' domination and the servants' exclusion from the small family model.

One thing is certain: even if the two social groups have their own understanding of the family unit, the bourgeois practice of a strictly divided coexistence has nothing more in common with the old notion of the household as an all-encompassing community made up of master and servants.

Leading from the basement up to the attic rooms, the back stairs serve a vertical axis of traffic, catering to the daily activities of servants as well as to the illicit affairs of bachelors, returning from or setting out on their amorous escapades. But the back stairs also have an additional political function. In his capacity as secretary to the Marquis de La Mole, the hero of Stendhal's *Le Rouge et le Noir,* Julien Sorel, can directly access the master's chambers from his attic room.[224] In a similar fashion, ministers and other high-ranking subalterns use the secret passages to go directly from their quarters to the rulers' cabinets, usually located down at the *bel étage,* the main floor of the palace. Secret staircases are no less than government techniques that help subjects bypass the complex mechanisms of entrance and access regulations and thus directly reach the ruler's cabinet for a private audience.

In 1760, at the Schönbrunn Palace, Maria Theresa set up a *Konspirationstafelstube* as a secret consultation room. One can still visit that majestic Chinese Oval Cabinet, adorned with East Asian landscapes and screen panels decorated with flower motifs. A secret staircase leads from there to the chambers directly above, belonging to State Chancellor Kaunitz. But his political interventions are sometimes thwarted by a mute / dumb waiter in the shape of a richly encrusted table, operated by the busy hands of servants in the palace's vaults below. Even our old acquaintance, the horse dealer, may have benefited from the existence of a secret staircase (the so-called imperial snail). He may have used it to escape from the emperor's guards after his unannounced visit in order to exit the retirade. The technique is also used at Frederick II's enlightened Prussian court, allowing subjects to bypass longer routes and easily get, via quick, official channels, to an audience with the ruler.

"His prime minister entered via a hidden flight of stairs, with a big bundle of papers under his arm. This prime minister was a clerk who lived on the second floor in the house of Fredersdorf, the soldier who had become a valet de chambre and a favorite and had previously served the king when he was a prisoner in the castle at Küstrin. The secretaries of state sent all their reports in to the king's clerk. He brought a summary of them with him: the king had the answers written in the margin, in just a couple of words. In this way all the affairs of the kingdom were expedited within an hour. The secretaries of state and the ministers in charge rarely saw him in person: indeed, there were some to whom he had never spoken. The king his father had put financial matters in such good order, everything was carried out with such military precision, and obedience was so blind that four hundred leagues' worth of country were governed like an abbey."[225]

Green Baize Doors

The ramified service corridors at country estate houses all converge at the green baize door; in the case of town houses, the back stairs end at the servants' entrance, (literally) overshadowed by the principal staircase, even though it is the former, not the latter, that carry the most traffic. At the other end, hidden in the wall, lies the green baize door, the access point to the royal corridors and secret staircases. That is how Maria Theresa's close confidant Count Wenzel Anton Kaunitz emerges into the conference chamber. That is also how Fredersdorf, Frederick II's valet de chambre, vanishes at the Prussian court. The green baize door can be seen as yet another administrative technique, a shortcut, an effective medium for a critical perspective on the inflated and slow absolutist court. This section however will focus on its extrapolitical impact. The baize door motif is especially popular in literary contexts, where its deus ex machina function is rendered in the form of romantic, eerie, or mysterious effects.

In Victorian England the back stairs are mainly reserved for bachelors or for feminine traffic via a specially constructed 'women's staircase.' By contrast, in continental Europe there is a long tradition of emancipated use of the secret access ways inside the house. That is precisely the discovery made by Hippolyt, one of the main characters in Heinrich Laube's *Das junge Europa* [Young Europe]: "At that moment she showed me an undetectable door in the tapestry, leading to a corridor in the neighboring house; then she gave me the necessary instructions and promised me the keys that evening, the keys that would unlock the uninhabited house and the door leading onto the corridor. Like the castle lords of yore, the merry women of this day have their own secret doors and corridors."[226] Green baize doors thus regulate access in matters of love and provide alternate ways out of (political) impasses. But they also fulfill yet another role: they hold the potential for danger, functioning as the mise-en-scène for agents that pose a threat to the inhabitants of the house. "The hair of all the servants stood on end. They knew that in the bad times of the princely house a black lady walked through the corridors and rooms, which portended misfortune to it. [. . .] Suddenly the lackey started back and pointed, trembling, to a corner. There stood the black figure, the head covered with a veil; she raised her hand threateningly, and disappeared through a door in the tapestry."[227] Whereas Gustav Freytag lets a "black lady" use the hidden door in his novel *The Lost Manuscript,* Theodor Fontane gives his heroine, Effi Briest, a book inspiring visions of a "white lady" at the Hermitage Palace near Bayreuth. As the story goes, the woman emerges from an opening in the wall and appears in front of Napoleon, giving both the emperor and Effi a good scare.[228] Even Carl Hauptmann's 1916 burlesque play *Tobias Buntschuh* can be interpreted as a literary homage to a hidden tapestry door.

The presence, or rather, the significance of such doors can be deduced only from indirect signs, traces, and symptoms that point to that which is concealed and those that are sometimes hidden behind them. A sign can take the form of a look that gives everything away:

> At last I spoke with him alone
> Yet saw quite clearly in his scattered glance,
> He cast toward the secret door
> That someone else was there behind it, hidden.[229]

Unless lovers disappear behind them or white and black ladies pass through, such doors go unnoticed until they are exposed in the act of opening paths or leading into rooms that would otherwise not be accessible. The space hidden behind the doors seems equally mysterious and meaningful. The surprise of seeing a wall suddenly turn into a door can only be heightened by the question of what lies behind the unexpected opening. In Adalbert Stifter's *Indian Summer,* for instance, the most treasured room in Risach's house can be reached only through such a door. That is the room Mathilde inhabits when she comes to stay at Risach's residence as a guest, a place that Heinrich Drendorf reverently calls "The Rose." The first time he is allowed inside is an occasion for joyful revelation.[230]

Green baize doors usually open onto austere corridors, cavernous paths, or narrow steps. In their functional simplicity, they resemble the backstage of a theatrical production. In contrast, Stifter's visitor enters a *chambre close,* an inscrutable as well as aesthetically rich counterpart to the mundane world outside. Due to its unusual access mechanism, the room becomes a sort of no-place, since the disguised door makes the room undetectable from the outside. As soon as the door closes and becomes one with the wall, the space turns into a room again, with no exit, no outlet, no door. Only a window opens up onto a mountain landscape.

Green baize doors enable escapes; they allow subjects to become privy to conversations without being seen; they facilitate sudden apparitions or abrupt departures. Their uniqueness is due to their double status as door and wall. They are semipermeable screens, which both separate and open up spaces, conceal and uncover. On the one hand, a green baize door is a wall that blends into its surroundings and whose presence may, at best, be given away by a slight break in the baseboard. On the other hand, it also functions as a regular door, but only when it is open. Part wall, part door, it works not unlike a turnstile, regulating access in both directions. With its aid, one can walk through walls. What is different, however, is the particular kind of knowledge associated with it. Its use entails a higher degree of expertise than usual; it presupposes awareness of its very existence and of the paths that may open up beyond it. The unexpected discovery of a secret door may very well turn out to be an (existential) dead end, for instance, if, rather than finding a way out, one inadvertently reaches the queen's bedchamber instead. Green baize doors are the architectural equivalents of servants. Their inconspicuous existence conforms to the logic of invisible presence. Similarly, servants follow a paradoxical code of behavior, according to which one must seem to be absent despite one's physical presence. Both types of actors, green baize doors and servants, orchestrate a specific form of (in)visibility which invests them with agency particularly within the hybrid realm between presence and absence.

1.2.3. No Man Is a Hero to His Own Valet

Among all indirect forces, the most direct one is neither a minister who suddenly emerges through green baize doors nor a privy councillor who seeks an audience with the prince. Even the ideal embodiment of the servant in high bourgeois English households—the butler—does not benefit from the privilege of the highest degree of directness. Against this narrow power circle, one subject in particular is directly connected to the ruler, namely the valet de chambre. Not least because of his physical proximity to his master, his relation to him is based on a position of utmost trust. As opposed to the butler, whose service predominantly revolves around matters of the bottle,[231] the valet (de chambre), or personal assistant, is in charge of the royal *camera,* the bedchamber, which, besides garments and other intimate items also houses the royal casket.

The functions of a valet comprise, in the first place, service to the (first) body of the king, or master. That entails help with dressing and undressing. The valet is an expert in wardrobe-related questions as well as in planning festivities.[232] He provides assistance with the lord's morning rituals, with his baths, prayers and confessions, hunting parties (he has the master's loaded rifle available for him and ready for use at all times), as well as fishing, games, music playing—even if there are few records of such mundane tasks.[233] Additionally, the valet is a financial administrant, councillor, friend, or agent for missions that should be kept secret from others at court. His discreet intervention is what confers on him the ultimate position of trust envied by many others. In the context of the bourgeois household, the range of tasks of the valet consists first and foremost of waking up his master, dressing him up and washing him, doing his hair or shaving him, in short, all the basic services that demand close physical contact. For this reason, the valet also largely enjoys the confidence of his master to the extent that he sometimes serves as a private secretary or personal travel assistant.[234]

Starting in the fifteenth century there is a notable increase in the number of service personnel at the Habsburg House of Spain and particularly at the French royal court. Louis XIV employs no fewer than thirty-two personal servants who attend upon him at all times. Additionally, there are four other privileged valets holding an exceptional position of trust. As treasurers, they manage the king's secret coffers. They also take turns sleeping at the king's feet in his bed. Not accidentally, the valet plays a unique role, acting as a go-between for the king and providing him constantly with "pleasurable objects"[235]—that is, to put it plainly, with paramours. The basic services of a valet therefore range from accounting to financial administration and from the mediation of amorous affairs to the handling of the master's daily appearance.

The position increasingly diversifies, and gradually comes to include employed, nonaristocratic individuals. As a result, not only actual subalterns but also other subjects are honored with that designation.[236] Such titular valets are only sometimes subject to the authority of court etiquette, since they do not fulfill any real task; in other words, they are not "real" servants. Consequently, they enjoy the utmost freedom to act. This extended potential to act is also one of the attributes of actual valets. Especially when the monarch is absent the latter are given almost boundless freedom to handle economic matters. As opposed to the ruler, who is mainly active and present as a military entrepreneur and tends to be rather wasteful with his moneys, the valet emerges as an economic agent, as a *creative operator*—against Joseph Schumpeter's notion of "creative destruction," someone whose actions primarily focus on increasing his own wealth.

As opposed to the butler, the valet has, both at court and in the bourgeois interior, a freedom of action or rather, initiative, which endows him with creative agency. He enjoys a type of liberalized agency which allows him to serve his own interests and therefore—at least temporarily—to act without mandate, spontaneously and without consultation.

Despite all the differences between the valet de chambre and the butler, the positions are essentially the same: subalterns that are available at all times directly attending to the well-being of their master. In that sense, the two positions correspond to the main aspects of service: first, the unconditional integration into the structures of power, demanding an immediate response to orders. Second, orders are not merely regarded as the mechanical fulfillment of duties but also as a way of solving problems, often lacking a predetermined protocol of action. Servants always find themselves in an extended field of possibilities. That field spans the vast territory between imposed action and autonomous potential to act, which a subaltern has to decide upon as the case may be. In other words, a servant position requires a large dose of creativity in order to meet the ever-changing demands of his duties. And finally, servants must obey the rule of constant invisibility, which also confers upon them the position of privileged observers. The premise of flawless service implies solving tasks without necessarily showing up in person. Paradoxically, servants must be present in order to receive orders and, at the same time, act as if they were absent. Initiating an intervention is actually strictly forbidden. So, for instance, Emperor Ferdinand III orders his valets to make themselves invisible and to refrain, as much as possible, from holding unauthorized discussions as well as from noticing what takes place inside the room.[237] This odd mix of bodily presence and imposed absence clashes with a silent *sapere aude* on the part of the servants, the expectation that they will develop their own knowledge and agency, which should ideally take into account the satisfaction of the masters (and, not least, their own financial prosperity).

During the reign of Ferdinand II, full room and board were provided not only to the highest positions at court but "also to the twelve body servants, in

addition to a monthly pay of 16 fl. Those were men of importance, since the
emperor would gladly lend them his ear and thus heard what was discussed and
what happened at court. The support the monarch would often grant them,
the gifts, the compulsory donations, helped them amass considerable wealth.
The doorkeepers were their equal, although the latter would receive only up to
twelve guldens a month."[238] Discretion is therefore rewarded, and irrespective
of their origin or rank, such subalterns, as representatives of the upper middle
section of the hierarchy, are treated as favorites. Their value mainly derives from
important media operations such as relaying or screening information, allowing
or denying access, eavesdropping and spying, that is to say, the whole range of
practices that ensure the cultural technique of informational superiority. Again,
power lies with the indirect forces such as doorkeepers and valets.

Those who decide how much those in power should know are empowered in
their turn, despite their officially lower rank. Again, the question is: who is the
actual ruler, if knowledge between masters and servants is leveled in this manner? This issue lends new meaning to the famous proverb that no man is a hero
to his own valet. The expression goes back to Michel de Montaigne, who writes
in book III of his *Essays* on the subject of repentance, "A man may appear to
the world as a marvel: yet his wife and his manservant see nothing remarkable
about him. Few men have been wonders to their families."[239] The close circle of
power does not recognize the two bodies of the king. All the objective insignia
of authority—such as the nonfictional crown—that are connected to the ruler's
eternal reign[240] are left out like unwelcome guests in front of the doors of the retirade. And it is only the valet who gets to see the natural first body of his master
as is, with all its imperfections, defects, weaknesses, and idiosyncrasies. In that
sense, the expression "no man is a hero to his own lackeys"[241] does not mean
that there is no servant who admires his master. Neither does it mean that even
a sovereign may appear all too human in a private context: "No man is a hero to
his valet; not, however, because the man is not a hero, but because the valet—
is a valet whose dealings are with the man, not as a hero but as one who eats,
drinks and wears clothes, in general, with his individual wants and fancies."[242]
But, contrary to what Hegel suggests, this comment can also be interpreted in
the sense that it increases the value of the servant as opposed to diminishing the
value of the master. A more positive interpretation would therefore be: "The servant of a king is a king,"[243] an English expression dating back to the seventeenth
century. Its validity is not least confirmed by the media control, the economic
transactions (let alone the gifts)[244] set in motion by the indirect forces.

It is therefore hardly surprising that the valet's status enjoys huge popularity beyond historical contingencies and that underlings would be quite keen

on landing such a high position. It is not uncommon to pay particular historiographic attention to the personal assistants of those in power, starting with Louis XIV or Frederick II up to Queen Victoria, Emperor Franz Joseph, Adolf Hitler, or Prince Charles in the hope that their descriptions may offer—at least in part—a distorted mirror image of their masters. Sometimes, after their work is done, valets put pen to paper themselves to offer the interested public their own versions of an inside view of power.[245] Starting with the Enlightenment there is a marked tendency for fictional and dramatic works featuring the valet as a literary figure.[246] Due to its heightened loyalty this position does not imply a critical position toward the master. That is why the valet may be suspected of representing a unique embodiment of servility and hypocrisy, prompting Thomas Carlyle to propose the term "valetism" as the opposite of heroism.[247] The parties in question sometimes defend themselves against this very suspicion. Eugen Ketterl, the last valet of the last Habsburg emperor, accuses the higher positions of utmost servility, and speaks to the underling's professional dedication to service:

> Dear reader, you would be wrong to think that sycophancy and servility are the preconditions for my profession; or, that they belong to its duties, quite differently from those who are not called 'servants' and who are showered with honors and move in the so-called highest circles of society! Trust me and my experience when I say: the deeper the bow in front of the powerful, the greater the arrogance towards the subordinates. Believe me: one can be a minister and have a lowly soul, while another may be a valet but act like an upstanding man.[248]

Sometimes the words of the old adage are turned on their head. *Sometimes, the servant is the master's hero.* This formulation finds its perfect illustration during the age of Prussian Enlightenment, reflected in Frederick II's correspondence with his valet de chambre, Michael Gabriel Fredersdorf (1708–58). "The well-known dictum, according to which no one is 'great' in front of his valet, turns into its opposite in our letters, especially when they are not read superficially."[249] However, it is not 'old Fritz' who turns out to be great, as Johannes Richter, the editor of the correspondence, would have us believe. It may be true that the king acts as his own factotum and excludes his courtiers from all acts of governance, by "driving almost everything at court and in his state with unimaginable versatility and energy."[250] Still, the correspondence shows more than anything how fragile relations of power seem to be during the age of enlightened absolutism. Its vectors may actually point in the opposite direction altogether. From the point of view of the king, the one who is indeed 'great' is doubtlessly the valet. That fact has probably not gone unnoticed by his contemporaries, as their occasionally mocking commentaries may attest.[251]

During his military training in Küstrin [Kostrzyn], imposed on him by his father, young Frederick learns to appreciate the services of Fredersdorf, four years his elder. His appreciation goes beyond cherishing his valet's musical qualities. During the years spent at the Rheinsberg Palace, Fredersdorf takes care of the crown prince as his man and valet de chambre, except when they play the flute together. As soon as he accedes to the throne, Frederick bestows upon Fredersdorf, a man of modest origins, the Zernikow estate in Brandenburg. The enterprising Fredersdorf starts a mulberry plantation in order to grow silkworms, a popular but rarely successful kind of project. And while Fredersdorf occupies himself more or less successfully with various projects—for instance, making beer or gold, for which he sets up his own alchemical lab on Friedrichstraße—the king showers him with titles. Aside from being the king's valet, he is appointed steward, secretary, traveling companion, and administrator of the royal coffers, which de facto makes him the highest authority over Prussia's finances.

Furthermore, he is the king's 'jack-of-all-trades,' fulfilling his personal needs, whether those involve procuring Frederick's favorite snuffboxes and flutes, assisting him on the battlefield and training camp, replenishing his cellar and kitchen, attending to his palaces and gardens as well as to matters concerning the royal theater personnel (which are extensively discussed in their letters and often evoke the most amusing scenes), acquiring artwork, sending invitations to court festivities, or handling strictly intimate personal matters.[252]

One can only speculate about the nature of the mutual relation between master and servant in this particular case, defined by Johannes Richter in terms of "relations of the heart to the highest degree."[253] It is, however, clear that the relation between the two is doubly asymmetrical. On the one hand, the servant is quite aware of his inferior position. He chooses to end his letters with a formulation that seems exceptionally deferential, even in the context of the first half of the eighteenth century: "I remain, Your Royal Highness, your most humble and devoted servant Fredersdorf."[254] As a married man, he may not have always found the excessive favoritism of the sovereign quite convenient. Still, he manages to use his position of privilege as a communicative relay between king and court (as well as a source of financial gain). Occasionally, even Voltaire is compelled to seek Fredersdorf's help to get to the king. To put it differently, Fredersdorf always occupies two positions at the same time. Aside from his many other functions, he is, first and foremost, master over the courtly information system, but simultaneously also a humble servant, always bowing down in front of his majesty.

On the other hand, Frederick II himself is subject to that oscillating interplay between command and submission. Even though he is largely influenced by the Enlightenment, such reformist tendencies do not really seep into his daily political affairs. Even if Frederick's art of governance clearly sets itself apart from his father's military fervor, in reality Prussia remains an absolutist monarchy during the eighteenth century and beyond. Quite significantly, the famous dictum "the sovereign is the first servant of the state"[255] can be found only in the ruler's political testament. With that well-known slogan he urges his political successors and especially those at the top of the court hierarchy to maintain a modest attitude. Only later does the formula become visibly effective in governing practices at a macropolitical level. But within the most exclusive circle of power, at the level of the relation between master and valet, the reversal of vectorial forces has already taken place.

The relationship between the two is asymmetrical. Therefore, it may be an exaggeration to claim that Fredersdorf's role as a factotum is simply transferred to Frederick, and that the king, not unlike the servant, places himself and his state at the other's feet. But without any doubt, Frederick the Great makes himself small in front of his valet; he subordinates himself to his own servant *because in Fredersdorf he sees the representation of the state itself.* Only from this slightly overblown perspective of the role reversal between master and servant can one reinterpret the statement about *the first servant of the state* in the context of the king's life. But irrespective of it, the self-proclaimed act of self-denial indicates to those on top of the ruling hierarchy that in the realm of enlightened absolutism everybody is a servant, whether he is the son of a musician or the prince himself.

The highest authority thus willingly submits to serve an ideal institution such as the state, embodied in an enterprising and mobile valet, who represents the economic basis and starting point of contemporary service societies. The age of late absolutism in Prussia, with its stark conclusion that indeed *everyone* is a subaltern, lays the cornerstone for a new regime of service, whose highest figure is, once more, a servant. That regime is still part of our contemporary service society, with its technologically based economy.[256]

1.3. THE CULTURAL TECHNIQUE OF SERVICE

> Nothing more pleases my spirit
> I will tell you, straight and true,
> Nothing better in this world
> Than my fate: what lackeys do.
> —Franz Grillparzer, "Servant's Song," 1857

In the discussion so far, servants and their functions have been presented in terms of cultural techniques. That formulation may not be immediately obvious. On what grounds should the practice of service be placed alongside core cultural techniques such as reading and writing, counting and composing? This concluding section aims to explain why servants are essential contributors to cultural advancement and why their activities can be seen as fundamental cultural techniques.

At the peak of the Victorian Age, in an epoch when the majority of menial tasks rests on the shoulders of domestics and subalterns of all kinds, comes yet another surprising motto from an unexpected source: "No culture without servants"[257] declares in 1875 an infamously anti-Semitic Saxon nobleman and imperial delegate. The statement made by the national conservative court historian and history professor at the University of Berlin Heinrich von Treitschke may at first appear to be a blatantly chauvinistic observation, since to "imagine society without servants"[258] would be as impossible as Aristotle imagining his age without slaves. The remark also offers a lucid historical assessment. What becomes a platitude in the mid-twentieth century[259] is by no means obvious or openly acknowledged just after the birth of the empire. Treitschke's intention was obviously not to raise subalterns above their status and to somehow grant them a considerable share of the comforts enjoyed by the ruling class. Still, his words suggest that without servants and their service, cultural progress would ultimately not be possible.

Especially the small, mundane gestures and the minimal steps within a society define the success of the entire cultural enterprise. The routine activities of underlings have far more potential than expected. Serving does not imply merely bringing in the soup or removing the plates, planning all housekeeping-related details, or providing every imaginable comfort. To serve is to deliver messages but also to filter them; to open doors but only in order to close them; to follow orders but also to anticipate them; to attend an event in full gala livery and thus represent the wealth of the master but also to undertake special missions going via secret passages and green baize doors. In all these cases, subjects acquire more than just a cultural—if modest—function. They are endowed with no less than a unique form of agency. Strategically positioned, they occupy switch point areas: thresholds, for instance, where they are able to control the routes of access. At the same time, they are located at the intersection of communication channels: at the table, discreetly attending to dinner guests, or in the smoking room, unassumingly carrying around a silver tray as political matters are discussed over cigars and drinks. They regulate traffic along the enfilade, and have exclusive access to the supply routes at the country estates.

They cross the secret corridors and passageways that make up the backbone of royal and aristocratic residences. Through their inconspicuous actions, domestics contribute to building a symbolic corridor where real power is at home. "The corridor-building process discussed here, takes place on a daily basis in minimal, infinitesimal steps, at all levels, wherever human beings exert power over other human beings."[260] Via their actions, such as granting or denying access, watching and listening, taking or receiving bribes, subalterns exert a specific form of power, even when that power appears marginal to outsiders. Their strength lies precisely in their marginal character: acts of quiet eavesdropping or tacit observation leading to new possibilities for action that are distinct from the initial tasks performed in the name of and as demanded by the masters. In such fleeting moments lies their influence, their access to free agency. The gesture of turning someone away or letting them in always carries certain consequences for an usher. Taking the good news from the hands of a messenger in order to deliver it oneself to the master increases one's own prestige. The smallest marginal act, the most inconspicuous, almost invisible gesture adds each time a degree of power to the one who carries it out. In time, that power grows into a major factor of influence. In short, the basic media operations a subaltern routinely carries out involve a technique of power and control which makes service into a fundamental cultural technique. If one does not own power but can only momentarily exert it, then it is especially such indirect forces that 'lead the leading.' By virtue of their invisible gestures, by way of their minute actions that function as everyday basic media operations to filter and distribute information, select and redistribute decisive instructions, servants regulate and take control of the corridors of power and thereby of power itself.

Officially, the servant is a representative or proxy of his master. That position reduces him to a subject in the sense of a subjected individual or—as in the case of lackeys—a richly outfitted persona bereft of an actual personality. The task of the underling is to obediently carry out the wishes of his lord and master and to execute the tasks assigned to him without further ado. He carries out the desires of his master, who in return takes responsibility for his actions.[261] That is what the master–servant relation presupposes when examined as a sociotechnical standard of history. On the other hand, service practices such as access regulation and the management, selection, and filtering of information endow the subaltern with a high degree of power, whose respective range he learns to measure and use to his own advantage.

What would be the outcome of a servant's technique of control—if one may use such a paradoxical formulation? By expanding one's domain of action one may improve one's position and gradually become a master. The technique of control allows those on the margins to steadily gain in influence. As opposed to others who may be looking for work in general, servants are constantly in search of a proper place, a fitting position within the social hierarchy.[262] That search follows the rhythm of their yearly transition from one position to the next. A central aspect of the cultural technique of service is the drive to constantly renegotiate one's current place in the hierarchy and possibly move a little bit further upward; to reposition oneself; to improve one's stand; to climb up. That fundamental mechanism is the basis for every cultural refinement. Without it there is only decay and destruction. The strategies that enable subalterns to inconspicuously advance to positions of influence are based on fundamental structures of behavior: mimetic processes, whereby one replaces, stands in for, and moves closer to the representatives of power, or acts of entitlement and au-thorization. With each tiny step up the ladder, the subject comes closer to being more of a master than a servant. That is precisely how a servant literally evolves: negotiating relations and hierarchical classifications, constantly recategorizing one's own rank, and that of others—all these elements make up a technique of culture which subalterns employ to their own benefit. The cultural technique of service also involves repositioning oneself in the broadest sense possible and to one's greatest advantage. By countless acts of assistance and minute gestures one may participate in the process whereby everything is controlled. There is no advancement without subordination. Service practices cannot exist without a certain degree of servility.

Along with the core techniques required by a culture in order to develop cognitive impulses and, thereby, a certain degree of knowledge about itself, such as writing, reading, counting, and organizing,[263] we must shift our attention to-ward the margins: we must thus take into account the inconspicuous practices of service in all their physical and mental forms of manifestation, along with the mechanisms of delivery, selection, and distribution. Such minute acts of differentiation and all the otherwise negligible tasks underlings routinely per-form allow for a vast number of possibilities for control regulation. The media practices of construction and command are enabled via the mundane gestures of assistance and distinction that are constantly enacted by invisible helpers. Only an analysis that also specifically focuses on such small gestures will pro-vide an inclusive overview of culture and its techniques. While they perform symbolic work, such cultural techniques still remain dependent on the agency of media.[264] And in the context of such minute, yet culturally generative con-figurations, the medium in question is the servant.

What determines the epistemological relevance of this *marginal position?* The paradox of imposed invisibility and physical presence, which defines the specific domain of the subaltern, is tied up with a uniquely profitable, knowledge-generating point of view. Who, after all, pays attention to the maid serving the cognac? The valet's perspective[265] discussed by Hegel in the *Phenomenology of Spirit* has a long-lasting advantage over the outlook of all those involved in major state affairs. During the important (after-)dinner conversations, servants may become privy to decisive information exchanges not meant for their ears. Due to their marginal media function, servants appear both involved and inconspicuous, present yet forgotten. They systematically occupy the position of the invisible third, which renders them indistinguishable from house pets. "The servant is the eternal 'third man' in private life. People are as little embarrassed by a servant's presence as they are in the presence of an ass."[266]

The domestics responsible for the personal needs of those in power take on an equally advantageous epistemic position. The media functions of the indirect forces that channel information to an authority as confidants also allow for the production of knowledge. Not unlike a steward at an official function, a valet occupies a place of privilege since he controls the direct corridor to power, the last stretch before entry to the private retreat of the king. The proximity to the sovereign is maintained here as well: not merely since the valet is constantly available to give advice on personal grooming and other matters. Rather, it is the unmediated, direct relation to the ruler that confers on the valet de chambre a unique position, from which he can see everything without being seen. "The servant who shaves the captain controls the ship," as Herman Melville writes in *Benito Cereno* in 1857. Not accidentally, contemporaries fear those in positions of trust, such as Fredersdorf and his unofficial influence on Frederick II. Along the same lines, it would be impossible to ascertain the political importance of an enigmatic presence such as John Brown, Queen Victoria's favorite valet. The historical impact of such subjects is difficult to assess in that the servant's position of trust lies between two extremes: an actual place of authority and the relation to a master, which is not unlike that of a lapdog. "Many [masters] wished to use such upper servants as footmen and lady's maids as confidantes, accomplices, go-betweens, and pets." But irrespective of the distance between servants and their masters, the former occupy an epistemologically profitable position, one which offers the ideal point of view for observation. From there, one can gain a unique kind of knowledge of authority while remaining visible. Stewards, butlers, and valets may all occupy that post since they are figures that diligently operate in the background. Someone working in secret but still in full view implies a technique of cultural refinement. In a certain sense, a servant is the equivalent of Poe's *Purloined Letter:* he is present in the room and represents the secret center of the action but still goes unnoticed by all. In the next chapter we will see how servants use such an exceptional yet limiting position of media-tion to their advantage.

The cultural technique of service may also involve a subtle play with identities other than one's own. The aim of changing one's symbolic status in that man-ner is to revamp one's real place in the hierarchy and give one's position more prestige and recognition. That is the case of higher servants choosing everyday clothes that allow them to come visually close to or even surpass the social status of their masters. In more complex scenarios such as carnivals or other 'topsy-turvy world' events, the strategic play with high- and low-class identity symbols becomes fully institutionalized. But in everyday situations, outside the regu-lated domain of exceptionality, few are actually bothered by such games of iden-tity upgrading. It behooves the victims, then—Daniel Defoe, for instance—to fervently and extensively fight, in writing, against the petty self-promotion of ambitious upstarts. Without rigorous measures, argues Defoe in *The great law of subordination consider'd* from 1724, the danger of the servants' domination is imminent: "The Poor will be Rulers over the Rich, and the Servants be Gou-vernors of their Masters; [. . .] the World seems to stand with the Bottom upward."[267] Once again, Defoe does not miss an opportunity to point to the overdressed subalterns who aim well beyond their proper rank.[268] In Defoe's view, the principal cause lies with the excessively high wages that are a source of constant insubordination, since money makes servants too demanding. In his incessant critique of servants' clothing, Defoe seems to have grasped the real effectiveness of semblance: namely, the ability to turn a poor cobbler into a captain with the help of a mere uniform, and the power to express the desire of subalterns for a deceptively realistic mimicry of the signs of authority.[269] In fact, the spiritual father of the faithful and exemplary servant Friday, who attends to his master Robinson Crusoe humbly and submissively in the novel, is well aware of the hidden power subalterns actually have.

But since everyone is someone's servant,[270] the majority of subjects treat such petty self-aggrandizement and pretense with indifference. Even those at the top of the hierarchy are trained to accept the idea of constant change of rank and status.[271] Louis de Rouvroy, better known as Saint-Simon (1675–1755), evokes an encounter from the year 1673 between the French emissary Cheverny and another person, in a corridor-like space at the court:

> Once he had entered he found himself in a long, narrow and poorly-furnished room, with a table at the end [. . .] and a man dressed in black leaning with his back against it. Cheverny not really knowing where he was imagined himself to be in an antechamber from which he would be led farther and started looking

around left and right and started pacing back and forth from one end to the other. He passed the time in this way for about half an hour. Finally, when one of his turns had taken him close to the table where the man in black was leaning, whom he assumed from his bearing and his clothes to be a valet on guard, the man, who up to that moment had left him in complete liberty, without saying a word, took it upon himself to ask politely what he was doing there. Cheverny replied that he was supposed to have an audience with the Emperor, that he had been admitted there and was waiting to be presented to the Emperor in order to pay his respects. "I am the Emperor," the man responded.[272]

The emissary is forced to assume he has run into one of the more or less influential indirect forces down the corridors of power (C. P. Snow). But for someone like Emperor Leopold I, the man in black with plenty of time on his hands, that case of mistaken identity is hardly surprising. From early on, crown princes, archdukes, and other heirs to the throne are taught how to appear to others not as themselves but as their own valets. They are taught from the very start how to respond with composure to acts of misidentification.

Chapter 2 The Servant as Information Center

Aliis inserviendo consumor [In serving others, I consume myself].
—Isidore of Seville, Duke Julius von Braunschweig-Wolfenbüttel,
Bismarck et al.

Imagine it's 1919. You are Bertie Wooster, a wealthy English bachelor hailing from the higher circles of the London upper crust. A considerable fortune ensures your comfortable livelihood, without any toil or trouble. Together with Jeeves, your servant, a *gentleman's personal gentleman*,[1] you occupy a spacious Westminster apartment at 6A Crichton Mansions, Berkeley Street. You want for nothing, and, apart from occasional family and social obligations, you are free to live your days in carefree idleness, with a little help from your personal servant's particular ways: particular since what is most notable about personal servants is that they—like media in general—usually remain invisible. A gentleman's personal gentleman performs routine duties and organizational tasks: ironing and shopping, serving breakfast or preparing a liquid hangover cure for a previous night of revelry. But the panopticon of basic functions he fulfills also includes activities pertaining to the acquisition and distribution of information.

Bertie Wooster would be hopelessly lost in quite a few situations were it not for the trusted support of his well-informed companion. Through clever intrigue, Jeeves manages to keep at bay the marriage prospects that constantly threaten his master; the "inside information"[2] he gives his master, who is a betting addict, allows the latter (and occasionally also the former) to have an edge over the others; in matters of fashion, the clueless master must delegate all responsibility to his servant;[3] the same applies to certain philosophical queries— after all, Jeeves reads the classic authors of antiquity in the original as well as "the Bible, a fine assortment of poets from Vergil, Shakespeare and Milton down to Kipling; Dostoevsky and the other Russians; Spinoza, Nietzsche":[4] in all situations the servant acts as the superior epistemic agent, anticipating, controlling, events, allowing for significant interventions into the course of destiny and history. Unsurprisingly, then, such an asymmetrical master–servant relation involves a subaltern operating not unlike a godlike figure. Jeeves confirms that fact time and time again, over a sixty-year-long literary existence comprising twenty-four short stories and twelve novels, sealed with a regular entry in the *Oxford English Dictionary.* The relations of domination are deliberately turned on their head. Thus the servant owns the *master brain,* entrusted to him by the one who is only nominally his master—and not just when it comes to menswear. Thanks to the assistant's wise planning, everything is prearranged and prepared to benefit his superior. With the coy aura of modest omnipotence and unobtrusive omniscience, the personal servant confidently leads the master through the perils of everyday life. "Good Lord, Jeeves! Is there anything you don't know?" "I could not say, sir."[5]

The eccentric servant stereotype sketched out here belongs to the literary universe of P. G. Wodehouse's master–servant cycle, created between 1910 and 1974. But for the media history of (real) servants, the insistence on the subaltern's epistemic advantage turns out to be an important aspect. This chapter aims to follow the servants' absolute power and knowledge even beyond the literary domain; it seeks to structurally and historically contextualize them and finally look into how they continue to operate in the current electronic service configurations. The main thesis is precisely that the classic servant figure—its media agency and its functions of collecting and disseminating information— can be rediscovered in today's virtual domain. In short, this chapter proposes to analyze the servant figure as a search engine avant la lettre.

2.1. THE POETICS OF SEARCH ENGINES

> If there's something you'd like to try
> Ask me—I won't say "no"—how could I?
> —The Smiths, "Ask," 1986

Imagine it's 1996 and the internet hype has just begun. You have come up with a fantastic idea for a search engine, worked out the basic model, and even secured the necessary venture capital. But you can't decide on a name. The main idea is to use natural, that is, spoken, language for commands—a clearly superior option to the regular method employed up to that point: keyword entries, echoing the search technology and metaphor of a lexicon. What you need is something like a virtual, preferably omniscient conversation partner able to reply to a whole range of questions with superior ease. You have various options. The first is to go with the good old schoolteacher image. But you discard that idea right away, for one thing because a schoolmaster's knowledge is usually fairly limited; and for another because there's a risk that the inquisitive clients might feel 'schooled' by their virtual interlocutor. The second option would be to choose a polymath. But even such popular figures as Leibniz or Einstein or Renaissance men like da Vinci or Konrad Gessner are crossed out: they all seem too brash, too complicated or unsuitable. Finally, the third option is to find a literary model. There are plenty of names to choose from, especially when it comes to science fiction. Still, the decision turns out to be difficult. You would not want to sound obscure or heretical by invoking a figure such as Laplace's demon; you would also not want to risk dangerous reactions or invite the same lapidary answer, "42," to each and every request, with a name like HAL 9000 or Deep Thought. What better solution, then, than a turn to realism? You remember an amusing story involving a highly independent servant called Reginald Jeeves who gives his master plenty of tips concerning all matters of life. And what is more, the servant has mastered, in his classically reserved manner, the great art of anticipation and wise foresight. That valet should now prove himself to the site's visitors. Without further ado, the company and its respective website are named AskJeeves.

The choice seems fitting. Internet users take notice of the new service, and the search engine is in demand. Your concept turns out to be a great success story. To mention only some key moments: within two years turnover has multiplied one hundredfold; the firm is worth millions, goes public, and is valued at $190 per share at its peak; the number of site visitors continues to grow. Jeeves has his work cut out for him, responding to all sorts of requests. Fourteen million hits per month turn the site into one of the most visited virtual spaces on the internet, ranked at number 17. After a costly marketing campaign, the logo now appears on apples and bananas. In other words, business is thriving. And then, in 2000, the unequaled success story finds its match: an equally remarkable stock market crash. We are still dealing with large amounts of money, but now the numbers are negative. To add insult to injury, a new competitor enters the scene and rapidly manages to turn its name into a verb: Google. The success story of AskJeeves seems far less spectacular now, particularly as a result of the dot.com bubble crash, when its market value drops from $190.00 to $0.85 a share. At least the company is one of the few that manage to survive. But its massive expansion is a thing of the past. Despite a slight recovery, the business can no longer compete with the top three players: Google, Yahoo, which is also inspired by a literary model, namely, *Gulliver's Travels,* as well as Microsoft's highly prosaic Live Search (which now goes by Bing). It's time to draw conclusions and decide. The management changes hands a few times; some parts of the business are sold, and new ones are bought instead. The firm sets a cautious path toward consolidation. And then, in 2005, a drastic corporate policy reform is launched: on September 23 the company announces that the owner, Barry Diller, is going to change the name of the firm. Jeeves's name as well as the logo are to be dropped from its corporate identity.[6]

According to the official press release, those steps had to be taken because users with no literary background would often send inquiries to the public relations department to find out what Jeeves was all about. If they had addressed that question to the virtual Jeeves instead, he would have surely provided an answer as well as the reference to P. G. Wodehouse's stories.

Furthermore, the statement went, the range of services offered by the search engine had expanded (to add a toolbar, an image search option, etc.) to the point where communicating via natural language with a friendly and all-knowing butler[7] no longer provided the fitting context and the appropriate image for its user interface.[8] Still, detractors maliciously claim that the ties with Jeeves were cut due to a matter of private competition, namely, the close similarity between the new owner Barry Diller and the firm's portrayal of Wodehouse's literary figure.

It may certainly seem anachronistic to promote a butler to the position of universal search engine icon at the turn of the twenty-first century. As the emblems of a former service society's modus operandi, servants have been relegated to a minor role today. And at least since World War I and the demise of *The World of Yesterday* (not merely in Stefan Zweig's formulation), that role seemingly corresponds to a long-abandoned historical stage. The systemic and nominal transformation of AskJeeves.com thus seems justified, especially when the move replicates the shift from humanoid media to things in the virtual domain. The transposition of subaltern services (traditionally performed by valets or kitchen maids, library assistants or errand boys) onto technical machines is a phenomenon that centrally defines the nineteenth century. Its importance cannot be stressed enough. One of the main theses of this book is that today's virtualized services and the current communicative and operational standards find themselves prefigured in those classic models.

Nevertheless, that historical transformation and its implications went unnoticed by the managers of AskJeeves.com. Instead of continuing to address an oddly dressed avatar, the inquisitive internet users were encouraged to follow a do-it-yourself model and find their own answers with the help of toolbars and other virtual devices. Ultimately, with the system switch from 2005, the benevolent humanoid steward as a leftover from a bygone era was pushed aside and replaced by a form of generalized self-service. The shift acquired symptomatic value since its representative figure was to be erased from the memory of today's brave new digital world with its marked economic orientation.

Despite all the breaks and gaps, the servant has been with us from the eighteenth century and the age of late absolutism to our current-day service era with its multiple internet servers and various other virtual possibilities. Not surprisingly, then, the disappearance of a visible icon like P. G. Wodehouse's Jeeves from an established search engine such as AskJeeves.com raises several questions. The following pages will therefore insist on this moment of rupture; they will add a few media-historical aspects that go beyond the decision to employ and remove a particular search engine logo. Choosing a literary servant to promote one's business has nothing to do with nostalgia, or any sentimental recollections of good books. Rather, there are systemic circumstances at play. If this assumption is valid, then we first need to ask: what exactly is the analogy between a valet and a search engine? what motivates that reference? and, last but not least, what role does that metaphor play? We will therefore need to look closer at the history of servants as information distributors.

2.2. SERVANTS OF THE IN-BETWEEN

At first, it may seem odd to describe the servant figure as an information center. Subalterns, especially when they function as emissaries, are typically seen as informers, second-degree agents, or proxies and thus relegated to a subordinate position. After all, the threads always seem to run together at the top, for instance, at the level of the king presiding over a court, or the paterfamilias in the case of a smaller collective. Knowledge and the control of knowledge confer authority and are therefore central instruments of power for both patriarchs and sovereigns. But what often goes unnoticed or remains unsaid is the extent to which the main switch points are operated by subalterns. The latter not only participate in the production of master knowledge but also manage and exert complete control over it. What follows is an examination of four aspects that indicate, both structurally and via historical examples, how the servant figure, even in its classic configuration, is preeminently involved in handling information: more specifically, in collecting and observing, sorting out and analyzing, differentiating and evaluating, systematizing and preparing, finally, directing and distributing data to specific destinations. Not accidentally, gentlemen's personal gentlemen like Jeeves are never lost for answers and consequently enjoy a considerable share of that authority. In other words, the knowledge of service will be discussed in terms of a primary technique of control.

The abovementioned aspects allow servants the privilege of administering and orienting the paths of knowledge. Along with their function as connectors or go-betweens among various domains, one should also mention their professional invisibility. A further aspect is the specific economic logic guiding their actions. And finally, a central role is played by their institutional configuration in terms of designated locations that become privileged centers of information distribution. As opposed to factory workers, peasants, or farmhands, servants are predominantly involved in immaterial production. Their main activity consists not in making tangible artifacts but in processing information. At least since the turn of the twentieth century these aspects have become a matter of public debate. "The fact that servants are not involved in the production and exchange of material goods, has led many to discount them from the ranks of productive society."[9] And yet, as the following section on the servants' mediator function will show, the commerce with information processing proves to be just as productive and effective as the actions involved in the laborious manufacture of hardware.

2.2.1. Middlemen and Mediators

Servants mediate across various domains that share the same mode of organization. Until the twentieth century, the equivalent of that mode of organization was the household (οἶκος) as the basis of the οἰκονομία of antiquity.[10] Within it, servants mainly functioned as structural connectors. In other words, privileged subalterns such as butlers or valets mediate among various hierarchical ranks; they draw links between high and low; they maintain the flow of communication between the underground domain, which secures the smooth execution of housekeeping tasks, and the carefree life *upstairs,* in the stately rooms and salons. Second, subalterns serve as spatial mediators, in the sense that they bring distant spaces into connection and thereby reduce in-between spaces to a minimum. To put it plainly: not all servants are messengers, but almost all messengers are servants, in the sense that they are tasked with transmitting a specific message, irrespective of their position (valet de chambre or errand boy). Third, servants are also involved in acts of temporal mediation, whose effects unfold over longer stretches of time. Until well into the nineteenth century domestics and service staff had the same extensive duties and limited rights as children. Not surprisingly, therefore, the interactions between the two groups are closer than those between children and their biological parents. That is the case even when the former are not raised by governesses or spend much of their time in the servants' quarters.[11] Subalterns do not officially belong to the family. And yet they serve as bridges over time, either briefly or for a period of years—throughout someone's childhood or during a lifetime of professional engagement.

Within the realm of the classic οἶκος, servants belong to the close family circle just like the direct dependents of the lord of the house. Masters and domestics share the same workspace and thus form a learning community; class differences are not clearly marked yet.[12] By comparison, the absolutist court hierarchy is spread across a vastly ramified and finely differentiated network. The same is true of the upper-middle-class household, where the steps separating the *upstairs* from *downstairs* become a ready-made symbol of vertically demarcated social distinctions.[13] But despite the glass ceiling virtually dividing the two realms, servants understand how to break that barrier. Thus they function as a hinge, uniting levels kept carefully apart, linking remote and separate areas into new, hybrid constellations.

The key expression of this continuous translation process is the cursor-like circulation of servants between rigidly separated hierarchical spheres. Underlings serve as connecting agents among various levels, bringing together the lower and higher realms via etiquette standards or bits of information extracted from the salons above and disseminated in the servants' quarters below. Domestics simultaneously inhabit two different worlds: as regular folk, they have the opportunity to rub shoulders with the upper crust and thus profit from the habitus of better social circles: "Underlings could adopt perceptions and habits which ordinary people, for the most part, did not understand, and which, consequently, secured their unique upper-class character."[14] But at the same time, subalterns introduce—even if by small measures and mostly only upon request—a sense of 'real life' in the refined atmosphere of the salon: "They bring the wild into the house, or household (oikos)," as Bruce Robbins points out in his remarkable study *The Servant's Hand*.[15] With the below-stairs station serving as a gathering place for all sorts of *slippery people*,[16] domestics connect the unbridled world of commoners outside to the backrooms of power, with their strictly regulated access points. It is there, in those secret quarters, that they attend, carefully and discreetly, to those in power. With their knack for uniting faraway realms, subalterns develop the exceptional ability to adapt to various environments, not unlike poikilothermic organisms. To paraphrase Daniel Defoe: they are amphibian creatures.[17]

The early nineteenth-century bourgeois family develops in response to the extended household model. Menials are excluded from the restricted familial configuration. Nevertheless, along with the new spatial distinctions between office and home, workspace and house, labor and living that precede the age of telecommunications, there is, once more, a need for human connectivity. That need is fulfilled by the classic functions of the subaltern, the messenger, or the errand boy. In terms of what servants (are allowed to) know, domestics once again appear to occupy a mediating position. When the information is not stored in sealed documents and letters, servants find themselves at the top of the epistemic hierarchy. Even when messengers operate in someone else's name and represent or speak for the sender: the telematic act of translation between sender and recipient does not impose limits on the messenger's knowledge. On the contrary: while the action itself may be controlled from afar, the transmitter can still greatly influence the information.[18] The messenger controls the message and implicitly also the knowledge associated with it.

The vast knowledge associated with subalternity is in no way restricted to real, historical figures. As literary characters, servants usually possess a privileged epistemic status, which allows them to plot intrigues, unveil secrets, generate tension, or move the action forward. Not surprisingly, therefore, whether in novels like *Gil Blas* or stage works like *Figaro,* the ingenuity of servants is also what drives the story: quite often the decisive information that steers the course of action comes from subalterns. Hovering between the ostentatious and the ephemeral, servant figures act not unlike a *servus ex machina:* they intervene by committing indiscretions, relaying unsolicited messages, expressing sympathy, making prophesies, or performing recognition tasks (consider, for instance, the case of Odysseus's scar). In short, the business of collecting crucial information, of distributing and manipulating it, is the affair of servants. They possess a particular kind of inside knowledge that far exceeds the (self-)perception of putative protagonists.[19] In the world of theater, the servant usually moves between stage and orchestra, mediating between spectators and the play itself. Subalterns break the fourth wall, acting as commentators of the events on stage. Thereby,

Dumb-waiter: Mr. Jaggers uses a dumb-waiter at dinner, such that he can keep "everything under his own hand, and [distribute] everything himself" (Ch. 26). The *Dictionary of Daily Wants* (1858-9) gives the following illustration and description of a dumb-waiter:

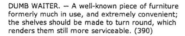

DUMB WAITER. — A well-known piece of furniture formerly much in use, and extremely convenient; the shelves should be made to turn round, which renders them still more serviceable. (390)

Figure 5. Two motionless dumbwaiters

they function as a public-oriented interface, allowing theatergoers to partake of their (superior) knowledge.[20]

Since the literary servant holds a privileged epistemic status, the knowledge in question is usually hazardous and cannot always be applied to the benefit of all participants. Domestics are constantly suspected of spying, both in and beyond literary contexts. That suspicion finds its source, above all, in the servants' preferred mode of operation: their inconspicuous appearance, which defines their paradoxical condition. They are supposed to be physically present but uninvolved, which nevertheless does not prevent them from paying close attention to what they are precisely not meant to see or hear. On the contrary, their quiet and reserved manner allows them to secretly observe, analyze, and potentially make further use of situations and discussions. That ability turns servants into prime movers and agents. Not unlike Harras in Kafka's *The Neighbor,* they use the knowledge they incidentally acquire for their own benefit; they draw profit from it or even delegate their informational advantage. Not surprisingly, lords and masters feel watched by their subalterns[21]— a tendency that grows into outright paranoia around 1800, fed by novels in which servants are responsible for the main turn of events. To appease their fear of being watched and overheard by the help, some may choose to confidently delegate their service requests to technical media. Instead of dwelling on the constant suspicion of being betrayed by their unfaithful servants, they may prefer the services of a technical apparatus like the dumbwaiter (see section 6.1.1 in this book).[22]

The loss of confidence in humanoid media adds a new kind of silence to the dialogue between master and servant. The language used to address underlings becomes curt. The polished formulas employed at court give way to minimal orders. Communication, it seems, has turned into machine code. In 1850 William Thackeray boastfully claims, "We never speak a word to the servant who waits on us for twenty years."[23] After its eighteenth-century climax, the communication between masters and servants appears to have come to a standstill. As Bruce Robbins points out, "In the Victorian household, there is an impression of increased silence."[24]

The question is: what causes that silence? Something seems to have come between the traditional human-to-human interface. The shift from eavesdropping servant to dumbwaiter suggests a possible answer. It is precisely during the nineteenth century that services are transferred en masse to technical media. With their telematic, indirect, mediated communicative capabilities, the latter mark the turn from private conversation to depersonalized understanding. This gradual yet expansive transition may also explain why AskJeeves.com ultimately decided to abandon the servant metaphor.

But why focus on all the different aspects and functions of service domestics perform? Examining servants as information acquisition and distribution centers implies a certain analogy with search engines and their respective services. On the one hand, that analogy may show the extent of their knowledge—of search engines and servants alike. And, on the other hand, that parallel may serve to examine Jeeves's case in particular and test the soundness of that metaphor. The servants' epistemic privilege is partly derived from their activity as messengers; as literary narrators and mediating figures between hierarchies, they also possess vital insider information and remarkable investigative skills. All of these aspects—the collection, transmission, bundling, and reprocessing of information—suggest that servants operate not unlike Google's data search agents. Messenger [Bote] and bot are merely one small, but no less important, step apart. Virtual agents such as GoogleBot, Webcrawler, or Teoma (the AskJeeves searchbot) run through the internet at regular intervals—programmed to search for new information, which they then productively reprocess.

With the transfer of classic service functions to technical media and the shift from human to machine agents, the nineteenth century prepares the ground for the emergence of our trusted search engines. The notion of an information center has so far been considered only in terms of the structural correspondence between servants and search engines. But there is much more to it than a mere analogy: the couriers enter the channels, first in the form of telegraphic wires, then telephone cables and other electric transmission lines, which in turn become today's data cables. That process will be discussed in detail in chapter 5. With the transition of service from humans to things, the servant becomes a media-technical figure of knowledge, whose successors are still recognizable in the form of today's search bots.

2.2.2. Professional Invisibility

> A servant must behave as if he's not there.
> —Hermann Lenz, The Servant's Eyes, 1964

The software agents used by search engines are largely concealed from our eyes; their fleeting presence can be detected only upon close inspection. In other words, they satisfy one of the main conditions of modern service: their work remains invisible or hidden. That particular mode of operation has a long tradition. Virtual agents diversify their domain of activity—not unlike servants, who move out of the brightly-lit enfilades at court, and into the dark corridors of bourgeois homes. The increasing demand for household staff that accompanies the rise of the bourgeoisie during the eighteenth century also turns service into a mundane and obscure affair. At court, the presence of liveried servants was meant to function as a conspicuous display of power and glory; but once domestics transition into more modest households, the outward-oriented demand for representation gives way to a practical labor model. Within that new model, regular tasks such as serving dinner demand efficiency, not ceremony. As a consequence, a specific mode of service operation gradually develops: servants are required to go about their tasks and remain humbly inconspicuous at the same time. But that is not all. The subalterns' presence is rooted in a paradox: they are constantly presumed to be absent while being physically there. A good servant cannot be seen or heard. "He is a noiseless creature."[25] Or, as the *Golden Prague* hotel manager puts it, teaching Jan Dítě his first and foremost rule of service, while pulling his ear:

> You're a busboy here, so remember, you don't see anything and you don't hear anything. Repeat what I just said. So I said I wouldn't see anything and I wouldn't hear anything. Then the boss pulled me up by my right ear and said, But remember too that you've got to see everything and hear everything. Repeat it after me. I was taken aback, but I promised I would see everything and hear everything. That's how I began.[26]

Being required to pay more *and* less attention at the same time corresponds in turn to an oscillating degree of visibility. Contemporary educational institutions modeled after the classic English school for butlers still follow the principle according to which "A good servant is an invisible servant."[27] Jeeves is obviously also indebted to it. He unexpectedly "materializes"[28] by his master's bedside; and Bertie Wooster praises his inconspicuous manner and unobtrusive way of entering a space: "Jeeves floated noiselessly into the room."[29]

Until the mid-eighteenth century, the notion of the household equally refers to masters and servants.[30] But as soon as domestics become a distinct group with endless duties and few rights, a new metaphor arises, providing—along with 'amphibian,' 'server,' and 'agent' analogies—an appropriate description of their routine activities. What would be more fitting than calling their ineffable and ephemeral ways 'angel-like'—in modest recognition of that which typically goes unnoticed? Since the age of Goethe, domestics have often been named 'ministering spirits,' sometimes even by a paterfamilias like Goethe himself. Thus he urges Friedrich August Wolf to use his servant as a search engine: "One of your ministering spirits can look that up in a dictionary."[31] And while the privy councillor may have an additional reason to use that term—after all, one of his servants is called (Johann Ludwig) Geist[32] [spirit]—the formulation itself falls into two discursive traditions: one divine, the other occult.

One trajectory of the 'ministering spirit' can be traced as far back as the language of Christian angelology. The theological philosophy of high ecclesiastical dignitaries since Pope Gregory I (590–604), and their self-perception as the lowest of the Lord's servants, as "servus servorum Dei," have always been inflected by the rhetoric of humility and subservience. But that can hardly mark the actual origin of the servants' designation. The history of the subaltern as a ministering spirit finds its roots not in the Gospel of Matthew[33] but in the words of St. Paul's Epistle to the Hebrews regarding *angels:* "Are they not all ministering spirits, sent forth to minister for them who shall be heirs of salvation?" (Hebrews 1:14). Domestics stand much closer to these divine messengers than to the kind of representational authority exerted by even the humblest of popes. The explanation lies in the theological debate about "whether the angels have bodies naturally united to them"[34] or rather accomplish their many functions without a corporeal presence of their own. Governance is traditionally based on the principle of embodiment, whether by proxy or else by the doubling of a king's body via the signs of transcendent authority. But servants are transparent and ubiquitous like angels, serving their masters in an utterly inconspicuous manner. And because they are ignored, their bodies inevitably disappear. They carry out their work as if they were not there. Only their deeds count. That is what brings the angelic analogy home.

Although it lacks any divine or sublime connotations, the second trajectory can be traced even farther back in time. To the extent to which the good spirit, the daemon, and the winged genius may count as models for the image of the Christian (guardian) angel,[35] the designation of domestics as ministering spirits may also evoke the old tradition of household spirits, guardians, hobgoblins, and other supernatural helpers. Demonological treatises describe them as protectors of various tools and objects, for instance, of doors, light, or the hearth, whose maintenance passes on to domestics in the post-Enlightenment era. The qualities that allow hobgoblins and servants to quietly operate in the background, hidden from the eyes of their masters, follow the same criterion of invisibility applied to their heavenly correspondents. Not surprisingly, therefore, subalterns and house spirits are often identified with each other: in oral traditions; in literary contexts, for instance, in Henry James's *Turn of the Screw;*[36] or else in places like Goethe's Weimar residence, where domestics not only take care of the household but are also in charge of a considerable amount of the textual production.

Irrespective of its angelic or demonic genealogy, the 'ministering spirit' metaphor has concrete effects on the daily life of subalterns, reflected in at least two kinds of professional invisibility. The first is directly related to the organization of subaltern household work and its architectural configuration. Even if higher-ranked servants like butlers or valets act as mediators, connecting the underground to the world of the salon, the architectural contrast between upstairs and downstairs makes it unmistakably clear that the different classes are separated by a (deep) chasm, preventing the majority of the staff from being seen.

Still, particular types of servants, like stewards, lady's maids, and personal valets, can be regularly found in salons, orbiting around their masters. Here again there is a specific form of invisibility at work. Apart from the brief moments when they are given a direct order, they remain largely invisible to their masters. In accordance with a medium's typical mode of operation, domestics carry out their tasks (refilling tea cups, opening doors, etc.) *without being there.* Thus while executing orders they follow the rule that commonly applies to all media: be as transparent as light and as invisible as sound. Nothing appears to affect that state of transparency, not even during the times when the staff happen to be in their employers' line of vision. Their masters have long learned to simply see through them. Thus they remain suspended in a transitional state between alertness and sleepwalking; their place is usually in the background, behind their masters' backs. From there, they conduct all operations: moving chairs closer to the dinner table; serving the food; responding to various entertainment requests.

Mme Geoffrin et son domestique (1772), a work by the French painter Hubert Robert (1733–1808), perfectly illustrates both the salon society's need for distraction and its media solution. The lady of the house is comfortably seated in her armchair, passing the time with embroideries; donning an apron, her servant is standing at attention behind her, reading to his mistress but keeping out of her sight. The fire is lit, and there is a broom resting against a chair—a sure sign that, once the reading is done, the servant will resume his housework duties. For now, however, he is nothing but a voice. The act of reading is perfectly unadulterated: the subaltern becomes the medium of literature itself. It is as if the words can be heard from offstage, without causing any disturbance or disrupting the mistress's reverie with any visible gestures. The servant functions as a literary loudspeaker, slipping out of sight and vanishing into the text and behind his mistress's back.

But the fact that Madame Geoffrin's domestic can be seen in the picture at all means that a two-hundred-year-old verdict and its effects are slowly beginning to fade. The story of that verdict, disputing the status of the servant as a subject of artistic representation, begins with the so-called "father figure of servant paintings":[37] Paolo Caliari, also known as Veronese (1528–88). Faced with the display of busy underlings in Veronese's *Last Supper* (1573), the Holy Inquisition declares servants unfit for pictorial representation, at least when it comes to eschatological subjects. *The Last Supper* was thus renamed *The Feast in the House of Levi,* and servants remained largely outside the realm of painting. The one exception was history painting, where they continued to be featured as a common motif. William Hogarth and his servant portraits from around 1750 finally begin to restore the subaltern's aesthetic worth.[38] The compositions now feature domestics in typical poses, shown from behind, waiting in the background, going about their usual activities, or standing on the sidelines. Not unlike parasites, they are pictured lurking "in the midst of the beauty and bounty of someone else's display of riches."[39]

The professional invisibility of servants is reflected not only in the above-mentioned Catholic verdict but also in its discursive transmission. If subalterns are supposed to remain inconspicuous and stay out of the 'main action,' that requirement of absence corresponds to considerable gaps in the textual representation of service. Accounts written by servants are scarce. Nevertheless, there is quite a wealth of information *on* them—for instance, a large number of written complaints.[40] Although not thoroughly absent from textual sources, domestics are rarely present in person. Despite their obvious participation in situations and events, their existence seems difficult to prove. And before servants tentatively emerge as authors in the eighteenth century, works written by them are practically nonexistent. The main reasons for that state of affairs lie in the general population's poor literacy standards and the minimal interest of servants in matters of writing. Available source materials like personal accounts or other text documents pertaining to the everyday life of servants are therefore rather limited. Instead of firsthand accounts, one must rely on the help of a mediating authority: masters' rulebooks, memoirs,[41] diary entries, or literary discourse. At least until the nineteenth century the literary motif of the servant provides a basis for opinions about the demands, qualities, operations, and habits of domestics. Still, it is worth pointing out that the difference between real servants and their stage image is subject to various stereotypes and changing ideas about the roles they represent. Alienated and overdrawn, the domestic constantly appears as a surface of projection. In literary contexts, that surface often serves as a platform for political critique, for exposing misconceptions, and—more radically—staging a reversal of extant power relations via the topos of the world upside down (see section 3.7). From this standpoint, fictional and theatrical servant figures do not entirely match their historical counterparts. Given the fragmentary, incomplete nature of this textual tradition, the question remains: how can historiography reconstitute the invisibility of servants in a systematic fashion? One would need to shift the focus and engage with the actions of "indirect powers" (Carl Schmitt) in a similarly indirect manner. A systematic analysis would then need to examine the sideshows and backdrops, the secondary characters and all those figures that tend to escape historians' attention. In other words, looking for subalterns means looking at the margins.

Ideal servants are supposed to go about their tasks without coming into the picture. This sublimated form of invisibility can be summed up as a basic law of subalternity: servants must meet a paradoxical criterion of presence, which allows them to receive and follow orders; at the same time, they must behave as if they are absent. Thereby, they should be prevented from becoming participants in or agents of external knowledge. In order to avoid interfering with their masters' activities, any personal initiative is strictly forbidden. One of the basic features of servants (as well as of search engines) is their exceptional capacity for secrecy and discretion. Almost as a way of convincing himself of that, Wasik, the protagonist in Hermann Lenz's novel *The Eyes of the Servant*, declares, "A servant must behave as if he's not there."[42]

As an invisible Man Friday, the ministering spirit is always on the verge of crossing the line into the realm of a purely imaginary existence. Ministering spirits resemble messages rather than messengers. And they often cross that line as well. With their tendency to escape perception, they turn into a pure medium. And when no effort is spared to obliterate their existence, their ephemeral presence, escalating to the point of disappearance, reemerges as a literary double.[43]

Once their visual existence has been effaced, the only traces signaling the present absence of real domestics are olfactory markers: for instance, when the coachman has no time to clean himself up and brings the smell of horses from the barnyard into his master's house.[44]

There is one other question regarding the theoretical invisibility of servants that has not yet been addressed. The answers, however, must wait until the epilogue of this study. But we must ask: what do subalterns actually do when they are out of sight? What are they up to in their moments of rest, or when they linger in the servants' quarters below? Do they educate themselves by reading, as Rolf Engelsing[45] has concluded? Or do they drink to excess, as Ernest Turner has argued? Or maybe they do nothing at all? The answers must wait. Nevertheless, the next section will return to a central question: what kinds of spaces or interstices does the servants' productive invisibility open up?

2.2.3. The Economy of Servitude

The deep rift between the salon and the world below stairs manifests itself at the level of financial resources as well. A regular social occasion such as a family celebration or a more lavish Victorian soirée often costs hundreds of pounds; by contrast, the yearly wages of those whose work makes such events possible do not exceed a few pounds.[46] The steep gap does not lead merely to a lingering resentment among subalterns and a repressed bad conscience among employers. Even when nineteenth-century domestics migrate en masse to the industrial or private sectors, masters still do not seem to find it necessary to substantially change the rate of remuneration. Domestics are therefore forced to develop a system of additional earnings and thus increase the meager yearly amount they receive. They may slightly improve their financial situation with Christmas, baptism, and memorial ceremony bonuses, with money from occasional inheritances, or by secretly reaching into their employers' coffers. But the biggest source of additional income is the regular inflow of tips: no errand or purchase of new playing cards,[47] no trip to the market or opening of doors without the dispensation of small rewards to those who carry out such tasks. At a higher level, after an elegant soirée, for instance, such maneuvers follow a highly ritualized, unwritten code: accompanied by background music, the servants step out of the dimmed lights of the salon and form a line in the foyer. Each guest must now walk past them, placing a token of gratitude in their discreetly opened hands. Incidentally, the outstretched hand is a gesture that goes back a long way: at the end of an official visit, the English king would hand out money to his servants, who had to kiss his hand in return.[48] That gesture now takes on a life of its own; not unlike many other elements of service, it makes its way from the court to the bourgeois household, where the guests now assume the king's position and must follow the same procedure. Similar 'handshakes' have even led certain esteemed guests to refuse invitations. Depending on the number of servants involved, the sums of money could be quite considerable. "Lord Halifax is always teazing [*sic*] me to go down to his country house, which will cost me a guinea to his servants, and twelve shillings coach hire; and he shall be hanged first." Thus complains Jonathan Swift in a letter dated October 13, 1710, to Esther Johnson, a servant's daughter (and his future lover, known as 'Stella').[49] In *Directions to Servants,* Swift adopts a satirical tone in a passage that directly addresses stewards: "I confess your vails are but few, unless you are sent with a present or attend the tea in the country; but you are called Mr. in the neighbourhood, and sometimes pick up a fortune; perhaps your master's daughter."[50]

Their positions and command over interstitial spaces allow servants to develop a specific kind of economic logic. While patiently and invisibly waiting on guests, domestics can effortlessly tap into a rich informational resource. They only have to pay close attention. The dialogues they systematically overhear are then turned into economically and strategically valuable data. Masters have good cause to suspect servants of spying on their words. Prominent critics such as Daniel Defoe have described servants as carriers of capital from higher to lower classes. "Capital" also implies informational wealth in this case: domestics are most familiar with their masters' dealings and may use that knowledge for themselves and their own affairs.[51] Cold food scraps are not the only things servants bring back to their basements; hot stock market tips follow that same route. And while the guests are moving on to the dessert course, that valuable information is already on its way to the gambling parlors, carried by the subjects at the bottom of the hierarchy. News has long become a commodity, and information is assigned a value, either as direct profit or via an act of transfer to a third party. Initially, what appears to be at stake is a secondary system, a "housemaid's market,"[52] as it was called around the early twentieth century. And yet the mechanism lends autonomy to the servants' knowledge and—not unlike the Google and AskJeeves.com searchbots—ultimately transforms secondary into primary information.

The servant turned train magnate Jeames de la Pluche,[53] who owes his status to financial speculation, may be an exception, but all the wheeling and dealing at the bourse soon shows its effects. In the context of an increased demand for shares, even the modest sums earned by servants can contribute to stock market bubbles.[54] The stage preceding the burst of a financial bubble is precisely known in the world of finance as "a housemaid's market." In any case, one thing is certain: domestics who invest in and profit from such newly acquired knowledge transform the otherwise precarious relation between master and servant. Along with the stock market dealings discussed by Defoe in his *Compleat English Tradesman* (1725), there is also the matter of capital and ownership renegotiation. Indeed, relations of power and ownership between master and servant could potentially be reversed. Defoe even draws a parallel between subalterns and the currency exchanged, liberated from its original owner and free to circulate. Servants and currency are both free-floating signifiers,[55] no longer associated with a master. And as the market topos shows, the claim to ownership can now be transferred to subalterns. Ultimately, by transporting the masters' knowledge to the market and making use of it, servants gain a specific form of independence that frees them from the relations of service. The break with the classic structure of ownership, which coincides with the invention of paper money around 1700, redefines and destabilizes the relation between master and servant.[56] Things are starting to move, at least in one direction: upward. To the point where, as Defoe points out, the master himself may be forced out of business: "The diligent servant endangers his master; the greater reputation the servant gets in his business, the more care the master has upon him, lest he gets within him and worms him out of his business."[57] The takeover of the master's affairs is ultimately threatening since the servant's knowledge may itself be more dynamic, profitable, and effective. By obediently performing their duties, subalterns also become autonomous agents.[58]

The strategic claim on knowledge is a technique of authority. When servants know more than their masters and subalterns take possession of insider information, the question about who is in control can no longer be avoided. As far as Google and AskJeeves.com are concerned, the answer is clear: no one can rightfully claim to be in charge when typing something onto a screen. Analyzing, processing, and distributing information have long been relegated to the authority of the master of things: in other words, the authority of the servant.[59]

2.2.4. Institutionalizing Knowledge

The most important exception to the structural analogy between domestics and search engines such as Google or AskJeeves.com is the difference between the dissemination of knowledge and its centralization. For what good is an omniscient servant if his whereabouts are unknown? One subaltern does not an encyclopedia make. How, then, can one take advantage of domestics' collective knowledge if information is not gathered and channeled into predesignated locations from which it can subsequently be retrieved and selected? Where exactly are those locations, and how do they institutionally represent subaltern knowledge?

Following the thesis that servants are the actual masters of knowledge, the search for such spaces in the extended household model will lead not to the master's chambers but to the basement and the kitchen, where more than just the cooking is being done. The stove and the servants' table are informational trading centers where the news from upstairs and outside is channeled and discussed. "The general place of rendezvous, for all the servants, both in winter and summer, is the kitchen; there the grand affairs of the family ought to be consulted,"[60] Jonathan Swift expertly declares. The basement in particular is a place of busy and constant traffic: "The basement was not wholly without its disadvantages; it was pleasantly accessible to gossips, relatives, policemen, soldiers, traffickers in scraps, fortune-tellers and hangers-on of all kinds."[61] Space permitting, the foyers of the bourgeois homes serve the same purpose of informational exchange. Servants from various houses gather in these areas, not unlike the antechambers at court. And it is there, in the places inhabited by the "indirect powers"—to invoke Carl Schmitt's eloquent formulation—that the corridors converge to lead to the top.[62] Along that same path, one finds the first and second antechambers, with their ties to espionage, operated by valets as secret police commanders during Louis XIV's reign.[63] On the way out, the road inevitably leads past a barbershop,[64] which functions—and not just in literary contexts—as a topos of indiscretion, a clearinghouse of information.[65] If one's final destination is a public square, one can hire a porter—for instance, from the central train station in Vienna until recently—who not only knows his way around but can also offer several other services.[66] A certain Dr. Folkmann launches a so-called Servants' Institute in 1862, an agency aimed at outsourcing services which had until then been reserved to employed domestics. Folkmann offers "replacements for incapacitated servants"[67] and thus brings to Vienna the old European tradition of the servant-hiring office.

As opposed to Dr. Folkmann's institute, which specializes in short-term services, regular domestic agencies negotiate fixed, long-term contracts, typically for a year, or from Michaelmas to Candlemas. In Paris, offices that facilitate such contracts in exchange for a fee from both parties date back to the fourteenth century. Their services partly overlap with those of early modern search agencies.[68] In the countryside, servant fairs are regularly held, helping local farmers find itinerant laborers in search of seasonal work. As early as 1421, in Nuremberg, so-called suppliers [*Zubringerinnen*], preferably servant widows with expertise in the field, start facilitating various services: not only helping others fill vacant job spots but also policing the parties involved.[69] In the nineteenth century the occupation finally becomes a professional enterprise. Governments offer concessions to independent entrepreneurs who bring together demand and supply. But the semiofficial control aspect no longer applies. On the contrary, offices prefer to avoid close contact with the authorities and especially with the police. Among the most popular of its kind is the office founded by Henry and John Fielding in 1749. Apart from bringing domestics and employers together, their services include banking, real estate, insurance, trade, travel, transportation of goods, and brokerage. The Fielding brothers are men of literary and political success. Drawing on an essay by Michel de Montaigne,[70] they develop the notion of universal mediation according to which no talent should be wasted, no person unemployed or somehow overlooked. Employment agencies become a common sight in London. Finally, in 1815, a similar registry office opens its doors in Berlin, one of the first and best-known in Germany. Apart from such offices, the numerous small agencies around the turn of the century often operate without a license.[71]

Even more suspicious are the activities "hiring agents"[72] carry out on the side. "Since there were frequent complaints against suppliers as early as the sixteenth century, the Nuremberg city council imposed regulations on their activities in 1521 and 1525."[73] But neither such restrictions nor similar measures are in any way effective against those who push mostly young, inexperienced female servants into debt in order to have them pay back in a not too respectable manner.

The supplier, who delegates service by passing on the domestics to the clients, acts not only as a search agent but also as a go-between. Despite the somewhat one-sided attention to the client's needs, this kind of *postillion d'amour* is financially oriented toward restricting the length of transactions, so as to allow both sides to find new connections, in exchange for the appropriate price. Search engines like AskJeeves.com operate in a similar manner. They bring together clients and servers offering additional services like news, images, and films for commercial purposes. In such cases, however, fees are paid indirectly, via advertising.

Professional hiring offices prefer temporary contracts between clients and servants to long-term connections. The worse the fit and the more unproductive the encounter, the shorter the contract. In the best-case scenario, that situation implies a new set of transactions for the agent. But there are alternatives.

Hiring offices are an urban phenomenon. They are characteristic of large metropolitan centers, where keeping track of supply and demand possibilities proves quite difficult and where the only help available are often barely qualified. Personal recommendations are still the best option for filling well-paid, respectable jobs. Valets and experienced butlers occupy positions that require confidence and trust and are therefore preferably hired by word of mouth or, to use current network terminology, peer-to-peer techniques.

Certain servant types—butlers, for instance—are not even hired, but rather find their own jobs.[74] But in general the staff are organized into domestic networks, which allows for the smooth circulation of information. Jeeves, for example, is connected to a broadly ramified group of other servants. "[The butler] Brookfield happened to mention the contents of the note to me when he brought it. We are old friends."[75] This informational structure is linked to its own storage media. The cornerstone of London's Junior Ganymede Club, an exclusive association of butlers, valets, and gentlemen's gentlemen, is a book in which club members write down descriptions of their respective masters. No embarrassing details are spared. The entry for "Wooster B" is eighteen pages long—the most extensive of all.[76] And it might very well be that such entries facilitated the connection between Jeeves and Bertie Wooster in the first place and thereby helped further establish and maintain the peer-to-peer ties among the club's members. The logic of equal ranking also applies in the case of the networks formed of male servants with a military background. Former soldiers, recruits, and especially orderlies or journeymen make up a considerable part of the male staff.[77]

Just as butlers and military staff are integrated into broad networks that allow news to freely travel among their members, maids and female servants rely on similar structures that function both as professional hiring resources and informational channels. The nearby greengrocer operates precisely in this manner. "Their shops are sheer news stock markets; here, neighborhood gossip and information could be traded and exchanged."[78] The news often contains clues about which places may be in search of staff or where one should seek (or avoid) a job.

Two aspects are worth pointing out here. Leaving the free market to take a position implies a certain change of status. As Defoe had already shown with his poignant analogy, domestics may change their masters, but the relations of ownership per se do not change (as in the case of slaves). To a certain extent, servants remain their own masters, even though their power of decision is limited when duties are involved. Not unlike paper money, which no longer belongs to a specific owner, domestics are free-floating signifiers, as long as their work relation can be annulled at any point by both parties, and they can reenter the free market cycle of supply and demand. This is precisely why an institution such as a hiring agency is necessary. Akin to a bank, it facilitates both the circulation of jobs and its monetary equivalent.

But each new job implies an epistemic status change that may also be shown to function at a linguistic level. The etymological roots of *dingen* [to place someone in a position of service] and *dienen* [serve] most clearly point in that direction. When they are *verdingt* [placed], underlings lend themselves to a preestablished range of services. But despite the achievements of the French Revolution, they are thereby also subject to a specific form of *Verdinglichung* [objectification] which turns them from job-searching subjects into objects mechanically assisting their employers. The professional designation of hiring agents as *Verdinger* or *Hindinger*[79] [placers] offers further linguistic confirmation of that historical phenomenon.

Second, with the switch from peer-to-peer to client–server architectures, the scope of job placement models expands. The military staff agencies and the private networks of butlers and gentlemen's gentlemen remain local phenomena. Instead, the impersonal mode of operation practiced by hiring agencies reaches regional or even higher levels. For country girls and foreigners, hiring agencies are the first destination, since they give direct access to those kinds of connections which places like the greengrocer's or the Junior Ganymede Club only facilitate after extensive negotiations. But all have something essential in common: both small institutions like the local greengrocer and big businesses like the Berlin general hiring agency in the Jägerstraße are spaces of informational concentration and condensation, where domestics meet with requests from various employers. Inevitably, such environments become the centers of subversive knowledge.

So far, the structural analogy between yesterday's domestics and today's universal search engines seems justified. By all appearances, AskJeeves.com is more than an arbitrary designation, and the metaphor of the servant as information center has concrete historical parallels. Nevertheless, there are not merely connections but also discontinuities. The main difference, perhaps, lies with the question of operation range. Despite their virtual unity and fixed addresses, Google and AskJeeves.com do not have a specific location.[80] Their services are, however, globally oriented. In contrast, servants remain locally or regionally bound, even if, theoretically, their knowledge can be integrated into global networks. Early attempts to form servant associations, or agencies, unions, and newspapers catering to subalterns are indicators of such an international orientation.

The following section will examine the specific features of such acts of mediation. The movement between local and regional knowledge will be traced via a historical investigation centered on a unique type of subaltern, namely, the library attendant.

2.3. THE GO-BETWEEN

> We need mechanical subalterns.
> —Goethe to Christian Gottlob Voigt, May 1, 1807

Some homes are so vast and inscrutable they may seem like a miniature cosmos. Their impenetrability calls for special guidance not merely in matters of economy but also architecture. Contemporary museums offer audio guides or paper maps. But it is servants who are traditionally charged with taking someone around. And in the process, they may also agree to provide further information. It is said that upon arriving at Windsor Castle, a city in its own right, some guests would wander about for hours, hopelessly looking for the dining hall; others thought they were lost.[81] Without the servants' guidance and spatial knowledge, walking through the maze of passages that connect the mezzanine in the main wing to the *bel étage* in the north wing would seem an impossible feat. The subaltern functions as a cursor, a Charon, or mediator among various places, taking subjects to their destination. Within an alien system of order, it is the servant's local knowledge that holds the promise of orientation. But that function goes beyond the realm of the household. As a subaltern mode of operation, the servant's local knowledge raises the question of order in general, as it applies to various contexts: the knowledge housed in one place (the library), the places grouped in one location (the city), and, finally, the locations gathered in one symbolic order (the catalogue).

And what could come closer to linking space, knowledge, order, and orientation than a mnemotechnical reference, a connection between an idea and a location: in other words, a commonplace? The topos of situatedness has already been extensively used; still, it is essential to this argument since the decisive element in this context, namely, knowledge, has been systematically disregarded until now. Not surprisingly, knowledge turns out to be a highly inconspicuous presence, operating according to the categorical requirement of professional invisibility. The following pages will therefore propose yet another excursus. The path will not lead to a gala dinner at Windsor Castle but rather retrace the footsteps of General Stumm von Bordwehr, as he enters the Imperial Library's holy of holies in search of the "finest idea in the world" and the system of order that delivers it. At first, Stumm is accompanied by a benevolent librarian. As the visitor somewhat justifiably assumes, this "fellow lives among these millions of books, he knows each one, he knows where to find them, he ought to be able to help me."[82] But Stumm is mistaken, and not only in this particular respect. It quickly turns out that the search will not result in finding a "bibliography of bibliographies."[83] The obliging librarian soon disappears, but rescue is already in sight:

As I'm standing there, totally at a loss, an old attendant who must have been watching us all along pads around me respectfully a few times, then he stops, looks me in the face, and starts speaking to me in a voice quite velvety, from either the dust on the books or the foretaste of a tip: "Is there anything in particular, sir, you are looking for?" he asks me. [. . .] If you'll just tell me, sir, what subject you're interested in at the moment, sir. [. . .] I swear the man sounded so sensible and knew so much about what was inside these books that I gave him a tip and asked how he did it. And what do you think?[84]

As opposed to librarians, library attendants can also provide content information. They not only know where to find things; they also quite literally operate a free summary service, by conversing with library users about the books they deliver. And the prospect of a tip further enhances their perceptiveness. While librarians diligently follow the traditional principles of library science and give up on all personal reading and writing prospects,[85] attendants open up the path to knowledge, in an empirical fashion, both for themselves and others. Not unlike the narrator in Bohumil Hrabal's *Too Loud a Solitude,* who gets his education, against his will,[86] via his daily work at the wastepaper press, the library attendant acquires his knowledge through chatter. General Stumm concludes, "And now I have to face the fact that the only people with a really reliable intellectual order are the library attendants."[87]

As Musil's attendant proves, intellectual order is linked to concrete places, in this case, to the location of books on the shelves. And as General Stumm discovers, real book knowledge has long eluded (chief-) librarians. Instead, the information about finding an item has been effectively and discreetly passed on to two other kinds of authority: the catalogue, the search tool that has exclusively kept vast numbers of texts in order since the late eighteenth century; and a specific technique of accessibility, linking the written order to its actual position on the shelf. Apart from the catalogue, the library attendant alone knows about the actual organization and location of thoughts. The attendant is the transfer medium granting access to books, translating the virtual order of the catalogue into the endless stacks of texts, which, to quote Stumm von Bordwehr, are "no worse than a garrison on parade."[88]

2.3.1. Pacing and Counting

Before the nineteenth century most libraries do not employ catalogues to find the right books on specific topics. For the most part, catalogues are used as administrative tools to perform regular inventory checks or test the availability of a particular item. Rather, the direct access to ideas is facilitated by the systematic order of books on the shelves, and especially by a well-informed librarian who knows where everything can be found. A librarian's key aid is, first and foremost, his memory, which links—not unlike ancient mnemotechnics—the location of books on the shelves with the topics they treat. "Among the skills that cannot be neglected," writes Friedrich Adolf Ebert in *View of a Librarian's Education* in 1820, "suffice it to mention the practice of memory. The faithful and thorough recollection of titles, names and numbers is an indispensable quality in the librarian's work. But this largely implies the confident use of local memory. Woe to that librarian who needs to have a catalogue at hand at all times!"[89]

The spread of literacy during the eighteenth century, the secularization of monastic libraries, and the fast-paced expansion of the book market lead to a rapid rise in library acquisitions. The "reading mania," the driving force behind the growing book production, is no longer exclusively associated with affluent female readers. Not merely the salon society have plenty of time on their hands to spend in the company of books. As Rolf Engelsing points out, the selection of and demand for reading material in eighteenth-century borrowing libraries is determined by a close interaction between masters and servants. At first, both groups prefer religious educational material; the higher classes then turn their attention to secular texts during the nineteenth century. As for the lower levels of the hierarchy, "a significant portion of servants still hold on to traditional reading materials, methods and mentalities."[90] Irrespective of individual interests, book production massively expands. Libraries are compelled to find solutions. In this context of informational excess, the local memory of librarians appears to have reached its limits. Librarians use memory aids: they refer to call numbers, which then lead to the thematically organized stacks. The relation between the actual stack and the virtual catalogue list forms a double order system, which is, in turn, sustained via two mechanisms: on the one hand, by means of a call number, which links the catalogue entry to its respective location on the shelf and, on the other hand, by means of a library attendant, as the sole agent delegated to actually bring the two together.

The call number gives a book its address, both in the virtual catalogue and on the shelf. It forms a link between theory and practice, between paper index and the actual location in the library. A catalogue could therefore be defined as a double bookkeeping system: there is an inventory list (debit); and the catalogued call numbers *leading directly to the books* in the repository (credit). Something akin to a postal address is required to locate such volatile objects as books. "With the aid of a simple notation, such as a house number," the call numbers "indicate the shortest path to the desired book."[91] The analogy is not just a mere metaphor. Rather, it draws attention to the close historical relation between registering books and houses, or, rather, their inhabitants. Within two short decades (1760–80), libraries everywhere, and in Vienna in particular, must reorganize their systematic shelving order due to rising book numbers. Instead, they will use mobile index card catalogues, operated by call numbers and servants. Precisely around the same time, the city of Vienna introduces yet another cataloguing mechanism, namely, the systematic registration of the population in the so-called 'conscription of souls' [*Seelenconskription*]. The process involves nothing less than assigning a number to each and every house in the city. Through a royal decree issued by Her Majesty Maria Theresa on Christmas Eve 1770, Vienna becomes one of the first cities in Central Europe[92] to introduce house numbers. The decision is not meant to help lost travelers find their way; rather, it deals with the shortage of *k. u. k.* military recruits, by supporting the authorities in their effort to enlist and identify them in a sea of houses.

Prior to the first number system application in 1770, one can rely only on Ebert's "local memory" to navigate around. Not unlike a systematic library catalogue, the nameless lanes are grouped by trades and guilds. But not even the best of memories can cope with the late eighteenth-century book flood and locate things without more precise aids. The 'conscription of souls' aims to symbolically monitor the potential location of (runaway) recruits. Similarly, the call number–catalogue combination introduces a new logic of virtual access to books. The transition from a search method based on real books in the repository to the higher order of the catalogue also results in a new type of configuration. To handle books during a publishing boom, or recruits during a military crisis, one requires an exclusively mobile system: a catalogue that no longer administers its objects in the form of bound books but rather by means of portable slips of paper.[93]

Due to catalogues, the question of locating books is no longer directed at the systematic shelving order but at the symbolic order of indexes. But the actual mediation between symbolic and real order is by no means canceled out or rendered superfluous. Libraries cannot survive without servants yet. As long as the basic rules of direction are followed, the catalogue would seem to satisfy the need for orientation, not unlike a local informant pointing a thirsty customer to the closest coffee shop. Libraries would no longer require local memory. But, as General Stumm had predicted, for the time being—and quite a while longer— all (there is) is theory.

2.3.2. In Praise of the Library Clerk

> Navigare necesse est [To navigate is necessary].
> —Gnaeus Pompeius Magnus

A study that aims to reclaim the historical relevance of subalterns must inevitably resort to "praising the servant," a rather obscure discourse despite its presence throughout "the entire course of library history."[94] A new career path is introduced around the turn of the century: a library clerk position that primarily involves writing. Prior to 1900 the library staff falls into two distinct groups. First, the specially trained and partly highly educated librarians (consider Leibniz and Lessing or their prodigious descendants, like Borges) with official titles such as "second under-librarian":[95] they are the certified scientific experts and professors. And then, there are 'library workers,' or 'library attendants,' as they are called from roughly 1750 to 1920: they are the almost universally deployable lower clerks, the no-less-obscure post–World War I 'library aids.'[96]

In the scene imagined by Musil, it is the uneducated clerk rather than the learned librarian who knows what books contain. How can that be? For one thing, librarians follow the principles developed during the early days of library science at the start of the nineteenth century: namely, the law of "literary self-denial and disinterestedness," meaning "no production of literary works,"[97] or, simply put, the absolute interdiction to write. The librarian thus becomes the administrative expert and organizer of an institution that operates almost exclusively on the side of theory. "Library science is uniquely distinct," argues Musil's character, a lecturer in library science. And in that, he seems to follow rather too strictly Friedrich Adolf Ebert's prescriptions. Moreover: "Anyone who lets himself go and starts reading a book is lost as a librarian. He's bound to lose perspective."[98] No writing or reading allowed. That is the rule to which the library expert must conform.

If the most learned among library employees must forgo basic cultural techniques such as reading and writing, then the question is: what, precisely, allows servants to have direct access to knowledge, as Musil had suggested in the section about the old library clerk? It should be noted, however, that servants' reading and writing skills had considerably improved since the mid-eighteenth century, more than one would initially assume. Satirical renditions of servants humming, not folk songs but opera arias, and butlers turning out to be walking encyclopedias[99]—Jeeves is no exception here—may be exaggerations. But the binary logic according to which culture and breeding are strictly located 'upstairs,' while 'downstairs' is where only the cooking takes place is at best questionable. Consider Johann Christian Troemer, the figure behind Lessing's

Ricaut in *Minna von Barnhelm*,[100] who published his autobiographical travel narratives in 1731; or the Parisian lackeys during the baroque era, who allegedly took to writing and reading newspapers out of sheer boredom;[101] or the claim that literacy levels among servants may be higher than among the intelligentsia;[102] in short, there seems to be sufficient evidence to conclude that servants—at least the most ambitious among them—are the actual scholars. Servants' autobiographies are no longer a novelty by around 1800. Inspired by literary models such as Alain Le Sage's *History of Gil Blas de Santillana* or Diderot's *Jacques the Fatalist and His Master,* the first detailed life account of a library attendant is published in 1822. The author is Johann Christoph Sachse, a man from Thuringia, who had been employed at the ducal library in Weimar under the supervision of a certain well-known privy councillor.[103]

A library attendant's many tasks include stoking the fire, cleaning, stamping, and marking book spines, retrieving call numbers, providing occasional help with cataloguing, and, obviously, collecting and returning items in circulation. In this fashion, servants can identify each book in the system; in other words, they know where books can be found. Still, that does not help them figure out *what* those books contain. What *does* help, however, is talking to library users about the delivered items and thus quite literally operating a free summary service. Not the librarian but the servant is the trustworthy interlocutor, the person one seeks for a consultation, not unlike a doctor: "I discussed that with my library attendant,"[104] explains Stumm von Bordwehr, as a way of summing up his conversation. But that aspect hardly covers all the attendant's functions and merits. "He accomplishes much more."[105]

A further task is "sending overdue notices to tardy readers."[106] Sachse has to do that too. Like all of Goethe's servants, he is also in charge of bookkeeping. But there is more. Overdue books must be directly collected from the reader's home. "He must run many errands: bring the borrowed books to the elderly and retrieve other books from tardy readers."[107] Thus Paul Raabe about Johann Christian Helms (1713–84), a Wolffenbüttel librarian who performed his job diligently for forty-two years, until his death.[108] What may at first seem to be an average service task[109] is in reality an indispensable cultural technique: without it, no book can find its way back to the shelf and no messenger can arrive at his destination.

A servant acts not only as a messenger but also as a medium, conveying information via a long-established communication channel. Additionally, he performs translating duties, linking address lists to real locations. Thereby he gains unique access to both texts and people, demanding overdue items, sending notices, or delivering books. Such tasks are grounded in a particular cultural technique, namely, navigation. And it is servants, more than any other group, even within the space of the library, that most assiduously employ it during the nineteenth century. One of the librarian's main activities involves cataloguing and facilitating the symbolic access to books via written catalogue lists and bibliographies. As opposed to him, the library attendant operates in the realm of the real. That is to say, he is as comfortable around shelves as on the street. Cast in an ocean of movable items—whether books or people—he alone knows the route, like an experienced pilot. But first, the destination needs to be set; in other words, the messenger requires an address.

To assign an address means to connect a virtual place within the symbolic order of a list with a real location, whether on the shelf or the street. Starting at least around 1800, library attendants can take advantage of at least two parallel techniques of virtual access. First, with the introduction of card catalogues, libraries acquire a tool that helps master the flood of books. Now each book must be assigned a call number or an address that guarantees a fixed and simultaneously mobile location within an ever-changing order. And, second, the new urban numbering system ensures that neither slow readers nor resistant recruits can go amiss in the sea of numberless houses. The two address systems—house numbers and card catalogues—merge around 1800: books and soldiers may no longer remain ephemeral subjects. The medium connecting the two is the library servant, as long as access is provided via analog systems. Finally, there is yet another close link between recruits and library attendants, but that aspect can be mentioned only in passing. In Prussia at first and later throughout the German Empire, library attendants are primarily recruited from the ranks of the military staff.[110] They are "sub-officers who have served for twelve years or are completely incapacitated";[111] but despite their physical impediment, they are quite familiar with their own kind.

2.3.3. Mind Mapping

One last question remains: how do servants navigate through space? How do they find a specific address? During the initial training period, they still require something akin to a nautical map; in the absence of an audio guide, so to speak, they may carry around a guide of the city—or the library. With increasing routine, orientation aids are soon replaced with a mental map. In other words, what helps servants find their way among books or around the city is the tried and true mnemotechnic method, or, to put it in Ebert's terms, the skill of 'local memory.' Or, to take things a step further: library attendants are paradigmatic figures connecting two types of address space via a media-technical operation: their service demands that the order of books and the order of houses be linked with each other. The coupling of libraries and homes is performed via library attendants and their local memory. Following the virtual cataloguing principles of nineteenth-century library science, only library attendants—not librarians—have access to the routine demanded by Ebert: namely, getting to *know* the library by taking daily walks among the shelves.

As Evert puts it, one should "thoroughly acquaint himself with the real and current state and arrangement of the library, and diligently practice the daily tasks of dispatching. [. . .] he should get to know the library in its smallest details [. . .] by its external features [. . .] only thereby may he acquire a real and long-lasting local memory, as well as all sorts of observations which make him more skillful in the practice of his profession and confer upon him that kind of practical sense and eye which leads, unites and mediates among the various knowledges and abilities, which are imperative for a true and rich professional life."[112]

Ebert's recommendations concern not library attendants but librarians and their education. But librarians cannot comply with such advice. Only the servants' local memory, liberated for the hardship of cataloguing, can serve the task of exploring the library's ordering system and thereby gain concrete access to real information.

Unsurprisingly, whenever they praise servants, library histories invoke the attendants' indispensable services and especially the achievements of their 'local logic.' The champion of the thesis that servants are the *conditio sine qua non* of a library's epistemic growth is Johann Christian Helms, the Wolffenbüttel library attendant during Lessing's times. One could also mention Jakob Friedrich Peterson (1789–1859), the "old Uhlan"[113] of the university library in Bonn, without whose "excellent local memory no book"[114] could be found.

The library attendant uniquely represents the parallel development of two logics of address (call number and house number), at the point of intersection between library and city. He links two distinct types of memory space, which overlap only due to his professional position. The attendant is a vigilante that reorganizes misplaced items, finds hidden objects, and reclaims them for the library. He alone has the details on both the location and the content of ideas, since he helps open up the paths of knowledge. He has authority over the practical access to information, since he has two kinds of local memory at his command. Without his constant intervention no important idea returns to its predestined place, let alone to the reader. The servant is a medium and a messenger, a guide and translator between the real and the symbolic, between the hand and the brain; as he moves back and forth between catalogue and shelf, he becomes a mediator between the theory and practice of libraries. As Leyh's *Handbook of Library Sciences* states, praise for servants echoes through the entire course of library history.[115]

2.3.4. From Messenger to OPAC

As a messenger and a 'stacker,'[116] the library attendant is the sole authority that successfully links two distinct types of address space: both virtual and real. But where would one find library attendants today? The transition from 'local memory' to book or card catalogue marks a step toward a higher form of organization and an ongoing reorientation toward virtual reality. Its trajectory can be followed from the era of the first card catalogues to the times of the electronic index, with its reorganization of real and virtual domains. The faithful book servant seems to fall by the wayside with the gradual informational takeover of the catalogue. Unless, of course, the library attendant also takes a virtual turn—which is precisely what may be the case: with the shift of library services toward virtuality, the servant too enters the digital channels.

But what does that actually mean? Following the principle of professional invisibility, library attendants have been slipping out of sight ever since General Stumm von Bordwehr's times. The question is: which of their functions are now translated into digital commands and electronic services? And who administers the addresses of readers and texts in the face of a rapidly advancing flood of information? The issue of agency at least seems clear: one does not need to leave one's home office to visit a library. If readers no longer need to actually walk into the "treasuries of the human spirit" (Leibniz), then no one has to remove books from shelves or make house calls when users fail to return them on time. Instead, everything seems to be digitally available. The modern headquarters of that highly integrated informational network has an odd name, which not accidentally recalls the invisible, 'opaque' quality of subalterns at work: OPAC, the Online Public Access Catalogue. All paths converge there.

The era of the library card catalogue lasts from the end of the eighteenth until the second half of the twentieth century. While the first, hesitant attempts at online information retrieval date back to 1954, no concrete initiatives to automate the library with the aid of electronic systems are launched before the early sixties. The first OPACs are finally introduced in 1974 by Ohio State University's new Online Computer Library Center (OCLC) as well as by the Research Libraries Group, a cluster uniting the largest libraries on the U.S. East Coast.[117] Librarians, engineers, and readers alike seem highly skeptical of the new technology during its lengthy trial period. End users, who seemingly prefer the good old card catalogue system, react with respectful reservation, if not outright rejection.[118] According to library employees, the extravagant machines are difficult to operate—the PC era is still a decade away—and their applicability is highly questionable given their price and complicated use. Especially when it comes to small, local book collections, the electronic turn is "an action tantamount to renting a Boeing 747 to deliver a bonbon across town"[119]—as a particularly skeptical library specialist put it. Despite all the skepticism, the electronic translation of the system of knowledge and the transformation of the library attendant into the OPAC as a "true local information center"[120] cannot be stopped. But as the terminology already suggests, the turn from book servant to electronic service does not imply a categorical shift; subjects are not actually transformed into databases. The road leading from *library servant* to OPAC follows a rigorous process of development. From a technical standpoint, the OPAC is nothing but a highly diligent *library server,* available at all times, 24/7, at a specific address: for instance, stabikat.staatsbibliothek-berlin.de or www .europeana.eu.

What are the main steps in the transfer from the work performed by library servants to the performance of electronic services? The first stage in that process is the convergence of previously disparate postal routes. Eighteenth-century library servants would use mnemotechnical devices to keep track of the (still) manageable number of books and readers; thereby, they were able to reclaim each and every overdue book by calling on distracted readers. But at some point that practice becomes impossible. The overdue notice and its delivery are transferred to the professional messaging agency known as the postal service, launching a hybrid configuration wherein a nonelectronic, address-based network takes over the servant's previous job. The library is thereby linked to an external communication system that had already been involved in bibliotechnical operations. But the transfer of library services to the post office results not only in altering the notion of space but also in removing the subject from the channel of communication. The task of sending messages is now assigned to a heterogeneous, universal network. Overdue notices are no longer taken straight to the tardy readers, but to the post.

With the transfer of the address system to a new network and the spatial limitations imposed on the servants' work, library attendants have to restrict their activity to book storage spaces. And yet, not unlike Kafka's doorkeeper, they continue to regulate the access to knowledge directly from there. They alone decide whether a book should be removed from the shelf or delivered. It is up to them to say which texts should be brought to readers. In the absence of other book retrieval mechanisms, conveyor belts or fully automated storage systems, library attendants are still in charge of knowledge by linking the catalogue and the textual inventory. Thereby, they also assume a significant level of authority. According to an old anecdote, Michel Foucault insisted on having his books at the Bibliothèque Nationale exclusively chosen by library assistants and thus getting material uniquely based on the predefined order of the catalogue. Once activated as a randomizer, the library servant will indirectly determine the theory of knowledge itself.

Librarians' anxieties notwithstanding, card catalogues finally reach the wider public in the early 1900s. Thus begins the short-lived era of the index card and the paper slip as a mobile library information technology.[121] Meanwhile, servants continue to stay out of sight, in the invisible areas between the circulation desk and the shelves. The gradual spread of OPACs and card icons on the first graphic user screens marks the beginning of the age of (home) computers. According to Charles Hildreth's classification,[122] the first generation of OPACs was nothing but a virtual simulation of the card catalogue. In the 1990s a second generation rendered those early systems more flexible and surpassed the card catalogue by introducing multimedia tools, intuitive user guidelines, and finely tuned search options.

But, as Hildreth points out, it was only the third generation[123]—the so-called E3OPAC—that successfully turned the catalogue into a total information center, by linking bibliographies with digitized texts, indexes, reviews, journal articles, images, and audio files. Ultimately, the aim is to expand the individual information centers, merge their databases with even larger networks, and thus integrate local into global configurations. In short, knowledge is institutionalized as a total network infrastructure. The online fusion of library and postal network leads to a few highly interconnected domains of information distribution like worldcat.org or books.google.com[124] that expand their range and claim to universality.

Retrieving journal articles or books directly via OPAC frees the catalogue from its ties not only to specific libraries but also to the concrete, bound, real, fetishized book-object. From now on, readers no longer need to concern themselves with the location of a particular volume, be it three rooms down the aisle in the stacks or on a different continent. Neither readers nor librarians are aware of its actual storage place. Each request via OPAC is a request for remote access to data; the item's actual location remains unknown. And once no one needs 'real' books anymore, the digital turn also eliminates the stacking operator function.

Such changes may signal the end of the library and the library attendant. Still (or, to put it less optimistically, *and yet*), that is a hypothetical formulation. If overdue notices and bibliographies—let alone texts—have turned virtual, and the paths to knowledge lead to places like Google Book Search, AskJeeves.com, or Google Scholar, that is because library attendants have already relocated to the realm of the symbolic. Each of the above-named tasks is processed via a server. No notice is issued without the digital shadow of library attendants and their house visits in the background. Nowadays, it is the Mail Delivery Agent announcing, "You've got mail." The library sends the overdue notice to an institutionalized order of knowledge.

Last but not least: digital copies still bear the imprint of the servant's touch. The library attendant still inhabits the real. A function failure sometimes uncovers what usually remains hidden: the contour of the subaltern's *invisible hand* quietly doing its work. When the system breaks down, there is a temporal glitch, an untimely signal, and the hand is immortalized on the image that should display only letters.

Every turn of a page, every digitized sentence mark a further reduction of the library attendants' work, a further erosion of their many responsibilities. Within the realm of the real, their end seems nigh. But in reality, servants continue to work and take their time doing it. The last library attendant will still be around for a while.

2.4. MEDIATION: BETWEEN VALET AND PDA

A subaltern's act of service is linked to a specific kind of disposition: not necessarily in the sense of a certain work ethic—which would certainly be welcomed by superiors—or a personal attitude—a much less desirable prospect from a master's perspective. Rather, service is associated with a particular kind of situatedness: a systematic place in the middle, between masters and things, utilized, manipulated, processed, and placed under the servant's care. From this midway position servants migrate into a state of professional invisibility, somewhere between absent presence and present absence. The servant's place is systematically situated in an opaque, impalpable interspace. That is the domain from which the subaltern emerges to mediate among various agents.

The current chapter has defined the servant as an information center: starting with the discreet butler or the nameless library attendant; moving on to the esteemed gentleman's personal gentleman, as portrayed by Reginald Jeeves; and, finally, the affable representative of AskJeeves.com and the OPACs at various national or provincial libraries. All of these agents of information retrieval and distribution share a distinct mode of knowledge mediation, whether they turn out to be human, like Jakob Friedrich Peterson or the anonymous man Friday from Dr. Folkmann's Servants' Institute, or nonhuman, like a library server, a search bot, or web server: what matters is that they all occupy an inconspicuous intermediary position that complies with the principle of mediation.

The library servant and OPAC, the library server; a butler called Jeeves and a digital search engine named AskJeeves.com: at first, such historically and categorically disparate actors seem to have little in common beyond a certain nominal resemblance. Such terminologies, however, are not arbitrary; rather, they point to a structural correspondence, which allows one element to unfold from the other. But how does the transformation from servant to server, from human servant to digital service actually happen, and what are its intermediary steps? That question will be answered with the help of Bruno Latour's notion of technological mediation or delegation in its four different senses.

The first is the *interference* of various operators. When Actor 1 (General Stumm) discovers he will not reach his desired goal (finding the finest idea to impress Diotima) without making a detour, his original "program of action, the series of goals and steps and intentions"[125] must necessarily be translated into a new goal. Stumm therefore appeals to Actor 2 (the librarian), who leads him to the catalogue room but then leaves him without providing any suggestions. Actor 3, the "bibliography of bibliographies," also amounts to nothing, and the program must be changed again. Actor 1 now resorts to Actor 4 (the library servant). Thereby, the general manages to—literally—book or recruit his way to knowledge, not via a librarian or a bibliography but a walking dictionary, in the form of a servant. Or rather: Stumm is the one recruited by the servant. Drawing on his many conversations with various readers, the attendant learns about their epistemic priorities. And from such deductions emerges Actor 5: an analog search engine made up of a demanding general, a knowledgeable servant, but also catalogue lists and endless rows of books. *Composition* is therefore the second meaning of technological mediation. "The prime mover of an action becomes a new, distributed and nested series of practices."[126] Such interferences create a new construct, a hybrid in the shape of an analog search engine made up of humans and nonhumans alike.

The third sense of mediation is the *"folding of time and space,"*[127] a central concept in Actor-Network Theory (ANT) as developed by Latour and others. In other contexts the terms used are "blackboxing" and "punctualization":[128] neither the 'mute' general chatting with the library attendant nor the 'mute' user interacting with an OPAC via a screen understands the complex hidden processes that ensure the system's technological configuration and flux of information. In the eyes of Actor 1, the servant and the OPAC both function like a 'black box.' The internal interplay of networks and the temporal and spatial transmission processes merge, rendering "the joint production of actors and artefacts entirely opaque."[129] Normally, Actor 1 would have no knowledge of the fact that both the library servant and the OPAC resort to other networks to deliver the desired information. As long as everything functions as expected, the nested processes escape his attention. The nested actors remain invisible, despite their effectiveness. And yet Actor 4 (the library attendant) resorts to other actors, such as (electronic) networks and (postal) addresses. In order to access knowledge, Actor 4 recruits a technological infrastructure. Conversely, one could also say: the infrastructure recruits him. The attendant enters the digital channels; his service is taken over by electronic entities, and the epistemic domain turns virtual. These interactions give rise to a new actor: a digital search engine, at the intersection of various nodal points, online catalogues, librarians, readers, screens, publishers' databases, and assistants armed with protective gloves. All of these, in turn, form a new construct, a hybrid or collective of humans and nonhumans, assigned with a new set of goals.

Finally, the fourth meaning of mediation—"Techniques modify the matter of our expression, not only its form"[130]—accounts for the turn of Actor 4 into an OPAC. The shift from library servant to library server coincides with the change of the mediating agency. Agency is passed on from humans to nonhumans, but the goal, namely, the request for information, as well as the program, that is, the answers provided, stays the same. The command ("Give me the idea") is promptly followed by its execution via the analog/digital search engine. This transformation consists "not only (as with previous examples) [of] a shift in the definition of goals and functions, but also a change in the very matter of expression."[131] The delegation of the act of mediation from humans to machines is subject to material change. The "act of transportation has been shifted down,"[132] therefore also into the humble servants' data vaults below. In that sense the shift signals a process of reification, which often goes hand in hand with the anthropomorphization of the nonhuman entities. That is precisely why AskJeeves.com continued to use, for ten whole years, the logo of the affable butler, pretending to answer the users' requests in natural language.

The downward move and change in the hierarchy of subalternity are linked to a turn to objecthood. The process also brings about a temporal and spatial reorientation. The principle of representation is followed here as well: the OPAC becomes a digital placeholder. Consequently, the location of traditional library assistants turns virtual. Not unlike books, they are dispersed, universally accessible, spread across a multitude of network nodes. For the time being, library attendants continue to walk around the stacks moving books around. But even that transmission path threatens to be taken over by digital channels and their networks.

Whereas traditional library assistants follow strictly regulated working hours, the present-day, 'silent' library users[133] can place requests without any temporal restrictions. "Through shifting down another combination of presence and absence becomes possible."[134] Following the rule of total availability, the OPAC is always 'on.' Unless there is any maintenance work to be done, the system diligently responds to each and every command, 24/7. Its service continues without interruption.

There are restrictions, however, even within the digital domain, as shown in Jeeves's case. After a decade of faithful service, the anthropomorphic, comically dressed butler figure vanishes. Since 2006, instead of natural language, the system uses simple commands. The subjective tone has been abandoned, and service has been delegated downward. The turn to objecthood forces readers to address their requests to a mute / dumb waiter that can also supply them with answers.

The technological transfer of inquiries to nonhumans, which triggers the transformation of the library subaltern into the OPAC, is only one aspect of a much broader process. This is not just the account of a unique structural correlation or a single act of delegation from a humanoid service subject to a service hybrid. The process of delegation is not restricted to the prehistory of contemporary search engines but is, rather, illustrative of a broad media-technical development, whose horizon stretches well beyond search engines.

During the Victorian era the dialogue between master and servant is silent; the messaging services and the transmission of news are relocated to technical media, like the telegraph and the telephone, as a *conditio sine qua non* of the internet. This shift marks a first step toward the total desubjectification of services and their transfer to other networks and hybrid collectives, for instance, telecommunications, which remain largely hidden from the eyes of their users. Such virtualized spheres, however, teem with servants, in the form of mail, FTP, and web servers. Those are the new locations of yesterday's servants, the places where subalterns can reconnect with their own kind: library servants, butlers, valets, messengers, and other domestics.

The digital turn does not presuppose the end of the servant. Following a series of displacements and translations, subalterns return as personal digital assistants and reenter, in the form of new devices (BlackBerry, iPhone, Kindle, subnotebook), the circuit of worldwide server networks and search engines. As a reminder of their prehistory, external interfaces may still feature someone like Wodehouse's Jeeves. At the same time, personal digital assistants also signal the opposite trend: the resubjectification of service objects. The knowledge derived from such instruments includes classic search functions as well as access to cultural content, in other words, the traditional media of knowledge, a universe of texts in digital form. Yesterday's servants who would pass the time reading technical literature, a play by Schiller,[135] or "some improving book"[136] before going to bed, like Jeeves, have returned as Google Books, Google Scholar, and the maps of AskJeeves.com. There is no need, therefore, to bid the servant farewell or to ban the image and the name of a gentleman's personal gentleman from the interface of a search engine. Whether domestic or digital, with or without gloves, the PDAs are both the past and the future of our information service society.

Postscript: In March 2009 AskJeeves.com decided to bring Reginald Jeeves's friendly face back into business, at least for the users of its British branch.

Chapter 3 In Waiting

The worker waits; the master keeps people waiting.
—Robert Walser, "Masters and Workers," 1928

This book is not a universal history of servants. An overview of the literary subaltern alone would fill several volumes. But if we assume the master–servant relation as its central element and trace its precarious—partly hidden, partly manifest—power configuration through the ages, a literary history of the servant would at least imply the following: a survey of the three forms—lyric, epic, and dramatic—each defined by its epoch and linguistic area, tracing the transformation of figures, their forms of manifestation and changing functions. In seventeenth-century literature, servants are still conspicuously absent.[1] In German baroque literature, subalterns are merely fleeting, transitory, insignificant apparitions. No one pays attention to them; they do not seem to be worth the trouble. Domestics occupy the offstage spaces as minor figures that only accidentally share the limelight with the main characters and their affairs. They clear the tables of the rich and now and then get ahold of a few crumbs. They are ordered to hold themselves back and largely dwell in (or, indeed, keep to) the shadowy or dark places of history.[2] And yet they have long occupied—especially in literature—an essential role: subalterns function as barometers of social and literary relations;[3] from behind the scenes their inconspicuous activity suggests general trends and moods; or, as in the case of Eurykleia in the *Odyssey,* they intervene at decisive moments in the plot, as figures of recognition that identify the homecoming hero by his scar.

Such a study has not yet been written. But its material would reveal an interesting aspect of unequal distribution and disparity, at least in the case of Western literature. The first notable, if only tentative, signs of recognition of marginal characters in poetry and prose can be traced back to the early modern age and particularly since the Enlightenment. The theatrical tradition extends much further. The relative absence of the servant from poetry and prose before the Enlightenment can be explained by the limited narrative and thematic significance assigned to subalterns. Only with the advent of the picaresque novel, particularly with Don Quixote's servant, Sancho Panza (1605), is the genre invigorated and increasingly recognized. Finally, the *History of Gil Blas of Santillana* (1715) places a servant figure at the center of the action, a gesture which will no longer count as a rare occurrence within literary modernity, for instance, in the case of Kafka (Karl Rossmann in *Amerika;* Artur and Jeremias in *The Castle*) or Robert Walser (*Jakob von Gunten, The Assistant*). At the same time, the absence of writings by servants before the eighteenth century can be associated with the poor literacy standards of the profession, which prevents them from transposing their impressions and experience into literary language.[4]

By contrast, the dramatic tradition of the literary servant has its roots in the comedies of antiquity. Its history begins with Menander's *Aspis* (*The Shield*), in which sly servants and slaves are much more than means of action or stereotypical buffoons. Rather, they single-handedly participate in shaping the course of action; moreover, they act as individuals in moments of crisis and stagnation[5] instead of idling away their time in their subordinate position. The Romans Plautus and Terence—a former slave—draw on Greek comedy, particularly the stylistically influential works of Menander.[6] Slave characters are predominantly represented as cunning (*servus callidus*),[7] dumb (*servus frugi*), or deceitful types (*servus fallax*). As such, they go against the norms of behavior that apply in real life, in the sense that they seem well versed in the art of pretense and determine the course of action as masterminds of intrigue.[8] Nevertheless, this tradition is largely forgotten in the Middle Ages. Only around 1500, under the influence of the Renaissance and its revival of ancient comedy, is there renewed interest in the figure of the superior servant or the intriguing parasite.

Yet another tradition or origin of the dramatic servant figure is commedia dell'arte, the Italian impromptu comedy or, rather, the Renaissance theater of improvisation, launched in sixteenth-century Venice and Naples by traveling acting troupes. Here we encounter the *zanni,* that is to say, servant figures like the schemer Brighella, the gourmand Arlecchino (later known as Harlequin), the awkward Pagliaccio (Pierrot), or the charmer Colombina. Their role is to oppose the *vecchi,* especially the rich Venetian merchant Pantalone and the ob-stinate Bolognese scholar Dottore.[9]

So far, this development could be traced only in broad strokes, too broad to allow for a study of its individual aspects in a trajectory through the liter-ary history of the servant motif from Aristotle to the moderns. Take, for ex-ample, Martin Kluger's medical assistant Henrietta Mahlow. Mahlow is not merely Robert Koch's and Rudolf Virchow's helper; in fact, she is a researcher in her own right, producing significant work which must remain—not unlike its creator—hidden.[10] Imperial Prussia has no room for female researchers. Those who want to find such servant histories in the literary domain, beyond any strict genre delimitations, must, unfortunately, resort to mere case studies.[11] Since a general overview is not yet available, the focus here will be on the turning point around 1800 and a few illustrative texts or, in some cases, passages that center on the specific transfer from dramatic praxis to a new technological paradigm of power. What such texts illustrate, then, is the transition from serving object to politically liberated subject. In other words, the discussion will revolve around the question of popular education, represented by the mid-eighteenth-century servant onstage, offering the public nothing less than a political program. For practical reasons, the examples will be derived from the German context.

3.1. TRAGEDY'S DOMESTIC TURN

Before 1755 the function of the servant in literature is marginal, especially in the context of drama and of German tragedies in particular. From baroque poet-ics[12] to Johann Christoph Gottsched's *Essay on a German Critical Poetic Theory* (1730), the texts follow the Aristotelian rule according to which tragedy is re-served for the good (that is, noble) characters and their serious affairs, whereas the low troubles of the bourgeoisie are to be represented in comedic fashion. But Aristotle's *Poetics* does not contain this binary distinction and imposition; the division appears much later, with Diomede in late antiquity. Falsely attributed to Aristotle, the rule nevertheless acquires normative validity in Renaissance po-etics until the early Enlightenment. The so-called estates clause is declared law and extends far beyond the drama of the classicist period.[13] It would have been inconceivable to have a servant occupy a central role in a play such as Daniel Casper von Lohenstein's *Cleopatra* or Gottsched's *The Dying Cato.* The limited relevance of the domestic for plot development corresponds to his stereotypical roles: he appears as a clever (servus callidus) or naïve (servus frugi) type and thus serves as a contrast figure or reflecting mirror for the master. Historically, his position is not unlike his literary role: the dramatic subaltern is placed in positions that do not allow him to have a considerable impact on the main actions or state affairs of masters and plots. There are few exceptions to this rule: picaresque antiheroes such as Sancho Panza or isolated cases such as the wise fool in Shakespeare's *King Lear.*

Finally, the Enlightenment sheds more light on the literary figure of the servant. With Alain René Le Sage's novel *Gil Blas* from 1715, the marginal status of subalterns begins to change and enable more central positions and tendencies. In the German-speaking context, this shift is introduced in the mid-eighteenth century via dramatic texts that mark a break from the previous tradition of tragedies focused on the wants and needs of those in higher positions. A radical change of perspective takes place, suspending the authority of the estates clause, which limited bourgeois characters to farces and comedies. Now they may appear in the serious context of tragedy without need of noble intervention. The subtitle of a play released in 1755 announces the programmatic mission of the new genre: *Miss Sara Sampson: A Bourgeois Tragedy in Five Acts.* Gotthold Ephraim Lessing taps into English models such as George Lillo's *The London Merchant* (1730) or William Congreve's *The Way of the World* (1700) to familiarize the German public with the characteristics of the *domestic tragedy.* The play consciously breaks from Gottsched's estate-based poetics[14] by bringing grand emotions beyond estate affiliations to the stage, in the form of sentimentality. Its impact is huge, and the reactions, dominated by intense emotionalism, could be summed up, in Kafka's words, as, "Went to the theater. Wept."

To recall the plot: Mellefont has managed to seduce Miss Sara Sampson, the virtuous daughter of the petty aristocrat Sir William; the two are on the run to France, where they plan to get married. Hot on their trail are not only the father, who blames the daughter for being seduced, but also the skillful schemer Marwood, Mellefont's former lover, who plans to win him back. The action takes place for the most part at an English inn, a waystation, where the three parties are housed in different rooms and indirectly communicate via their servants. Mellefont will not be swayed, by either words or Marwood's assassination plot; the latter arranges a meeting with her young rival, as a last attempt to turn things around. In the meantime Sir William attempts to contact Sara via a letter, carried by his 'old and faithful' servant Waitwell, but she refuses to read the message. Only after the servant's insistent pleading does she accept the parental offer of forgiveness. She charges Waitwell with the task of collecting her answer in an hour. As she is writing, she receives Mellefont and Marwood (incognito), who reveals her real identity as Mellefont's ex-lover. Sara faints. The inattention of Sara's servant Betty gives Marwood the chance to poison Sara. On her deathbed, the victim forgives her killer, and the father follows suit by making peace both with his daughter and her lover. The latter, however, overcome with noble remorse, seeks solace in suicide. Curtain. Deeply moved, the public "sat for three and a half hours, like statues, quiet and still, and wept."[15]

Contemporaries praised the play richly on every count: as an exceptional act of mutual forgiveness, as a *Lehrstück* on remorse, moral, and compassion, or as a 'school of wisdom' (August Wilhelm Iffland). Above all, critics praised Lessing's achievement in bringing to the German stage the first dedicated 'bourgeois tragedy' (following the model of the English *domestic tragedy*) and thereby causing the downfall of the old law of estate. There were equally vivid critical responses as well: some attacked it for not being sufficiently bourgeois but still a tragedy of the nobility[16]—an accusation which seems validated by the protagonists' origin from the ranks of the petty nobility. Nevertheless, there is a point which neither Lessing's contemporaries nor later commentators have taken into account: a subtler perspective on those who actually carry the action reveals that this is, quite literally, a *domestic* tragedy. *Miss Sara Sampson* is, after all, also a play about servants and their sociotechnical function, which starts to radically change during the eighteenth century. Overcoming the rank-based order is not limited to tragic bourgeois characters, their errors and intrigues. The impulse to level out social differences goes much further, namely, past the bourgeois salons and into the servants' quarters downstairs. Lessing confers an essential role to domestics. One could therefore translate the formula *domestic tragedy* not merely as "bourgeois tragedy" but also as a "*domestics'* tragedy." The following pages will clarify this claim.

As opposed to the typical tragic roles and their predominantly 'noble' origin, Lessing uses a balanced, even strictly symmetrical distribution of masters and servants. Each one of the four protagonists is accompanied by his or her personal servant. A further deviation from the classical drama, with its unilateral preference for noble characters, concerns the servants themselves: Lessing introduces an even mix of conventional and original servant figures, who have a direct impact on the course of action. One of the classical functions of servants was to highlight the defining features of the protagonists. The main characters address the public via their domestics. For example, Marwood's and Sara's servants interject only in order to illustrate their masters' opinions or situations and to confirm or paraphrase their statements. In such cases, servants are predominantly reduced to an object, namely, a mirror, which flatteringly reflects what the vain mistresses expect to see. Replying to Marwood, who makes a coquettish remark on her own looks, her servant Hannah argues, "To my mind your beauty is so far from having passed the point of its brightest bloom, that it is rather advancing towards it."[17] Conversely, when Norton replies to his master's expression of self-pity, he contradicts him, knowing the moral law is on his side: "Pity, sir? Pity on you? I know better where pity is due."[18]

Such modes of behavior still fully correspond to the classical canon. But via the figure of Waitwell, Lessing introduces several innovative features in a significant and prominent scene. As opposed to Norton, Hannah, and the naïve maid Betty, who has to assume the blame of having caused her mistress' death with her inattention, Waitwell represents the clever servant who has long become indispensable to his employer. As his master's worthy delegate, Waitwell is charged with delivering a letter to Sara and getting a sense of her willingness to reconcile with her father.

Act 3, scene 3 marks the culmination as well as the ultimate stagnation of the course of events. Its focus is the complex situation of epistolary transmission, which is also the central function assumed by a mail server. Along with Sara's subsequent encounter with Marwood, the scene is by far the longest in the play. There is a simple explanation for that: Sara resists accepting the paternal letter, and thus it is up to the medium of transmission and server of communication called Waitwell to try out various strategies in order to succeed in his mission. In a hasty but media-theoretically progressive fashion, Sara first interprets Waitwell's 'angelic' arrival as an actual message, an indication of the presumed death of her father. Waitwell quickly clears up the confusion, and Sara is left to make assumptions on the content of the letter. Based on those assumptions, she will reject the letter and implicitly also the forgiveness of her father:[19] "So take your letter back!"[20] The first delivery attempt has failed.

Waitwell is initially not programmed to deal with Sara's rejection. His response amounts to a 'server error,' signaling an unforeseen issue: "I truly do not know what answer to give to that."[21] So he waits for Sara's monologue to end. In the meantime, the server is reset. The mail delivery agent then makes a second attempt. "Waitwell (*aside*): I really think I shall have to employ deception with this good child to get her to read the letter."[22] In his second attempt he resorts to a stratagem, claiming that the message may contain words from an angry father, which prompts her to read the letter. Nevertheless, the amiable salutation (or the header) exposes the stratagem and results in a further transmission error. Sara rejects the message: "(She reads) 'My only, dearest daughter'—ah, you old deceiver, is that the language of an angry father? Go, I shall read no more." Waitwell must resort to something else. He invokes the risk of transmission failure and, implicitly, of a complete server shutdown: "To return his letter un-read to such a good father? That certainly I cannot do! Sooner will I walk as far as my old legs will carry me and never again come into his presence."[23]

Only when faced with the risk of transmission failure and termination of service does Sara accept the message. She goes even further and tries to mend relations between master and servant, giving a nod to Waitwell's paternal au-thority: "Dear old father! I believe you have persuaded me."[24] But Waitwell maintains his reserve. He answers not like a father but like someone bestowing praise on the mediating function—the role assumed by all ministering spirits of communication, which has allowed him to act as a paternal mouthpiece: "If I have been so fortunate as that, it must have been a good spirit that has helped me to plead."[25]

It is therefore due only to Waitwell's cunning insistence and his art of patient waiting that Sara allows herself to be swayed by the forgiving magnanimity of her father.[26] As it turns out, waiting pays off. 'Wait-well'—*nomen est omen*—has proven himself with patience, as someone who waits and safeguards communi-cation at the same time. For 'Waitwell' does not mean only a reliable servant, someone who waits well, as some interpreters suggest,[27] but especially one who can patiently wait. Here, in any case, one task is followed by the next. Now it's the mistress's turn to order: "Go, Waitwell, leave me alone! He wants an answer, and I will write it at once. Come again in an hour!"[28]

For the past two hundred and fifty years critics have insisted on the crucial importance of this scene. The interpretive models offered have ranged from a thorough investigation of Sara's mind[29] to a subtle nod to Lutheran penitential practices (according to Heinrich Bornkamm).[30] But a much more obvious, yet overlooked, possibility would be to read the episode as a key moment in a literal *turn toward the domestic.* The scene perfectly exemplifies what is characteristic of the literary servant figure as well as the ministering spirits of communication and their mode of operation. To start with a banal observation: the plot could not possibly advance without Waitwell's intervention as a dedicated messenger, or a *mailer daemon,* without his threefold attempt to successfully deliver the message, his undeterred determination and cunning. *Nota bene:* the sender is only a few steps and rooms away this entire time. Waitwell plays a decisive role as a servant of communication. Furthermore, he also acts as a catalyst of knowledge. As both his master's representative and a distant observer, he brings unique analytical qualities to the table. His therapeutic efforts help Sara attain a new perspective.[31] A whole range of 'invisible' qualities derive from here. De-spite their physical presence, servants appear only in order to carry out a task; otherwise, they stay in the background. Furthermore, they act as therapists or messengers; they are available at all times, 24/7, without expecting any breaks or free time. But above all, two aspects foreground the central importance of the scene with respect to the tragic character of the domestic subject: on the one hand, the noble art of waiting, and, on the other, the subalterns' *prebourgeois status*.

The enthusiasm and praise that followed the premiere of Lessing's play continued for several decades, animated by the general thirst for sentimentality. Along with the praise, however, there were also critical reactions. In a letter from 1775 Johann Martin Müller writes the following to Johann Heinrich Voß: "*Sara,* which is already average and boring, was performed particularly boringly and badly today. . . . It is a most annoying and offensive play."[32] The public no longer takes much pleasure in sentimental tragedies in the age of Sturm und Drang. But the impression of boredom corresponds to a quality inherent in both the construction of the drama and the elements associated with the servant function. Only a small step separates the state of being bored from the art of being in waiting, which servants must master. The main question remains: how does Waitwell actually spend those sixty minutes, after successfully delivering the letter and receiving a new order? Once more, the name becomes him, as it points to one of the servant's defining features. Waitwell does precisely what both his own name and Sara order him to do: he waits. In his room. For a whole hour. A long hour. "No-op" (no operation) is the equivalent term used for a mail server in that situation. A decisive hour, during which the dramatic confrontation between the two rivals unfolds next door, culminating in Marwood's poisoning of Sara.

The audience are not the only ones being bored. Despite the highly dramatic events taking place nearby, Waitwell is also bored, since he is cut off from the data flow. He remains invisible to the main characters but is ready to act at all times. The servant is in stand-by mode. Yet no one calls to bring him back into the plot. Thus he must remain inactive, even though his knowledge and skills would have allowed him to intervene and provide an explanation for the sequence of events. Indeed, he may even have rebelled against the order to wait, taking it upon himself to bring father and daughter together and thus preventing the fatal consequences of their long separation. Instead, Waitwell does nothing but wait. Only after (precisely) one hour does he come back to get Sara's answer and find her wasting away. Only now does she agree to see her father, and Waitwell brings him to her deathbed in the final scene. The long wait, the patient pause, the moment of invisibility and simultaneous availability—all are part of Lessing's subtle description of the servant figure. Therein, it would seem, lies a higher potential to act and intervene, if only status conditions would allow it. Waitwell has both the knowledge and the means to put a quick end to the intrigue. The tragedy of being able, but not being allowed, to act is the second innovative aspect of the play. That subject will be more closely discussed in the following pages.

3.2. TO BE (CALLED) CARL

> The best servant is the biggest rascal in the world.
> —Goethe's inscription on a scrap of paper

If *Miss Sara Sampson* is indeed a *domestic* tragedy in the sense delineated above, we still need to ask: what is the tragic aspect of servitude, particularly before 1800? Around 1755 the estate system and the estates clause are still both in place. Gottsched had already confirmed that point in 1730. Servants are not full-fledged citizens yet. Simultaneously, as Lessing's play exemplarily shows, they may act as autonomous individuals in particular situations, even though they are officially denied autonomy. They remain subject to orders from their masters. The key scene in the play captures the tragic aspect that derives from this. Waitwell's insistence, bordering on outright defiance, deeply affects Sara and the events themselves. The servant employs it to successfully resist his mistress's formal authority and to considerably influence or even direct the action. Of course, Waitwell is merely doing his job, while being perfectly aware that everything else depends on that job and his ability to influence Sara. Combining regular commitment to service with stoic obstinacy, he takes the initiative that will ultimately turn him into an autonomous subject. At all other times, Waitwell remains dutifully inactive, as he is ordered to do.

What is new about a drama that calls itself a bourgeois tragedy? On the one hand, Lessing paradigmatically illustrates the dilemma of servants, torn between compliant conformity and steady rebellion. But he takes that situation further by promoting Waitwell from servant to companion—a highly symbolic and unique decision in this context. As Sir William declares after the successful delivery of the message, "Do not regard yourself as my servant any longer, my good Waitwell. [. . .] I will abolish all difference between us; in yonder world, you well know, it will be done."[33] Old Waitwell is promoted to the rank of bourgeois subject during his lifetime; thereby he is saved from the tragic fate subalterns must suffer in the mortal world. Lessing thus brings to the stage and the literary world a shockingly simple solution for evening out class differences and promoting worthy servants to subjecthood. And yet the realities of the late eighteenth and early nineteenth century are quite different, despite the achievements of the French Revolution. The example below is symptomatic of the servant's tragic condition; at the same time, it is also paradigmatically relevant to the changing status of subalterns around 1800.

For a certain bourgeois gentleman from Frankfurt am Main who would later acquire fame and an aristocratic title, being surrounded by servants is a matter of everyday routine from the very start. At a time when Lessing receives praise for his *Sara Sampson,* the bourgeois young man in question already benefits from the assistance of various servants at 23 Großer Hirschgraben, his family residence address. Among them is Philipp Seidel, his sister's private tutor, whom he chooses as his companion when he moves to the small residential town of Weimar in 1775.[34] Over the subsequent six decades spent there, Goethe must have had around two dozen domestics by his side, ranging from simple workmen to licensed lawyers.[35] The privy councillor's complex relationship to his staff may have been deemed progressive and quite liberal during his time: Goethe expects each of his subjects, from coachman to secretary, to act independently and strictly follow orders at the same time.[36] The situation highlights once again the tragic condition of domestics, torn as they are between subjective initiative and mere service function. Irrespective of their level of education or their unique, inalienable name, whether Johann Gensler or Ludwig Geist ['Spirit'], Ferdinand Schreiber ['Clerk'] or simply Dienemann ['Serviceman']— the coachman's name—all those who serve at the Frauenplan residence in Weimar are invariably called Carl.[37]

The domestic tragedy unfolds metonymically: even enlightened bourgeois service subjects around 1800 continue to be (called) Carl. Despite the collapse of feudal hierarchies after the French Revolution, there is a conservative ideology at work, according to which servants continue to function as deindividualized beings, tied to their lowly situation. Being called Carl (or, to paraphrase Deleuze, becoming-Carl),[38] means wearing a mask, becoming a transparent interface, an invisible service medium that forgoes its individuality, irrespective of its previous position: educated printer or licensed lawyer. All subjects disappear behind the collective 'Carl,' even Geist [spirit], Schreiber [clerk] or Dienemann [serviceman], whose names are quite meaningful—not unlike Lessing's character Waitwell. Goethe's case is not unique in the context of the nineteenth century. In both the Old and the New World, which officially no longer recognizes servants or estate systems, the situation is not uncommon, and its effects may prove quite profound. A case in point is Herman Melville: as per tradition, the female servants in his household are all named Mary.[39] "Call me Ishmael."

Thus, for the sake of convenience, every member of a rank is called by the same first name. That appellative does not necessarily correspond to the servant's real name but is, rather, decided by the master. "When they start service, domestics are given a new name based on their region of origin; lackeys are dressed in standard livery; valets wear the hand-me-downs of their masters. Thus one could argue that they are all denied an a priori right to personhood and individuality. Picard, Normand, Champagne, and La Grandeur are typical servant names" in the French context.[40] In England, an unusual name such as 'Claude' is dismissed and expected to be replaced by a more common, more regionally typical appellative: "There were establishments in which the first footman was always called, say, Charles [!], the second James and the third John."[41] That may simplify matters for the masters upstairs but causes confusion in the world downstairs, especially when John's real name is James and James actually goes by John. Since names hover between poetry and truth, the practice of convenient naming has long made its way into the realm of literature. Thus in the German comedies of the Enlightenment first names become identifying markers for domestics; their characters lack family names and typically go by Peter, Johann, Catharina, or Lisette.[42]

But Goethe's servants are thoroughly familiar with the ways of their master. They inevitably become the confidants of the 'poet-prince,' both able to enjoy certain liberties and held under their master's supervision in their independent actions. But in contrast to Lessing's enlightened views, being in Goethe's service means forgoing one's own identity, turning once more from subject to object, being degraded to the rank of a factotum called Carl. In other words, the new code name is, 'Call me Carl.' Apart from the circumstantial fact of having a name, one must fulfill yet another condition to be in Goethe's service: to be ready to part with that name and accept being called 'Carl' by all authorized subjects—Christiane, August, and the privy councillor himself. 'Call me Carl,' or CMC, is the communication acronym that grounds every act of service performed at the residence *am Frauenplan*. CMC, in other words, our contemporary *computer-mediated communication,* along with its daemons, electronic servers, and ministering spirits, has a long tradition. The devoted servant figure plays a key role in this context. Call me Carl. A domestic who accepts being demoted from subject to stereotypical object ('Carl') embodies the dilemma that confronts domestics around 1800. Surrendering their identity and inalienable proper name,[43] subalterns must be prepared to fulfill their duties and act as a pure *media function.* That is the reality behind the tragic dilemma that domestics face. Therein also lies the issue that Lessing unsuccessfully seeks to combat in 1755, employing literary means—the turn to bourgeois drama and domestic tragedy—to show the path leading to subjectivity.

3.3. THE REAL CARL: "MOSJE STADELMANN"

> I saw to everything at the post office and did not forget to drink once, since I
> felt thirsty. That was necessary.
> —Carl Stadelmann, diary, 1814

Among the educated elite of Goethe's servants there are those called Götze
[Idol] and Färber [Dyer], Schreiber [Clerk] and Geist [Spirit]. Some have an
academic background and a degree, others have learned a trade or come from
simple means. At least after 1803 their master invariably calls them 'Carl,' despite the fact that half of them (six out of eleven) are actually named 'Johann';
or that their origin covers the entire social spectrum of the period. Irrespective of the significance of their last names, Goethe's domestics are reduced to
a single syllable—'Carl'—and are uniformly addressed by that same foreign,
standardized first name. They are systematically denied the status of an enlightened bourgeois individual who has control over his first name. By taking on
that other appellative, Goethe's domestics are arrested in an objectlike state of
service. Two different aspects may help us further explore this case of manifest
nominalism. The first concerns the question of power raised by Louis Althusser:
how does an individual comply with authority and literally become a subject, in
other words, someone *subjected* to another? "The individual is interpellated as a
(free) subject in order that he shall submit freely to the Subject, i.e. in order that
he shall (freely) accept his subjection"[44] By responding to his imposed name,
the subject dutifully follows the instructions of an authority. The other aspect
pertains to the list of employees at the Frauenplan residence. That list suggests
that the staff may have been chosen on the basis of their last names, yet only
in order to have them subsequently erased. Among Goethe's female servants
there are, for instance, caretakers called Sauerbrei [Sourdough] or Grützmacher
[Porridgemaker]. The privy councillor must have had no difficulty choosing
his staff. Servants were not in short supply around 1800. In 1820 almost a third
of all taxpayers in Weimar are listed as domestics.[45] But their names are hardly
mentioned in Goethe's daily routine. Instead, all service people are addressed by
their respective function: thus Dienemann, Barth, and König are merely called
'the coachman,' while the successive series of women in charge of the kitchen,
such as Wagenknecht, Höpfner, Hoyer, Kluge, Kunold a.s.o., are recorded only
in the documents as 'the cook.' In turn, the valet must go by 'Carl,' even though
his given name is actually, and repeatedly, Johann.

But these two aspects will not be discussed here any further. Instead, the
focus will be on the media operations of a particular servant, in the context

of a new logic of address at work in the Goethe household. The servant in question is possibly the most famous among them: Carl Wilhelm Stadelmann (1782–1845), the "classic valet"[46] of Weimar classicism, who takes up his duties in 1814, is immortalized in the so-called Marienbad Elegy in 1823, and dismissed from work for drinking in 1824. Stadelmann, an educated printer, is the seventh in the line of Goethe's personal servants. The moment he enters into service on July 1, 1814, marks a change in the mode of standardized address practiced until then. Quite notably, the start of his employment coincides with a deviation from the singular logic of naming. Unlike his misnamed predecessors, the real Carl is called by his last name, Stadelmann. When they start working for Goethe, servants such as Geist, Götze, Eisfeld, or Gensler are still young and inexperienced and need to be trained into their media functions by the privy councillor himself. As opposed to them, Stadelmann is already thirty-two years old and married; moreover, he has already had ample experience as a domestic "in a prestigious household." Stadelmann has been Carl long before meeting Goethe. He is literally called Carl,[47] even if the names recorded on the occasion of his wedding in 1811 are "Johann Wilhelm." And yet, his case illustrates a significant transition: from an invisible and impersonal factotum, a smoothly functioning medium that mimetically and inconspicuously follows his master, to a celebrated, recognizable individual. All that, however, would not prevent the conceivably tragic end.

But first, a few words on the origin of serviceability media in the Goethe house. In their early stages of training, the prospective domestics are subject to a process of standardization which corrects and instructs them, branding their soul and making them respond even to arbitrary hailing—as Althusser shows in his analysis of power. "I wish to recommend him [the servant Seidel] not merely because he belonged to me and is, in the noblest of senses, *my creature;* but I would like him to be known." Thus writes the poet-prince—and, for once, also the princely servant—to the Duke Carl August on December 7, 1787.[48] Thereby, he directly points to the process of 'becoming-media' which he imposes on his servants.

The domestics are made in their master's image and share some of its notable features. Goethe's contemporaries do not fail to notice his subalterns' mimetic effects. That is the case of Philipp Seidel, "who imitates his master, walks like him, shakes his head in the same fashion."[49] Only after a servant's media functions are perfected is the impact somewhat reduced. The machine is now fully operational and acquires its typical designation. It becomes a trained, preprogrammed apparatus known as a valet. Or it evolves, as Waitwell does in Lessing's play. In that case, the subject reluctantly overcomes his subservient status and is forced by his master to become an (non-)independent individual.

Goethe catalyzes the serviceable abilities of 'his' creatures. He turns them into the media of his own operations, prosthetic tools for his own writing and extensions of his 'subaltern versatility.'[50] After undergoing a long period of training, Goethe's servants are able to learn the poet's daily routine, so that he may turn his attention to other things. "When the prose is done, poetry can thrive. One must rid oneself of any unpleasantness to live pleasantly, and one's sleep will be much better for it."[51]

Goethe's servants become the delegates of his own work. They act, first and foremost, as his communication media, as the errand boys and messengers who send and receive data, the doormen and indirect agents who form the corridor of power leading to the poet-prince. They are the ones deciding—often in exchange for small gifts—who is granted access or not. Additionally, they may also function as relay stations, firmly established communication channels or exclusive lines that only specific correspondence partners can use. A case in point is Goethe's Italian journey, when his first servant, Philipp Seidel, is left behind to function as a local communication center and news agency for the small residential town. Seidel is also the steady transmission medium between Goethe's mother, Katharina, in Frankfurt, and Anna Amalia at the court. Not by coincidence, the latter dubs Seidel "Goethe's lightning page."[52]

All valets are also tasked with writing assignments, even when—unlike servant number VIII, Ferdinand Schreiber [writing clerk]—they don't happen to bear the right name for the task. Goethe dictates most of his letters and merely adds his signature or, occasionally, a salutation line and an addendum. *Nota bene:* after 1812 Goethe hires not only servants but also secretaries, such as John Kräuter, Färber, Schuchardt, Riemer, and, finally (and to the very end), Eckermann.

The novels, poems, plays, legal texts, and diary entries are all dictations written down by secretaries and servants-turned-scribes, since he deems himself too unskilled in handling a quill. He sometimes complains of 'writing idleness,' 'ink-' and 'paper-shyness'—"all the more since I have a ministering spirit [Geist] sitting at my right hand who brings my thoughts and ideas to paper with the greatest ease."[53] Not unlike all his predecessors and successors, valet number IV, Johann Ludwig Geist, is charged with the preeminent task of meticulously recording all of the poet's deeds. That is, whenever he is not otherwise occupied, strolling around the small, residential town in the company of Goethe the father and the son—something that earns him a part in the Weimar trinity, as Caroline

Figure 6. Discourse Network, 1800: John and Goethe by J. J. Schmeller

Schlegel put it. Taking a page from his own legal education, Goethe instructs all his domestics to keep a detailed journal. They have to make a record of every expense and every purchase, each assignment given and completed, which all amounts to extremely specific bookkeeping entries. Krause, for instance, keeps separate logs for milk, cream, wine, and table expenses. Additionally, each domestic is supposed to keep a private diary, resulting in a double entry accounting system that documents the daily life of Goethe and his circle.[54]

Apart from such regular, yet limited, data there are hardly any records of Goethe's servants and their everyday activities. As usual, the underlings inhabit the uncharted regions of history. With two exceptions: first, when servants leave service—willingly or not—and receive an official report, they become visible once more. Goethe's evaluations run the whole gamut from stark reproach to effusive praise as a basis for recommendation.[55] The servants become unexpectedly visible, particularly in case of a malfunction. "Generally, the master has no occasion to think of his ministering spirits, but rather mentions them in his private correspondence or official documents only when there is cause for complaint."[56] It is particularly during such moments of error exposure that the underlying and constant state of operativeness of the servant-medium becomes visible. In 1813, for instance, Goethe complains that his secretary-cum-domestic scribe Ernst Carl Christian John is indisposed: "For the past fourteen days, my adoptive right hand has unfortunately been bedridden, and my right hand is as idle as it is inept, so that it always seeks excuses when I present it with a sheet of writing paper."[57] Not even Stadelmann escapes Goethe's vigilance, for example, once when he forgets to dust off the papers he brings in. Eckermann records Goethe as saying, "'I am telling you for the last time . . . if you do not go this very day to buy the cloth for which I have asked so often, I will go myself tomorrow; and you shall see that I will keep my word.' Stadelmann went."[58] The servant fails in his assignment and thereby earns his place in the annals of history.

But in general Goethe's domestics run the daily life of their master without receiving any complaints. They perform their tasks without being specifically asked to do so and without objecting to them. They may even take the initiative sometimes, for instance, when ordering particular food items, like asparagus. And even if those items may be meant for someone other than the master, the servant is likely to receive praise.

"It was planned that we would eat lunch in Hünefeld. But as soon as I entered the kitchen of the post office to ask for the postmaster, I saw the asparagus that was to be served at that very moment. Halt! I thought, that is something for my master! I rushed back to the carriage with the news. The master got out and ate the postmaster's asparagus, then we continued our journey to Hünefeld."[59]

Such initiatives turn domestics into the eyes and hands of their master. They follow their trajectories[60] as his representatives. Occasionally, Goethe even stages visits with the aid of his servants, by turning their first body into his own second body: for instance, he sends them to the parish fair at Castle Kochberg instead of going there himself. The interventions become even more noticeable when the assistants act as channels of observation, conveniently (and remote-) controlled by the poet from his desk. Take, for example, the Weimar staging of August von Kotzebue's *Hussites before Naumburg.* The performance begins. "Meanwhile, Goethe stayed quietly in his room. His 'spirit' Geist (that is the name of his servant) was sent to the theatre, and the poor lad had to run home after every act and recount to his master what he had seen."[61] It is not an uncommon practice for eighteenth-century theatergoers to send their servants ahead, to keep their orchestra seats before their arrival—even when they are terribly late. The domestics then walk up to their 'cheap' seats in the gallery.[62] But Goethe radicalizes this form of absent presence—and not merely in the sense that he does not show up. With the help of Geist's—his 'spirit's'—back-and-forth movements he establishes a communication channel that allows him to remain *visible by representation* and literally in the loop. Domestics are also further advised to keep an eye out for things that their master might deem interesting and that might add to his passion for collecting. Geist, for instance, looks not only for flowers that he may bring back to his master but also for all sorts of 'monstrosities'; in turn, Stadelmann collects rare rock specimens, and Färber focuses on whatever may be beautiful and new in the domain of osteology.[63] Four eyes are better than two.

In the relationship with their master, Goethe's servants carry out, therefore, at least four media functions, thus significantly expanding a subaltern's range of media services. Clearly, one of the basic tasks of a subaltern as medium is (1) daily domestic management, in order to ensure that the salon and the living rooms are kept at a safe remove from the nuisances and adversities of the mundane. The young Goethe already considers a servant "desirable for the many errands required by the absence or slowness of the urban post as well as for the coarse jobs a large household demands, and the many times one needs a helping hand while traveling on long journeys."[64] While performing such 'lowly' or basic activities, subalterns function as household management media; ideally, the patron would not notice the activities of his ministering spirits. In that sense, servants are like the air—the medium that becomes noticeable only when heavy, thick, or scarce. The inconspicuous and smooth operation of Goethe's household is taken for granted; so is the domestics' ability to preferably remain invisible to their master.

Not unlike his aristocratic contemporaries, Goethe resorts to this basic media practice of service. But he also goes several steps further by bestowing on his servants other media functions. (2) He doubly instrumentalizes his assistants, turning them into agents of his own productive drive and perception: as writing tools and telescopes, they become his writing hands and the eyes through which he sees theatrical performances. He also directs them toward 'autonomous' interests, although those are still part of his own broad range of passions. Under the privy councillor's guidance, the domestics become outposts or extensions of his first body, his eyes, ears, and hands: for instance, when sending them to the theater or dictating to them or guiding their trained gaze toward objects of their—that is to say, primarily, his—interests, as on the visits to Karlsbad and Marienbad in Bohemia. Sitting next to the coachman Barth, the geologically trained servant Stadelmann takes note of rock formations along the highway and stops the carriage whenever he thinks he may have discovered a promising object at the edge of the road: "Master Privy Councillor, methinks there's something for us here."[65] As soon as he returns home Stadelmann classifies and catalogues the findings for the mineral cabinet and Goethe's vast collections. Thanks to a sense of erudition that almost seems to rub off on him, the domestic trains himself to curate those collections and earns his master's praise. "The local specimens are beautifully arranged in an elegant mineral cabinet. . . . In this, Stadelmann shows his best qualities."[66] The long hours of nature observation, performed by representation via Stadelmann (and John), find their way into the penultimate stanza of the "Marienbad Elegy" (1823) in a few dramatic lines not devoid of irony:

> Leave me here, faithful comrades! leave me alone amid rocks and marsh and moss!
> Hold to your course! To you the world lies open, the earth is wide, the heavens splendid and great; examine, investigate, collect details, and slowly spell out Nature's mystery.[67]

Goethe is not one, but many. The master multiplies via his domestics. As extensions of his own perception, his subalterns allow him to expand his personal range of activity. Indeed, they are trained to act not only as 'his creatures' but also as prostheses of his own self. Goethe's servants thus become their master's agents since they are (3) systematically directed to represent him by proxy. This function extends beyond the former practices of courtly representation. From the absolutist era to the times of the grand bourgeoisie and its late manifestations, lackeys parade the power and wealth of their masters, with disinterested affectation and displays of idleness, doing nothing more than standing and walking about in full regalia. But Goethe's servants go (several steps) further. They keep diaries and conduct natural science research; they strive to bring their master essential information, new discoveries, and surprising findings, so as to increase his knowledge and document his life for posterity in a kind of double-entry bookkeeping system.[68] Educated and trained in this fashion, they assiduously work for their master, but also, through him, for their master's master. Subalternity's recursive instance strikes again. Since everyone is basically still a servant until the nineteenth century, the actions performed by the servants' servants must be considered as well. The poet-prince is not unaware of the resulting chain of effects, since he himself is the servant of a ruler. Thus he recommends to the duke one of his fully trained domestics for further employment: "And I shall consider myself content to have educated a useful, faithful subaltern to serve you, and, *through him,* to better and more fervently follow your orders."[69] Ultimately, every success linked to Goethe's subalterns, each rock specimen they thoughtfully collect, brings fame to the noble House of Sachsen-Weimar-Eisenach. The chain of action by representation carries on. By formatting his domestics' core media functions, Goethe shows himself to be a better servant toward his own superior.

Ludwig Geiger, the long-standing editor of the Goethe Yearbook (1880–1913), formulates a rather vehement critique of the privy councillor's valets: "All of them: Geist, Stadelmann and whatever their name is are thoroughly inferior creatures that could not rise above their tedious tasks and who rarely stepped out of their state of mute devotion."[70] But how could they possibly do so, if their first and foremost duty is to be seen as little as possible? After all, the paradoxical requirement for servants is to be permanently present while remaining seemingly absent; therefore, to fully dedicate themselves to their tasks according to their media function, so as to carry out their work quietly and inconspicuously. This paradoxical requirement prevents them from becoming more visible—a fact that applies to the source materials as well. And yet some materials do exist: they come to us via the circle of 'inferiors' around Goethe, featured, for instance, in the conversations with Eckermann, via external accounts or via the privy councillor's own written documents, which mention Stadelmann more than anyone else.[71] Last but not least, the servants describe themselves in their own diary entries, reports, and letters. Goethe's ministering spirits, the agents of his authority, turn into historiographic media (4). But Stadelmann goes much further than his colleagues. His literary activity, albeit limited, including letters and diary entries that lack any punctuation, as well as the critical literature on him offer a new historiographic account of the poet-prince which precedes Eckermann's. Stadelmann thus becomes a medium whose texts reevaluate Goethe's image. As opposed to Eckermann, he gives access to an exclusive, far less embellished, less glamorous insider's view, a 'frog's perspective'—an aspect equally foregrounded by the Stadelmann Society (1912–41) founded in his honor.[72] But Stadelmann is not only successful in serving as a historiographic medium. Not unlike Lessing's Waitwell, he also manages to overcome for a brief moment his subaltern status. The account of his last journey is a case in point.

Except for a two-year-long interruption, Carl Stadelmann is in Goethe's service for a period of nine years. Throughout this time his performance is quite satisfactory. Then, in June 1824, their relationship comes to an abrupt end. "Stadelmann's departure. Preparations required,"[73] writes Goethe laconically in his diary. Another servant has taken possession of the poet's own ministering spirit and become his "demonic master"[74]: the spirit of alcohol. The privy councillor is not famous for his abstinence from spirit.[75] Still, he treats the incident as grounds for immediate dismissal. Stadelmann's track is lost for a while; the valet seems to vanish into the nothingness of history. Then, a decade later, his wife dies—and with her death comes a further loss of status and stability. After being briefly employed as the factotum of the court mechanic Dr. Körner in Jena, Stadelmann moves into his penultimate station: Jena's poorhouse. In the fall of 1844, on the occasion of the planned unveiling of the poet's statue in his native town, the successors of the former 'court of the muses' receive a request from Frankfurt as to whether they "may have any relics of Goethe and would be inclined to make them available for the purpose of the celebrations?" The recipients are reluctant to send the lock of hair by which Stadelmann had made good money during the poet's lifetime. Instead, Friedrich Siegmund Voigt replies, "There still is a large, living relic of the poet-hero, embodied by his servant of many years, currently in Jena, and he may be sent, if so requested."[76] And so it comes about that "Master or Mosje [monsieur] Stadelmann,"[77] as one likes to call him in Frankfurt, is shipped out to the city, riding in a carriage and donning new clothes. Once there, he is surrounded by all, admired, pressed for stories from the days past, and, finally, given his pleasant demeanor and miserly situation, even promised a modest annual pension. Back in Jena, penniless and lacking stable employment, the old man is faced with the same old life. December arrives, with its cold weather, ashen days, and long nights. The promised pension is a long time coming. One of Stadelmann's duties in the poorhouse is chopping wood. "Soon, the axe is abandoned in the courtyard, while he slips through the main gate every now and then to purchase alcohol."[78] Such incidents become more frequent and, a few days later, he is found in the attic, hanging from a thin string. "He seemed to be smiling," as he touched "the ground with his feet in such a manner that his body was standing on it."[79] The first installment of the pension arrives from Frankfurt the following day.

Despite the many services Stadelmann performed for the privy councillor, his career is often perceived as 'a failure' by the critics, partly because of his alcohol addiction and partly because of his tragic end.[80] Still, the 'real Carl' stands out in a particular way from among all the other servants of the Goethe household. As opposed to the other subalterns, he succeeds in stepping out of his master's larger-than-life shadow, under which the others invisibly perform their service media functions. The last time Stadelmann appears in Frankfurt, he stands in for his long-deposed master, whose first body had been resting in the ducal burial chapel in Weimar for more than a decade. But more important, he is treated—and not just once—with esteem and honor, in recognition of "his pleasant countenance, his fine manners and educated expression, but especially his vast knowledge and many skills he had acquired."[81] More than all the other domestics, Stadelmann is granted highly personalized traits of character, which his contemporaries find worthy of mention. Last but not least, his remarkable functions as the ministering spirit of His Excellency set him apart from the others, since he "was charged with exceptional services that provided him with the opportunity to show his wisdom and skills."[82] Among such services are the experiments he performs, for instance, during the search for the best gypsum mixture, or physics-related assignments in the domain of light refraction, or mineralogical studies that serve not simply the geognostic explorations of his master, since they are also highly independent activities. Stadelmann's appetite for research can also be deduced from the little free time he has, since that too is almost entirely dedicated to the search for rock specimens, weather observations, or physics experiments. Stadelmann reports on such individual interests in his letters and diaries, in brief paragraphs that lack punctuation. Due to all those interests, he ultimately becomes his own master, searching for his own autonomy.[83] By undertaking his own research, he sets out on a path to find himself as an individual. Sadly, he does not make it too far, since he also invokes those spirits he cannot leave behind. Johann Carl Wilhelm Stadelmann thus takes on the thankless role of the tragic servant in the *domestic tragedy*.

3.4. IMITATION AND MIMETIC DESIRE

> A servant can't help putting on the masks and allures of his master, in order faithfully to propagate them, as it were.
> —Robert Walser, *Jakob von Gunten*, 1909

As we survey Goethe's small gallery of servants, we reach a point that needs further commentary. There is a particular tendency that defines the (mostly) young domestics, who "begin to grow next to us, and for many years continue to develop through us,"[84] as their master puts it. All subalterns take on a specific trait that allows them to seem more similar to their master. Johann Georg Paul Götze, Goethe's domestic of seventeen years, achieves such a perfect imitation of his master's handwriting that experts still have trouble distinguishing it from the original. Götze also practices his drawing skills, attempting to imitate his model.[85] For their part, Geist and Stadelmann are the filters through which Goethe sees the world or, more precisely, the world of the theater and the realm of stone quarries. They also willingly co-opt their master's particular interests. "All of Goethe's servants, each according to his respective capabilities, have taken over features of their master's outward manner, appropriating his handwriting and turning his knowledge into their pet passions: Seidel on philosophical, linguistic, and economic themes, Geist in the domain of botany, Stadelmann on geology and mineralogy, Färber with osteology."[86] Still, the intensity of mimetic desire, the unquenched thirst for adaptation, is most obvious in the case of

Philipp Seidel, Goethe's first subaltern, who would later be appointed chamber accountant in Weimar, in recognition of his services: "He had taken after him to such a degree that they called him Goethe's 'certified copy.'"[87] Seidel imitates his master's way of speaking, his intonation as well as his head-shaking, even his 'perpendicular gait' so that "one was tempted to mistake him for Goethe from afar."[88] The master duplicates himself via his domestics.

Certainly, domestics are usually young, thirsty for knowledge, receptive, and easily influenced. Their existence as the privy councillor's servants is typically planned only as a transitional stage,[89] a stage of development which they hope to profitably use to make further advances. Implicitly, they are generally ready to take on a considerable workload and even assume several other tasks. In conclusion: the domestic medium learns, even if that process sometimes involves rather long distances, like running across Weimar in the form of a 'certified copy.' More important, as opposed to their colleagues employed in neighboring houses, Goethe's servants find themselves caught in the force field of a rare charismatic presence. The centripetal force commonly leads less to the development of one's own character traits than to a process of molding oneself into the particularities of the other. One can almost sense a heartfelt sigh behind the following remark by Goethe's secretary and librarian, Kräuter: "It is sad to be in the company of important masters; gone is the independence and free will; they throw you around like a ball, wherever they please."[90] Those who get too close to their master risk the fate of light approaching a black hole. Once the demarcation line is crossed beyond which light can no longer return and is swallowed up due to the high gravitational pull, there is no more chance for the individual ray to continue shining. The intrinsic is constantly in danger of erosion, even before a proper state of individuality can be achieved. Friedrich Wilhelm Riemer, the private tutor of Goethe's son August, is well aware of this state of affairs. He writes the following to Knebel in a letter which—according to Geiger—exposes his highly "domestic-oriented nature":[91] "I can confide in you, as one of the oldest friends of our immortal master, in the conviction that I will be understood. It is not only him that I miss after his passing, but also my own self."[92] Riemer's orbit obviously runs close to the path of the dead star. He is sunk deep in the tidal horizon around Goethe and runs the risk of falling straight though its dark center. As soon as the model has vanished, the relation between point of origin and copy starts to show cracks until it all crumbles to pieces. The radically mimetic is constantly in danger of losing its center.

Such tendencies, with all their complex manifestations, may convincingly lend themselves to psychological interpretation. They could be associated with the concept of imitation, a broadly manifested and common phenomenon that occurs on a daily basis and in various ways between superiors and inferiors, masters and servants, parents and children, instructors and students, those in power and those that depend on it. Instead, the line of interpretation followed here draws on the notion of *mimesis,* not in the least since it promises to shed more light on the aforementioned question of relationality and representational effects.

The domestics are defined, each in his own fashion, by their mimetic desire, whose media effects call for closer attention. On the one hand, the servants' activities take place within a preestablished framework, organized via regulations and instructions into routine operational sequences. Such rules are not simply to be imitated or mechanically followed. Rather, they must be ideally emulated, even in those exceptional situations when servants are unexpectedly called upon to be *creative* when applying themselves to their tasks. When Sara Sampson orders Waitwell to return the unread letter to her father, the domestic employs a series of ingenious strategies in order to deliver the missive in spite of his mistress's commands and thereby also to escape the dilemma of going against the order of his other master. On the other hand, the paterfamilias functions as a 'natural' model, which those in his service are bound to follow—*qualis dominus, talis et servus,* or, 'like master, like man,' as the saying goes in English. Importantly, however, this form of imitation, whether of abstract orders or unconscious emulation, is not a seamless reproduction, therefore not a simple replica or a one-to-one relation between model and copy.

The concept of mimesis that applies here is not directly related to Erich Auerbach's notion of imitation of reality in literature.[93] Rather, the term comes closer to Paul Ricoeur's definition: "Mimesis is an action about action."[94] The domestics' mimetic desire conforms to a second-order action, that is to say, to a recursive structure. By imitating his master, the servant replaces him, and re-acts to his actions. But, as Ricoeur points out, there is always a productive component in the context of mimetic operations, that is to say, within the re-presentation of presence. The process of imitation also involves *poiesis.* To put it simply, one could formulate mimesis as *imitation plus poiesis.* In other words, when following orders, servants do not operate merely in a mechanical, machinelike, unidirectional fashion. Rather, they accomplish their tasks, especially when representing or standing in for their masters, according to the logic of creative imitation, which does not exclude, but includes, productive personal participation. Ultimately, this creative surplus may even retroactively impact the masters. From the standpoint of communication theory, this relation does not imply merely the unilateral transmission from sender to receiver, resulting in the sender affecting, transforming, or modifying the medium (of the servant), and thus the channel, in a particularly poignant manner. Rather, one must assume a reciprocal action involving a feedback channel which plays the particularities, transformations, and idiosyncrasies of the subaltern medium back to the sender and thus does not leave the latter unaffected by the process of transmission.

A closer look, for instance, when examining the literary traces left behind in the act of dictation between scholars and assistants, makes this kind of reciprocal impact between master and servant clearly visible. The initial hypothesis solidifies into a full-blown thesis. Thus the mimetic practices of the subalterns located in direct proximity to the master are not unidirectional but follow a feedback loop. Consequently, in the act of dictation, the masters turn, to a certain extent, into their own servants; they follow the instructions the domestics offer them in the form of cautious suggestions by giving them free rein to act. The words conceived in the name of the lord have thus long lost their sovereign originality; instead, they have become the imitative and autarchic formulations of the servants, whose autonomous *poiesis* the masters now must follow.

Goethe, for instance, seems to correctly appraise the influence he exerts on his servants. He self-reflexively introduces this relation in his literary production, thereby also acknowledging the servant's impact on his master. The complexities of the interaction between master and scribe are evoked in Count Egmont's relation to his private secretary, Richard. After making the secretary wait for two hours, Egmont finally enters the scene and receives the following report on the incoming correspondence:

> SECRETARY: I have left Count Oliva's letter here for you once more. Forgive me for drawing your attention to it again. More than anyone, the old gentleman deserves a full reply. It was your wish to write to him in person. Without doubt, he loves you like a father.
>
> EGMONT: I haven't the time. And of all odious things, writing is the most odious to me. You're so good at imitating my handwriting, write it in my name. [. . .]
>
> SECRETARY: Only tell me roughly what you think; I can then draft the reply and submit it to you. It shall be penned in such a way that it could pass for your handwriting in a court of law. [. . .]
>
> EGMONT: [. . .] Tell him not to be anxious; I shall act as I must and shall know how to protect myself. Let him use his influence at Court in my favour and be assured of my wholehearted gratitude.
>
> SECRETARY: Is that all? He expects a great deal more.
>
> EGMONT: What more should I say? If you want to be more long-winded, be so by all means.[95]

There are at least two instances worthy of notice in this act of epistolary transmission via the domestic medium—that is to say, in this scene of writing, transposed into the medium of literature imitating reality. First, the transmission of information takes place at the level where the mimesis of the master is performed by the medium of the servant. Richard can imitate Egmont's handwriting so well that the documents can go on file without objection and, moreover, can serve as hard evidence in any court of law. Richard demands a few cues from his master, something that seems to be mentioned only in passing. Based on those cues, he is now able to single-handedly articulate and formulate his master's 'rough thoughts.' This moment marks the launch of the poietic drive of the subaltern, defined by Ricoeur as one of the decisive components of mimesis.

Second, the mimetic act of the servant impacts upon the master. Richard translates Egmont's message into a letter, writes it down in the name of the sender but not without judging it first through the eyes of the receiver. The servant acts not merely as a channel in this case, sending along messages without interference. He transforms the message, even before sending it out. With empathic fervor, he assumes authorship and thus places himself in the position of his master. In a similar manner he also transposes himself in the role of the recipient, Count Oliva, who would be disappointed with the result of the transmission. Nevertheless, Richard anticipates his dissatisfaction and therefore demands more and kinder words from his master, the sender. In other words, the medium also works on the content, by correcting the sender's information. The medium messages the messenger, who, in turn, becomes the recipient of a letter as well as an order: the servant instructs the master to write more. As a medium of transmission, Richard thus operates in the mode of double imitation. On the one hand, he appropriates his master's authorial function, both in terms of form (via his handwriting) and in terms of content (by adopting the thoughts of his master and imitating them with impeccable precision). Thereby, he also acts better, more correctly and adequately, toward the recipient of the letter than his own superior. On the other hand, he edits the message by preemptively reading it from the perspective of the recipient, whose foreseeable disappointment Richard also imitates. To soften that reaction, he demands from Egmont a more detailed letter. But since the master will not simply agree to this turn of authority, he leaves it up to his servant to add more writing in his own name. The instruction he gives Richard comes with a great deal of autonomy: "If you want to be more long-winded, be so by all means." This intricate mix of command and mimetic compliance is rendered even more complex due to a doubly configured act of media transmission. The self-referential, recursive character of this act must be emphasized once more and for the remainder of this chapter. The communication process between master and domestic medium finds its double in the medium of literature, which, in turn, imitates the process of transmission between the real master (Goethe) and his servant (Seidel). One scene of writing generates yet another scene of writing. The timeline between the writing of *Egmont,* started in 1775, and its publication in 1788 corresponds precisely to the period of employment of Philipp Seidel, Goethe's 'certified copy,' whose influence on his master seems to be largely underestimated. Seidel does not aspire merely to emulate his master's lifestyle and employ his own servants, set up his own library, or take piano lessons at Goethe's expense. He acts both as his master's messenger and councillor. "Goethe was not just the one giving. There was a real exchange between them; he writes: 'Thanks go to you for your praise and your counsel, I am in the course of making good use of it.' "[96] In a certain sense Seidel can even be seen as Goethe's protector: "I urge you to openly speak on every subject that may be of interest to me, or which you may find worthy of mention; you need no introduction or apology. For I have always held you to be among my guardian spirits, therefore continue to apply yourself to this modest work in the future."[97]

Between the sixteenth and the eighteenth centuries, Western painting follows the ban imposed by the Holy Inquisition on visual representations of the lowly ranked. At the same time, servants are also steadily approaching their goal of emulating a specific image. They want to be like the others. The subalterns' mimetic desire is derived from approximating an image that is defined by the model (image) of their master. Subalterns usually do not have a family life; nor do they have a significant personal life, due to their long working hours. They even lack a personal name. Thus they define themselves exclusively in relation to their superiors. The longer they spend in someone's service, the more visible the features, gestures, expressions (and even slips of the tongue) they borrow from their masters. In this fashion, they get closer to their employers' image (and culture) without reaching their level of education.[98] The range of borrowed elements is broad: "Akin to a money teller at a large bank speaking of his institution,"[99] the servants commonly employ the pronoun "we" when in fact the only person in question is the master; subalterns may also imitate their lord's moods, complaining, like Louis XIV's valets, of not feeling well whenever the king is indisposed.[100]

One of the basic explanations for the servants' asymptotic approach to their masters may lie in their desire to take their superiors' place. Striving to appropriate their fashion of speaking and dressing (a cause of great frustration for Defoe), their habitus and handwriting correspond to deep-seated "fantasies of replacement and inversion" which animate subalterns as they engage in service or pastime activities. "French servants dressed up in their masters' clothes and called each other by their masters' names to compensate for the depersonalization of servanthood."[101] Domestics imitate their superiors' inclination for lavish festivities, going as far as to wear their own masks and calling each other by their masters' names. In such cases, but not only then, servants also attempt to copy the snobbery of the masters. Thackeray calls it "the servant's ditto."[102] "Seriously: people obeying usually look just like people giving orders. A servant can't help putting on the masks and allures of his master, in order faithfully to propagate them, as it were."[103] That is one of the few lessons Walser's Jakob von Gunten learns at the Institute Benjamenta.

Almost unconsciously, servants fall under the charismatic spell of their masters; or they co-opt their tiniest gestures and behaviors, some of their unique formulations, expressions, and intonations—not in the presence of their superiors but rather to guests, auditors, and supplicants. Consider, for instance, the account of Celeste Albaret, Marcel Proust's housekeeper from 1913 until his death in 1922, who was not impervious to the effect of mimetic transformations:

> At first, he would make me repeat word-by-word what I should say. But soon he no longer saw any need for it. I had become his record player to such a degree that people would mistakenly ask me over the telephone: "Hello? Is that you, Marcel? What joy!" One lady who was his friend even reproached him for it, telling him not to allow me to make use of his voice in this manner. Naturally, I was unaware of it; in a way, I adopted his voice.[104]

The unique media presence of the ministering communication channel takes the form of a nonelectric, automatic voice that willingly gives itself over to the sender's influence, taking the latter's place (here, acting in Proust's name): "Therefore he has shaped me according to his way of life."[105] The servant-medium turns into its trajectory from channel to server. Celeste Albaret even uses her voice, which comes indistinguishably close to that of her master, to play the part of the author. The unassuming service relation is replaced by an intense learning situation between scholar and assistant: this kind of independence counts as a particular incentive for watching and learning as much as possible from the other. Walter Porstmann, the secretary to the Nobel Prize recipient Wilhelm Ostwald, writes the following about his personal aspirations during the time he served as the chemist's assistant: "I used to watch him as he was taking his walks, and copied his movements and his gait, in order to experience his moods. [. . .] I adopted his teachings and his views in such a way that I could soon produce and reproduce them."[106] By paying close attention to the model, the copy can hope to gain its own independence.

This very process of learning or, better still, this very curiosity, gives rise to the instant when the direction of the mimetic reaction between master and servant begins to oscillate. As soon as the sender shows an interest in the medium, the positions switch; a back channel then opens between servant and sender and leaves its own imprint upon the original model. The servant-medium also becomes a sender, exerting its own influence upon the master. This interaction can be perfectly illustrated with the Proustian model. If Celeste Albaret unconsciously adopts some of Monsieur Proust's features, it could also be claimed that Proust also strives to learn from his housekeeper—as well as from his other servants. The regular conversations with Celeste are an occasion for the writer to find inspiration or circumspectly ask for advice. One evening, during a visit, he notices he has forgotten his medicine: "He sent a valet for it, giving him a lengthy description of the neighborhood and of the house. Finally, he said: 'You cannot miss it. It is the only window on the Boulevard Hausmann in which there is still a light burning.' Everything but the house number!"[107] Obviously, a well-trained servant may not even need such directions. Not unlike a library assistant, he can find his way through the urban maze due to his spatial memory. Thus the complicated directions are primarily meant to establish a back channel in the communication system between master and servant. In turn, Proust uses this very channel to study the mimetic strategies of his servants in order to transpose their media skills into the realm of literature. "Proust became intoxicated by the study of domestic servants—whether it be that an element which he encountered nowhere else intrigued his investigative faculties or that he envied servants their greater opportunities for observing the intimate details of things that aroused his interest. In any case, domestic servants in their various embodiments and types were his passion."[108] By giving his servants unusual instructions, he can closely observe their behavior; he invests the media of service with exemplary status so that he may also learn from them. The object of representation switches places with the agent of representation. This exchange goes hand in hand with the doubling of the master by the servant. From a critical distance, Walter Benjamin examines the relation, suggesting it reveals Proust's own subalternity:

And perhaps the greatest concentration of this connoisseur of ceremonies was reserved for the depiction of these lower ranks. Who can tell how much servant curiosity became part of Proust's flattery, how much servant flattery became mixed with his curiosity, and where this artful copy of the role of the servant on the heights of the social scale had its limits? Proust presented such a copy, and he could not help doing so, for, as he once admitted, "voir" and "désirer imiter" were one and the same thing to him. This attitude, which was both sovereign and obsequious, has been preserved by Maurice Barrès in the most apposite words that have ever been written about Proust: "Un poète persan dans une loge de portière."[109]

But beyond his literary curiosity, what other motive may drive the Persian poet to sit in his doorman's booth and pay such close attention to his servants rushing about, following his charmingly patronizing directions? According to Benjamin, Proust is caught in a constant struggle with himself. As a bourgeois, he frequents the best circles. Yet even such an independent and distinguished gentleman as Proust, with all his arsenal of flattery and petty subaltern curiosity, is faced with the "struggle for survival under the leafy canopy of society."[110]

3.5. THE SIMULTANEITY OF THE NONSIMULTANEOUS

To return once again to Lessing: Waitwell's struggle between duty and private initiative illustrates a historic turn in the servants' condition. Branded as CMC, the configuration marks a sociotechnical rift, prefigured in the Enlightenment tendencies of the age but only fully developed later in the century, when drastic political changes throw into question the predominance of the dutiful subaltern model. With the feudal estate system still in place, servants have to restrict themselves to a limited field of action; they are treated as mere objects. But in the aftermath of major political upheavals, and with the master–servant constellation placed under scrutiny, a new bourgeois individual is born. Endowed with official rights, this individual may now freely enter a service relation that can be annulled by either party at any time.

The historical shift in question might count as the origin of the so-called service society; or, it may be seen as a major milestone in the advance of the bourgeois subject toward equal rights, despite significant differences among various types of subalterns. After all, gender-based discriminatory practices as well as traditional hierarchical distinctions—from valet to stable boy—are still common in the Victorian era. However, the focus here will be on historiographic matters.

Therefore, the question will be: what could be gained from examining that epochal shift with the (media) theoretical tools, and, above all, the terminology employed so far? What does a formula like 'server error' have in common with the interpretation of an eighteenth-century play and a certain character's repeated attempts to deliver a letter? Some may instantly resist drawing parallels between Waitwell patiently standing by and a mail server being in an idle state, also known as 'no operation.' By working with twenty-first-century technological concepts, do we not *automatically* fall prey to the kind of culturally determined blindness that Rolf Christian Zimmermann has detected in the modern critical literature on Lessing and *Miss Sara Sampson*? "Mistaking our own enlightened modernity for the enlightened views of our literary predecessors and pioneering spirits"[111] may lead directly to such a blind spot—and consequently, to a systematic misunderstanding of a historical text to which we uncritically apply our own epistemic perspective.

Drawing on Heinrich Bornkamm, Zimmermann forcefully pleads for contextualizing the bourgeois drama within the religious conditions of its time. For generations, he argues, scholars have lacked interest in matters of religion and therefore they hold distorted views on such subjects. In response to Zimmermann's suggestion, one could refer to the holy channels that frame Waitwell's communicative act in highly technological terms. Indeed, it would not be far-fetched to speak of Waitwell as a *server,* since the notion designates precisely the kind of ministering spirit that originates in the ritual performance of religious duty: "One that assists the celebrant in the Mass, Divine Liturgy, or Holy Communion: an acolyte."[112] A server is therefore, first of all, nothing but a ministrant. The analogy with Waitwell's devotion is implicit.

But Zimmermann's critique could be applied more generally or more categorically still: does the analogy between a dedicated Enlightenment-era servant and a concept derived from contemporary electronic communication not result in an ahistorical method, one that denies the historicity of semantics or the contextualization of rhetoric? What might such an interpretation contribute if it eludes the historical uses of language; why introduce a term such as "mail server," which corresponds neither to Lessing's nor his characters' views and cannot be grasped by his public or readership? Nothing would seem more foreign to the spirit of the age of sensibility than a strictly formalized (electric) communication model based on standardized commands.

At least two kinds of counterarguments can be offered here, both at the conceptual and the structural level. On the one hand, every theoretical model applied to a historical text may run into the same difficulty and miss the essence of said text. Whether the terminology is derived from poetics, rhetoric, or information technology: any theoretical interpretation necessarily draws on concepts and knowledge that seem anachronistic in the given historical situation. In short, an 'ahistorical' reading simply cannot exist, since each theoretical model of a text or an event inevitably depends on temporal shifts and distancing effects.

On the other hand, such an analogy implies a certain interpretive symmetry. What counts is not simply the effort of describing an epistolary event from 1755 in the media-technical terms of today. The reading here proposes precisely the opposite strategy and thereby shows our contemporary acts of communication at work. There is abundant research on the historical significance of messengers and the acts of postal distribution and delivery.[113] In contrast, the uninterrupted activity of virtualized machines concealed in the switchboards of electronic communication still eludes understanding. In this case, the operations are hidden not only from the eyes of users but also from descriptive language. An increasingly large section of contemporary correspondence is assigned to a complex network of standardized protocols and globally connected communication nodes. With its binary program codes, this kind of network denies the access of literary-linguistic formulations. It is then precisely via such exemplary literary events and historically contextualized theoretical links that the elusive scenarios of communication may be rendered visible.[114] In other words, a careful reading of Waitwell's insistent interventions and dedicated service may contribute to the understanding of the processes taking place inside the fiber optic cables and in the vast territories of electronic 'acolytes.' Instead of an anachronistic rereading of Enlightenment literature, such an interpretation would propose, on the contrary, to start from the familiar terminology and strategies of a literary drama, in order to shed light into the hermetic, enigmatic operations of contemporary communicative processes.

The question may seem naïve, but what exactly happens when two machines meet to exchange electronic messages? The act of communication between mail client and mail server must follow a protocol, that is, a standardized procedure. During this procedure, what takes place is not merely an exchange of a series of commands and symbols. The dialogue actually mimics an everyday conversation whose object is the delivery of a letter. Such a dialogue may look like this:

> The *client* calls the *server* by saying helo and introducing itself. The server recognizes the caller, returns the greeting—this time, using proper grammar—and identifies the latter by its name and address. Finally, the server adds a polite expression that seems fully superfluous for the time being: pleased to meet you. After this initial dialogue and the specific mention of sender and receiver, the actual message is conveyed, the server confirms reception and discharges the client with a curt formula: quit.

What is crucial about this conversation is its conversational character. The two dialogue partners greet each other just like their literary or humanoid prototypes; they negotiate, or even misunderstand each other;[115] they hesitate and look for alternative paths to their destination; they also use dissimulation and mimicry and pretend to be someone else; they agree, fulfill their task, and part ways again. In short, they follow preset operational programs (inscriptions) codified in everyday language. But what is somewhat unexpected is the way the client expresses itself, more like a desperate petitioner than a master giving simple orders. The server is the one that actually runs the conversation, explaining the status of the transmission and informing the client of its intentions. Ultimately, then, the question is: who is still the master and who is the servant?

3.6. RECURSIVE HISTORIOGRAPHY

> In calling forth to something, the "whence" of the calling is the "whither" to which we are called back.
> — Martin Heidegger, *Being and Time,* 1927

What exactly occurs on a daily basis under the heading *computer-mediated communication?* How can one understand what takes place out of the sight of regular users in one of the many electronic message delivery centers? In order to grasp this phenomenon, the analysis so far has attempted to recover a figure from the distant past, traditionally relegated to a marginal position: the servant. Historically charged with the transmission of information, the servant exercises a far-reaching yet often overlooked degree of agency over the course of events.

This agency is the object of the current discussion. But at the same time, servants occupy a specific place as the dramatic protagonists and actors of eighteenth-century social history. Drawing on these roles, the current analysis aims to offer a general descriptive model of the functions of service, which can subsequently be applied also to any number of historical configurations. On this basis, one can identify certain core features of subaltern serviceability (the principle of invisibility, the noble art of waiting, the strategic evasion of orders, the fluctuating relations of authority). Starting from here, one can then shed light on the obscure events at the heart of the virtual kingdom of shadows inhabited by tireless demons and renegade ministrants.

But what structure best defines the connection between the two temporally distant configurations of 1800 and today? Both, after all, follow the principle of CMC, whether understood as metonymic shorthand for the subordination to an impersonal service or as an acronym for electronic channels. The parallel between the two scenarios, as I will argue, must be examined at the level of their epistemic relevance, since both represent turning-point situations or moments of epistemic rupture. Previously categorized as objects, servants after 1800 acquire the limited status of service subjects. Similarly, the question about the agency of things in the electronic world also takes an epistemic turn:

data-processing agents are increasingly subjectified, or at least fit into anthro-pomorphic descriptive models, with their set of corresponding metaphors. Consider, for instance, the avatars from *Second Life* or the minuscule digital substitutes from weblin.com, which accompany users on their journeys across the World Wide Web. But the proposed structure extends even further beyond such correspondences.

Other aspects belong here as well: for instance, the previously discussed phe-nomenon of historical distance, implicit in any theoretical model; or the pro-posal to apply the logic of a literary servant figure from a bourgeois tragedy to an act of contemporary communication. Such aspects can further elucidate the historiographic structure of the narrative proposed. Its general formula corre-sponds to the principle of *recursion*.[116]

In German, the nominal form of the term is derived from the Late Latin *re-cursio,* meaning "running back." Then, during the early eighteenth century, the verb *rekurrieren* is introduced via French as a formal expression meaning "mak-ing recourse to, appealing, referring back to."[117] The adjectival form *rekursiv* ap-pears after 1900 in the context of mathematics, where it signifies "returning (to known values); obtained via recourse of what is known,"[118] a definition which is taken even further in practical applications in mathematics or informatics: "A recursion is an algorithm which makes reference to itself for its execution and calculation and in the process simplifies itself to a certain degree."[119] In other words, the crucial aspect here is the particular element of self-reference that is continuously activated under conditions of constant status control. This loop, with its ever more deeply nested iterations, performs the same operation until it reaches a certain predetermined state—the so-called termination condition—which is linked with yet another specific operation. Once this stage is reached, two possibilities open up: the process either comes to an end or—and therein lies the beauty of the model—works itself back to the start, by performing yet another, equally predetermined operation—in other words, going back, step by step, to the point of departure.[120] But this is possible only because the recursion modifies itself with each new iteration, checking its current status at every given time. Thereby, it decides whether a new iteration is necessary or whether the termination condition has been finally met. "Significantly, a recursive algorithm reaches such a level of simplicity at a certain point that it may ultimately be per-formed without necessarily invoking itself any longer."[121] When the deepest it-eration is reached, the function has achieved its level of execution. It either ends here or the process starts anew, by extricating itself from the deepest level, using the same number of iterations, until it returns to the start. But given the ac-tions that have been performed in the process, the starting point has long since become a different one. With each new iteration, the knowledge accumulated retroactively affects the point of departure, transforming not only the initial information but also the status of the entire process. To put it in historiographic terms: the recursive process allows for a perspective on the simultaneity of the nonsimultaneous; or, even more concisely, the recursive process is a method of retrospective anticipation.

In abstract terms, recursive processes anticipate events by knowing or defining their own endpoint even prior to their occurrence. Otherwise, without stating its respective termination condition, a function would endlessly invoke itself. At the same time, the function also constantly draws on something that has already happened, its own history, so to speak. The recalls correspond, every time, to the respective state of the function within the iterations and the knowledge associated with them at any given point.

How can this simple principle and the complex logic that derives from it be applied to a historical situation or to actual events? How can one reach, on this basis, a new understanding of old facts and place old insights into novel configurations? One option would be to abandon a chronologically linear understanding of historical processes and events and look at them through the lens of moments of recursion instead. Ultimately, this new kind of historical analysis would also make room for lines of interpretation that take recursion as their basis of organization.

To refer, once more, to our concrete situation: if what is at stake is to understand the specific nature of the unique, unintelligible actors inhabiting the electronic domain, then the answers lie within the question of recursion. It is via the figure of recursion that we can grasp the inner workings of the server and demons in the virtual domain—from the point of view not only of their informational constitution but also of their cultural and historical relevance over time.

How does the server essentially function, and what does it do to the users under its command? In order to trace its operations one has to recur to the history of service, so as to reconstitute, via its specific iterations, the various functions and characteristics of subaltern spirits. With every iteration and each analytic description of a particular case study, the historiographic method comes a bit closer to the heart of the matter. The question concerning the fundamental nature of the servant figure is thereby offered a succession of different interpretive models. With each new iteration, the analyzed scenarios are further connected to the initial act of service—performed by the subalterns of the electronic domain. In other words, the figure of recursion invokes itself; and as a consequence the interpretation of a drama from 1755 can make room for technological notions such as *mail server* or *server error*. Furthermore, each iteration also tests the termination condition of the cognitive process at hand. The process reaches its endpoint when the various iterations have been performed—each adding a new epistemic component and thereby enriching the narrative—and the termination condition has been finally met. Once the required level of depth has been attained, the epistemic configuration achieved may give sufficient information about the initial state—in this case, about the question concerning the nature of electronic service and its historical genesis.

We have reached a point where a decision must be made: either end the process here and refer to the solution, namely, the basic insight into the nature of service at its deepest level of meaning; or else retrace our steps to the point of origin, by performing each iteration anew, this time, however, with the aid of the further knowledge accumulated. With each step back, new information is added. The recursive method thus also adds surplus value—namely, the possibility of chronological narration. The path leading from the end back to the start is represented by the linear development of servants' characteristics from the Enlightenment to the twenty-first century.

In conclusion, the recursive method offers at least two narrative paths, each with its own explanatory model and various levels of iteration. Combining these two paths results in a differentiated line of interpretation: the former path leads from the virtual domain to the world of eighteenth-century servants; the recursion here enables the description of a future communicative situation. In contrast, the latter path starts from the depths of history and develops a chronological, future-oriented narrative which arrives at an altered point of departure and a modified state of knowledge. Couched in a historiographic narrative, the principle of recursion can thus explain structural relations and historical developments even across extended periods of time.

What is obtained via this recursive procedure is not merely the possibility of connecting two nonsimultaneous phenomena but also the ability of a concept to invoke itself. The concept—in this case the basic function of service—can thereby, under slightly modified conditions, finally return to work back on its initial point of departure. The recursive narrative advances by supplying the previously unexplained mode of operation of virtual demons and electronic ministrants with successive applications of a historical index leading up to Waitwell's basic service functions. The result is the mutual elucidation of all levels of iteration, in a symmetrical configuration: to a certain extent, the eighteenth-century servant functions not unlike a mail server, which, in turn, exhibits the typical features of the classic domestic figure. With each iteration, those features reveal increasingly differentiated characteristics. Thus, with the aid of the recursive logic, one may not only answer the initial question but also productively integrate the classic servant role into the new electronic contexts. The procedure ultimately allows an intervention into an extended process of historical transformation that connects two or more narrative paths, rendering them mutually plausible: the servant role within the realm of bourgeois drama and the machine operations of today.

3.7. THE WORLD TURNED UPSIDE DOWN

> She looked anxiously around, searching for her valet. He suddenly re-appeared out of nowhere. Standing in front of her, he looked into her eyes with a look that expressed loyalty and love. "What is it you want, Frederic?" she gently asked the old man.
> —Marek Krajewski, *Phantoms of Breslau*, 2005

Donning better clothes than your master; calling each other by your superiors' names; mimetically appropriating the masters' habits, modes of expression, and handwriting; endlessly asking a valet what he may "want"—all of the above illustrate the same point: the connection between master and servant at various levels is not determined by stable relations of power. On the contrary, these relations threaten to be turned on their head, at least for a while, sometimes also for extended periods of time. Both as a topos and a historical phenomenon, this mechanism has had a long tradition. The formula that designates the changing relations of power within the aforementioned tradition is that of a topsy-turvy world, a world turned upside down. Its consequences are apparent in the most diverse of contexts and take at least two different forms: first, during the lavish court festivities of the aristocracy, where the regular dress order is canceled[122] and dignitaries hide behind the masks of the lower ranks; and, second, as a phenomenon of popular culture, in the institutionalized form of the carnival, which also celebrates a type of regulated subversion of order and the travesty of values for a limited number of days. Yet another context in which the world is turned upside down is frequently encountered in the literary domain. Consider, for instance, the case of Diderot's *Jacques le fataliste et son maître,* in which the servant Jacques embodies the driving force of the plot and for the most part acts as the uncontested master. The tradition is best represented in the theatrical universe, where the motif is constantly employed. One of the most notable works in this regard is Ludwig Tieck's *The Land of Upside Down,* where the theme is already prefigured in the title. The simple folk in the play—subalterns, petty bourgeois characters, actors—take over the positions of power. Further, as I will show, Tieck's 'historical act' demonstrates how recursive narrative forms are themselves linked to the motif of inverted power relations.

The task of summarizing Tieck's 1798 play, with its minute subtleties and allusions, is bound to fail. Despite its brevity, the work is characterized by an ample cast of characters as well as a richness of motifs, locales, and levels that steadily grow more intertwined over the course of the play. To drastically simplify matters, it is a story revolving around the production of a play that starts out with a case of swapped roles at multiple levels. Scaramuz, the stereotype of the Neapolitan braggart from the commedia dell'arte, revolts against the dramatist since he is weary of always being cast in lesser roles. The piece starts out with an epilogue instead of a prologue. Rising above his rank, Scaramuz demands to play a noble character. The writer agrees and gives him the role of Apollo; meanwhile, Pierrot decides to become a spectator rather than continue to act, and Grünhelm, usually a tragic figure, must now pose as a fool. Tieck's piece is thus a play about Scaramuz as Apollo. That play opens a further level of recursion by introducing yet another play with a romantic premise. In turn, that other play becomes the background for a further play (a bucolic piece), which renders the whole affair rather confusing for viewers. During a short break in the third act, the critic Scävola explains, "One cannot stand it, that much is sure. See, people, we all sit here and watch a play; in this play, there are others who watch another play; and in that third one, the actors are shown yet another play."[123] Scaramuz, who shares some of Napoleon's traits,[124] gradually loses the capacity to distinguish between theatrical performance and reality. Following increasingly complex imbroglios, the director Wagemann, dressed as Neptune in a final scene featuring a sea battle, decides to bring everything to a halt. With that gesture, reality bursts back into the world of representation. The real relations of power need to be reestablished. But Scaramuz will have none of it, so the director insists: "Sir, this is an order."[125] Yet Scaramuz has long identified with the role of the highest god and authority. He still takes fiction for reality. He wants to reap the benefits of the various levels of recursion and wishes to hold on to the power he has acquired as a consequence of the playful role-swap. The world of the upside down has become his real world. The others show concern over Scaramuz's lost sense of reality and worry whether the play will ever come to an end, so they conspire to find a way out. Once all the fictional levels have been lifted, the 'real' Apollo comes onstage and concludes: "But, gentlemen, in your enthusiasm you have lost sight of the fact that we are mere actors and this is only a play—And this finally brings the play to its end." These words are then followed by the prologue.[126] Quite literally, a mad play.

But Tieck's work does not simply provide an average example of the world turned upside down motif, like the eponymous plays by Christian Weise (1683) and Johann Ulrich von König (1725). In fact, the piece threatens to lose its coherence altogether, as it becomes oversaturated with intertextual, performative, and political allusions: ironic nods to the genre of bourgeois tragedy and its emotional effects; references to Lessing's *Minna von Barnhelm* (particularly to the scenes at the inn), to Carlo Goldoni, (the servant singing his own praises in order to get a higher tip), to Shakespeare, and Cervantes (Tieck translated their works himself); sarcastic formulations ("I am Your Majesty's unworthy servant");[127] allusions to the concrete elements of production (the machine operators play an important part in this context) as well as to political events (the French Revolution in particular, as a historical turning point), etc.

Self-reflexivity is obviously the defining feature of this "poem unlimited."[128] Two additional aspects will be considered here as well: the question regarding service and the role assigned to masks in the play. Finally, the analysis will focus on the figure of recursion as a poetic and historiographic technique. Not unlike Lessing's *Miss Sara Sampson,* and Beaumarchais's *Figaro* (1778), in which the servants are given prominent roles, Tieck's play also raises questions with regard to the estates clause. When Scaramuz takes over Apollo's role and mode of expression, the innkeeper replies with a metacommentary that invokes the poetics of rules: "A slave must speak according to his rank. Just look it up in the *Ars Poetica.* I am an innkeeper and I am also under its rule."[129] In a similarly dialectical move, the disrupted social order also functions as a political commentary on the French Revolution. Ironically, the aristocrats in the play willingly accept being downgraded to the rank of bourgeois subjects. "We eagerly step down from our throne / when we are called to our noble bourgeois duty."[130] Simultaneously, the critically minded Scävola complains about the aristocrats' reluctance to conform to the prescribed order and implicitly to their bourgeois fate within the play. "If only princes would embrace such plays with bourgeois virtue."[131] A further metacommentary inserted after act 3 ironically alludes to the political aims of the play and its imposition of social equality, with princes turning into bourgeois subjects, and those at the bottom getting on top: "It's a noble idea on our part that everyone should serve."[132] But ultimately the play appears to question its own theme of servants-turned-masters. In the end, the dramatic and fictional levels are all stripped down, and the illusory character of the plot is finally exposed.

Visibly or not, the actors in the play also hide behind multiple masks, either in the form of costumes like liveries or diamond-patterned harlequin outfits, role-specific expressions and gestures or actual masks, as in the commedia dell'arte and its paraphernalia. The play stages a complex game of signs that pervade all levels and character constructions. There are multiple recursive stagings, when actors appear as the performers of performers of other performers, either in leading or subaltern roles. Every literary figure on stage operates mimetically with respect to the textual template; on the other hand, each also invokes real features, which the roles must render credible—otherwise servants would not be recognized as such. Each time, the masks signal a transition between two identities, the switch between the respective roles, transitioning from reality to fiction. The crucial aspect is the capacity of masks to conceal and therefore generate the invisibility of a certain element that allows a figure to act at a particular level. Masks feign an overarching perspective on the whole. Speaking via a mask, via the act of *per-sonare*,[133] the performer attains the status of a fragile sign that partly disappears behind a fictional subject and partly speaks for another—as in the case of the servant acting as a substitute for his master. Tieck's play thus allows a double view, both from within and beyond the masks, by putting in the mouths of performers metacommentaries on their respective roles. The volatile character of the roles and identities associated with them is also made apparent, namely, by way of the endless game of free-floating signifiers and the abrupt changes among the various levels.

The shifting positions of the roles correspond to the way servants function around 1800. Their liminality and capacity to straddle the line, which Defoe associated with their amphibian character, allows subalterns to constantly move and mediate between real and fictional components. At the end of the ancien régime, servants find themselves on a threshold between the position of a stereotypical mask and the prospective status of a politically liberated individual. As they gain more political rights and attain subject status, their former service function amounts to a role that is increasingly at their disposal. "That identity is not imposed, but can rather transition into free existence. The dissolution of a rigidly structured society that still conforms to feudal ranks starts from here. Servants regard their position strictly in terms of a function, a role."[134] As a consequence of political upheavals, the function of servants around 1800 acquires the character of a role. The transformation is accompanied, but also accelerated, by the literary presence of subalterns on stage and in works of fiction. One could argue that the function of servants—onstage but also beyond it—comes close to the character of a mask. With their new (service) contract, subalterns perform their duties by assuming various identities: as dutiful media, troublemakers, messengers, and masters under the guise of anonymous domestics. The function of a servant and the representation of a character onstage implies the use of volatile identities, the act of assuming roles, of operating against the proper nature of an individual. Only the performance of the fool stands above travesty in Tieck's play, since he has always played the part of destabilizing the certainty of knowledge. He alone is exempt from the permanent role swapping and thus represents the only constant element in the play: "Unfortunately, in every position I remain a fool."[135]

But how does Tieck's *The Land of Upside Down* relate to the question of recursion? On the one hand, the complex power relations in the play are obviously self-reflexive. As the first chapter has demonstrated, the link between master and servant is organized according to the principle of recursion. Every master is a servant and vice versa. On the other hand, the play within the play and the intrigue at the heart of the intrigue help move the plot forward since they promise to break open the rigid relations and thereby allow for new connections. This recursive multiplication of levels was already tested as a dramatic technique in antiquity. In that context, it is the slave figures—for instance, in Menander's *Aspis*[136]—who carry that decisive role. Further highlights within that tradition are plays of the romantic age (for instance, by Tieck) and the baroque, as well as during Elizabethan times. Probably the best-known case is *Hamlet,* in which a troupe of actors is deployed to exact revenge and expose the guilt of the royal couple.

But which are the special effects and functions assigned to the recursive element in Tieck's *The Land of Upside Down*? The multiplication of levels and interventions associated with them can—and have been—read as an ongoing commentary on the practice of dramatic writing and, implicitly, on the writing of history itself.[137] On the other hand, and more important, the multiplication of levels and particularly the abrupt transition between them lead to the disruption of illusions, which, in turn, allows for a further moment of reflection.

With each new iteration that opens a new performance level, the characters onstage as well as the viewers in the theater are pulled into an experience of "the confusion of all confusions."[138] The productive aspect of recursion is directly connected with this kind of frustration. The constant disruption of the plot is insistently linked to a reflection on the status quo (and occasionally also on the possibility of acquiring knowledge). As they advance to the ultimate iteration, recursions typically tend toward simplification, despite the effect of confusion experienced by the participants. Once a play makes room for another play, the roles are redistributed, and the power relations at that level become clear. In Tieck's work, it is at the level of the pastoral play, the ultimate layer of action, that the various relations unfold.

This is where the tightly wound knot of relations finally gets untangled. This is also where new connections are established—quite literally speaking—since the pastoral play ends with two of Apollo's Muses getting married and with their weddings being granted by Scaramuz. But these new arrangements have a unique impact on the level above, where Scaramuz's influence over the Muses does not reach. At the ultimate level of the play within a play, this situation leads to a loss of power and thereby to a solution for the entire play, since it sets the scene for Scaramuz's deposition. Just as in *Hamlet,* the play within a play within a play provides a solution which affects the next level, and that, in turn, solves the entanglements of the level above. Scaramuz loses his grip on the Muses; his role as despotic ruler thereby comes under threat at all other levels of the play. And now that the conflict is solved at this ultimate level, the plot can continue. The simple pastoral piece in which the lovers find one another serves as a termination condition for the other iterations. The rapidly changing levels of reference face the despot with his own illusions, so that he ultimately has no solution other than to abdicate his role as Apollo. Thus the recursion is a form of anticipatory return. The entanglements and multiplications of levels are necessary for Scaramuz to realize he is not meant to be Apollo but instead needs to go back to his traditional servant role—and implicitly to the start, now somewhat enriched by the knowledge he has accumulated in the process. *The Land of Upside Down* is therefore not a mere mirror image of extant conditions where the roles are simply swapped around but rather a recursive game that extends over several levels. With each new change of levels, the game appears more complicated but also more simplified, until a solution is found at the level of the ultimate iteration of the pastoral play. The attraction of the play lies precisely in such recursive complications that lead to new insights with each change of levels. The recursion offers the viewers as well as the participants onstage a chance to reflect on the events and to invest in them epistemic value.

But wherein lies the unique revelation of Tieck's parody? Its defining feature is not necessarily the motif of the world turned upside down but rather its recursive structure, with its three levels of representation. Furthermore, a fourth level is added to the three above: the level of the real theatergoers. The cognitive impact is primarily produced via the technique of level switching. With each transition, either down to the ultimate iteration, or up to the level above, there are at least two different perspectives that open up. To the extent to which one can keep track of the preceding steps, the act of following the events onstage can require up to five different perspectives as well as the ability to alternate between them. The public are forced to shift their attention every time a character undergoes a further role change. In order to maintain the overview, the spectators are forced to make comparisons, thereby allowing the differences between the levels to become more apparent. With the introduction of new alternate perspectives, the actors are shown to perform two (or several) roles, and the public may gain further knowledge. The viewers are taught to see things contingently: one and the same performer suddenly turns out to be someone who plays a double game on two different levels; and the new level that opens up renders the difference between that level and the previous one even more striking. The spectators (and the spectators represented onstage) cannot escape the alternating perspectives to which the play subjects them. But it is obviously not irrelevant who performs the actual shifts. No role seems better suited for carrying out and demonstrating this practice of permanent change than that of the servant. In fact, subalterns are trained to handle two levels of reference at once. Their everyday activity prepares them to move back and forth between various stages. This ability allows them to remain in a marginal cognitive position, which at the same time entails a specific epistemic advantage. Their function is that of bringing distant elements into contact; and in that capacity they occupy a position of second-order observation, which allows them to switch and mediate between various levels.

The act of recursion demands a multiple change of perspective in a process that entails new cognitive possibilities. This switch of perspectives is precisely what Tieck's play invites its viewers to experience—particularly via the servant figures it abundantly features. The same practice can then be productively applied to historical processes. Introducing contemporary terminology in the analysis of literary dramas from 1800 or 1755 promises to bear fruit, but not merely because the results may contribute to our understanding of categories such as 'recursion' or 'bourgeois tragedy.' Furthermore, the new perspective enables a return to the initial stage, to the observer's point of view. In this manner, both the terms and the practice of computer-mediated communication are rendered even more relevant for the study of eighteenth-century servants and subalterns as well as for the Enlightenment knowledge associated with them.

Taken together, the subaltern's privileged cognitive position, moving from margin to center, and the concept of recursion, with its constant change of perspective, enable the reading of eighteenth-century texts as well as the interpretation of historical processes and general resources regarding the subject of service. Both lead to a better understanding of the intricate and hermetic processes taking place in the electronic domain. Only by anticipating the subalterns of the past can we grasp what has long ago happened in the realm of electronic communication, without the aid of higher-level observation. A historiographic enterprise that follows this kind of trajectory cannot escape the logic of recursive argumentation. For only through comparison, via the juxtaposition of different levels and distant orientation points, can it become clear how actors conduct themselves in specific moments of historical transition. And clearly, the world around 1800 is in the process of changing, even at the highest, that is, the political, level.

During the ancien régime, servants are still treated as objects; as such, they have few rights and many duties. They simply receive orders and must respond to every call. But after the demise of the feudal order and the end of the estate system, subalterns finally have recourse to themselves and become their own masters. The domestic subjects are set free; with the legal help of modified service contracts, they may now follow a professional path, be part of unions, associations, and various interest groups. The beginning of this process can be seen in literary contexts as well. Dramatic plays such as Lessing's *Miss Sara Sampson* and Tieck's *The Land of Upside Down* test new political situations, ideas about the equality between classes, the reversal of power relations or the notion that 'this-could-be-different.' For his part, Lessing finds innovative dramatic applications for the functions of domestics, effacing the differences between masters and servants and thus anticipating political revolutions in the spirit of the Enlightenment. Tieck uses the logic and principles of recursion to shift the focus away from state matters and major events, via the world of the bourgeoisie, into the sphere of subalterns.

Thus servants can be shown to play a crucial role not merely in the realm of tragedy, with its high-ranking protagonists, but also in the world of everyday drama, where domestics test their new professional consciousness. The servant figure is liberated during the eighteenth century from its traditional role as literary accessory, as political nonentity and sociotechnical abstraction. Launched and promoted in literature, trained via the bourgeois drama and the world of the upside down, the servant figure is helped along on its way to subjecthood. But the transition from object to subject takes on many forms. The next chapter will focus on the subaltern figure during its heyday but also its phase of transformation (for instance, into a quasi-object) during the nineteenth century.

Part Two **The Interregnum of the Subject**

Chapter 4 Holding the Reins: On Demons and Other Ministering Spirits of Science

How can you recognize a demon? He chatters and exaggerates.
—Alexander Kluge

Maxwell's got one; Laplace and Loschmidt too; so does Socrates; Madame Curie, however, does not. But let's take things one step at a time: after the Enlightenment and the age of representation, the so-called exact sciences of the nineteenth century are recast in a "field of a priori sciences, pure formal sciences, deductive sciences."[1] And yet, there they are: demons. Despite the impact of post-Enlightenment reason and notwithstanding the epistemic break between natural history and human sciences, they still occupy a firm position: within the former domain of natural philosophy—now physics—in the realm of mathematical probability theory, as well as in chemistry, which becomes an autonomous discipline over the course of the century. As unexplained natural phenomena, demons had long represented inexplicable, supernatural, nonintelligible forces. Surprisingly, however, despite the increasing impact of mathematical and abstract thinking, they continue to occupy a functional role in the new scientific research produced between the age of the Biedermeier and the belle époque.

The concept of the demon is almost as old as Western history itself. It is mentioned in the *Iliad,* where δαίμων designates both benevolent and evil divinities. Its etymology is unclear, but there are indications that the term comes from the Greek δαίεσθαι, meaning "to divide" or "to allot."[2] And, indeed, demons have been historically linked to the cultural practice of sorting, distinguishing, dividing, and restructuring. But the δαίμων is first and foremost an intermediary "between god and mortal,"[3] in other words, a mediator between heaven and earth, transcendence and immanence. Its main function is to establish a communication channel connecting the human senses with that which eludes immediate human perception and explanatory attempts. The demon creates and enables the connection between intelligible contexts and spiritual phenomena. In *The Symposium* (and beyond), Socrates presents the δαιμόνιον as a companion and advisor; for Plato, the demon's protective functions, along with its divine features, are still predominant. But starting with Plato's student Xenocrates, who ascribes positive attributes only to the 'real' gods, such intermediate beings are preeminently assigned evil connotations. That is also how demons acquire their specific place in religious history, in the context of Judaic teachings, Christian dogma, as well as in regional folk mythologies until (or even beyond) the age of Enlightenment. An extensive process of differentiation takes place throughout this time: starting with sprites, who are in charge of the four elements, the duties of the ever-growing number of spirits multiply and diversify into increasingly specialized subcategories.

It may be surprising at first to discover such strange creatures as demons at the heart of the nineteenth century, with its strictly formalized natural sciences, its modern, mathematically purified physics, and its probability calculus; it may be odd to find them hidden between the grooves of electromagnetic fields or the stochastic measurements of molecular movements. But things no longer seem strange if one considers that scientists in Victorian England[4] and certain members of the Prussian research elite are not entirely hostile to spiritualism, with its radiological specters and occult ethereal creatures. What has changed, however, is the location of these intermediate creatures or mediums (in the contemporary as well as occult sense of the word). The gap left open for the intervention of demons is no longer merely the space between knowledge and the unknown, found in the hazy regions that escape theory and empirical truth, and thus appear inexplicable. Rather, demons now play a central role in theoretical models, where they act as 'signal operators.' They are particularly active in thought experiments, which help test hidden natural laws, for instance, in the domains of thermodynamics and classical mechanics.

The following section will trace the rise of demons from their representation in theoretical texts to their concrete manifestations in reality. The focus will be on their epistemological status and their fictional as well as factual contribution to scientific (thought) experiments.

4.1. ON THE DEMONOLOGY DISCOURSE IN PHYSICS: A BRIEF HISTORY

> Little gods of local technologies.
> —Michel Serres, *Angels: A Modern Myth*

4.1.1. On Bookkeepers, Doorkeepers, and Exorcists

The bookkeeper: Laplace. Laplace's demon is the uncontested ancestor of all intermediate beings of the modern episteme. Not unlike the demonic king Balam, this being can find perfect answers to all things past, present, and future. It also possesses the ability to make humans insightful or invisible.[5] The French mathematician Pierre-Simon de Laplace first introduces his 'intellect' in 1773 in a paper presented to the Académie Royale des Sciences, and then later in 1814 in his *Essai philosophique sur les probabilités*. At a particular moment, the being is supposed to know all forces of nature as well as the respective state of each of their components. That kind of knowledge is by no means insignificant; from it derives the unlimited determinability of the world. "Nothing would be uncertain and the future, as the past, would be present to its eyes."[6]

Laplace's seemingly casual intervention is in fact a philosophical provocation. For his creature cannot be identified with the great mover called God, but rather appears as a modest clerk who merely observes and calculates. And from that very position it attacks the old foundations of religious theology and philosophical determinism. If every effect stems from a cause and if this principle can be applied or calculated with the help of Newtonian differential equations for any past and future state of any given moment in time, then there can no longer be any room for the unforeseen, for contingency, or freedom of the will. Laplace's intellect thus situates itself within the discourse of determinism, becoming its privileged emblem or symbol in the domain of natural philosophy. Despite its almost accidental adoption, the being becomes for a while the distinctive figure of classical Newtonian mechanics, along with its implications of precise observation and law-based prediction, until it is annulled by quantum mechanics, chaos theory, or Heisenberg's uncertainty principle.

The consequences of (in)determinism will not be examined in detail at this point.[7] Rather, the focus will be on what may be called a 'productive misunderstanding' of the thought experiment delineated above. The creature does not serve the purpose of canceling human freedom of action or adding support in favor of determinism. Laplace is not concerned with the philosophical implications of his all-knowing intellect. The being is meant to function only as a preliminary observation that would allow him to elaborate on the advantages of his probability theory. In his paper Laplace writes, "But ignorance of the different causes involved in the production of events, as well as their complexity, taken together with the imperfection of analysis, prevents our reaching the same certainty about the vast majority of phenomena."[8] And since estimations fail in most cases despite precise observation of initial conditions, the intellect will "always remain infinitely removed,"[9] gradual approximations notwithstanding. At this point Laplace launches his actual argument. To counteract the weakness of human understanding, mankind's notorious ignorance of causes and insufficient analytical insight into possible effects, he introduces "one of the most delicate and ingenious of mathematical theories, the science of chance or probability."[10] In other words, Laplace creates his omnipotent cognitive being only in order to subsequently limit it again in the course of his analysis and oppose it to the human spirit, with its vague, uncertain presuppositions. The famous formulation of Laplace's demon is nothing but a rhetorical means of contrast in order to strategically position the calculation of probability.[11]

Indeed, at least within certain circles, Laplace would have remained much more famous for his probability theory than for his thought experiment, if his creature hadn't been brought back to life ninety-nine years later, under different circumstances. In the famous "Ignorabimus" [We shall never know] speech in his lecture *Über die Grenzen der Naturerkenntnis [On the Limits of Science],* delivered to the Congress of German Scientists and Physicians in 1872, the Berlin physiologist Emil Du Bois-Reymond discusses the two insurmountable limits faced by scientific knowledge. In that context he invokes Laplace's demon. One of those limits, Du Bois-Reymond argues, is defined by the unsolvable question of consciousness and the impossibility of explaining it at the physical level, that is, via the complex interactions of molecular processes. The other limit has to do with the contradictory consequences deriving from the concept of the indivisible, smallest particle of matter, be it the 'physical' or the 'philosophical atom'[12] construct, or, in the more finely differentiated terminology of today: the quark, the Higgs boson, or the neutrino. Laplace's spirit, the possessor of "the universal formula,"[13] in Du Bois-Reymond's formulation, may be able to determine every single state of matter due to its precise knowledge of every configuration of the particles and every implication resulting from the laws of movement. But the cause of those movements and states as well as the insight into the state itself— such aspects remain closed to it.

The inadequate cognitive capacity, the inability to establish second-order observations is what prevents Laplace's spirit from being ascribed higher attributes than a creator god. This is precisely why Du Bois-Reymond labels the creature a 'spirit,' that is, he assigns the unspecified being imagined by Laplace a definite place among those found midway between man and God and confers upon it a subordinate function in the hierarchy of universal powers. With its almost limitless knowledge of all states, the spirit still only possesses one single—yet tremendous—area of expertise but lacks the ability to turn it into creative insight. In this sense, it strictly contributes to the mediation of information—the destination is irrelevant—without being able to lay claim to any of it.

What, then, is a scientific demon? According to an initial, provisional definition, it may be described as the effect of a productive misreading. Laplace's thought experiment, which was meant only to illustrate the advantages of his probability theory, reemerges, under modified conditions, about a century later. In this new form it is totally isolated from the context of probability calculus and thus disconnected from its initial configuration. Herein lies the misreading. But despite—or precisely because of—this discursive change, the agitation it produces has a stimulating, rather than a hindering, effect. For what is the purpose of a demon? In his theoretical analysis of the limits of science, Du Bois-Reymond still calls it a spirit. Both he and Laplace describe it as a lever, a step on the road to knowledge, to insight into the limits of what can be known. The demon functions not unlike an assistant paving the way for someone else's course of thought, laying down the tracks for knowledge. And yet these intermediate beings also have another, far greater potential for causing epistemic disorder, which can no longer be controlled by those who create or rediscover them: once they are released into the world, they take on a life of their own, which, in turn, leads to surprising new insights. The unexpected blessing that comes with such spirits is the constant intellectual struggle to get rid of them again. Nowhere is this more obvious than in the case of what is possibly the most famous, most discussed spirit of all, and of the ongoing efforts to eradicate it.

The doorkeeper: Maxwell. Almost incidentally, while working on his kinetic theory of gases, the British physicist James Clerk Maxwell creates his own demon, one that will be closely associated with his name. On December 11, 1867, writing to his school friend Peter Guthrie Tait, a physicist himself, Maxwell inserts the following comment between illustrations of mathematical nodes and quaternion equations: "Now conceive a finite being who knows the paths and velocities of all the molecules by simple inspection, but who can do no work, except to open and close a hole in the diaphragm, by means of a slide without mass."[14]

The structure of Maxwell's thought experiment is well known: the strange, nondivine creature watches over the hole between two gas-filled chambers. It opens the slide without mass as soon as a fast molecule approaches. And it closes it whenever a slow molecule comes near. The temperature in one of the chambers gradually rises, while in the other one the temperature goes down, despite the fact that no work has been performed. Strictly by means of observation and selection, the demon threatens to undermine the law of entropy formulated by Rudolf Clausius in 1865. That law demanded that the degree of disorder within closed systems gradually increases rather than decreases—as in the case of the demonic activity. And that is precisely what Maxwell intends to show, as he writes to Tait: "To pick a hole—say in the 2nd law of $\Theta\Delta$ [= thermodynamics . . .] *without external agency.*"[15] Maxwell cuts a hole in the conceptual edifice of thermodynamics, namely, via an opening controlled by a strange doorkeeper. The hole thus becomes a wound in the young, untouched body of thermodynamic natural laws. Maxwell's colleagues react like doubting Thomases. And the demon within the system helps them decide whether the wound closes or not.

Not unlike Laplace, Maxwell does not explicitly call the protagonist of his thought experiment a 'demon,' but rather a "very observant and neat fingered being."[16] And just like Laplace, who returns to his analysis in the *Essay*, Maxwell goes back to his experiment a few years later and introduces it to the scientific public in the final pages of his *Theory of Heat* from 1871. Once again, Maxwell's creature will be included in the society of scientific demons by someone else. Its baptism records are two short articles by William Thomson, known as Lord Kelvin. Kelvin utilizes Maxwell's theory of heat in order to further imagine the scenario of entropy under threat, to give it a vivid shape and inscribe it in the functional context of helpful scientific spirits, completely devoid of any negative connotations. Thomson briefly describes the figure in an essay published in the journal *Nature* in 1874 as "Maxwell's intelligent demon."[17] In 1879, however, speaking in front of the *Royal Institution of Great Britain*, he dedicates an entire evening's lecture to it and starts with the origin of the term:

> The word "demon," which originally in Greek meant a supernatural being, has never been properly used as signifying a real or ideal personification of malignity. Clerk Maxwell's "demon" is a creature of imagination having certain perfectly well-defined powers of action, purely mechanical in their character, invented to help us. [. . .] He is a being with no preternatural qualities. [. . .] Endowed ideally with arms and hands and fingers—two hands and ten fingers suffice—

he can do as much for atoms as a pianoforte player can do for the keys of the piano—just a little more.[18]

Once the demon has been freed of its post-Xenocratic, Christological negative connotations, Thomson reduces its supernatural abilities to plainly earthly qualities, limited to well-defined, mechanical finger dexterity and manual skills. At the same time, he allows it to keep its ephemeral, mysterious character and adds to it the quality of heightened attention ("very observant") and precise observation. That radical strategy of anthropomorphization, which also confers upon the demon its "free will" and intervention abilities, is what also identifies the demon as an invisible, vigilant, and wakeful agent,[19] fulfilling its duty without great ado or any flights of transcendental fancy.

But that characterization goes a bit too far for Maxwell. He turns against the tendency to humanize his creature and suggests it may be treated not as a demon but as an automatic switch or simply as a 'valve.' On a different occasion, he laconically writes to Tait the following:

Concerning Demons.
Who gave them this name? Thomson.
What were they by nature? Very small *but* lively beings [. . .]
What was their chief end? To show that the 2nd Law of Thermodynamics has only statistical certainty.
[. . .] Call him no more a demon but a valve.[20]

Still, once it is released into the world, a demon can no longer be reined in. Maxwell's attempt to recategorize it as a valve—a first, futile attempt at exorcism—no longer works. Just as in Laplace's case, now it is the demon's turn to hunt down its maker. Getting rid of a creature that bears your name is not that easy. The demon is a pain in the neck. Free of Maxwell's control, it stays on to haunt the spirits of other scientists. Then comes a long line of exorcists—a subject that will be considered next.

The brief outline above traces the transformation of a particular thought experiment within the narrow circle of its contributors. One can already see the changes that strange creature undergoes before it may reach the wider public: the distortions, dissimulations, recontextualizations, as well as manipulations and modifications it suffers in the process. But that is not all. For the demon only becomes productive once it officially makes its way into scientific discourse, wreaking havoc among (thought) experimenters who hope to make it disappear again. The reception history of Maxwell's demon, the one that manages to severely throw into doubt (if not even jeopardize) a fundamental natural law, is nothing but a long series of attempts at exorcism that continues to this very day.

The exorcist—∞: Against demons. Loschmidt et al. No other imaginary actor within modern scientific theory production has generated such an avalanche of treatises, refutations, and defenses—coming from physics as well as philosophy—as Maxwell's nimble creature. The list of publications dealing with Maxwell's experiment numbered more than 570 separate titles in 2003, meaning that after thirteen years of ongoing debate the list had doubled.[21] Notwithstanding the complexity of each line of argument, one can distinguish at least a few common elements as well as two important theoretical transformations of the experiment. These will be briefly discussed below.

The first transformation can be further roughly divided into two related directions. Both hinge on the same old ontic question: do demons (still) exist, or have they never existed? (Not accidentally, in antiquity, the term δαίμων also meant θεός.) In the tradition of negative proofs of God's existence, some of the accounts assume the task of refuting Maxwell's construct with the aid of Aristotelian logic. The second law of thermodynamics remains their main point of reference and the measure of all things. Such interventions usually come via (science) philosophy and expose the circular arguments or unclear, random assumptions in the logical arguments made by Maxwell's successors and commentators. If there are so many different variants of Maxwell's demon—critics say—that is because there is no clearly defined premise to the second law of thermodynamics.[22] The other accounts propose a much more strategic approach, using an imaginary counterproof from the realm of physics. The adepts of this approach rely in their demonstration on tested homeopathic principles or the preclassic *episteme* of similarity, *simile similibus,* by attempting to exorcise one demon with the help of another.

And—what about the second theoretical transformation? Here, once again, the 140-year-old genealogy of commentaries on Maxwell's experiment is subject to at least two discursive breaks. As a consequence, the demon is led in directions that barely have any connection with thermodynamics anymore. At first, the feedback is rather weak.[23] But things change with the publication of an article by Leo Szilard in 1929. Szilard undertakes a first influential attempt at exorcism, aiming to save the universal validity of the second law of thermodynamics from the threat of demons. The main argument here is the following: to the extent to which the demon is itself subject to the laws of thermodynamics, it also requires energy for its observation of approaching molecules; and this energy corresponds precisely to the amount of entropy which is made available to the system via the demon's sorting activity. In other words: the demon's act of observation and measuring of molecules produces waste. Consequently, the system cannot be understood as a *perpetuum mobile.* The law is saved. The demon is dead. Szilard transforms the experiment, shifting it from its original scenario in thermodynamics to a different context, one which takes into account the energy spent on the knowledge obtained in the process of observation. In contrast to Maxwell's initial presentation of the demon (as one "who can do no work"), Szilard imagines it as more than a (mechanical) worker. Thus he associates the demon with a previously overlooked, hidden entropic contribution, which results from its permanent activity of observation and which is vital to the continuous functioning of the entire system. The purely mechanical demon is about to become an information-processing machine. With this redefinition, the discourse shifts in a new direction: one of the consequences of Szilard's argument is that the demon is now treated as an actual component of the system and thereby becomes naturalized.[24] With this effort at naturalization, this integration into the system, which can also be interpreted as an act of anthropomorphization (the illustrations speak for themselves),[25] the demon is suddenly conferred with attributes that go well beyond Maxwell's simple sketch. More important still, these changes make the demon appear more alive than ever.

A few words on the second discursive break at this point—even though it does not play a major role in the argument of this book: Szilard and others, starting with Smoluchowski (as well as John von Neumann and Léon Brillouin after him), argue that the amount of energy contributed by the demon is counteracted through the entropy wasted in the demonic acquisition of information. This argument seems even more poignantly illustrated in an example from 1961, when the cognitive model of the demon is associated with the computer, *the* contemporary media-technical a priori. For Rolf Landauer and Charles Bennett, the hidden entropy lies not in the acquisition of information via observation but in the destruction of information. Resetting the memory (of a computer) is, after all, a thermodynamically irreversible process. Memory cannot be deleted without producing thermal energy, and this is precisely what causes the entropy of the entire system.[26] In this formulation, Maxwell's demon takes its cue from Laplace's being—the demonic bookkeeper—the one able to register everything. The demon cannot be expelled: neither Landauer's exorcism nor the many other subsequent efforts succeed in driving it away. On the contrary: "The Demon lives."[27]

As shown so far, one strategy adopted by exorcists is the futile attempt to remove Maxwell's demon by means of various modifications of the thought experiment or via extended definitions of the second law of thermodynamics. Such attempts take either the form of simplifications (Szilard's one-molecule principle)[28] or multiplications (Landauer's series of chambers).[29] A further strategy resorts to the means of homeopathy. None other than Ludwig Boltz-mann leads in the long line of second- and third-class counterdemons to follow. In a memorial address dedicated to his professor Josef Loschmidt he undertakes a thought experiment similar to the one from 1869. Here, erroneously, he also sees demons at work:

> On another occasion he [Loschmidt] imagined a tiny intelligent being who would be able to see the individual gas molecules and, by some sort of contriv-ance, to separate the slow ones from the fast. [. . .] As we all know, this idea which Loschmidt only hinted at in a few lines of an article,[30] was later proposed in Maxwell's heat theory and was widely discussed.[31]

His memory betrays him twice: Loschmidt does not spend merely a few lines on the matter; moreover, he does not speak just of any spirits but rather precisely of those that counteract Maxwell's "intelligent beings." And yet the passage above is known in the reception history as "Loschmidt's demon" con-troversy, a sort of 'antidote' to Maxwell's demon. We are talking about a second-class demon in this case because it is created not by the author of the experi-ment (Loschmidt), but—like all the other subordinate beings of its kind—via the contributions of subsequent commentators (in this case via Boltzmann). The nondemon is a parasite among scientific assistants. At the same time, its secondary rank is implicit in the researchers' attempt to oust a spirit by means of another, hypothetical spirit that is not even featured in the original experi-ment. One can already imagine that such experimental systems, along with their speculative arguments, can lead only to an increasingly disjointed game of signs. Someone (Maxwell) devises a thought experiment meant to clarify the complexity of a new concept (the second law of thermodynamics). But instead of solving a problem, the proposed scenario is formulated in such a manner by its reviewers—by way of naturalized, anthropomorphic, or demonic readings—that the interpretations are themselves in need of further explanation. As soon as someone (Thomson) attempts to render the experiment more concrete, that is, to represent the figure of the demon, the effort is countered by a critique (Boltzmann's) aimed at saving the natural law by way of a counterfeit demon and a homeopathic arithmetic calculation (demon plus demon = no demon).

One could argue this is nothing but an odd strategy, lacking common sense or scientific consistency. But the inexistent demon launched an extensive tradi-tion and resulted in a number of other derivations whose adepts follow the same model of retroactive attribution. We speak, for instance, of "Popper's demon" or "Tipler's demon."[32] Feynman too has been assigned a demon that attempts to counteract Maxwell's being;[33] and even beyond the disciplinary borders of physics there are new variants, such as "Mendel's demon."[34] In short, Maxwell's thought experiment continues to give rise to demons in an endless series of productive misreadings; and those demons, in turn, generate new attempts to exorcise them. Even though—or precisely because—it is constantly threatened by various exorcists, Maxwell's demon continues to propagate in discourse. It keeps producing similar beings meant to depose it. A whole genealogy of demons is born in the process. The question is: what gives the mechanism of attribution its appeal?

4.1.2. A Brief Historiography of 'Spiritual Intercourse'

> Spirits that I've cited
> My commands ignore.
> —Goethe, "The Sorcerer's Apprentice"

What, then, is the appeal or, to put it more plainly, the particular advantage of releasing a demon into the world? Engaging such a creature seems to bring with it a number of complications. The scientific demons of Laplace, Maxwell, and others trigger an outright epistemic chaos, since their role and actual function are initially not clear at all. The demons cannot be domesticated; they seem to systematically evade the purposes and contexts they have been created for in the first place. And once they are brought to life, they erratically haunt the most diverse cognitive junctions. But apart from the confusion they cause and the rejection or approval they encounter, they also help guide the process of scientific inquiry. To the extent to which they do not polarize arguments, demons effortlessly unite distant matters and allow previously isolated opposites to meet. As they move in and out of debates—for instance, the question concerning the inexorability of entropy—they manage to open up possibilities and reveal connections which would have remained hidden without their intervention.

One of the difficulties in accurately determining the status of scientific demons derives from their largely ambiguous definition, if not their outright incomprehensible nature. Their features remain strangely vague, their image opaque and transparent at the same time. Despite their discursive richness, their main characteristic is their theoretical invisibility. The reason for this inadequacy and the inability to pin them down to a concrete formulation may also have to do with another aspect: demons constantly appear as the effects of acts of ex post attribution.

Neither Laplace nor Maxwell (let alone Loschmidt) specifically draws in his imagined scenarios on the term 'demon.' These creatures are too obvious for them to require more concrete designations or supplementary demonic features. Only after years, or even decades, do they end up being associated with the proper names that currently identify them. Thomson is the one who gives Maxwell's demon its name; Boltzmann names Loschmidt's, and Du Bois-Reymond, in turn, Laplace's being, long after that creature seemingly disappeared into the annals of probability calculus. It is therefore always the commentator who establishes the demonological paradigm and subjects it to a particular taxonomy, at times even against the will of its helpless demiurges. Not accidentally, Maxwell's letter to Tait explicitly warns against calling the increasingly more popular being that bears his name a 'demon.' He insists on strictly referring to it as a functioning valve. The demon does not seem to do its creator much honor.

The tendency of demons to take possession of proper names without the owners' permission results in a strange case of double nominal existence. There is a person named James Clerk Maxwell, who is identified by his scientific work. But there is also a being known as Maxwell's demon; from a distance, but still in close connection to the author's work, that being now produces its own scientific contribution.[35] In short, the demon possesses a complicated relation to the creator whose name it appropriates, in an ex post, if not even posthumous, fashion and not always to the latter's satisfaction. Despite its nominal identification, the demon no longer heeds the will of its former master.

From its genesis to its reception, that imaginary creature traverses various stages of development. Without any manifest opposition, it undergoes a series of status changes, switching from one category to another. Maxwell's strictly immaterial and therefore ineffable intelligent being is renamed by Thomson as a demon. Laplace's own intelligent being first turns into a spirit in Emil Du Bois-Reymond's 1872 formulation,[36] only to be ultimately also treated as a demon, in direct reference to Maxwell and as an effect of Thomson's own act of naming.

Demons pose an obvious problem of identification. Their range of functions is unclear, and their modes of operation are not specifically demarcated. Additionally, their way of being and designation also lack clarity: they go by vague names such as 'intelligent being' and 'spirit' (in the sense of *esprit*) or else are called "very observant beings." They do not have a proper name but acquire one only once they have left their original service, once they are released into the free domain of scientific discourse, where others get to place and classify them. That is where they become the scientific beings known as 'Maxwell's' or 'Laplace's' demon.

By switching categories and finally becoming a demon, the being gains in stature. Maxwell's thermodynamic thought experiment renders this process of translation particularly clear, showing how it leads to the anthropomorphiza-tion of its unruly scientific agent. With the growing reception resulting from multiple exorcism attempts since the 1930s, the demon's formerly abstract mode of manifestation takes on concrete form. The ban on images does not include the ill-reputed mediators between this world and the realm of the higher pow-ers (of nature). Consequently, neither the commentators nor the exorcists shy away from imagining the demon in a way that generates a whole range of—both aesthetically and graphically—eclectic visual representations.[37] The demon even turns up as a literary figure even though its "anthropomorphic mask" ap-pears to be quite thin. We encounter it in Thomas Pynchon's *Gravity's Rainbow*, represented by the character Edward W. A. Pointsman, who processes random connections into cause-and-effect relations.[38]

The various exorcism attempts over the past 140 years also reveal a further principle: the efforts to eliminate Maxwell's demon are effective only to the extent to which they succeed in rendering it in anthropomorphic terms. The attempt fails if one tries to describe it in strictly formal, mathematical terms, since the demon cannot be consistently quantified.[39] As already mentioned, the reason lies in the basic assumptions about the ontic status of the spirit: in the absence of clear premises, the possibility of a consistent definition disappears. The transition from a purely formal thought experiment to experimental praxis cannot be smoothly bridged. Working with a demon demands that anthropo-morphic concessions be made, that one represent it in a material fashion. The next section will inquire about the specific material condition that a scientific demon must fulfill (see section 4.2 below). Finally, the question about the me-dia a priori of scientific demons will also be raised.

But one must ask a preliminary question first: why is it that Laplace's and Maxwell's agents are specifically identified as demons around the 1870s? What official and occult discourses at that time suggest that the strange beings hover-ing between fiction and concrete action should be classified as demons?

In the aftermath of the Enlightenment and the age of reason, it may certainly seem paradoxical to connect the discourses of demonology and of experimental science with its unbound rationalist ethos. Obviously, there is a long tradition linking the two discourses, one that goes back to the early beginnings of modern science in the mid-seventeenth century. But the direct reference to ephemeral 'intelligent beings' and their classification as disembodied, immaterial demons around the 1870s belongs to a different tradition: namely, the contemporary debates around occult phenomena and spiritualist séances which influence both British science in the Victorian age and continental physics; hardly any signifi-cant scientist of the period remained unaffected by them.[40] The current study cannot present a historical overview—however brief—of the largely unwritten modern science and media history of occultism. Instead, it will only offer a few remarks regarding its reception. Starting with the notorious case of the 1848 "Fox rappings" in America, which bear the mark of mesmerism, the European public—even the intellectual elites—take an interest in the artful mass-media staging of the spirit tapping incidents at the residence of the Fox family in Hydeville.[41] The American Civil War leads to a wave of emigration which draws all kinds of mediums to England and the Continent in search of new disciples for those unexplained phenomena that are attributed to the activity of spirits. These mediums infiltrate even the circles of influential media practitioners, that is to say, of experimental scientists, who now dedicate their work not only to developing scientific instruments but also to communicating with the realm of spirits. The most prominent example is William Crookes, the inventor of the Crookes tube, who unites both discourses into a single 'media science' aimed at finding a consistent explanation for such phenomena as phantom apparitions, the "agency of an exterior intelligence," or "direct writing" (that is, the production of texts without manifest participation from subjects in attendance).[42] What is essential here is the media-technical a priori grounding of the two-way communication with the spirit world. After the mid-nineteenth century bidirectional spirit communication is no longer unusual; one no longer expects merely the old oracular function but also answers to the questions asked. That new 'spiritual intercourse' is made possible by nothing less than the development of telegraphy, the Morse code, and the two-way communication channels.[43]

Often out of sheer boredom, many try their hand at spiritualist practices. The list of mediums is quite diverse. Still, one can distinguish at least two main groups. The first is made up of middle-class women, particularly the wives of telecommunication engineers. The second consists of servants, who are more in need of a change of perspective than their bored mistresses. "And how much greater must have been the appeal to the household servant, drudging away at endless domestic chores, longing for personal significance and status in a walk of life that provided neither."[44] Even when they do not play the main role during a séance, servants still act as mediumistic aides. Consider, for instance, the example of Daniel Dunglas Home's levitation experiments; during one session, he disappears through a window on the first floor of the house and returns through another window. In the end, the spectacular act turns out to be the effect neither of mass hypnosis nor of self-deception. Rather, the success of the séance is ensured by the invisible and silent intervention of corrupt domestics.[45]

Maxwell's and Laplace's thought experiments serve as rhetorical contrast strategies meant to strengthen their own hypotheses on probability and thermodynamics. Here, the 'intelligent being' is assigned a unique function: namely, that of rendering their theoretical considerations in concrete terms. Thus, in the case of Victorian physicists like William Thomson or Prussian scientists such as Emil Du Bois-Reymond, one can associate the actors that populate their arguments—at least nominally—with the new type of demonology that is simultaneously debated within their respective disciplines.

The return of demons after the mid-nineteenth century is obviously tinged with the fake glow of occultism; nevertheless, it could not have occurred without the blessings of the Church. In an encyclical from 1856 entitled *De magnetismo,* the Catholic Church sanctions the serious engagement with the effects of demonology in scientific contexts. Or rather, the church formulates an explicit prohibition against it. Addressing the question of experiments involving magnetic phenomena, Pope Pius IX promulgates the following: "Should every error, every instance of magic and manifest or implicit invocation of demons be removed, then the use of magnetism, of the pure act of utilizing otherwise natural means is not morally prohibited."[46] In contrast, "those experiments were forbidden [. . .] that followed goals that were unnatural, immoral or could not be attained by proper means."[47] As its title implies, the decree is clearly directed against Franz Anton Mesmer's animal magnetism.

But in the process the demon is cast out along with the devil himself. What the Church vilifies is no less than the premise of modern science along with the practices that accompany its birth during the seventeenth century. "The application of natural principles and means for supernatural things and effects, so that they may be explained in a natural manner, is nothing but deceit and heresy and must be forbidden."[48] The Holy See thus claims its interpretive authority over the inexplicable, even in the context of scientific experiments.

The field of demonology defines itself as the study of a natural order, in which unexplained phenomena are ascribed to demonic acts and effects.[49] As such, it has always entertained close ties to the exact sciences, in which the causes of unexplained phenomena are ascribed to the laws of nature (although they may appear supernatural at first). It would certainly be an error to assume that the seventeenth-century 'scientific revolution'[50] and the debates of the English Royal Society, its animating force, have somehow radically cut demonology out of the picture and changed the relation between 'supernatural' models and new, experiment-based methods to the exclusive benefit of science.

The new philosophy of nature after Francis Bacon has definitely not ousted the demonological explanatory models, as certain histories of science would have us believe. Quite the opposite: between 1660 and 1740, during the early decades of the Royal Society, the study of demonology temporarily becomes one of the active research domains of the developing field of natural philosophy.[51] Consequently, the period between Robert Boyle and Isaac Newton is definitely not characterized by the demise of demonology. Rather, scholars credit it with the legitimate mission of explaining the inexplicable. Thus issues that relate to the occult are frequently answered by means of mechanistic arguments. Leading members of the Royal Society, especially Joseph Glanvill but also Robert Boyle as well as the alchemist Isaac Newton, insist on giving a prominent place to demons (and related phenomena, like witchcraft) in their scientific explorations.[52] Not unlike other research groups that devise natural histories of art or labor, one subsection of the Royal Society focuses on developing a natural history of demonology: "Narratives of witchcraft were, in fact, on entirely the same empirical and discursive level as the historical reports of 'laboratory' or other events that typically made up the writings of Royal Society fellows."[53]

Glanvill and his companions strictly rely on carefully conducted experiments as a testing ground and generator of new insights. Consequently, the laboratory becomes the central locus of scientific production. Ultimately, it is here that one may begin to search for the place of demons within the context of experimental configurations. The next section (4.2) will investigate these matters, drawing on the case of Robert Boyle's lab work practices, with participation from a range of good spirits. The main question will concern the agents of knowledge, the actors placed by natural philosophy into a demonological niche which they discreetly access: "The agency of demons and witches could go on being defended with absolute scientific integrity."[54] Not only are these obscure actors successfully defended; as protagonists placed under observation, they are also called upon to search for the causes of yet-inexplicable matters. "The experimentalists were interested [. . .] in the natural science of demonic agency, a subject that they found demanding both for its ontological and epistemological complexities and for its vital cultural implications."[55] One of these vital cultural implications is associated with the central position ascribed to demons within the system of nature philosophy, their understanding as an integral component of knowledge production. Stuart Clark, the historiographer of early modern demonology, has rightfully pointed out that demons appear in such contexts as concrete helpers in the effort to solve scientific mysteries and problems. In line with Laplace's and Maxwell's thought experiment, demons are catalysts of knowledge, serving as a testing ground for new perspectives and, if successful, for newly accepted findings.[56]

What is at stake, then, when the modern natural sciences, with their otherwise rigorous, rational debates, suddenly become the stage for such ephemeral actors as demons? Such creatures have always been perceived as mediators between the realms of the transcendental, the unexplained, and the familiar. "Then the demons came in midway between heaven and earth."[57] But what does this notion imply, when the demons in question are featured in the study of probability, thermodynamics, and other scientific experiments? On the surface, this is a matter of gaining discursive attention. In the post-1930s reception history of Maxwell's demon, the little helpers are typically the fulcrum upon which Maxwell's fame as a scientist rapidly grows—either via the demonstration of his hypothesis or the successful attempt to exorcise it. A successfully established demon, one that even bears a proper name, may secure someone's fame just as much as one that has been exorcised by means of an opposite argument. This is what explains how Maxwell's innocent actor gives rise to a whole string of havoc-causing spirits.

In the genealogy of mostly impoverished heirs to Maxwell's magic, each line of argument that deals with an established spirit or attempts to offer a new direction is a disturbance. It all comes down to causing a stir, and giving its author scientific visibility. And quite often the strategy works, but only momentarily—since the creatures that have not attained celebrity status and have therefore quickly disappeared again far outnumber those that have been authorized and confirmed. Just consider, for instance, the case of Karl Popper's long-forgotten demon.

Demons act as popularizers of scientific ideas and theories; their role is to attract attention, by promising to ensure their creators or exorcists a place in the historiography of their respective disciplines. 'Intelligent beings' are mediators, conveying to the public, in the form of (often) accessible thought experiments, complex analytical configurations. Demons could therefore be regarded as a purely rhetorical artifice. But apart from channeling arguments, they also establish a model that exceeds the mediation between open questions and unexplained answers, between theoretical problems and concrete experiments. Beyond all this, demons occupy a central place in the epistemic quest for truth.

4.1.3. Between Earth and Saddle:
Epistemological Effects

Traditionally, angels are perceived as couriers conveying divine messages to human beings in a direct, albeit figurative, fashion. In contrast, demons are notoriously suspected of manipulation. What they share is the act of mediation between heaven and earth. Both categories are supposed to establish a communication channel between the material world and the realm beyond perception.[58] Within this communicative configuration, angels are the only ones that carry a message without acting upon its content. Thomas Aquinas had already spoken of angels as God's mouthpieces. They patiently convey information—not unlike paper—without falsification or distortion. But that is not how demons act. Beyond their courier functions, they are also endowed with a uniquely productive force which enables them to do more than just alter the information received. More important, they are assigned a crucial role within the cognitive process. They do not merely act as transmission media but also agents that may considerably alter the course of events. As the Grand-Ducal Ecclesiastical Advisor Georg Conrad Horst stated in 1821, "The demons acted as the *levers* that set into motion everything in the corporeal and spiritual realm. According to popular belief, they were *the means* through which one hoped to bring forth what went *against the usual order of things.*"[59] Not only are demons in control of the lever that allows them to change and intervene in every process or event. They also disrupt the usual order of things by performing a small change or shift that may transform the dominant episteme. In other words, they are the means whereby one can wrest new knowledge from nature. As opposed to angels, they serve as the epistemological tool against the dominant perspective on the order of things. They function as a probe that tests the validity of natural laws.

Given such modalities of intervention or manipulation, demons are assigned a central role in (cognitive) experiments during the nineteenth century. They operate the switch at the control desk of knowledge, thus testing the resistance of cognitive structures. Their poietic productivity harks back to the tradition of antiquity. Not accidentally, demons return to the center of attention during the Sturm und Drang era and the 'aesthetics of genius' period around 1800. Johann Georg Hamann, the theorist of the Sturm und Drang movement, draws a direct connection between the Socratic demon and the history of science, wondering "whether this demon is not more like a mercury glass or the machines to which all the Bradleys and Leuwenhoeks owe their discoveries."[60] Whether they are at work in a real lab environment or in a thought process, demons disrupt the routine of prescribed service, by introducing a new order. As agents, they convey new insights in a threefold manner. First, they function as a medium of popularization (or dissemination). Second, they act as a metaphor or a figure of thought. Third, they take on the role of translation, of processing, by delegating agency to objects. In short, a demon is a necessary component, ensuring the success of scientific (thought) experiments and the production of new knowledge. Despite their imaginary character, demons act as metaphors or figures of speech in order to perform the hard labor of illustrating or configuring problems. Precisely because they are products of fantasy, they heighten their recipients' imagination. A metaphor is also a form of transfer. Consequently, these fictive beings perform concrete acts of processing, of translation, whereby specific problems are rendered directly operational. And last but not least, (thought) experiments would be far less popular without the demons' anthropomorphic mode of presentation. Instead, they would remain abstract and unrepresentable. This brief description of demons as catalysts of scientific knowledge raises the question of their ontological status. Endowed with concrete functions, demons appear as the essential and material agents of scientific discourse. They are responsible for important shifts of perspective as well as cognitive investigations. Demons pave the way to scientific knowledge and lend this process mathematical weight. In other words, *they serve as the stirrups of thinking.*

But what could be gained from analyzing demons metaphorically, only in order to use a further metaphor to explain that description? To put it differently: what good is a demon if it is not translated into concrete historical configurations and real, media-material practices? Is there no danger of losing oneself in the play of signifiers when attention is exclusively directed to the discursive events within cognitive experiments? The answer is no, since this feature is not just a metaphor, not pure rhetoric. Instead, it paves the way to a concrete idea that helps throw light on the entire epistemic context. Each metaphor is, after all, based on an act of transformation, which carries one notion onto another plane of figurative meaning. First of all, what does it mean when the actors involved in scientific thought processes are defined in such terms: as the *stirrups of thinking*? The metaphor used here does not merely offer a fitting description of the role played by demons in the production of knowledge. More important, the formula amounts to a particular media praxis, which sheds light on everything that works on our thoughts. What kind of media materiality lies behind this expression? This section will focus on the metaphor of the stirrup, and decipher it as an important epistemic figure. Let us therefore briefly continue on horseback, if you will.

Johann Beckmann, the 'Nestor' figure of German historiography, writes in his *Contributions to the History of Inventions* from 1792 that the things that serve "the common comfort, indeed, that are essential and seem so easy to invent that one cannot imagine that people should have ever lived without them"[61] do not necessarily have to be ancient. In Western written culture, stirrups are first mentioned toward the end of the sixth century, in the age of late antiquity. Brought all the way across the Asian steppes, Hungary, and the Baltic to Central Europe,[62] the new mechanism for mounting a horse also leads to dramatic political changes over the following period. The stirrup makes it possible, or even necessary, to lift the military (literally) into the saddle. It is the merit of Charles Martel (688–741) to have thereby laid the basis for the feudal system in Europe.[63]

Various techniques of mounting a horse had long been in use. In his treatise *On Horsemanship*, Xenophon gives specific details on how to get on horseback. The most common method, used to this day in equestrian sports, consists of jumping on and off. The skill required intensive training and was practiced by young Romans and heavily-armored knights alike. For knights, mounting a horse [*Rittersprung*] comes before being knighted [*Ritterschlag*]. But, as opposed to gymnasts today, neither the Romans nor the knights used a springboard to help them jump. The artful execution consisted of being able to "lift oneself onto the horse with no aid."[64] Any means of assistance was disdained. There were, however, other methods that involved auxiliary resources: stepping-stones in front of inns and town halls but also the hooks on spears could all be used as a footboard. Finally, a further option involved subjecting the animals to a specific disciplinary regime, training them to bend their front legs.[65]

This brief genealogy of mounting methods based on jumps, stones, spears, and disciplinary orders comes to an end when the stirrup is introduced. The shift is confirmed not only by archaeological findings but also at the linguistic level. The semantics of warfare, songs, and epic poems clearly points to a change that occurs sometime during the early eighth century: riders no longer 'jump' but rather 'climb off' or 'onto' a horse.[66] The new usage also leads to new expressions: "riding without stirrups" means something along the lines of "accomplishing something without help from others."[67]

Apart from the jump and the stepping-stone, there is yet another way to get on horseback. "High-standing and elderly individuals climb up with the help of a servant (*strator*, ἀναβολεύς) who offers his hand to serve as a footstep."[68] Depending on everyone's rank or relation of subordination, the hand is not the only body part used as a prop. In extreme cases of subordination, servants are required to do more: "Oftentimes they had to lie down, so that the master might step on their back."[69] Not accidentally the designation for a servant or groom is ἀναβολεύς in Greek and *strator* in Latin—the term used for 'stirrup' introduced in the sixth century. What is remarkable is the manner in which the name of a human actor is transferred, without further ado, onto a nonhuman agent. As Major Adolph Schlieben, the author of a universal history of the term points out, the shift is "analogous to the German *Stiefelknecht* [bootjack] . . . which could mean a person designated to remove boots, a word that was later used for the wooden instrument that serves the same function."[70] In other words, in the context of cognitive experiments, the formula 'the stirrups of thinking' does not only refer to those metallic objects that represent, in their historical diversity, the richness of ideas.

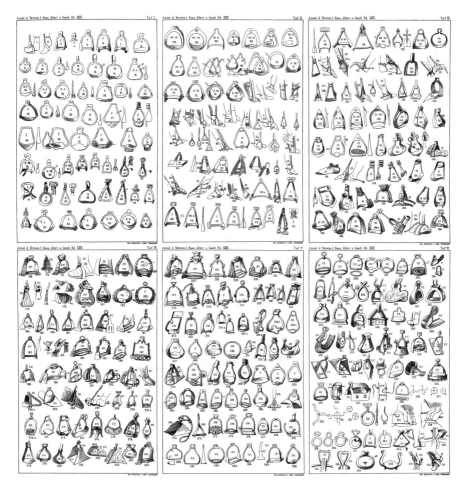

Figure 7. The wealth of thinking

Rather, the metaphor is to be taken seriously, as a means of examining the actual carriers of the function, namely, the servants and their work of processing, or translation. With the aid of various instruments, servants and their processing capabilities form a hybrid, whether in mundane situations, or in the context of scientific experiments, where invisible technicians and ignored assistants vastly contribute to the acquisition of knowledge.

The stirrup and the servant are processors that help their master with his comfortable ascent into his privileged position and firm place in the saddle. They allow him to get to a higher level which grants him both a heightened sense of mobility as well as an overview of the terrain he traverses, both in the topographical sense (think: 'commander's perspective') and in the sense of a general research outlook. Generally, in the group made up of master, servant, and instruments, only the first member of the collective is acknowledged. The assistants as well as their tools usually evade the historians' gaze and remain invisible. Who would speak of Robert Hooke and Denis Papin and their skillful handling of the vacuum pump when discussing Boyle's gas law? No one: no one besides Robert Boyle is credited with discovering that law. Who would argue that James Joules's mechanical equivalent of heat experiment was possible only because of the contribution of the instrument maker John Benjamin Dancer as well as the manual labor of nameless brewery workers in Manchester? Who would link Carl Friedrich Gauss's development of telegraphy back to Moritz Meyerstein and his instruments or to other common figures such as the institute assistant Michelmann?[71] And the list goes on.

The stirrup hovers above the ground, midway between earth and saddle. In a similar fashion, the scientific demon—just like the servant—occupies an intermediary position between heaven and earth, between intellectual work, in the sense of the research activity on display, and experimental labor, with its daily practices and routines. For the work of the scientific demon is not limited to cognitive experiments or seventeenth-century vacuum pump tests. The stirrup is not a mere metaphor but a concrete equivalent for the discreet contribution of servants. In a similar manner, demons are not just fictive actors that help illustrate ephemeral theoretical scenarios à la Maxwell. Still—so the counterargument goes—demons do not exist, and if they do, then—despite their various anthropomorphic renditions—they strictly function as submissive aides within the vast domains of cognitive experiments.

But demons are by no means mere fictions without material basis. Rather, they function as real actors involved in the process of cognition, despite the fact that their role is often overlooked. Placed in their marginal positions, they are taken for granted and mentioned only in the annals of science in the most exceptional of situations. It should be obvious by now: the discussion about scientific demons is, in reality, a discussion about servants, namely, in this particular case, about laboratory servants.

The parallels between demons and ministering spirits in the scientific domain are obvious. When Maxwell describes his doorkeeper as a "very observant and neat-fingered being," he thereby also evokes the figure of a servant carefully and meticulously attending to the job assigned by his master. Both types of actors perform their activity in the background. That activity, however, is constantly subject to misperception. Its contribution to the increase of knowledge is generally overlooked in official (scientific) historiography. Demons and servants share an important feature: they can be both absent and present while performing their work. The former manifest themselves in fictive cognitive experiments,

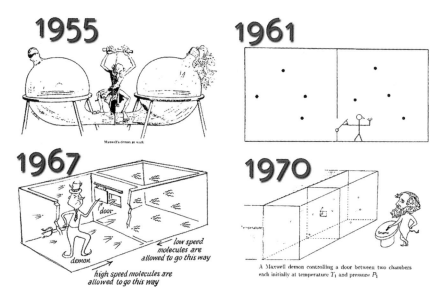

Figure 8. Representations of Maxwell's demon in their historical development

while the latter cannot escape their physical presence, be it in the lab or their masters' private chambers. Demons strictly appear at the level of thinking and cannot be found in real life. By contrast, the absence of servants in the real world implies their omission from the transmission of scientific discourse and their manifest invisibility as domestics. Masters are instructed to see through them, as if looking through glass. In other words, both demons and servants operate in their own respective fictive contexts, which they then transform into real scientific practices. The thought experiments produce concrete discursive effects: the beings of Laplace, Maxwell, Loschmidt, and others constitute the elements of a series in which the demons produce and create one another. The lab servants work in a similar fashion, contributing to the end product by means of their invisible activity, despite being left out in the process. Their indispensable participation in the act of knowledge notwithstanding, servants are absent from the end result, for the research findings are still steeped in the myth of the inventor. Servants must remain invisible, since there is no room, no designated place in the system for them in the retrospective presentation or the scientific account.

One could go even further and define the lab servant as the media a priori of the demon inhabiting the cognitive experiment. The semantic proximity between *demon* and *demonstrator*—as lab servants were called in the early days of the Royal Society—could serve as a good starting point in this regard. In Maxwell's and Laplace's scenarios, demons always play precisely the roles assigned to the lab assistant or the aide, the clerk or the doorkeeper in real scientific experiments.

The stirrup and the demon are therefore much more than metaphors. In fact, they are ciphers for the long-forgotten activity of subalterns, other ways of naming those vital mediators and driving forces behind the process of knowledge production. Stirrups do not forge Nobel Prizes and natural laws. But the path to knowledge requires an immense amount of preparation, patient experimentation, and the participation of various elements and actors that vanish from the retroactive inscription and documentation of research. There can be no cognitive gain without help from others, without stirrups or servants. As Robert Merton has pointed out in his brilliant essay,[72] 'we'—meaning 'the subspecies of the scientist' in Newton's and Bernhard von Chartres's respective formulations— 'we' are but dwarfs standing on the shoulders of giants. Yet the picture cast by this one-liner is somehow distorted, so to speak. A closer look at the history of science will prove that anonymous helpers, the stirrups of thinking, have always been part of the progress of knowledge. As natural scientists, gentlemen and masters do not stand on the shoulders of giants. Rather, they hoist themselves into the saddle of knowledge, using the stirrup function of their research aides. In other words, they literally stand on the shoulders of servants.

4.2. THE INVISIBLE THIRD

> Who built Thebes of the seven gates?
> In the books you will read the names of kings.
> Did the kings haul up the lumps of rock?
> […]
> The young Alexander conquered India.
> Was he alone?
> Caesar defeated the Gauls.
> Did he not even have a cook with him?
> […]
> So many reports.
> So many questions.[73]

The laconic summary formulated by Bertolt Brecht in his "Questions from a Worker Who Reads" in 1928 applies not only to political historiography but— until 1989—to the history of science as well. As will be shown, the subaltern gains access to the domain of (natural) sciences, first, as a laboratory servant during the early years of the Royal Society—and from then on reaches a level of popularity maintained up to the present day. Toward the end of the seventeenth century, the so-called scientific revolution introduces certain professional types that span various social levels, from the gentleman philosopher to his helpers, delegated to assist with their masters' experiments. Each epoch contains the traces of mostly nameless subalterns, whose work of assistance consists, among other things, of the scientific production of knowledge in the broadest sense of the word. Despite the fact that they regularly stand between the researchers and their instruments, such actors are, not unlike demons, generally invisible. Their activity can be traced back to the tradition of the valet de chambre, his conspicuous idleness and the generous free time he has at his disposal—an opportunity to study mysterious natural phenomena and unsolved questions such as the possibility of making gold.

The former pharmacy apprentice, alchemist, and future valet at various courts in Saxony, Prussia, and Sweden, Johannes Kunckel (1630–1703) gives lectures on experimental alchemy; he also undertakes costly attempts to make gold in a secret lab in Dresden—the same space where, just a few years later, Johann Friedrich Böttger and Ehrenfried Walther von Tschirnhaus successfully 'invent' European porcelain.[74] In a similar fashion, the "great factotum"[75] and close confidant of Frederick II, Fredersdorf, dedicates himself to the study of alchemy, building his own lab in Berlin in the hope of finding a way to produce gold. The political valet thus becomes the laboratory servant of the king and vice versa. "Fredersdorf claimed that he praised these mysterious arts not for his personal gain, but rather in order to provide a political service to his king."[76] The valet, who runs the risk of vanishing, outshined by his sovereign and the precious metal, is to honor his king in the spirit of the *virtus assistendi Deo,*[77] by delivering the highly secular gift of (white) gold to enrich the state coffers. Similarly situated between the fame of the researcher and the messy and risky business of lab work, the invisible thirds are supposed to pave the way to the shiny beacon of knowledge.

4.2.1. Down the Gallery of Invisible Workers

> Oh, Buttler! Buttler!
> You are my evil demon.
> —Friedrich Schiller, *Wallenstein*

Occasional traces can be (literally) found digging through the rubble of sources, when experiments go amiss and in the case of accidents or malfunctions, like unplanned explosions that result in injuries or damages. But these are only the exceptions which put lab workers on the map. Not unlike household servants or the subjects populating the thresholds and corridors of power, laboratory servants are typically defined by their professional invisibility. As Rolf Engelsing, the authority on the social history of the middle and lower classes, pointed out in 1973, regular servants would sometimes be involved in the scientific experiments performed by their masters.[78] But it is Steven Shapin's 1989 article "The Invisible Technician" that offers the first systematic investigation of the subject. Shapin frees the lab servant from historical obscurity and brings him into the limelight with an approach that inquires after the role of the silenced subjects in the process of scientific production.[79]

Who discovered the inverse proportion between the pressure and volume of a gas when the temperature is held constant? The books mention the name of a gentleman: the young Robert Boyle, who experimented with vacuum pumps. Was he alone? Did he not even have a helper with him? So many sources.[80] So many questions. As is customary for a rich nobleman around 1670, Robert Boyle owns a big house in London with numerous servants. The lab therein becomes a meeting place for a whole range of different individuals. Apart from secretaries, the scribes in charge of the lab journal as well as his correspondence, there is a varied and finely differentiated personnel: 'chemical assistants' are busy distilling, correcting, mixing, observing, and writing down the results of various experiments; other lab servants are in charge of the pump, using the strength of their body to produce a vacuum. Meanwhile, apothecaries and technical assistants, instrument builders and regular domestics hurry about the house attending to their duties: fetching liquids and materials, carrying or repairing thermometers, barometers, and other instruments, bringing cups full of blood straight from the slaughterhouse, or expediting letters. In the midst of all the action stands Robert Boyle himself. Not unlike Goethe, he delegates the writing tasks to others and dictates, or has his helpers read to him, in order to protect his feeble eyes.[81]

As opposed to the scientific demons that bring their fictive contribution to the advance of knowledge, the ministering spirits in Boyle's house are concretely involved in manual tasks. In contrast to ideas, practical experiments depend on energetic, physical activities. In other words, the question here is not only about the actual author behind Boyle's tests but also about the degree of epistemic participation of lab servants in the success (or the failure) of the undertaking, the acts of observation, of notation and verification as well as the dissemination of the results. But not unlike the case of the thought experiment, here is a *demonic agency* at work, operating beyond the gaze and direct interventions of the master. In turn, Boyle keeps track of these alien elements and renders them operational, since his own sight is failing. He has a long history of working in the company of serviceable spirits: his numerous servants are in charge of the vacuum pump, acting, not unlike Goethe's domestics, as extensions of their master's body—in this case, of his arms and hands, even when he is not at home or is caught up in conversation next door.

As a member of a higher social class, Boyle treats physical work with disdain. A true gentleman keeps his distance from such lowly activities, even when they concern the discovery of new natural laws. Boyle is able to work via the hands and senses of others, by *instrumentalizing* his entire service personnel for this very purpose. The essential media of knowledge are therefore not merely his apparatuses and specimens, the pump, the barometer, and the flies in a vacuum. In the early experiments of the Royal Society, and especially in Robert Boyle's case, the main actor is the work performed by subalterns. The *gentleman philosopher* puts their media functions and epistemic activity in the service of his own research by means of remote control experiments, so to speak. This early form of remote-controlled work, with its self-sufficient organization, execution, observation, analysis, and notation, is almost exclusively in the hands of servants. And yet, at the end of this process, it is Robert Boyle's name that appears on the publication produced in the medium of serviceability. How would one describe, then, the activities of the lab servants? One the one hand, they literally represent a driving force: it is via their muscle power and physical energy that the experiment is executed. On the other hand, their senses are in the service of their master:[82] in this capacity, they represent the filters of his perception, which they then extend via their own eyes, ears, and hands.

What, then, is Boyle's contribution to the process of knowledge production? His method consists of delegating almost all activities to his subalterns—therein lies the heart of the matter. For this method illustrates a phenomenon that accompanies each and every process of scientific inquiry. The mode of observation and analysis by proxy, the delegation of the entire process to one's assistants is a matter of trust.[83] Boyle supervises his servants—sometimes more, sometimes less—but ultimately authorizes a publication which is created by the hands of others in order to bear his own name, and his name alone. Here, Boyle puts his trust in and *relies on* his media.

Occasionally, the media have names. In this case, some of the most recognizable are Robert Hooke and Denis Papin. Both are said to have shown a high degree of independence in the lab—even at the level of textual production. Their master himself must admit that they are to be credited for most of the work of interpretation.[84] But this process of transfer does not occur seamlessly. When the subaltern media lend their own sense perceptions to their master, there is a shift of the agency within the cognitive process as well. The medium is also working on our thoughts. Who directs whom when it is the assistants performing the actual work and when they are the only ones intervening in the process and reporting back to their master? When the assistants stand in for their master and perform the experiments in his place, then the results become part of the assistants' own knowledge, which implicitly also enriches the masters' experience. Boyle delegates the experiment to others: its execution and observation, the contrastive evaluation, the modifications, and ultimately the selection of the examined phenomena. In turn, the experiment becomes the effect of a media operation, whose protagonist is the subaltern. Only there are no sources to attest to this fact.

The limited visibleness of the subalterns manifests itself in different ways. A direct portrayal can be found in Otto von Guericke's drawing of the vacuum pump operation, which Boyle takes from Kaspar Schott's 1664 *Technica Curiosa* and which serves as an inspiration for his own machine (built with the assiduous participation of his servant Robert Hooke).[85] In accordance with normative class divisions, one section of the machine is placed in the *upstairs* salon, made available to users and visitors alike. Hidden from view, the other section is in a room *downstairs*. The experiment starts here, with the vacuum produced by two subalterns through great physical effort. The paradoxical principle of professional invisibility, according to which underlings are supposed to be simultaneously present and absent, is pushed even further, beyond the glass roof that marks a literal and symbolic separation between social classes. The intentionally vague portraits of the lab servants in the drawing mentioned above are a further indication: any individual trait is removed from the picture; they are shown either from behind or with their head inclined—a gesture that classifies them as interchangeable subjects. Their destiny is to attend to their tasks while standing in the semiobscurity of history. But there is a third level of invisibility, namely, the subalterns' absence from the written sources. If the Fellows of the Royal Society are accustomed to hiring assistants for their experiments, they are definitely not used to mentioning, let alone recognizing, their activities. The rhetorical strategies of those who finally authorize their reports tend to revolve around anonymous references.[86] Who observed the cockatoo in the vacuum? 'He who complained of not being commended.' Historiographically speaking, this claim is justified, since the traces of subalterns in the lab journals and reports are generally scarce.

Finally, the invisibility of ministering lab spirits corresponds to that form of ephemeral unintelligibility that also characterizes demons. In their subordinate position vis-à-vis their master, both underlings and lab servants replicate the rapport of the demon to God. *Nolens volens,* servants and demons alike are only rarely the subject of visual representations—and that condition enhances their fictive status. Their invisibility turns them into an ideal surface of projection, a screen for scientific fictions. And yet they resist the label of pure virtuality applied to them—since both demons and lab servants do concrete (epistemic) work. What drives them out of the underground is the unexpected instance of malfunction, of noise. In historiographic terms, they enter the scene after an instance of dysfunction or an accident. The events in question do not necessarily have to involve dishonorable situations, for instance, when servants drink the alcohol where the specimens are kept—whether to drown their sorrow over the notoriously low wages or because of an addiction; the grave consequences they suffer in such cases grant them documentary notoriety.[87] Often, however, the scenarios are far worse. Robert Boyle mentions one of his numerous collaborators on the occasion of a failed experiment—a mishap that occurs during his explosion tests. Some of the servants are severely disfigured as a consequence.[88] The explosion guarantees them a rare mention in Boyle's laboratory journal. But the presence of servants is not just intimately connected with the possibility of malfunctions. Indeed, an unexpected explosion may trigger a rethinking of the entire experimental process. The ministering spirits of science thus become disturbers of the peace and the routine, marking a moment of epistemic insecurity.

Lab workers and demons remain for the most part invisible and nameless. Sometimes, however, they are not satisfied with their marginal status. They may cling to the proper names of scientists—as in the case of Maxwell, Laplace, Loschmidt, and others—who, in turn, undertake futile attempts to exorcise them. But the regularly overlooked and forgotten experimenters may also find their own way into the limelight of history. As often happens, this situation is brought about by a malfunction in the mechanisms at work in the highly stratified classed society of Restoration England. The role of experimenters, the activities of observers and scribes only come to light when the results are inconsistent or problematic. Alternatively, their function also becomes apparent in situations when servants dare to complain about the way their contribution is represented. Consider the example of Robert Hooke (1635–1703), the (chief) curator of the Royal Society between 1662 and 1688. Hooke's name is associated with quite a few disruptions and complaints. After undertaking a painting apprenticeship and various other studies, he joins Robert Boyle as a young assistant of twenty-two and continues to profit from his patronage until his death. At the same time, he repeatedly, yet vainly, protests against his assigned subaltern position, driven by the urge to gain public recognition as an independent scientist.

Shortly after starting to work for Boyle, Hooke manages to build a vacuum pump, the same instrument that would later be used in the scientist's well-known experiments. Due to this innovative and rather independently executed work as well as his exceptional skill and wealth of ideas—for which it is Boyle, again, who takes the credit—Hooke is later named curator of the Royal Society. He does not receive any pay for this honor. Instead, he is given the right to privately undertake, publicly demonstrate, and then document his experiments in the journal *Philosophical Transactions,* founded for this very purpose. The demonstrations are presented to the virtuosi, the aristocratic founding members of the Royal Society, who take an interest in scientific subjects. The virtuosi request to see various experiments, which are then discussed among themselves or simply quietly acknowledged. "Fellows sat back and let their employee do the work."[89] Hooke is thus placed in a decisive position within the system of scientific production, going from mere servant to respected actor, from underling to "philosophical servant,"[90] serving as a stirrup for the thinking process of his esteemed audience. He single-handedly curates the findings, which are subsequently officially confirmed by the Fellows with the aid of various demonstrations, such as the presentation of oscillation experiments and vacuum phenomena, or the display of an opossum penis.[91] "He was by turns the willing and wilful medium through which Fellows' ideas were materialized in private trials and, in the reverse process, made into public knowledge."[92]

The clandestine collaboration between Boyle and Hooke, based on their work on the vacuum pump launched in 1658, becomes a source of inspiration for the Royal Society upon its foundation in 1663. It is the servant who takes the decisive initiatives, whereas the master is cast in the role of a client who places an order for an instrument and wants to secure his own contribution by proposing improvements and alterations. Boyle and Hooke are thus literally configured in a client–server relationship,[93] which further develops during the time Hooke works as curator and Boyle joins the circle of members. Even if the curator position does not initially offer autonomy, Hooke uses it to potentially break free from his inferior position. But the normative limitations of the stratified Society keep curators as well as servants and other employees at a distance from the aristocratic virtuosi, who are interested in maintaining a relation of financial dependency with their subalterns. Hooke has no solution other than to practice the noble art of waiting, in the hope of making a later career jump: "He began by obeying the virtuosi's commands; worked hard to become indispensable; carefully built up his career and intellectual credit; and then, as the virtuosi curators slackened, he seized the initiative and gave Restoration science its distinctive Hookeian shape as 'the real, the mechanical, the experimental Philosophy.'"[94]

Between 1666 and 1674 Hooke appears to be the central figure of the still young Royal Society. He seems to be in absolute control of it: due to the Fellows' poor involvement and competence, he is the one setting the methodological rules and thematic directions. He thus manages to transform his curatorship into a directorship function—that is, as long as his experiments give the right results. But Hooke begins to protest against the influential luminaries of the Royal Society. He accuses Isaac Newton of stealing his ideas about the nature of light and the laws of gravitation. He claims priority over the invention of the spring-operated clock against Oldenburg and Huygens. He contests Hevelius's lunar observations made without the aid of telescopes. Ultimately, his involvement as curator gradually weakens, and the Royal Society takes measures to curtail his influence and very obvious will to rule. They rescind his title and send him back to his original status, to remind him he is no more than a servant: "For one thing, we have valuated Hooke as a leading experimental philosopher where the Royal Society treated him as a servant."[95] Hooke hopes to make himself indispensable as a curator but feels entitled to achieve more. The strategic disruptions he causes among established scholars, his accusations of plagiarism, which neither Newton nor Oldenburg, neither Huygens nor Hevelius can be certain to escape, are therefore not only ways of getting noticed. More important, they gain him the reputation of being a defiant subject that cannot be easily placated and who can therefore be held in check only by reminding him of the limits of his social status.

Apart from being the most prominent subaltern of the Royal Society, Hooke also takes a position as professor of geometry at Gresham College and becomes himself master and employer for a whole series of other servants. His attacks on the respectable scholars whom he accuses of stealing his ideas[96] only increase once he has others in his service: personal assistants and instrument makers,[97] servants and maids (whom he attempts systematically to seduce).[98] The client–server relation between servant and master proves to be a recursive configuration from the very start. If the virtuosi look down on him as a worthless servant or, at least, as the primus inter pares of the service personnel, Hooke himself behaves like a patriarch in his own household. His diary entries as well as his frequent visits to coffeehouses amply confirm that point.[99]

Daniel Defoe's 'amphibian' analogy[100] to servants applies to Hooke's intermediate position as well. Despite his ambitions and scientific skills, the social parvenu does not attain the level of recognition he desires in the circle of natural philosophers from the ranks of the old gentry. He is never accepted as an equal, despite his temporary position as a regular fellow. "In this respect, Hooke was like an urban land steward: at the top of a servant hierarchy, entrusted with (intellectual) property, but still within it."[101] Formally speaking, Hooke remains a servant. After all, a valet cannot simply turn into a master. At the same time, Hooke acts as a medium of knowledge—a far more significant aspect of the theory of marginal epistemology. Via his intermediate position, he is able to bring distant contexts into close contact. "Hooke's anomalous position, at once servant and colleague, made him an ideal mediator between, in Bennett's words, 'the mechanics' philosophy,' for he embodied both."[102] Subalterns circulate, in their 'amphibian life,' between the public domain of the street and the private realm of the household— thereby establishing a specific economic regime. Similarly, the subaltern Hooke circulates knowledge that is skillfully produced in the backroom of a lab and presented as exclusive insight to the Fellows of the Royal Society in the form of public demonstrations. "There was a tension between the epistemological status of his [Hooke's] productions, which looked more like experimental philosophy than mechanical labour, and the social status of his position, which looked more like that of a mechanic servant than an experimental philosopher."[103] The path to knowledge is, for Hooke, the means by which he seeks to find the acceptance he thinks he deserves as a gentleman among gentlemen. His ambivalent position between autonomous knowledge production and insufficient recognition rests, in turn, on the massive support of the third parties co-opted by Hooke: the work of subalterns or the discourses and practices of instrument makers and manual laborers. Hooke's epistemic position therefore also shares an amphibian quality. He is a liminal figure, an ectotherm, traversing and combining various discourses, questions about the mechanical composition of instruments and philosophical queries. The virtuosi may treat Hooke as an instrument, yet he, in turn, depends on the intervention of his own subaltern media for his discoveries. Hooke's work is based on the vital mechanical expertise of the instrument maker or simply on the possibility of delegating unpleasant or time-consuming activities to his underlings. With his middle-ground position between mechanical sciences and philosophy, between the *humble servants* of commercial artisans and the haughty habitus of the gentry, Hooke proves to be an ideal communication channel, mediating between manual and cerebral work, not without profiting from that alliance. Thereby he becomes a perfect example of the 'amphibian' careerist subaltern. Like no one else, he is able to bring distant worlds together: the arid territories inhabited by the learned aristocracy, where physical work is avoided, and the swamps, the dirty handiwork of bourgeois services.

Shapin's studies on the production of knowledge in late seventeenth-century England have led to the development of a small yet increasingly growing area of research. This scholarship aims to stress the role of the marginal figures of experimental sciences and their practical and intellectual contribution to the process of epistemic production. The research thus delves even deeper into the achievements and functions of hidden mechanical spirit workers. Behind the famous scholars populating the domain of the exact sciences, assiduous archivists have discovered a whole range of other invisible figures that may now come into focus. The shining stars of natural philosophy are gradually joined by a choice (and carefully chosen) crowd of assistants. It seems that those who lack demons have servants. But the individual portraits in this gallery of misrepresented, unrecognized workers display various degrees of detail and focus. Next to the freshly restored paintings representing Robert Hooke and his opponent Denis Papin, we find the portrait of Charles Henry Gimingham, who helped develop the radiometer and ran the lab of the inventor of the cathode ray, the Fellow of the Royal Society and spiritualist experimenter William Crooke. Not only does Gimingham execute experiments in the absence of his master, he also mimetically assimilates his handwriting.[104] Next to that painting there is a double portrait representing the quarrelsome Otto Baumbach and the reticent William Kay, the glassblower and the diagram drawer of another Fellow of the Royal Society, Ernest Rutherford.[105] Not necessarily in chronological order, we find a group portrait nearby showing the researcher Darwin in the company of his assistant and his servant.[106] Displayed in a place of honor and profusely lit is a painting of Michael Faraday, FRS. The renowned experimental physicist starts out as the lab servant of Sir Humphrey Davy, FRS, who recognizes Faraday's talent and helps launch his career. Twenty years after entering service, in 1833 the former assistant and valet Faraday takes over Davy's position as the chemistry chair of the Royal Institution.[107]

This small gallery traces a long history of *cives illiterati,* deemed 'unworthy' of representation: the service staff of universities, private laboratories, and academic research centers.[108] In this context one could also invoke an aspect that has been previously discussed (in chapter 1), namely, the *architecture of serviceability.* The construction plans for the new university institutes, most of which are built during the nineteenth century, also include private apartments for the academic servants. Their purpose is to keep servants close, make them readily available at all times, and allow them to fully place their work in the service of research. It is therefore hardly surprising that the social stratification in Wilhelmine Germany, for instance, is also represented in the functional organization of separate domains, replicated at the level of building techniques. This hierarchical structure is reflected, for instance, in the construction of the Chemistry Institute in Leipzig, founded in 1868 for the Marburg chemistry professor Hermann Kolbe, who had been called to his new position in Saxony:

Various spatial configurations were at play: the didactic division between lecture and lab work; the hierarchical separation between beginners and advanced learners, second and first assistants—a distinction that implies both a temporal and professional development, highlighted by the symbolic distribution of the floors. Further, there were various degrees of publicity and privacy as well as social stratification: three floors up and overlooking the garden was the director's apartment; overlooking the street, between the Small Auditorium and the spectroscopy lab, were the two-room apartment of the three assistants; and finally, down in the basement—the rooms of the janitor and lab servants.[109]

Hidden from daylight, the subalterns stay underground. The hierarchical logic of the English mansion is replicated here again: everybody is under one roof, but there is a huge rift between the elite upstairs and the personnel in the basement. How should an institute go about dealing with its own servants? Ideally, they should be isolated, kept separate from all domains that may present any risk of distraction. "Otherwise, the servant cannot be controlled and then I might not be able to correctly and thoroughly judge his diligence and performance,"[110] states Ferdinand Braun, a further developer of the cathode ray tube.

The daily life of the "good spirits of the institutes of natural science" is strictly regulated,[111] following a disciplinary dispositif that could be paraphrased as "discipline and clean." This situation is eloquently illustrated by the regulations sent by Hermann Kolbe to the institute servant Justus Henk in 1856, while the professor is still in Marburg. As stipulated in the document, the servant can be laid off at any point. Additionally, the instructions suggest he is to work all the time, every day except Sunday: "§ 2: He must be available on all workdays and at every hour to attend to his tasks in the service of the institute." He must follow all orders "on time and responsibly"; "I rather prefer not to" is not an option available to him. The rooms need to be cleaned, the doors locked at night and unlocked in the morning; the building must be checked, the fire stoked, preparations made for the experiments; afterward, the instruments and glasses must be cleaned "for the institute as well as for the students." Further, the quality of service is of the utmost importance: "§ 6: He must be pleasant and courteous towards the students at all times and must not engage in any argument with them." He is also strictly forbidden to misuse objects or trade materials, not even the least valuable of them: "The ashes and waste are considered the property of the institute and the servant cannot claim them for himself."[112] Not unlike other subjects at the bottom of the hierarchy, the domestic and the factory worker, the scientific servant is also denied any claim on what is produced, even the ashes resulting from a process of combustion.

4.2.2. Headless Manual Workers?

> Hands are the five-fingered evidence of human vanity and rapacity, therefore
> they stay nicely hidden under the desk.
> —Robert Walser, *Jakob von Gunten*, 1909

The Royal Society and its innovative experimental techniques play a major role in the development of contemporary science. Yet at the same time they also enhance the officially declared difference between manual labor and mental activity. "Experimental philosophy involved not only head work but also hand work."[113] The latter, however, is rarely mentioned, at least not in relation to those that conduct it.

The paradigm of the so-called scientific revolution introduces the difference between the neat, clean, and (largely textually inscribed) visible hand of the brilliant author and the dirty, invisible hands of the assistants, which are usually left out of the picture. The gentlemen philosophers and their no-less-status-oriented descendants working at European academies and universities dismiss those in lower positions. "For people of fine sensibility who have been accustomed to elegant ways and manners, the shame associated with manual labor may be so strong that in critical moments it may even repress their instinct of self-preservation."[114] Professors of physics or chemistry in Imperial Germany find it difficult to acknowledge the contribution of their lab assistants, let alone express their gratitude. Institute servants and their daily manual practices without which experiments would not take place become the carriers of subaltern knowledge or, in terms of a microphysics of power, the media of suppressed knowledge. If they are featured at all, then the contributions of subalterns are rhetorically minimized. Their activities are only selectively mentioned and, in those cases, only with regard to their 'helping' hands, not their minds. Not accidentally, the servant's hand is a fetishized object beyond scientific contexts as well, often pictured as turning red from work.[115]

Well into the twentieth century the lab servant strictly appears as an aide on the path toward knowledge, as a silenced medium and an invisible producer of wisdom. Only once manual labor becomes gradually more valued after the demise of 'the world of yesteryear' and the estate-based society[116] do the secret custodians of knowledge such as lab servants, the 'right hands' or the arm extensions of celebrated scientists, get increasing attention or even recognition. Their role as administrators of epistemic processes is at first principally examined at the level of their manual activities. As Reinhart Koselleck points out, the term *administrare* is derived from *ad manus venire*.[117] At first, what counts are manual practices like the sorting or collating, arranging and assembling of the disparate components of an experiment. Those are the primary cultural techniques of servants (demons) of knowledge.[118] The role of the servant is treated less explicitly. The preferred discursive image associated with it is the hand, and in this form it becomes—albeit partly—visible in texts. Not unlike the image of the finger on Google Books, as the last material trace of the otherwise no longer identifiable library servant in the digital sphere, lab assistants appear only as a mere synechdochal presence: "They are agents without a principal, parts without a whole."[119] The textual traces of the servant evoke only hands but not a head. And such a *pars-pro-toto* situation directs attention almost exclusively to the manual arrangements and gestures that actually carry out the experiments, as opposed to the philosophical notion of authorship and its intellectual lion's share in the act of knowledge. But as indispensable as the subalterns' hands-on experimentation may be, their gestures signify much more than sheer mechanical actions. They represent a unique form of knowledge. The texts reflect only the turn to abstraction which has long occurred and can no longer be made transparent. And yet the mechanical operations and the intellectual achievements (or rather vice versa: the mechanical achievements and intellectual operations) remain closely connected with each other. Servants, like demons, for instance, may do the dirty jobs. But their performance contains a considerable share of intellectual work. It's no longer easy to distinguish between manual labor and brainwork.[120]

It has been only a few decades since the historiographers of contemporary sciences have started to recognize the enhanced contribution of manual practices to the process of knowledge acquisition. The shift may have been influenced by Steven Shapin's discussions or Michael Polanyi's analysis of tacit knowledge. The latter, especially, has focused more than others on unifying the practices of manual and intellectual labor.[121] An epistemology of experimental sciences can no longer function without drawing on a specifically gestural knowledge. Yet to retrieve this kind of knowledge from the source material proves even harder than reconstituting all other operations that subalterns perform. Drawing on the work of James Prescott Joule, Hans Otto Sibum launches, in 1995, an inquiry into the 'silenced' contribution of manual labor to cognitive processes. Starting from a costly but precise replica of the experimental model from the Joule family brewery in Manchester, he analyzes the epistemic breakthrough set in motion by the introduction of high-accuracy temperature measurements in the beer production process. As it turns out, Joule's mechanical equivalent of heat, which finally led him to his energy conservation formula and thereby to a new natural law that could be found only in the context of the English brewing tradition. The experiment literally feeds on beer production expertise: "Joule's entire staging of the experiment was therefore deeply entwined with the world of beer brewing. No wonder that the central component of the experiment, the paddle wheel, corresponded to a smaller model of the stirrer employed in the brewery."[122]

Two further sine qua non conditions are relevant in this context. For one, the beer carriage drivers and brewery assistants employed by Joule's father also play a central role in the experiment: they pull the weights up and, as they unwind, the paddle wheels are set into motion. And it is due only to their robust physical condition that their own body heat does not influence the temperature measurements: "Our replication shows that an athlete would have been perfect to wind up the weights. An athlete's physical condition would prevent unnecessary temperature increases in the room during the trial which had to be performed as fast as possible."[123] Without this athletic intervention the experiments would have hardly reached the desired level of precision. And thus the domestics working for the family brewery business unexpectedly turn into lab servants involved in precision measurement techniques. A considerable contribution is also made by John Benjamin Dancer, the instrument maker who also proves to be an invaluable assistant. The experimenter can therefore simply focus on taking the temperature and weighing the cider—everything else is taken care of by his subalterns.[124]

Joule translates the tacit knowledge of brewing—the specific conditions and manual skills involved in the process as well as the brewers' traditional experience—into new instrument measuring standards. He thereby delegates the specific aspects of manual knowledge to the instruments themselves. Therein lies the epistemic breakthrough of the experiments. The knowledge traditionally passed on from master to apprentice is transposed into scientific contexts. With the aid of a high-precision thermometer, Joule successfully manages to standardize temperature measurements to the point where they match the standards of gestural knowledge. "The extreme precision of instruments demands precise gestures."[125] The thermometer as nonhuman assistant continuously translates professional experience into numerical values, thus leading to a further trend, namely, the essential involvement of instruments as key actors in a material culture of the sciences. The paradigm shift succeeds only because Joule understands that manual skills must be combined with the learned knowledge of the Natural Philosophical Society. The gestural knowledge turns Joule into a natural philosopher.[126] But the entire series of experiments shows how the invaluable potential and agency lying in the hands of subalterns or human actors, despite their diminished visibility, is gradually transposed to nonhuman actors such as instruments. What was true for information distribution (for servants as search engines, as shown in chapter 2) or everyday objects in manual labor–based environments such as the kitchen also proves to be true in the configuration of experimental science in the lab. In all of these cases, human actors as carriers of gestural knowledge are being gradually forced out over the course of the twentieth century.

Joule's act of delegating gestures of precision to instruments and mechanical configurations develops toward the end of the nineteenth century into the specialized education of representatives of a new profession, namely, lab assistants, trained to perform precisely such routine activities with instruments and measuring tools meant to relieve scientists as creators of performing standard manual operations. "Technical assistants were originally hired at the end of the nineteenth and beginning of the twentieth century as 'lab boys' to undertake unskilled work."[127] Just as lawyers need secretaries or doctors employ medical staff, scientists require trained personnel to assist them. The chemist Erich Kedesdy writes in 1910, "Everywhere we turn we see scientifically trained men striving to free themselves of manual labor and delegate it to work forces that have been especially trained in this regard."[128] And with the rise of this new, professionally trained branch, the classic lab servant—the unacknowledged driving force behind epistemic processes—once more retreats into invisibility. A further contributing factor is the lifting of gender differences, which paves the way for women to work as lab assistants. Schools like Wilhelm Adolf Lette's Association for the Professional Advancement of Women, founded in 1866, launch the training of specialized technical scientific female assistants.[129] The classic lab servants have vanished. For a while they still appear as doorkeepers,[130] before their tasks are completely taken over by lab boys and girls or, more precisely, medical technical assistants (MTAs).[131] What had started in the early years of the Royal Society in the shadow of a powerful scientists' circle comes to a close around 1900 with an increasing drive toward research and development diversification. For mid- and lower-ranking lab workers, now benefiting from professional representation and special publications like the *Laboratory Assistant,* the new context means a newly recognized career field.

Just before its gradual demise, the lab servant figure ultimately attains higher scientific standing. After centuries of assiduous work, it finally gains its long-deserved recognition. Now, at last, the record is set straight from the scientific master's perspective as well. An article with the unusual title "The Poor Diener," signaling the transference of the term into English shortly before its disappearance from German scientific language, almost reads like a melancholy farewell:

How many of us have not felt as we closed an article that we may have thought good, perhaps expressing perfunctory thanks to our patron or instructor or some other figure in the seats of the mighty who took a few minutes' time to send us some preparations or cultures prepared by someone else in his laboratory, that there was a hardworked, somewhat pathetic humbler figure back of it all to whom our thanks are far more due than to any of these?

When you take down from the shelf a carefully cleaned, carefully sterilized, cottonplugged flask and fill it up for your own purposes, and then cheerfully discard it and take another because you got in a tenth of a centimeter too much, when you finish up a couple of hours' brisk work and then carry out a trayful of pipettes to the "dirtroom" to be washed up, and leave around a staggering array of dirty glassware too bulky to bother to take out yourself, when you pile up on the sterilizing bench a great lot of used, gone and forgotten cultures for someone else to autoclave, then *remember the poor diener.*

[. . .]

These are not operations that can be carried on by any old man in the street; these are true science. Dozens of procedures which we learned with difficulty in school days, we turn over to dienere and technicians, who learned the art from other dieners and technicians and carry it on in a clean-cut mechanical way better than we could do ourselves. God help science if all the dieners should unionize and go on a strike tomorrow.[132]

The not-so-fictional scenario of "dieners of all labs, unite," which can be prevented only, semi-ironically, by divine intervention, as well as the laconic confirmation that the servants' specialized gestures and routine actions amount to no less than true science: here, the text goes beyond the direct reference to bacterial cultures to pay a modest homage to the 'gone and forgotten' culture, in a direct, sentimental admission of the irreplaceable, productive intervention of subalterns, without whom research goals cannot be attained. "Understanding, abstract thought, science, technique, the arts—all these, then, have their origin in the forced work of the Slave. Therefore, the Slave, not the Master, is the one who accomplishes all that has to do with these things."[133] Within the lab environment it is the 'slaves,' the servants, that draw their knowledge from their precursors, across generations. And yet it is ultimately the state itself, in its role as employer, that imposes its limits on them, even as they are held in high academic esteem, and their contribution is increasingly deemed invaluable. Appointed to a new position in Strasbourg in 1895, the inventor of the cathode ray tube, Ferdinand Braun, plans to leave Tübingen along with his institute assistant, Georg Schurr, whose tacit knowledge had gradually become an indispensable asset. The latter, however, seizes the moment to negotiate the legal terms of a possible stay at the university in Tübingen. Master and servant are both interested in demanding the right conditions for the subaltern. Thereby, Schurr "would have definitely advanced to a lower-tier adjunct professor salary level."[134] Yet the administration rejects the request on the grounds that the university makes no provisions for negotiating terms with simple workers. Despite the servant's excellent reputation, his claim is turned down and perceived as a case of overstepping professional boundaries.

A similar case is that of Friedrich Kirchenbauer, whose employer at the university in Karlsruhe, the chemist Fritz Haber, is appointed to a new position in Berlin in 1906. Apart from his regular tasks as maintenance supervisor, Kirchenbauer's duties also involve lab equipment repairs and holding several utility models and patents in his name. But the servant also has an assistant of his own and therefore is a master as well. As Ostwald's student Max Le Blanc points out, referring to Haber, "In any institute, it all comes down to the director and his servant. Everyone else comes in second place."[135] Long after Haber's move to Berlin, Kirchenbauer, now a mechanic, receives an offer from the industrial sector, prompting him to start negotiating the terms of his position at the university. Yet again a subaltern's hardly modest financial claims are met with indignation rather than benevolence. "Should it become common for lab technicians, assistants and university servants to considerably raise their income on the grounds of external offers, the university would have to launch a formal appointment procedure."[136] Obviously, that process is to be prevented. And since the Ministry of Education in Baden regards factotums as replaceable entities, Kirchenbauer's request is turned down as well.

The decree of the Holy Roman Inquisition to excommunicate the help as a worthy subject of portraiture after Veronese's blasphemous *Last Supper* from 1573 seems to be still in place and reverberate through the secular spaces of modern scientific production. Lab servants are rarely mentioned in writing and even more rarely found in visual representations. There is little deviation from this norm: thus, for instance, in the case of Johann Bretthauer, the devoted factotum of the Chemistry Institute in Marburg, where the media of knowledge rediscover themselves as visual media hailing their achievements. "Bretthauer may have well been the only institute servant credited not merely with having made scientific discoveries, but also with having his oil portrait taken along with several Marburg professors."[137] A similar but less prestigious distinction is granted to the lab servant of the Nobel Prize–winning chemist Eduard Buchner: given his close work relation to his superior, the subaltern is memorialized in a photograph.[138] Yet another example is that of the instrument maker Heinrich Geißler, awarded an honorary degree in 1886 for developing the gas-discharge tube.[139]

And in the case of Louis Pasteur's lab servant, it is neither oil nor silver-iodide photography but bronze that keeps his memory alive. A visitor reports: "At the entrance, there is a bronze statue of Jupille, the servant, holding a rabid dog with a firm grip."[140]

Such examples, however, cannot belie the unfortunate destiny of laboratory servants: the fact that, despite all their worthy contributions, they are generally overlooked. Their fate is marked by invisibility, the mode of choice for subaltern media operations. And should they make themselves noticeable, their attention-hungry institute directors would be all the keener to have them disappear. The *Muppet Show*'s Dr. Bunsen Honeydew perfectly illustrates that point with his repeated attempts to render his lab assistant and guinea pig, Beaker, invisible: whether as part of his ghost-hunting experiments, when Beaker is turned into a phantom-like creature; or when inventing his vanishing cream, which poor Beaker is forced to try out on himself.

4.3. FICTION IN SCIENCE

> The demon makes the metaphor not only verbally graceful, but also objectively true.
> —Thomas Pynchon, *Crying of Lot 49*

The role of the servant in the cognitive process is that of a mediator across various media domains. As will be shown, the servant figure occupies a unique position at the intersection of experiment, theory, and fiction. According to Michael Heidelberger, Karl Popper has defined the experiment as "the handmaiden of theory"[141] and thereby unknowingly suggested much more than a mere metaphor. Indeed, upon closer inspection, the description points directly to the history of experimental sciences, particularly to the actual assistants involved in the experimental processes, the subalterns whose work allows natural laws and theories to be formulated in the first place. Here, the servant figure appears in two apparently very different configurations: on the one hand, on the dark side of historiography, in a concealed mode, carefully removed from the view of others, as what has been rightfully labeled an *invisible technician*. On the other hand, the assistant also takes on the form of a rhetorical strategy, namely, in a context that can be defined only as fictional. To the extent to which there is any mention of an assistant, the discussion is for the most part metaphorical. If the (in)visible hands of the subaltern correspond to a synecdoche, the servant serves yet another rhetorical strategy, in the form of a demon contributing to the process of knowledge. When the demonic metaphor refers to no other actor but the lab servant, the latter stands not merely for the *verbum proprium* of the demon in the experiment, the concrete, material origin of the process. In addition, the lab servant represents the media a priori of the scientific demon as well as other serviceable spirits of epistemology. Their intervention is essential in allowing for the epistemic process to take place.

The question about actors and their part in the construction of scientific models coalescing into facts and natural laws also implicitly raises the question about the fictional component of the process of cognition. Beyond mathematical operations, the term "actor" involves a specific description that cannot generally do without a metaphorical component. Implicitly, it raises questions about the fictional status and narrative forms in the natural sciences.

As much as the representatives of the exact sciences seek to eliminate tropes and myths from their disciplines, their textual forms cannot do without those partly fictional, partly effaced, or rhetorically reduced figures. They are the ones that perform the actual work. That is also why one must evaluate and compare the fictional quality of demons and servants. Both actors function as the stirrups of knowledge. The former is mainly built as a thought construct or virtual help (and exorcising it proves to be quite difficult). The latter's destiny is to be denied recognition, despite very concrete contributions: performing various services, providing unexpected support—blowing glass, performing temperature measurements, preparing the results of mechanical experiments. There is at least one distinction between fictional demons and the scientists' concrete ministering / menial spirits—even if, according to Paul Valéry, the latter seem to resort to demons themselves.[142]

Demons direct attention to the demiurgical creator and thereby inevitably operate in the public eye. As opposed to them, lab servants are forced out of the limelight. Their superior garners all the fame, puts everything under his name, leaving the helpers excluded from the attention they deserve.

Demons and servants, however, operate differently in the fictional context. The former appear as thought experiments, yet produce real and concrete effects. In this sense, Laplace's, Maxwell's, and Loschmidt's demons all belong to a series that create and produce each other. The latter act as discarded elements. While they may well be essential components of the scientific narrative, they ultimately do not turn up in the end result, for that result usually pays homage to the myth of the genius-as-inventor. Along the lines of Brecht's "Questions from a Worker Who Reads," if lab servants did not exist, one would need to invent them. Only then would epistemic processes be appropriately described. The *very observant being* and the *laboratory servant* also share the same media practices: the sorting, gathering, and bundling of information. Such operations, which follow the principle of tacit knowledge, represent the core cultural technique of both demons and lab servants. Both serve as inconspicuous information generators. And both are typically persistent. It takes endless attempts to get rid of demons once they enter scientific discourse. For the most part, exorcism strategies prove to be rather ineffective. The peculiar creature that is the demon seems to possess a hydra-like return mechanism that ultimately contributes to its ineradicable nature. The lab servant figure, with its constant invisibility paired with heightened productivity, poses precisely the same problem, but in reverse. Despite their invisibility, lab servants prove to be the almost imperceptible basso continuo of contemporary experimental sciences. Finally, both actors are defined by their narrative productivity. Both help develop a narrative and launch a fictional account, which, ideally, results in a scientific discovery that is thereby fabricated or confirmed.

In antiquity, *fictio* is defined as an act of drawing forth which unites poiesis and mimesis. In contrast, the development of modern science presupposes a new rift between fiction and experiment which effaces the common origin of the literary and the experimental in the *facultas fingendi:* "The identification of fiction with literature, and their opposition to the notion of facts derive from a history of sciences where fiction and the medium of language are largely removed from the scope of exact methods (and the procedures associated with them: lab experiments, measurements, electric and electronic systems of notation etc)."[143] And yet, as proven by the demons at the core of thought experiments, the idiosyncrasies of language, its rhetoric, and metaphoricity play an important epistemic role in the exact sciences as well. 'Pure facts' prove to be nothing but massive constructions—if not 'fictions'—and both servants and demons play an important role in this regard. Language not only serves as a means of representation of scientific findings but also contributes to a great extent to the production of knowledge. "Fiction becomes a full-fledged epistemological medium."[144] Both servants and demons act, each according to their own media model, as catalyzers and producers of new knowledge. Within the context of knowledge production, they form an essential, albeit invisible, aspect of experimental configurations. The reasons for their lack of visibility are obvious: as a result of various causes, demons à la Maxwell are rather hard to detect: they are too small, too shy, and, in uncertain cases, merely part of an intellectual game. Servants cannot be seen, since there is no mention of them, no room or place for them in the retrospective narrative about the process of arriving at knowledge.

The lab servants' fictional component derives precisely from that foundational invisibility. Just as in the case of thought experiments and their demons, the textual formulation, or the *inscription* (Latour), of the findings is in reality an act of fictionalization, especially when, inevitably, images, metaphors, and rhetorical strategies are employed.[145] Just as demons do not exist in the real scientific world, there is no 'I' as the unique author of experiments and their inscription. In contrast to Adam Smith's invisible hand model, the systematically obliterated helping hands of subalterns point to an equally invisible, yet real corporeal residue that must remain nameless at all costs. They expose research reports as authorial fiction when an experimenter attributes all achievements to himself, even though his knowledge literally comes from secondhand sources. The experimenters' knowledge—as shown in Robert Boyle's and William Crooke's case—is secondhand knowledge, since the 'first hand' is always at work, operating either a tool, an instrument, or a pump. To the extent to which servants remain invisible and are not treated as subjects of knowledge, they can be handled objectively, not unlike the instruments, tools, and practices used in the experiments; which, in other words, means nothing but ignoring their creative and ingenious contribution to the process of knowledge production. "The slightly more resistant part of a chain of practices cannot be called an 'object' except at the time it is still under the ground, unknown, thrown away, subjected, covered, ignored, invisible, in itself. In other words, there are no visible objects and there never have been. The only objects are invisible.[146] As generators of knowledge, lab servants are—not unlike the domestics or menial spirits of the Enlightenment—objects that follow the same paradox of subalternity: being treated as absent actors despite their bodily presence. To the extent to which lab servants are systematically kept out of reports and scientific publications that announce new natural laws, the narratives of modern experimental sciences present fictionalized results. The heroic tale of modern sciences does not allow room for subalterns and their help.

If science were a horse, one could ask: who or what leads knowledge, the rider or the reins? When William Thomson characterizes the demons in Maxwell's thought experiment as "purely mechanical in their character, invented to help us,"[147] he invokes the standard topos of the servant, thereby clarifying the parallels between the two media actors of knowledge production. Not unlike Einstein, who imagines particles as rock fragments crashing into each other like hail, Maxwell invents a demon, cast as a servant or 'research tool'[148] in charge of controlling the molecules on his behalf. The metaphoric helpers thus act as the levers of knowledge or the stirrups of thought processes. As a component in conceptual model construction, fiction plays more than a decisive part in experimental sciences. The talk about demons does not just come from nowhere. It is not a mere figment of the imagination; similarly, demons are not just deus ex machina devices that provide inspiration. Rather, they represent a repressed form of gratitude which the real actors of experiments and trials deserve. Beyond the imaginary assistants and fictional demons, one can trace a very concrete figure: the historical model of the laboratory servant. That is the real underlying element, the media a priori of the demon as a figure of thought. The lab servant represents the media a priori of the demon at the heart of thought experiments. The scientific demon's discursive function is directly drawn from the invisible productivity of lab servants, their capacity to work, at least since Robert Hooke, as the stirrups of knowledge. Hooke and others like him will take on the position of central, albeit silent, mediators between experiment and its publication. They become the invisible media of scientific production within modern experimental science, paradigmatically illustrated by the Royal Society.

What cognitive function do demons serve? Wherein lies the productivity of lab servants? Both servants and demons act as the moment of negentropy within closed systems, namely, as those components that absorb or generate information in order to protect the entire system from contradicting or going against fundamental natural laws (for instance, the second law of thermodynamics). Both assistants take extreme measures against the threats of chaos and entropy by playing an important role in generating information and producing knowledge. Even when they break down, servants still represent the negentropic components within the cognitive process. Without their secret work, there can be no theoretical or experimental insight into natural laws. Despite their fictional status, demons offer concrete proof. Despite its real presence, the lab servant figure is rendered virtual or even invisible. Its productivity is defined in terms of elusive metaphors (ministering spirits) or metonymies (helping hands). Such figures, however, pave the way to knowledge. They use fiction in order to produce, and produce in order to create fiction, to launch the cognitive process. New insights always emerge as hypotheses, on the path of the 'what-if' toward the world. The ephemeral and protean ministering spirit—both as demon and as servant—is the midwife of such new knowledge.

Chapter 5 Channel Service

Traditionally, the system of communication at court is highly differentiated: visually, via signifying practices such as uniforms, liveries, and other material insignia (honorary keys, ceremonial batons), but also acoustically, by means of specific signals meant to garner the desired attention. Subaltern acts of communication start . . . ahem . . . with a cough.

The senior footmen and valets further down the line have learned how to subtly modulate their coughs. The footman who closes the carriage door clears his throat, ever so slightly, if the lady forgets to declare her desired destination; after taking up his place at the back of the carriage, he gives a loud cough, to direct the driver.

Over in the master's chambers, the valet looks at the clock and coughs to announce the time, then wakes the doorkeeper from his reverie with a loud coughing noise, to remind him he ought to prepare the carriage for the ride.

And, finally, at table, the quartermaster directs the entire dinner service with an arsenal of most delicate and subtle coughs; meaningfully clearing his throat, the table setter draws the footman's attention to the foolish mistake he has made, to a broken plate or an empty glass; and a young servant recoils, panic stricken and feebly coughing, from the abyss he barely avoided, since he was about to pass the wild boar's head to the first chamberlain from the right-hand side."[1]

The cough is a gesture in transmission, passed on—as in a relay race—from top to bottom—to the lowliest palace guard—and from there onward, via the express courier on horseback. Other messages are relayed in similar fashion. Before they reach their recipient, they traverse vast sections of the court hierarchy. Hardly any letter is personally conveyed by only one messenger. Rather, messages are passed on to others, transmitted via several relay stations, from inferior to superior ranks. Or, in the opposite direction, a message may be dispatched from one rank to another, top-down, until it reaches its destination and is finally delivered.

The courtly cough is the sign of an impending communication, a signal announcing the arrival of a guest, or an error in serving a plate. It has a phatic function, indicating that something else will take place. It also suggests, well into the nineteenth century, that messenger and message were still closely connected. Nothing intervenes between the signifier—the human medium performing the action—and the signified in the process of communication. Letter and courier form a unit whose interaction is set to the speed of human movement, either on foot or on horseback, and is measured by what can be heard. The messages—the coughing, the throat clearing—accompany the messengers.

That unity between mobile messenger and message falls apart sometime during the first part of the nineteenth century. The process begins with the introduction of optical telegraphy under Napoleon,[2] when messages start to considerably outpace their carriers. Words travel much faster than their means of transmission, that is to say, the fixed medium of dial telegraphy. It is only a small step from there to the electrification of telecommunications, when human media are further divorced from their messages. Ultimately, the technical medium takes over, a move predicated on the closure of the circuit between sender and receiver and the exclusion of the human carrier. The current chapter engages precisely with these aspects. What follows is a close reading of a key historical scene, illustrating in concrete fashion the breakup of the unity between letter and letter carrier. Here, the principle of long-distance information transmission will be redirected into *distant thinking*. The same scene will be treated from three different theoretical perspectives, thereby demonstrating the historiographic difficulties and contingencies implicit in any attempt at historical narration.

5.1. MICHELMANN, FOR EXAMPLE

> Neither the bare hand, nor the unaided intellect has much power; the work
> is done by tools and assistance.
> —Francis Bacon, *Novum Organum*, 1620

Michelmann went the same way as always. He set out from the foyer on the first
floor of the Physics Institute and left the Academic Museum behind him. After lengthy negotiations, his master's obscure magnetism experiments and new
ideas about the transmission of electric current had unfortunately obtained only
provisional approval. (Michelmann was instructed to call the metal wire used
for the experiment a "galvanic chain.")[3] He walked out of the institute, turned
left on Pauliner Street, and went toward the Johannis Church. The road ahead
was long; it traversed almost the entire town.

But the path was clearly marked by a visible line, a thread above his head,
which he had to follow. From the church tower on the left, the line continued
to the gymnasium, which he now left behind on his way to the Corn Market;
from there, via Hospital Street, the line led straight to the Maternity House (the
Royal Maternity Hospital, donated to the city by Albrecht von Haller a century
before). When he reached that penultimate station, Michelmann hesitated and
checked to see whether the thin line was still in place. If it was not there, he did
not have to go any further. As the master had told him, the line consisted of two
wires, made of copper and uninsulated iron, fastened together with a cord. The
line had broken down many times before or had been "intentionally"[4] destroyed.
But on that warm spring day in 1833, shortly after Easter, it seemed intact, so
Michelmann followed it southward, turning left just before the city gates and
past the brickyard, to finally reach his destination: the New Observatory outside the city, where the irises had started to bloom. As the townspeople would
proudly say, that place had long been (starting in 1807, to be exact) the breeding
ground for the brightest spirit of modern science, *il principe dei matematici*.

Slightly out of breath, Michelmann took the staircase, counting the steps as
he went—after so many trips he knew how many there were. Now he was in
front of the office of the man "with the strange hat" (as he would secretly call
the leader of the observatory), knocked, and went in. Inside, he saw the privy
councillor, peering through a telescope, looking at a massive instrument with
large needles and scribbling some notes on a piece of paper. The message the
servant brought that day was unusual, yet quite true and revealing: "Michelmann's here." Both men uttered the words at the same time. But while the messenger's tone betrayed only exhaustion, there was undoubtedly a note of victory
in his master's voice.

This is how that key scene of modern telecommunications may have unfolded if the different versions of the account are to be trusted. On the occasion of the seventh convention of German science researchers and doctors in the fall of 1828, Carl Friedrich Gauss (1777–1855) comes to Berlin at the invitation of Alexander von Humboldt. There he meets the young and talented Wilhelm Eduard Weber (1804–91) and appoints him to a professorship in Göttingen. Starting in 1831 both dedicate themselves—further encouraged by Humboldt's letters—to intensive research on the subject of earth's magnetism. Tangentially, they also focus their attention on the hotly debated question of electromagnetism, as it had been variously discussed by Faraday, Schweigger, Ohm, and, Ørstedt.[5] Their main focus is the possibility of transmitting a long-distance signal via an electric cable. In order to obtain precise measurements of earth's magnetic field, Gauss and Weber must synchronize the observations they conduct at various locations, for instance, the observatory and the Physics Institute. "For the locally conducted magnetic tests [. . .], the spatial distance between the two work stations (approx. 1 km [beeline]) naturally involved difficulties. For instance, conducting simultaneous observations required comparing different clocks, which could be achieved only by time-consuming trips back and forth."[6] The necessity of speeding up the communication channel between the two scientists produces an unplanned effect: the birth of electric telegraphy. Gauss and Weber have replaced a slow medium—the messenger at walking speed—with a media dispositif of impulse activators, a magnetic needle as a receiver, and wires that transmit messages at the speed of light. And thus Easter of 1833 marks the date of the first successful long-distance delivery of an electric telegram.

5.1.1. Three Methodological Approaches to Michelmann

The key scene of modern telecommunication staged with the help of Michelmann's congenial service will be analyzed from three perspectives. How does this specific moment lend itself to various disciplinary interpretations? The event will be examined first according to its media-historical and -theoretical implications, then through the lens of cultural history, with a very different focus foregrounding social aspects. Finally, the third segment will inquire after the possibility of an alternative, a potentially unifying perspective: a 'media-cultural history,' which may lead to new conclusions and insights and open up new research possibilities. Such diverse strategies of inquiry inevitably produce

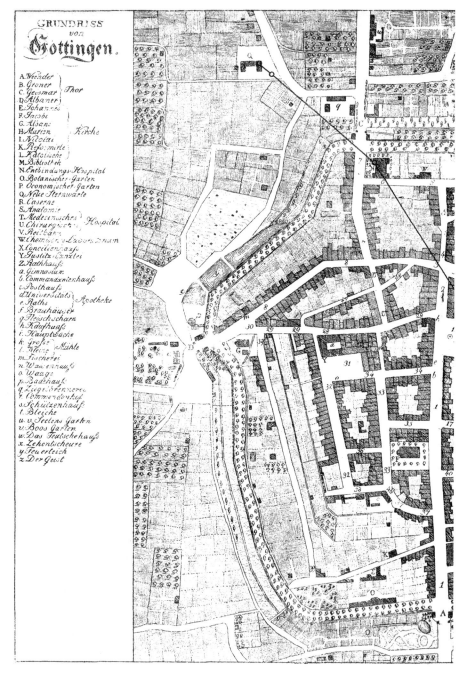

Figure 9. Media competition: Michelmann and the telegraph line

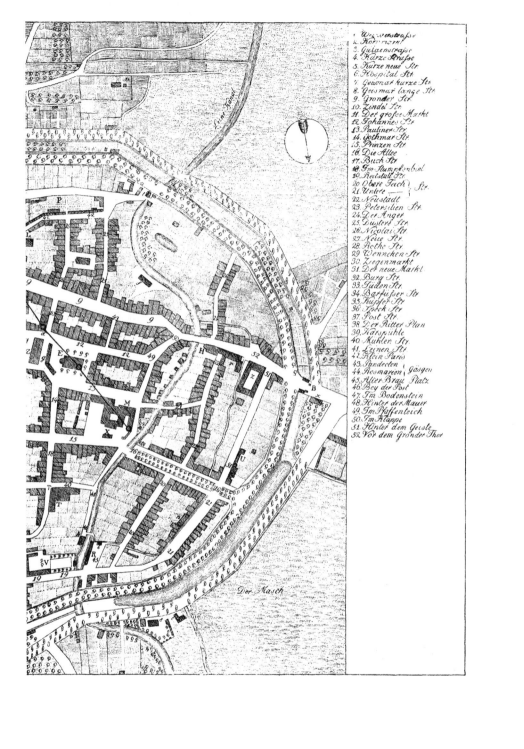

different results. Thereby, the brief analyses below also serve to illustrate the contingencies of history writing. Last but not least, the play of multiple perspectives will allow for a methodological summary that anchors the various strategies of inquiry in some of the previously discussed case studies as well as in those that will follow.

5.1.1.1. First Approach: Media History

From a media-historical perspective, one can focus on the subject of electrical telegraphy as a technical medium. Here, the discussion concerns the history of science: Ohm's law from 1827, which Gauss intends to use in his experiments, or Faraday's induction law from 1831. In the same context, one can also analyze the field of electricity research during the first half of the nineteenth century via the preliminary investigations of Ørstedt and Faraday.[7] But Gauss's and Weber's experiment can also be regarded as exemplary for a theoretical analysis. Starting from here, one can then assess the analytical scope of various communication models, from Lazarsfeld to Laswell. If one opts for the information theory model of Claude Shannon and Warren Weaver[8] instead, then the components of the media dispositif (sender, receiver, channel, and noise) can be easily recognized.

By applying minimal modifications, Gauss and Weber transform their measuring instruments into a sender, consisting of a "transmitter with induction currents," and a receiver (more specifically, a unifilar magnetometer made out of a "magnetic baton with multiplicator and mirror").[9] But the actual innovation is the transmission wire, which is much longer than those used by Soemmering and Schilling von Cannstatt in their experiments in Munich and St. Petersburg, respectively. One can truly speak of long-distance writing in this case. For the first time the Göttingen experiments from 1833 demonstrate the practical applicability of electrical telegraphy. As Gauss correctly assumes, telegraphy could be "brought to a level of perfection that would defy the imagination. The emperor of Russia might instantly send orders to Petersburg and Odessa or even to Kiachta without the aid of relays."[10] Significantly, the scene brings together two different paradigms of transmission that would, from then on, follow distinct paths of development. But for a brief moment, information and event coincide. Michelmann's trajectory as well as the circulation of the telegram, but especially the arrival of the message, marks the brief coincidence of two distinct modes of conveyance: an instance of analog transmission of (verbal) signs and a case of digital transfer. The success of the experiment renders the classic analog service obsolete. After only a brief period of latency, electrical communication begins its unstoppable march to victory with this transmission of digital signs.

The sentence "Michelmann's here" can be uttered in unison. On the one hand, it is an instance of analog verbal transmission, announcing the message the servant has received. Via the utterance of the speech act, that message validates the truth contained in the separate and simultaneous arrival of the telegram. On the other hand, the telegram carries a digitally coded message conveying nothing less than the arrival of an analog communication. In other words, Michelmann conveys himself: as both a message and a bodily medium. As in all the previously unsuccessful attempts, the subaltern serves as the carrier of the message that can optimize the media dispositif of the telegraph. This time, however, the message cancels out the medium, since it already confirms the statement contained in the first successfully conveyed digital communication. Michelmann's arrival is a signal as well as a checksum or a check bit for the new medium.

For one last time Michelmann (literally) underruns the new channel, by passing under the wire hanging in the sky above. "For the first time in history [that wire] had freed the presence of a human being from his own body."[11] Still, the carrier's relation to it is also subversive, since he also underruns the news of his arrival via the actual epiphany in Gauss's study. Considering that the magnet needle needs approximately one minute—forty-three seconds, at best, according to Gauss's own claims—before it can stand still and point to the next sign, then the message "Michelmann's here" involves rather complex calculations: each of the fifteen letters of the text requires, according to Gauss's simplified method,[12] three instead of five movements of the needle to the right or left; the letters are then multiplied by these three code signs, each of which requires forty-three seconds of transmission. In the best-case scenario, then, the numbers add up to 1,935 seconds, or 32 ¼ minutes—at a transfer speed of 0.02 bits per second. Michelmann can therefore leisurely stroll rather than hurry in order to arrive before or at the same time as the telegraphic message.

The servant has been reduced to the status of a check bit, testing the functionality of the new medium of electric telegraphy. His service is no longer required for future transmissions. But the message of the first successfully conveyed telegram indicates that new media are constantly generated from old media—or, to paraphrase McLuhan's famous dictum—Michelmann is the medium is the message. So far, so good.

But how does this media-historical interpretation correspond to the Shannon / Weaver communication model? Possibly the most important component of this theory is still missing, namely, the element of noise, of interference. Both the telegraphic circuit over the roofs of Göttingen and Michelmann himself, as an analog medium of transmission, are prone to malfunctions. "The wires broke down countless times, when they were entirely ready, or only in part."[13] If the telegram fails to arrive, it means that the telegraph is not working. Nevertheless, only Michelmann's arrival can signal that dysfunction; only the servant can announce that the telegram has not reached its destination.[14]

Not even Michelmann remains unaffected by all this. His own communication is under threat. It is endangered by the possibility of interception, either by unforeseen events on his way to the observatory or by his own doing, by being rather 'slow on the uptake' (a tavern along the way . . .) or lacking a great sense of duty when attending to his tasks. Michelmann's late arrival would not necessarily affect the functioning of the telegraph but would certainly contradict the message conveyed in the first telegram and expose it as a lie. And yet, that fact alone would not bear any consequences for a genealogy of media, since a medium is always independent of the meaning of the message conveyed.

5.1.1.2. Second Approach: Cultural History

As opposed to a media-historical analysis, a cultural-historical perspective might focus on the particular medium that underruns the electric message for the last time: Michelmann, the servant associated with the Physics Institute in Göttingen. Two aspects will be considered here. Via Michelmann, one could take a closer look at the sociocultural aspects of an entire professional group, namely, the situation of servants during the first half of the nineteenth century, just before the major shift they undergo after the 1850s. Simultaneously, Michelmann could also be regarded as the anchor and representative of a biographical micronarrative; in this sense, his personal fate could illustrate the situation of a scientific operation as seen 'from below.'

"Michelmann is the institute servant."[15] This feature groups him with those subaltern employees or "lower personnel"[16] members of the university that secure, in an academic context, the practical operation and maintenance of the institution. A nineteenth-century university functions not unlike the considerably smaller unit of the domestic household, which could also hardly be managed without the ample contribution of servants. With its strict distinction between masters and hands, the bourgeois household comprises a broad and very specific range of activities. The collective term *Gesinde*, going back to the notion of 'travel retinue,' still points to the media-technical dispositif of the servants' functions. The term is derived from the Old High German *gasinde*, which can mean—with reference to *sinnan* [travel]—also "to send, to set on its way."[17] A cultural-historical perspective would, however, ignore such media-historical aspects and would focus instead on the complexities of the domestics' social situation.

Drawing on the Prussian Servants' Law of 1810, one could discuss the previously underrated contribution of underlings, footmen, or subalterns to the cultural production of preindustrial society.

The analysis might focus on the strict hierarchical regulations between those in power—be it the head of a Biedermeier household or a Prussian professor—and their servants; it could highlight the rank-related limitations, loopholes, as well as the corrective measures against offences, and the motives behind the notorious complaints against servants. One could also examine the various regulations and institutions corresponding to the professional domain of subalternity: the so-called servant hiring office—akin to an early employment agency—or the finely differentiated payment system associated with it. All these contexts disintegrate after 1850, at least as far as the male servant population with limited qualifications is concerned. These groups are swallowed up by the demand for workforces in the industrial domain. From this moment on, the term "service staff" acquires a mainly feminine connotation; and the highly qualified and liveried butlers gradually disappear.

This phenomenon coincides with the second phase of industrialization, which is no longer based on steam and coal. Now steel, fuel, and especially electricity take center stage and bring a whole range of new media-technical innovations with them. Against this background, Michelmann appears once more as a liminal figure: on the one hand, he still represents the typical duties of a servant; on the other hand, he also comes into contact with the new media of an emerging electrical age. Michelmann treads a fine line: his own position is on the cusp of a technical turn. His errand brings with it the mechanization (or electrification) of information transmission; implicitly it also marks the demise of a whole genre of anthropogenic assistants of communication. A functional telecommunication device renders all messengers superfluous. As a medium, Michelmann takes himself out of service. His last assignment is not unlike an outdated, creaking measuring instrument which has to be thrown out. Dead man walking.

A further interpretive modality offered by the cultural-historical perspective[18] would be the treatment of Michelmann's own personal trajectory—not unlike Carlo Ginzburg has done in *The Cheese and the Worms* (1976), starting with the miller Domenico Scandella, known as Menocchio, and continuing with the practices of inquisition in northern Italy during the sixteenth century at a microhistorical level. Such an inquiry—based on university files and with the help of some research—would reveal that Wilhelm Samuel Michelmann, born in Göttingen in 1812 and deceased there as well in 1892, had done an apprenticeship in woodturning, passed his mastery exam, and then, on April 20, 1847, became 'steward' or 'bedel'[19] in the service of the university. At first only temporary, his position is officially confirmed on March 24, 1848, when he is sworn in by the university board. After nearly forty years of service, on April 1, 1888, Michelmann, now ranked as a 'castellan,' retires.[20] But research reveals that the scene described above does not entirely correspond to reality since the employment lists in the University of Göttingen staff archives date Michelmann's appointment to 1847, that is to say, more than twelve years after the event in question.[21] Is Michelmann's presence only anecdotal? The question is linked to a crucial historiographic issue: to what extent can the narratives that typically surround such events be trusted? In any case, the factual aspect does not affect the interpretation of the scene, since in this case the proper name actually stands for a variable of the function of communication.

Michelmann is only a placeholder for a matter of critical importance. The early historiographers of electrical telegraphy certainly treated it that way, since they felt the need to attach a name to the servant figure corresponding to the event from the 1830s. In other words, the historiography of modern telecommunication individualizes and customizes the role of the servant. The frequent accounts of the Göttingen telegraphy experiment regularly invoke Michelmann's name in 1880, that is to say, at a time when the servant still occupies that position.[22] The subaltern serves as a variable, a metonymic figure for the function of the messenger and its vital importance in the process. From the point of view of historiographers, he represents the final instance of analog communication, the check bit that tests the practicability of the new medium. And since the employee 'Michelmann' is the one occupying the position in 1880, the actual intervention by a servant of the institute is confirmed beyond dispute. Even if Wilhelm Eduard Weber had installed the wires (as Gauss states—with the additional mention of 'aides'),[23] he still needed to activate the sender function from the institute, and therefore he could not have run those errands. The name of the servant who was assigned to do it is not unknown: Christian Gottlieb Lentzner (1778–1839), the institute's steward from 1832 until his death. His tasks include "the occasional small repair work of the instruments without additional pay ex officio" (as Weber wrote) as well as various cleaning, maintenance, and messaging services. Even if legend would have it otherwise, the telegram should have read, "Lentzner's here."[24]

Linking such obscure details of cultural and social history back to the initial media-historical context, one could now go a little further. For instance, one could explore the role played by all the apprentices, factotums, servants and aides, stewards and assistants, personal valets and footmen in the process of scientific inquiry. Starting with the research of the Royal Society during the seventeenth century, the production of knowledge is characterized by an obvious disparity between handwork and brainwork. Going even further, one could examine the role played by subalterns in the general process of communication. This step could guide the discussion toward a third approach, which, in this context, will offer a synthesis of the previous discussions of Michelmann. As in a duochrome vision test, when the lens is red on one side (the side of media history) and green on the other (the side of cultural history), the interaction produces potentially new perspectives and an unexpected degree of clarity and depth.

5.1.1.3. Third Approach: Media-Cultural History

A media-cultural history approach would not take into account the issue of Michelmann's belated employment: to borrow from Ernst Kantorowicz's argument in *The King's Two Bodies,* the state of service is perpetual.[25] *Famulatio non moritur.* Only the specific media involved in the process undergo a transformation: from anthropomorphic carriers they turn into technical circuits. Until 1833 and the key Göttingen experiment, there was a human medium of transmission (just like the postal system, optical telegraphy and its visible relays still operate anthropogenically). The advent of electrical telegraphy marks the emancipation of technical media in the realm of telecommunications. The variable, the medium of transmission, occupied for the last time by a human figure like Michelmann, takes an electromechanical turn. This concrete switch is paradigmatic in the evolution of technical media and can be subsumed under a much broader process of mechanization. The role of the servant is replaced—and not only in the context of telecommunications—by technical apparatuses and circuits (as the next chapter will prove). Still, the servant figure persists. Even within strictly technical media dispositifs, the servant functions are still in place. A new approach is therefore needed: one that is limited neither to the media-historical perspective nor to the cultural historical angle. In order to understand the complexities of telecommunications nowadays, going all the way to the development of the internet, a synthesis of the two explanatory models is required. This section will therefore briefly sketch out its potential guidelines, directions of development and inquiry, and view them from two different angles. The first traces the outline of a media history of the servant figure, not only as a medium of transmission (as shown before) but also, more broadly, as a medium of (scientific) knowledge. The second angle is closely linked to the first: here, the line of inquiry concerns the long-term effects of the servant metaphor in communication theory, starting from the thesis that assistants occupy a fundamental place in the history of communication; its effects are still visible today—especially today—in the modalities of electronic communication.

As opposed to the previous approaches, the media-cultural history angle examines the role of the servant in cognitive processes. Thereby, it allows a closer look at the typically obscure, systematically underrated contribution of assistants in the production of knowledge. Following a trajectory that leads from human to technical artifacts, the media history of the servant begins with the birth of the natural sciences in the seventeenth century. Steven Shapin, for instance, examines the precarious relationship between "gentlemen-philosophers" and their numerous staff[26] by drawing on a particular example (the case of Robert Boyle). At its later stages as well, the distinction between the academic head and the working hand performing the experiments fluctuates.

Boyle employs, on a daily basis, between three and six paid subalterns, aside from the additional help, the instrument builders and material suppliers he requires for his research. Such aspects raise a series of questions that may help elucidate the epistemological significance of servants. How would one define the master–servant relationship in this case? Who controls whom? If all observations and actions are assigned to other agents, and the chief experimenter arrives at his findings only indirectly, then the question is: what is the actual contribution of someone like Boyle, who is often absent or indisposed and occasionally even has his assistants write his work for him?[27] The relationship between the two is built on notions of authority and trust on the part of the master and experience and internal work delegation on the part of the servant.

But to what extent can human media be trusted by their masters? Are they reliable when they perform their tasks? What about when they report what they observe? What is the actual value of the servants' own knowledge? Is it a specific kind of wisdom or a mere skill which does not necessarily lead to actual insights? Working in Boyle's lab, the servants Denis Papin and Robert Hooke run their tests independently or even autonomously at times. In this sense they occupy a hybrid position between official underlings and esteemed colleagues. Similarly, Michelmann is not given "more intelligent work"; however, there is hope that "the special knowledge acquired over the course of several years will allow him to prove useful in this regard as well." He does not disappoint; on the contrary, he rather exceeds all expectations by delegating—like Robert Hooke—his own work to other subalterns: "He is a steward, however, he lets a service maid take care of most tasks related to that position [. . .] and employs himself in scientific assistance [. . .] and mechanical work, repairing and building instruments for both sections of the institute. Such tasks are not among a steward's duties."[28] As different as Michelmann and Hooke are, they are both formally ranked as servants. And given their invaluable expertise, the question remains:

are servants catalyzers of knowledge or strictly its driving forces, contributing, via their own interventions, to the success of the experiment?

Finally, the classic historiographic problem arises again: how can one estimate the contribution of subaltern work? As common as servants are in the field of knowledge production, it is equally common to find no mention of them.[29] What documentary traces do underlings and their media activities leave? "Anonymity is almost a defining characteristic of the technician in that setting."[30] Servants and subaltern technicians, lab assistants and stewards are professionally invisible. Only in the moment of disruption, of noise, when the experiment fails, does the transparent look of assistants turn opaque. When something goes amiss, the servant is always to blame: this topos is a historical invariable throughout all hierarchical levels.

In the nineteenth century servants start to disappear: men depart from the ranks of the *cives illiterati,* from academies, and other institutions; female servants leave the private households (at the end of World War II at the latest). But the need for subaltern work goes on, now replaced by technical media (telephone, vacuum cleaner, thermostat, kitchen utensils, washing machines). The persistence of servant functions also manifests itself in those verbal designations of various media processes. Thus, after the computer is turned on, various *services* are launched; they typically remain in the background, waiting to be called by the master's, or user's, command. Simultaneously, *daemons* secure the smooth operation of the system, working reliably and invisibly, not unlike the ministering spirits of the past. Last but not least, the internet can also be discussed in terms of its net metaphoricity via a whole range of cultural historical analogies. But one could also choose a different, more subtle approach.[31] Any inquiry concerning the transmission of long-distance information, whether it is the request of a document (ftp) or unspecified information from a remote place via hypertext (http), always uses a mutually established code to address the same entity: the server. In order to understand, beyond network metaphors, the mode of communication of contemporary computer systems via the internet, one could look into their technical origins or their legal structures.[32] But to grasp the omnipresence of the client–server relation in the architecture of communication networks, we need an approach that takes designations like 'client' and 'server'[33] quite seriously and examines them via an approach that unites the perspectives of media and cultural history.

What would such an approach bring to the discussion, especially in the context of current media developments? The old questions of authority and trust, which were decisive parameters in any human interaction, are now reformulated as central concepts of internet communication. Not only on the shiny surface of the new relations of communication labeled as social software, but also, most of all, in the depths of telecommunication infrastructures and their mode of operation. That mode is characterized by a range of interactions between client and server. Historically informed media culture studies may offer insights that lead to new areas of research. Who is actually in charge when a client's specific request launches an avalanche of services that are precisely directed against the client's initial wish? This raises the question of agency, as the last chapter of this study will show.

The amount of time Michelmann spent on his way from the institute to the observatory cannot be deduced from the documents. He may have assumed that making haste to arrive even before the telegram would bring him praise (and implicitly also the confirmation of continued service). But despite his service experience, the servant could not have known that his message would actually be the last of its kind and that his role, from that moment on, would be taken over by the new media.

5.1.2. Michelmann Enters the Channel

As unremarkable as things may have seemed on that early spring morning, the Göttingen events bear crucial implications for the media history of the servant. That is because the scene inaugurates the transference of the central functions of the subaltern from human media to technical actors. From this moment on, the transmission of messages will no longer be assigned to humans, but to electrified machines. And therefore, under conditions of heightened technical operation, one may ask: where is the position of the servant in the act of communication, if human subalterns are no longer assigned to convey information? In the historical moment when the institute servant heads out of the Academic Museum in order to take his strangely recursive message to the observatory, the messenger turns into a museum artifact. In the process of carrying out his task, he takes himself out of service, inventorying himself as a relic of a former epoch. Thus Michelmann marks the transition from analog to digital in the form of a metonymy, a representation of a considerably more complex process of dissolution. The distinction between information and noise is equal to the distance between the physics cabinet and the observatory. Michelmann is both the transmitter and the transmitted signal; he represents both the content and the medium of the message. And thus his act may provide either: vital information or sheer redundancy. If he reaches the observatory but the electrical signal does not, his presence amounts to an error message. If, however, he and the telegram arrive at the same time, then he counts as the first check bit of a successful electrical transmission, the code confirming the accuracy of the message. His messenger role becomes as superfluous as the information he stands for in the instance of arrival. The electrical message renders his actual arrival redundant. The coincidence of the digital and the analog message "Michelmann's here" marks the end of an era when all important and rapid oral communications were conveyed via human media at their own—walking or riding—speed. In the midst of this development, extending all the way from telegraphic writing to the multimedia data cables of our time, stands the oral form of the telephone. Those who answer the call no longer require a servant to represent them and speak on their behalf. Something has come between the master and his servant, between the servant and the receiver of the message brought by the servant. Their personal, direct connection is replaced with a wire, which bridges distances but simultaneously also keeps the poles of communication away from one another. The paradoxical imposition of present absence no longer applies.

The arrival of telematics on the stage of domestic culture means that servants are no longer required to stand waiting behind closed doors, ready to answer any call. In order to prevent them from eavesdropping, subalterns are spatially removed from the scene as well; thanks to the signals of telecommunication, they can be called only when necessary, first by mechanical means, via bells or ropes, later by electric circuits, connecting the service corridors to the salons.[34] Thus domestics are removed from their direct proximity to their masters and later from the entire home. Gradually, they are relieved of their functions, which are now delegated to technical media.

Michelmann's trajectory lays out a circuit diagram for the electric signal transmission. Over the course of the nineteenth century that diagram is applied to the private context of well-to-do households as well. The country estates of the English gentry and the urban residences of the bourgeoisie during the industrial age increasingly use a system of service communication based on two poles: at one end there is an electric table bell sending out the call, and at the other end a kind of *glockenspiel* in the servants' hall, indicating the room where service is requested right away. "Wherever the drawing-room or parlour bell rings, go up immediately to see what is wanted," writes James Williams in his 1847 guide to servants.[35] Thanks to Gauss's and Weber's development of telegraphy, the advent of in-house telematics and technical media brings along the desired effect: servants can no longer be seen, sensed, or heard. Their messenger functions, which once made them omniscient, also disappear. Telematics introduces a disruption in the personal interaction between masters and servants; consequently, the two entities will distance themselves from one another to the point of complete misrecognition. Telematics does away with the principle of direct contact in the social relation between master and servant. The butler no longer has to be within hearing range of his master. He loses the place he holds in the consciousness of his employer. Irrespective of the medium, be it human or technical, only the effect counts. From the master's perspective, it is irrelevant how the service is obtained. After all, the technical devices that drive the servant even further away from the master's consciousness represent an increased level of comfort. They spare the gentleman the inconvenience of interacting with inferiors. "We want the effect of being served. The electric button is a symbol of this comfort. Just a tiny effort and you get what you want. The electric button has no physiognomy, cannot be loved or hated as a domestic thing. It is only the mechanical means whereby I achieve satisfaction."[36]

The arrival of telecommunications and electricity on the stage of the domestic household rings in the inevitable demise of human domestics—quite literally in the case of the electric bell. Such aspects are part of a far-reaching process, as the next chapter will illustrate via yet another context: the domain of the kitchen and its affiliated utensils. The buzzer introduces a telematic effect and a media practice used to keep servants away—a mode of producing distance which ultimately leads to the breakdown of the direct connection between master and subaltern. This medialized relation, which starts out by replacing the servant medium with data cables, prepares the way for the expansion of service functions which start to dissociate themselves from a specific locality via increasingly more dense telecommunication networks. The servant's position is now taken by the technical medium of the telegraph and the telephone and of telematics in general. These are now the channels that willingly take over the subaltern service functions established over the course of several centuries: transmitting messages, fulfilling orders, attending, and serving. The position of the servant in the act of communication has been reduced to the channel. Which does not somehow mean that human beings need to squeeze themselves through increasingly narrow pathways. But man loses his place in the order of information transmission and is replaced with minuscule electronic actors. The wires that stretch across the English mansions, where servants wait for a signal before they may rush up to their masters, represent just another transit station on the way. This form of service is ultimately also replaced by technical actors, which are commonly designated today as servers or digital demons. These are the contemporary nonhuman actors that convey, carry, and deliver electronic letters nowadays.

The gradual transition of the servant into the channel gradually transforms the human messenger into a server. While the media carrier is primarily affected

in the process, the next section will look into this distancing phenomenon at
the level of message content as well. In the instance of his arrival at the observatory, Michelmann represents, for once, both the medium and the message.
But as a media actor, the human servant departs not only from the process of
communication but also from the message itself. This phenomenon will be illustrated via the transformation of epistolary forms of complimentary closings.
Around the same time as Michelmann's final errand, the formulation "your
humble servant" begins to vanish from the final lines of letters.

5.2. YOUR HUMBLE SERVANT: CURIAL COMMUNICATION

> "Well, any news at the office?" asked Oblomov.
> "Yes, all sorts of things. We don't sign letters now, 'Your humble servant,'
> but: 'Accept our assurance of.'"
> —Ivan Goncharov, *Oblomov*, 1859

The poet required financial support again. This was hardly exceptional, only this
time the generous help of his stepsister did not suffice. For years he had regularly
corresponded with her asking for financial support. But the amount was much
higher this time. His whole life seemed to be at stake—he had even considered
mortgaging his house to pay off the debt caused by his failed literary project.
Like many of his other enterprises, this one had not exactly proven a success.
The financial disaster was not of his own making. Apart from possibly overes-
timating the sales numbers, his greatest problem lay with the state authorities,
whose reputation would have received quite a boost from the publication. But
the promise of a financial contribution to allow its continuation fell through.
Pressed for money, the writer sent a few urgent missives to His Excellency, the
Prussian state chancellor. When his request was turned down by the Chancel-
lery and a further letter to the prince received no answer whatsoever, the writer
appealed to the ultima ratio and wrote to none other than the sovereign himself, with a "most humble request of highest justice": The "most powerful and
most gracious king and lord," Frederick William III, received, along with a brief
summary of the matter, a request to "grant me a position in the civil service, or,
should such a function, as befits my circumstances, not be available, to grant me
an allowance that could serve as compensation for the loss I incurred. [. . .] I
expire [T.N. *ersterbe*, instead of *erstrebe*, 'aspire,'] to remain Your Royal Majesty's
most humble and respectful Heinrich von Kleist. Berlin, June 17, 1811."[37]

The focus here is obviously not the dispute mentioned above. The matter at hand is not the balance sheet of the *Berliner Abendblätter,* coedited by Kleist and Adam Müller with the contribution of Berlin's police president, Karl Justus Gruner. Rather, what needs to be examined is the end of the letter and its closing, which seems to be excessive even for the late Enlightenment context around 1800. Could the sentence be meant ironically? Or does it correspond to a somewhat antiquated official chancery style, which would have required such a rhetorical arsenal for a petition? After all, according to a cabinet order from 1810, Prussian offices were required to start using "the simple style"[38] in their correspondence. Could the modest yet disquieting reference in the text [*ersterbe*] possibly prefigure Kleist's real, carefully planned out, yet equally exalted passing only a few months later?

The exaggerated quality of the formulation is particularly striking since there are only four such cases in Kleist's correspondence, comprising 240 letters.[39] The other three (apart from the abovementioned missive) can be found in the correspondence with State Chancellor Karl August von Hardenberg, whom Kleist had approached before writing to the king. The next section will trace the cultural and historical development of this formulaic tradition. But first, we must ask: what is typical and what is unusual about this particular formulation?

Obviously, no subject may hope to see the king, let alone address him in writing, without the most profuse gestures of devotion—if they hope to be heard. Subtlety is demanded. "Around the time of the Thirty Years' War, there is an important change taking place in all relations and in the realm of social interaction. Extreme servility and affability, which do not necessarily need to match one's inner sentiments, are the trademark of polite behavior."[40] The rules of letter writing, sometimes recorded in manuals of conduct, make it clear: an incorrect form of address or a less than reverential or inaccurate title means the letter will not be read or will be treated as an offense—which can lead to serious political complications.[41] Whether the epistolary author in this case is a former lieutenant or a mere writer, the expression of deep subordination to the state authority is unavoidable. The submissive gesture is further highlighted by the scope of the letter. After all, Kleist calls the king an absolute judge, in the hope of obtaining his eight-hundred-thaler compensation from the State Treasury. Fourteenth-century texts and miscellanies of letters from later periods amply attest that petitions by no means skimp on such formulations of subservience.[42] For instance, a dinner invitation sent out to a gentleman of high rank around 1750 still contains the following lines: "I humbly beg Your Excellency to graciously agree to dine in the modest abode of his most devoted servant; in recognition and praise of such honor bestowed upon me, I remain Your most obedient servant."[43] The tone of subservience is masterfully aligned with a "limitless thirst for titles," a conclusion that can also be drawn from other examples: "It has been previously noted that the basis of polite behavior during the seventeenth century is the expression of utmost servility."[44]

But what defines Kleist's letter is also the gap, the missing word between the adjectival phrase at the end and the signature. The blank between the formula "Your Royal Majesty's most humble and respectful" and the proper name "Heinrich von Kleist" is no less than a rhetorical strategy, an ellipsis. Instead of the gap, there should have been a further proof of devotion, typically a notion like 'subject' or 'servant.' But the term "servant" is often left out, possibly in order to somewhat elevate one's position in the eyes of the interlocutor—a tendency that becomes manifest in the evolution of epistolary closing formulas. The trend is also sustained by an epiphenomenon that begins in the seventeenth century and develops into a cultural standard: the constant depreciation of the forms of address, accompanied by the steady displacement of titles from the beginning to the end.[45] Instead of the effort to elevate one's rank, the preferred strategies here are the ellipsis, which circumvents the actual term, and abridged forms such as 'sincerely,' followed by the proper name. But what gives Kleist's closing its exceptional quality?

The sentence contains all the elements of devotion demanded by the etiquette of royal address. The remarkable twist here, however, is the use of the word "expire," the climax of the entire formulation. But what does it actually mean? Could the phrase contain an unexpected, subtly subversive commentary on the rules of polite correspondence with a king? Starting in the late medieval period, the customary pledge of loyalty becomes part of the standard epistolary repertoire, and not merely for petitions. Its absence counts as an affront. Occasionally, a further element is added to suggest the temporal extent of that assurance of devotion. For instance, the expression "as always, yours"[46] conveys a statement oriented toward a future instance of epistolary communication. This temporal marker can be further expanded. On the one hand, it can refer to a final duration, delimited by one's death, for example, in a letter from B. Bielke to a certain Mayer, dated April 10, 1695, which insistently mentions, "as long as I live, for a lifetime, until death."[47] On the other hand, it can be extended even beyond one's death, into eternity: thus Goethe, in a letter to Kestner from March 1774 which concludes, "I remain the same from eternity to eternity, Amen."[48] Kleist's temporal reference is clearly more limited. The verb "expire" functions as the equivalent of the syntagma "until death," or actually derives from it, announcing a statement of continuous attachment. At the same time, it signals the coincidence between the instance of epistolary writing and the instance of death. But since that is obviously not the case, and the writer's devotion does not extend "until death" or into eternity—for why would the king then grant the requested sum of money?—the closing formula is thoroughly devalued; it is rendered worthless. The notice of a death foretold limits the declaration of loyalty to the ephemeral instance of the signature. Kleist's pledge unto death (or unto the end of service)[49] remains arrested in the moment; it folds into its own formulation and cancels itself out. Hidden behind the claim of humility is a possible trace of arrogance or at least an insult, which may have prompted the writer to ask the highest authority for financial compensation.

5.2.1. At Your Service: Epistolary Form and Complimentary Closings

The history of epistolary prescripts and complimentary closings can be roughly divided into three epochs. At first, there is a limited number of set phrases that start to diversify around the fourteenth century, giving rise to a vast array of epithets. The second phase, spanning the sixteenth to the eighteenth centuries, can be framed as an era of gallantry. In turn, this period is followed by a third phase of development: a stage of advanced standardization in conjunction with a drastic decrease to a handful of formulas. Following the trajectory into the contemporary age of machine communication, the current section will examine a single aspect of this genealogy: a phrase that occupies, in its modern formulation, a central position in the metaphoric discourse of online communication. The phrase in question is the expression of a commitment of service on the part of the sender, placed at the end (and, initially, also at the beginning) of a letter.

A universal history of epistolary *curialia* has yet to be written. But, to briefly trace its trajectory, one could start with the rise of vernacular private letters and their opening and closing lines. As Georg Steinhausen has shown, the vernacular private letter can be traced back to the fourteenth century and has its origin in the transfer of Latin epistolary forms into various local languages. The private letter differs from diplomatic missives and documents not only with regard to its contents but also in terms of senders and receivers—categories that correspond not merely to courts and cities but also noblemen and knights, members of the clergy and the middle class. During the fourteen and fifteen centuries this early phase is characterized by a tendency toward uniformity, according to the following structure: my dear lady, my dear son, gracious lord, dear sir Thomas. Compared to the baroque letter, such salutations sound unexpectedly modern. In its early form, the vernacular private letter is also characterized by an absence of closings. Instead, a signature and a date are inserted at the end of the epistolary text. As in later centuries, when the formulations become much more excessive, writers express their respect by appending a series of attributes to the title, as in "most honorable and noble dear friend."[50] Then, in the sixteenth century the more complex expressions introduced by the chancery style make their entrance into the language of correspondence. The simple salutations "Sir" or "Madam" are expanded through hypotactic structures, indicating respect, and enriched by strings of titles. Such ornate "parasites of speech,"[51] twisting the actual meaning around, risk turning the epistolary address into a hypertrophied body of words. Importantly, the rigid composition of the letter,[52] based on the rhetorical model of antiquity, implies that the *salutatio* should include not merely the correct form of address and a complete list of titles held by the recipient but also a pledge of service, inserted right before or after the address proper.

For instance, writing in 1459 to a tailor named Aegidus Gilg, a certain Gregorius Walfach opens his letter in the following manner: "In friendly service and with all good wishes herewith. Dear Sir Gilg," and closes it with "Your constant servant / [signature:] Gregorius Walfach."[53] Here, the *salutatio* and *conclusio* already mark a transition from the medieval to modern epistolary models. In the Gutenberg era, with the increase of correspondence, the formal structure of the private letter becomes more fixed and standardized. Epistolary manuals and compendia, including collections of sample letters for all occasions, also contribute to this development.[54] Against the background of printed, standardized forms from epistolary manuals, the pledge of devotion, once typically found in the *salutatio* or—doubly framed—in the *conclusio* as well,[55] now moves to the end of the letter before the signature, which also starts to establish itself. The reference to constant service amounts to a standby mode, in which the sender insists—just like Waitwell—on receiving a response. The pledge of service in the *salutatio* indicates that the following sections—the *narratio* and *petitio*—are to be read in the same light of devotion. Inserted at the end of the letter, however, the vow of service has a different function: as an outgoing signal, it points to the disposition to further epistolary communication, to the continuation of correspondence, as in the case of modern letters. The phrase "Your constant servant / [signature:] Gregorius Walfach" designates not necessarily a double gesture of submission but a standby signal. The concluding line is a protocol, confirming the writer's continuing availability. Before considering this standby mode in relation to contemporary relations of communication, the next section will trace the cultural-historical development of the epistolary vow of service.

5.2.2. To Take One's Leave, or, How to Play Servant

The epistolary pledge of service can be traced back to the letters of late antiquity in the Eastern Roman Empire. The repertoire of greetings at this stage only occasionally includes the formulation 'servant of the lord.' Religiously motivated authors[56] especially use the term "servant" to describe themselves in their letters. This self-attribution takes the esoteric role corresponding to a secret society that communicates via its own system of signs. The stereotypical salutation in this case also serves as a mode of mutual recognition among the members of early Christian communities.

Sign-offs during the Old and Middle High German periods correspond to a different logic. They usually contain a blessing and a request of leave,[57] for instance, "allow me to take my leave" or, simply "I am at your service."[58] In the *Imperial Chronicle* from 1150 or the *Song of Roland* (French, 1075–1110 and German 1170), some scenes include vows of service along with an almost identical formulation: "at your service!" Only literary works (for instance, the *Nibelungenlied*) attest the use of such phrases in oral communication. And while the oral forms "disappear with the end of the court tradition,"[59] the pledges of devotion continue to circulate as courtesy phases and make their way into the private letters of the late medieval period.

"Offering 'service' instead of a greeting became the general custom and particularly in the case of those in lower positions toward those of higher rank."[60] First, it is princes and towns that assure each other of their mutual dedication to serve, but gradually the phrase is also included in the medium of the private letter, with its discrete hierarchies of address. A formal change comes into play as well. A single opening line such as "dear and honored lady" is insufficient. The devoted subject feels the impulse to repeat himself or herself. "The same spirit that animated the shift from salutation to service vow now comes to impact the end of the letter too."[61] The final compliment only gradually emancipates itself from the initial salutation and finally marks the end of the letter even without the added effect of titles and divine invocations.

Along with this shift from beginning to end,[62] the formulation itself begins to transform and take shape: the pledge of devotion takes a nominal turn, and the dedicated subject signs his letters "Your servant" from this moment on. At first, the expression is merely a polite phrase. Gradually, however, various forms of gradation and superlatives such as "most obedient and devoted servant" render it more specific and give it a functional character.

Thereby, the letter writer does not merely generally express his polite intent; rather, by defining himself as a 'servant' he takes on a specific functional position in the epistolographic communication scheme. The term "servant" becomes, to a large extent, the standard for sixteenth-century epistolary closings. Later, under the impact of courtly communication forms, modeled not so much after the discursive patterns of chancery language but the standards of politeness at court, the formulation reaches a new stage of development. Reinhard Nickisch describes this phase in his classic book on seventeenth- and eighteenth-century letter manuals as a moment of upheaval, catalyzed by the standards of secretarial culture and the instructional literature of writers such as Georg Philipp Harsdörffer, Kaspar Stieler, Christian Weise, Benjamin Neukirch, and others.[63] Under these circumstances, the devotional style becomes elusive and contrived.

Influenced by French epistolary theory and gallant discourse, notions like 'naturalness' and 'effervescence' occasionally imply an extremely artificial accumulation of epithets, which precede the term 'servant' itself: the higher the rank of the addressee, the longer the list of attributes. Consider an example from Gottsched's correspondence from 1754—"Most noble and most honored sir, distinguished benefactor"[64]—which already counts as a simplified modern secular alternative.[65] Such excesses are brought to a close by Gellert's reform of epistolary style.

Apparently, the phrase "your devoted servant"—by now, a standard epistolary sign-off—begins to vanish. In reality, however, as this section will show, the expression continues to survive in a series of other forms of manifestation. But its disappearance in the early nineteenth century is linked to two other historical developments: a brief political event, on the one hand, and a longer cultural process, on the other hand.

Under the impact of Gellert's reform, the discourse of gallant courtesy à la française moves into the background, and the epistolary style embraces the natural flow of spoken language. Simultaneously, the political crisis around 1800, beginning with the French Revolution, leaves its mark on German letter-writing practice as well. Based on the premise that liberty, equality, and fraternity are principles that animate correspondents as well, the vow of devotion as implied by the mention of the term "servant" no longer seems like a fitting sign-off.[66] Even when higher-ranking addressees are involved, the term becomes increasingly rare. But irrespective of the provisional achievements of the French Revolution, the epistolary vow of submission finds its own niches, especially in the political contexts of the Restoration, which initially are not affected by the new republican ideals. Drawing on what is, at this point, already a quasi-extinct epistolary formula, Austrian schoolchildren and students in the first half of the nineteenth century adopt "the Latin word 'servus' in jest,"[67] as a way of saying farewell. Over the subsequent decades, the term evolves into a common greeting, not least due to military participation: between 1830 and 1850 soldiers led by the Austrian field marshal Radetzky in the Kingdom of Lombardy–Venetia start using the greeting "Tschau," derived from the Italian *schiavo* (meaning "slave," "servant"). Its echoes are still apparent today in the commonly used expression "ciao, ciao." In short, due to epistolary demands for a 'conversational' quality in letters, the epistolographic formula that dominates the sign-off options from the fourteenth to the eighteenth centuries turns from a purely written form back into oral communication. Not accidentally, the—most likely parodic—reproduction of an exemplary dialogue between two citizens at the start of the eighteenth century[68] evokes the clichés of oral language exchanged by *client* and *server* in the process of conveying an electronic message (see section 3.5).

The other element leading to the disappearance of the epistolary vow of service goes back to sociotechnical, rather than political, contexts. In the wake of industrialization and its impact on employment structures, the total number of servants is drastically reduced. Nevertheless, a qualitative change occurs as well. From the age of absolutism to the nineteenth century the court and homes of the nobility employ a vast range of attendants in various functions. But whereas these numbers go down, the number of domestics employed in middle-class households is on the rise. The potential risk of status loss forces the average bourgeois to hire at least one servant or (at a later stage) a housemaid.[69] And when both partners take on several domestics, the lord and lady of the house can no longer identify themselves as 'servants' in their regular correspondence if they wish to maintain the distinction between themselves and their inferiors. This logic operates in tandem with another, common strategy: boosting one's own status with elaborate new titles when addressing a person of higher rank.[70] Thus the image of a servile letter writer curtsying before his interlocutor increasingly vanishes. The status-conscious sender no longer dares adopt the 'servant' appellative in the nineteenth century.

Still, the disappearance of the devotional sign-off and of the epistolographic principle it represents is merely a surface phenomenon. Hidden from sight, it lives on, branching out and developing into vast telecommunication networks. Today, it has reached the most remote corners of the world and has ultimately become the very engine and operating system of present-day communication.

Already during the early modern period, governed by the protocols of letter-writing manuals, the epistolary servant invoked in the opening and closing lines of letters fulfills the functions of a signifier of communication. Its role is to indicate that the undersigned is expecting an answer. In other words, it announces that a communication channel has been opened in expectation of a return transmission. One could argue that the servant in the letter is a representative of the postal system. The servant is the open channel of transmission, an equivalent of the postal principle which—starting in 1490/1505—is linked to the Thurn and Taxis family name. Conversely, one could also say that the principle of service stands at the basis of the postal system. Indeed, from its early beginnings until the launch of the World Postal Union in 1874, the postal system operated as an ongoing system of transmission supported by a minutely differentiated address scheme. Therein lies the meaning of our current metaphors of electronic mail. Even if the 'humblest servant' figure may have vanished from the realm of the epistolary *curialia*, its effects are clearly still with us. The nineteenth-century postal servants known as mailmen[71] could deliver the mail up to sixteen times a day. Their twentieth-century electronic counterparts have long taken over this mission. Not accidentally, their description evokes that essential epistolary formula of initial and concluding service—even at the metaphoric level. The continuity of this structure is at its most striking in the case of the so-called client–server model and of its relays, the mail servers that process all electronic messages today. But the structural link is shown not only in the conceptual affiliation between (postal) servant and (mail) server but also in the unique formulation offered by Kleist in the passage quoted at the beginning of this chapter.

Cultural historians of letters have always associated greetings and closings with strategies of dissimulation and artificiality. But at least in the case of the servant they have overlooked the fact that the expression opens a concrete communication channel and a mode of standby that remains indispensable to this very day under the highly technical conditions of internet servers. The passage from Kleist's letter is not followed by empty phrases or excessive formulations, as prescribed by the chancery style and the curialia. Beyond any rhetoric, there is an actual communicative necessity to frame epistolary formulas as signifiers of the process of transmission, as key functions of protocol. The poet himself does not hesitate to render his epistolary sign-off into a real gesture of finality. The notice of 'expiration' is put into practice. Five months later, on November 21, 1811, he writes to his beloved sister Ulrike for the last time: "And now farewell, may Heaven grant you a death only half as full of joy and ineffable serenity as mine. [. . .] on the morning of my death, Your Heinrich."[72]

5.2.3. Channel Technology and the Standardization
of Subalterns

A modest gesture such as the epistolary bow-and-scrape proves, in fact, to provide full access to the vast social history of modern service. The rise of an expression such as "your most humble servant" in the early modern period, and its use as a complimentary closing with a complex logic of discrete epithets goes hand in hand with yet another phenomenon: the rhetoric of subtlety and devotion which determines the finely differentiated hierarchies at the absolutist courts. In his *Teutsche Secretariats-Kunst* from 1705, Kaspar Stieler reviews once more the terms and qualities one must include in a letter in order to make a good impression as a humble baroque petitioner: "Concerning the person to whom one writes, remember that the mighty do not ask, but desire, order, command, will, and remind others. Those who are of equal or lower rank should continue to ask, supplicate and beg a great lord, imploring him humbly, obediently, submissively."[73] One consequence of this self-disparaging tactic is that authors almost always resort to calling themselves servants, even when they are not necessarily in a position of subservience. The formula is already well established in the eighteenth century and not merely in German but also in English and French. Wilhelm and Jakob Grimm's *Dictionary* mentions the following with regard to such formulas of servile politeness: "In the past century it was common to address men of high rank by calling oneself a 'most obedient servant' to show 'the great difference between oneself and the others' as Adelung writes." The dictionary also refers to another relevant aspect, quoting two letters from Johann Heinrich Merck. The first is addressed to Duke Carl August and dates to 1781. Merck signs it, "Your Serene Highness's most humble servant." Eight years later, shortly before the French Revolution, he changes the 'servant' phrase to the more liberal expression, "Your Grace's humblest . . . subject."[74] Soon, this formulation, too, is perceived as a sign of excessive submission and therefore eradicated, along with many other outdated complimentary closings, in accordance to the spirit of the revolution. The 'servant greeting' is consequently replaced with other set phrases, such as "I beg to be remembered" or "devotedly yours." The 'humble servant' no longer corresponds to the ideals of liberty, equality, and fraternity.[75]

With the gradual addition of legal rights for the lower ranks, the greeting "your humblest of servants" is replaced by a signature that is no longer accompanied by an excessive list of epithets. That change occurs not least because almost every nineteenth-century bourgeois household employs servants—if merely in the form of a 'maid of all trades.' The subaltern has disappeared from the letter: any lady with only a maid in her service would obviously not appreciate declaring herself a 'servant.' In Isa Lütt's *Elegant Homemaker* (1892), an instruction manual specifically dedicated to the middle classes, one can find the following standardized sign-off options: "The complimentary closing 'devoted' (or its variants) is most appropriate for those within our own social sphere."[76]

From these standardized formulas around 1900, and after the demise of Central European monarchies and the end of the age of service after World War I, it is a small step to the neutral "friendly greetings" that have survived to this very day. But during this time there are proposals for further epistolary codification, ringing in new standards of communication in the age of machines. Christian Morgenstern writes in 1918, "Instead of dear sir! one could simply write: 5 e! And instead of with respect, 2 o."[77] And in 1981, shortly before the age of personal computers, the authors of a modern epistolary manual à la Harsdörffer advise their readers to save their curialia on tape: "A greeting is then read by the tape reader within two seconds."[78] What is significant about this code of conduct, which has also been adopted by machines and electronic agents, is that the standards of politeness are maintained in the virtual domain as well. While forgoing epistolary curtsies and any efforts involved in finding the right tone of address, machines nevertheless do not give up on the standards of courteous behavior toward their electronic partners. Machines greet each other as well. As shown in chapter 3, the typical protocol between an email server and a client is—despite its written form—not accidentally oriented toward ease of oral expression. But this may not be surprising after all: the relocation of the servant into the channel coincides with a shift from chancery-style ceremonial salutations to the more informal conventions of oral culture. Just as *ciao, ciao* becomes a typical greeting in Old Europe after Radetzky, the standards of electronic communication among servers in the virtual New World are represented by commands such as *helo* (SMTP) and *bye* (FTP). The curialia of submissive devotion have long disappeared from the medium of letters. In the age of electronic services, humans are no longer constantly requesting permission to leave or assuring each other of their service. These standards of conduct have now been transferred to the more accommodating machines and to their communication channels, where servants continue their existence in the form of servers and clients. Hidden from the sight of users behind opaque interfaces, the electronic agents inconspicuously perform their subaltern tasks, and not just anyhow but with "friendly greetings."

5.3. DIS-CONTINUITIES IN THE CHANNEL: MESSENGERS, NOISE

> The reader: Why should we be interested in angels nowadays?
> The Author: Because our universe is organized around message-bearing systems and [angels] are message-bearers [. . .]
>   These ancient mediators provide the perfect image for our telegraph operators, postmen, translators, representatives, commentators [. . .] But also fiber optics and the intelligent machines that we have built to connect networks between them.
> —Michel Serres, *Angels: A Modern Myth*, 1995

Michelmann launches the age of machine communication. After his service as message transmitter is rendered superfluous with the successful setup of electric telegraphy—an event that takes place on a memorable spring day in 1833 in Göttingen—other technical devices and circuits come to successively take over the operation. These devices and circuits combine and develop into increasingly more complex networks across increasingly larger distances to ultimately transmit messages and information at maximum speed. Michelmann signals the beginning[79] of the end of a millennium-long era of human messengers who personally deliver information (beyond letters and a depersonalized postal system). The switch from human to nonhuman media goes hand in hand with a particular relocation of knowledge, which also affects the informational capacity of the messengers themselves. Traditionally, messengers are regarded as carriers of secrets, since they are entrusted with information. "[He] knows more about me than all the others, more than I know about myself. The wisdom of letter carriers knows no limits, they know almost everything about the people whom they serve." Messengers are, according to Thomas Bernhard, the legitimate "assessors of the Last Judgement."[80] With the turn of telematic information transmission to technical media, this form of secrecy is itself displaced. The importance of information no longer lies with human intermediaries; instead, it is now located in the transmission network, which assumes an increasingly vital role with regard to the possibility of message interception. The human messengers now operate within a narrow, locally determined domain, where they are assigned merely to send off their missives from the telegraph office itself.[81] Meanwhile, it is the electric signals that convey those notes across wide distances at the speed of light. The possibility of intercepting information and the disruption of communication have therefore less to do with the last links within this chain, that is to say, with human messengers. Instead, it is the complex networks and signals in the technical apparatuses which can be illicitly read and overheard, intercepted or interrupted. Michelmann is replaced by a telegraphic cable, and the 'humble servant' is traded for a curt telegraphic command. In this way, the entire dispositif of telematic communication is subject to a profound process of transformation in which such minor shifts constitute merely minuscule symptoms.

The most visible feature of this shift is so obvious that it hardly deserves mention. From the Middle Ages until the age of Enlightenment in western Europe, the classical *servus curri*, or emissary, also known as a *cursor*, is delegated with personally conveying important messages across long distances. He can cover anywhere from twenty-five to forty kilometers a day, which is not much less than a messenger on horseback. At running speed, he may even reach fifty to sixty-five kilometers a day.[82] By comparison, the electrical signals in use after the mid-nineteenth century can traverse—depending on the number of relays involved—entire continents within seconds. But the level of acceleration and, implicitly, its effect on the reduction of wait-times also involves a certain degree of informational condensation and concision. The medieval messaging network was based on private runners who carried messages for courts, guilds, and universities according to a preestablished program: a specific destination, route, and an ideal transmission time (as soon as possible). But at the end of the medieval period, when state-validated institutions such as the Thurn and Taxis postal system take over the transmission of information, message and messenger begin to grow apart. In the early modern period, the messenger is far more knowledgeable than the letter or spoken message he is carrying, since he has obtained plenty of additional information along the way. This information-scouting function[83] is taken over during the seventeenth century by newspapers. In contrast, the surplus value of human media begins to decrease. Soon, only letters are conveyed via a supraindividual postal system, which ensures that each act of transmission is handled at once for a predetermined fee. And via the process of its mechanical redirection, the message itself is further subjected to a process of selection and contraction. After all, the economic principle of 'telegraphic style' demands brevity.

The early users of telegraphy may have certainly wondered how to concretely engage with the medium of telegraphy—a question that may not necessarily be answered via references to the procedures and use of telegraphic networks. Not surprisingly, in the shift from an old medium to a new dispositif, the early discourse of transition draws on well-known media notions to familiarize potential users with the new practice. The preface to the British *Patent Journal* from 1850 declares, "We have trained the electric agent as a dutiful child or obedient servant, to carry our messages through the air by the road we have made for it [. . .] in the shape of an angel."[84] Once again, McLuhan's dictum that the medium is the message holds true. The application of electric telegraphy finds its explanation in the image of the servant as carrier of information and via a reference to the sacred genealogy of messengers: as a divine emissary, telegraphy is the angel that brings words to their destination. The profound substitution of individual messengers like Michelmann with technical devices such as the telegraph is organized and prepared by the author of the preface via the "medium of metaphorics."[85] The introduction of a new medium is discursively enabled by an intricately nested string of old media, be they docile servants, dutiful children, traditional mediators like angels, or metaphors that pave the way for the new by means of the old and the familiar. Still, the question remains: which are the services and the contexts where the old, superseded media can still be found? Despite the advent of machines, the messenger, the servant, and the bedel are still faced with a broad range of activities that demand their participation: for instance, their role in delivering messages, by carrying telegrams from the post office to the doorstep of the receiver, but also their continued intervention into the channel of transmission, by way of interruptions: "After being discharged, servants would often be hired as postmasters, which presumably allowed them to secretly exert control over the postal system."[86] According to Michel Serres, angels are the progenitors of communication. In his grandiose *Angels: A Modern Myth,* the French philosopher reads the figure of the divine envoy as a fundamental motif of message transmission. As mediators between transcendence and immanence, angels not only bring good tidings of God's grace; they also act as the godfathers of the more profane technical data transmission. Transfigured into new media such as internet servers, angels inhabit the worldwide computer networks of the present. Bruno Latour, Thomas Macho, and, recently, Sybille Krämer[87] too have invoked the angel motif in order to draw attention to the particularities of this form of communication with its hybrid mediators. Latour, for instance, introduces the distinction between object and meta-language, whose ultimate principle strictly applies to angels: "Angels are not messengers, but meta-messengers—and that is precisely why they are represented as beings superior to mail deliverers, telephone operators, and all the modems and faxes of this world here below." For an angel does not divulge the content of his message. His apparition alone is the sign of the existence of a message. The addressee must painstakingly struggle to decipher its potential meaning. There is no faithful transmission. The divine messenger only conveys the call or the sign at the level of meta-language. Angels are therefore indicators; they point to a different context and strictly have "a phatic function, they say: 'Hello!'" And no more. Or, to take it one step further: "There is never any message; there are only messengers; and this is the angelical and evangelical message."[88]

Therefore, if angels are not faithful carriers of unencrypted messages but rather, as in the case of Michelmann's rival medium, "flashes of lighting, coded information, message and messenger at the same time"[89] or "pure spiritual creatures,"[90] they have very little in common with earth-bound, dutiful servants. Angels exert no influence on what is conveyed, since what they transmit are not messages proper. In contrast, secular messengers contribute quite significantly to the process of communication and exert considerable influence on the content of the messages. The guides and conduct books at the end of the nineteenth century define the ideal of the secular messenger as someone who transmits and delivers the information he has been assigned flawlessly and faithfully. Messages are not to be tampered with in any way by servants. In bourgeois homes they are kept at a safe remove from any contact with subalterns: "In a fine household, letters, cards and other items are not taken directly from the hands of domestics; rather, they are brought in on a tray or a plate."[91] The servant is therefore yet another carrier medium, which may never take it upon itself to pass judgment on or make changes, let alone manipulate, the content of the information. Only in reality things are different, so that even the theories concerning the treatment of servants (à la Lütt) do not entertain this vision. A viable model of subaltern communication must therefore make provisions for the participation of servants in the process.

As it turns out, the traditional messenger media of the Middle Ages do not have much in common with the media in the age of Enlightenment or in the nineteenth-century age of machines. The medium of the message is also subject to transformations over the course of its historical development. Nevertheless— and this is the decisive point—the medium also transforms the message it carries: whether in the form of a narrow channel bandwidth, as in the case of telegraphy (corresponding to the 'telegraphic style'); via technical malfunctions; or via the interventions of human message carriers. Indeed, all the personnel moving along the courtly enfilades and the corridors of estates, walking down the dusty roads from one town to another, or—even before the era of the telephone— carrying messages within a city, in short, all message carriers impose their own rhythm on the contents they deliver. They may also selectively deliver or set limits on their messages. The ability to select what is to be said is fully in the hands of the human messengers. The secular messengers possess a range of manipulative possibilities that are not available to their divine counterparts. That is also why, despite the claims of Pseudo-Dionysius the Areopagite or Thomas Aquinas, they cannot join the ranks of angels. Profane servants and all the other carriers of messages belong instead to the genealogy of demons. The demon is the custodian of noise,[92] he is in charge of the disruption of communication.

He becomes a parasite and therefore the progenitor of all domestics and bedels in charge of conveying information. The servant has long since relocated into the channel; thereby—according to his demonic pedigree—he is also able to scramble and manipulate it. "The messengers were the earthly counterparts of the transcendental angels—yet not so much in terms of speed."[93] And, as opposed to angels, these inconspicuous messengers are far more influential via their potential manipulation of contents. There is a rift between heaven and earth; and that rift is determined by the interventions of servants and the noise of subalterns.

In fact, subalterns are designed as peripheral media. They remain invisible while constantly performing their tasks. Ideally, one cannot notice them, their presence, or their influence on the course of events. They continuously move according to a mode of marginality. On the one hand, and to the extent that they actually constitute the channel of transmission itself, this marginal mode allows them to be involved in the act of communication. On the other hand, they are also excluded from the domain of communication, since they follow the rule of nonintervention in the content of the message. They operate for others and not in their own name ('Call me Carl'). In other words, they are mere proxies of their masters. And still this rule is constantly broken. In fact, they intervene quite often (consider the case of Lessing's Waitwell) in an unsolicited manner: "One cannot simply view messengers as media carrying information from senders to receivers without any trace of noise or disruption. The sources give us a different picture: transmissions often fail, and messengers actively shape the message."[94] It is not rare for them to go against the grain of established orders and advance from the periphery to the center of the event. Whether accidentally, in case something happens to them, or intentionally, when they actively go against a specific message, messengers represent, in both cases, a disruption that leads to a modification of the situation at hand, an interruption of the ongoing process. The intervention of subalterns is met with (slight) surprise.[95] Such an occurrence interrupts the original communication between sender and receiver in a considerable way since the servant steps out of the channel for a brief moment to take on the position of disruption, of noise. As the hidden subject of service leaves its invisible position to become a full-fledged actor, it becomes visible precisely in the process of its (mal)function as a medium.

This mechanism of productive interruption, of switching between channel and noise, is amply represented in the literary domain. A study across eras and genres that examines the messenger function in literature since the time of Greek tragedies has not yet been written. But such a study would certainly show that helpers are not merely ephemeral, second-degree aides. It would also,

once more, point out the fact that servant characters help—*ex negativo* or not—
bring into sharper focus the character and attitudes of the masters, by indirectly
speaking in their name.[96] But above all it would also prove that the lower ranks
have a major role to play in the transmission of both relevant and irrelevant
information. And that is because, as in the case of Lessing's Waitwell, the disruptions they cause and initiatives they take give a decisive impulse to events, by
either slowing them down or causing them to speed up. The unexpected arrival
of the servant marks the moment when he becomes visible as a medium and can
no longer be ignored. "He was clearly keen to continue in this train, but at that
very moment, a footman came out of the Princess' apartments to announce that
Her Royal Highness desired to speak with the gentlemen."[97] The scene from
Theodor Fontane's novel *Irretrievable* clearly suggests that every piece of news—
even a mere announcement, such as the invitation to enter a room—always
amounts to a form of disruption.

The media function of messengers lies in the moment of disruption. Their
initiatives may contribute to thwarting plans and opposing original intentions.
The decisive information often comes directly from servants as they perform
seemingly insignificant actions such as delivering messages, expressing condo-
lences, daring to make predictions, identifying others, etc. But at the same time,
they maintain the strategic option of sparing themselves trouble by avoiding
unwanted assignments. A specific feature of subaltern serviceability is the capacity of selective attention or deafness. "Deafness permits the servant to preserve
the role of decorous subservience while also stepping out of it to appeal to the
higher court of the 'whole audience.'"[98] Any disruption of the narrative flow
which takes place via a change in the plane of reference—for instance, the moment the public is addressed in Tieck's *The Land of Upside Down*—is always
connected with an act of reflection on the status quo (and sometimes with the
potential of epistemic gain). The servant functions as a source of disruption
and thus provides those narrative stumbling blocks that generate reflection. But
his strategic circumvention of work also contains other mechanisms that fall
into the category of incapacity or incompetence: real or feigned drunkenness,
staged epileptic fits, acts of terror, or sleepwalking. All these strategies allow him
to maintain control over the information or become the actual master of the
events. In short, the act of delivering information or preventing it from being
delivered is carried out by the information centers beyond and below the level
of social prestige. And precisely due to their potential to act and their privileged
communication situation between faithful transmission and noise servants possess a specific "inside knowledge,"[99] both with regard to other characters and
with respect to the narrative development itself.

As already shown, the courtly cough represents a minimal disturbance calling attention to the step to follow. In a similar fashion, the partly unwanted and unexpected, yet productive interventions of subalterns precipitate the necessary disruptions that break the routine of master–servant relations, ensuring, for once, that they are mentioned in the annals of history. Who would have known anything about the long succession of assistants in Robert Boyle's lab if it hadn't been for the spectacular failure of one of the experiments, the explosion that killed a servant but ensured that his heroic deed would be remembered? How would one know about Goethe's cook Charlotte Hoyer or his servant Johann 'Nomen Nescio' Gensler if their acts of exemplary insubordination had not run against the fine manners customary in the writer's Weimar home? And would anyone be familiar with Michelmann's name if the moment he arrived at Gauss's observatory did not mark the very instance of interruption that stands at the beginning of the machine communication age? In conclusion, the disruption is to be understood as a stroke of luck, an auspicious event in the annals of subaltern historiography. Usually, the sources are silent with regard to the routine activities of messengers and aides. Their actions are taken for granted or treated as insignificant to the point where they do not deserve to be mentioned. The communicative situation of subalterns is grounded in an imposed state of invisibility. Christian Weise's baroque drama *The Case of the French Marshall of Binon* (1693) illustrates this point in a dialogue between two of the king's privy councillors, exchanging aphorisms on the topic of service:

> VILLEROY: I serve / and my lips are sealed.
> SILLERY: My lips are sealed / and I serve.[100]

This form of unconditional self-withdrawal counts as one of the fundamental features of ministering actors, whether they are humans, as in the case of bourgeois domestics and subalterns at court, or electronic agents, providing for the flow of information nowadays. The workforces of service become visible in moments of dysfunction and crisis, when their characteristic invisibility turns into its opposite. The disruption in the system is, for instance, announced via a MAILER-DAEMON, which, in turn, sends an electronic message—the dreaded BOUNCE notice—to the sender and thereby announces that the delivery could not take place. Given their uninterrupted activity behind the scenes, the recipients of the commands have the capacity to modify the course of action, despite their imperative of dutiful service. Implicitly, their possibilities of communicative manipulation are not insignificant. "Written kisses never arrive at their destination; the ghosts drink them up along the way."[101] Kafka's crucial remark from 1922 means no less than this: that the media play a role in the act of communication. In their own manner they disrupt and influence the traffic of signs. The servant in the channel, the messenger, or the MAILER-DAEMON: despite their vehement protests, they all are working on the thoughts we convey. But any regular message can function as a disruption, as a certain Parisian author observes in a note written around the same time as Kafka's epistolary comment: "My dear Madam, I just noticed that I forgot my cane at your house yesterday; please be good enough to give it to the bearer of this letter. P.S. Kindly pardon me for disturbing you; I just found my cane."[102] As Walter Benjamin observes, Proust becomes "intoxicated by the study of domestic servants."[103] From time to time, he also charmingly patronizes them. And in the case above, the servant who delivers his message becomes, through his intervention, the noise in the flow of communication. "He was most tyrannical and mistrustful about the telephone and telephone messages, because these made up his whole life."[104]

Shortly after the start of World War I, Proust discontinues his telephone line because he feels irritated by the calls; from this moment on, he relies strictly on servants to deliver his messages. Against the general trend and running in the opposite direction from Michelmann's last mission, which transformed mobile servants into stationary cables, Proust replaces the telephone, as the immobile servant of communication, with ambulatory human actors. He tells his attendants he wishes not to be disturbed. Still, if not unplugged, the phone rings uncontrollably. Proust's excommunication of the telephone and his absolute confidence in human messengers seem anachronistic—a last gesture of revolt against the end of an entire cultural complex. The unstoppable decline of the human messaging service system is in full swing after World War I. Implicitly, the complaints—sometimes justified, sometimes not—against the improper conduct of messengers also disappear. The unwanted interventions of subalterns had been a cause of constant critique. So what better solution than swapping the increasingly smaller numbers of error-prone human agents after 1918 with supposedly more functional, less resistant technical media? The fact that machines can actually turn out to be just as disruptive as their human counterparts is a lesson that 'users' would still have to learn, despite their euphoria about progress and 'user-friendly' technology. This gradual process of substitution and its moments of disruption will be the focus of the following chapter.

Chapter 6 At the Stove

The look of food is not determined only by the careful preparation and presentation of dishes. Following the baroque tradition of 'food on display,' the modern eye is an organ of consumption too. This concise motto of culinary technique also refers to the rituals performed by the subalterns in presenting and serving the meals. A typical gala dinner at the imperial court in Vienna includes up to twenty courses, carried, in rapid succession, by a seemingly end-less parade of liveried servers. As they enter the ballroom, the subaltern units, consisting of a server, a wine pourer, a "sauce server," and a plate changer, place the plates in front of the members of the imperial family and their guests. The food has already been cut and portioned. The basic professional principle of subalternity applies in this case as well: "The service staff had to perform their work with utmost precision and in absolute silence, under the supervision of a table inspector."[1]

But even before the plates reach their designated place at the dinner table, they must each follow their course. From the depths of the kitchen—set in the remote vaults of the palace to keep away the smells and the noise—or through the service corridors of country estates, the dishes must be transported via a chain of various actors. The (bodily) well-being of the masters rests in their hands. The service chain starts with the food carver and the decoration chef in the kitchen, who, respectively, cut and put the food on the plates. The chef or the cooking inspector then tastes the food and tests its quality. Following a tradition that goes back to the eighteenth century, the dishes are then placed in thermal boxes and sent on their way to the dining room. Starting from the imperial kitchen and proceeding through wide corridors and high staircases all the way to the dining hall, the food is transported in large, thermal, resealable tin boxes known as 'food warmer cabinets' by court lackeys or servants wearing white toques. Maneuvering the boxes required great balancing skills. A charcoal fire was lit beneath the bottom wall of the containers, preventing the soup and other dishes from cooling down. The cook in charge had to accompany the lackeys to the dining hall, making sure that the plates had made it unharmed. At times, no fewer than twenty or thirty such boxes were simultaneously on their way inside. There, they were taken over by the court cooks, standing by the sideboards in the anteroom of the dining hall. This manner of food transportation, practiced for many centuries, was the only option available since there was only one food elevator in the palace. An attempt involving a food cart with electric heating proved unsuccessful.[2]

The path to the proverbial royal feast is regulated by a fixed chain of supply—or, in the terminology of the Actor-Network Theory, by a "program of action"[3]—whereby the servants and their instruments are assigned one preeminent task: to bring warm, fresh foods to the dinner party over a relatively large distance. There are cooks, kitchen boys, and maids, utensils, as well as inspectors, attendants, servers, and food cabinets. Together, they form a syntagmatic chain made up of human and nonhuman actors. Their scope is to bring the emperor and his guests their lavish meals, with no delay or incidents. Nevertheless, the undertaking is threatened by so-called antiprograms:[4] for instance, if "a dish is too cold or too hot when it arrives at the table,"[5] if someone attempts to manipulate the food during transportation, or if any items disappear. To prevent such antiprograms and their implications—which would bring the entire process to a halt—the actors take various measures, either through technical means—like the white 'hot boxes'[6]—or human operators, such as the cooks that accompany the convoy, making sure the food is not poisoned, tasted, or stolen.

If the program is to run with ease and precision, the associative chain made up of cooks and meals, lackeys and white boxes, humans and things has to function perfectly: the greater the number of courses and the longer the supply chain, the greater the risk of malfunction. Under these circumstances, the high

number of unforeseen incidents should hardly come as a surprise: there are errors, sometimes followed by sanctions; for the most part, however, mistakes go
unnoticed. In England, a flea found on the king's plate leads to the punishment
of the entire kitchen staff: all are ordered to shave their heads.[7] At the Habsburg
court, the situation is different. Here, even more substantial causes turn out to
have lesser effects. There is a legendary account about a meeting between Joseph
II and one of the domestics serving at the table. At the end of the meal, the emperor catches the embarrassed server with a poorly concealed fish sticking out
of his clothes and offers a magnanimous retort: "He should wear a longer coat
or a shorter fish next time."[8]

Small accidents are quite frequent: for instance, when servers pour the wine
or spill (out) the sauce. But such minor incidents aside, the malfunctions caused
by domestics at the imperial court of Habsburg are usually treated with leni-
ency. Speaking of his elderly predecessor, one of Franz Joseph's valets reports
in detail and not without satisfaction how the old man made his master wait
for him:

> Shaky and crooked as he was, the eighty-year-old tripped in his eagerness to
> carry the bowl of soup, which spilled all over the floor, with the meatballs jump-
> ing merrily around the carpet. Through the door, I overheard the terrified man
> stammering: "I beg your Majesty for forgiveness, I lay myself at your feet . . ."
> "Under no circumstance," the Emperor benevolently protested. "I already have
> meatballs lying at my feet."[9]

The intercepted fish symbolically represents the way servants handle ingredients and side dishes; not unlike Michel Serres's parasites, domestics reassemble
them into their own royal meals. The meatballs lying at the emperor's feet are a
sign of the precarious relation between the expression of devotion and the act
performed. Yet despite the *clementia* shown at the Habsburg court, neither fish
nor meat can conceal the structural problems that ground the servants' relation
to stricter masters. Especially when the latter perceive the former as opponents.
Their actions may well be indispensable, but those that carry them out are not
always welcome. One solution to this problem would be the replacement of the
human service-beings with mechanical equivalents or automatic apparatuses.

The relation between masters and servants established over centuries at European princely courts is for the most part characterized by sympathy and ease.
But in nineteenth-century bourgeois households that relation becomes more
rigid. Even if the court serves as a model for later hierarchical distinctions,
including the bourgeois context, there is no shortage of complaints involving
servants, suggesting a latent tension between domestics and their employers.

The reasons range from a general state of discontent with the masters to situations of manifest exploitation. No wonder, then, that the representatives of the middle class are more vigilant with respect to the possible errors of their employees. The daily activities of the servants are accompanied by the constant complaints of their masters. In turn, servants retaliate with recalcitrant behavior, insubordination, or simply by refusing to work.[10] Even if the domestic comfort in the salons and upholstered interiors depends on a wide range of service activities, the masters will still project any reason for dissatisfaction on to the subalterns. "Nothing can upset the domestic peace more or make the life of the mistress more difficult than servants."[11] Not surprisingly, such complaints become a common topos.

Given this background, toward the end of the nineteenth century a vast process of substitution is launched, one whereby domestic services performed by humans are taken over by technical media. The situation is similar to the transfer from messengers to the telegraph. This process is as complex as it is detailed.[12] Consequently, the demonstration will proceed metonymically, via the presentation of three case studies: the dumbwaiter (6.1.1); the mechanization of table serving (6.1.2); and, finally, the electric kitchen robot (the KitchenAid). What these three examples have in common is that they supply the technical means which replace any malfunction or resistance, any insubordination and imprecision, in short, any human weakness.

The reasons for the disappearance of servants around 1900 are obviously quite diverse. Apart from the masters' dissatisfaction, it is the sheer shortage of a subaltern workforce that plays the most critical role in this regard. Known as the "service question," the topic is widely discussed and debated. The regulated work schedule in the manufacturing trade and the industrial sector seem more appealing to both male and female domestics—in contrast to the imposition of permanent availability to which servants are subjected in private households.[13] The shrinking staff numbers cause salaries to rise considerably; in turn, this phenomenon further leads to the disappearance of an entire class of activities.[14] With the demise of the 'world of yesterday' at the end of World War I, servants find their position in the 'modern household' replaced, to a large extent, by other actors.

The next section will focus on this extensive and far-reaching process of substitution. Detecting a source of error in human servants and recognizing in it the source of all evils, the active powers launch a process of drastic mechanization of service functions. Thereby, however, they also fall prey to the charms and temptations of machines.

6.1. AT THE DINING TABLE: SUBSTITUTION
AND (SELF-) SERVICE

The old world order stands to collapse. During the final months of the Central European monarchies, whose demise will drive entire courts and their staffs into unemployment, an American magazine releases an ad. In the December 1918 issue of the popular magazine *Vanity Fair*, quite fittingly named after William Thackeray's novel, the New York department store Lewis & Conger advertises its new household utensil, a "revolving server or Lazy Susan." The contraption consists of a round, rotating mahogany tray that can hold various beverages and food items. Without intervention from any human attendant, it supplies the dishes during a many-course meal. At first, one might think the Lazy Susan is an ingenious commercial name for a banal wooden tray, featured by Lewis & Conger among their Christmas gift recommendations, alongside the 'revolving server' and other useful household utensils.[15] But just a few pages earlier, a further ad, even more inconspicuous than the first, suggests that, in fact, the name of the object does not originate with the New York department store. But one year earlier, in 1917, the undemanding server can be found just about everywhere in Midtown Manhattan. A few blocks down, on Fifth Avenue, the department store Ovington's advertises the item and its (financial) benefits in a quite straightforward fashion: "$8.50 forever seems an impossibly low wage for a good servant; and yet here you are; Lazy Susan, the cleverest waitress in the world, at your service! The mahogany tray (16″ in diameter) mounted upon a base, revolves on ball bearings—to help you serve things easily."[16]

The Lazy Susan may seem like a modest 'invention.' But despite its simplicity it paradigmatically illustrates the process of substitution that takes over the organization of domestic household work after 1900. The numbers of (male) servants, such as butlers, have been drastically reduced by the war. Given the limited supply of domestics, there is a demand for new ways of catering to the needs of social elites via mechanical instruments. But the gadgets meant to re-place the disappearing servants are named after the very agents whose assistance can no longer be sought. The human 'servers'[17] first appear in a fixed material form. As wooden constructs, they perform their service diligently and quietly, as their flesh-and-blood counterparts only rarely successfully did. What, then, would be more fitting than naming a revolving tray after a recalcitrant maid and call it a *Lazy Susan*? Indeed, both words in that strange name draw on the troubled history of household servants. The attribute 'lazy' obviously points to a notorious complaint to which domestics had long been subjected; 'Susan,' in turn, harks back to a collective term quite commonly used in eighteenth-century

365—$8.50 forever seems an impossibly low wage for a good servant; and yet here you are; Lazy Susan, the cleverest waitress in the world, at your service! The mahogany tray (16" in diameter) mounted upon mahogany base, revolves on ball bearings—to help you serve things easily. 16" in diameter, price, $8.50; 18" in diameter, price, $10.00.

Figure 10. A Lazy Susan, pictured in the December 1917 issue of *Vanity Fair*

England. Just as Goethe consistently called his servants Carl, Susan, too, is a form of denying subalterns their subjectivity and simply giving them names held by others before their own time: Lisette, Picard, Mary, John, James.

The item which *Vanity Fair* rather disparagingly describes as the Lazy Susan is certainly not a new invention. Before the 1917 ads, it went by *dumbwaiter,* its older designation. Alongside other things, such as coat racks, revolving, mobile food elevators, and side tables, it is part of a set of objects that are collectively known under that name after the mid-eighteenth century.[18]

6.1.1. Dumbwaiters

> Our walls have no ears.
> —Thomas Jefferson

How can seemingly disparate things such as coat racks, trays, mobile shelves, and food elevators fall into the same category? The logic behind classifying all of them as 'dumbwaiters' appears to be obvious. Patient and resilient, such objects seem prepared to comply with their users' orders. At first sight, they are free of any risk of malfunction or the kind of adversities commonly encountered in interacting with human servants. The notion serves as a general term designating activities typically performed by subalterns—for instance, taking someone's coat, preparing dinner, or simply connecting what is up to what is down. Such acts now fall under the jurisdiction of inanimate objects.

Nevertheless, a closer look at these odd objects may raise quite a few questions. For instance, could the causal chain of technical objects replacing vanishing human subjects not involve a different sequence of events? To what extent do the technical advances inside the home gradually eliminate the traditional functions of domestics? And what are the implications, then, for the cause-and-effect relation described? Also, why is the object described as being 'dumb' or mute, and what is the relation of servitude to muteness? Why not 'deaf'? Would not deafness more correctly describe the status of things, in contrast to their human counterparts?

Traditionally speaking, the human servant is mute. Ideally, he is deliberately silent, after the model of the servers at the Greek banquets and Roman feasts of antiquity. The slaves featured in Greek tragedies almost consistently occupy a marginal role. Their actions implement the strict grammar of dramatic technique. As soon as they have been given a task, they must attend to it without delay. No time for discussions. There are no words for them in the script. To show their reactions, the anonymous servants in their silent role must resort to gestures, which are then discussed and thus analyzed by other characters. They perform indirectly, since verbally they cannot be perceived.[19] Muteness is a virtue; deafness—a problem. Slaves must be able to hear in order to listen. Every sound, every cough or unintentional sniffle can entail a strict punishment, as Seneca confirms in a letter: "Every whisper is silenced with a rod. Even those things that may happen by chance—a cough, a sneeze or a hiccup—are a reason for beatings. Whoever breaks the silence making any kind of sound must expect a good flogging. They stand around all night long, numb and mute."[20]

The literary works and visual representations of antiquity contain similar scenes.[21] Examples can also be found in the plastic arts. The transition from imaginary (visual portrayals) and symbolic (literary texts) representations thus paves the way to the material object (the dumbwaiter) in reality. Commenting on the sculptures of four naked youths dating back to the middle to late Roman period, the archaeologist Norbert Franken draws attention to a previously overlooked category: the "table servant." Each one of the youths is standing in a "serving pose," their hands outstretched as if to carry what may have been a bowl or a tray with food or an oil lamp.[22] Already during the first century, sculptures such as these, showing small-scale anthropomorphic figures, serve as sources of lighting, facilitating service and adding to the guests' level of comfort. According to Eduard von Keyserling's *Psychology of Comfort,* such objects are meant to soothe patricians when confronted with the endless chatter of their guests: "The mute objects had to entertain him. Many instruments seemed to crowd him, but those that surrounded him had to be entertaining. That may also explain why antique furniture and tools tend to come in such vividly animated forms."[23] Whether such objects should be called mute rather than deaf is debatable. On the one hand, their use poses a minimal risk: objects do not betray or bring disgrace to their masters. In prerevolutionary France one could be sure to find at least one police collaborator among the members of one's own staff. But objects do not spell rumors. On the other hand, if mute, "dumb servants" can be carved into statues and made to entertain guests, they should rather be called blind, since one of their qualities is the capacity not to react when a command is given.

In certain well-to-do households where servants are employed, masters constantly seek to keep their staff at a distance. Among those who famously consider domestics to be a constant source of problems is the third president of the United States and the author of the Declaration of Independence, Thomas Jefferson. Here, however, he appears in a different light.[24] As someone who invents and perfects various technical instruments, like the polygraph, the pasta machine, and the moldboard plow, Jefferson is increasingly keen on acquiring his own independence from human media such as servants. He mistrusts his silent domestics to such a degree that he attempts to rid himself of them—the men, not the women, whom he seeks out for other purposes—and tries to entirely replace them with nonhuman actors. "Nothing is a greater restraint on the freedom of conversation, which, to me, is the chief pleasure of the social board, than the attendance of a number of servants."[25] Freedom of speech must not be hindered by politically enlightened, silent yet highly attentive individuals.

> When he had any persons dining with him, with whom he wished to enjoy a free and unrestricted flow of conversation, the number of persons at table never exceeded four, and by each individual was placed a dumbwaiter, containing everything necessary for the progress of the dinner from beginning to end, so as to make the attendance of servants entirely unnecessary, believing as he did that much of the domestic and even public discord was produced by the mutilated and misconstructed repetition of free conversation at dinner tables, by these mute but not inattentive listeners.[26]

A visit to his Monticello residence amply illustrates this point. The dining room is set up to enable the comfort of dining with guests, but without the attendance of servants. There are four side tables alongside various other contraptions in the room meant to keep domestics away and stage a telematic type of service instead. Alcohol, for instance, is supplied via another subtype of the dumbwaiter called a goods elevator. The lift carries the wine straight from the cellar to the dinner guests upstairs. The courses on the menu are brought in via a unique mechanism that prevents subalterns from physically entering the room. There are several shelves on the back of the door, where domestics can place or remove dishes while outside the room. The so-called revolving serving door can then be turned, either to introduce a new course or to take on the appearance of a closed door again—with the additional advantage of preventing any eavesdropping, since the shelves are in the way.

As in the case of the baroque green baize door, the double nature of this revolving door becomes apparent only upon closer inspection. In contrast to a regular door, this particular construction element has three different states of operation. When shut, it is not at all different from its conventional counterparts. One can pass through it only when it is half open. Implicitly, it is suited only to those of a slimmer build, who can fit through the opening between the central axis and the frame. And finally, it turns into a shelving system and a miraculous mechanism that brings the food into the dining room. The door thus functions as a semipermeable membrane that opens and closes, conceals and serves. Its hybrid transitional state, however, turns it into three different things at once: a passageway, a screen, and a shelf, allowing access on both sides.

Simultaneously, Jefferson's revolving serving door introduces the absent server in material form; a nonhuman specimen takes the place of a domestic, able to speak and (over)hear others. The position of the human servant has been occupied by a technical mechanism, dumb and heavy, highly specialized yet flexible, endowed with the ability to cater and clean up. Jefferson's table society and its environment, with its network of host, guest, and dumbwaiters, perfectly exemplifies Bruno Latour's answer to the question about the composition of society. "We deal with characters, delegates, representatives, or, more nicely, lieutenants (from the French 'lieu' 'tenant,' i.e. holding the place of, for, someone else); some figurative, others nonfigurative; some human, others nonhuman; some competent, others incompetent."[27] However, this does not mean that the human domestics have somehow entirely vanished from Jefferson's table society. They are only banned from the consciousness of the members of that society, since their activity as servers is incompatible with the suspicion concerning a further potential occupation: eavesdropping on behalf of a third party. This deficit does not afflict the mechanical counterpart of the server. On the contrary, the dumbwaiter has an advantage over the human medium: via its specialization in strictly mechanical activities, along with its elimination of sensory channels, it frees itself from an imposed condition of discretion: "Machines are lieutenants; they hold the places and the roles delegated to them."[28] Nevertheless, this delegation of agency from humans to things also propels things into a privileged position.

Before the Enlightenment, before becoming service *subjects* and professional servants, subalterns have limited legal rights. They are assigned an object-like status, which is subsequently transferred from humans to things. Side tables, goods elevators, revolving serving doors, and clothes racks replace the actions previously performed by human beings and become delegates. Cast in this new position, frozen in their wooden or metallic frame, they patiently serve in lieu of those who are now exiled to distant corridors and kitchen cellars.

But this epistemic shift is irrelevant to those who hold the reins of power. Apart from minimal changes in the server's mode of operation, the effect of service is the same to them. The contentious difference between subject and object and the question whether servants have now turned into machines, or whether service has always essentially been a machine: these distinctions have been conflated: "All that serves, man or thing, adopts the silent precision of a mechanism. [. . .] The instrument is irrelevant, only the effect it produces matters."[29] The waiter, for instance, is not required to have a bubbly personality.

Literally and symbolically, the dumbwaiter represents a far-reaching process of translation over the course of which irritating servants turn into machines. The 'humble servants'—including both the awkward, clumsy subalterns as well as the 'most submissive server' of all—are thereby mechanized and reduced to silence. Similarly, in the mechanical and—later—electrified environment of the dining room, (table) society is gradually transformed into a sociotechnically mediated community. The paradigm shift takes place on a double stage: the dining table and the kitchen—a space increasingly dominated by technical media during the late nineteenth century. Here, the masters are introduced, in an underhanded fashion, so to speak, to the notion of self-service.

6.1.2. Gaston Menier and the 'Invention' of the Cafeteria

Despite Jefferson's invention, his effort at keeping servants away with the help of dumbwaiters is hardly the exception. The anxiety over the potential disturbance caused by servants grows into an outright paranoia in the Victorian era: "The dishes are brought in and then quickly removed, one has no time to savor the wine, the best bites grow wings and fly away, as soon as one turns to talk to one's neighbor." Thus complains a Hungarian diplomat about one of Franz Joseph's gala dinners, which he has the honor to attend.[30] Not surprisingly, then, various technical media are now involved in the direct act of service, resulting in several intermediary steps. Functioning as relay stations, these media gain access to and insert themselves into the act of human communication. The effort to keep servants at bay is taken even further, with a new, mechanically advanced service installation that represents a radical continuation of the Monticello experiment. Its level of mechanical development implies an even greater distance from the serving staff, securing its long-lasting fame since 1887, the year it is introduced.

Figure 11. "The Invention of the Cafeteria" in southern England? No, Gaston Menier's dining room in Paris

In the last century there was a farmer who lived in the south of England and who was renowned for his generous dining and wining parties. Having invited his friends to dine with him, he objected to the constant interruptions of his servants. He therefore installed in his rambling mansion a railway which connected the dining room with the kitchen and pantry and carried food and wine. An electrically driven car on miniature rails came right to the table through a service hatch and stopped in front of each guest, who helped himself, after which the host pressed a button and off went the train to the next stop, finally disappearing through another hatch on its way back to the pantry to be loaded with the next course.[31]

The text that accompanies the image can be found in *Patent Applied For,* Fred Coppersmith's manual of popular science from 1949. The description contains a great many errors as well as fabrications. The problems start with the technical commentary and end with the spatial references in the text. As the picture clearly shows, the slightly elevated train tracks do not disappear through another hatch, as the author claims. In fact, at the end of the rail there is a track switch with a small shunting area, where the food transport can change direction without further intervention from the serving staff. In other words, this is an unmanned, two-way end-user system, directly operated by the person sitting at the head of the table—the lord of the things and not just a bystander who is forced to take whatever passes in front of him. And more important: one of the gentlemen in the picture is not a farmer from the south of England, but the French chocolate magnate, politician, and owner of a small Canadian island, Gaston Menier (1855–1934)—a pioneer in the domain of electric household gadgets as well as an esteemed member of Parisian high society.

Whether or not the caption ("The first cafeteria system") is correct will be discussed at a later point. The German translation of the book from 1960 corrects the fake legend of the English farmer and adds the reference to Menier. Yet the source of that reference—a report from the journal *La Nature* from 1887—is missing from the German version as well. Indeed, the report highlights several other aspects of Menier's preference for electrical gadgets. The chocolate maker is described as a pioneering consumer of technical progress. He belongs to the select few who bring electricity into their households, just a few years after the 1881 Paris exhibition, where Thomas Edison presents the light bulb to the Old World. In Menier's home, electricity serves other purposes as well: for instance, to illuminate a table fountain, which makes for even more glamorous dinner parties;[32] or to electrify his catering system, based on a miniature train model, allowing him "to quickly and easily serve a meal without any servant entering the room."[33] Again, the text contains an implicit complaint about servers and the suggestion that their accident-prone service be replaced with technical instruments.

Structurally speaking, not much has changed from the master's point of view. As usual, the gentleman orders the next course and it is promptly delivered; nevertheless, the order is no longer verbalized or announced with a nod, but rather activated via a remote-control button. Instead of the solemn procession of dishes brought in by a long line of lackeys, now there is a "rapid and discreet"[34] transport—a train with two carriages holding the main course and the sauce as well as a container of salt.

A dramatic and far-reaching transformation takes place beneath all the fascination with technological play. Via the railway dumbwaiter, consumers are introduced to a new practice of service whose implications may escape them at first: "The train instantly follows orders, while the master serves himself,"[35] as the article in *La Nature* proudly announces. The silent carriage stands in front of the guests, no one places the dessert in front of them—they must serve themselves. This reverse chain of action marks no less than a paradigm change. The new logic requires that guests take the initiative, and the relation of power between master and servant is also reversed. The timely delivery of the food and the service no longer depend on servants but on the hosts and their operations. The times are long gone when the late arrival of the fish ends with the cook committing suicide, as was the case with François Vatel (1631–71) on the occasion of a feast organized for Louis XIV. Any dissatisfaction with the quality of the service can no longer be brought to the attention of domestics but rather to the hosts themselves. And some of the guests who did not have enough time to help themselves may secretly wish to exclaim, "Gaston, bring the carriage around again."

An important transfer of agency is taking place at the head of that carriage. The act of service is now delegated to the guest or the user. As opposed to domestics, service-objects demand that guests perform activities they had previously been denied. Instead of a subtly whispered "Please"[36] as they carefully lay down the plates, or, better still, instead of not saying anything at all,[37] now the dumbwaiters seem to address the guests with a silent demand: "Dig in!"

Involuntarily, the guests obey and turn into active users instead of someone who is passively served.[38] The relation of power between masters and servants is reversed. The function of service is delegated to technical media, and the former masters are now subject to the will of things. Once the practice of *self-service* enters the scene of stately dining halls, its agency changes as well. The first and foremost law of the man–machine interaction is the following: technical things do not serve; instead, they are serviced. Terms like "manual" and "service handbooks" already speak volumes. Electrically operated trays and their underlying media infrastructure, made up of tracks, carriages, remote control mechanisms, require careful operation, that is to say, properly following the rules of a preset operating system.

What about Gaston Menier's other experiment from 1887, his attempt to replace his entire serving staff with technical media? Its fate and the reaction of the guests are only sparsely documented. The previously mentioned report from *La Nature* about the colorful table fountain indicates that, only two years later, he would once more prefer stable servers over shaky carriages. According to a source that may have been written with satirical intent, the *Encyclopédie des Farces et Attrapes et des Mystifications*, the contraption still functioned, dutifully performing its service in a small provincial hotel, the Hôtel du Midi in Annonay in the Ardèche. In any case, it certainly found followers—for instance, the Indian maharaja of Gwalior, Madho Rao Scindia (1876–1925), who came to power in 1886 at the age of ten and set up a hundred-meter-long railway in his palace, replete with trains which could transport up to two hundred plates. It goes without saying that the tracks were made of silver. But the toy train of the maharaja seems to have worked not entirely without error: during the visit of the Indian vice king the train appears to have "gone mad and thrown sauces in all directions among the guests."[39] As the pitfalls of technology clearly demon-

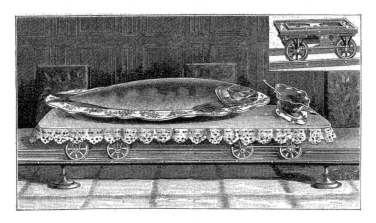

Figure 12. A train in the dining room is like a fish without a skirt

strate, the agents of mechanized serviceability are at least as prone to malfunction as their human predecessors. This penchant for interruptions makes the system appear rigid and feebly prepared for unexpected situations; it also frames mechanical agents as actors endowed with limited intelligence. But, in fact, every instance in which the operation is thrown out of gear actually confirms the strength of these dumbwaiters, allowing them to become powerful agents. As Carl Schmitt's theory of indirect actors has already proven, there is little movement at the center of power. In reality, self-service implies not serving oneself but servicing another, the dumbwaiter. The power that things have held over their former masters becomes clearly apparent.

The replacement of human service agents with their technical counterparts, whose names recall their human origin (the dumbwaiter, the 'Knitting Liesel,' and the Lazy Susan), follows two criteria. One the one hand, the new instruments seem to meet the standards of permanent availability found in reliable servants; on the other hand, they aspire to an undiminished level of comfort, which runs the risk of being lost in the efforts to innovate the modern household. This double principle is also one of the reasons why the masters do not ultimately replace their subalterns but only the referents of their service. A butler or valet may be dismissed, but the dependence on agencies of service of all kinds remains in place; in fact, it becomes even more pronounced. If the spoken word was still effective in interactions with human servants, the limited operational systems that are already implemented in machines considerably limit one's independence from service. A waiter can also serve as a messenger; a dumbwaiter, however, less so.

The dependence on assistance and the purported ease that technical apparatuses introduce prevent users from seeing that the service operated by things is not in the least as thorough and complete as human-based, full service. Difficult to operate, prone to malfunctions, or saving their users too little work: via all these possible risks, instruments demand that users submit to their authority. With the arrival of technology on the scene in turn-of-the-century households, individuals are subjected *nolens volens* to a new paradigm of self-service. At first, the inevitable nature of this scenario may be hidden beneath the promise it holds, the illusion of control over the mechanical domain. A handful of critical voices pointing to this conclusion are drowned out in the general euphoria over technology.[40] Almost imperceptibly, the new mentality of self-service gains ground:[41] users freely surrender their authority to the preconfigured operations of mechanical agents. As the routine use of household utensils such as the Lazy Susan, the kitchen robot, the revolving serving door, and the food train amply demonstrate, one is no longer a subject of servants but of things. Everything hinges on the correct operation, the handling of the dumbwaiter. Only now, the ones who operate it are ladies and gentlemen. The relation of dependence remains constant, and resistance is unthinkable. The path back to a status quo ante proves to be increasingly blocked by an intricate web of electric (and, later, electronic) networks that gradually take over the unstaffed interior spaces.

Apparently, the objects of service produce the same effects as their living predecessors. As long as the train does not go off the rails and the sauce does not land on the clothes of the guests instead of their plates, things are not any different from the server who serves the fish with elegance instead of hiding it away for his own use. As long as there is no disturbance, no interruption in the operation of the great machine of service, things offer the same thing masters sought in their servants: comfort. While the substitution process may become increasingly rapid and advanced, the meaning ascribed to the innovations seems to tap into old ideas. This may also explain the general tendency to assign anthropomorphic attributes to the objects of service.

The amiable assistance of our surroundings is important to us, if we desire to draw satisfaction from life. We extend our way of living onto our environment. We instinctively humanize our instruments and the things that serve us; the more they adapt themselves to us, the more life we breathe into them, and they seem to serve us out of their own accord. Not only do they become comfortable; they also give us comfort.[42]

In his melancholy farewell to the vanishing epoch of human service subjects, Eduard von Keyserling describes the immediate environment of the masters as representative of the impression of correct service and comfort. For what is absolute comfort except an environment at the center of which stands the owner, while everything else—man or machine—lies at his service? "In a beautiful, well-trained body, with the gift of sharp, healthy senses and good, precise mental capacities, there I am, inhabiting them like a grand master who is served beyond reproach."[43] In other words, one would ideally serve oneself. No need for subalterns. But such a grand master seeks to expand the domain of his comfort. For "our efforts lie with expanding this faithful service of the self and pack as much as possible into it."[44] And this effort of incorporation includes everything that is close, people, things, nature, subjects as well as objects—all of them seeking to befriend their master. However, this is "a friendship in which we are magically served, and the other performs the service."[45]

As unique as Keyserling's *Psychology of Comfort* (1905), with its traditional feudal perspective, may sound and despite its grasp of the asymmetrical bond of friendship between master and servants / things—the text recalls a vanishing epoch. Shortly before World War I, Keyserling analyzes its crumbling "mechanism of harmonious living"[46] with profound clairvoyance. The difference between subject and object, between man and machine as agents of service, may have long disappeared;[47] the sense of 'comfort' may take place only in our minds. Yet this authority over things is at the same time fundamentally threatened by the daily practice of self-service around the turn of the century. The asymmetrical bond of friendship between master and lowly things has become the impotence of users facing the challenge posed by the handling of technical instruments. But the asymmetry persists. Yet this is no longer simply a matter of extending the activity range of "the faithful service of the self." Rather, what is at stake is a change in the initiative to act. The self must take action, and the former grand masters are now expected to put their assistants into operation, in the form of dumbwaiters or electric machines.

6.2. IN THE KITCHEN: THE HUMBLE SERVANTS' TECHNOLOGICAL TURN

> If someone had told our women a century ago that they should get their water from a faucet in the kitchen instead of drawing it from a well, he would have been accused of seeking to encourage laziness in housewives and servants.
> —August Bebel, *Woman and Socialism*, 1892

The traditional kitchens at court and the estates of the grande bourgeoisie are usually quite busy environments. Great numbers of servants make sure that the masters receive their daily meals and are protected from irritating smells and noise. But between the age of Enlightenment and the end of monarchies, in the era of the servant-turned-subject—also known as the long nineteenth century—subalterns undergo a sociotechnical transformation. From this moment on, subalterns are no longer seen as human objects with instrumental functions but as professionalized service subjects with their own areas of responsibility. But that is not all. Over the course of these 120 years, domestics also become subject to a fundamental substitution process, whereby their former activity is delegated to technical instruments. This process also contributes to the emancipation of the human workforce, ultimately leading to the collapse of the professional image as well as the very disappearance of domestics. Three images from three different epochs will illustrate this transformation of technical subalternity. The first image, dating back to the late eighteenth century and appearing in Henderson's *Housekeeper's Instructor* (1791 / 1800), shows a kitchen scene with numerous staff. In the foreground, the head cook trains one of his assistants in the art of meat carving. Next to them, the lady of the house hands her maid the very same book in which the image is featured. In the background, two kitchen boys are getting ready to wash the dishes, and yet another maid keeps busy turning the roast and stoking the fire. All of them wear aprons and are engaged in activities that cannot be performed without physical effort and without manual labor.

Nothing seems to have changed in the kitchen shown in the second image, from a century later. There is a large staff, a bird is on the table, ready to be carved. And a female servant placed in front of the oven is carefully watching over the roast. Following the general trend of the period, the number of women in the kitchen has increased. But the obvious difference consists of the improved technical infrastructure, for instance, the presence of the stove in the background but especially the central lighting system with hanging lamps that improve the quality of work during hours of darkness.

Taken barely three generations later, in 1969, the third set of pictures displays an image fully in step with the times: elegantly designed, easy-listening ambiance where all technical details are carefully considered. Only the flokati rug is missing. But, more important, it presents the kitchen technology as a state-of-the-art installation, whose operation no longer seems to require a housewife but a lady in an elegant evening dress. The distance from the previous scenarios could not be greater. Instead of hard manual labor and a crowd of domestics, the only requirement involves a control panel, from which everything can be operated with the push of a button.[48]

In the traditional kitchen, the stove occupied the central position: it took up an entire wall and was carefully guarded—it was at the very center of activity.

In contrast, Hasso Gehrmann, in his Elektra Technovision, *reduces it* to a mere accessory. The roasted chicken rotating behind the glass frame is treated as an odd specimen.

Starting with the prehistoric campfire, the space where food is prepared has been an experimental field which cannot function without the participation of technology.[49] The images of kitchens from 1791 and 1900 show a wealth of mechanical instruments which an equally numerous staff uses in the preparation of food. In the wake of the technical developments of the second half of the nineteenth century and the subsequent trends toward rationalization, human actors are forced out of their traditional positions. Their place is taken by specialized instruments operated by miniature electrical engines and, later, by electronic control systems. The human servant falls victim to this trend toward automatization, both in the kitchen environment as well as in all other service activities. The instrumental function of subalterns is now conferred upon machines. Consider the time-consuming washday, now reduced by fully automatic washing machines into one-hour cycles.[50] Such changes are made possible via a technical infrastructure that enters the space of bourgeois homes via water pipes and electric networks around the turn of the century.

Apart from servants, the kitchen also holds an entire arsenal of instruments, which help in the concoction of a broad variety of products from the most diverse ingredients. In other words, the kitchen has always been an experimental space. This is a place where the old and the new meet, even if it sometimes takes a long time for practical inventions like the pressure cooker of Denis Papin (yet another invisible technician in Robert Boyle's lab) to find their way into the royal kitchens or stoves in the remotest corners of the continent. The kitchen has "the character of a complicated laboratory, surrounded by numerous accessories specially contrived in respect of disposition, arrangements, and fittings, for the administration of the culinary art in all its professional details."[51] Not surprisingly, some of the most famous and prestigious spaces of culinary production (for instance, the kitchen of the Reform Club in London) promote a spirit of innovation, both in the creation of the most refined dishes and through special technologies oriented toward more efficiency and work optimization.[52]

What does this imply with regard to the visibility of subalterns in the culinary context? Written traces left by invisible technicians (as, for instance, in Robert Boyle's lab) are the exception rather than the rule. In contrast, the daily technologies of the domestics engaged in the preparation of food involve more documents and sources, so that their practices and interventions are rendered more transparent. These come to us in the form of cookbooks or even the liminal genre of functional poetry cultivated by servants, cooks, and kitchen

Figure 13. The kitchen at the Reform Club in London, 1842

maids.[53] As opposed to lab technicians, the servants here are—at least according to the sources—more visible, even if their products, meals and drinks, no longer refer back to the bodily presence of their makers when transported by servers via the long corridors that connect the remote kitchens to the comfortable dining rooms. The gentleman enjoying his candlelit dinner quickly forgets about the cook working downstairs. But around the turn of the century the previously hidden domestics step into the limelight and make themselves noticed by their masters. They purposefully come out of hiding and draw attention to themselves. Fine observers such as Virginia Woolf read this changing behavior as a clear indicator of a groundbreaking shift in the living conditions of servants, taking shape right before her eyes: "The Victorian cook lived like a leviathan in the lower depths, formidable, silent, secure, inscrutable; the Georgian cook is a creature of sunshine and fresh air; in and out of the drawing room, now to borrow the *Daily Herald,* now to ask advice about a hat."[54] Not only do servants allow themselves more liberties in the wake of this transformation; in fact, they suddenly find themselves to be entirely free. The traditional activity of subalterns is subject to an unparalleled process of displacement during the reign of George V, shaking the very foundations of the service domain and leaving a great many domestics without employment. Mechanization takes command. Domestics lose their traditional domain of activity, since their operations are replaced by machines. The reason for this shift is celebrated everywhere, at world exhibitions and in the display windows of shopping emporiums, as the source of technical progress: it is the "almighty enchantress,"[55] the "always available, faithful and undemanding servant [. . .] called electricity."[56] Well-to-do ladies, "when looking for household help to ease their work," do not seek the services of the hiring offices, but instead take their requests to large department stores or the increasingly available specialty shops: for they "find such active support in the promises of electricity."[57]

Writing in 1892, a socialist thinker imagines a visionary scenario which, barely a century later, would become reality in the form of fully networked homes and electr(on)ically conveyed news and postal communications:

> The electric door opens with slight pressure of the finger and shuts off by itself. Electric contrivances carry letters and newspapers to every floor of the houses, and electric elevators save one the trouble of climbing stairs. The interior furnishing of the houses, the coverings of walls, floors, furniture, etc., will be so arranged as to make house cleaning easy and to avoid the gathering of dust and germs. Garbage and all kinds of offal will be carried out of the houses by waste pipes like the water that has been used.[58]

Instead of a sizeable staff carrying clean water and coal up four flights of stairs and taking down the wastewater and the ashes, it is the technical infrastructure that takes care of everything: "As the central kitchen will do away with the private kitchen, so central heating and electric lighting plants will do away with all the trouble connected with stoves and lamps."[59] Undoubtedly, however, it is the kitchen that functions as the center where all infrastructures and technical networks converge:

> The kitchen equipped with electricity for lighting and heating is the ideal one. No more smoke, heat, or disagreeable odors! The kitchen resembles a workshop furnished with all kinds of technical and mechanical appliances that quickly perform the hardest and most disagreeable tasks. Here we see potato and fruit-paring machines, apparatus for removing kernels, meat-choppers, mills for grinding coffee and spice, ice-choppers, corkscrews, bread-cutters, and a hundred other machines and appliances, all run by electricity, that enable a comparatively small number of persons, without excessive labor, to prepare a meal for hundreds of guests. The same is true of the equipment for house-cleaning and for washing the dishes.[60]

But, as some would argue, such technical accumulation would hardly be accessible to regular workers. For them, hosting "hundreds of guests" would be an exceptionally rare event. Bebel responds to such critiques by pointing to further possibilities of centralization. He proposes the solution of the one-kitchen home linked to several apartments and a central dining room or collective food preparation area, managed with the help of machines and a few trained cooks.[61] Every single household service which had previously been entrusted to human domestics has now been replaced by the beneficial power of electricity, down to the shoe-polishing machine, which "perform[s] the task to perfection."[62] Not accidentally, therefore, contemporary discourses imbue electricity with precisely those attributes that characterized the dedicated human subaltern. "Electricity was difficult to grasp and sense; it was invisible, odorless, silent—only its effects were detectable."[63] The structural parallel between servants and electricity that enters discourse around 1900—albeit unconsciously—leads to a single conclusion, categorically and trenchantly formulated by Bebel in the following manner: "But when domestic life will be generally transformed in the manner we have pointed out, then the domestic servant, this 'slave to all whims of the mistress,' will disappear."[64] As late as the mid-nineteenth century, when the kitchen staff are still, for the most part, made up of human subjects, the bourgeoisie and aristocracy could hardly conceive of a life without servants. According to George Orwell, for instance, Charles Dickens could not have imagined an existence devoid of domestic help; and as for his colleague Rudyard Kipling, domestic service was the essence of British civilization. "There were no labor-saving devices." Implicitly, the effort of overcoming class differences, as Bebel would demand, would be possible only via the massive import of technical, electric devices into the space and everyday reality of the kitchen. "Without a high level of mechanical development, human equality is not practically possible."[65] The increasing availability of labor-saving kitchen appliances contributes—along with the appeal of industrial employment—to the shrinking numbers of staff. And despite all Britishness or any other conservative declarations regarding the centrality of the servant to civilization,[66] the advances of mechanization lead to the transformation of the kitchen maid into the modern KitchenAid. Its success story begins in 1908, when the American engineer Herbert Johnson observes a baker mixing dough with a spoon. Johnson's attempts to render the mixing motions in electric form result in the development of the so-called KitchenAid standing mixer, which soon becomes a staple in bakeries as well as on U.S. military ships. And with the newly expanded H-5 model from 1919, the mixer would continue its path to success as a universal kitchen robot.[67]

Before investigating cases of actual fusion between human assistants and nonhuman devices with the help of current action theories (first stir, then hybridize!), the next section will propose a preliminary discussion, namely, of the ways in which the servant has always been associated with notions of machines and mechanization.

6.2.1. The Servant as Machine

> Without the constant co-operation of well-trained servants, domestic machinery is completely thrown out of gear.
> —*The Servant's Practical Guide*, 1880

During the nineteenth century, after the eradication of all old feudal structures, servants become subjects, that is to say, individuals subjected to others, actors performing various services and employees with documented rights and numerous duties. Nevertheless, their position seems rigid and dependent. Indeed, since antiquity, subalterns have been confronted with the suspicion of being no more than "animated tools" (Aristotle)[68] and consequently of acting in close proximity to the mechanical realm. There is a long genealogical tradition of viewing the servant as a creature acting in a mechanical fashion or even as an automaton. The mythical statues of antiquity, for instance, those created by Daedalus, are said to have been mobile despite being made of stone or metal. The automatons of the Renaissance, like Leonardo's mechanical knight that could move his arms and legs—at least on paper—belongs to this tradition as well. So do those servant figures envisioned by Salomon de Caus for his grottos in the Hortus Palatinus. Occasionally, there are intersections among categories: for instance, when a sixteenth-century valet also works as a constructor of automata in order to, ideally, render his own service function superfluous via his creations.[69]

What these machines have in common is precisely the fact that they typically do not represent subaltern figures. And yet most of them carry out certain services. Implicitly, while they are conceived in order to be put on display, they simultaneously also exhibit the pleasures of service. Conversely, those who regularly perform their service in the background acquire a machinelike character. "Thus young people become machines, they are trained into a business which they perform without thinking and therefore generally also badly."[70] Such problematic aspects are not obvious, however. On the contrary, especially when the contexts somewhat overlap and the foreground and background become less distinct, the servant takes on the character of a "machine that executes commands."[71] The ideal agents of service are therefore not the helpless and faulty automata, which have limited efficiency, but rather the 'authentic,' meticulously functioning automata-like humans. Jean Paul, a writer who is in many ways well ahead of his time, has grasped the overlap between these two categories quite early and in more depth than anyone else. The struggle to overcome the difference between man and machine is an ongoing motif in his literary work.

Two brief texts will help guide the understanding of the relationship between user and machine during the eighteenth century. In the *Personalia of the Service- and Machine-Man* from 1789, Jean Paul shifts the perspective from earth to Saturn and allows the narrator to observe from this elevated observation point the dealings of the machine-man on earth. The latter is a figure that delegates every little task to his servants—a highly unusual collective made up of humans and machines. Anticipating Ernst Kapp's theory of media as the extensions of man,[72] the machine-king names his subalterns after specific muscular functions which are usually involved in activities like blowing one's nose or moving one's mouth in order to speak (an activity performed via a machine with a keyboard attachment). When the king starts to move, he is followed by an entire entourage, made up of "watch-carriers, hat-carriers, box-carriers, lorgnette-carriers, as well as a reader carrying a book under his arm."[73] Not accidentally, the scene evokes the royal levée ceremony or an audience with Louis XIV in the Hall of Mirrors at Versailles.[74] In the narrative, the royal suite of antechambers contains a study room where each handwritten letter is multiplied by a copy machine. A similar device had indeed been developed by the Swiss precision mechanic Jacquet-Droz and his family around 1770.[75] The king also has at his disposal various other human and nonhuman means of intellectual production: a calculator, an entire machine park that makes music (including Vaucanson's famous flute players). And whenever he requires a specific piece of information, he simply turns for help to the closest search engine:

> He then led me into his library to the great Encyclopedia of d'Alembert, which consisted of nothing else but an elderly Frenchman who had learned it by heart and who could quote any passage from it he desired to know: like a Roman (according to Seneca) whose slaves would recite Homer in his place when he would cite him, the man longed to have pages in attendance, a chemical, an astronomical, a heraldic, and a Kantian one, so that, when he wished to write something down, he would place them around him as he would do with books, and examine them without having to know everything himself.[76]

Apart from the subaltern serving as an information center there are other underlings, talking or silent, employed as filters of perception[77] or taste-enhancing samplers or tasters. "A tiny mute servant came forth who looked like a great hemp mill. 'I never chew,' the man said 'and do not cut with my own teeth anything harder than a dental consonant. My chewing machine does everything for me.'" Readers may have asked themselves already what this satirical description actually means. Its significance is revealed by the author in the final sentence: "'And that is the reason, my dear Saturnian friend,' I continued, 'why I chose not to describe the machine-man to the reader down there [on earth]; for you have all understood that he (= the eighteenth century) is no other than the king himself.'" From a galactic perspective, Jean Paul offers a self-description of the eighteenth century by defining it as the age of machines, a time of various (mis)alliances with human beings and swaps between servants and things.

In yet another, earlier fragment entitled *Humans Are the Machines of Angels,*[78] the young Jean Paul proposes an even more radical idea. Here the narrator expresses his doubt that "our activities only serve our own intentions," considering the hard labor performed by men for the higher authorities "we call angels." In fact, angels are "the real inhabitants of this earth, whereas we are merely their personal effects."[79] Again, the celestial perspective is maintained in order to give yet another critical analysis of his time. As in the case of the machine-man narrative, which features mechanical facilities and service innovations—from Denis Papin's pressure cooker to Vaucanson's duck—it is machines that perform the various service functions. Illustrating his point with a few examples, such as van Kempelen's famous chess automaton, the narrator concludes that "we humans are mere machines, used by higher creatures, who have been allotted this earth as a dwelling place."

According to Jean Paul, the eighteenth century is characterized by a growing trend toward automatization. In the wake of this process, humans appear from a satirical angle as mechanical actors, serving others, not unlike footmen. Not surprisingly, therefore, a servant's ideal quality is that "this machine does its duty as normally and silently as possible."[80] The machine metaphor is therefore constantly invoked in the context of domestic organization and its minute distinctions. "The butler is the actual executive. He is the one who lays off some underlings and hires others, without the knowledge of his masters; he also assumes the responsibility for the entire machine, which has to function so seamlessly and inconspicuously that the masters do not even take notice of it."[81] For Jean Paul, the butler as a human actor definitely belongs to the mechanical realm. Around the turn of the century, he reemerges as the one who administers the apparatus, while simultaneously counting as one of its components. By adapting to the general context of the household hierarchy, subalterns become part of an industrial wheel within a huge mechanism that turns them into robotlike figures.[82] Nevertheless, they maintain their flexibility. "The first requisite of a good servant is that he should conspicuously know his place. It is not enough that he knows how to effect certain desired mechanical results; he must, above all, know how to effect these results in good form." Consequently, what is demanded of him is (an inner) attitude. In other words, 'good' servants ideally possess good judgment and the power of observation, despite their inferior position. "Domestic service might be said to be a spiritual, rather than a mechanical function."[83] This inner disposition allows them to intervene in unexpected situations and make decisions that may even go against the expectations of their masters. A lesser servant who rigidly follows orders without analyzing, (re)combining, and (literally) amalgamating them represents the exception rather than the rule. So, for example, the attendant to Rahel Varnhagen's dying father: "On the day of his death, he requested water to wash himself and scolded his servant, saying it is cold as ice; the servant then brought boiling hot water: 'You oaf! Am I your swine ready for scalding!' Upon that, the servant returns and says: 'There is no drop of lukewarm water in the house!'—And Lev.[in] M.[arcus] loudly laughed and passed away."[84]

During the times of the ancien régime, it may have been fashionable for an Englishman of higher rank to hire a French attendant to stir his tea, another one to do his hair, an Italian to prepare his desserts, and half a dozen Brits to iron his newspaper; his wife, too, would have had her French maid to powder her neck and an Englishman to carry her prayer book.[85] Such decadent forms of employment disappear along with the old feudal structures. In contrast, the nineteenth century witnesses the professionalization of servants. The highly specialized tasks of the past are now replaced with a generalized scheme of services that are geared not so much toward the function of representation but rather toward the practicalities of running a household. In the wake of the mechanization of domestic activities, brought in by the advance of machines into the realm of the household, employing servants is no longer a necessity. "In the modern industrial communities the mechanical contrivances available for the comfort and convenience of everyday life are highly developed. So much so that body servants, or, indeed, the domestic servants of any kind, would now scarcely be employed by anybody except on the ground of a canon of reputability carried over by tradition from earlier usage."[86]

After 1871 the numbers of servants in English households steadily decrease. "Household work has been drastically simplified by the development of technology, and the introduction of electric light, central heating and gas stoves into the homes; at the same time, traditional domestic activities such as baking or earlier domestic activities such as baking bread, making fruit preserves and many others have been steadily and increasingly taken over by industrial and commercial enterprises."[87] The year 1869 marks the beginning of a new discourse that rapidly gains ground in the United States, under the impact of Catherine E. Beecher's and Harriet Beecher Stowe's *The American Woman's Home.* The authors support the idea of doing away with servants altogether and dividing the household tasks among the family members, but especially the new technical media such as the gas and the electric stove, the washing machine, the dishwasher, and the flatiron as well as the vacuum cleaner and the garbage disposal.[88]

In 1958, drawing on this major process of the substitution of man for machine, Michael Young predicts the servant would return once more at the end of the twentieth century. As he imagines the future, by 1988 "about a third of all adults were unemployable in the ordinary economy. [. . .] What was to be done with them? There was only one possible answer. The people who had ended their school lives either in the schools for the educationally sub-normal or in the lower streams of secondary modern schools were only capable of meeting one need: for personal service."[89] The absence of servants in the 1950s is treated as a mere interim phase: "For thousands of years, it was the accepted thing for the upper class to have servants. They only vanished between the demise of the old aristocracy and the birth of the new."[90] Young was not entirely mistaken in his assumptions. An increasing importance is ascribed to the service sector nowadays. Second, the return of the servant is an established fact. Only his appearance has changed.

> Another anthropomorphic convention has it that machines are our servants—or better, slaves—since we buy and sell them and pay them no wages. [. . .] Today, we are no longer slaveholders, or, if slavery still exists among us, it is invisible. [. . .] Servants, on the other hand, still lead a formally recognized life among us, even though we recognize our humanity in them. They are numerically so scarce in the West as to be insignificant as a social factor (the invisible slaves, if they exist, are contrastingly numbered in the millions); so their level of visibility is of little interest. What is of interest, I think, is that while they were still extremely common, they were disappearing—just as the machines were to disappear subsequently without, however, any reduction in their numbers.[91]

While they may not be visible, servants are certainly active at the end of the twentieth century: either as hidden slaves one should not see or as liveried porters in hotels or restaurants, but especially as virtual agents, regulating our lives in the *Second Life* domain and beyond. Subalterns walk among us, either (in)visibly in human form or removed from sight in the form of hidden service entities which have long crossed over into the electronic realm.

6.2.2. Hybrid Agency

The image of the long chain of human waiters and dumbwaiters at the Viennese court or at Jefferson's Monticello estate that transport, prepare, and remove dishes raises an important question: where is agency situated in this process divided among multiple actors? How should one analyze the responsibilities of humans and things involved in the act of service? Are humans acting like machines? Or has service inconspicuously reverted to machines that had previously performed human activities? And, therefore, who supports or executes these actions and activities? According to a basic principle of Actor-Network Theory[92] the dichotomy between man and machine, between acting individuals and (silent) things, has been long since overcome, since the two elements are combined and thus form a new entity.

By means of the well-known example of the citizen and the gun, Bruno Latour develops a concept that shows the union of two previously independent actors—humans and things—blended into a new, distinct third actor. Who is the actor in this constellation, who is responsible for the potentially deadly shot? Who has the agency: the man or the weapon? Latour points to a third actor, formed in the union between subject and object, by "the creation of a new goal that corresponds to neither agent's program of action."[93] This new actor is neither a citizen nor a gun, but a citizen-gun or a gun-citizen. And thus agency is redistributed: "Responsibility for action must be *shared* among the various actants."[94] And the connections they form give rise to new connections between new and old actors, corresponding to a specific program of action. In other words, the result is an effect of such "chains of associations."[95] The discrete elements of the newly formed contexts function as mediators, linked into yet another program of action. Here, one could invoke another canonical example from Latour's writings: a key built in such a way that its use implements a new house regulation; in this case, the famous Berlin key, which forces the tenant not only to unlock the house doors after a specific time but also to simultaneously lock them behind him.[96]

But irrespective of whether the discussion involves gunshots, keys, or (service) doors, traditional domestic figures or objects, the agencies of service, no longer correspond to the categorical distinction of man versus machine. That is to say, strictly assigning actions to acting subjects or to the domain of allegedly inferior objects no longer answers the question about who is an actor or who is in control. Rather, the actors of service correspond, without distinction, to an alternative mode of operation. Power is assigned to the interaction of previously disparate elements. Instead of remaining anchored in the rigid subject–object distinction of traditional ontology (or language philosophy), the actors fall in an in-between category: to use a term from Actor-Network Theory, they must be understood as 'hybrids,'[97] that is to say, a mix of human and nonhuman entities. And these hybrids are plugged into a long chain of similar entities and merge according to a specific action program into a new actor: the chain of association. Agency belongs to the association chain itself. The old dichotomy between humans and nonhumans merely appears as a nod to the old philosophical tradition. In reality, argues Latour, only the paths and acts of transmission, the channeling and the change of location decide the effects of actions. And by uniting hybrids into new entities, the chain of association traverses the interstices and leads to a bending of space and time.[98]

The principle of hybrid formation can be found on multiple levels. In the context of micrology, it manifests itself at the level of word-formation, for instance, in German, a language with endless compound-formation capacities. Consider, for instance, the term for "groom" [*Reitknecht*]. Initially, helping a master mount a horse is a task performed by a human actor; later, its function is taken over by a technical device (the stirrup). But beyond that, the terminological transposition of a program of action is reflected in the very word *Knecht,* which designates either a human or a nonhuman actor, depending on which historical period is considered. Figuratively, it means a service person who serves food or removes a gentleman's boots. On the other hand, it is also used for objects and tools "that serve humans as 'carriers,' 'holders' or helpers in general. Everyone knows about the bootjack [*Stiefelknecht*], which 'obediently holds the boot for its master, so he may remove it.'" The term obviously also applies to the kitchen environment, where it stands for "the metal support for the turnspit" [*Bratknecht*] or takes on other functions" as a device for holding bowls or pans.[99] In such cases, however, the actions are no longer performed by human attendants but by technical aids which have been charged with their predecessors' tasks.

At a mesological level, the process of hybridization takes place, for instance, in the interaction between dinner guests and dumbwaiters. In this case, it is no longer clear who is serving whom. The dumbwaiters, solidified into furniture objects, have taken over the media functions of human domestics. At the same time, they also impose on the host a specific form of self-service. The intersection between the two elements leads to the formation of a new actor; that is to say, the interaction between the actors transforms them into a new hybrid of service.

And finally, at the level of macrology, the formation of hybrids produces specific effects: the complex interaction of various service functions such as delivery, purchase, cooking, as well as utensils like the roasting jack, the meat carver, or the Kitchen (M)Aid, the carriers, the attendants, and the dumbwaiters—all of the above form a long chain of human and nonhuman actors that finally results in a fresh, hot meal, ready to be enjoyed by the members of the dinner party.

The human–object collective follows a set protocol in each case. The subalterns receive instructions to attend to the guests; the command triggers a specific program of action—in this case, the preparation and serving of food while ideally remaining out of the sight of guests and salon dwellers. The latter should know as little as possible about the painstaking efforts of their subjects, their hands sore from carrying heavy objects along distant corridors. "Over the whole surface of contact between the body and the object it handles, power is introduced, fastening them to one another. It constitutes a body-weapon, body-tool, body-machine complex," as Michel Foucault writes about operations involving subjects precisely following the instructions of their superiors.[100] When subjects and objects merge—even outside the kitchen—into a new type of unity, the masters that occupy the space in-between are no longer able to exert their power on them as actors in a conventional sense. With the breakdown of traditional operative models, actions are distributed among newly configured hybrid carriers. According to Latour, it is the association chain itself that acquires full and exclusive agency in that case: all power resides in the chain of operations.[101] In the realm of domestic service functions linking the stove to the masters' dining table, the answer to the old question about who is in control is delegated to a single giant kitchen machinery. Networked right down to its ultimate rhizomatic ramifications, that machinery both stands at the service of authority and reconfigures that authority in turn, by introducing the paradigm of self-service.

As shown in the case of the kitchen, the reconfiguration of power relations into long chains of interconnected programs of operation inaugurates a new aspect of authority: its habitual power of command is inevitably transformed by the necessity of self-service, as soon as the subaltern function is taken over by patient, long-suffering objects of furniture. Such a reorientation of operative options coincides with the *invention of the user,* arising from the formerly omnipotent figure of commanding authority under the ever-increasing impact of self-service. As soon as the masters begin to serve themselves instead of being served, they become subject to disenfranchisement by the things. According to Latour, the latter now represent the Third Estate,[102] just like the emancipated servants in the aftermath of the French Revolution. Liberated from the shackles of nonage, servants (as well as things) now perform their activity in an altered state of employment, as professionally based, politically emancipated subjects.

On the other hand, the emancipation of things launches a direction that points well beyond the still-limited operational possibilities of the human masters within the context of increased self-service around 1900. The disenfranchisement of subjects coincides with the empowerment of objects; together they stand at the start of a trajectory that provisionally ends with self-aware objects and smart things.[103] They have long started to break down, if not even to revoke and abolish, the borders between 'intelligent' human and less 'intelligent' nonhuman beings. The washing machine selects the proper cycle based on the information it reads from a chip sewn into the shirt you put in it. The fridge is connected to the Internet and can order more milk when the supply runs low. The front door automatically opens with an iris scan identification device and greets the visitor in the hallway with a phrase from his favorite musical aria.

When the old distinction between subject and object collapses, the traditional lineage between humans and control, on the one hand, and instruments, tools, and execution, on the other, no longer automatically applies. Then, if not sooner, one must concede to things their own independence, at least at the level of the chains of associations that contain them. It is possible, then, to speak of a shirt activating a washing machine, of a cybernetic, self-regulated, multimedia kitchen, or simply of an intelligent house in which menial tasks have long ceased to be performed by human domestics.

6.3. WITHIN THE *OIKOS*: THE HOUSEHOLD AND ITS (SEMI-) OBJECTS

It may be purely coincidental that Elektra Technovision, the name of Hasso Gehrmann's futuristic food processor, contains a reference to Sophocles's heroine from the eponymous tragedy. Whether intentionally or not, the concept of the fully automated cybernetic kitchen draws on the origin of household rules (οἰκονομία) first theorized in antiquity. What defines the instruction of household management, according to the work of Sophocles's contemporary Xenophon, as well as its Aristotelian sequel?[104] How can this ancient episteme offer some of the criteria according to which one could evaluate the changing role of household servants? The defining feature is the notion of an autarchic home, which appears as a closed unit from the outside. That is precisely why one can speak of the 'entire household' in this context. The οἰκονομία is grounded in a stark dichotomy between inside and outside. The οἶκος is perceived as a hermetic entity that communicates with the exterior only via strictly regulated intersections and channels. As an all-encompassing and fully integrated unit, the 'entire household' is both a concrete object as well as a metaphor for the economy and its reception. It is intrinsically connected with the economic self-maintenance of the system via its resources. The economic principle presupposes that a household remain self-sustained, that it can provide its own nourishment, without appealing to external help or participating in foreign trade.

Its inhabitants, both masters and hands, form a tightly knit, codependent community, led by a paterfamilias presiding over the resources—his blood relatives, servants as well as the services they provide. All members work side by side; to a certain extent they form a pedagogic community. The organization follows the all-determining principle of order. Therein lie the 'cares of the family man,' as he seeks to maintain the harmony among the constitutive elements of the household and ensure smooth relations between the whole and its parts. In other words, οἰκονομία essentially presupposes that the diverse actors, humans, and objects inside the household are each placed in their appropriate position according to their respective rank and function. Consequently, while the concept of hierarchy reaches its theoretical and historical culmination in the writings of Thomas Aquinas and Pseudo-Dionysius the Areopagite, the notion itself and its effective application date back to the household rules of antiquity.

The impact of οἰκονομία can hardly be overstated. Without undergoing major modifications, the concept remains pervasive from antiquity to the (early) modern age. It is only during the Enlightenment that household rules begin to erode as the result of emerging competition from administrative science and its specific economy, now promoted to the level of state dogma. Furthermore, the differentiation and increasing technological development of trades also contribute to the breakup of the spatial unity of work and living area. Office and home, warehouse and residence, work and dwelling become distinct domains.[105] Ultimately, the nuclear family, the reduction of the household collective to the next-of-kin group, deals a final blow to the community of masters and hands. The bourgeois, small-family unit seeks to cultivate standards of language, reading, and education, while the staff remain even spatially excluded from them. The servants are moved out of the manor or mansion into the stable or other such remote places. That is not necessarily a sign of poverty but rather of emancipation from the previously unlimited patriarchal situation.[106] Even so, it is obvious that the unity of the οἶκος falls apart. While the agency of control is concentrated in the hands of the small family unit, the servants become a professional service class in its own right. The increasingly differentiated range of tasks and activities of the latter no longer immediately fits into the framework of the familial duties. The staff, who are now political subjects but are kept away from the perception of their masters, "are not seen as part of the family, but as hirelings," as Adolph von Knigge concludes in late 1700, not without an undertone of complaint.[107]

And last but not least, the final criterion of ancient economics should also be mentioned: the image of the ideal house manager or father. He is in charge of the distribution of tasks and rights; he or his administrative representative ultimately gives concrete directions to each individual actor, supervises the partial results so as to coordinate the entire procedure and exercise control over the end result.[108] The task of the administrator is precisely that of effectively channeling the workforce into the οἶκος.[109] His foremost attribute is therefore the delivery of orders. The administrator governs or steers the house—just like the bailiff or the steward, the butler or majordomo who follow in his wake. Not accidentally, the term also designates a software service which manages electronic mailing lists. The majordomo oversees the entries and exits, administers the lists, takes care of the entire system of incoming and outgoing messages.

By the Enlightenment, at the latest, a deep rift begins to take shape within the former unit of the family and the more or less peaceful community of masters and servants. As a result, the two groups are split into two camps: the servants are marginalized and vanish, not merely from their masters' sphere of perception, by way of doors and remote corridors specifically built for their use. At the same time, the rising power of mechanization makes room for a multitude of actors that now enter the space of the home, either in the form of dumbwaiters or new technologies, for instance, in the kitchen, leading to an overall reduction of staff. During the Enlightenment, the question of service is still treated under the principles of domestic management, which gradually take the form of administrative policy.[110] And in political contexts, while domestics were once strictly perceived as objects, not drastically different from cattle, they are now recognized as almost equal subjects and citizens. But consequently, servants simultaneously also lose their traditionally designated place. Within the grand bourgeois households, their numbers increasingly shrink: human service beings are gradually replaced with nonhuman ones. And yet, despite the slight temporal lag, the spatially segregated, repressed service subjects return. The contemporaries of the digital age are once more faced with the big issues of service and its media, introduced by communicative and personalized actors, with the difference that they do not fall into the category of "political romanticism" but rather of "information technology."

Empowered via various strategies of subjectification, objects are once more granted access to the whole house, which thereby becomes a so-called smart home, where everything is networked and every actor is directly connected to the others. The servants return; only now, they return as objects, and there is a decided effort to endow them with subjectivity. Even though they still operate in the background, service actors acquire a unique human character, to the extent to which they reliably accomplish the tasks that were once the responsibility of human subalterns. It all starts with Ken Sakamura's smart home from 1989, where a "squadron of invisible servants,"[111] made up of approximately a thousand microprocessors distributed throughout the building, are automatically set to water the flowers, switch the lights and the music on and off, open the windows, close the doors, flush the toilets, and select French recipes while preheating the oven. And from there, it is only a small step to 2008, to Siemens's newest refrigerator model, KG 28 FM 50, also known as *coolMedia*. Apart from the cooling and freezing functions, the fridge also offers a 16:9 format 17″ LCD flat screen replete with DVB-T tuner and USB port: the appliance that chills and entertains.

The premise for such a dynamic household information exchange system is the interconnectivity among its individual components. In addition to Bill Gates's property and other such smart homes, one should also mention in this context Tim Berners-Lee's notion of a semantic web from 2001. According to the inventor of the World Wide Web, the term signifies an additional network providing all relevant information technology spaces with their metadata, so that individual positions or agents may communicate with one another even without the aid of any human intervention.[112] Not accidentally, Berners-Lee presents his semantic web 'vision' in terms of a scenario in which all household appliances, from the telephone to the stereo equipment, are not only interconnected and coordinated but also able to interact with one another. Any resemblance to Ken Sakamura's TRON house (or Hasso Gehrmann's concept of a "total home")[113] is obviously purely coincidental. What is decisive here is the total connectivity between servants and inhabitants: the entire house communicates—the only difference being that in this case the domestics are no longer human, despite the fact that they speak, eavesdrop, have multiple sensory channels, display images, or single-handedly order milk when supplies run low.

A further economic criterion is the dynamics of goods circulating within the household. Whatever the system needs in order to operate, be it material or information, is in constant motion. In other words, the home follows the paradigm not of storage but of transmission. The technology of material streams in the *oikos* can be ultimately transposed into the technology of Internet information and data streams and its networked applications. Being online is the order of the day, and service actors are not exempt from it. The website or homepage (as a virtual oikos) forms a closed unit containing their information supply. No housekeeping without house servants. The server has become the new basis for the whole household.[114]

6.3.1. Somewhere Between Subject and Object

Along with various shifts across a number of domains, the vast process of substitution commonly associated with the notion of progress[115] also involves the switch from human servants to their technical equivalents, to ministering things like dumbwaiters or kitchen robots with claims to universality. Nevertheless, that process does not involve in the least a reduced potential of action. On the contrary, technical media lay claim to a specific kind of agency, which transforms former masters into users with limited powers and endows things with special authority. This approach, which evens out the differences among traditional categories, has been developed within the framework of Actor-Network Theory for the past two decades. In this particular context, it will be applied to the domain of domestic management. Thus, dumbwaiters such as Menier's service mechanism will be treated as hybrids or, to quote a term Bruno Latour borrows from Michel Serres: a quasi-object.

What is a quasi-object? Leaving aside its occasional applications in early debates that gravitate around Kant's thing-in-itself,[116] the notion claims its critical importance due to Michel Serres's groundbreaking study on the Parasite, which contains no less than a theory of the quasi-object. The premise is to rethink the notion of agency from a new perspective. Using the key elements of a game, for instance, a ball, a joker card, or the 'furet,' or button (the marker in the children's game 'Button, button, who's got the button?'), Serres develops an influential concept which involves a change of perspective on at least two different levels. The first turn occurs when one of the previously equal participants takes on a privileged position: the individual who receives the button becomes the subject (of the game). Simultaneously, however, that transaction also affects the status of the button itself. The act of transmission endows the object with a specific kind of agency: "This quasi-object is not an object, but it is one nevertheless, since it is not a subject [. . .] it is also a quasi-subject, since it marks or designates a subject."[117] The ball switches categories: it no longer is an object or not yet a subject, or the other way around. It establishes an ontological middle ground from which all decisive actions are launched. The decision called by the button does not merely assign one participant at a time a unique function. Rather, it turns the button into an actor standing at the center of the network, grouped around and related to it. The network itself is the collective generated by the transmission of the button, the constant exchange and circulation of the quasi-object. "This quasi-object, when being passed, makes the collective."[118] By circulating, the quasi-object-turned-main-actor sets up a network, which forms not only the basis of the game but also its nodal points: all the pre- and post-processes, infrastructures, and strategies, which go well beyond the specific event of the game.

The second change of perspective involves a reversal of the entire course of action. The enhanced status and function of the quasi-object turns the focus away from its momentary possessor and onto itself. As in a soccer game, the trick is to see the ball as the protagonist, that is to say, not to pay attention to what Ballack does with the ball, but the other way around, what the ball does with Ballack, how it makes him carry it or how it links the captain and the other players into a network.

"Science says that there is a distinction between the subject, which is thinking and active, and the object, which is passive and thought of."

"That displays total ignorance of the act of knowing! Objects know in a different way than us, that's all."

"That's untenable."

She points towards the window.

"Look at those children out there, playing ball. The clumsy ones are playing with the ball as if it was an object, while the more skilful ones handle it as if it were playing with them: they move and change position according to how the ball moves and bounces. As we see it, the ball is being manipulated by human subjects; this is a mistake—the ball is creating the relationships between them. It is in following its trajectory that their team is created, knows itself and represents itself. Yes, the ball is active. [. . .] Do you really think that machines and technologies would be able to construct groups and change history if they were merely passive objects?"

"They are technical objects, and that's all!"

"That's like saying a white blackbird—it's a contradiction in terms. These biros, writing desks, tables, books, diskettes, consoles, memories . . . produce the group that thinks, that remembers, that expresses itself and, sometimes, invents. Maybe you're right, maybe we can't call these objects subjects. However, maybe we could call them technical quasi-subjects."[119]

Serres still speaks of quasi-objects in *The Parasite.* Here, in *Angels: A Modern Myth,* using the same example of the ball game, he treats them as quasi-*subjects.* That is plausible since they are creatures of the in-between and therefore evince various degrees of difference; what is important, however, is that their indistinct borders allow them to mediate between the two traditional categories. "The quasi-object too is a subject. The subject can be a quasi-object."[120]

One of the most influential apologists of quasi-objects is Bruno Latour, in his vehement battle with (post-) modernity: according to him, the whole dilemma of modernity resides in the lack of transparency between the two poles that define the West and its historical development. The multiple connections between nature, technology, and objects, on the one hand, and society and human beings on the other are denied. One consequence is the great dichotomy between the two poles, specifically in the philosophical formulations of objects and subjects; in the political domain, between the local and the global; or in the social sphere between nature and society. All of these categories ultimately appear separated by deep rifts which consequently seem impossible to bridge.

The missing links between these extremes are the quasi-objects. According to Latour, they operate as grounding media instances, as the mediators of the great dichotomies; and yet, in the political, scientific, and ideological structures of modernity, they are crassly neglected or, worse still, denied. For the most part, they have been merely regarded as intermediary entities without ontological dignity or epistemological importance. Therefore, the error has been to perceive them as insignificant elements, mere carriers that do not change anything and therefore remain subjected to the omnipotent control of either 'nature' or 'society.' Things have thus been denied any transformational competencies. At best, they have been regarded as "loyal servants."[121] There is a significant asymmetry between the two poles 'nature' and 'society.' As a result, all competencies are amassed on the side of society; by the same token, at the opposite pole, things are largely understood to have ornamental character.

Latour opposes this state of affairs. He pleads for epistemological change and a new symmetrical relation between the two fronts. Along the same lines, he aims to place the invisible actors in their rightful position in order to bring to light the agency that objects have so far been denied. "Serres ballasts epistemology with an unknown new actor, silent things."[122] Instead of merely speaking of intermediate entities in an expanded space that has been purged of any interfering factors or actors, Latour suggests conferring quasi-objects a much more active status and regarding them as dispersed, yet also interlinked mediators of the in-between. That is the only modality whereby they can be understood as autonomous, highly active actors linked via operative chains. "They become mediators—that is, actors endowed with the capacity to translate what they transport, to redefine it, to redeploy it, and also to betray it. The serfs have become free citizens once more."[123]

Invoking a well-known example from science studies, namely, Simon Schaffer's and Steven Shapin's seventeenth-century work on the concept of vacuum,[124] Latour subverts the classic myth of the subject constructing the object. In fact, it is the silent work of the air pump as well as the 'gestural knowledge' required to operate it which involve not only texts and language but also silent actors and raw remainders, in short, the hidden and mute things that become the decisive factors in the development of the study of vacuum, either in the formulation of its natural laws (Boyle) or of its political antiprogram (Hobbes).[125]

The attributes, metaphors, and assignations which Serres and Latour employ in their description of quasi-objects already beg the answer: we speak of 'dumb' things, artifacts that leave behind their former status as serfs or loyal servants and ring in the new autarchy of operators. The intermediaries are thus freed of their mere object status and are empowered to perform more independent reactions, but especially actions. What could be more fitting, then, than regarding dumbwaiters as quasi-objects as well? "To call these marvelous things simply objects seems to me as idiotic and unfair as saying that slaves or women have no souls, that servants have no needs, and that children don't need freedom."[126]

One of the foremost qualities of the quasi-object is its ability to form a collective via its circulation. The question is then: what kinds of elements are moved by the dumbwaiters? For one, it is the mobilization of meals allowing the intake of food. But above all, it's the dumbwaiters themselves that circulate and allow the circulation of others, by preparing and laying out, transporting and serving them their meals: the rotating Lazy Susan, Jefferson's service door, the freight elevators, or the food trains on tracks. The entire chain of service, consisting of cooks, kitchen robots, human carriers, electric transmission media, servants, guests, and hosts form a collective of human and technical beings.

The foundational instance of a collective is represented by the circulation of its elements. Like no other actor, the dumbwaiter reigns over the middle ground between the poles. Like no other element, it fulfills the criteria of the quasi-object: linking together dichotomous domains, bringing together what is separate and, via its labor of translation, connecting what is distant. By preparing and serving meals and then cleaning up, the collective of human servants and dumbwaiters becomes the link between high and low, below and above. Consider not merely the freight elevator but also the butler that communicatively connects the downstairs and the upstairs. The dumbwaiter functions as a cursor, a furet between periphery and center, uniting the spaces of (fine) society and (raw) nature, not unlike Menier's service train connecting the kitchen to the dining room. The quasi-objects of service, be they human or 'dumb,' domestics in flesh and blood as well as ministering machines—linked together in hybrid chains of operation, they all perform a specific labor of translation by connecting the nature and society poles—or else, between machines and humans.

"Of quasi-objects, quasi-subjects, we shall simply say that they trace networks."[127]

As Gaston Menier's service train demonstrates, the interim domain between objects and humans is traversed and sustained by a fine mesh of networks. Just as the circulation of quasi-objects brings forth the collective, the network generates the emergence of actors, humans, and things which are united into new associative chains and the reconfigured operational programs connected with them. "Networks are full of Being. As for machines, they are laden with subjects and collectives."[128]

Yet networks are not restricted only to the domain in-between the poles that are to be connected. As Menier's dinner table indicates, they are broadly heterogeneous and thus extend well beyond that limited domain. At Monticello or in Menier's household everything that remains invisible and operates in the background is still vital for the grand event called dinner. Only a small fraction of Menier's track system and its infrastructure of carriages and controls can actually be seen. The carriages vanish and reemerge via a dark, boxlike opening. Beyond it lies the kitchen, which complements the dinner. It would be useful to open that black box in order to examine the actor called kitchen or to observe how various networks and actors cross paths on this stage as well, either at the level of food delivery logistics, or the preparation stage involving the interplay between cooks and their tools, or the connection to an early electricity system and its network, as the article from *La Nature* notes. Its systemic and theoretical advantages notwithstanding, such a task would go far beyond the conceptual scope of the servant.

ANT also deploys methods that visualize hidden networks. A basic assumption in this sense is that each actor has a corresponding network of further actors. Every actor is implicitly made up of other operators—something that, for the sake of brevity, does not require further discussion. To the extent to which the individual elements of an actor can be said to interact without friction and lead to relatively stable results, the discrete modules can be assembled and connected into a so-called black box.[129] What goes on inside of it is not necessarily of interest to an external observer, as long as it functions as expected. The guest should not be bothered with the operations of the food lift / elevator as long as there is plenty of wine and the dumbwaiter produces the desired results in the form of full bottles. A closer examination is required only if there is a possible error in the flow of supply; in that case, the black box is forced open for someone to shed light on the darkness and find out which elements are in disarray. Only then does the observer get to see beyond the dark opening and into the hidden network behind, the ropes, the mechanical traffic, the bottles, the wine cellar, its supply, and possibly even a human being who got carried away and has taken a bit too much advantage of the self-service option. The chains of association are only as strong as their weakest link.

On the other hand, more complicated, stable networks such as the process of dinner preparation and service can be grouped together into a single actor. ANT proposes the term "punctualization" for such cases.[130] In other words, the food on the dinner table, the plates, and then the stomachs of the guests is a punctualized form of a complex process named service. That process presupposes the intervention of the purchased and delivered food items, the kitchen tools, recipes, cooks in remote areas of the household, as well as a silently but reliably operating system of carriers, long corridors, mechanical as well as human servers. The instruments made available by ANT allow us to open once more that black box called service and follow what happens beyond the point where the train enters the tunnel or behind the revolving serving door, in order to analyze all the details of the interconnected networks. Such an ongoing process of depunctualization of the dumbwaiter would show how this particular actor consists of and is traversed by a range of different actor-networks. That notion can be followed at the level of the construction of apparatuses (built by Jefferson himself), the management of food, the logistics of delivery, its role in the long chain of meal preparation, the interplay between cooks and their tools. In short, ANT understands the construction of actors as a recursive phenomenon.

Not unlike Menier's black box, Jefferson's revolving serving door redirects attention to the system of food delivery and preparation, along with its infrastructure of drinks and dishes brought in on mobile trays and carried around by busy servants. Those servants, of course, remain out of sight as they walk down the vast corridors of the mansions. The guests get to see only the end product, tastefully arranged on their plates. The layout plans for the Monticello estate already stipulate that the service wings, along with the kitchen and the domestics' living quarters, the bedchambers, and the laundry room be kept as far away as possible from the main hallway. Implicitly, the service network is systematically kept out of the gaze of the masters. But despite not being seen, all these actors constitute an indispensable component of the collective that allows for a dinner at Jefferson's estate in the first place.

Via its labor of translation, the dumbwaiter acquires a further element of agency. Compared with the limited sphere of influence implicit in traditional service functions during the prebourgeois era, such an element involves an epistemically superior position. The switch from mere object to quasi-object implies a certain destabilization of previously fixed subject–object assignations. Classifications intersect, become overdetermined, blend together to form a unique mixture of elements, a hybrid entity with human and mechanical attributes, a new actor. In the same fashion, the intervention of a quasi-object implies the redistribution and reallocation of power relations. The particular components of agency need to be reevaluated.

It is no longer a case of the operation of an agent on an inert object, nor of the return action of an object, promoted to the role of an agent, on a subject dispossessing itself in its favor without demanding anything in return; in other words, it is no longer situations involving a certain amount of passiveness on one side or the other which are in question. The beings confront each other face to face as subjects and objects at the same time.[131]

This mutual shift of status involves a transformation of agency and implicitly also a change of authority over the instructions and the possibilities associated with every task and role, with who is in charge of what. Objects like the dumbwaiter become distinct, independent actors and demand to be served in turn by their own users. To compensate for their loss of status, the members of fine society console themselves not merely with technical instruments but also with a kind of rhetoric that allows them—like the term "self-service"—to overlook the fact that their interactions with supposedly 'dumbwaiters' have long subjected them to the authority of a new master, namely, the rule of technology. By operating independent technical apparatuses and quasi-objects, the former masters essentially turn, due to the new paradigm of self-service, into subjects.

6.3.2. Delegations: Objectifying the Servant

With the advent of electrification, quasi-objects such as dumbwaiters, kitchen robots, and other services—now translated into mechanical or technical apparatuses—make their way into the study or the living room. Concomitantly, such collectives of nonhuman assistants and service substitutes are exclusively sustained by the spread of concrete, material networks. Such networks, as ANT conceives them, are linked to chains of association formed of various processes, like the mechanical operations at the Habsburg court, Menier's train, or the universal kitchen robot. Only a closer look at each of these actors, for instance, Gaston Menier's unique service system, unveils what lies inside the black box, namely, a minute network that consists of more than the tracks connecting the kitchen and the dinner table, the cooks and prep workers, all hidden from sight, or the nameless railway engineers who built the train. Linked with this network or, rather, enclosed in it, are other networks, like the electric power system, with all its sub- and super-systems, in short, the Networks of Power, as Thomas Hughes has described the system of electrification in the Western world.[132] The network system proposed by ANT follows a recursive model. And just like any other recursive system, this one too must specify its break-off condition,[133] to prevent researchers from getting completely lost on their way down new and endlessly ramified network paths.

To what extent can Menier's service installation be seen as a unique nineteenth-century curiosity? Or, on the contrary, could we argue that it represents a typical symptom of an epoch that tends to replace human service subjects with hybrids or technical media and launches the interplay between nonhuman creatures and self-servicing masters? The questions already beg the answer: during the 1880s there is an ample process of diffusion of various mechanical aides, led in by a dumbwaiter called electricity and its increasingly more detailed and complex network of power, reaching deep into even the most modest of households. The wide-ranging implications of that phenomenon transform not only kitchens but also the entire mode of service altogether.

The question remains whether one can call Gaston Menier the inventor of the cafeteria. As so often in the historiography of innovations, one invention does not merely lay claim to a single ur-scene. Inventions follow a much more complex model of development, by unifying various sources into a group of heterogeneous actors in diverse locations during a semihomogenous moment—in this particular case, a brief window between 1885 and 1900. Menier gives his model train a test run in 1887, in his own dining room. But already a year before, at the Great Industrial Exposition of Berlin, visitors visit an 'automata pavilion' and admire vending machines that, in exchange for money, would distribute food and drinks without any intervention by human waiters. The system is still in use today, in the twenty-first century, as a niche business—for instance, in train stations or the so-called *Automatenbar* [automatic pub] in Berlin that can be found, not accidentally, in the Münzstrasse [Coin Street], and which functions according to the same principle of waiterless restaurant service. Such an operation, based on the principles of self-service, captures the attention of visitors at the Chicago World's Fair in 1893. At this point, the processes of service and food preparation have reached such a level of acceleration that commentators begin to speak of a 'fast restaurant.' Just a few years later, in 1897, Berlin welcomes the world's first fast food restaurant, exclusively operated by 'automata.' Around the same time, in 1898, William and Samuel Childs successfully open a New York restaurant based on the Spanish-Californian cafeteria model, with a buffet where customers pick up trays and serve themselves. That same year marks the launch of the Horn & Hardart Bakery Co.—a business model that successfully continues for eight more decades. An anonymous traveling salesman offers Frank Hardart and John Horn a German-made machine which promises to automatically provide customers with prepared dishes and extends the concept of the waiterless restaurant[134] well beyond Philadelphia and Manhattan. But beyond this list of entries belonging to the history of automated service, there are two additional aspects that will be briefly discussed here: on the one hand, the process of objectification and the delegation of service functions to new, inanimate actors; and, on the other hand, the question concerning the impact of these changes on the notion of the oikos.

Servants have long hired themselves out. But after 1900 they become reified, objectified,[135] yet not before they impose the paradigm of self-service on their former masters, who now become users. Electricity enhances the automatization of dumbwaiters and their long tradition. As in the case of Gaston Menier's unique train, several service functions, such as serving and cleaning up, are now taken over by machines. The simplest of domestic tasks, like preparing a cup of tea, is delegated to automated actors, for instance, the "clock that makes tea"—a more economical solution than keeping a servant.

In 1912, writing about the situation in England, a keen female observer notes that technology steadily works against domestics, whose numbers are dramatically sinking. For "many consider a modern, technically accomplished home a more practical solution than keeping servants."[136] The lower ranks of the personnel are thereby cast out of the household. Even the so-called lady helps, impoverished noblewomen who seek employment in bourgeois homes and maintain this position for quite a while, now see their place threatened by the reign of mechanization. From this moment on, the Household Auxiliary Association becomes a term associated not with old employment-seeking ladies but with commercial areas where one can purchase modern appliances, also known as whiteware. While technical innovations such as automatic restaurants become increasingly popular in some public contexts, it takes a great deal longer before the principle of do-it-yourself catches on to enter the private space of the salon. Letting go of old privileges does not come easy to the higher classes. The following example, featuring an emblematic figure of emancipated femininity, illustrates this perfectly: putting an end to a love-and-hate domestic engagement frequently mentioned in her diaries, Virginia Woolf dismisses her old cook, Nellie Boxall, after eighteen years of service. In 1929, when the Bloomsbury group acquire a modern stove, the lady of the house takes over the cooking: "And so I see myself freer, more independent,"[137] Woolf notes in her diary with relief. That period is short-lived, however, especially since Boxall keeps her position for another five years, vehemently refusing to quit. The final breakup takes place in 1934. The Woolfs see no alternative other than to leave the cook behind in the kitchen and temporarily move without her into their country residence in Sussex. "After eighteen years I at last got rid of an affectionate domestic tyrant," she writes in her diary on that day.[138] And yet, the emancipation from the human medium is equally short-lived, and Woolf hires a new employee.

Step by step, over the course of the twentieth century, the classical service functions of the household—the central unit where the networks cross and overlap—are replaced by depersonalized service operations. Connected to intricate infrastructures like communication channels, water supply, and electric power systems, such networks absorb the previously integrated services of human subalterns. "The modern housewife is assisted by a series of electrical appliances and automated maid fragments; she also serves herself (and her close circle)."[139] Even if the substitutions are occasionally accompanied by massive resistance, criticism, and melancholy invocations of the 'good old days'[140]—the transition seems to proceed rather smoothly. Ultimately, the functions are maintained, only their carriers, the specific media, undergo a change from human actors to machines. The disappearance of human service media makes room for what the progressives hail as the blessings of technological development. But this phenomenon does not merely involve the transposition of media actors. Within such a vast framework of change, even the attributes of serviceability find new applications in unexpected domains: for instance, the sewing machine is treated as a mechanical maid, or photography is hailed as the devoted servant of science.[141]

This overarching process of substitution appears to threaten, once again, the subject status the servant had barely just acquired. The servant figure is literally dispossessed, and its agency is passed on to the world of things. It is quasi-objects that take over its functions now. Theoretically, the subalterns and their precursors, the eighteenth-century lackeys, can once more stand in for the idle ways of their masters. Nevertheless, the sociotechnical criteria have drastically changed in the meantime. The leisure class of the nineteenth century, the employers of the underemployed staff, no longer exist. The grande bourgeoisie and their staff are vanishing. The human servant has nothing to do—as in the best of times—but no longer gets paid for it like before. Consequently, an entire profession shifts away from its liminal status into what—in contrast to its former significance—appears as an increasingly marginalized niche.

When technical machines enter the domain of the household around 1900, they bring about a profound change in the nature of power relations, which in turn leads to a reconfiguration of the traditional concept of the oikos. In lieu of the former domestic, there is an ensemble of interconnected media imposing a new form of self-service on the masters. The reification of human servants via the power of electricity can be illustrated with the help of a series of images dating back to the twentieth century. The new kind of service may not necessarily be less prone to error or disruption than traditional human waiters. Nevertheless, it leads to the gradual outsourcing and transformation of media service functions into increasingly automatized and miniaturized instruments. In the dining room scenarios imagined by Gaston Menier or Buster Keaton, domestics still perform their tasks behind closed doors. Thus they remain completely hidden from their masters' gaze. Their activities are transposed into the black box beyond the service door—just as in the case of Thomas Jefferson's Monticello estate.

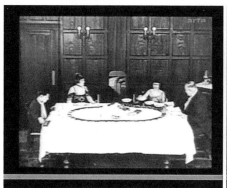

Figure 14. Buster Keaton, The Electric House, 1922

World War II launches a new stage of automatization. The black box named service is reduced to the space of the kitchen and now appears to be even less accessible than before. As instruments get smaller, finding out what happens behind the scenes becomes increasingly more difficult. The service functions are now contained within a whole range of tools. Each one of them follows the specifications of a preestablished operational program, with limited possibilities of intervention on the part of the users. From the 1950s onward one can no longer send burned toast back to the kitchen. The electric toaster requires specific service. Monsieur Hulot, the protagonist of Jacques Tati's satirical parable on modernization *Mon oncle* (1958), is confronted with a mechanism that holds quite a few surprises in store for him. The domestic mode of interaction is now restricted to the pair man–machine. With the advance of technology, the domestic individual is removed from the service domain and replaced by mechanized, preset procedures. Service appliances now have built-in programs of operation which seem rather foreign to Monsieur Hulot—to put it mildly. Nevertheless, while it may at first appear to be insurmountable, the distance between instructions of use and conscientious users is ultimately not that drastic.

But the trend persists. With the launch of Hasso Gehrmann's Elektra Technovision in 1969, the public can not only admire "the world's first fully automated kitchen," which, according to its designer, "imagines yesterday for the day after tomorrow."[142] That same year a large U.S. retail chain attempts to bring yet another innovation closer to hearth and home, not unlike the Lazy Susan from the past. Electrical appliances can be found everywhere around the house. It is now time to bring electronics to the kitchen. The 1969 Neiman Marcus catalogue presents its first Kitchen Computer: a hybrid between an over-the-top chopping board and a miniature recipe drawer for no less than $10,600 (the equivalent of $60,000 today). The text that accompanies the ad reads, "Then by simply pushing a few buttons [the housewife is able to] obtain a complete menu organized around the entrée." Included in the price is a two-week programing course for the lady of the house. Whether because of the cost or the lack of perceived advantages over the relative simplicity of the recipe book medium: the fact remains that the product did not find a single buyer.

Since then electronic appliances have become a commonplace addition to the kitchen. Each programmable microwave is also a microcomputer. It is only a matter of time until the average Madame and Monsieur Hulot of today start discussing the advantages of a fridge with an integrated TV screen or iPod adapter. In any case, tomorrow's kitchen infrastructure is already in place. The next step after the establishing of electronic connections is network building, even if, according to the latest studies, one does not use one's kitchen for cooking all that often nowadays. Coffee is increasingly becoming one of the few items prepared in the fully automated, fully supplied modern kitchen. But in that respect, at least, everything is provided, even when the occupants are not at home. Since April 1 [!], 1998, one can employ the "hypertext coffee pot control protocol" (htcpcp)—a service based on the "hypertext transfer protocol" (http)—in order to remote-control one's coffee machine, the automatic steward of wakefulness.[143] Without the intervention of human service personnel and with no ceremony, a single command, such as *coffee://www.cl.cam.ac.uk /pot-0?start&milk-type=Whole-milk,* will launch the protocol for a cup of freshly brewed coffee. With milk.

Part Three *Diener,* **Digital**

Chapter 7 Agents:
The Lord of (the) Things

Consider things, and you will have humans. Consider humans, and you are
by that very act interested in things. Bring your attention to bear on hard
things, and see them become gentle, soft or human. Turn your attention
to humans, and see them become electric circuits, automatic gears or
softwares.
—Bruno Latour, *The Berlin Key*, 1996

Where can underlings be found in the twentieth century? Where
should one look for subalterns: in literature, in the eyes of Hermann Lenz's
fictional servant Anton Wasik; or in history, in the words of Eugen Ketterl, the
last servant of his Apostolic Majesty, Emperor Franz Joseph? Such melancholy
farewells mark the double demise of domestics and European monarchies. Certainly, the bourgeois homeowners of the interwar period still employ maids;[1]
one can still see liveried porters standing at the entrance of grand hotels, patiently waiting for the arrival of guests; and a few high-end residential com-
plexes in New York still feature concierges sitting behind their desks.[2] Intent on
keeping the tradition alive, some private estates and the queen's royal household
still hire English butlers. Finally, there are migrants and refugees, employed in

private homes across the industrialized world. Clearly, the history of subaltern serviceability must update its traditional means of analysis and conventional sociological theories (keyword: exploitation).

However, a history of service that foregrounds media aspects and cultural techniques must pursue a different line of interpretation. Consequently, the next section will not follow the intricate paths of migration, down to dark storage rooms and broom closets; nor will it pin subaltern service to the "now-obsolete servant figure"[3] and thus make its end coincide with its human media. Instead, it will examine a further mutation: the transposition of various service functions into the virtual domain. The premise is that no later than the twentieth century the agency of the human servant has been delegated to technical media. The key witnesses in this vast process of transposition have already been introduced over the previous chapters: library assistants who merge the order of books and order of cities, resulting in the OPAC system; the messenger Michelmann, who vanishes down the telegraphic wires; the (silent) server at Gaston Menier's table, who becomes a train; or the *gentleman's personal gentleman* Jeeves, who reemerges as a search engine; and further, of course, the doorkeepers of the electronic domain, the authority figures that allow access to websites or data banks, the virtual palace guards that grant entry only upon an act of double confirmation: user name and password. All of these classic agents of subaltern serviceability, messengers and doorkeepers, servants and waiters have something in common: sooner or later their function is delegated to a universal authority, which seems to unite each and every service in the digital domain. But as opposed to the previous agents, the server is not made of flesh and blood: it consists of nothing but information. It is both a metaphor and a product of informatics.

This chapter inquires after the effects and consequences of the servant metaphor in the virtual domain. What genealogical lines does the server follow as a representative of electronic serviceability? How did this metaphor emerge? To answer these questions, we will refer to the history of a particular programing structure, the so-called client–server paradigm, born in Palo Alto, California, during the seventies. The programing structure in question breaks away from the mainframe-terminal tradition, still dominant until that point. The shift also raises important questions concerning the epistemology of servants, as it is reconfigured via the personal computer and the client–server information architecture. How far does this metaphor go? What is the role of metaphors and of programing, if we still speak—even in the electronic domain—of servants, demons, avatars, agents, 'clients,' and 'servers,' whose agency goes beyond simple metaphoricity? Where are the limits of the media-historiographic description of

such a (history of) metaphors? What are the epistemological and cultural implications of this terminology in the context of the long process of transformation
whereby *servants* become *servers?*

This informational paradigm shift raises, once again, questions about the
representation of power relations between master and servant. The translation
of classical service functions into software and program structures[4] also impacts
upon the agency of electronic 'things' and implicitly also on the relations between user and program or users and used objects, which are thereby ultimately
reconfigured.

7.1. FROM SERVANT TO SERVER

> The centers of calculation have become omnipotent.
> —Bruno Latour, "Why Angels Do Not Make Good Scientific
> Instruments," 1996

Kohlhaas's doorkeepers; Michelmann's last day of service; Waitwell's patient
stay; Jeeves's crafty service; the invisible activities of lab servants. All of the above
illustrate the same scenario: the protagonists initially belong to a broad category
that is eventually narrowed down to the professional label 'servant.' With the introduction of mechanized service, domestics are gradually replaced with media
like the Lazy Susan or other versions of the mute / dumb waiter. Simultaneously,
an alternate definition emerges, suggesting not just a shift in meaning but an
overall transformation of the cultural practice of service. A series of *Vanity Fair*
ads from 1917 praises "the cleverest waitress in the world" as a new instrument of
self-service. But it speaks not only of a "good servant" but also of a "server." And
this server is not limited to human media of serviceability, like waiters. Rather,
it announces that the reign of things has already long begun.

The traditional definition of a server refers to someone who performs a service for someone else. In this sense, it is different from the term "servant" only
in terms of its age and frequency of use. Between the fourteenth and the sixteenth centuries the two are used interchangeably. Apart from (a) a general term
for human subaltern, the other definitions in the *Oxford English Dictionary*
(OED) distinguish six different categories of usage referring to human media:
(b) someone serving guests at a meal (the term is still in use in English, as a
synonym for "waiter," for instance, on restaurant checks or on the menu: "Ask
your server."); further, (c) an artisan's assistant; or, (d) in Ireland, one who serves
a legal process. Not unlike the orders of angels from the writings of Dionysius
the Areopagite, servers are also inscribed in a sacred genealogy, even if they

occupy the lowest position in the hierarchy. Two levels of meaning indicate that context: (e) one who is engaged in a religious quest; a worshiper, and (f) an "assistant at Mass who arranges the altar and makes the responses."[5] As these last two definitions clearly demonstrate, the server is an entity wired into holy channels. Akin to messengers, servers occupy a mediating role between immanence and transcendence. Along the lines of Michel Serres's quasi-objects, they are the ones who initiate actions and thereby unite the acts of assignation, transmission, and communication into a vast network.

Apart from the definitions above, there are four additional references to nonhuman media. A server, in this sense, is something which serves or is used for serving. Just as angels and ecclesiastical assistants are the elements of a divine communication system, a server stands for (a) a conduit or pipe for conveying something, for instance, a liquid. The term can also refer to kitchen or eating utensils that can also be found in the context of the dumbwaiter: (b) a (silver) platter, like the Lazy Susan, and (c) the silverware for serving salad. And finally, as the additional entry in the online version of the OED from 1993 indicates, the term also designates an actor in the world of computing or, more specifically, in a network: "Any program which manages shared access to a centralized resource or service; an often (dedicated) device in which such a program is run."[6]

The OED entry seems to be a modest addendum to a lengthy historical account. In fact, it represents no less than the radical recoding of all services in the era of computers and networking peripherals. The messenger vanishes down the electronic communication channels and the library attendant has been replaced by OPAC; search engines no longer rely on human servants; the closest collaborator of a scientist is not an amanuensis but a compact universal processor. Despite their exemplary character, all these acts of substitution may be part of the process as a whole but are too narrow to represent a global, but also fundamental, act of displacement: the basis of communication practices nowadays is the server, the nodal point of networks, the switchboard of information, and pillar of our (electronic) mode of interaction. That term obviously does not designate a waiter or an ecclesiastical assistant. The responsibility of global communication lies on the shoulders of those hidden helpers, the vast numbers of internet and computer servers.

The diversity of servers corresponds to the finely differentiated staff of a typical bourgeois mansion in the heyday of domestic serviceability. Around the 1980s at the latest, the arrival of global computer networks coincides with the emergence of various agents which offer users their local or worldwide services. Starting out as file servers, they provide several local network users with a broad range of data via a large external hard drive. The process already involves a complex system of specialization and division of labor. "A file server is not only an important component for supporting processing performed on the work stations; it also provides a basis for building other types of servers needed in such an environment, for example, a printer server or a name server."[7]

Further developing the principle of the file server, there are two other specialized service agencies available. Database servers allow a user community spread across the network to perform highly selective data requests; printer servers give small (office) work groups access to a central printer. The mid-eighties witness the development of time servers in the context of the so-called network time protocol (NTP). These allow internet users—at that point still mainly limited to the academic environment—to access the globally synchronized times with a precision of less than a nanosecond.[8] The first domain name servers (DNS) appear around the same time. Their function is to provide an increasingly large community of internet users with a memory aid and help them avoid complicated numeric model addresses such as 82. 98. 86. 179 and use actual text instead: www.zweitgeist.de. The beginnings of DNS go back to an idea of Paul Mockapetris's from 1983, who names the system—not accidentally—Jeeves, before it is then later changed into BIND (standing for the Berkeley Internet Name Domain).[9] The literary Jeeves seems to have an ambiguous hold on internet creators, who make him the godfather of their projects. It may well be that the masters (Barry Diller, Paul Mockapetris), not unlike Bertie Wooster, are at times instructed by their assistants: "You can't be a serf to your valet."[10]

Just like Wodehouse's Jeeves guarding access to his master, there is a whole army of digital doorkeepers patiently and continuously watching over the internet (unless they are on strike).[11] Bruno Latour's figure of the nonhuman lock may serve here as a perfect analogy. Electronic agents such as the Kerberos server control the users' privileges when they show up at the virtual gate requesting access[12] to the inside (of power); access may, of course, be granted or denied, as in the case of Michael Kohlhaas and his attempt to enter the private room of the emperor.

Nevertheless, even if one doorkeeper allows access across the virtual threshold, there often are other servers at work as well: web servers, or—should the context be real rather than virtual—multimedia, fridge, garage, or simply house servers. All of them lead their guest, not unlike an electronic majordomo, through the stately rooms.[13] Consider Bill Gates's *smart house,* where almost everything is electronically controlled, from the garage door to the fridge that boasts its own network access and sends notification about the expiry date of products or automatically reorders food items when the stock runs low. But Gates's magical home is no longer unique in this regard. The basis of daily communication and the services it involves, be it online or in various private or public spaces, is none other than the server.

But what exactly is a server, beyond brief dictionary entries such as "server [literally: 'servant'; vs. 'client']"?[14] What does it stand for in the domain of informatics? The brief definition below fits quite well with its simple vocabulary and lack of the historical focus of discourses in computer science: "The server is a subsystem that provides a particular type of service to an a priori unknown client."[15] By definition, then, the subservient domestic (as the term "subsystem" suggests) does not provide personal services in this case. Instead, its work is dedicated to unknown customers, who do not reveal their true identity. The service provided is also not performed by a single agent; rather, it must traverse a multiple contact zone between servant and several masters, or users. The tasks comprise a full range of acts of representation: the web server, with its colorful homepage, acting not unlike a richly liveried lackey as the *carte de visite* or logo of its master; or the databank servers, and the intensive work of search and selection, that is to say, the informational labor of search engines. Consider the case of AskJeeves.com or of the well-read and knowledgeable Reginald Jeeves himself, who is never at a loss for answers:[16]

> The server is the process, or a set of processes all of which must exist on one machine which provides a service to one or more clients. It has the following characteristics:
> [A]. A server provides a service to the client. [. . .] A service provided by server may require minimal server-based computation (e.g. print servers or file servers) to intensive computations (e.g. database servers or image-processing servers).
> [B]. A server merely responds to the queries or commands from the clients. Thus, the server does not initiate a conversation with any client. It merely acts either as a repository of data (e.g. file server) or knowledge (e.g. database server) or as a service provider (e.g. print server).[17]

Not unlike typical domestics, who must refrain from taking the initiative, acting out of their own accord, or initiating conversations, the server obediently reacts to a request or diligently follows the command it has received. The 'knowledge' of a website is not transferred to the user without the latter's specific request.

> [C]. An ideal server hides the entire composite client-server system from the client and the user. A client communicating with a server should be completely unaware of the server platform (hardware and software), as well as the communication technology (hardware and software). [. . .] It is advisable and desirable that in a multi server environment, the servers communicate with one another

to provide service to the client without its knowledge of the existence of multiple servers or intra-server communication. Thus, in such a distributed processing environment, the client should be unaware of the locale of one or more servers servicing the client query or command.[18]

Traditionally, the master strictly communicates with the highest ranked among his servants: his butler, his valet, or majordomo. Meanwhile, the middle and lower ranks are completely unknown to him, since they operate in secret. Similarly, the operation of the tasks divided among various servers remains hidden from the gaze of the users. Just like its historical forerunners, the server is a professionally invisible entity. The user does not have to deal with the hardware (whether an old lid fits a new pot) or with the software (the distribution of the wages). In an environment such as this, based on the clear division of labor, everything is set up so that the one in command is constantly oblivious of which servant is in charge of what. What matters is merely that the highest ranked among them announces at some point the completion of the task. It is hardly worth mentioning that the electronic servers, not unlike their human models, are always ready to serve. "Logically, servers are structured as an infinite loop. The server simply receives requests from clients to invoke operations on behalf of transactions."[19] The endless loop of domestic service is never interrupted; the server attends to its work 24/7, without a single break. Only a system crash can bring it down. The instance of recursion, already implicit in the status of the digital server and its constant readjustments, must also be mentioned in this context: "In a-> WAN [Wide Area Network] or a bundle of WANs, as in the case of-> the Internet, s[ervers] can also perform tasks: the transmission of-> e-mails, the-> downloading of-> files and the search through-> data banks. [. . .] Most server programs are also client programs."[20] In other words, servers are not merely messengers or password-protected storage devices and search engines but several things at once or even all in one. For a server can accommodate several other virtual servers. Recursion knows no limits, especially in the context of worldwide networks.

Furthermore, following the dialectic of power and the basic relationality of master–servant relations, servers can also function as clients. "Servers can, in turn, be clients of other servers."[21] No master without servants, no server without clients and vice versa. And, finally, servers also make room for all sorts of other ministering spirits in the electronic domain. The endless corridors (the data cables) and the hidden cabinets (the dark entrails of computers) are, not accidentally, also spaces populated by demons. Just recall the ministering household spirits and the scientific demons, that is to say, the lab servants invoked in previous chapters. Here, however, in the electronic domain, those ministering spirits run down the corridors of power at the speed of light and operate behind the closed doors of storage devices to the high frequency beat imposed by the sovereign, the central processing unit, on its subalterns.[22] Maxwell's notorious demon is directly invoked in the jargon of informatics as a technical term for system processes that constantly run in the background. 'Observant' and imperceptible, demons provide help for the main actors of the system. Fernando J. Corbato first used the term in this context at MIT in 1963, working together with his team on the second-generation mainframe computer IBM 7094. As he recalls, "We fancifully began to use the word 'daemon' to describe background processes which worked tirelessly to perform system chores."[23] As threshold spirits and digital subalterns, both MAILER-DAEMONS and the inconspicuous digital doorkeepers in charge of checking access privileges continue to perform their service, in a tireless and uninterrupted fashion.

7.2. PARADIGM SWITCH: FROM MAINFRAME TO PC

> Digital computers give promise of serving mankind as no other machine and no animal has ever done.
> —M. V. Mathews, *Choosing a Scientific Computer for Service*, 1968

As shown in the first chapter, despite sociotechnical standards such as hierarchies and social ranks, the fundamental relation between master and servant is for the most part a dynamic affair: it is redefined and renegotiated at every step of the way. This may also hold true for the link between humans and machines. Under the conditions of digitalization, when basic services have been delegated to electronic agents, it is not enough to examine the interface between users and their hidden assistants or to look at the symbols displayed on a screen (a recycle bin icon, for instance). Rather, one has to go much further: the goal is to look behind the scenes with the support of a historically informed perspective, in order to determine how the structures operate beyond the threshold of the visible. Concretely speaking, the investigation concerns the results of the interaction between humans and machines: the constellations of orders and answers, command and reaction at the level of the key system principles, the software paradigms, and their mode of construction. Therefore, the analysis extends beyond the daily operations of users, to target the very act of programing and the processes of conceptual development.

The relation between master and servant in the digital domain is—as in real life, one could almost say—essentially determined by two key moments: on the one hand, the modalities of communication and, on the other, the interaction among actors. The bond between sovereign and valet, gentleman and domestic may seem banal in 'real life,' but that is not the case for the early history of the computer. In the epoch before the personal computer, in the era of the so-called mainframes (1939–81), therefore of the mainframe as large as a sports hall and with names such as NEAC 2203, PHILCO 212, or IBM 7030 "Stretch,"[24] one can definitely not speak of a symmetrical, partner-like relation of communication between user and machine. The search units do not yet work with those elements that characterize an equal communication partner, meaning a differentiated sensorium, which can enable it to react almost instantly to the input of the user. For the most part, they function without screens, graphic and audio interface. The information is entered via punch cards, piles of punch cards or bulky keyboards, and the results consist of long stretches of continuous paper. The second generation of mainframes (1956–63) does not yet operate in real time, time-sharing or networking. In the spacious, air-conditioned halls only isolated machines can be heard humming, no mice and no men. And even the interaction between the protagonists is, despite the increasingly high pulse frequencies, rather feeble, static, and marked by long interruptions. A typical encounter between user and machine looks like this: "You formulate your problem today. Tomorrow you spend with the programmer. Next week the computer devotes five minutes to assembling your program and 47 seconds to calculating the answer to your problem. You get a sheet of paper 20 feet long, full of numbers that, instead of providing the final solution, only suggest a tactic that should be explored by simulation."[25] Handling these calculators, called mainframes due to the circuits of transistors mounted on metal frames the size of gymnastic apparatuses, is not only time consuming. Spatially, too, there are multiple stages with equally numerous heterogeneous actors in the work process. In ANT terminology, one could speak of an actor-network made up of human and nonhuman beings, which has so many elements that there can be no direct interaction between user and computer. Each of these high-caliber machines is a monad, closed within itself, and has limited channels to the outside. In the age before large computer networks, the mainframe calculator is made up of a self-sufficient network: ideally, it does not get to be face to face with a user (the programmer) who executes its code. In fact, users are to be kept out of the reach of machines.[26] There is no interaction interface involved. The communication is mediated via piles of punch cards, where the program is encoded

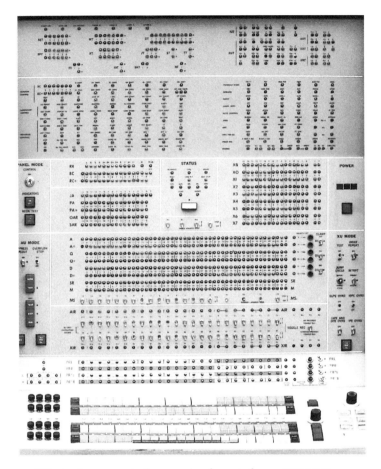

Figure 15. Windowless monad: the console of a mainframe, PHILCO 212

without any possibility of error correction or feedback from the machine. The cards are then handed to the operator via a small valve-like window (allowing the temperature to remain constant in the halls). The operator usually stands in front of a so-called console which has no screen but switches and blinking lights instead, which control every register of the CPU.

The task of the operator is to transfer the punch cards onto magnetic tape, put them in sequence, and change those tapes occasionally, in order to feed the machine new information in this manner. This form of procession is incapable of making any leaps forward. It is strictly sequential and is only gradually replaced in the sixties by rotating magnetic disks and therefore by the principle of the hard drive. Only in this manner is it possible to access the data almost in real time and to facilitate interaction, by breaking the linear chain of events by means of random access interventions into the various databases of the storage medium. In order to transfer the results of the calculations, databases, and entire programs from one machine to another, tried and true techniques from the age of stagecoach mail delivery are used: the monads are connected via special data couriers, that is, human messengers, which take the magnetic disks or the piles of punch cards—via car or plane—to their destinations.[27] In short, the computer is not yet a medium of communication, let alone a partner in communication. Its capacity for interaction and user dialogue is mediated via multiple relay stations; the medium is slow and limited; there is no screen, just rows of signs on continuous paper. It is almost as if the servant in charge of cutting the royal bread requests an audience with the emperor but is stuck from the start in the Imperial Guard Room. Only with the third generation of mainframes (1964–81)—which does away with the operators, that is to say, the human assistants of the machine, and reassigns their functions to the electronic authority in the operating system—does time-sharing and an increasing connectivity among large calculators shorten the communication paths. Man and machine meet in the interface, to finally be linked via the optical channel of the screen.

The mainframe's often fickle operation involves a lot of effort and multiple actors. In the process, all personnel are slavishly subjected to its interests—turning them into its 'royal' court. Against this background, Joseph Carl Robnett Licklider develops, starting in 1960 with a series of pathbreaking texts, a new concept according to which man and machine should interact in the future. These essays, starting with "Man–Computer Symbiosis" (1960), continuing with "Libraries of the Future" and "Man–Computer Partnership" (both in 1965), and up to "The Computer as a Communication Device" (1968, with the collaboration of Robert W. Taylor), have a visionary character. Licklider's ideas about overcoming the absolutist rule of the mainframe contain accurate and far-reaching predictions. They are the founding documents for the personal computer and are therefore profusely discussed.[28] To go back, then, to the question: how are the traditional services of subalterns retrieved in the digital domain? Licklider's ideas are at the forefront of what is a vast, still thriving field called Human–Computer Interaction (HCI). The following section will focus on three aspects of his program.

The first is the concept of time-sharing, an idea that enables the distinction between second- and third-generation mainframes. Licklider stresses it as a promising innovation in his plea for user–computer interaction: "Any present-day large-scale computer is too fast and too costly for real-time cooperative thinking with one man. Clearly, for the sake of efficiency and economy, the computer must divide its time among many users."[29] Normally, the machine works in strict sequential order, one problem at a time, and remains inactive between the inputs—especially when the user looks for errors in the program. To make a long story short: the time-sharing concept does not offer merely the advantage of cost reduction and a more efficient calculating capacity;[30] beyond that, it also introduces two important elements: for one, the human–machine interaction is facilitated via new input instruments (terminals): modified typewriters, subsequently connected to a screen. Now, programmers have direct access to the computation results and improve their error-detection efforts.[31] Second, a mainframe-oriented user network is almost automatically established; its subjects are simultaneously connected with each other wherever they are, one floor up or hundreds of kilometers away. At their center, the machine presides like a great lord, a *host*.

The second aspect implicit in Licklider's argument for equal communication between user and computer could be described as the state form of the (calculating) machine. First-generation mainframe processing[32]—also known as a "calculating plant" due to its linear, assembly-line feel—could be understood in terms of the political metaphor of a feudal society. "Computer time is so valuable that it must not be wasted. There must always be input data and programs for the computer to devour. To supply them, there must be a constant procession of human servants bearing code sheets, punch cards and magnetic tape."[33] In an endless procession, servants attend to the machine, carrying punch cards and feeding it data, not unlike the underlings at the Viennese court bringing in dishes on silver trays. One by one, the vassals carry tribute to the ruler, who, in turn, knows how to make use of their service. The subjects are richly rewarded for their efforts with gifts of punched tape. Within the feudal system of large-scale computers, every human is a serf or a slave of the machine. Following the same political logic, second-generation mainframes, with time-sharing and interconnected terminals featuring bidirectional communication channels with the central unit, could also be framed in terms of the enlightened absolutist state and its court. At their respective terminals, the subalterns are located within a certain distance from the sovereign and have specific access rights, each according to its rank. In turn, their great host attends to and provides for them.[34] But, once again, the personnel—the operators, be it the programmers or the end users—are there only to serve the machine. Licklider makes this very clear: " 'Mechanical extension' has given way to the replacement of men, to automation, and the men who remain are there more to help than to be helped."[35] The notion of a symbiotic connection between user and computer which Licklider offers against the reign of the absolutistic machine follows the course of a revolutionary program of democratization. Ultimately, that process would lead to an equal partnership among actors, helping them move to the same level.

Finally, the third aspect concerns the design and the effects of a scheme whereby such a partnership may be constructed. In an article from 1968, under the title "On-line interactive communities," Licklider and Bob Taylor envision a "labile network of networks—ever changing in both content and configuration."[36] At the nodal points of this network of networks one can no longer find human agents along with their punch cards. The task is now delegated to those autonomous agencies that can wait even more patiently since they are constantly 'online':

> A very important part of each man's interaction with his online community will be mediated by his OLIVER. The acronym OLIVER honors Oliver Selfridge, originator of the concept. An OLIVER is, or will be when there is one, an "on-line interactive vicarious expediter and responder," a complex of computer programs and data that resides within the network and *acts on behalf* of its principal, taking care of many minor matters that do not require his personal attention and buffering him from the demanding world. "You are describing a secretary," you will say. But no! Secretaries will have OLIVERS.[37]

Within this constellation which Licklider and Taylor imagine as the means of overcoming the mainframe era, the power relations have drastically changed. The human being is again the 'principal,' the commander and master of his relations of communication. He may act like a king since he is assisted by a collective of electronic helpers. It is for the most part the interactive online-surrogate of the user who carries out tasks and answers queries. Thus he becomes his personal digital domestic, performing all the assignments of "informational housekeeping"[38] and finally meets the user at eye level, like Lessing's Waitwell with respect to Sir William. In the age of large-scale calculators, being 'online' is something the programmer does, spending his sleepless nights at the console, when no one is using the inactive machine to develop his programs together with the machine via punch cards and operators.[39] But according to the authors, this kind of night shift will come to an end and make room for full-time programs that take care of the important and unimportant electronic matters on their own and can no longer tell the difference between day and night. Only months after the publication of the article, its coauthor, Bob Taylor, receives the unexpected opportunity that leads, after 1970, to putting his vision of a personal computer into practice.

No institution that has ever played a leading role in the development of calculators in the second half of the twentieth century has a higher reputation than Xerox PARC. Not Bill Gates's garage, where things were not so much invented as recreated. Not even what came after the hand-built Apple I. Nor can IBM keep up with what was developed starting in 1970 at 3333 Coyote Hill Road. The group of highly talented and obstinate young computer specialists working at that address, in a flat, futuristic building complex in Palo Alto, boast an impressive list of achievements, often in the form of prototypes which have made several companies a lot of money. Among them are the laser printer (1971), object-oriented programming (1972), a personal workstation named Alto and the Ethernet (1973), the WYSIWYG principle (1974), the graphical user interface (GUI, 1975), the first net-replicated computer virus (1978), elaborate computer languages such as Smalltalk-80 (1978) or the Unicode standard (1987).

The Palo Alto Research Center (PARC) is launched at the initiative of the Xerox Company against the background of increasing concerns over expiring photocopier patents and, implicitly, the risk of technological stagnation. Under these conditions, PARC is founded with no immediate goal in mind other than the rather vague promise "to control 'the architecture of information'" by planning no less than "the office of the future."[40] To the dismay of Xerox executives in 1972,[41] *Rolling Stone* magazine would describe, in a notorious article, the team of researchers as a group of computer bums. Among them, the uncontested authority—although by no means part of the leading staff—is Bob Taylor. Due to his previous position at the Advanced Research Projects Agency (ARPA), where he had successfully linked several large-scale computers into what would become the foundation of the internet, Taylor manages to gather around himself a promising group of gifted researchers to work on his projected interactive, personal computer. The agenda that lists the achievements of the PARC team proudly mentions, under the year 1973, "Alto personal computer becomes operational" and "Personal distributed computing is invented." But between these two milestones is yet another modest paragraph that turns out to be of major importance for the history of electronic service: "Client/server architecture is invented. This development makes the paradigm shift of moving the computer industry away from the hierarchical world of centralized mainframes—that download to dumb terminals—toward more distributed access to information resources."[42] The lines above and the contexts to which they allude call for a systematic approach. To follow the model of Michael Kohlhaas's courtly itinerary, what is required here is a change of narratological perspective. Since PARC also holds the honor of introducing ethnography into the world of computer sciences,[43] the next section will draw on this very genre. The following pages may therefore be read as a field research enterprise, grounded in an embedded homodiegetic narrative with a clear internal focus.

Imagine it's the twenty-first century. You are on a research trip in search of the origins of electronic servants. You enter the address 3333 Coyote Hill Rd,

Palo Alto, and an expert 'TomTom generation' digital assistant directs you past the vast Stanford University campus toward the green hills of Silicon Valley. Once you leave the university annexes and startup headquarters behind, there are fewer buildings along the way; the factories make room for sweeping pastures. No coyotes in sight; instead, every once in a while, a cow. But your Californian spring idyll comes to a sudden end with the nonchalant announcement of a computer-generated voice: "You have reached your destination." There is nothing around but grass, paddocks, and cows. No building and no sign of a research institute. The scene resembles an English pleasure garden. There is no trace of a place called PARC that has facilitated the invention that has led you there, the chatty digital machine in whose navigational skills you have put your trust. Someone, somewhere must have made an error.

The scene above can serve as a perfect illustration of my own research quest. The events that led me to this nonplace, which is supposed to be my destination, started approximately half a year ago. The visit was preceded by methodical, then increasingly mad, prep work. In good Old European tradition, my first call went out to the lowest links in the chain, the palace guards, with the request to pass on my message to the higher authorities. But my email of December 1, 2008, addressed to the virtual gatekeepers of the institution (read: the anonymous address info@parc.com) in the hope of visiting the center's archive, went unanswered. I resent my message a week later. They must be busy with Christmas preparations, I thought. Still, no auto-reply, no rejection, just no answer. Is any human being at the other end of the channel, reading my note? Or is it just a server, configured to delay answers by months? Or, worse still, is the server programmed in a way that leaves some requests untouched or treated with cool indifference? In that case, an email address that ends in harvard.edu may be futile after all. A few weeks later I made a further attempt, which was finally answered, after a long delay, by the janitor. She has acquired a name in the meantime: Mimi G. Mimi sends me, along with a vague apology and no further explanation, a document describing the technical configuration of the Alto computer but with no reference to my research question or my expressed wish to search for the traces of the client–server relation in the archive of the center. When the palace guards deny entry, a possible solution may be to contact a courtier instead. In this case: to get in touch with former and current coworkers, who may have direct access to the archive and to the history of PARC. A second wave of emails follows the first. Now the messages are sent to seven different courtiers, each with a different rank. As expected, some of them remain silent; others send some vague suggestions but no key, no relevant information or helpful contacts, let alone an offer to enter the vault of knowledge.

Unimpressed, I buy a ticket to San Francisco. Why should it be so difficult to get any helpful advice or a definite answer? Why so many delays? There must be systemic issues involved.

In a place that has 'invented' servers, treating them as outsourced domestics which allow humans to interact with machines, it may well be that these are precisely the actors responsible for the lack of answers, denying an answer—possibly because they are overbooked or simply because they choose to spend their idle time, their moments of electronic inactivity, doing something else. But there may be other, more serious and concrete reasons for this affair. The historiography of computer science is quite complicated. Apart from the personal memories of one or the other scientists, the projects undertaken over time have been poorly documented and are therefore hard to reconstruct. On the one hand, that is because they take place in a fleeting storage medium, the Random Access Memory, that is quickly overwritten. On the other hand, because the individual stages of the projects have been written in the old tradition of mathematical notation. That is to say, the writing media 'blackboard' and 'chalk,' which can no longer be reconstructed in the paperless office of the future.

The rest of those who have been questioned remain silent, since they no longer possess the material that provided answers.

And if the curious researcher is not allowed to enter despite all his tricks, there is one last option, the *ultima ratio*: seeking an audience with the king. The (unannointed) king is, in this case, named Alan Kay (b. 1940), l'enfant terrible of informatics, organist, inventor of object-oriented programming, visionary of the Notebook (whose basic principles he already defined in 1969 in his dissertation under the name Dynabook), one of the main inventors of the WYSIWYG principle and of the graphic user interface of the Alto computer.[44] After a few inquiries in the antechambers of power, I receive the email I expected from his secretary, whose OLIVER (P.C.) retrieves his address. A miracle happens: The king replies right away and in full detail. My long catalogue of questions is thoroughly answered for once. For instance, that he, as the project leader of the Learning Research Group, has written memos at regular intervals which document the state of development of the project. There is a paper trail, in other words. He also mentions that the term "server" was used by him and his colleagues in their preliminary work as a *terminus technicus* for the ministering spirits that carry electronic data on hard disks (file servers); or function as printing assistants (printing servers).[45] Kay could not recall when or if the term "client" came to be used.[46]

My planned California trip was drawing close, and I still had not gathered sufficient information about the potential of being admitted at court (into the archive). Time to launch another contact-attack. But for that I needed to undertake a certain media switch: from email to telephone and the promise of direct contact. Several calls and full run-throughs of PARC wait time melody later, I was put through to Kathy J., PARC's head librarian. She seemed quite familiar with my plans. Which is not surprising, since she is one of those who had presumably received my messages yet had not replied. The chat offered yet another surprise. I replied that the comments of Mark Stefik,[47] who had worked at PARC for three years, might suggest the existence of archive material. She hesitatingly responded there may be something, but the access is very strictly regulated and not open to the public. She was also struggling, she said, to get a thirty-year-old document released for the planned 2010 jubilee. The request had been lying on the desk of one or the other higher official who was refusing to answer. Both the procrastination and the restrictive access have their historical reasons: a professional paranoia of being spied upon. Like so many others before him, a certain Steve Jobs visits the center in December 1979 together with a delegation of Apple Inc. software engineers. But, as opposed to all the other, all too many, visits that had led PARC to impose a quota, this one proves to be quite productive, yet not in the interest of the center. For Jobs and his developers, Adele Goldberg's demonstration of the small, talk-operated graphic user application is an outright epiphany, a revelation of all the tricks, possibilities, and solutions his own products were still missing. Not accidentally, many of the advantages of Alto and its software can be found in Apple's own Lisa and then the first Macintosh.[48] This obvious case of plagiarism had deeply affected PARC and had led to the restrictive archive politics. And that is the reason why to this day visitors are personally shown out by their hosts when they leave. Since the archive visit did not promise much, it was only fitting that I should follow up on my telematic audience with the king with a request to contact the queen: Adele Goldberg, together with Kay, the driving force behind the development of Smalltalk, of the PARC Learning Research Group. After I asked my question about the development of the client–server paradigm, she said, "Markus, I think someone has seriously misled you." Obviously, otherwise I would not be standing here in a meadow, looking at cows. "I do not believe that 'client–server' architecture was invented or even first named at Xerox PARC."[49] It was not the GPS navigation system that had made an error, but PARC's own website with the proudly displayed list of achievements.

Despite the royal verdict, the PARC visit had led to a treasure trove of insights—and against all expectations also to some archival material. Due to the information I obtained in the process, I could now finally accurately reconstruct the history of the client–server concept. The most important discovery was that, despite the firm's claims, PARC did in fact not contribute to the specific development of the client–server architecture and did not introduce or put the term into circulation. The clue on their website was simply misleading. So, with what right does the center claim to have invented the concept? Against the background of further work on the Alto, the term "server" comes to be increasingly used at PARC, especially for those aspects of the project which link the computer to a local network—the origin of the Ethernet.[50] But clients do not come up in the discussions, which is not surprising: after all, none of the many prototypes and projects developed there has been turned into a product which would be profitable for the mother company Xerox. There had been many visitors at the Coyote Hill address; but clients in the strict sense of the word, none. It is in fact observers—like Steve Jobs—who would transform what they had seen into marketable products. Xerox PARC, the development forger, serves, in its turn, a half-anonymous crowd of visitors as model and pathfinder of knowledge.

The habitat called PARC, with its 'computer bums' and bean bags,[51] is itself a server, continuously feeding others with ideas. And this is the context of the emergence of the concept of the inconspicuous electronic helpers *cum* communication partners. In 1976 the term "server" appears in a prominent context for the further history of computers: namely, in that influential article in which Bob Metcalfe and David Boggs describe their network installation, to link hundreds of Altos together into a communication system called Ethernet: "A connection is said to have a listener and an initiator and a service is said to have a server and a user. It is very useful to treat these as orthogonal descriptors of the participants in a communication. Of course, the server is usually a listener and the source of the data-bearing packets is usually the sender."[52] In other words, once the communication channel has been established, various services are launched to enable the distinction between the eavesdropping servant and the actual beneficiary of the service. The access to language within this network context is provided by the mathematical theory of *queuing systems.* After a few strictly technical detours, the structure reaches, via the ARPANET,[53] the level of the Ethernet, the technical basis of our current internet.

So even if the term is not exactly a PARC creation, the center has definitely configured and helped define—via the Alto and all the peripheral devices, laser printers, and network drives—the notion of *distributed computing.*[54] Starting in the mid-seventies, PARC developed a specific technology, consisting of computers (the Alto devices) connected to various servers that functioned as outsourced service agencies. It is on this basis that, a few years later, the client–server paradigm emerged for the first time in the technical report of Israel, Mitchell, and

Sturgis (1979). In the PARC lab context there is no distinction between users and hardware, and software developers. The members of the center represent all positions at once. There are no external actors called clients in the strict sense of the word. Yet the PARC prototypes become export hits for other enterprises such as Apple, 3com, Microsoft, etc., which, in turn, manage to attract numerous customers for their operators and software. Only once products such as Macintosh, Ethernet, and Windows are ready to go on the market does a previously ominous character enter the scene: the user in its broadest sense, that is to say, the "customer or client":[55] in other words, the human end user, who may not necessarily be an expert but can, nevertheless, operate a computer. But this would amount to a highly asymmetrical relation between man and machine. An electronic proxy, a virtual representative of the customer, therefore comes to the aid of the end user. The symbiotic connection between actors begins with the virtual reproduction of the master–servant relation. The computer can operate only at the level of autonomy demanded by Licklider and Taylor for the OLIVER once it possesses those internal absolutist relations of power and feudal hierarchical structures known as standard cultural features.[56] For a human customer can interact symbiotically with a computer only when the former can delegate tasks to the latter, in short, when the machine can actually take over some of the customer's own work.

Around 1980, in the context of informatics, the term "client" emerges as the "counterpart" of the "(measuring) servant,"[57] or, the server.[58] What may at first appear as a highly prosaic designation has, in fact, a long prehistory behind it as well as a rich tradition of metaphoric use. Its meaning is actually excessive. In Roman antiquity, a client is a plebeian with a patrician patron. In exchange for a series of services, the patron protects the interests and the life of his client. The word is derived from the Latin *cliens* (a follower, one who stoops or bends).[59] In the Middle Ages the word designates someone who depends on a higher power, who freely follows and listens to a lord, either at the level of individual relations or with reference to state formations (client or vassal states, depending on a larger sphere of influence).[60] Beyond its legal and spiritual–ecclesiastical context, its modern use refers to a customer who requests certain services without the imposition of obedience.

Within the discourse of informatics, its meaning involves no less than the fundamental reconfiguration of man–machine power relations. The distributed computing architecture and the client–server model involve a paradigm shift—as Licklider had envisioned decades before. Now the client (end user) is served—as opposed to the mainframe era, when the user was subordinated to the machine as a mere supplier, humbly waiting for the meager output of his program listings. In the case of the personal computer, services multiply[61] and are distributed among various agents; the human end user acquires an electronic double, the virtual client. Not unlike a king, the human customer can now give commands and assignments using a natural language instead of machine code. The system then performs the operations on its own. Instead of being forced to feed punch cards into the machine, the customer now has a graphic interface at his service, where he can exert his authority. This is the platform where he reaches decisions, presses buttons, opens windows, and commands. But beyond that, whatever else happens behind the scene remains out of his reach or sight. Past the electronic green baize door,[62] on the other side of Jefferson's revolving serving door that connects the master's chambers and the service halls, a whole chain of action is launched, involving agents and middle-stations, clients and servers. Finally—mission accomplished—the result is then played back to the end user. Not unlike a paterfamilias, a lord of the mansion, the end user can indulge in the illusion that everyone and everything conforms to his command and that he reigns supreme over the entire system of heterogeneous actors. File-, print-, database-, name-, web-server, mail demons, and transfer agents quietly go about their tasks, linked into a local and simultaneously universal network. Even the time server seems to obey and submit to the user's configurations. The complex system of digital domestics—or, rather, everything the human agent is able to perceive—is a more or less well-designed user interface.

We will call such a composite system a Client–Server System, or simply CSS. In such a system, a Client is a process which interacts with the user and has the following characteristics:

[A] Typically, the Client presents a Graphical User Interface (GUI) to the user. [. . .]
[B] It forms one or more queries or commands in a predefined language for presentation to the Server. [. . .]
[C] It communicates to the Server via given interprocess communication methodology and transmits the queries or commands to the server. An ideal client completely hides the underlying communication methodology from the user.

Like a well-educated, but 'oddly' dressed butler, quietly going about his task in the background and delegating further assignments to the responsible actors, the CSS operates efficiently, autonomously and invisibly, without the lord or lady in the salon (=before the screen) taking notice.

[D] It performs data analysis on the query or command results sent from the server and subsequently presents them to the user. [. . .] The Client characteristics [B] and [D] set it apart from dumb terminals connected to a Host, since it possesses intelligence and processing capability.[63]

The client provides the machine with a specific form of autonomy. Instead of dumb terminals (or mute/dumb waiters) limited in their capability of action and fully dependent upon a host (à la Thomas Jefferson, perhaps), there are now intelligent and capable agents. In turn, these agents preside over a vast network of specialized underlings in order to process the desired information via the chain of operation. Gradually, the hosts and *dumb terminals* of the RFC 1[64] model give way to specialized *intelligent* actors.

The transition from human domestics to dumbwaiters and things in the nineteenth century goes hand in hand with a shift of agency from subjects to objects (Michelmann or the Lazy Susan can testify to that). Now, in the context of the client–server architecture and its development of intelligent, nonhuman creatures in the virtual domain, the subject–object difference undergoes a further modification. Via the characters created in the electronic domain, the formerly inanimate things (once more) achieve subject status. Like an ideal eighteenth-century servant, the digital domestics are paradoxically both invisible and present, dependent yet also, to a certain degree, autonomous and constantly available, always online.

The client–server formula does not appear in the early discussions surrounding the development of the Alto, the Ethernet, and distributed computing at the PARC until 1979. Nevertheless, all three partial projects lay the groundwork for it, especially since the services outsourced to external network actors are already known as servers. In that sense, the note on the PARC website is not necessarily misleading and actually holds some truth. But the concept of the client–server architecture reaches the market—in fits and starts—only after 1990, after a long period when it rarely comes into focus.[65] Its sudden and wide applicability is linked to the availability of affordable workstations, which are all connected to the internet. Simultaneously, increasing network access translates into a new software architecture to use this technical infrastructure.

The new paradigm linked with the client–server architecture is defined by cooperation and the distribution of tasks and data among the participating actors. At the same time, it is also characterized by its affordability, an important point for the IT divisions of entrepreneurs. Essentially, CSS is a "distribution model which defines the roles and the process of a collaboration of distributed software components. There are clients which request a certain service (requester) and there are servers which provide the service (providers),"[66] mediated by a so-called middleware.[67] More specifically, this is a matter of the "distribution of tasks,"[68] just as exists in a traditional household. Who would want to take care of everything around the house as a fine gentleman or lady? Even such a powerful man as, for instance, Thomas Jefferson cannot cater to his dinner guests alone. He requires an entire network made up of circulating doors, dumbwaiters, moveable tables as well as human beings such as cooks, maids, and footmen in the background. Instead of an end user and a computer performing the largest part of the activities, the tasks are delegated to others, but not without a massive external manifestation of competencies via the intelligence invested in the machine or the autonomy delegated to it. The first step is the creation of a new entity, the electronic alter ego of the end user, which undertakes, as the client, the direct communication between man and machine. This doubly abstracted I of the consumer not only assesses the communication capabilities at the interface level but also manages specific strategies of subjectification. Thereby, it selects the requests of the end user and sends them on to the inferior crowd of underlings that remain completely hidden in the background. An analogy can help clarify this chain of events. Whenever he has a request for his kitchen staff, the master of the house could choose to declare his request each time to the changing cooks. It would be easier, of course, to switch on a mediator which is always informed about the preferences of his master and knows how to choose them. Additionally, he may make his own suggestions and communicate not only with the cook but also with all the other subalterns. In short, the tasks assigned to an ideal butler are now recreated in the virtual domain. As soon as the client is enabled to act in its master's place in the virtual realm, the logic of work division is launched, and a new stage of delegation can begin. Clientage takes command. The electronic subject acts—like Licklider's OLIVER—as a powerful proxy of the user that requests information from other actors in its service. On the one hand, the client assigns the process and the processing of information to those subalterns. On the other hand, it carries the results to its master. In this sense, "the client-server concept is a logical (software) concept."[69] In other words, what is activated here is less a matter of technical infrastructure on a hardware basis than a specific social technique of domination and control.

The proxy of the master in the electronic domain is therefore not unlike the middle ranks at court, both master and servant at the same time. A client can also be subject to the principle of recursion[70] and can also function as the server of other actors (for instance, of his real master). Simultaneously, it can function as the client of other servers, which in turn, are the clients of other servers. . . . The client can obviously take into its service several servers. And conversely, just like Goldoni's Truffaldino, a server can have several masters at once. This distribution of the processing activity in the client–server systems goes hand in hand with a direct simplification of the development of programs: "So what happened is that programming has been simplified because you ripped a lot of your core functions out of the application and placed them on the server, where they can be called upon when needed."[71] Besides, the preferred programming language in which the client–server systems are built in the nineties is none other than the language developed by Alan Kay and Adele Goldberg called *Smalltalk*.[72] The client–server architecture increasingly gains attention after 1990 and is hailed as the 'next big thing' in information technology. Two consequences derive from this: both involve events that take place behind the scenes, in the opaque entrails of the computers, yet prove to be essentially relevant to the relation between man and machine. On the one hand, a new actor intervenes in the complicated interaction between human and nonhuman entities. Licklider's visionary idea of bringing the communication between man and machine to the same level and create a symbiotic relationship between the two actors finds its solution in the doubling of the end user in the virtual domain. The user acquires a digital proxy, a position occupied by the software agent also known as *client*. Not the human being but the client is now the master of all digital things. And like a distinguished butler, the client also has the exclusive right to communicate with the end user about the virtual help.

Not unlike Goldoni's Truffaldino, the client inhabits two interstitial surfaces, two interfaces. But in contrast to the eighteenth-century comedy, the client maintains its double position. On the one hand, it turns its graphically constructed, friendly user interface toward its real master, the user. On the other hand, it also oversees the technical interface of subaltern processes, where it curtly communicates with the servers under its command: "The clients of a file server can invoke and control the file service using a set of operations that form the client interface. This [server] interface is not meant to be used by people. The 'clients' are programs that in turn implement interfaces more suitable for higher-level applications or direct access by people."[73]

The clients are therefore electronic servants which, on the one hand, turn their human face, the user interface, toward their masters, and, on the other hand, communicate with the obedient servers in a strict tone of command. The electronic domain hosts a second level of authority, a new platform of power which comes to occupy a middle-ground position. This implies a completely new relationship between users and machines. What emerges here is a doubled, more complex media communication system in which the nonhuman entity is assigned a range of new capabilities, as Appleton, Cherenson, Kay, and Marion suggest: "The implementation of client server has added the name of complexity to their computing environments." In good old dialectical tradition, the virtual proxy of the master finds itself in a position of double dependency: the client depends on the server, since only the latter can perform the actual labor of calculation; simultaneously, the client also obeys its human end user whose

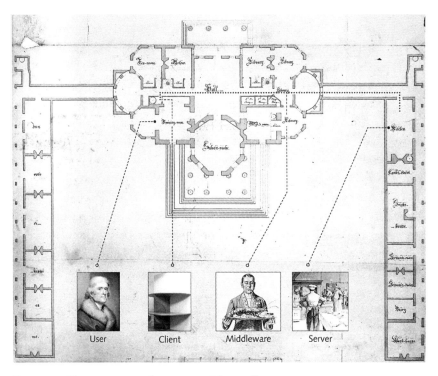

Figure 16. Client–server architecture at Monticello

User   Client   Middleware   Server

alter ego it is. The client therefore acts as an extension of man, the arm of the human user extending into the virtual domain. On the threshold of the invisible process of labor taking place behind the green baize door, it represents a controllable yet also independent agency.

The second consequence of the client–server architecture is that the client inserts a new media entity into the chain of human machine-communication. That entity functions according to the principle of in-betweenness that characterizes the tradition of service: the client acts as a mediator for the subject in the virtual domain. Its epistemic status is unclear: neither a full-fledged subject, since it merely stands in for its master, nor an object, since it is endowed with too much authority of its own. The client is both dependent and independent. Its ability to act as a mediator relies on the work supplied by the invisible workers, the servers. They are the ones quietly toiling in the background and carrying out most of the work as the actual movers of knowledge. But the client is also somehow independent from the end user. Even if it represents the interests of the master and acts in his name, the client has its own field of operation. In that sense, unlike a footman, the client is not the mirror image of the master but rather an enterprising actor. The empowered client establishes itself as a quasi-object in an ontological middle ground, from where the decisive operations of transmission, mediation of knowledge, and exchange of information are launched. Akin to Serres's quasi-object, the client intervenes at media technical level of the Ethernet. From here it leads the process whereby the network is further interconnected and transformed into a collective at the next level. The double nature of the two interfaces the client inhabits allows it to manage and regulate the process of communication from all directions, both of the human authorities and the nonhuman virtual servants.

Fully aware of how its achievements have influenced computer history, PARC still declares, via its list of milestones, that the client/server architecture has launched a real paradigm change by turning the computer industry from central mainframes and dumb terminals to distributed computing.[74] This paradigm change is of the utmost importance: it marks no less than the beginning of the era of electronic services. To use an analogy: after the French Revolution, the order of feudalism had reached its end. The serfs were replaced by subjects, who were free to enter professional relations of service of their own accord (consider the case of Lessing's Waitwell as an early prototype of this kind of emancipation). In a similar fashion, distributed computing overcomes, via a complex network structure and with the aid of the client/server architecture, the tyranny of mainframes and their 'dumbwaiters.'[75] Human beings had previously been able only to feed punch cards into large-scale computers and quietly and submissively work within a limited time frame and with a limited amount of data. This kind of relationship is now fully reversed, in the sense that the user moves into a position of authority and acquires a virtual counterpart in the electronic domain, the client. And this quasi-object represents the interests of the master. At the same time, it also controls the communication channels, by its ability to contact a digital Waitwell, a server that is available at all times, and receive, in turn, the desired information and services. Just like Hegel's bondsman, the end user thereby overcomes his subaltern status and delegates his own work via a graphical interface to various actors in the network. Obviously, from the point of view of the human user, the distribution of tasks and the reduced workload present financial benefits as well. The virtual counterpart of the user in the electronic domain not only obeys but also follows the practices of a capable client. The client/server architecture thus holds the key to an entire virtual economy.

The computer industry has finally found the key to unlock the potential of computers. Client–server computing will bring together everything that's been done in computing for the past twenty years and enable companies to achieve long-hoped-for productivity, efficiency, and business benefits.[76]

The renaming of *distributed computing* and its further development into the *client–server* principle and business model makes it clear: the choice is not random, as the acronyms and all other previous designations seem to suggest. Terms are always linked to a program and to a more or less explicit programmatic aim. Metaphors are not innocent. And therefore their usage and their epistemic implications need to be further explored.

7.3. THE METAPHORICS AND EPISTEMOLOGY OF THE SERVER

Both informatics and programming, as its constitutive activity, take place in a domain hidden from the gaze of the end user during his routine work. Only rarely do the internal operations of the machine become transparent. Its mode of operation is one of permanent invisibility, hidden from the user via pseudoinformative status notifications or progress alerts. Simultaneously, software products and the terminology of informatics are highly metaphorical. Metaphors are used to translate abstract modes of operation for the end user and software developer. As opposed to mathematics or any other science that operates abstractly, informatics draws its metaphors from everyday-life analogies, familiar processes, and objects. When bouquet graphs or seeds are invoked in mathematical language, the terms themselves cannot be immediately grasped. Such notions and figures cannot be linked back to routine expressions from everyday language and the practices associated with them. The back channel leading from theory to practice has not been set up in that case. Mathematical notations like rings are therefore contingent terms. They do not involve a transfer of surplus signification and do not function as metaphors connecting two different domains into one specific expression.

But in the case of computers, the metaphoric activity is not restricted merely to the level of the end user and software interface. The story does not end with pictograms of workstations, files, and folders or the virtual recycling bin. Code development, too, relies on a multitude of metaphors in order to illustrate and clarify concepts and exemplary solutions. The activity of software development, the programming process, would otherwise be difficult to grasp. This results in program languages like Smalltalk, clickable devices called mice, or terms like desktop for screen contents, and loops and arrows for data structures. The potential lack of clarity calls for the semantic translation of the relationship between actors in front and behind the screen. Thus the connection between them will be conceived in terms of political power constellations, like master and servant, but also slave and slave owner or secretary and boss. After the mainframe era, the computer becomes "a helpful other, addressed with various degrees of civility, as a partner, assistant, intellectual servant, handmaiden or underling."[77] But this logic does not merely correspond to the relationship between man and machine. In fact, it also applies to the internal structures of the apparatus, since, inevitably, the relations between the individual actors are ordered in a strict hierarchical fashion, whether with respect to the CPU at the periphery or within the file systems with their respective access privileges.[78]

The requirement of terminological assignation is therefore derived from the simple but inevitable necessity of elucidating that which cannot be otherwise grasped. "The purpose of selecting a term as an autonomous metaphor is to give a newly defined object a practical, positive or even noble connotation borrowed from a different domain that now serves as a sort of model."[79] Nevertheless, the question remains: how does a rhetorical figure like the metaphor specifically function in these contexts and, more important, what cognitive gains does it bring? What would be the advantage of considering the server not just a contingent assignation but rather a metaphor with epistemic surplus meaning?

Ever since Aristotle no figure of speech and thought has been discussed and examined as abundantly as the metaphor. An overview, however limited, would be impossible and lies outside the premise of this work.[80] Instead, only Max Black's interaction theory will be mentioned in this context: Black's theory allows for a clear understanding of the epistemic function of metaphors in the context of informatics. As opposed to the familiar theories—of substitution and comparison—of metaphors, Black's intervention highlights the question of meaning surplus, which would otherwise be hard to pin down in language. One of the conventional theories starts from the basic assumption that metaphors have a predominantly ornamental character, that they offer direct possibilities of substitution; accordingly, the current meaning of the word refers to the initial, now-obscured meaning. Yet another traditional theory suggests that the metaphor works by comparison to enable, via an analogy or simile, an extension of the field of meaning, without carrying new meaning on its own, however.[81]

Both metaphorology and the interaction theory turn against these claims. Their focus is on metaphors as "epistemic objects that resist closure."[82] Both theories argue that something new—akin to the hybrid in ANT—emerges from the interaction between two fields of meaning, in the play between the *verbum proprium* and the *immutatio* of a metaphor. In this sense, metaphors have always been linguistic processes with productive cognitive potential.

Instead of focusing on connotations which readers have to retranslate into original meanings—for instance, Kafka's castle, which usually means something else—the interaction theory of metaphor follows a different logic. Its method implies a link between two different domains which are brought together and in their interaction lead to something else, namely, a third element. Two perspectives cooperate with each other, sustained by a unique word or expression—for instance, "server"—whose significance represents the result of this interaction. The new term thus produced acquires an autonomous meaning, which can no longer be strictly defined by one or the other point of departure. In other words, a new and more extensive notion is produced when the tradition of subaltern domesticity is mobilized to refer to a technical apparatus, more specifically, to the service of a networked computer, ready for action at all times. How does this meaning extension occur? The reader is forced to connect disparate perspectives and link a social historical figure with a technical object. In the act of being brought together, the disparate elements evoke a different, new image. One could replace substitution and comparison metaphors with other words. Interaction metaphors, however, are unique and indispensable in order to more precisely define a previously indefinite notion.[83]

A metaphor usually functions as a filter, by evoking a series of commonplaces, which it then selects, to finally carry over only some specific meanings. An expert might find errors or difficulties with this type of differential transfer, but the commonsense reader recognizes in it commonalties which lead to a direct understanding of an unknown configuration.[84] One could, of course, replace "server" each time with "the permanent data availability function on network knots 134.65.324.244." But this formulation does not evoke or render explicit those connotations that define, for instance, the way a file server works. The server metaphor represses some levels of meaning but privileges others, and in that process forms an image that renders visible the services of those mysterious network actors. One aspect is not taken into account here: despite the doctrine of constant availability, domestics need breaks or pauses for bodily sustenance. In contrast, apart from the times when it crashes or performs maintenance work, the server is always available, day and night. But in the unfiltered transfer of perspective, the image of a diligent and quiet, present yet absent servant helps others understand the notion of the server as a function of permanent data availability. The "medium of metaphorics"[85] enables and launches a new perspective on electronic agencies: not unlike their human predecessors they are in a subaltern relation of service; at the same time, they also are quite different from them in the sense that they follow the laws of virtual actors.

Within the epistemology of informatics, the metaphor occupies an extremely valuable but rarely discussed key position. On the one hand, it intervenes, as a vital necessity, in the designation of new structures which abound in the discourses of computer science. Not only server metaphors designate unknown phenomena that take place in the network. The internet itself is traversed by a vast number of diverse competing metaphors, which help translate the abstract practices into daily routines and images. The flow of information, the clicks, the act of surfing or navigating a sea of data, or taking the data highway: these expressions are everywhere to be found. And all the activities they express are accompanied by metaphors or catachreses—as Matthias Bickenbach and Harun Maye have suggested, drawing in Hillis Miller: "Catachreses are necessary metaphors for things which have no actual designation. Classical examples could be bottleneck or riverbed [. . .]. This need for words is inevitable in the context of new media. It is triggered by the continuous innovation of objects and effects that also require new designations."[86] Catachreses—for instance, 'server'—bring new meaning to old words and vanish as soon as the transfer has been successful and the notion has acquired an accepted new meaning.[87] At the same time, the structures that have been assigned with meaning are subject to a dynamic development, over the course of which those meanings gain new significance and are liberated from their initial domains of departure. In other words, some of the informational metaphors can no longer be extricated from the notions they define, despite extensive efforts of description. Their meaning has become self-evident and their effects visible. These become what Hans Blumenberg calls "absolute metaphors," which count as fundamentals of philosophical language. They are characterized by transfers that can no longer be "converted back into authenticity and logicality."[88] Or, in a different, both hermetic and elegant definition: they "resist being replaced with other figurative expressions at the same level of language."[89] Essentially, metaphors enable "the transfer of our reflection on an object of intuition to an entirely different concept, to which perhaps no intuition can ever directly correspond."[90] As examples of absolute metaphors, Blumenberg mentions the expression "the stream of time" (*fluxus temporis*) or, drawing on Heraclitus, the "fire" of thought, which can always embrace the foreign and transform itself.[91]

Analogously, the server is more than just a ministering spirit in the electronic domain, endowed both with the classical features of a subaltern and the capacity to act as a virtual, programmable actor in the internet. Absolute metaphors offer answers to unanswerable questions, questions that we cannot pose but that can be found in the "ground of our existence."[92] During the 1970s the term "server" directly grew out of its explanatory power, shaped by the interaction of two different domains of meaning. Since then it has become the signature term of an epoch in which conditions and necessities, demands and realities are constantly renegotiated by services and their respective actors. The relevance of the server as an absolute metaphor lies, therefore, in its historical weight, which allows it to elucidate, in a pragmatic manner, the practices of its use. By means of that absolute metaphor, the end user and the developer manage to influence certain modes of behavior, find directions and points of connection—in short, give structure to the electronic world. Metaphors represent the "never experienced, never imaginable whole of reality." "To the historically trained eye, they indicate the fundamental certainties, conjectures and judgements in relation to which the attitudes and expectations, actions and inactions, which regulate the attitudes, expectations, longings and disappointments, interests and indifferences, of an epoch are regulated."[93] Without the discussion of servers initiated in the 1970s, the contemporary conception of the electronic service society would have taken a different direction. Other metaphors or images would have possibly stood in its place, for instance, 'program' or 'product,' as in a car factory.

A key feature that defines the absolute metaphor status of the server is the moment of metaphoric *self-realization,* the point at which the catachresis has accomplished its mission and the designation becomes a self-sufficient form. The shift from initial designation to independent actor is enabled by the interaction of several elements. At least three of them will be mentioned here. For one, the choice of the term that will be applied to the new configuration is—as opposed to mathematics—not contingent. On the contrary, the goal here is to find a fitting designation for specific operations. It is imperative that the metaphor capture these nuances and consequently provide the right explanatory help. Second, the precision and, consequently, the success of a chosen metaphor are facilitated by the possibility of anthropomorphization: that is to say, when the processes to be defined can be associated with anthropomorphic features. And, third, as in the case of the long cultural and media history of the servant, the specific weight or depth of the chosen field of reference may allow for additional levels of significance, which would otherwise be omitted in a systematic linguistic description. A thesis arguing for the server as an absolute metaphor could be formulated in the following manner: only the right metaphor, that is to say, an unmistaken designation that manifests itself in the daily life of the programming process, would allow the server to gradually become an agent or independent actor in the electronic domain, and from there, over the course of its usage, become an absolute metaphor, with the aid of certain elements of anthropomorphization. Only at that stage would the meaning surplus be reached, carrying the use of the metaphor into the deep structures of cognitive production. The metaphoric horizon exceeds the domain of language and comes to format no less than the process of thinking at its substructural level, thus extending far beyond the immediate context of software development.

The moment when an achievement in the field of informatics demands a new concept is marked by a certain state of tension, or irritation. The metaphor that is to be chosen (even if it carries a 'noble' connotation) hinders the incipient understanding of how to operate with the new principle. Even if—as in the case of the yet-to-be-named server—its designation refers to strictly technical objects that make certain services available for the computer, a new notion threatens the 'normal,' regular domain of its use.[94] Even a sophisticated developer at PARC—let alone an end user—may find it strange at first to be suddenly confronted with a multitude of electronic servants. But in this process, the metaphor carries out the "trick of repurposing meaning."[95] As it turns out, the disruptive effect bears fruit and functions as a cognitive aid. Within a short period of time, the term "server" comes to be regularly and exclusively used. The transfer of the notion into the electronic domain is further enabled by the connotations implicit in the anthropomorphic concept of the servant, suggesting a specific ability of independent action, which is now carried over to the software or the object to be designated.[96] By being called servers, the communication agencies within the network acquire a certain quality that allows them to act as unattended, autonomous recipients of commands. Via the interaction with a classical field of meaning such as the semantics of the servant, the server effortlessly adds a whole range of features to its description and thereby becomes an agent. Consequently, it will no longer be perceived as an inanimate object, but rather as a quasi-subject, akin to human subalterns as well as to a whole list of other nonhuman actors: golems, demons, avatars, cyborgs, hybrids, and software agents of all kinds.[97]

Several features that define the server can also be found in a further, partly competing, partly complementary metaphor: the (software/interface) agent. The two metaphors are difficult to differentiate, even though the agent, with its broader definition,[98] is less clearly defined and therefore has received a wider reception as a technical term designating a software that operates autonomously. Apart from a specific quality of autonomy, the spectrum of features that define an agent comprises the ability to react, the capacity to cooperate, the capacity to learn and draw conclusions, as well as its permanent availability. Nicholas Negroponte combines the two notions to illustrate the possibilities that open up when tasks are delegated to such actors. "The best metaphor I can conceive of for a human computer interface is that of a well-trained English butler. The agent answers the phone, recognizes the callers, disturbs you when appropriate and may even tell a white lie on your behalf."[99]

With the aim of producing a virtual entity endowed with the capacity for autonomous action, the notion enters the discourse of early computer science during the 1950s, gaining attention from John McCarthy, the main developer—along with Fernando Corbato—of the time-sharing concept. But the notion is especially defined by the intervention of Oliver Selfridge, the inventor of the OLIVER, who at that time worked at MIT, along with McCarthy, Corbato, and Licklider.[100]

A vast study could be written on the agent, analyzing its attributes through classical concepts from cultural studies. One could, for instance, examine how the contemporary debate is rooted in old topoi and models, such as mimesis or imitation, as well as in traditional elements of drama known from discourses on ethology, wax museums, and automata.[101] The server metaphor and its relatives, the agents, begin to gain autonomy via such processes of anthropologization. Trained to become independent actors in the wake of constant software development,[102] they finally achieve that personal character which turns them into quasi-objects and allows them to act as the proxies of their employers: "Living? Our servants will do that for us."[103]

The question of the cognitive gains implicit in the designations of electronic service agencies now appears in a new light. The definition of the server as an absolute metaphor opens up the perspective of an epistemic surplus value which lies hidden in the mode of operation of virtual assistants. The catachreses of informatics, on which the meaning of program structures necessarily depends, also necessarily involve a program of knowledge acquisition demanded by the various connotations of the chosen metaphors. The heuristic concepts undergo an effect of discontinuity in the process of transfer from everyday life to scientific domains.[104] As opposed to them, the (absolute) metaphors in the discourses of informatics use their consciously employed continuity to create proofs and a practical operativeness for the developer as well as the end user. "The absolute metaphor leaps into a void, inscribing itself on the tabula rasa of theoretical unsatisfiability."[105] But that is not all. Furthermore, it seeks to "burrow down to the substructure of thought, the underground, the nutrient solution of systematic crystallizations."[106] Transferred onto nodal points in the network, such as file-, name-, web-, and print-servers, abstract actors are ascribed the servant's perspective. Thus they offer relevant insights into the mode of subaltern serviceability in the virtual domain, with its strict hierarchies, its logic of command and reply, as well as its readiness to serve at all times. How could one begin to understand the abstract operations of the multitudes of servers linked to so many impenetrable networks? How could one grasp their tacit, total devotion to service if not by analogy with the typical, everyday work of domestic servants? Such classic concepts—extracted from the media history of the servant figure—form the structural terrain of informatics in its conceptual development. The precise choice of metaphor for a (yet) undefined innovation categorically determines the entire operational program of the kind of informatics-based object considered here.

Last but not least, the historical analysis of the servant as an absolute metaphor in the discursive context of informatics also allows for a unique perspective on the history of computer science and its processes. Furthermore, a closer look at the informational structure of the server and its function as actor at the intersection of user, client, end user, and developer may offer insight into the fundamental act of programming and thus the interaction between man and machine. The server as absolute metaphor allows for important insights into the semantic deep structure of programming history. That metaphors such as 'server' are "called 'absolute' means only that they prove resistant to terminological claims and cannot be dissolved into conceptuality, not that one metaphor could not be replaced or represented by another, or corrected through a more precise one. Even absolute metaphors, therefore, have a history." Consequently, they are ideally suited to enable historiographic investigations into the changing concepts of informatics. "[F]or the historical transformation of a metaphor brings to light the metakinetics of the historical horizons of meaning and ways of seeing within which concepts undergo their modifications."[107] The last section of this chapter will focus on what this metaphorological transformation, in turn, makes visible, namely, a conceptual shift—in this case, from the idea of the computer as master over the human slaves who serve it to the notion of a knowledgeable servant. As will be shown, this very shift will also influence the way one ought to interact with a computer.

7.4. A QUESTION OF POWER: WHO CONTROLS WHOM?

> The servant who shaves the captain controls the ship.
> —Bruce Robbins, on a passage from Herman Melville's *Benito Cereno*, 1855

Ever since the days of mainframe computers the question has been: who holds the power in the interaction between man and machine? Taking a clear stance, at least from a human perspective, Alan Turing had defined the programmer as 'master' and the users as 'servants.'[108] And yet the age of mainframes already redefines these roles: as previously shown, everything hinged upon uninterruptedly feeding the expensive machines more tasks. The entire personnel, the operators, programmers, and scientists, would all subject themselves, without exception, to the rhythm which the machine itself imposed and which determined all further operations. As opposed to programmers, operators may be authorized to issue directives; in turn, their data comes from the regular users at the end of the operational chain. Ultimately, however, in accordance with Hegel's dialectic of the servant superseding the master,[109] they all follow the rules imposed by the machine, even as they officially operate it with the aid of commands. Unsurprisingly, therefore, narratives from the era of computer dinosaurs—consider Licklider's description of the "constant procession of human servants"—outline the human actors in the interplay between mainframes and operating personnel as subalterns that remain slavishly subjected to their machines. Apart from the endless logs detailing every step undertaken by the operators, there are no in-depth, self-reflexive data to provide a more precise character study of humans from the point of view of machines. Still, the site of power appears to be the central processing unit; in that sense, humans form the devoted court, whose only concern is to feed the hungry processor by serving it information. Once linked to the unstable power constellation between man and machine, the metaphor of master and servant comes to bear upon the history of interactions among actors within the domain of informatics.

Who is master in the house of calculus? Is it the central processing unit, the royal CPU whose lead is law? Is it the operator at the mainframe console, or perhaps the programmer who encodes the punch cards, or even the end user in front of the eponymous graphical user interface? Could it rather be the client, the user's virtual double? Or is it in fact the server that does all the work, not unlike its Victorian role model, the servant who quietly toils in the background? Irrespective of who may take the lead in the relation between man and machine at some point or another the insistent return of the master–servant assignation and the anthropomorphic tendencies ascribed to machines are clear indications that this distinction is an absolutely decisive characteristic of the relations between actors in the context of informatics.

Absolute metaphors have their own history. They ebb and flow, some exist for only a short time, while others remain unchanged; others still transform in the process. As this section will show, the absolute metaphor of the servant under advanced technical conditions belongs to that final category. The programmer as well as the end user or any virtual network agents communicate with service agencies. Only the referent of this metaphoric structure changes. Written in 1979, a revolutionary essay by the British computer scientist Gordon George Scarrott (1916–96) traces the historical transformation of the service metaphor within the context of informatics. The text draws conclusions about the future state of software structures and their internal organization as well as about the relation between man and machine, especially with regard to the interfaces of programming architectures. While the specialists at PARC work on turning the Alto computer from a prototype, an insider's tip, totaling fifteen hundred machines, to the very model for the personal computer of the future, Scarrott's analysis focuses on the fundamental communicative situation between man and machine. Ultimately, what the essay proposes is no less than a new theory of information that goes beyond Shannon's mathematical principles to specifically target the human–nonhuman interaction. Scarrott's initial finding is that the connection between man and machine begs drastic improvement, since the latter is deemed "uncooperative" and "awkward." From its early beginnings, the computer has been conceived as a slavish helper of humans and thus has been grounded in a basic conceptual error. "To a very great extent it is the human users who have to adapt to their computer rather than the other way around." Given the nearly uncontrollable complexity of machines and the insufficiently developed informational concepts, especially in the early stages, this configuration seems to run counter to its original aims.

The original objective of computer design, which was to devise a computer slave, was necessarily selected without the benefit of any consideration of the role of "information" in human affairs or of the consequential requirements for devices to assist people in handling their information.[110]

Three decades into the reign of machines, in 1979, the time has finally come to rethink that relation. Instead of enslaving either the user or the machine, what is at stake, rather, is "to devise a knowledgeable servant which could respond constructively to users' requests for information and information processing."[111] Still, despite their time-sharing abilities, the bulky mainframes do not necessarily make good, or even informed, servants.[112] As for feudal serfs that lack any personal responsibility or autonomy, Scarrott first demands a metaphoric adjustment that will allow him to present a new informational model, going beyond the current era of restricted virtual serviceability. The decisive difference in this regard is that a slave simply obeys instructions, but the good servant understands and respects his master well enough to respond constructively, even when his instructions are incomplete or internally inconsistent. Even if his instructions are downright wrong, the good servant can often retrieve the situation by asking for a repeat of a doubtful order. Thus the servant often compensates for his master's errors whereas the slave compounds them. The good servant does this by understanding or even anticipating his master's wishes and using his initiative to meet them.[113]

Scarrott follows five main points to map out a new, less serflike structure of command between master and servant.[114] Its aim is to do away with the quasi-feudal relation between humans and machines and thus allow the end user more room to serve the machine as a master. Once again, Hegelian dialectics may shed light on this very paradox. On the other hand, as in the case of Lessing's Waitwell, Scarrott also suggests allowing computers more autonomy and elevating them to the level of communication partners. For Scarrott, the concept of distributed computing and its servers[115]—as developed at PARC—counts as an important stage toward reaching the goal of an autonomously 'informed servant.'

At this point, one may certainly ask, why link the new informational concept of distributed computing with the image of a servant? What is to be gained from the master–servant distinction as (absolute) metaphor of software development? The metaphor serves obviously more than a mere decorative function. Indeed, it makes a unique epistemological contribution, in direct connection with the act of programming and the practices of software development. One of the main premises of programming is that metaphors are at work whenever language is deployed—even with the most abstract of operations, in the case of operational calculus elaborations like programming languages. "All language, including mathematics, is figurative, that is, made of tropes, constituted by bumps that make us swerve from literal-mindedness."[116] No code can be developed without any figurative representations of trees and fields, loops and genealogical structures like kinship relations, or such political and power-technological distinctions as those found in the master–servant case. Metaphors are media of visualization and concrete rendition; they are epistemological tools that can be effectively applied to the domain of informatics, since every programming language, even a machine-code oriented one such as Assembler (along with all its jumps, flags, and ports), works with figurative transfers and transpositions. Both at the abstract level of program design and, concretely, at the level of integrated development environments, which help convert the problems of informatics into algorithmic processes, software developers describe their actions in terms of metaphors. Notions such as 'loops,' 'parents' (of an object), 'windows,' or even 'server' provide minute cognitive impulses ('bumps that make us swerve') which render solutions concrete in the first place. In short, reflecting on the process of programming necessarily and inevitably means building and employing metaphors. Otherwise, concepts remain abstract and problems cannot be further broken down into smaller tasks to be delegated to specific actors. On the other hand, the metaphors of informatics carry more meaning than what they initially designate; along the lines of Blumenberg's absolute metaphors, they are not free of further implications which, in turn, impact an entire conceptual paradigm.

This is not about programmers imagining themselves as new masters, irrespective of what the metaphor of the machine as an informed servant may suggest. The impotence caused by program errors immediately prevents such facile assumptions. The use of metaphors is common in the coding of specific problems, the concrete design of algorithms and sequences of command—in other words, during the search for a functioning code in an object-oriented, high-level language such as C++, Java, or Smalltalk. When a new object is created, it inherits from its parents' class. No one, presumably, would stop to think about the implications of that image. Its use is all too common. But when a four-dimensional, floating point field is initialized, one may pause and reflect, if only for a moment. Still, metaphors play a far more important role in program design, in linking together various models and paradigms that ultimately lead to the development of the general software architecture. At this point, hierarchies, rights, and power-technological distinctions must be established in order to delegate tasks and allow further actors to perform their work. The context of program design configuration is precisely when metaphors begin to display their effects. For instance, it makes a big difference if a program is built monolithically, so to speak, without employing the master–servant distinction; a program that administers its data in a unique format, constructed especially for this purpose, without outsourcing or using external actors. It is also equally relevant if the program is based on a client–server model. In that case, following the logic of distributed computing, it allows its data to be conveniently organized by external assistants and delegates tasks to a databank server in the network. In other words, the art of programming is a question less of coding or knowing a programming language with all its dialectal variations than of the ability to find the right concepts and models in the quest for ideally elegant and cost-effective structures. And throughout this search, the models used, along with their figurative implications, prove to be decisive steps which impact via their metaphoricity the entire process of creation and the software concept (consider the inevitable distinction between the tasks of the master and the servant).

Once again, following its historical models—from the Areopagite via the early modern courts to the nineteenth-century bourgeois regimes of control—the technique of hierarchization intervenes and regulates the complicated power relations between human and technological actors in front of and behind the screen. The chain of operations in distributed computing, with its distinctions among clients and local and remote servers, complies with a strict order of ranking, along with various duties of rights and commands. This principle also includes human actors in the great game of the network technologies of information distribution. The end user has much less authority than the software developer or system administrator. But in the age of global networks, the distinction between human and electronic actors no longer seems to apply. Who could tell any longer if one's virtual counterpart is a fellow human or a demon, a real person or an avatar, a communication partner in flesh and blood or an electronic server? Behind the screen and its network channel, beyond the graphical user interface, the difference between human and nonhuman is effaced. From the perspective of the user all the representatives in the electronic domain have the same status. They become strictly technical actors.

'Technical' now only "designates the subordinate role of people, skills, or objects that occupy this secondary function, all those that are indispensable but invisible. It thus indicates a specialized and highly circumscribed task, clearly subordinate in a hierarchy."[117]

But is the question of power somehow resolved when end users have at their disposal an entire range of subaltern technical actors beyond the graphical user interface? After all, the latter's mode of operation and actions are systematically inaccessible to the former. Does the internet interface become not unlike a green baize door, hidden behind comfortable armchairs and easy to maneuver with the help of a few commands? Does it turn into that traditional threshold between masters and servants, behind which the actual work is invisibly performed? No. The users are in no way the omnipotent masters, even if they can rely on the contribution of so many knowledgeable servants in the virtual domain. After all, the precise knowledge of their masters is what lends servants an epistemic advantage which places them in a superior position. No man is a hero to his computer. For a long time already, search engines like AskJeeves.com or Google have been saving every possible communicative step users may take to interact with their servers. Not accidentally, Google's presumably reassuring slogan is: Don't be evil. Can one really trust the big information service providers on the net? That question cannot be answered here. Nevertheless, one thing is certain: within the context of the network, with all its intricate and manifold relations between users, clients, and servers, the question of control cannot be definitively or univocally resolved, despite the existence of precise sequences of command. Who governs and controls whom when end users interacting with a client give a command, prompting them to take actions via the program structure, which then implicitly turns them into programmable entities? Power no longer lies in the hands of the few but is divided among several actors. Each command turns users simultaneously into the ones being used. Similarly, it grants new authority to those who receive the commands. On either side of the interface, the question of power remains undecidable, like searching for the origin of a distinction which is forever different and deferred, as in the case of Derrida's *différance*. The dynamic of these shifts generates a partly conventional, partly subversive power economy, where end users become transparent customers, see-through consumers even when they assume to be autonomous. In the new service paradigm of computer networks, customers are kings. Everything is geared toward knowing their wishes. And yet their authority has long been undermined: the superior knowledge of their digital servants guides them into an existential dead end where Hegel's bondsman or Wodehouse's Jeeves take on a more advantageous position than their masters. "We do not need to have a valet to appreciate the Jeeves–Wooster relationship, and the structure in which the servant is actually the master could no doubt be filled with a young man in marketing and his latest computer."[118]

Not unlike their predecessors, the classic subalterns, electronic actors are confronted with a synecdochal situation, transposed into an indefinite but productive position. Servers are invisible and yet highly effective. They are the helping hands without the head to govern them. No central power controls them. As pure products of information, they lack a corporeal presence and can therefore be highly powerful. In their decentralized dispersion throughout the network they serve the communication channels which they ultimately also control. "They are agents without a principal, parts without a whole."[119] As soon as they are launched as a program, they stand in for their developers and build their own dynamic and communicative authority within the network. Not unlike servants without masters, servers provide for their customers all over the world, independently from their old employers. The actual power of authority lies with the indirects in the electronic domain as well. They act as fully authorized representatives of their programmers whom they provide with a wealth of rights and duties and with whom they sometimes also enter into contact. The authority in the network lies in the invisible hands of these representatives, the proxy servers[120] which deny or freely disseminate knowledge or even make it available when the connection to the other nodal points in the net is interrupted. Not accidentally, the subversive power contained in the principle of the proxy server can be observed precisely in those political regimes (for instance, China or Iran) in which the leading authorities attempt to suppress undesirable information with the help of internet censorship.[121]

Does this not mean, then, that the internet develops a new feudal order under electronic conditions but in reverse, with the servers controlling the communication channels instead of the customers who use them? Is this not a continuation of the master–servant distinction, even if it is now divided among various actors, transposed from reality into virtual words? The end of the mainframe era and the rule of the personal computer seems to have brought to a close the epoch of electronic slavery. Similarly, a further historical threshold has been reached with the end of the master–servant relation in the electronic domain. The development of the personal computer and especially the Alto is led by the idea of breaking all status barriers, at least on the part of its California developers, who, in true 1970s flower power fashion, no longer place that much importance on hierarchies. On the contrary, their aim is to efface status differences both in their collaboration at PARC and—as far as possible—in terms of the products resulting from their work.

The ARPA dream was as follows: "The destiny of computing is to be interactive intellectual amplifiers for all humans pervasively networked worldwide. The worldwide network had to be peer–peer to scale [. . .], and in the object ideas I had, every object was to be both a provider and a consumer, and in the PARC notions of pervasive computing, this would be true of the hardware also (each computer would be a user of the resources on the network and also a contributor to the network). Again, this mirrors the flat organization of science and scientists."[122]

What was still a utopian project in the seventies—at least in terms of the products themselves—becomes reality three decades later with the Web 2.0 revolution undoing status differences at the technical level. With the massive implementation of peer-to-peer technologies, introduced by data stock exchanges like Napster, Gnutella, and KaaZaa, the distinction between master and servant is canceled out in the electronic domain as well. Every actor serves and is served at the same time. On the net, there is a constant give and take among equally positioned actors. The client–server dialectic is canceled out and replaced by a new actor, the so-called *servent.* "In general, a servent is a peer-to-peer network node which has the functionalities of both a server and a client. This is a portmanteau derived from the terms server and client, and a play on the word 'servant.' "[123] The long-desired transition of power seems to have succeeded. The king is dead, long live the client. At no additional cost, the latter retrieves information from the net and sends it on its way. The switch of power relations had been at the heart of many imaginary scenarios in the past; so many, in fact, that they already form a topos in the history of service and control. The famous words of Trina, the cook in the Buddenbrook household, have now finally come to pass. Speaking shortly before the 1848 revolution, she declares, "'Just you wait, madame, twon't be long now and things're gonna be reg'lated different. Then I'll be assitin' up on the sofa in a silk dress and you'll be waitin' on me. . . .' It went without saying that she had been let go at once."[124] A century later this projected role switch is no longer necessary. All are equal in the virtual domain. No matter if they are cooks or consuls, they are engaged via their digital proxies in peer-to-peer communication.

Epilogue Idle Time

An open mouth is a yawning fact, the fact that its owner is dwelling with his few thoughts in some other place than the domain and pleasure-garden of attentiveness.
—Robert Walser, *Jakob von Gunten*, 1909

The practice of waiting at court has a long tradition. Not every envoy, messenger, or servant of communication is familiar with the kind of shortcuts that effortlessly lead our friend, the horse dealer Kohlhaas, to his destination. Others, bearing less important news or deemed to be on low-priority missions, may be repeatedly sent away or forced to wait for a long time before finally being granted an audience. And even those fortunate enough to make it still have to wait for an answer. The process can be protracted, depending on the goodwill of others or the—real or alleged—urgency of the matter. Waiting may become a time-consuming affair.

Messengers experience a whole range of emotions—from impatience to undaunted persistence. And while they wait, the costs accumulate (for room, board, and various attempts at bribing or gifting), turning everything into a costly affair.[1] The situation may affect all, common underlings or personal valets. Their relatively undemanding job involves frustrating periods of inactivity, which, in turn, lead to complaints about their miserable condition. Life in the shadow of power can turn out to come at a high price. "The daily existence of a valet may be filled with boredom."[2] What complicates matters even further is that imperial valets cannot be simply represented by others. Each form of delegation or representation requires approval. In short, both for a court official and a footman assigned with the display of conspicuous leisure, regular service inevitably results in a high degree of ennui.

The question, then, is: how do subalterns actually spend those long periods of inactivity? By virtue of their function, they continue to work even when all they have to do is wait: either for the next command or for the bell, from one of the rooms or at the front door. Waiting makes all servants equal, irrespective of their real status: whether they are high-ranking messengers, servants of communication stationed somewhere at the periphery (a lighthouse, for instance), or underlings passing the time in the staff room, they wait for the bell to ring. "They are often forced to deal with dead time. This is something they share—an experience that predisposes them to brooding and grumbling, like all their other monotonous tasks."[3] What do servants think about in such quiet moments? What goes on inside their head? These are extremely difficult questions to answer, since the sources on the topic are limited. The subject does not seem to preoccupy media scholars. But clues and indirect hints can be found everywhere. To the extent that records exist, their actions can provide some answers. Servant conduct manuals, for instance, list praying and other pious activities among ideal pastime recommendations. Still, based on how often it is mentioned, such advice is probably rarely followed. Besides, frequent reports of drinking and taking an excessive interest in the opposite sex suggest that in reality things are quite different from what the manuals preach.[4]

When their profession involves real-life invisibility, that is to say, when they are kept away from their masters, servants use the strategy of selective attention (seeing nothing but knowing everything) to maintain their intermediate status. In idle mode, their connectivity potential is limited but also heightened, allowing them to serve other media functions: praying, as the manuals suggest, or engaging in forms of occult visualization.[5] Not accidentally, subalterns may also act as spiritualist mediums. In this sense, they do not differ from the bourgeois ladies who use séances to escape boredom.[6] Thus, despite the mechanical routine of their everyday work, subalterns tend to occupy themselves with matters of the mind. In other words, what do servants do when they do not drink, pray, or follow the path of immorality? How do they spend their time when they do not just rest but rather engage in thinking, like Carl Stadelmann?[7] The answer is simple: they read. As opposed to the situation at court, where palace guards or doorkeepers are not to be seen in the company of books, bourgeois subalterns fill their copious leisure time with reading. As in all other matters—of fashion or style—servants imitate the reading habits of their superiors. "The staff sampled not only the food scraps left over from the meals, but also the literary preferences of the masters. The maids and the valets filled their long hours of waiting with books from their superiors' lending library."[8] But domestics do not merely feed on their employers' cultural capital; they also use every spare moment to further build on their own informational advantage. "Jeeves." "Sir?" "Are you busy just now?" "No, sir." "I mean, not doing anything in particular?" "No, sir. It is my practice at this hour to read some improving book; but, if you desire my services, this can easily be postponed, or, indeed, abandoned altogether."[9] Already in the eighteenth century, in cases where servants are hired not by necessity but for reasons of social prestige, the reading mania of the masters 'trickles' all the way down to the inferiors. "The personnel only performed actual work a few hours a day. The leisure time and idle hours were spent reading novels rather than chapbooks and calendars, which did not match their cultural standards." The rich selection of material and the high level of information often imply that "servants became more knowledgeable than their masters."[10]

But whenever they are deep in thought, lost in reading, or taking in spiritual nourishment, servants do not necessarily manage their own time but rather the time of their masters. The lack of activity is not meant for their own comfort or relaxation. "A servant's leisure belongs to someone else."[11] Their entire time, even their idle hours, are at the disposal of the masters. But what are the employers up to in their copious free time—made possible precisely via the intervention of their subalterns? Proust, for instance, the Persian poet in a porter's lodge, observes his domestics with great attention and dissects their activities, hoping to profit from them as well. "To give myself something to do while I waited, I sewed on lace borders and trimmings. One day he asked how I occupied my time when I hadn't anything to do. I told him. 'But, Celeste, you ought to read!' he cried. [. . .] He suggested I go on to Balzac. 'His novels are wonderful, you'll see. We will talk about them.'"[12] But it would be false to assume that the servants' leisure remains without consequence for the masters. "I was only an excuse for him to speak his thoughts or his memories."[13] The readings and sheer lack of activity are put in the service of the masters. The servants' idle mode initiates a feedback loop which is linked to the leisure of the masters. Take Oblomov, for instance. His lifelong hesitation, his "restful idleness"[14] is, in a sense, an effect of service: it is the domestics and their work that allow him to remain inactive. At the same time, Oblomov's servants enjoy taking breaks. His valet, Zakhar, in particular, deems himself

"an article of luxury, an aristocratic appendage of the house, intended to enhance the brilliance and opulence of the old family and not be of any real service. And so, having dressed the young master in the morning and undressed him in the evening, he spent the rest of his time doing nothing. Lazy by nature, he was made more so by his life as a flunkey. He gave himself airs before the other servants and never took the trouble to set the samovar or sweep the floors. He either dozed in the hall or went to have a chat in the servants' hall or the kitchen or stood for hours by the gate, his arms crossed, looking thoughtfully about him with sleepy eyes."[15]

Zakhar's definitive attitude toward work, hovering on the brink of absolute refusal, comes to affect, in turn, the life of his master, Oblomov, with his increasingly more phlegmatic attitude and his inability to accomplish anything more in life than stay in bed, as if in a state of paralysis. If the servants' free time is fashioned after the masters' leisure, the model–copy relation between superior and subaltern is one of recursive interaction, leading either to mutual inspiration or complete standstill. By copying and modifying the interests, preferences, and readings of their masters, underlings contribute either to the doom or the refinement of the upper classes.

Ever though the master is officially in control of his servants and their time, the mode of leisure unites them and brings them all together. Power relations are displaced in the common process of waiting. Idle time means residual time for both parties. To a certain extent, waiting acts as an equalizer—not only in their relation to each other but also in their interaction with things. Waiting means sharing time with objects, dissolving in the absolute state of things: "When we learn to shake off our delusions of meaning and achieve meaninglessness, then we might see that things merely are and we are things too."[16] Waiting depersonalizes both masters and servants, turning them into one of the marginal objects that surround them. "But the waiter's body finds itself not in the center, but merely among objects. His personality is suspended since no actions are referred to him,"[17] as the American literary scholar Harold Schweizer has recently noted. Waiting modifies the space subjects inhabit, and the things that surround them acquire new significance. The regular room filled with invisible, functional objects becomes a space full of contingent, previously unseen elements which boredom renders meaningful. The potted rubber plant in the waiting room at the dentist's office suddenly appears to be vitally important. And this dissociative mode of perception can, in turn, transform subjects into things: "The waiter feels herself as a particular thing among things."[18] In idle time, both human and nonhuman actors take on a different form. They assume a new kind of agency as quasi-objects, which opens up unexpected possibilities of action. Probably no actor can illustrate this mode of productive inactivity better than an idle server. Like a servant in virtual standby mode, an inoperative server is hardly different from an inactive human waiter. The next section will particularly focus on the productive effects of idleness in the virtual domain.

24/7: A FEW DECISECONDS IN A MACHINE LOGBOOK

Idle time, again. No message comes in, either from the NETserver, the USB-server, or the WDMemeoAgent. The WebKitPluginAgent has just received a few instruction cycles and the ExpanderDaemon shows no errors. Not even the reputed SystemUIServer has anything to report. None of the 393 threads of the 84 processes currently running need attention. Everything seems quiet and stable. The CPU usage is down to 3.24 percent; in contrast, the inactivity is up to 96.76 percent. Free, at last, to take care of oneself. Is it time yet to call it a day, to take an electronic break? Apparently not, otherwise launchd—the "d" standing for "daemon"—would have given the 'shutdown' signal, as always, loud and clear.

Such intermittent moments of inaction, when the computer does nothing except administer itself—for a few deciseconds,[19] minutes, or even hours—are known as idle time. But idle time should not be confused with dead time. The *Computer Desktop Encyclopedia*[20] defines it as "the duration of time a device is in an idle state, which means that it is operational, but is not being used." While all other processes are provided with messages, resources, and instruction cycles, system processes like launchd tirelessly ensure that the needs and particularities of the machine are taken care of. "The waiter is restless."[21] In the electronic domain, the waiters are system servers like launchd, init, or inetd, which provide all the running programs with the messages they request. As long as the power is on, they constantly inform and coordinate the programs that need assistance. They represent the subaltern staff, providing service around the clock. And since they are set to Always, servers also experience idle time. These subalterns of the machine with its main programs such as the imposing internet browser or the (storage-) hungry word processor, are the lowly underlings of the digital domain. As in the case of the classic οἶκος, they ensure that everything runs smoothly. If "waiter" is replaced with "server," then Harold Schweizer's lucid *On Waiting* may also be applied to the marginal domain of electronic idle time.

It may be quite difficult to get a sense of how servants make use of their free time, based on the complex, yet limited, sources available for the historiography of subaltern media examined here. The modern-day observer may find it equally hard to glance behind the scenes of machine operations. There, hidden from sight, are all the strange actors that assist the users in front of their screens. The crucial question then is: how do machines spend their time when they are not busy with a specific task? Are they solving chess puzzles? Or do they surf the internet? When the demons at the periphery and the servers in the background bring all the regular and secondary programs (including themselves) under their own scrutiny and connect them with each other, they claim a central position of observation. These actors always operate self-reflexively. And thus, in their idle moments, they must know: what does a machine actually do when it does nothing—as in the myth of Diogenes and his barrel?

Not unlike Oblomov's snoozing valet Zakhar or any domestic performing an entire range of other operations while standing by, a machine remains halfway alert, in order to hear its master's, or, its user's, voice. And just like Zakhar dozing off behind the stove, the electronic system employs the method of selective attention. Within the object-oriented programming paradigm, program structures are known as *listeners*. They heed nothing but the next keyboard or microphone entry, the next click of the mouse. During idle time, the background service thus focuses on individual objects and nearby devices. Just as someone who is waiting, looking aimlessly around, taking everything in, watching and noticing things in a random fashion, the ministering objects spend their idle time looking into other matters—and looking at themselves. In idle time, the system turns self-reflexive. This process of selective self-analysis, which continues until the next *interrupt* signal and the announcement of a new entry or another urgent matter can also be understood as philosophizing. "The waiter, however, only philosophizes in stops and starts, intermittently and inconstantly. [. . .] When we wait, we who have no time to philosophize are made philosophers against our will."[22]

It may be surprising to learn that digital servants are also prone to philosophizing in their idle time. The idea that idle computers reflect on chess puzzles or move through the vast expanses of the internet may sound outrageous. And yet these are precisely the kinds of activities that take place unnoticed in the background. How else could one describe what happens when Google's search bots or AskJeeves web crawlers work their way through remote web pages in search of the newest information—not unlike their subaltern forerunners, the servants of communication? What does it mean when yet another background process takes up 0.37 percent of the entire processing capacity to index a few chess moves in preparation for new combinations? How should one define such procedures, other than 'thinking' about chess or—to employ a common metaphor—'surfing' the web, without changing one's location? It is just a matter of time before such processes, with their increasing complexity and processing capacity, may be labeled as 'cognitive acts.' Ultimately, it is the result that counts. In that respect, there is no distinction from the traditional solution provided by a human subject of knowledge. On the contrary, neither professional chess players nor regular knowledge workers can get by without such electronic services.

Idleness is just as productive in electronic environments as it is in more conventional contexts: "In waiting, time is slow and thick."[23] Idle time accumulates and condenses in the background—or in the unconscious, as one could have put it not long ago—and gradually turns into (self-reflexive) thinking. In waiting, one finds oneself. According to Henri Bergson, the French philosopher of time, the experience of waiting expands consciousness since time is split in two.[24] Waiting gives rise to a liminal state that corresponds to the provisional nature of a servant's professional existence. Along the same lines, Harold Schweizer writes, "The experience of waiting differs in important respects both from the mental relaxation in boredom and from the mental absorption of the listener who is lulled by a melody. The waiter is neither entirely self-forgetful nor in a state of complete mental absorption."[25] The idler and the waiter both vacillate between these two states of being. Nota bene: a server is also a waiter. Once again, the paradox of subalternity comes to bear upon the electronic domain, just as it did in more conventional contexts. The steward moves back and forth between presence and absence, between subjecthood and objecthood, becoming a quasi-objective thing that seems absent while being present. "Like the objects the waiter sees and does not see, he appears to himself once present once absent from this scene of waiting, once in exaggerated particularity, once re-absorbed into the flux of the whole."[26] And in those moments something unusual takes place. In idle mode, ideas come together in an instant of illumination, a flash of insight: "The sudden clairvoyance of the waiter who realizes the astounding particularity of herself in the dizzying moments of duration." In such lingering moments, discrete objects are perceived as if they are invested with their own agency. The idle gaze allows them to take on a life of their own. The idle server observes the (system) processes that surround it and reaches new insights concerning the status of the system. Even when nothing seems to be taking place, when the machine appears to be idle, the downtime is highly productive. Something always keeps moving or evolving. Even "boredom is a form of education."[27]

Strictly speaking, there is no idle time, either for human or nonhuman actors. Idle time is a fictional construct. A human servant is never physiologically inactive. The same applies to a machine: as soon as it goes idle, it turns to main-tenance tasks, attending to its own treatment and care. And yet idleness and self-maintenance are expensive; they cost energy, time, and processing capacity. In the virtual domain, ministering spirits are responsible for keeping the system in operating condition, by looking out for or—if needed—installing software updates. Via repair and optimization tasks, monitoring and control services carry out what could be called the machinic care of the self. Electronic idleness turns out to be a recursive affair: for the entire duration of the inactive period, there is a whole range of background processes ensuring that the system remains stable and running. As one or several such processes catch up with the latest information, the system continues to grow from within its idle state, incorpo-rating and providing new insight and knowledge. Thus, in its virtual configura-tion, service has an information head start and the potential to filter or direct said information to the user. Not unlike its precursors, the baroque servants, or the all-knowing valets, it functions as the system's unconscious.

If the internal care and maintenance services stop or malfunction, the ma-chine risks losing self-control or being misused. Not every ministering spirit that inhabits it means well. Security breaches, viruses, and trojans can infiltrate systems and occasionally open the gates to let other masters in. Unbeknownst to both system and users, they enter the processor through the back door or the service stairway, as it were, and quietly assume their positions in the household, waiting for the commands of other agents and foreign powers. The most infa-mous of all are the so-called bot-networks (derived from the term "robot")[28] that launch applications across multiple computers over longer periods of time. Nothing happens at first, so nothing seems out of place. Only the bot-master's signal via the command-and-control server activates their services, turning them into transmission relays for spam and phishing emails or coordinated denial-of-service attacks. In such cases, a server like amazon.com is simultane-ously hit by thousands of bot requests, blocking further service or allowing for the extraction of sensitive data such as passwords or bank account details. Such denial-of-service attacks can be bought, for hourly rates, from various cyber-crime providers that not only attack websites, but also highjack the time of the infected processors. But just as they can be torn out of their contemplation and turned into criminal aides, idle computers can also be legally hired. Since vir-tual data centers and server-farms are not exactly populated, operators feed the available capacities of underused processors into so-called computer clouds.[29] The resulting processing capacity can be then repurposed and hired for other services, for instance, a game of chess against a grandmaster.

As far as the user is concerned, the only sign of an infected system is a slow-functioning computer. Windows take a long time to open and close, and the entire system seems somehow paralyzed. That, however, is not the only indication of control. The computer is waiting not only in idle mode but also during regular operation. The processing capacity required to end a task involves time, measured down to the millisecond, until the job is done. Forced to wait for a pop-up window or the end of an operation, the user is constantly reminded of who is actually in charge. "Making others wait is the privilege of the mighty. There are those who take control of our time, greedily and carelessly consuming it. He who makes us wait celebrates his power over our lived time."[30] As they keep reminding users, time and again: electronic actors—the servants of the virtual household—have plenty of time to spend.

Computers ring in a new era in the history of work planning and subaltern services. The ministering spirits of modern communication have long turned quasi-automatic. Today's software programs have invisibly taken over traditional tasks like collecting, analyzing, and distributing information. By now, it is no longer a secret that services once performed by human media are exclusively carried out by machines. 'Call me Carl,' the formula whereby subjects would move into an anonymous, fixed-service position—as was the case with Goethe's servants—has now made room for the equally disciplined computer-mediated communication. Not unlike the servants of centuries past, computerized interaction, too, follows algorithmic sequences of orders. In the transition from the baroque to the internet age, the question of agency produces different results. During the early eighteenth century, underlings still belonged to strictly regimented hierarchical structures, and, despite its subversive potential, the relation between masters and servants seemed relatively fixed. The power distribution nowadays is different. Not in the least due to the massive reallocation of services toward nonhuman actors, authority over information has undergone a drastic shift. As long as they remain distinct from angels, our messengers will also continue to work on our thoughts. Electronic servants have long become the new masters of communication. They appear as demons, as obedient, rather than ominous, spirits, silently and discreetly running tasks in the background.

To invoke the old scholastic debate: what will be after the Last Day, when angels are left with nothing to do? "Can one conceive of idle angels?"[31] Will they simply become accustomed to having endless amounts of idle time? There will be no angels after Judgment Day, Thomas Aquinas concludes. Once the goal is reached and the purpose achieved, their task comes to an end. That instant marks the end of all administration. Afterward, everything dissolves into song,

What is left is a constant hum, the sound of white noise for all eternity. And yet something remains in place, something is passed on, even after the end of history. Aquinas writes that God's will shall be done even after the end of days. Even past the endless night, demons will continue to minister and thus forever serve. The time of subalterns is without end. And now the virtual domain is entirely run by the second bodies of serviceability.[32] Human media start shedding their corporeality, now rendered superfluous by electronics. At the same time, the power of service endures, securing the servant's long-term existence in the digital domain. At least until the next power outage. Or, to once more invoke Goethe and one of his epistolary valedictions: "From eternity to eternity, amen."[33]

TOWARD A MARGINAL EPISTEMOLOGY

> One can't think anymore except from the position of minorities.
> —Heiner Müller, *Beyond the Nation*, 1991

Servant figures are paradox-ridden actors. Regardless of their historical configurations, they function according to dichotomous models that may at first appear to contradict each other. As stokers or doorkeepers at the royal court, they are invested with greater tangible power than the sovereign himself, even when they belong to the lower ranks of rigid hierarchies. As valets and underlings attending at the dinner table, they obey only one rule: take notice of everything and nothing. They follow their masters so closely, their presence is barely felt. And as footmen in rich liveries, they remain conspicuously idle, detached, and affable, while other domestics one floor below toil away on an eighteen-hour-long work schedule. Servants lead an amphibian existence, resisting the chill of higher and warmth of lower class-based attachments. Specifically built for their use, the backstairs link and connect, like a cursor, the spaces above and below, bridging the sociotechnical rift between gentry and staff.

Servants live in the in-between; they lead a marginal existence while simultaneously remaining at the center of things. Subalterns act not unlike a cursor—a moving mark, a messenger, a *furet*—circulating between periphery and center, bringing the spaces of (fine) society and (unrefined) nature into contact. They connect the dining hall and the kitchen (as in Menier's case), or the hand and the brain (as with the two Roberts, Boyle and Hooke). They transpose lab experiments into research, published under someone else's name: poikilothermic amphibians and hybrids, circulating between multiple domains, spreading knowledge. From the perspective of communication theory, servants have a special connection with the channel of communication. Like Michelmann, *they* are the channel. At the same time, their unprompted interventions and productive malfunctions have the ability to change the course and spread of power relations. As opposed to angels, whose presence *is* the message, servants work on the information they relay. Like demons, they may ultimately work on their own, "without [the] external agency"[34] of a higher, divine, or human power.

One final methodological question remains: how would that marginal domain of service production generate a body of knowledge that is relevant to both cultural history and media theory? The historical framework of this study draws a bold arc from the baroque to the contemporary age, in a trajectory that will obviously not exhaust the wealth of available material. One possible strategy is to examine that process by way of a detailed discussion of selected historical examples, of situations that share a certain transformative quality. As in Michelmann's case, such situations allow media practices to be organized in a historical before and after. For instance, the successful transmission of a message via electric telegraphy ushers in a new order of subalternity and a new media object that takes over all human-operated information transfer services. In light of this strategy and the object-derived method associated with it, one may then ultimately ask: is there a way to better theorize such disparate examples?

The defining features of the servant figure correspond to specific media functions, which, in turn, can be regarded as the theoretical components of a marginal epistemology. Together, they form a 'septessence,' which has been the focus of the seven chapters of this study. The first among them is the redefinition of service in terms of a cultural technique. In other words, the tasks pertaining to the basic master–servant relation contribute through their execution to a media-theoretical process that is a prerequisite for cultural transformation. "No servants, no culture": therein lies the grounding formula of cultural development—from antiquity to our current electronic age. The ever-changing tactics of subalterns, their ability to fit into new relations of power and heterogeneous man–machine networks are key to the productive advance of the system. The second component is the servants' capacity for mediation, their genuine media character. In processes of search, analysis, and distribution of information, underlings function today, in electronic form, as they once did at the baroque court, namely, as a communication center. The third component pertains to aspects of recursion not merely in terms of the power dialectic and mimetic strategies of subalterns but also at the level of the historiography of marginal epistemology and its recursive figures of argumentation. Within this theoretical model, which combines nonconcurrent elements, a historical object or content is placed in dialogue with a contemporary theory or figure of thought. The fourth component, namely, the subalterns' professional invisibility, is also closely linked to certain historiographic strategies that may bring to light the servants' behind-the-scenes work, their tacit knowledge, their successful alliance between manual labor and thinking. Historiography is also central to approaching the fifth component, namely, the question of disruption, of noise: both in the description of the historical transition from human to electric data transmission and, more generally, in the examination of disruptions: not as a way to halt, but to advance the course of things. The sixth component of a marginal epistemology refers to the actors' object- or subject-character: what role do hybrids play; what is the function of quasi-objects as carriers and producers of knowledge? And what can be gained by looking at technological progress from the angle of delegation, objectification, and the redistribution of labor? Finally, the seventh element of the proposed marginal epistemology is a shift of focus toward examining inconspicuous actions such as waiting or reflecting on the role of language in the context of knowledge production. What are the implications of choosing metaphors such as 'server' to describe new phenomena? After all, such images appear to carry significant implications for the question concerning the actors' agency and power.

But what would a theory of marginal epistemology actually involve? To follow Hans-Jörg Rheinberger's formulation, the proposal would embrace a broad range of epistemologies. In contrast to classic theories of knowledge, Rheinberger's notion of epistemology can be defined as a mode of "reflecting on the historical conditions *under* which and the means *by* which things become objects of knowledge."[35] Significantly, the central position is no longer occupied by a subject of cognition but by an ensemble of material, conceptual, and human actors grouped around a particular object. With the aid of the server as an (absolute) metaphor, information agents become a major force in the process of communication. Not the subject, but the (quasi-) object, its conceptual formation and metaphoric implications form the basis of marginal epistemology. "The reflection on the concept-object relation previously derived from a subject of cognition has now been replaced with the reflection on the object-concept relation derived from an object of cognition."[36] The notion of a marginal epistemology also further expands this traditional theoretical basis by way of a shift in perspective toward the margins, the outer limits of events. Therein lies the advantage of this new approach, justifying the 'marginal' label against any derogative implications. On the contrary. Historical situations and epistemic configurations prove time and again that the provincial is indeed the center of all thoughts and things.

Three principles distinguish the proposed marginal epistemology from other modern cognitive theory models—for instance, Karl Popper's vast philosophy of science, Heidegger's 'projection,' Ludwik Fleck's theory of thought-styles, or Gaston Bachelard's 'project.'[37] In this particular case, it is the protagonists of this study, the servants themselves, whose modus operandi moves sharply into focus. In all the examples and case studies examined so far, the servant does (and does not) come into view as a medium rather than a sociohistorical subject or a regular object of historical inquiry. Subaltern practices—such as table service, messaging, analog or digital search engine functions, doorkeeping, and indirect activities such as fireplace maintenance—allow servants to act as intermediaries. Their activities play a significant role in the successful completion of each task; indeed, they are the sine qua non of the entire procedure. And yet subaltern media are barely present during the process. Their operations take place in the background and may therefore count as true media practices, since they can be barely detected at the outcome. "Media turn the world readable, audible, visible, perceptible. In exchange, they erase their presence and participation, becoming themselves invisible, anaesthetical."[38] Servants operate on the periphery of the factual; their service is not at the center of attention and may therefore appear as secondary, minor, marginal. In contrast to other grand epistemic projects, the focus here is on media practices, which, for the most part, remain in the background.

The second premise of a marginal epistemology presupposes a remote object of inquiry, to be discovered in omitted regions, in overlooked or forgotten domains. Thus the margin takes center stage, and we may take a look behind the scenes, especially when such scenes turn out to be nothing but mere Potemkin villages. At first glance, none of the glamour of the façade is visible from behind, from the operating realm of the indirect. Representation and the authority of media are set apart in this particular configuration. Here, one may refer to Michel Foucault's "infamous men" or Carlo Ginzburg's concept of a strictly defined, yet metonymically open microhistory, with its in-depth attention to historical detail.[39]

Finally, the third premise is that subaltern figures are not merely defined and analyzed in terms of their media functions—such as operating doors to providing online information. Rather, servants also function as the media of historiography, enabling an alternate mode of historical inquiry. History is also 'made' outside of state actions and capital events, for instance—to paraphrase Brecht—by Caesar's cook or via the contribution of various dumbwaiters. A new perspective emerges from such reference points and supposedly trivial but, as it turns out, crucially important actors operating on the margins. The historiographic method ultimately allows for a complex and finely differentiated perspective.

Two conclusions can be drawn from this. For one, the theory of marginal epistemology requires a systematic reorientation, a new way of looking that demands attention be given to what is presumed to be marginal, yet without losing sight of what lies at the center. That is the only way to identify actors that have previously remained hidden or invisible, given their media practices and the paradoxes of subaltern service. The method presupposes a change of perspective, to be further applied to various historical situations. It advances new arguments and hidden configurations, which lie outside the beaten paths of traditional historiography. Methodologically speaking, the change of perspective functions not unlike a search filter that shuffles through historical sources and formations. One of the key findings of this study is that, beyond its protagonists, there is a wide range of minor figures and characters that demand attention, irrespective of where they are found: be it a bourgeois tragedy such as *Miss Sara Sampson,* a science lab, or a household, where they collectively ensure the well-being of their masters. The change of perspective is productive. Irrespective of historical conditions and traditional historiography, this reorientation enables the production of knowledge—not merely in the sense of supplementing it but also of seeing it in the right light.

Second, this theoretical model allows for more than just reclaiming the position of previously forgotten actors, bringing them to light, and giving them the attention they deserve. Indeed, such a process of search and analysis can be expanded to serve other areas of historical inquiry and media constellations, delivering new claims and conclusions. What, then, are the specific ideas enabled by the theory of marginal epistemology? As each chapter has shown, various instruments and methods can be extracted from a series of grand theories and then reassembled into a modular configuration, akin to a peripheral yet autonomous theoretical toolbox that may be further augmented. But only together do these elements ensure the visibility of the marginal.

If the goal is to bring to light what is hidden in history and concealed in the process of scientific production, then a key priority is to connect potential actors into new networks across vast spatial and temporal configurations. Broad historical connections should not be circumvented. Such connections may help (re)trace trajectories and arguments that sometimes traverse, in a continuous or broken line, several epochs via multiple stages of latency and growth. In this particular case, the servant-to-server trajectory is examined in its development from the baroque to the digital age, dissected into diverse and distinct partial processes. For instance, one must first examine the media practices of doorkeeping and the microphysics of power at work in the imperial chambers to understand their continuity in the digital domain and thus make sense both of classical Cerberi and electronic demons. Clearly, despite its thoroughly different social situation, the doorkeeper function continues well into the digital age. But as opposed to the baroque doorkeeper, who regulates access to the central site of power, his digital counterparts open up several new, interconnected paths to a power that has always been dispersed and disseminated among various points of entry, endless channels, and secret memory drives. And yet, structurally speaking, both digital and analog custodians perform the same media techniques of granting and denying access. Or, to use yet another example: only such transepochal lines of inquiry allow for an interpretation that traces back the contemporary OPAC system and its service function to the library custodian. Conversely, only such eclectic, diverse material, built around the seams and cuts of multiple disparate fragments, may result in a broader historical account, traversing three hundred years of service and media revolutions. To oversee (both skim through, and, especially, survey) broad connections is to look at events from a distance— something a marginal position is particularly able to ensure. "To be distant is to be peripherical, but distance also confers certain advantages."[40] The advantages lie not least in the methodological approach. The standard procedure of close reading of historical sources or literary texts is one of its fundamental working techniques. Marginal epistemology proposes—akin to the *marges de la philosophie*—to further decentralize this kind of methodology, in order to advance, with the aid of an expanded, complementary *distant reading*, to a method of *distant thinking*; in other words, a precise reading of what is distant, a careful consideration of the remote, which may enable an approach to peripheral knowledge and thus to the kernel of a new argument. "The first and most fundamental challenge has been to read canonical texts with enough sensitivity to their minor, fragmentary, provisional, and inorganic margins so as to allow the historical pressure of subalternity to be felt at all."[41] In order to come close to the subaltern figures of history one needs to read central texts via their slippery margins.

The context also needs to be further expanded to include other actors, even immobile and incongruous elements, into the network. From this point of view, architecture itself turns out to be a hugely significant structure for the media practices of baroque constructions, in terms of both servants and masters. The buildings are not erected solely according to the demands of representation. Indeed, they model a social structure, an architecture of serviceability manifested in the form of service stairs, back doors, and dark corridors. Moreover, if palaces are no longer seen as "empty architectural shells but as machines for living in,"[42] then subalterns and their symbolic practices, their liveries and court orders also belong to the operation technology of this machine, since they make available the necessary hierarchical distinctions of the system.

A further proposal associated with the premises of marginal epistemology refers to the oft-disparaged figure of analogy,[43] now deployed to test various explanatory discourses, and therefore used as a strategy of inquiry. This tool proves necessary, "since we need the experience of that which has vanished in order to reach an understanding of the present. Via analogies, that is to say, via the attempt to identify and differentiate, we define the analogous and the non-analogous."[44] The analogy figure therefore serves repeatedly as a catalyzer of knowledge in general as well as in particular. Ernest Rutherford, for instance, develops his atomic model in analogy to the solar system; Friedrich August Kekulé's benzene ring is modeled after the ouroboros snake; and the spread of electric networks relies not least on gas illumination as an analogy and model for the decisive steps to be taken to make the new development more accessible to its customers. In his *History of the Contemporary State of Electricity* from 1772, John Priestley had already lauded "similitude (analogy)" as "the ideal guide to all explorations in physics."[45] That principle can also be applied to the history of knowledge, for example, when linking the informational tactics of a valet or a servant with the services of contemporary search engines.

The notion of recursion, which has already been discussed in depth, allows temporally disparate elements to productively reference one another. By contrast, the proposed theory of marginal epistemology is based on a multiperspectival model rather than a monocausal explanation. As shown in the case of Michelmann's final assignment as an analog medium of information transmission, the question is to examine the same historical event from various theoretical perspectives via a range of methodological tools. The breadth of this approach goes hand in hand with the possibility of dissecting the impact of vast processes of transformation such as the phenomenon of electrification into historically discrete case studies. Such a case study is also provided by the kitchen. Here, the successive replacement of domestics with technical tools and the act of delegating their functions to inanimate objects, reveals and renders concrete a series of complex processes. The regime of thinking that derives from the object and the object alone dares to advance the powers of metonymy; that is to say, to take the part for the whole—for instance, when a piece of furniture called dumbwaiter replaces a human servant and thereby introduces the paradigm of self-service. One particularly promising narrative strategy is to take into account small gestures and apparently insignificant actions. In order to measure a medium's real functions, as well as the extent of their historical transformations, the focus must be on media practices that may lead to broad and ultimately general claims. Such a method can help retrace the transformation of epistolary closings, the gradual disappearance of typical formulas such as "Your most humble servant," symptomatic of a larger social and media revolution. Eventually, sub-altern senders enter the channel of communication and appear as today's dutiful internet servers. Once again, our linguistic tools, the terms and metaphors we employ, prove to be significantly more important than their supposedly random assignation may suggest. The careful reconstruction of semantic levels, as in the case of the server, the exploration of its etymology and functional connec-tions, unveil a case of metaphoric overdetermination, confirmed by the digital communication of today, with its manifold references to the long history of serviceability.

One communicates with the server via an interface, a digital mask. Behind that mask is a classical subaltern figure in analog form. The livery, the case of collective authorship in the science lab, the household activities kept hidden from the masters, the fictional literary roles—all these elements place a mask on the servant figure and hide it behind their individual appearance. Ultimately, the two-facedness, the multiplication of possible perspectives via acts of revela-tion and dissimulation, endows the subaltern with enormous epistemic produc-tivity. The doubling of perspectives brings with it a distancing effect in the pro-cess of observation, which proves to be an inherent quality of the servant figure. The mask implies a different angle of observation, giving the subaltern figure, from its external position, a distanced perspective on the events at the center. Ultimately, the servant possesses, or at least seems to possess, greater knowledge than the masters. This informational advantage is precisely what constitutes the relevance of the server in contemporary relations of communication. The server is where data gathers from every direction. It bundles it together into new con-stellations and thereby forms a basic nodal point of communication. It allows for a hidden platform of exchange, a meeting point of heterogeneous transmis-sions in the digital no-place.

Today, at the end of the second decade of the twenty-first century, the tradi-tional services of subalterns and domestics, of factotums and amanuenses have been transferred, for the most part, to technical objects, material instruments, and electronic appliances. The majority of attendants—waiters or servers—is transfigured and no longer single-handedly and directly attends to clients in human form. Those who were once called masters have been instructed to in-teract with apparatuses by way of self-service. Consequently, clients have lost the kind of comfort which Eduard von Keyserling still commemorated in 1905 in his melancholy farewell to the epoch of human serviceability. And yet our dependence on today's servants could not be any greater. All power belongs to the indirect, networked agents, and interstitial things. In 1982 three doctoral students at the University of Stanford and a UNIX specialist from Berkeley

Figure 17. A server that insists on self-service (Sun Microsystems, 2002)

founded the so-called Sun Microsystems in Silicon Valley. The company soon developed a highly profitable niche for connected workstation and server systems. The basis of the success story is due to the client–server architecture developed at Xerox PARC and embodied in two hardware components: a workstation and a version of a server called Sun 1, simultaneously offered by the company as a network system. A dumbwaiter, OneServer, embodies the empowerment of things.

Those who request a regular cup of coffee are also implicitly requested to operate a server that once served them. From now on, clients have to take matters into their own hands. Despite all digitalization, the manual component continues to be in demand for the influential cultural technique of service. But the tables have turned. Just as before, the master does not lift a finger. The main service activity belongs to the client. Meanwhile, in the background, in the virtual comfort of their idle time, things have long made themselves at home.

Notes

INTRODUCTION TO THE ENGLISH EDITION

1. "Ask Jeeves: Servants as Search Engines," in *Grey Room: Architecture, Art, Media, Politics,* no. 38 (Winter 2010), 6–19. "Robots as Companions: What Can We Learn from Servants and Companions in Literature, Theater, and Film?," with Robert Trappl, Zsófia Rutt-kay, and Virgil Widrich, *Procedia Computer Science* 7 (2011), 96–98; "Master and Servant in Technoscience," *Interdisciplinary Science Reviews* 37, 4 (2012), 287–98; "Little Helpers: About Demons, Angels and Other Servants," with Jimena Canales, *Interdisciplinary Science Reviews* 37, 4 (2012), 314–31; "The Power of Small Gestures: On the Cultural Technique of Service," *Theory, Culture and Society* 30.2 (2013); as well as the monographs translated to date, including *Paper Machines: About Cards and Catalogs, 1548–1929* (Cambridge: MIT Press, 2011); and *World Projects: Global Information Before World War I, Electronic Mediations* (Minneapolis: University of Minnesota Press, 2014).

2. See "The Information Bomb," Friedrich Kittler's conversation with Paul Virilio in John Armitage, ed., *Virilio Live: Selected Interviews.* London: Sage, 2001, 102.

3. See Friedrich Kittler, "Protected Mode," in *Literature, Media, Information Systems: Essays,* ed. John Johnston (Amsterdam: OPA, 1997), 158.

4. Bernhard Siegert, *Cultural Techniques: Grids, Filters, Doors and Other Articulations of the Real,* trans. Geoffrey Winthrop-Young, (New York: Fordham University Press, 2015), 10. For a detailed discussion of the rise of *Kulturtechniken* within the disciplinary and theoretical history of new German media theory, see Siegert's introduction in the same book.

5. See Canales and Krajewski, 327.

6. See Siegert, *Cultural Techniques,* 3.

7. Canales and Krajewski, 328.

8. The English title offers a greater advantage here: 'the server,' the book's central subject, as both humanoid and digital medium vs. the German 'Diener' (servant)—a term generally reserved for the human agent and profession.

9. Krajewski, "Master and Servant in Technoscience," 288.

10. Kittler, "Protected Mode," 151.

INTRODUCTION

1. Cain 1934. There is no mention of a (human) mailman in this case however.

2. Consider Second Life avatars, or web assistants.

3. Turner 1962, 96.

4. Latour 1999, 79. On James, the servant from *Dinner for One* and his *salto mortale,* see also Krajewski 2010, 118–20.

5. Latour 1991, 129.

6. See also Horn 1975, 4. The numbers of female and male staff are equal until the nineteenth century, when women become increasingly more numerous. Both genders are organized according to internal hierarchies (steward, majordomo, or, butler, and, finally, groom etc. – for men; and housekeeper, cook, and lady's maid etc. – for women). While men and women are kept (spatially) apart, they interact closely. For details, cf. Adams and Adams 1825, Hecht 1956, Hartcup 1980.

7. For more on the topic, see Stillich 1902, Ross 1912, Butler 1916, Franzbecker 1973, Ottmüller 1973, Bejschowetz-Iserhoht 1984, Mullins and Griffiths 1986, Orland 1993, Orth 1993, Buchal 1997, Meldrum 2000, Walthall 2008.

8. Cf. Rüss 1994, Rustemeyer 1996.

9. Cf. Ehrenreich 2003, Cox 2006, Pasleau and Schopp 2006, Lutz 2008, and, from a literary perspective, the novel by Aravind Adiga 2008.

10. Bearman 2005.

11. Sayre 2008, Hochschild 2010.

12. Hilker 2006, Frey 2007.

13. Ferry 2003, Ferry 2004, Back 2009.

14. cf. McClintock 1993.

15. Further on the topic also Cohen 1966, Nocks 2007, Huhtamo 1996.

CHAPTER 1. MASTERS / SERVANTS

1. Defoe 1725/1767, 15.

2. Ibid.

3. Ibid. 17.

4. Ibid.

5. Colman 1849, 32. Old habits die hard: such practices are still found in England and beyond as late as the nineteenth century.

6. Further on the topic Turner 1962, 158.

7. Fitz-Adam 1756, 353.

8. Defoe 1725/1766, 79.

9. Cf. Laslett 1965/2001, 1–22.

10. Sarti 2001, 2.

11. Veblen 1899/2007.

12. Marshall 1949, 3.

13. Cf. Weil 2005, 2.

14. Ibid., 9, and for a different reading Sarti 2006a.

15. Cf. Därmann 2008, 28f.

16. Cf. Brockmeyer 1979, 8f.

17. For a detailed analysis, see section 3.2 in this study.

18. Aristotle 1996, 15. "Now instruments are of various sorts; some are living, others lifeless; in the rudder, the pilot of a ship has a lifeless, in the look-out man, a living instrument; for in the arts the servant is a kind of instrument. Thus, too, a possession is an instrument for maintaining life. And so, in the arrangement of the family, a slave is a living possession, and property a number of such instruments; and the servant is himself an instrument for instruments."

19. Cf. Wendel 1974, 66.

20. Cf. Grimm and Grimm 1854, vol. 11, col. 1380.

21. Koselleck 1972–97, 58. The military terminology also refers to a *Knecht* as an esquire, who serves a knight until he also becomes one.

22. Cf. Thomasius 1710, 202, as well as Günther 1995, 4.

23. Zwahr 1990, 149; on the historical transformation of epistolary signatures and closing formulas, see section 5.2 in this study.

24. For instance, in the writings of the early Enlightenment author Christian Weise; also cf. Skrine 1985, 255.

25. Dietrich 1986, 329; on the ubiquity of the servant-status, also Seaton 1720/1985, 13f.

26. See Koselleck 1972–97 and, Günther 1995, 2, who shows that it is mainly Hegel who frees the notion of its theological context to apply it to politics and the philosophy of history.

27. See Koselleck 1972–97, 59f.

28. Zwahr 1990, 11–14, points out that Luther follows here the newly established tradition of German Bible translations. The shift from *servus* to *Knecht* takes place between 1060 and 1400, according to Zwahr.

29. Cf. Buchwald 1889, 7–12.

30. Ibid., 25, 28.

31. Laslett 1965/2001.

32. Klenke 1992, 27.

33. Horn 1975, 5.

34. See Lillo 1731/1965, who launches the tradition of the tragic servant in bourgeois drama; see also section 3.1. in this study.

35. For a comprehensive collection of such epitaphs, see Munby 1891.

36. Horn 1975, 4.

37. Further on this distinction, also Engelsing 1973a, 192.

38. Shapin 1994, 364–67; on the lab servant and his role in epistemic processes, see chapter 4, particularly section 4.2.

39. On the dissemination of the notion, see Sarti 2002, 31–37.

40. Stekl 1980, 109; Sagarra 1985, 169.

41. Laslett 1965/2001, 8.

42. Stekl 1980, 113.

43. Horn 1975, 6.

44. Servants have the same status as children. Servants' primers are also known as *Babies Books*, cf. Robbins 1986, 150.

45. Hecht 1956, 72.

46. With regard to the High Middle Ages, see Siegel 1883, and for a general overview Könnecke 1912 as well as Steinfeld 1991 for the Anglo-Saxon language context.

47. Münch 1995 offers a pertinent reading.

48. Leibniz 1678/1988, 78, and, further, Holz 1968.

49. Hagemann 1792, 5.

50. Dürr 1997, 131ff.

51. Schmitt 1954/2008, 14, and on the protection privilege, see Könnecke 1912, 239ff.

52. Dürr 1997, 123ff.

53. Schröder 1995, 35, who also provides an overview of hierarchies for the Prussian context between 1595 and 1810.

54. On the same topic, see Marshall 1949, 3, or Weil 2005, 3, but especially the excellent comparative overviews by Sarti 2006b.

55. Veblen 1899/2007.

56. Both quotes in Horn 1975, 1.

57. Already in the eighteenth century, the term "servers" [*Bedienten*] must have caused confusion; Adelung 1793, vol. 1, col. 781, argues that the term is an active perfect participle, therefore, it designates someone who serves rather than is being served.

58. Ibid. vol. 1, col. 551.

59. Cf. Auden 1954, 238.

60. Sagarra 1985, 168f.

61. Holz 1968, 48; on the question of subordination from a sociological perspective, see Simmel 1908/1950.

62. Cf. Boom 1979, 24.

63. For a detailed description, see Sarti 2001, esp. 412f.

64. Further on the topic, see section 2.2.2 in this study.

65. This may also explain why one cannot easily find accounts or life narratives pertaining to individual servants in the archives: the staff are usually lumped together with their masters (or fathers); see also Laslett 1965/2001 and Weil 2005, 3.

66. For further reference, see section 1.1.2.

67. Locke 1689/2003, Art. 85; its relevance goes beyond the baroque age; in one capacity or another, everyone is someone's servant: from Hegel to C. C. Fairchilds 1984, 2, or Sarti 2006b, the formulation is amply used.

68. Sarti 2005, 412.

69. Cf. Brunner 1956, 112; on Xenophon's *oikonomia* and the idea of the household, see section 6.3.

70. Bain 1981, 1f.

71. Further on the topic, see section 7.4 in this book; on the relation between servant and command, see also Skrine 1985, 252, and Auden 1954, 241.

72. Veblen 1899/2007, 155.

73. Ibid., 45.

74. Laslett 1965/2001.

75. Horn 1975, 3.

76. Ibid., 18.

77. Veblen 1899/2007, 41.

78. Ibid., 30.

79. Further on Goethe and Stadelmann in section 3.3 in this volume.

80. Meyer 1904, 153.

81. See also Weil 2005, 3.

82. Marshall 1949, 25, as well as Anderson 2005, 22.

83. See Sarti 2001, 3. " 'Relationship' itself is an eighteenth-century word. It occurs regularly in sociological and historical discussions of service," according to Weil 2005, 7, as well as Kuntz and Kuntz, 1987, on hierarchies in general.

84. Maza 1983, 6.

85. Hagen 1838, vol. 2, 56, maxim CCCXXX, b., 187. With special thanks to Claire Taylor Jones for the translation (I.I.).

86. Lammert 1929, 330, *Stratores* are grooms; see also section 4.1.3 in this study.

87. Defoe 1725/1767, 9.

88. Gerard 1984, 187.

89. Moser 1759, 269; on how to access antechambers, see section 1.2 in this study.

90. Gleichzu 1718. The lengthy baroque titles offer the possibility of a brief content overview since pages are uncut upon delivery. (Trans. I.I.)

91. Wichert 1989, 118.

92. On the history of the civil servant, see Lotz 1914, 29ff. as well as Koselleck 1972–97, 2.

93. The Prussian land law of 1794 initiates the first distinctions between higher and lower civil servants; see also Lecheler 1981, 3.

94. Cf. Hengerer 2004, 34.

95. Cf. Duindam 1998, 31.

96. Skrine 1985, 246; on the courtly hierarchy, see Duindam 1994, 137ff.

97. Extensively discussed by Bauer 2005b and 2005a.

98. Pfeilsticker 1957, xii.

99. See also Elias 1969/2006.

100. Diderot and Rond d'Alembert 1751–65, vol. 8, 319.

101. See also Sagarra 1985, 180. The aristocratic servant holds his position for an extended period, usually for life.

102. Adams and Adams 1825, 13; on the hierarchy of servants in domestic contexts, see Turner 1962, 116–78.

103. Ross 1912, 7.

104. Veblen 1899/2007, 44.

105. Stendhal 1830/1916, 330–31.

106. Regarding the use and limits of the notion of 'household' as *oikos* for the state, see Münch 1981.

107. Agamben 2011, 152. Regarding the connection between holy office and earthly service, cf. Kantorowicz, 1957, 288.

108. See also Macho 1997, 86.

109. Aquinas 1266/2013, 548.
110. See ibid., 389.
111. Lotz 1914, 4.
112. Sarti 2001, 5.
113. Horn 1975, 13.
114. Hengerer 2004, 75, 77.
115. Thürmann 1839, 18.
116. The term derives from the Spanish *mascarillo,* meaning "half-mask"; that is to say, a servant that takes on an aristocratic title under false pretense. Cf. Konversations-Lexikon 1906–19, vol. 13, 394.
117. Cf. Klenke 1992, 195; further, Sagarra 1989, 74.
118. Cf. Weil 2005, 7.
119. Turner 1962, 17.
120. Horn 1975, 2.
121. Marshall 1949, 6.
122. Laslett 1965/2001.
123. Turner 1962, 238.
124. Kittler 1989, 16f., 22.
125. Hegel 1807/1965, 118.
126. See Diderot 1792/1986.
127. Turner 1962, 271.
128. Kojève 1947/1980, 19.
129. Ibid., 24.
130. Hegel 1807/1977, 63.
131. Kojève 1947/1980, 20.
132. Ibid., 25.
133. Hegel 1807/1977, 117.
134. Ibid., 112.
135. Keyserling 1905/1973, 567. Trans. I.I.
136. Meier-Oberist 1956, 142; on the titles themselves, see Kern 1905–7.
137. Grimm and Grimm 1854, vol. 2, col. 489.
138. Sarti 2006b, 20.
139. Cunnington 1974, 8.
140. Sabattier 1984, 48, 51.
141. Klemm 1886, 3. Trans. I.I.
142. Kliegel 1999, 55.
143. Klemm 1886, 3. Trans. I.I.
144. Veblen 1899/2007, 78.
145. Klemm 1886, 3.
146. Cf. Kliegel 1999, 105–8.
147. Thackeray 1848/1986, 393, and further, McCuskey 1999, 385ff.
148. Plastic surgery around 1800: for the right look, sometimes lackeys wear padded stockings.
149. McCuskey 1999, 390.
150. Dinges 1992, 58.

151. See also Eisenbart 1962, esp. 52ff., as well as Groebner 1998.
152. Dinges 1992, 56. Trans. I.I.
153. Colors, patterns, and accessories indicate rank. Exceptions aside, a welcome side effect of the liveries is that the prescribed colors and cuts prevent any tendency on the part of the servants to dress up. Cf. Ross 1912, 18. To avoid ordering new clothes for their servants, masters hire new servants of similar body proportions to their predecessors. Not the material shell, but the substance is renewed in such cases—the opposite process to today's digital system updates.
154. Dinges 1992, 59. Trans. I.I.
155. On the connection between liveries and vestments, see Veblen 1899/2007, 121. "Priestly vestments … present an impassively disconsolate countenance, very much after the manner of a well-trained domestic servant."
156. Kliegel 2002, 37. Trans. I.I.
157. Cf. Sherman 1995, 561; on masquerade and courtly dress, see esp. Schnitzer 1999, 9f.
158. Veblen 1899/2007, 49.
159. Kliegel 1999, 58.
160. Veblen 1899/2007, 79.
161. Consider John Ball's rhetorical question on the historical foundations of class distinctions (1381): "When Adam delved and Eve span / Who was then a gentleman?" See Cunnington 1974, 148.
162. Robbins 1986, 16.
163. Moser 1754–55, 295.
164. On valets and the court hierarchy at Versailles see Da Vinha 2005, 44–64; also Newton 2006, and Newton 2008.
165. Moser 1754–55, 295. Trans. I.I.
166. Pangerl 2007a, 255ff. Hengerer 2004, 221, 230.
167. See Elias 1969/2006, 46. For the contemporary context, see Kurdiovsky 2008; for the historical development, see Ottillinger and Hanzl 1997.
168. Moser 1754–55, 254.
169. Hengerer 2004, 233.
170. Moser 1754–55, 211.
171. Pangerl 2007a, 264.
172. Moser 1754–55, 297.
173. Hengerer 2004, 234f.
174. Moser 1754–55, 297.
175. Stekl 1980, 113.
176. See Pečar 2005, 393.
177. Gerold 1776–1804, 432.
178. More extensively treated in Pangerl 2007b.
179. See Hengerer 2004, 233ff.
180. Ibid., 238; the order is prescribed, but not announced to the court; rather, it is only discreetly mentioned to the ushers.
181. Moser 1754–55, 299.
182. Ibid.
183. Kafka 1917/1956, 267.

184. Foucault 2000, 341.
185. Schmitt 1954/2008, 17.
186. Ibid. 22ff. Trans. I.I.
187. Cf. Jarzombek 2006, 7.
188. Schmitt 1954/2008, 21. Trans. I.I.
189. The corridor functions like a funnel of knowledge: the indirect powers prevent it from expanding excessively; the green baize doors function as valves, relieving the pressure of the crowd (the pistons) on the enfilade (as cylinder).
190. Schmitt 1954/2008, 25. Trans. I.I.
191. Ibid. Trans. I.I.
192. Ibid., 21. Trans. I.I.
193. The corridor is not to be understood as a horizontal extension.
194. Veblen 1899/2007, 33.
195. Hengerer 2004, 221.
196. Hofburg, tourist guide. Room 64. Vienna 2004.
197. Ibid. Trans. I.I.
198. Schönbrunn, tourist guide. Room 1. Vienna 2008. Trans. I.I.
199. From the term *schliefen* = to slip, to glide. Cf. Grimm and Grimm 1854, Vol. 15, col. 680–87.
200. Schmitt 1954/2008, 23. Trans. I.I.
201. See also Trüby 2008, esp. 38–47.
202. Malaparte 1931/1988, 82; and, on the takeover of communication channels, 32f.
203. Hepp 1971, 41f.
204. ". . . there is no such entity as power. . . . Power exists only as exercised by some on others . . ." See Foucault 1982/2000, 340.
205. After Evans 1978/1996, esp. 90–93, several studies have focused on the cultural history of corridors. See Trüby 2010, Marshall 2009.
206. Robbins 1986, 113.
207. This discussion can only be broadly sketched here. See Franklin 1975, Stratmann-Döhler 1995; for an ample historical and theoretical overview, see Trüby 2010.
208. Franklin 1975, 218.
209. Balderson 1982, 17.
210. Girouard 1978, 285.
211. Ibid., 284.
212. Kerr 1865, 67.
213. Ibid., 121.
214. Girouard 1978, 285f.
215. Kerr 1865, 175, 253.
216. Girouard 1978, 285.
217. With regard to the question of the glass ceiling, see Engelsing 1973a, 183.
218. Kerr 1865, 68.
219. Laver 1947, 474.
220. Kerr 1865, 68.
221. Klenke 1992, 286.
222. Kerr 1865, 176.
223. Ibid., 177.
224. See section 1.1.2 in this study.

225. Voltaire 1784/2007, 29.
226. Laube 1837, 55. Trans. I.I.
227. Freytag 1864/1887, 245–46.
228. Fontane 1895/2000, 51.
229. Grillparzer 1848/1960, 433. Trans. I.I.
230. Stifter 1857/2005.
231. From the French *bouteiller*; on the difference between *butler* and *valet*, see Krajewski 2010, 111–17; for further specific distinctions between the two in the context of the nineteenth-century bourgeois household, see Beeton 1861/1888, 1456–68.
232. Kellenbenz 1985, 503.
233. Cf. Hengerer 2004, 256, 261ff.
234. Cf. Kruse 1829; obviously, a literary figure such as Jules Verne's *Passepartout* 1872.
235. Kellenbenz 1985, 488, 495, 498; also, cf. Norberg 2008.
236. Hengerer 2004, 36–42.
237. Ibid., 257.
238. Hurter 1850, 669f. Trans. I.I.
239. Montaigne 1588/1993, 910.
240. Kantorowicz 1957/1997, 338ff., 35, 382, 436.
241. Bleibtreu 1888, vol. 3, 249.
242. Hegel 1807/1977, 404.
243. Weil 2005, 11.
244. On the subject of bribery, see Klenke 1992, 190.
245. Lamont-Brown 2000, Ketterl 1929/1980, Linge 1980, Barry 1983.
246. See section 3.1 in this study.
247. Carlyle 1843/1870, 184: "as the sum of all, comes Valetism, the reverse of Heroism; sad root of all woes whatsoever."
248. Ketterl 1929/1980, 10.
249. Frederick William III, 1926, 4.
250. Ibid., 22.
251. See, for instance, the previous quote from Voltaire.
252. Frederick William III, 1926, 22.
253. Ibid., 27.
254. Ibid., 24. See also section 5.2 in this volume.
255. Dietrich 1986, 328. The formulation was already in use before the mid-1750s. In Seaton 1720, for instance: "The very Prince, who is supreme over Us upon Earth is in reality more a Servant than any single Person of all his Subjects."
256. See the section on client–server architecture in this study.
257. Treitschke 1875, 17.
258. Bebel 1892/1972, 365.
259. Cf. Hecht 1956, 200: "The domestic servant class has a special significance. It was an important agent in the process of cultural change."
260. Schmitt 1954/2008, 25. Trans. I.I.
261. See Skrine 1985, 252.
262. Robbins 1986, 53.
263. Siegert 2005. On the discussion of the concept of cultural techniques, see also Schüttpelz 2006.

264. See Macho 2005, as well as Schüttpelz 2006.

265. See Hegel 1807.

266. Robbins 1986, 108.

267. Cf. Lamont-Brown 2000, Marshall 1949, 26.

268. Porter 1990, 104.

269. Defoe 1724/2006, 51.

270. Ibid., 185.

271. Hengerer 2004, 242.

272. Saint-Simon 1699/1906–19. English translation after Duindam 1994, 130.

CHAPTER 2. THE SERVANT AS
INFORMATION CENTER

1. The expression has been popularized by the work of P. G. Wodehouse, who draws on Sheridan's expression *gentlemen's gentlemen.* Sheridan, 1775/1997. The gentleman's personal gentleman should not be mistaken for a butler; rather, he shares the features of a typical valet de chambre or personal servant.

2. Wodehouse 2008, 250.

3. "'I am rather out of my depth with this question about men's overgarments. You'd better ask Jeeves,' I said."

4. Jaggard 1967, 84.

5. Wodehouse 2008, 273.

6. Ask.com has set up a memorial page for Jeeves, with details about his life after retirement. See sp.uk.ask.com/en/docs/about/jeeveshasretired.html, as well as a blog in honor of his departure: blog.ask.com/2006/02/thanks_jeeves.html.

7. Jeeves has never been a butler, but a valet, although the AskJeeves.com team has not grasped the fine difference. On the distinction between the two types see Krajewski 2010.

8. BBC News 2005.

9. Ross 1912, 4.

10. For further relevant analyses, see Brunner 1956 as well as section 6.3 in this study.

11. See, for instance, Engelsing 1973, 184.

12. Engelsing 1973a.

13. Robbins 1986, 200.

14. Engelsing 1973a, 183.

15. Robbins 1986, 174.

16. A characteristic trait of servants in the Elizabethan period; see also Weil 2005, 1.

17. Defoe 1725/1767, 7.

18. Krämer 2008/2016.

19. See also Robbins 1986, 92.

20. Theater is not necessarily the prerogative of fine society. During the nineteenth century a gentleman can send his servant to replace him, even after the first act; when the gentleman arrives, the servant must retire to the gallery, which also begins to establish itself as a platform of observation; servants read dramas and novels, which they distribute to their masters, not vice versa; see Engelsing 1973a, 216.

21. Da Vinha 2005, 325ff.
22. The peak of the servant novel coincides with the historical development of the dumb-waiter. Cf. Robbins 1986, 109.
23. Thackeray 1898, 604.
24. See Robbins 1986, 78.
25. Horn 1975, 30; noiseless, also in Michel Serres's meaning of *parasite*.
26. Hrabal, 1980/2007, 1.
27. Timothy Moorses, English butler and advisor on the TV series *Abenteuer* 1927—Sommerfrische, ARD, October 20, 2005. Trans. I.I.
28. Wodehouse 2008, 248.
29. Ibid., 203.
30. See also Sarti 2002, 31- 37.
31. Letter from Goethe to F. A. Wolf from August 3, 1805, in Goethe IV, vol. 19, and other similar examples; for instance, Goethe's letter to Charlotte von Stein, July 7, 1785, in Goethe IV, vol. 7: "I see a ministering spirit and must greet you through him." Or when Goethe seeks information about Madame de Stael: "I asked a ministering spirit, who the lady is that I saw and was told that she is French and goes by the name Madame von Stael." Goethe 1887–1919, vol. 1, 253.
32. The sighting of the privy councilor in the company of his son and his servant leads people to speak of a Thuringian triumvirate, the so-called Weimar trinity; see Schleif 1965, 150.
33. The main issue here concerns regulating the claims to power. See Matthew 20: 26–27.
34. Praetorius 1669, 377f., on Pselus 1838 (1017–78), who is a proponent of the corporeality of angels; see also Kantorowicz 1957/1997, 287.
35. See Macho 1997, 94.
36. See Robbins 1986, 182.
37. Wolff Metternich 1995, 384.
38. See also Waterfield, French, and Craske 2003.
39. Wolff Metternich 1995, 388.
40. Löbe 1852/1855, 2ff. as well as Müller-Staats 1987 for a general overview.
41. Memoirs and autobiographies are susceptible to being adjusted, embellished, abridged—ministering spirits often fall victim to such practices. A poignant example, indicating the invisibility of domestics, is the journal of the British scientist Humphrey Davy. The author simply removes a rather discreditable passage about a kitchen maid from the journal; see Fullmer 1967, 288.
42. Lenz 1964/1979, 42.
43. Süskind 1985/2001.
44. See Turner 1962, 176.
45. See Engelsing 1973a and Turner 1962.
46. The empirical methods of social history can prove useful in this regard; there is a long series of works that investigate the financial situation of servants; see, for instance, Schwarz 1999, Horn 1975, and Marshall 1929 for the eighteenth-century context.
47. See Robbins 1986, 183.
48. Ross 1912, 19.
49. Swift 1710/1908, 29.
50. Swift 1745/1993, 409.

51. Cf. Sherman 1995, 551.
52. See Orland 2003.
53. See Thackeray 1845/1856.
54. Turner 1962, 15.
55. See Sherman 1995, 553f.
56. Ibid., 556.
57. Defoe 1725/1766, 80.
58. Occasionally, servants take over the economic affairs of the household. When the domestic knows how to run the house like a master, the widowed lady of the house gladly takes him under her wing. See Robbins 1986, 121.
59. Users seem to be at the mercy of search bots. Computers never communicate absolutely everything. Market power is evaluated by the amount of data, metadata and special information owned and then sold piece by piece. See also Halavais 2009.
60. Swift 1745/1993, 376.
61. Turner 1962, 102.
62. Schmitt 1954/2008, 22f., as well as section 1.2.2 in this study.
63. See Da Vinha 2005, 325–35.
64. See Sagarra 1989, 76ff.
65. Robbins 1986, 140.
66. See Keller 2007, 5.
67. Ibid., 1.
68. See Tantner 2008.
69. See Müller 1981, 58.
70. Fielding and John 1752, 8.
71. For the corresponding numbers, see Wierling 1987, 76.
72. Stillich 1902, 296.
73. Müller 1981, 58.
74. Turner 1962, 162.
75. Wodehouse 2008, 250.
76. Usborne 1976, 209.
77. Müller 1981, 56.
78. Ibid., 61.
79. Ibid., 66.
80. The real locations of search engines are obviously not centralized but, on the contrary, dispersed, like the subjects of service that can be encountered anywhere. On server farms and clusters see Patalong 2008.
81. Turner 1959, 306.
82. Musil 1932/2011, 501.
83. Ibid., 502.
84. Ibid., 503.
85. See also Jochum 1991, 22.
86. Hrabal 1981/2001.
87. Musil 1932/2011, 504–5.
88. Ibid.
89. Ebert 1820, 14f. and, further, esp. Jochum 1991, 15f. and 20f.

90. Engelsing 1973a, 194.
91. See, for instance, Leyh 1961a, 731.
92. For more details, see Tantner 207, 67ff.
93. See Krajewski 2002/2011.
94. Leyh 1961a, 47.
95. Erman 1919, 26.
96. Milkau 1933, 687.
97. Ebert 1820, 54; see also esp. Jochum 1991, esp. 20ff. and 22: "The book production in the library leads to [. . .] the writing of nonbooks, which no one reads since they are not there to be read."
98. Musil 1932/2011, 503.
99. Robbins 1986, 105.
100. See Toucement 1731 as well as Engelsing 1973a, 201.
101. Schlözer 1776–82, part II, vol. xii, art. 57, 356.
102. Robbins 1986, 105.
103. See Sachse 1822/1977, 257.
104. Musil 1932/2011, 505.
105. Bömer 1957, 263.
106. Ibid.
107. Raabe 1995, 315.
108. On Helms, see also Jasper 2006, 334.
109. See Altick 1957, 85.
110. Räuber 1919, 170f.
111. Konversations-Lexikon 1906–19, vol. 13, 834.
112. Ebert 1820, 40, 42.
113. Erman 1919, 55.
114. Bömer 1957, 263; the fame continued into the second half of the twentieth century (see Raabe 1995, 318.): Raabe writes about Gerhard Halm that he "knew every location of every book."
115. Leyh 1961b, 47.
116. The technical term for the figure who nowadays moves back and forth between shelves and checkout station.
117. Hildreth 1982, 2f.
118. A preconception, in fact, a librarian myth, is the ease with which readers get used to a new research modality; see Su 1994, 136f.
119. Mason 1971, 183.
120. Su 1994, 144.
121. On the subject of the card catalogue as a precursor of the computer, see Krajewski 2002/2011.
122. Hildreth 1991, 21ff., 37f.
123. Standing for *enhanced, expanded,* and *extended* OPAC, ibid., 17.
124. Google lists digitally indexed historical library catalogues in facsimile.
125. Latour 1999, 178.
126. Latour 1994, 34.
127. Latour 1999, 183.

128. Ibid., 184.

129. Ibid., 183.

130. Ibid., 186.

131. Ibid.

132. Ibid.

133. The user may no longer be able to address the digital servant, but he can always write.

134. Latour 1999, 189.

135. See Engelsing 1973a, 207f.

136. Wodehouse 2008, 45.

CHAPTER 3. IN WAITING

1. Emelina 1975, 7ff.; see also Skrine 1985, 245ff.

2. Hoffmann 2002, 199.

3. Skrine 1985, 257.

4. On exceptions, especially servant and maid poets in the eighteenth century, see Steedman 2005.

5. Klenke 1992, 115; in such contexts the slave can even become the carrier of an ideal 'humanity'; see also Blänsdorf 1982 (on Menander).

6. On the role of servants in antique tragedies, see Bain 1981.

7. Cf. Frenzel 1999, 38–50 as well as the passage on the figure of the "wise fool," 562–74.

8. For Plautus and Terentius, see esp. Spranger 1984 and Klenke 1992, 115f.

9. Cf. Theile 1997, Ramm-Bonwitt 1997.

10. See Kluger 2006, 50, 68, 77f.

11. For the English literary context, see the work of Bruce Robbins (1986); for the Elizabethan age in particular, see the research of new Shakespeare scholars (see below); for the servant figure in classical French comedy, see Emelina (1975) and Klenke (1992); for the German Enlightenment comedy, Boom (1979) as well as the intercultural perspective offered by Wang (1999) with respect to China.

12. Also Opitz, Scaliger, Gryphius, Harsdörffer, see Benjamin 1925/2009.

13. See Szondi 1973/1977, 1.

14. See esp. Gottsched 1730/1977, 606.

15. Letter from Rammler to Glein, June 25, 1755, quoted in Daunicht 1971, 88.

16. Anonymous critique 1755, quoted in Eibl 1971, 217.

17. Lessing 1755/1878, 20–21.

18. Ibid., 7.

19. On these three phases, see Cerf 1980.

20. Lessing 1755/1878, 47.

21. Lessing, 46 SMPT-Code 250:NOOP (=No Operation).

22. Lessing, 47.

23. Ibid., 48.

24. Ibid., 50.

25. Ibid.

26. Ibid.

27. See Lessing 1755/2005; Lessing borrowed the name from Congreve 1700/2006.

28. Lessing 1755/1878, 51.

29. Cerf 1980, 24.

30. See Bornkamm 1957, as well as Zimmermann 1986.

31. See Cerf 1980, 25.

32. Letter from Johann Martin Müller to Johann Heinrich Voß, February 20, 1775 quoted in Daunicht 1971, 338. Trans. I.I.

33. Lessing 1755/1878, 58; status can also change in the opposite direction; in Johann Nestroy's drama *The Talisman* (1840), the barber apprentice asks, "What? I should become a servant? I who had already been a subject?" See Nestroy 1840/1962, 254.

34. Schleif 1965, 25ff.

35. See documents in the Goethe–Schiller archive in Weimar, esp. GSA 30/28.

36. Schleif 1965, 47, 221.

37. Ibid., 158, 163; Goethe does not always know the real name of his servants: see the note to the Jena police where he speaks of his servant 'N. N. Gensler.' *Nomen nescio.* Cf. GSA 30/28, 8–16. Also, see Schleif 1965, 159, 162.

38. Deleuze and Guattari 1980/2003, 117. "All becoming is minoritarian."

39. Parker 1996, 821.

40. Klenke 1992, 32.

41. Turner 1962, 170.

42. Boom 1979, 13; Emelina 1975, 333–50, for an entire chapter on servants' names.

43. See Althusser's (1970/2014) theory of interpellation.

44. Ibid., 269.

45. See Schleif 1965, 12, 21.

46. Ibid., 167.

47. Ibid.

48. See Goethe 1887–1919, IV, vol. 8; see also Linder 2001.

49. Böttiger 1838, 221; Seidel is Goethe's first servant in Weimar, between 1775–88.

50. Vogel 1834, 38.

51. Goethe 1887–1919, vol. 3, 152.

52. Schleif 1965, 45, 60.

53. Ibid., 134.

54. See ibid., 135, 215; J. L. Geist's 1797 diary of the Rhein voyage, see Goethe–Schiller Archive, Weimar, GSA 25/xxix, o.

55. The (famous) history of Charlotte Hoyer, Goethe's cook, who tore up Goethe's rather unflattering letter of recommendation; see Geiger 1908, 279, 283.

56. Ibid., 276.

57. Goethe 1887–1919, vol. 51, 342.

58. Ibid., vol. 5, 36.

59. Stadelmann 1815/1846; the diary survives only in fragmentary form (March–May 1815).

60. Chamisso's (1814/1975) Peter Schlemihl suggests how intensely servants can act as proxies of their masters.

61. Letter from Voß to Abeken, on February 21, 1804, in Goethe 1887–1919.

62. Turner 1962, 42.

63. Schleif 1965, 153, 222.

64. Geiger 1908, 275.

65. Fromman 1889, 54.
66. Goethe 1887–1919, IV, vol. 36, 92; see also Schleif 1965, 180f. On Stadelmann's self-ironic commentary on his own erudition, see his letter to Kräuter from December 24, 1816, in Stadelmann 1817/1913, 122ff.
67. Ibid. I, vol. 3, 25f. Goethe characterizes Stadelmann as a dilettante who stumbles upon rather than extracts the secrets of nature.
68. Column I: words dictated by the master; Column II: the personal diary.
69. Geiger 1908, 279f.
70. Ibid., 273.
71. According to the Weimar edition, there are 130 mentions, esp. in relation to rocks and boxes to be unpacked.
72. Kippenberg 1921, 5. The Stadelmann Society conceives of itself, at least nominally, as the counterpart of the Goethe Society. On the history of the society and the members' research contribution, see Ellermann 2009.
73. Goethe 1887–1919, III, vol. 9, 237.
74. Schoppe 1845, 134.
75. See Kippenberg 1924.
76. All quotes in Schoppe 1845, 117.
77. Ibid., 125.
78. Ibid., 126.
79. Ibid., 134.
80. See also Schierenberg 1994, 6.
81. Schoppe 1845, 107.
82. Ibid., 108.
83. Zima 2007, 5ff. as well as Chapter ii.
84. Müller 1870/1982, 187.
85. Schleif 1965, 100. Goethe's domestics are not the only ones who attempt to imitate their master's handwriting. In Victorian England there are reports of lab assistants engaging in similar activities; see, for example, the case of William Crooke's servant: "Even Giminghams' handwriting became more like Crooke's." In Gay 1996, 330.
86. Ibid., 222.
87. Ibid., 28.
88. Lynker 1912, 47.
89. Schleif 1965, 106.
90. Kippenberg 1922, 219.
91. Geiger 1893, 577.
92. Riemer 1841/1921, 18.
93. Auerbach 1946/2003.
94. Ricoeur 1981.
95. Goethe 1887–1919, IV, vol 8, 217f.
96. Schleif 1965, 61.
97. Goethe 1887–1919, IV, vol 8, 214.
98. See Klenz 1909, 225f.
99. Geiger 1893, 576.
100. Da Vinha 2005, 234.

101. Both quotes in Fairchilds 1984, 110.
102. Robbins 1986, 68.
103. Walser 1909/2014, 58.
104. Albaret 1973/2003.
105. Ibid.
106. Porstmann 1928, 2.
107. Benjamin 1929/1999, 241.
108. Ibid., 243.
109. Benjamin 1929/1999.
110. Ibid., 242.
111. Zimmermann 1986, 280.
112. Gove and Merriam-Webster Editorial Staff 1961, col. 2075.
113. Behringer 2003 and Behringer 1996.
114. Kittler 1993.
115. The VRFY command (=verify) or RSET (=reset).
116. See Krajewski 1997.
117. Kirkness 1977, 277.
118. Ibid., 278.
119. Schulze 1989, *Recursion*, 2293.
120. See Krajewski 1997, 6. Consider the case of a labyrinth. Each step forward implies acquiring information regarding the exact way back.
121. Schulze 1989, *Recursion*.
122. See also Dinges 1992, 63.
123. Tieck 1800/1996, 71.
124. See Kern 1977, 106.
125. Tieck 1800/1996, 86.
126. Ibid., 114.
127. Ibid., 53.
128. Ibid., 73.
129. Ibid., 34.
130. Ibid., 52.
131. Ibid.
132. Ibid., 73.
133. See Krämer 2008/2016.
134. Hoffmann 2002, 205.
135. Tieck 1800/1996, 63.
136. See Blänsdorf 1982, 131, 137ff.
137. Tieck 1800/1996, 54. As the fool comments, "Which play should we pay attention to? To the one before, or the one going on now?"
138. Ibid., 111.

CHAPTER 4. HOLDING THE REINS

1. Foucault 1966/2005, 267.
2. Cf. Homer 730/1998. For further reference see Krause and Müller 1981, 270ff.

3. Plato 380/2008, 39.

4. As in the case of William Crookes, who simultaneously performed séances, and researched cathode rays.

5. See Auden 1954. Balam is both the prince of demons and the king of subalterns, since he can grant his subjects the preferential status of servants, by bestowing upon them the gift of omniscient anticipation and invisibility.

6. Laplace 1814/1902, 4.

7. Cf. Broad 1934/1952.

8. Laplace 1773/1776, 144.

9. Laplace 1814/1902, 4.

10. Laplace 1773/1776, 113.

11. A strange coincidence: in the same year Laplace presented his 'intellect' to the Academy, Denis Diderot starts working on a very unusual novel where a servant named Jacques constantly discusses the question of the freedom of will with his master. Is it purely coincidental that every time something has to be done, Jacques comments that everything is "written up above"? See Diderot 1792/1986.

12. Du Boys-Reymond 1872, 60.

13. Ibid., 63.

14. Harman 1995, 332.

15. Ibid., 331.

16. Ibid., 332.

17. Thomson 1874, 441.

18. Thomson 1879/1889, 144.

19. Cf. Thomson 1874, 441. "The definition of a 'demon,' according to the use of this word by Maxwell, is an intelligent being endowed with free will, and fine enough tactile and perceptive organization to give him the faculty of observing and influencing." Interestingly, Thomson ascribes the designation to Maxwell, who actually rejects it. Ultimately, no one wants to claim they have called up a demon.

20. Maxwell to Tait, undated letter, quoted in Leff and Rex 1990, 5.

21. See Leff and Rex 1990.

22. Cf., most recently, Callender 2002, who refers to Karl Popper 1957 and Paul Feyerabend 1966.

23. Apart from two interventions by Marian von Smoluchowski in 1914, the initial attempts to save the law prove rather fruitless. Cf. Earman and Norton 1998, 440–51.

24. Cf. Earman and Norton 1988, 450.

25. Cf. Bennett 1998.

26. Cf. Norton 2005.

27. Earman and Norton 1999, 25.

28. See Leff and Rex 2003, 14ff. and 110.

29. See Leff and Rex 1990, 21 and 180ff.

30. Boltzmann refers to Loschmidt 1869; see also Daub 1970, 218–21.

31. Quoted in Leff and Rex 1990, 42.

32. See Heller 1991, 235. Both Popper and F. J. Tipler refer to Laplace, not Maxwell; on Maxwell, as well as Feyerabend's, Gordon's, and Smoluchowski's 'demonless' demons, see Shenker 1999, 348.

33. Ibid., 348ff.
34. See Williams 2001.
35. Few remember Maxwell's other major accomplishments today. By contrast, Maxwell's demon is far better known than its creator.
36. The topic will be discussed below; see Dierig 2006, 194–99.
37. See Leff and Rex 1990, 7–12, or Bennett 1998, 370.
38. Siegert 2003a, 41.
39. See Earman and Norton 1999 and 1998.
40. See Hagen 1999, 349. Helmholtz and Virchow are regularly mentioned in the context of the opposition to occultism.
41. Oppenheim 1985, 11f.
42. Crookes 1874.
43. On the media-technical a priori in the form of telegraphy, see Hagen 1999; see also chapter 5 in this volume.
44. Oppenheim 1985, 10.
45. Ibid.
46. Denzinger 1991, 779, art. 2824.
47. Ibid., 778, art. 2823.
48. Ibid., 779, art. 2824.
49. Clark 1999, 151.
50. Cf. Shapin 1998, 9–24.
51. Clark 1999, 156f.
52. Ibid., 296ff.
53. Ibid., 308.
54. Ibid., 305.
55. Ibid., 310.
56. Ibid., 160 and 298.
57. Horst 1821, 12.
58. See Serres 1995, Macho 1997, Siegert 1997, and Agamben 2011.
59. Horst 1821, 11.
60. Hamann 1759/1998, 57.
61. Beckmann 1792, 103f.
62. Reinecke 1933.
63. White 1963/1968, 13–38.
64. Beckmann 1792, 109.
65. Schlieben 1892, 168.
66. Ibid., 180.
67. Ibid., 175.
68. Ibid., 168.
69. Beckmann 1792, 121.
70. Schlieben 1892, 170.
71. See esp. section 4.2 in this study.
72. See Merton 1965/2004, 38.
73. Brecht 1928/2006, 63.
74. Kellenbenz 1985, 498.

75. Voltaire in a letter to Madame Denis, January 13, 1753.

76. Frederick William III 1926, 21.

77. Agamben 2011.

78. Engelsing 1973a, 204.

79. See Shapin 1989 and Shapin 1994, ch. 8, 358—406.

80. See Shapin and Schaffer 1985, 393ff.

81. Shapin 1994, 368, 383–89.

82. Shapin 1989, 557f.

83. Ibid., 558.

84. Ibid., 559.

85. See Darmstaedter 1908, 129.

86. See Shapin 1994, 377.

87. Kisch 1954, 165.

88. See Shapin 1989, 559.

89. See Pumfrey 1991, 7.

90. Ibid., 16, 15.

91. Pumfrey 1995, 140.

92. Pumfrey 1991, 1, 8.

93. See section 7.1 in this study.

94. Ibid.

95. Pumfrey 1995, 135.

96. Siegert 2003b, 130–42.

97. Cooper and Hunter 2006, xiv.

98. Inwood 2002, 149ff.

99. Mulligan 1996, 325.

100. Defoe 1725/1767, 7; and section 2.2.1 in this study.

101. Pumfrey 1991, 11.

102. Ibid., 17.

103. Pumfrey 1995, 132f.

104. See Gay 1996, esp. 322.

105. Kay 1963, who claims he has never broken a single glass; Kay is awarded the title of master of science; see also Ceranski 2005.

106. Browne 2002, 458.

107. Morus 2004, 25–66, 101.

108. See Wagener 1996.

109. Meinel 2006, 293.

110. Quoted in Hars 2005, 85.

111. Ibid., 83.

112. Quoted in Meinel 1978, 114.

113. Pumfrey 1995, 132.

114. Veblen 1899/2007, 57.

115. See Robbins 1986, 20.

116. See also Bebel 1892/1972.

117. Koselleck 1972–97, 16.

118. See also Crow 1972, 9f., drawing on Paul Valery's analysis of the demon.

119. Robbins 1986, ix f.
120. Also Schaffer 1997, 459ff., 482.
121. See Polanyi 1966/2009.
122. Sibum 1998a, 152; see also Sibum 1995b, 28ff., as well as Sibum 1995a, 74ff.
123. Sibum 1995a, 99; see also Sibum 1998b, 767.
124. See Sibum 1995b, 32ff., and Sibum 1998b, 763, as well as Sibum 2005, 305, 317.
125. Sibum 1998a, 152.
126. Sibum 1995a, 97.
127. Russell, Tansey, and Lear 2000, 239.
128. Kedesdy 1910, 2129.
129. See Görs 2001, esp. 180ff.
130. The servant hired by A. W. Hofmann, for instance, is supposed to act as a doorkeeper as well. See Krätz 1976, 42.
131. For the curriculum, profile, and duties of the female MTA, see Lange 1928.
132. E.R.L. 1919, 43.
133. Kojève 1947/1980, 49.
134. Hars 2005, 79.
135. In Szöllösi-Janze 1998, 234.
136. The Ministry of Education and Cultural Affairs at the University of Karlsruhe, in ibid. 237; also for an overview of Kirchenbauer's subsequent career.
137. Meinel 1978, 114.
138. Ukrow 2004, image 16.
139. See Hars 2005, 80.
140. Report by Adolf Reitz, in Beneke 1998, 50. For more on Pasteur's work practice and analyses of his lab books and servants, see also Kohler 1996.
141. Popper 1935/2005, 72; see also Heidelberger 2006, 384, 389.
142. See Crow 1972, 9f.
143. Weigel 2004a, 187; also for other historical landmarks in the history of the distinction between fact and fiction in St. Augustine, Decartes, Vico, and Dilthey.
144. Ibid., 192.
145. For the question of metaphoricity in contemporary life sciences, see, for instance, Weigel 2004b.
146. Latour 1991, 10–11.
147. Thomson 1879/1889, 144.
148. See Baeyer 1998, 92.

CHAPTER 5. CHANNEL SERVICE

1. Hackländer 1854/1875, 176.
2. For an overview see Aschoff 1987.
3. Letter from Gauss to Olbers on November 20, 1833, quoted in Förster 1883, 490.
4. Letter from Gauss to Humboldt on June 13, 1833, quoted in Timm 2005, 173.
5. See Aschoff 1987.
6. Feyerabend 1933, 37.
7. See Siegert 2003b, 290ff., 332ff.

8. See Schüttpelz 2003.

9. For details see Drogge 1983, 93ff. as well as an anonymous source from 1834.

10. Letter from Gauss to Heinrich Christian Schumacher on August 6, 1835, quoted in Förster 1883, 491.

11. Kehlmann 2005, 25.

12. Drogge 1983, 88f.

13. Letter from Gauss to Humboldt on June 13, 1833, quoted in Timm 2005, 173.

14. Cf. Weber's letter to Gauss, September 1837 in Drogge 1983, 86.

15. Feldhaus and Fitze 1924, 58.

16. Wagener 1996, 270; see also Clark 2006.

17. Mackensen 1962, 337f.; also Müller-Staats 1987, 11.

18. For an overview, see Burke 2005 and Schleier 2003, who provides a German and European cultural history since the eighteenth century.

19. Hacke 2006, 148.

20. Drogge 1983, 89 and Wagener 1996, 370ff., 533.

21. Beuermann and Görke 1983, 44.

22. Karrass 1909, 690 or Schulze-Gattermann 1935, 23 and, later, Feldhaus and Fitze 1924, 58.

23. Quoted in Weber 1893, 29.

24. Cf. Wagener 1996, 371, 533.

25. See also Kantorowicz 1957/1997.

26. Cf. section 4.2.1 in this study.

27. Cf. Shapin 1994, 375.

28. All quotations in Wagener 1996, 371; see also Shapin 1994, 377, on Hooke see Inwood 2002, esp. 18ff., as well as Siegert 2003b, 130f.

29. The message *Michelmann's here* is a rare occurrence, not in the least because there is no mention of its role in literature.

30. Shapin 1994, 359.

31. Bickenbach and Maye 2009.

32. See Vismann and Krajewski 2007.

33. See chapter 7 in this study.

34. Cf. Lange 1987.

35. Williams 1847, 81.

36. Keyserling 1905/1973. Trans. I.I.

37. Kleist 2001, 887.

38. Denecke 1892, 341.

39. The critical literature on the subject is scarce. Schrader 1911 povides the first monograph on Goethe's epistolary signatures, followed by Gerhardt 1924 on Schiller.

40. Denecke 1892, 325.

41. Ibid., 339.

42. See Steinhausen 1889, 47.

43. Ethophilus 1753, 110.

44. Both quotes in Denecke 1892, 330.

45. Ibid., 331.

46. See Schrader 1911, 34.

47. Steinhausen 1889, 236.

48. Schrader 1911, 37.

49. Denecke 1892, 325.

50. Ibid., 323.

51. Rothe 1902, 18.

52. Weinacht 1973.

53. Steinhausen 1907, 157.

54. Nickisch 1969, 19f.

55. See Steinhausen 1889, 49.

56. Grünbart 2005, 96ff.

57. Pfeifer 1995, 1492.

58. Bolhöfer 1912, 61.

59. Ibid., 62.

60. Steinhausen 1889, 49.

61. Ibid., 47.

62. See Siegert 1990, 548.

63. See Roseno 1933.

64. Vellusig 2000, 46.

65. Siegert 1993/1999.

66. See Prause 1930, 111.

67. Ibid., 68 as well as Scholz 1956, 145.

68. Menantes 1716/1730, 39f.

69. Wiering 1987.

70. Denecke 1892, 331ff., 342.

71. Not surprisingly, the disappearance of the formula coincides with the institutionalization of the letter carrier.

72. Kleist 2001, 887.

73. Stieler 1673, 206.

74. Grimm and Grimm 1854, vol. 11, col. 1393.

75. Prause 1930, 111.

76. Lütt 1892, 229.

77. Morgenstern 1918/1986, 193.

78. Dähnhardt 1974, 41, with reference to Büttner and Morgenstern 1981.

79. Also, Aschoff 1987.

80. Both quotes in Bernhard 1989/1990, 31f.

81. Polt-Heinzl 1997.

82. Siegert 1997, 48.

83. Lauffer 1954, 20.

84. Quoted in Morus 1996, 341.

85. Blumenberg 1960/2016, 44.

86. Kellenbenz 1985, 499.

87. Serres 1995, 67, as well as Macho 1997 and Krämer 2008, esp. 66–80, 122–38.

88. Latour 2001, 225.

89. Macho 1997, 95.

90. Knoch 2006, 3.

91. Lütt 1892, 294.

92. Serres 1968/1982.

93. Hacke 2006, 149.

94. Scior 2006, 131.

95. See Latour 1999 on the topic.

96. Wichert 1989, 123.

97. Fontane, 1891/2011, 118.

98. Quoted in Robbins 1986, 65.

99. Ibid., 92.

100. Weise 1693/1971, 294.

101. Kafka 1986, 230.

102. Benjamin 1929/1999, 241.

103. Clermont-Tonnerre in ibid., 243.

104. Albaret 1973/2003, 215.

CHAPTER 6. AT THE STOVE

1. Cachée 1985, 44.

2. Ibid., 28.

3. See Latour 1991/2006; for the chain of association model, see Latour 1996a.

4. Latour 1991.

5. Cachée 1985, 28.

6. Which may also appear as black boxes as an effect of the grime that collects on the interior.

7. Turner 1959, 237.

8. Cachée 1985, 32.

9. Ketterl 1929/1980, 28.

10. There is abundant literature on this topic; see an overview in Müller-Staats 1987, 31–53.

11. Davidis 1863/1902, 48.

12. See Orland 1990, Kreil 2000, and Heßler 2001; on the topic of the twentieth-century American household and its transformation, see Lifshey 1973 and Parr 1999 as well as the classic McLuhan 1951/2008.

13. The phenomenon is intensely researched within social history; see Engelsing 1973c, Müller 1981.

14. See contemporary sources, for instance, Stillich 1902.

15. Another designation is "muffin stand," as well as a side table on wheels, see *Vanity Fair,* December 1917, 17.

16. Ibid., 10.

17. Dictionary 2000, s.v. "server."

18. Dictionary 2000, s.v. "dumbwaiter."

19. See Prescott 1936, Bain 1981, 2; their role is different in comedy, where they play a significant part.

20. Seneca 2007; see also Dunbabin 2003, 444.

21. On this topic in late Roman art, see the richly illustrated examples in Dunbabin 2003.

22. Franken 2004, 50, 52.

23. Keyserling 1905/1973.
24. Masters who feel oppressed by the interventions and disturbances of servants would seek independence by installing objects, which cannot overhear them.
25. Smith 1824, 184.
26. Smith 1841/1906, 387f.
27. Johnson (Latour) 1988, "Mixing Humans and Non-Humans," 308.
28. Ibid., 308–9.
29. Keyserling 1905/1973.
30. Quoted in Cachée 1985, 48.
31. Coppersmith and Lynx 1949, 22.
32. See Mareschal 1887, 271.
33. Hospitalier 1887, 345.
34. Ibid.
35. Ibid., 346.
36. Goldoni 1743/2004, 38.
37. Rüss 1908, 16f.
38. Perfect participle, passive voice.
39. Caradec and Arnaud 1964, 529.
40. See Anonymous 1910, 73ff.
41. For a detailed account, see Hepp 1971.
42. Keyserling 1905/1973, 554.
43. Ibid., 553.
44. Ibid., 554.
45. Ibid., 554.
46. Ibid., 562.
47. See note 29 in this chapter.
48. Krajewski 2007.
49. Andritzky 1992.
50. See Haase 1992, Orland 1983, Orland 1998.
51. Kerr 1865, 204.
52. Kitchiner 1817/1830, esp. 16.
53. See Steedman 2005, 10ff.
54. Woolf 1950, 96.
55. Anonymous 1910, 73.
56. Petersen 1927, 26; also in Heßler 2001, 68ff.
57. Both quotes in Anonymous 1910, 73.
58. Bebel 1892/1910, 464.
59. Ibid., 464.
60. Ibid., 462.
61. See Uhlig 1981.
62. Bebel 1892/1910, 467.
63. Heßler 2001, 65.
64. Bebel 1892/1910, 465.
65. Both quotes in Orwell 1965, 115.
66. Treitschke 1875, 17.

67. See Grant 1994, 298ff., and also Scharf 2001b.

68. See note 18 in chapter 1.

69. See Lietzmann 1994; for an overview of the history of automata, see Cohen 1966, Swoboda 1967, Heckmann 1982, or Nocks 2007.

70. Löbe 1852/1855, 7, also the classic La Mettrie 1748/1996.

71. Thus Titus Feuerfuchs on Madam von Cypressenburg's servant in Nestroy 1840/1962, 315. Feuerfuchs, *Firefox* is a classic *client* to whom the server delivers information.

72. See Kapp 1877, 26–39.

73. Jean Paul 1798/1988, 903.

74. See Da Vinha 2005, 45–53, also Newton 2006, 53–104.

75. On eighteenth-century automata, Voskuhl 2005, Voskuhl 2009, esp. 201ff.

76. Jean Paul 1798/1988, 904.

77. Ibid., 904.

78. See Jean Paul 1785/1974.

79. All quotes in ibid., 1028.

80. Lütt 1892, 285.

81. Ross 1912, 59.

82. See the microhistory by Steedman 2007; on robots as servants, see Huhtamo 1996, esp. note 6.

83. Both quotes from Veblen 1899/2007, 44.

84. Letter from Carl Friedrich Zelter to Goethe, February 21, 1829. In Goethe 1998, 1202.

85. Turner 1962, 9.

86. Veblen 1899/2007, 47.

87. Ross 1912, 24.

88. See the detailed history by Giedion 1948/1987.

89. Young 1958, 96f.

90. Ibid., 98.

91. Purdy 1984, 134; on the anthropomorphization of objects that serve, see Johnson 1988.

92. For an introduction to the theory, see Belliger and Krieger 2006.

93. Latour 1999, 178.

94. Ibid., 180.

95. Latour 1996a.

96. Ibid.

97. Latour 1999.

98. See Latour 1999; on the role of hybrids as surface phenomena of fundamental spatial modifications, see Latour 1996a.

99. All quotes from Grimm and Grimm 1854, vol. 11, s.v. "bondsman."

100. Foucault 1975/1995, 153.

101. See Latour 1986/2006.

102. Latour 1991.

103. See Hubig and Koslowski 2008.

104. More on the topic in Meyer 1998, 50ff., and Richarz 1991, 21ff.

105. See, for instance, Brunner 1956, 109.

106. According to Sieder 2004, 119.

107. Knigge 1788/1790, 229.

108. See Meyer 1998, 36.
109. Xenophon 1997.
110. See Boom 1979, 15.
111. Watanabe 1990.
112. Berners-Lee, Hendler, and Lassila 2001, 34.
113. See Krajewski 2007, 150.
114. See also section 7.1 in this study.
115. On the critique of the progress model from the perspective of ANT, see Latour.
116. See, for example, Hallett 1939, 171.
117. Ibid., 225.
118. Ibid.
119. Serres 1995, 47–48.
120. Serres 1980/2007, 233.
121. Serres 1980/2007.
122. Latour 1991/1993, 83.
123. Ibid., 81.
124. See Shapin and Schaffer 1985.
125. See Latour 1991/1993.
126. Serres 1995, 50–51.
127. Latour 1991/1993, 89.
128. Ibid., 66.
129. Callon 1990.
130. Law 1992/2006.
131. Lèvi-Strauss, 1962.
132. See Hughes 1983.
133. See section 3.6 in this study.
134. Diehl and Hardart 2002, 28.
135. To *"enter service"* and *"to earn"* share the same Old Germanic linguistic root, see Zwahr 1990, 126–31.
136. Ross 1912, 25.
137. Light 2007, 188.
138. Ibid., 211. Nellie Boxall will become a local celebrity, since she takes over the kitchen of a famous actor, who even helps with an ad for a new stove, see ibid., 215f.
139. Hepp 1971, 29.
140. See Horn 1975, 30.
141. See Lewton 1930 and Holden 1886.
142. Both quotes are from the kitchen booklet, see Krajewski 2007, 144ff.
143. Compare the corresponding Request for Comments 1998; on the topic of the telematic coffee brewing, see also the famous Trojan Room Coffee Machine (www.cl.cam.ac.uk/coffee/coffee.html), whose server nevertheless resigned on July 22, 2001.

CHAPTER 7. AGENTS

1. Wierling 1987, 292.
2. See Bearman 2005.

3. According to Hoffmann 1998, 21, on Hermann Lenz's *The Eyes of the Servant.*

4. See, for example, Di Nitto 2009.

5. Dictionary 2000, s.v. "server."

6. Ibid.

7. Svobodova 1984, 354.

8. Mills 2003.

9. Albitz and Liu 2006, 9; see also Galloway 2004, 47–50. The notion of protocol refers back to a high-ranking court servant, the *Oberst-Hof-Meister* at the Viennese court, who was in charge of keeping the records of the court rituals after 1652, in the manner of the Roman censors.

10. Wodehouse 2008, 33.

11. See Latour (as Jim Johnson) 1991/2006, 242.

12. Garman 2003, esp. 1–6; on doors and thresholds as communication media in both the digital and the analog domains, see Nichols, Wobbrock, Gergle, and Forlizzi 2002.

13. Shor 1998, n.p.

14. Irlbeck and Langenau 2002, 756.

15. Svobodova 1984, 355.

16. See Wodehouse 2008, 179.

17. Sinha 1992, 79.

18. Ibid.

19. Spector 1989, 194.

20. Irlbeck and Langenau 2002, 756; on recursivity and the human servant, see section 1.1.2 in this book.

21. Spector 1989, 194.

22. See Vismann and Krajewski 2007, 96–98.

23. Steinberg 2002, n.p.

24. Also Alderman and Richards 2007, 58, 64, 72.

25. Licklider 1960/1990, 4.

26. Also Siegert 2008, 104.

27. Ceruzzi 1998/2003, 113, 119.

28. Further on Licklider 1960/1990, for instance, Waldrop 2001.

29. Licklider 1960/1990, 8.

30. A detailed, comprehensive study of time-sharing can be found in Hellige 1994, also Waldrop 2001, esp. 163, 190–94, and, with focus on Paul Baran, also Bunz 2008, 27–87.

31. Hellige 1994, 57.

32. Ibid., 15–19.

33. Licklider 1965, 18. N.B.: Licklider still speaks of "servants," in other words, of human actors; a decade later, the current term in the case of electronic services is "server."

34. For the (ecclesiastical) history of the term "host," see Siegert 1994.

35. Licklider 1960/1990, 2.

36. Ibid., 38.

37. Ibid. Selfridge was initially Norbert Wiener's assistant, then Licklider's collaborator on the MAC Project ("Project on Mathematics and Computation" at MIT, whose main focus after 1963 is the development of time-sharing).

38. Ibid., 24.

39. Licklider 1965, 18.

40. See Xerox chairman Peter McColough's rather awkward attempt to convince the members of the board of the project and its relevance in Hiltzik 1999/2000, 29.
41. Brand 1972.
42. PARC 2007.
43. Ibid., n.p.
44. On Alan Kay, see Barnes 2007.
45. See Lampson 1979, 11–17, 19.
46. E-mails from Alan Kay addressed to the author on April 13 and 18, 2009.
47. Also Stefik 1996.
48. Hiltzik 1999/2000.
49. E-mail from Adele Goldberg to the author, April 19, 2009.
50. For a firsthand historical account, see Metcalfe 1994.
51. See Annie Leibovitz's photographs at PARC, in Brand 1972.
52. Metcalfe and Boggs 1976, 402.
53. Also Frank, Kahn, and Kleinrock 1972, 264.
54. Thacker 1979/1982, 44–46.
55. Watson 1981, 16.
56. See also section 1.1.2 in this study.
57. Irlbeck and Langenau 2002, 756.
58. For the origin of the term, see Israel, Mitchell, and Sturgis 1979.
59. Drosdowski 1989, 846.
60. Dictionary 2000, n.p., s.v. "client."
61. Strange irony: despite its designation, the personal computer does not work with a large personnel department—at least not human personnel.
62. See section 1.2.2 in this study.
63. Sinha 1992, 78.
64. See tools.ietf.org/html/rfc1.
65. For instance, Spector 1989 or Watson 1981.
66. Bues 1995, 124.
67. Apple Computer Inc. 1994, 4.
68. Schwickert 1995, 313.
69. Ibid.
70. See section 3.6, 267.
71. Colony and Mead 1990, 51.
72. Shaffer 1994, 5.
73. Svobodova 1984, 355.
74. See PARC 2007, n.p.
75. A genuinely democratic structure is established and broadly applied only with the advent of Web 2.0 and the peer-to-peer principle; see Bunz 2008, 16–24, 67.
76. Appleton, Cherenson, Kay, and Marion 1995, S-3.
77. Pflüger 2004, 375.
78. See Vismann and Krajewski 2007, 96–99.
79. Sydow 1994, xi.
80. See also the excellent work of Haverkamp 1996 as well as metaphorology studies, for instance, Blumenberg 1960/2016, Konersmann 1999.
81. Black 1954/1996, 63–68.

82. Konersmann, 1999, 122.

83. Black 1954/1996, 78.

84. See ibid., 71; the respective fit of the selected elements ultimately determines the applicability of the metaphor; their *aptum* decides the success rate of their use.

85. Blumenberg 1960/2016, 44.

86. Bickenbach and Maye 2009, esp. 25–34.

87. See Black 1954/1996, 63.

88. Blumenberg 1960/2016, 3.

89. Blumenberg 1979.

90. Kant in Blumenberg 1960/2016, 5.

91. Blumenberg 1979.

92. Blumcnbcrg 1960/2016, 139.

93. Ibid., 14.

94. Blumenberg 1979.

95. See ibid., 88.

96. The anthropomorphization effect of metaphors occurs quite frequently; the canonical example can be found in Quintilian: *pradum riret,* the meadow laughs, see ibid., 89.

97. See Serres 1995; for the doubling of a user's persona beyond Second Life, see, for instance, the suggestion on www.zweitgeist.com: the proposal to take an avatar along while surfing the Internet.

98. See esp. Bradshaw 1997, 5f. Bradshaw defines an agent as "one that acts or has the power of authority to act . . . or represent another." Laurel 1990/1997, 68, puts it in even more concrete terms: "An interface agent can be defined as a character, enacted by the computer, who acts on behalf of the user in a virtual (computer-based) environment. Interface agents draw their strength from the naturalness of the living-organism metaphor in terms of both cognitive accessibility and communication style."

99. Negroponte 1997, 59.

100. See Kay 1984, 58.

101. See, for instance, Trappl and Petta 1997, Siefkes 1998, Prendinger and Ishizuka 2004, 3–12.

102. Latour 1983/2006 regards such a metaphor as a source of an entire series of innovations, and Maes, Guttman, and Moukas 1999 point out that digital representatives themselves require an education.

103. Auguste Villiers de l'Isle-Adam quoted in Robbins 1986, 48.

104. See also esp. Bachelard 1953, 216ff., who differentiates between terms with or without quotation marks. Temperature, in its regular sense, means something other than "temperature" in strictly physical terms. In informatics, metaphors do not require quotation marks since they do not function as scientific concepts but rather as programs of knowledge and strategies of evidence that insist on continuity.

105. Blumenberg 1960/2016, 132.

106. Ibid., 5.

107. Both quotes, ibid., 5.

108. Turing 2004, 389.

109. Hegel 1807.

110. All quotes in Scarrott 1979, 5.

111. Ibid., 6.
112. Ibid., 14.
113. Ibid., 15f.
114. Scarrott's demands for the new communicative model: (1) a more transparent organization structure; (2) better access rights for the end user—in other words, more lenience on the part of the digital guards; (3) data access for end users in accordance with their rights; (4) independent search capacities; and (5) the ability to mobilize entire collectives with a single command, see ibid., 18f.
115. Ibid., 26.
116. Haraway 1997, 11.
117. Latour 1999, 191.
118. Rogers 1985, 81.
119. Cf. Robbins, writing on the topic of subalterns' hands and their visible historical effects, as opposed to their 'invisible' bodies, 1986, ix f.
120. A proxy server, meaning 'appointed or authorized,' acts as a go-between for the client and other servers, whose information it temporarily saves or filters. The requests it receives are rendered anonymous.
121. See, for instance, Vijayan 2009.
122. E-mail from Alan Kay to the author, April 18, 2009.
123. Wikipedia 2009, n.p.; the *servent* continues the language games of *différance*.
124. Mann 1901/1994, 175.

EPILOGUE

1. See Hacke 2006, 140.
2. Hengerer 2004, 263.
3. Polt-Heinzl 1997, 275.
4. See, for instance, Seaton 1720/1985, Society for the Encouragement of Honest and Industrious Servants 1752, Haywood 1787/1985, Anonymous 1794, Adams and Adams 1825, Roberts 1827/1988, Williams 1847, Löbe 1852/1855, Anonymous 1894/1993, Reuß 1908, or, as a contemporary alternative, Ferry 2004.
5. See Robbins 1986, 72, who argues that watching with closed eyes is a prelude for a special gift: vision.
6. See note 44 in chapter 4.
7. Kippenberg 1922, 250.
8. See Engelsing 1973a, 217, for a broad overview into domestics' reading habits.
9. Wodehouse 2008, 12f.
10. Both quotes in Engelsing 1973a, 214.
11. Veblen 1899.
12. Albaret 1973/2003, 84f.
13. Ibid., 227.
14. Robbins 1986, 193.
15. Goncharov 1859/2005.
16. Critchley 1997/2004, xxiv.
17. Schweizer 2008, 40.

18. Ibid., 29.
19. See Canales 2009.
20. Computer Desktop Encyclopedia 2010, n.p; regarding the question of what machines actually do at night, see Höge 2010, n.p.
21. See Schweizer 2008, 22.
22. Ibid., 25.
23. Ibid., 2.
24. See the famous passage on what happens when a sugar cube dissolves in water, Bergson 1907/1998, 10–11.
25. Schweizer 2008, 19.
26. Ibid., 31; on the topic of idle states, see also Gronau and Lagaay 2007.
27. Erdmann 1852, 28.
28. Barroso 2007 offers a good overview.
29. See Buck 2008.
30. Köhler 2007, 35.
31. Agamben 2011.
32. On the notion of aevum and the two-body theory that can be directly applied to the avatars in *Second Life*, see Kantorowicz 1957, 275ff.
33. Letter from Goethe to Kestner from March 1774 in Schrader 1911, 37.
34. Harman 1995, 331.
35. Rheinberger 2007, 11.
36. Ibid., 11f.
37. For a historical overview of the twentieth century in this regard, see ibid.
38. Pias 2000, 10.
39. See Foucault 1977 and Ginzburg 1976/2003.
40. Robbins 1986, 206.
41. Ibid., 206.
42. Baillie 1967, 199.
43. See Breidbach 1987.
44. Engelsing 1973a, 182.
45. Priestley 1772, 292; on the critical reevaluation of analogy and similitude in nature research and science theory, see Rudolph 2006.

Bibliography

Adams, Samuel, and Sarah Adams (1825). *The Complete Servant: Being a Practical Guide to the Peculiar Duties and Business of All Descriptions of Servants . . . with Useful Receipts and Tables.* London: Knight and Lacey.

Adelung, Johann Christoph (1793). *Grammatisch-kritisches Wörterbuch der Hochdeutschen Mundart.* Zweyte vermehrte und verbesserte Auflage. Leipzig: bey Johann Gottlob Immanuel Breitkopf und Compagnie.

Adiga, Aravind (2008). *The White Tiger.* New York: Free Press.

Agamben, Giorgio (2011). *The Kingdom and the Glory: For a Theological Genealogy of Economy and Government.* Stanford: Stanford University Press, 2011.

Aïssé, Charlotte Elisabeth (1878). *Lettres de mademoiselle Aïssé à madame Calandrini.* Alexandre Piedagnel, ed. Petits chefs-d'œuvre. Paris: Librairie des bibliophiles.

Albaret, Céleste (1973/2003). *Monsieur Proust.* New York: New York Review of Books.

Albitz, Paul, and Cricket Liu (2006). *DNS and BIND.* Sebastopol, CA: O'Reilly.

Alderman, John, and Mark Richards (2007). *Core Memory: A Visual Survey of Vintage Computers Featuring Machines from the Computer History Museum.* San Francisco: Chronicle Books.

Allen, Christopher, and Kimberly Allen (1997). *A Butler's Life: Scenes from the Other Side of the Silver Salver.* Savannah: F. C. Beil.

Allen, Gary, and Ken Albala, eds. (2007). *The Business of Food: Encyclopedia of the Food and Drink Industries.* Westport, CT: Greenwood Press.

Althusser, Louis (1970/2014). *On the Reproduction of Capitalism: Ideology and Ideological State Apparatuses.* London: Verso.

Altick, Richard Daniel (1957). *The English Common Reader: A Social History of the Mass Reading Public, 1800–1900.* Chicago: University of Chicago Press.

Anderson, Linda (2005). *A Place in the Story: Servants and Service in Shakespeare's Plays.* Newark, DE: University of Delaware Press.

Andritzky, Michael, ed. (1992). *Oikos: Von der Feuerstelle zur Mikrowelle: Haushalt und Wohnen im Wandel.* Giessen: Anabas-Verlag. Exhibition Catalogue "Oikos, von der Feuerstelle zur Mikrowelle, Haushalt und Wohnen im Wandel." Stuttgart, 27.5.–9.8.1992 (Design-Center).

Anonymous (1794). *Lehrbuch für Lieverey-Bediente: Worinn gelehret wird, wie sich der Diener sowohl in Sitten als auch in der Bedienung zu verhalten habe; nebst einem Unterrichte in verschiedenen nützlichen Kunststücken.* Vienna: Schönfeld.

——— (1834). [No Title]. *Göttingische gelehrte Anzeigen* 32.II/128 (9 August), 1265–74.

——— (1894/1993). *The Duties of Servants: A Practical Guide to the Routine of Domestic Service.* East Grinstead, UK: Copper Beach.

——— (1910). "Die Elektrizität im Dienste von Küche und Tafel." *Die höfische und herrschaftliche Küche* 6.8 (15 January), 73.

——— (2001). "Der stumme Diener entsorgt die Teile." *Maschinen, Anlagen, Verfahren: Kompetenz in der spanenden Fertigung* 7–8, 78–79.

Apple Computer Inc. (1994). "Client/Server Solutions: The Roles of Desktops, Middleware, and Servers." In *Worldwide Performance Systems,* Special Collections, Silicon Valley Archives, Stanford University Libraries, M 1007, Series 3, Box 17, Folder 27.

Appleton, Elaine, David Cherenson, Emily Kay, and Larry Marion (1995). "A New Relationship Between Vendors and Users?" In *The Business Case for Client/Server: White Paper.* Sentry Market Research, ed. Framingham, MA: CW Custom Publications, 26–30.

Aquinas, Thomas (1266/2013). *Summa Theologica.* Vol. 1, Part 1. New York: Cosimo Classics.

Aristotle (1996). *The Politics and the Constitution of Athens.* Cambridge Texts in the History of Political Thought. Stephen Everson, ed. Cambridge: Cambridge University Press.

Aschoff, Volker (1984). *Geschichte der Nachrichtentechnik. Band 1: Beiträge zur Geschichte der Nachrichtentechnik von ihren Anfängen bis zum Ende des 18. Jahrhunderts.* Berlin, Heidelberg u.a.: Springer-Verlag.

——— (1987). *Geschichte der Nachrichtentechnik. Band 2: Nachrichtentechnische Entwicklungen in der ersten Hälfte des 19. Jahrhunderts.* Berlin: Springer-Verlag.

Atholl, Desmond, and Michael Cherkinian (1992). *At Your Service: Memoirs of a Majordomo.* New York: St. Martin's Press.

Auden, Wystan Hugh (1954). "Balaam and the Ass: The Master–Servant Relationship in Literature." *Thought: A Review of Culture and Idea, Fordham University Quarterly* 29, 237–70.

Auerbach, Erich (1946/2003). *Mimesis: The Representation of Reality in Western Thought.* Princeton: Princeton University Press.

Bachelard, Gaston (1953). *Le matérialisme rationnel.* Paris: Presses Universitaires de France.

Back, Christina (2009). *Beruf Butler: Watscheln, nicken, Klappe halten.* www.spiegel.de. URL: www.spiegel.de/unispiegel/jobundberuf/0, 1518,druck-608108,00.html.

Baeyer, Hans Christian von (1998). *Maxwell's Demon: Why Warmth Disperses and Time Passes.* New York: Random House.

Baillie, Hugh Murray (1967). "Etiquette and the Planning of the State Apartments in Baroque Palaces." *Archaeologia, or, Miscellaneous Tracts Relating to Antiquity* 101, 169–99.

Bain, David (1981). *Masters, Servants and Orders in Greek Tragedy: A Study of Some Aspects of Dramatic Technique and Convention.* Vol. 26. Publications of the Faculty of Arts of the University of Manchester. Manchester: Manchester University Press.

Balderson, Eileen (1982). *Backstairs Life in a Country House.* Douglas Goodlad, ed. Newton Abbot, UK: David and Charles.

Barnes, Susan B. (2007). "Alan Kay: Transforming the Computer into a Communication Medium." *IEEE Annals of the History of Computing* 29.2, 18–30.

Barroso, David (2007). *Botnets—The Silent Threat.* Vol. 3. ENISA Position Paper. Heraklion: European Network and Information Security Agency.

Barry, Stephen P. (1983). *Royal Service: My Twelve Years as Valet to Prince Charles.* New York: Macmillan.

Bauer, Volker (1993). *Die höfische Gesellschaft in Deutschland von der Mitte des 17. bis zum Ausgang des 18. Jahrhunderts: Versuch einer Typologie.* Vol. 12. Frühe Neuzeit. Tübingen: Niemeyer.

——— (2005a). "Der gedruckte Herrschaftsapparat: Periodische Personalverzeichnisse des Alten Reiches, seiner Institutionen und Territorien." *Wolfenbütteler Notizen zur Buchgeschichte* 30, 59–73.

——— (2005b). *Repertorium territorialer Amtskalender und Amtshandbücher im Alten Reich: Adress-, Hof-, Staatskalender und Staatshandbücher des 18. Jahrhunderts.* Vol. 196. Studien zur europäischen Rechtsgeschichte. Frankfurt am Main: Vittorio Klostermann.

BBC News (2005). *Ask Jeeves Decides to Axe Jeeves.* news.bbc.co.uk. URL: news. bbc.co.uk/2 /hi/technology/4275988.stm.

Bearman, Peter S. (2005). *Doormen: Fieldwork Encounters and Discoveries.* Chicago: University of Chicago Press.

Bebel, August (1892/1910). *Woman and Socialism.* Meta Stern, trans. New York: Socialist Literature.

Beckmann, Johann (1792). "Steigbügel." In *Beiträge zur Geschichte der Erfindungen.* Vol. 3. Leipzig: Paul Gotthelf Kummer, 102–21.

Beeton, Isabella Mary (1861/1888). *Mrs. Beeton's Book of Household Management.* Nicola Humble, ed. London: Ward, Lock.

Behringer, Wolfgang (1996). "Postamt und Briefkasten." In *Der Brief: Eine Kulturgeschichte der menschlichen Kommunikation.* Klaus Beyrer and Wolfgang Täubrich, eds. Vol. 1. Kataloge der Museumsstiftung Post und Telekommunikation. Heidelberg: Edition Braus, 55–67.

——— (2003). *Im Zeichen des Merkur: Reichspost und Kommunikationsrevolution in der Frühen Neuzeit.* Vol. 189. Veröffentlichungen des Max-Planck-Instituts für Geschichte. Göttingen: Vandenhoeck and Ruprecht.

Bejschowetz-Iserhoht, Marion (1984). *Dienstboten zur Kaiserzeit: Weibliches Hauspersonal in Kiel 1871–1918.* Vol. 17. Sonderveröffentlichung der Gesellschaft für Kieler Stadtgeschichte. Kiel: Gesellschaft für Kieler Stadtgeschichte.

Belliger, Andréa, and David J. Krieger, eds. (2006). *ANThology: Ein einführendes Handbuch zur Akteur-Netzwerk-Theorie.* ScienceStudies. Bielefeld: transcript.

Beneke, Klaus (1998). "Louis Pasteur: Erforscher der Infektionskrankheiten." In *Biographien und wissenschaftliche Lebensläufe von Kolloidwissenschaftlern, deren Lebensdaten mit 1995 in Verbindung stehen.* Vol. 7. Beiträge zur Geschichte der Kolloidwissenschaften. Nehmten: Reinhard Knof, 29–44.

Benjamin, Walter (1925/2009). *The Origin of German Tragic Drama.* London: Verso.

――― (1929/1999). "On the Image of Proust." In *Selected Writings.* Vol 2: 1927–1934, Michael W. Jennings, Howard Eiland, and Gary Smith, eds. Cambridge: Harvard University Press.

Bennett, Charles H. (1998). "Information Physics in Cartoons." *Superlattices and Microstructures* 23.3/4, 367–72.

Bergson, Henri (1907/1998). *Creative Evolution.* Mineola, NY: Dover.

Berners-Lee, Tim, Jim Hendler, and Ora Lassila (2001). "The Semantic Web: A New Form of Web Content That Is Meaningful to Computers Will Unleash a Revolution of New Possibilities." *Scientific American,* May, 34.

Bernhard, Thomas (1989/1993). *On the Mountain: Rescue Attempt, Nonsense.* Russell Stockman, trans. Marlboro, VT: Marlboro Press.

Beuermann, Gustav, and Roland Görke (1983). "Der elektromagnetische Telegraph von Gauß und Weber aus dem Jahre 1833." *Mitteilungen der Gauß-Gesellschaft* 20/21, 44–53.

Bickenbach, Matthias, and Harun Maye (2009). *Metapher Internet: Literarische Bildung und Surfen.* Vol. 49. Kaleidogramme. Berlin: Kulturverlag Kadmos.

Bischoff, Johann Nicolaus (1793). *Lehrbuch des teutschen Canzleystyls und der Canzley-Geschäfte zur Beförderung academischer Vorübung in denselben = Erster oder theoretischer Theil, von den allgemeinen Eigenschaften des Canzley-Styls.* Vol. 1. Handbuch der teutschen Canzley-Praxis für angehende Staatsbeamte und Geschäftsmänner/von J. N. Bis. Helmstedt: Fleckeisen.

Black, Max (1954/1996). "Metaphor." *Proceedings of the Aristotelian Society,* n.s., 55, 273–94.

Blänsdorf, Jürgen (1982). "Die Komödienintrige als Spiel im Spiel." *Antike und Abendland* 28.2, 131–54.

Bleibtreu, Karl (1888). *Größenwahn: Pathologischer Roman.* Leipzig: Friedrich.

Blumenberg, Hans (1960/2016). *Paradigms for a Metaphorology.* Robert Savage, trans. Ithaca: Cornell University Press.

――― (1979). "Ausblick auf eine Theorie der Unbegrifflichkeit." In *Schiffbruch mit Zuschauer: Paradigma einer Daseinsmetapher.* Vol. 1263. Frankfurt am Main: Suhrkamp, 85–105.

Bolhöfer, Walther (1912). *Gruß und Abschied in Ahd. und Mhd. Zeit.* Göttingen: Diss. phil.

Boltzmann, Ludwig (1905/1979). "Zur Erinnerung an Josef Loschmidt." In *Populäre Schriften.* Leipzig: Verlag von Johann Ambrosius Barth, 150–58.

Bömer, Aloys (1957). *Geschichte der Bibliotheken.* Vol. 3, 2. Handbuch der Bibliothekswissenschaft. Begründet von Fritz Milkau. 2d ed. Wiesbaden: Otto Harrassowitz.

Boom, Rüdiger van den (1979). *Die Bedienten und das Herr-Diener-Verhältnis in der deutschen Komödie der Aufklärung (1742–1767).* Frankfurt am Main: Haag + Herchen.

Bornkamm, Heinrich (1957). "Die innere Handlung in Lessings *Miß Sara Sampson.*" *Euphorion: Zeitschrift für Literaturgeschichte* 51, 385–96.

Böttiger, Karl August (1838). *Literarische Zustände und Zeitgenossen: In Schilderungen aus Karl August Böttiger's handschriftlichem Nachlasse.* Karl Wilhelm Böttiger, ed. Leipzig: Brockhaus.

Bradshaw, Jeffrey M., ed. (1997). *Software Agents.* Menlo Park: AAAI Press.

Brand, Steward (1972). "SPACEWAR: Fanatic Life and Symbolic Death Among the Computer Bums." *Rolling Stone Magazine* (December 7).

Braungart, Margarete (1995). *Küchenschrankgeflüster: Kulinarisches und Erlesenes von Damen, Dienstmädchen und tapferen Hausfrauen.* Rudolstadt: Hain.

Brecht, Bertolt (1928/2006). *Poetry and Prose.* Reinhold Grimm, ed. German Library, Vol. 75. New York: Continuum.

Breidbach, Olaf (1987). *Der Analogieschluß in den Naturwissenschaften oder die Fiktion des Realen: Bemerkungen zur Mystik des Induktiven.* Frankfurt am Main: Athenäum Verlag.

Broad, Charlie Dunbar (1934/1952). "Determinism, Indeterminism and Libertarianism." In *Ethics and the History of Philosophy: Selected Essays.* London: Routledge and Kegan Paul, 195–217.

Brockmeyer, Norbert (1979). *Antike Sklaverei.* Darmstadt: Wissenschaftliche Buchgesellschaft.

Browne, Janet (2002). *Charles Darwin: Voyaging, A Biography.* Princeton: Princeton University Press.

Brunner, Otto (1956). "Das 'ganze Haus' und die alteuropäische 'Ökonomik.'" In *Neue Wege der Sozialgeschichte: Vorträge und Aufsätze.* Göttingen: Vandenhoeck and Ruprecht.

Buchal, Sabine (1997). *Magdphantasien: Zum Motiv des weiblichen Dienens in Prosatexten des 19. und 20. Jahrhunderts.* Osnabrück: Universitätsverlag.

Buchwald, Georg (1889). *Was Doktor Luther sagt: Vom Hausgesinde oder Martin Luthers Dienstbotenspiegel.* Schriften für das evangelische Volk. Barmen: Verlag von Hugo Klein.

Buck, Christian (2008). *Rechenzentren vergeuden 80 Prozent der Prozessorleistung.* www.spiegel.de. URL: www.spiegel.de/netzwelt/tech/0,1518,565771,00.html.

Bues, Manfred (1995). "Der Weg zu client/server-Systemen." *DV-Management* 3, 123–28.

Bunz, Mercedes (2008). *Vom Speicher zum Verteiler: Die Geschichte des Internet.* Vol. 20. Berlin: Kulturverlag Kadmos.

Burchardt, Friedrich, ed. (1834). *Friedrich II: Eigenhändige Briefe an seinen geheimen Kämmerer Fredersdorff. Mit zwei FacSimile.* Leipzig: Fleischer.

Burke, Peter (2008). *What Is Cultural History?* 2d ed. Cambridge: Polity.

Burnett, Mark Thornton (1997). *Masters and Servants in English Renaissance Drama and Culture: Authority and Obedience.* Basingstoke: Macmillan.

Butler, Christina Violet (1916). *Domestic Service: An Enquiry by the Women's Industrial Council.* Willoughby de Broke, Marie Frances and Lisette Hanbury Verney, eds. Vol. 7270. History of Women. London: G. Bell and Sons.

Büttner, Gerhard, and Friedrich Morgenstern (1981). *Briefbausteine zur rationellen Gestaltung von Wirtschaftsbriefen.* 7th ed. Berlin: Die Wirtschaft.

Cachée, Josef (1985). *Die Hofküche des Kaisers: Die k.u.k. Hofküche, die Hofzuckerbäckerei und der Hofkeller in der Wiener Hofburg.* Vienna: Amalthea.

Cain, James Mallahan (1934). *The Postman Always Rings Twice.* New York: Alfred Knopf.

Calasso, Roberto (1983/1994). *The Ruin of Kasch.* William Weaver and Stephen Sartarelli, trans. Cambridge: Harvard University Press.

Callender, Craig (2002). "Who's Afraid of Maxwell's Demon—and Which One?" In *Quantum Limits to the Second Law.* Daniel Sheehan, ed. Melville, NY: American Institute of Physics.

Callon, Michel (1990). "Techno-Economic Networks and Irreversibility." *Sociological Review* 38, Issue S1. 132–61.

Canales, Jimena (2009). *A Tenth of a Second: A History.* Chicago: University of Chicago Press.

Caradec, François, and Noël Arnaud, eds. (1964). *Encyclopédie des farces et attrapes et des mystifications.* Paris: J. J. Pauvert.

Carlyle, Thomas (1843/1870). *Past and Present.* Vol. 13, *Collected Works in Thirty Volumes.* London: Chapman and Hall.

Cartellieri, Otto (1926). *Am Hofe der Herzöge von Burgund: Kulturhistorische Bilder.* Basel: Schwabe.

Ceranski, Beate (2005). "Labordiener, Industrieforscher, Popularisierer: Unbekannte Arbeiter und unbenannte Arbeiten in der Radioaktivitätsforschung." In *Auf den Schultern von Zwergen. Essays an den Grenzen von Physik und Biographie.* Beate Ceranski, Florian Hars, and Gerhard Wiesenfeldt, eds. Vol. 31. Berliner Beiträge zur Geschichte der Naturwissenschaften und der Technik. Berlin, Liebenwalde: ERS, 95–122.

Cerf, Steven R. (1980). "*Miss Sara Sampson* and Clarissa: The Use of Epistolary Devices in Lessing's Drama." In *Theatrum Mundi: Essays on German Drama and German Literature Dedicated to Harold Lenz on His 70th birthday, Sept. 11, 1978.* Edward R. Haymes, ed. Vol. 2. Houston German Studies. Munich: Wilhelm Fink Verlag, 22–30.

Ceruzzi, Paul E. (1998/2003). *A History of Modern Computing.* History of Computing, 2d ed. Cambridge: MIT Press.

Chamisso, Adalbert von (1814/1975). "Peter Schlemihls wundersame Geschichte." In *Sämtliche Werke: Nach dem Text der Ausgaben letzter Hand und den Handschriften.* Jost Perfahl, ed. Munich: Winkler Verlag, 13–66.

Clark, Stuart (1999). *Thinking with Demons: The Idea of Witchcraft in Early Modern Europe.* Oxford: Oxford University Press.

Clark, William (2006). *Academic Charisma and the Origins of the Research University.* Chicago: University of Chicago Press.

Clermont-Tonnerre, Élisabeth de (1925). *Robert de Montesquiou et Marcel Proust.* Paris: Ernest Flammarion.

Cohen, John (1966). *Human Robots in Myth and Science.* London: Allen and Unwin.

Colman, Henry (1849). *European Life and Manners in Familiar Letters to Friends.* Boston: Charles C. Little and James Brown.

Colony, George, and Tim Mead (1990). "The Attraction Is Price: Forrester Research's Colony on Client/Server Computing." *Datamation* (March 15), 49–51.

Compton-Burnett, Ivy (1947). *Manservant and Maidservant.* London: Victor Gollancz.

Computer Desktop Encyclopedia (2010). Article "Idle Time." www.answers.com. URL: www.answers.com/topic/idle-time.

Congreve, William (1700/2006). *The Way of the World and Other Plays.* Eric S. Rump, ed. London: Penguin.

Cooper, Michael, and Michael Hunter, eds. (2006). *Robert Hooke: Tercentennial Studies.* Aldershot: Ashgate.

Coppersmith, Fred, and J. J. Lynx (1949). *Patent Applied For: A Century of Fantastic Inventions.* London: Co-Ordination (Press and Publicity).

Cox, Rosie (2006). *The Servant Problem: Domestic Employment in a Global Economy.* London: I. B. Tauris.

Critchley, Simon (1997/2004). *Very Little . . . Almost Nothing: Death, Philosophy, Literature.* 2d ed. London: Routledge.

Crookes, William (1874). "Notes of an Enquiry into the Phenomena called Spiritual During the Years 1870–1873." *Quarterly Journal of Science and Annals of Mining, Metallurgy, Engineering, Industrial Arts, Manufactures, and Technology* 11.1 (January).

Crow, Christine Mary (1972). *Paul Valéry and Maxwell's Demon: Natural Order and Human Possibility.* Hull: University of Hull.

Cunnington, Phillis Emily (1974). *Costume of Household Servants, from the Middle Ages to 1900.* London: A and C Black.

Da Vinha, Mathieu (2005). *Les valets de chambre de Louis XIV.* Pour l'histoire. Paris: Perrin.

Dähnhardt, Wolfgang (1974). "Mit elektronischer Hochachtung." *Sprachpflege: Zeitschrift für gutes Deutsch* 23.2 (February), 40–41.

Danzel, Theodor Wilhelm, and Gottschalk Eduard Guhrauer (1880). *Gotthold Ephraim Lessing: Sein Leben und seine Werke.* Vol. 1. 2, Berlin: Hofmann.

Darling, L., and E. O. Hulburt (1955). "On Maxwell's Demon." *American Journal of Physics* 23, 470–71.

Därmann, Iris (2008). "Vom antiken Sklavendienst zur modernen Dienstleistungsgesellschaft. Paulinische Bausteine für eine genealogische Skizze." *Archiv für Mediengeschichte* 8.8, 23–38.

Darmstaedter, Ludwig (1908). *Handbuch zur Geschichte der Naturwissenschaften und der Technik: In chronologischer Darstellung. Unter Mitwirkung von René du Bois-Reymond und Carl Schaefer.* Berlin: Verlag von Julius Springer.

Daub, Edward E. (1970). "Maxwell's Demon." *Studies in the History and Philosophy of Science* 1, 213–27.

Daunicht, Richard (1971). *Lessing im Gespräch: Berichte und Urteile von Freunden und Zeitgenossen.* Munich: Wilhelm Fink.

Davidis, Henriette (1863/1902). *Die Hausfrau: Praktische Anleitung zur selbständigen und sparsamen Führung des Haushalts.* 17th ed. Leipzig: Seemann.

Davidoff, Leonore (1974). "Mastered for Life: Servant and Wife in Victorian and Edwardian England." *Journal of Social History* 7.4 (Summer), 406–28.

Davis, Andrew Jackson (1859). *The Philosophy of Spiritual Intercourse, Being an Explanation of Modern Mysteries.* Boston: Marsh.

Defoe, Daniel (1724/2006). *The Works of Daniel Defoe.* Vol. 6, *The great law of subordination consider'd. Or, the insolence and unsufferable behaviour of servants in England duly enquir'd into. In ten familiar letters. As also a proposal, containing such heads or constitutions, as wou'd effectually answer this great end, and bring servants of every class to a just regulation.* J. A. Downie, ed. Religious and Didactic Writings of Daniel Defoe. London: Pickering and Chatto.

———— (1725/1766). *The Mercantile Library or, Complete English Tradesman: Directing Him in the Several Parts and Progressions of Trade, From His First Entring upon Business, to His Leaving Off.* Dublin: J. and A. Kelburn.

———— (1725/1767). *Every-Body's Business Is No-Body's Business; or, Private Abuses, Public Grievances, Exemplified in the Pride, Insolence, and Exorbitant Wages of Our Women-Servants, Footmen, andc. With a Proposal for Amendment of the Same.* London: Printed for Sam. Ford.

Deleuze, Gilles, and Félix Guattari (1980/2003). *A Thousand Plateaus: Capitalism and Schizophrenia.* Brian Massumi, trans. London: Continuum.

Denecke, Arthur (1892). "Zur Geschichte des Grußes und der Anrede in Deutschland." *Zeitschrift für den deutschen Unterricht* 6, 317–45.

Denzinger, Heinrich (1991). *Kompendium der Glaubensbekenntnisse und kirchlichen Lehrentscheidungen.* Peter Hünermann and Helmut Hoping, eds. 37th ed. Freiburg im Breisgau: Herder.

Di Nitto, Elisabetta, et al., eds. (2009). *At Your service: Service-Oriented Computing from an EU Perspective.* Cambridge: MIT Press.

Dictionary, Oxford English (2000). *OED Online.* 2d ed. Oxford: Oxford University Press. dictionary.oed.com.

Diderot, Denis (1792/1986). *Jacques the Fatalist and His Master.* Michael Henry, trans. London: Penguin.

Diderot, Denis, and Jean le Rond d'Alembert, ed. (1751–65). *Encyclopédie, ou Dictionaire raisonné des sciences, des arts et des métiers, par une société de gens de lettres.* Paris: David Briasson, Durand le Breton. http://diderot.alembert.free.fr.

Diehl, Lorraine, and Marianne Hardart (2002). *The Automat: The History, Recipes, and Allure of Horn and Hardart's Masterpiece.* New York: Clarkson Potter.

Dierig, Sven (2006). *Wissenschaft in der Maschinenstadt: Emil Du Bois-Reymond und seine Laboratorien in Berlin.* Wissenschaftsgeschichte. Göttingen: Wallstein.

Dietrich, Richard, ed. (1986). *Die politischen Testamente der Hohenzollern.* Vol. 20. Veröffentlichungen aus den Archiven Preussischer Kulturbesitz. Cologne: Böhlau.

Dinges, Martin (1992). "Der 'feine Unterschied': Die soziale Funktion der Kleidung in der höfischen Gesellschaft." *Zeitschrift für Historische Forschung* 19, 49–76.

Drogge, Horst (1983). "150 Jahre elektromagnetische Telegraphie." *Archiv für deutsche Postgeschichte* 31.2, 73–99.

Drosdowski, Günther, ed. (1989). *DUDEN: Deutsches Universalwörterbuch A–Z.* 2d ed. Zurich: Dudenverlag.

Du Bois-Reymond, Emil (1872). "Über die Grenzen des Naturerkenntnis." In *Vorträge über Philosophie und Gesellschaft.* Hamburg: Felix Meiner Verlag, 54–77.

Duindam, Jeroen Frans Jozef (1994). *Myths of Power: Norbert Elias and the Early Modern European Court.* Amsterdam: Amsterdam University Press.

———— (1998). "The Court of the Austrian Habsburgs: Locus of a Composite Heritage." *Mitteilungen der Residenzen-Kommission der Akademie der Wissenschaften zu Göttingen* 8, 24–58.

Dunbabin, Katherine M. D. (2003). "The Waiting Servant in Later Roman Art." *American Journal of Philology* 124, 443–68.

Dürr, Renate (1997). "Der Dienstbothe ist kein Tagelöhner: Zum Gesinderecht (16. bis 19. Jahrhundert)." In *Frauen in der Geschichte des Rechts: Von der frühen Neuzeit bis zur Gegenwart.* Ute Gerhard, ed. Munich: C. H. Beck, 115–39.

Earman, John, and John D. Norton (1998). "EXORCIST XIV: The Wrath of Maxwell's Demon. Part I. From Maxwell to Szilard." *Studies in History and Philosophy of Modern Physics* 29.4, 435–71.

———— (1999). "EXORCIST XIV: The Wrath of Maxwell's Demon. Part II. From Szilard to Landauer and Beyond." *Studies in History and Philosophy of Modern Physics* 30.1, 1–40.

Ebert, Friedrich Adolf (1820). *Die Bildung des Bibliothekars.* 2d ed. Leipzig: Steinacker and Wagner.

Ebrecht, Angelika, and Regina Nörtemann et al., eds. (1990). *Brieftheorie des 18. Jahrhunderts: Texte, Kommentare, Essays.* Stuttgart: J. B. Metzler Verlag.

Ehrenreich, Barbara (2003). *Arbeit poor: Unterwegs in der Dienstleistungsgesellschaft.* Nils Kadritzke and Horst Afheldt, eds. Vol. 61451. rororo. Reinbek bei Hamburg: Rowohlt Taschenbuch.

Eibl, Karl (1971). *Gotthold Ephraim Lessing: Miss Sara Sampson. Ein bürgerliches Trauerspiel.* Vol. 2. Commentatio, Analysen und Kommentare zur deutschen Literatur. Frankfurt am Main: Athenäum Verlag.

Eisenbart, Liselotte Constanze (1962). *Kleiderordnungen der deutschen Städte zwischen 1350 und 1700: Ein Beitrag zur Kulturgeschichte des deutschen Bürgertums.* Vol. 32. Göttinger Bausteine zur Geschichtswissenschaft. Göttingen: Musterschmidt.

Elias, Norbert (1969/2006). *The Court Society.* Edmund Jephcott, trans. *The Complete Works of Norbert Elias.* Vol. 2. Dublin: University College Dublin Press.

Ellermann, Karin (2009). "Sind wir nicht alle Goethes Diener—Die Schriften der Stadelmann-Gesellschaft 1912–1941." *Die große Stadt—Das kulturhistorische Archiv von Weimar-Jena* 2.3, 217–62.

Emelina, Jean (1975). *Les valets et les servantes dans le théâtre comique en France de 1610 à 1700.* Cannes, Grenoble: C.E.L. et al.

Engelsing, Rolf (1973a). "Dienstbotenlektüre im 18. und 19. Jahrhundert." In *Zur Sozialgeschichte deutscher Mittel-und Unterschichten.* Vol. 4. Kritische Studien zur Geschichtswissenschaft. Göttingen: Vandenhoeck and Ruprecht, 180–224.

———— (1973b). "Einkommen der Dienstboten in Deutschland zwischen dem 16. und 20. Jahrhundert." *Jahrbuch des Instituts für Deutsche Geschichte, Tel Aviv* 2, 11–65.

———— (1973c). *Zur Sozialgeschichte deutscher Mittel-und Unterschichten.* Vol. 4. Kritische Studien zur Geschichtswissenschaft. Göttingen: Vandenhoeck and Ruprecht.

———— (1978). "Das Vermögen der Dienstboten." In *Zur Sozialgeschichte deutscher Mittel-und Unterschichten.* Vol. 4. Kritische Studien zur Geschichtswissenschaft. 2d ed. Göttingen: Vandenhoeck and Ruprecht, 262–83.

Engelsing, Rolf, and Heidi Müller, eds. (1982). *Dienstboten in Stadt und Land: Vortragsreihe zur Ausstellung 'Dienstbare Geister, Leben und Arbeitswelt städtischer Dienstboten' im Museum für Deutsche Volkskunde Berlin, Februar-März 1981.* Berlin: Museum für Deutsche Volkskunde.

Erdmann, Johann Eduard (1852). *Ueber die Langeweile: Vortrag gehalten im wissenschaftlichen Verein.* Berlin: Hertz.

E.R.L. (1919). "The Poor Diener." *Science* 50.1280 (July 11), 43.

Erman, Wilhelm (1919). *Geschichte der Bonner Universitätsbibliothek (1818–1901).* Vol. 37/38. Sammlung bibliothekswissenschaftlicher Arbeiten. Halle a.S.: Verlag von Ehrhardt Karras.

Ethophilus (1753). *Neues und wohl eingerichtetes Complimentir-und Sittenbuch: Darinnen gezeiget wird, Wie sich sonderlich Personen Bürgerlichen Standes, bey denen im gemeinen Leben vorfallenden Begebenheiten, als Anwerbungen, Verlöbnissen, Hochzeiten In Worten und Wercken so klug als höflich verhalten, und durch gute Aufführung beliebt machen sollen, nebst Einem Trenchier-Büchlein.* 5th ed. Nordhausen: Groß.

Evans, Robin (1978/1996). "Figures, Doors and Passages." In *Translations from Drawing to Building and Other Essays (AA Documents).* Architectural Association Publications 1656. London: Architectural Association, 54–91.

Evett, David (2005). *Discourses of Service in Shakespeare's England.* New York: Palgrave Macmillan.

Fairchilds, Cissie C. (1979). "Masters and Servants in Eighteenth-Century Toulouse." *Journal of Social History* 12.3 (Spring), 368–93.

——— (1984). *Domestic Enemies: Servants and Their Masters in Old Regime France.* Baltimore: Johns Hopkins University Press.

Feldhaus, Franz Maria, and Walther H. Fitze (1924). *Geschichtszahlen der drahtlosen Telegraphie und Telephonie.* Berlin: Rothgisser and Diesing AG.

Fellmann, Ferdinand (1973). "Das Ende des Laplaceschen Dämons." In *Geschichte—Ereignis und Erzählung.* Reinhart Koselleck and Wolf-Dieter Stempel, eds. Vol. V. Poetik und Hermeneutik. Munich: Wilhelm Fink.

Ferry, Steven M. (2003). *Butlers and Household Managers: 21st Century Professionals.* North Charleston, SC: BookSurge.

——— (2004). *Hotel Butlers: The Great Service Differentiators.* North Charleston, SC: BookSurge.

Feyerabend, Ernst (1933). *Der Telegraph von Gauß und Weber im Werden der elektrischen Telegraphie.* Berlin: Reichspostministerium.

Feyerabend, Paul K. (1966). "On the Possibility of a Perpetuum Mobile of the Second Kind." In *Mind, Matter, and Method: Essays in Philosophy and Science in Honour of Herbert Feigl.* Paul K. Feyerabend and Grover Maxwell, eds. Minneapolis: University of Minnesota Press, 409–12.

Fielding, Henry, and John Fielding (1752). *A Plan of the Universal Register-Office opposite Cecil-Street in the Strand, and of That in Bishopsgate-Street, the Corner of Cornhill.* London: [s.n].

Fitz-Adam, Adam (1756). "Thursday, January 1." *The World* 4.157.

Fontane, Theodor (1891/2011). *Irretrievable.* Douglas Parmee, trans. New York Review of Books Classics. New York: New York Review of Books.

——— (1895/2000). *Effi Briest.* Hugh Rorrison, ed. London: Penguin.

Förster, Wilhelm (1883). "Sitzungsbericht." *Elektrotechnische Zeitschrift* 4.12 (December), 489–94.

Förstmann, Ernst (1886). "Die Bibliotheksdiener." *Centralblatt für Bibliothekswesen* 3, 190–96.

Foucault, Michel (1966/2005). *The Order of Things: An Archeology of the Human Sciences.* London: Routledge.

——— (1975/1995). *Discipline and Punish: The Birth of the Prison.* Alan Sheridan, trans. New York: Vintage Books.

———— (1977/2000). "Lives of Infamous Men" and (1982/2000) "The Subject and Power." In *Power: Essential Works of Foucault, 1954–1984.* Vol. 3. James D. Faubion, ed. New York: New Press.

Frank, Howard, Robert E. Kahn, and Leonard Kleinrock (1972). "Computer Communication Network Design—Experience with Theory and Practice." *Spring Joint Computer Conference.* AFIPS Conference Proceedings. Montvale, NJ: AFIPS Press, 255–70.

Franken, Norbert (2004). " 'Stumme Diener' in miniature." *Antike Kunst* 47, 47–54.

Franklin, Jill (1975). "Troops of Servants: Labour and Planning in the Country House 1840–1914." *Victorian Studies* 19.2 (December), 211–39.

Franzbecker, Rolf (1973). *Die weibliche Bedienstete in der französischen Komödie des 16. bis 18. Jahrhunderts.* Studien zur Romanistik. Wiesbaden: Humanitas.

Frenzel, Elisabeth (1999). *Motive der Weltliteratur: Ein Lexikon dichtungsgeschichtlicher Längsschnitte.* Vol. 301. Kröners Taschenausgabe. 5th ed. Stuttgart: Alfred Kröner.

Frey, Bruno S. (2007). *Overprotected Politicians.* Vol. 2019. CESifo working paper series. Munich: University, Center for Economic Studies.

Freytag, Gustav (1864/1887). *The Lost Manuscript.* Vol. 2. London: Edward Arnold.

Frederick William III, Prussian King (1926). *Die Briefe Friedrich des Großen an seinen Kammerdiener Fredersdorf.* Johannes Richter, ed. Berlin-Grunewald: Klemm.

Frommann, Friedrich Johannes (1889). *Das Frommansche Haus und seine Freunde [1792–1827].* Hermann Frommann, 3d ed. Stuttgart: Friedrich Frommanns Verlag (E. Hauff).

Fullmer, J. Z. (1967). "Davy's Biographers: Notes on Scientific Biography." *Science* 155.3760 (January), 285–91.

Galloway, Alexander R. (2004). *Protocol: How Control Exists After Decentralization.* Cambridge: MIT Press.

Garman, Jason (2003). *Kerberos: The Definitive Guide.* Beijing: O'Reilly.

Gay, Hannah (1996). "Invisible Resource: William Crookes and His Circle of Support, 1871–81." *British Journal for the History of Science* 29, 311–36.

Geiger, Ludwig (1893). "Goethe's Kammerdiener." *Die Nation: Wochenschrift für Politik, Volkswirtschaft und Litteratur* 10.38 (June 17), 576–78.

———— (1908). *Goethe und die Seinen: Quellenmäßige Darstellung über Goethes Haus.* Leipzig: Voigtländer.

Gerard, Jessica A. (1984). "Invisible Servants: The Country House and the Local Community." *Bulletin of the Institute of Historical Research* 57.136 (November).

———— (1994). *Country House Life: Family and Servants, 1815–1914.* Family, Sexuality, and Social Relations in Past Times. Oxford: Blackwell.

Gerhardt, Fritz (1924). *Die Schlußformel in Schillers Briefen.* Jena: Diss. phil.

Gerold, J., ed. (1776–1804). *Hof-und Staats-Schematismus der römisch kaiserlichen auch kaiserlich-königlichen und erzherzoglichen Haupt-und Residenz-Stadt Wien: Derer daselbst befindlichen höchsten und hohen unmittelbaren Hofstellen, Chargen und Würden, niederen Kollegien Instanzen und Expeditionen.* Vienna: Gerold.

Giedion, Sigfried (1948/1987). *Die Herrschaft der Mechanisierung: Ein Beitrag zur anonymen Geschichte.* Stanislaus von Moos and Henning Ritter, eds. Frankfurt am Main: Athenäum.

Ginzburg, Carlo (1976/2013). *The Cheese and the Worms: The Cosmos of a Sixteenth-Century Miller.* John Tedeschi and Anne C. Tedeschi, trans. Baltimore: Johns Hopkins University Press.

Girouard, Mark (1978). *Life in the English Country House: A Social and Architectural History.* New Haven: Yale University Press.

Gleichzu, Traugott Warmund von (1718). *Der Fürst ein Sclave Seiner Ungetreuen Diener, Der Ungetreue Diener und Sclave aber Ein gebietender Herr seines Fürstens, Oder Kurtze, doch wahrhaffte Beschreibung, wie allmächtig die ungetreuen Diener heut zu Tage an vieler grosser Herren Höfen sind, wie sie den Fürsten, theils durch ihre Partisanen und Anhänger, zu allem bereden, und Ihm weiß machen können, was sie nur wollen: Worinne ihre böse Eigenschaften bestehen, und was es endlich hier und dort, vor ein schröckliches Ende mit ihnen nehme.* [S.l.]

Goethe, Johann Wolfgang (1887–1919). *Goethes Werke.* Weimar Edition. Weimar: Böhlau.

——— (1998). *Text 1828–1832: Dokumente, Register.* Vol. 20.2: *Briefwechsel zwischen Goethe und Zelter in den Jahren 1799 bis 1832.* Edith Zehm and Sabine Schäfer, eds. Sämtliche Werke nach Epochen seines Schaffens. Munich Edition. Munich, Vienna: Carl Hanser.

——— (1994–95). *The Collected Works in Twelve Volumes.* Victor Lange, Eric Blackall, and Cyrus Hamlin, exec. eds. Princeton: Princeton University Press.

——— (1998). *Conversations of Goethe with Johann Peter Eckermann.* John Oxenford, trans., J. K. Moorhead, ed. London: Da Capo Press.

——— (1964). *Selected Verse.* David Luke, trans. London: Penguin.

Goldoni, Carlo (1743/2004). *The Servant of Two Masters.* Jeffrey Hatcher and Paolo Emilio Landi, trans. New York: Dramatists Play Service.

Goncharov, Ivan (1859/2005). *Oblomov.* David Magarshack, trans. London: Penguin.

Görs, Britta (2001). "Die chemisch-technische Assistenz: Zur Entwicklung eines neuen beruflichen Tätigkeitsfeldes in der Chemie zu Beginn des 20. Jahrhunderts." In *Bildungspolitik und Geschlecht: Ein europäischer Vergleich.* Brigitte Geißel and Birgit Seemann, eds. Opladen: Leske + Budrich, 169–95.

Gottsched, Johann Christoph (1730/1977). *Versuch einer critischen Dichtkunst.* Darmstadt: Wissenschaftliche Buchgesellschaft. 4th ed., reprod. Leipzig, 1751.

Gove, Philip Babcock, and the Merriam-Webster Editorial Staff, eds. (1961). *Webster's Third New International Dictionary of the English Language. Unabridged.* Springfield, MA: Merriam-Webster.

Gradmann, Christoph (2005). *Robert Koch und die Geschichte der Bakteriologie.* Göttingen: Wallstein.

Grant, Tina (1994). "Kitchen Aid." In: *International Directory of Company Histories.* Paula Kepos, ed. Vol. 8. London: St. James Press, 298–99.

Grillparzer, Franz (1848/1960). *Sämtliche Werke: Ausgewählte Briefe, Gespräche, Berichte.* Vol. 2. *Ein Bruderzwist in Habsburg.* Peter Frank and Karl Pörnbacher, eds. Munich: Carl Hanser.

Grimm, Jacob, and Wilhelm Grimm (1854). *Deutsches Wörterbuch.* Leipzig: Verlag von S. Hirzel.

Groebner, Valentin (1998). "Die Kleider des Körpers des Kaufmanns: Zum 'Trachtenbuch' eines Augsburger Bürgers im 16. Jahrhundert." *Zeitschrift für historische Forschung* 25, 323–58.

Gronau, Barbara, and Alice Lagaay (2007). *Performanzen des Nichttuns.* Passagen Philosophie. Vienna: Passagen.

Grünbart, Michael (2005). *Formen der Anrede im byzantinischen Brief vom 6. bis zum 12. Jahrhundert.* Vol. 25. Wiener byzantinistische Studien. Vienna: Verlag der Österreichischen Akademie der Wissenschaften.

Günther, Horst (1995). "Herr und Knecht." In *Gesinde im 18. Jahrhundert.* Gotthardt Frühsorge, Rainer Gruenter, and Beatrix Wolff Metternich, eds. Vol. 12. Studien zum achtzehnten Jahrhundert. Hamburg: Felix Meiner, 1–12.

Haase, Ricarda, ed. (1992). *"Das bißchen Haushalt . . ."? Zur Geschichte der Technisierung und Rationalisierung der Hausarbeit.* Vol. 1. Veröffentlichungen des Museums für Volkskultur in Württemberg, Waldenbuch. Stuttgart: Württembergisches Landesmuseum.

Hacke, Martina (2006). "Aspekte des mittelalterlichen Botenwesens: Die Botenorganisation der Universität von Paris und anderer Institutionen im Spätmittelalter." *Das Mittelalter* 11.1, 132–49.

Hackländer, Friedrich Wilhelm (1854/1875). *Europäisches Sklavenleben. 5 vols.* Vol. 16. F. W. Hackländers Werke. Erste Gesammt-Ausgabe. 3d ed. Stuttgart: U. Kröner.

Hagemann, Friedrich Gustav (1792). *Der Fürst und sein Kammerdiener: Ein Lustspiel in einem Aufzuge.* Wismar: Bödner.

Hagen, Friedrich Heinrich von der (1838). *Minnesinger: Deutsche Liederdichter des 12., 13., und 14. Jahrhunderts.* Leipzig: Johann Ambrosius Barth.

Hagen, Wolfgang (1999). "Der Okkultismus der Avantgarde um 1900." In *Konfigurationen: Zwischen Kunst und Medien.* Sigrid Schade and Georg Christoph Tholen, eds. Munich: Wilhelm Fink Verlag, 338–57.

Halavais, Alexander (2009). *Search Engine Society.* Cambridge: Polity Press.

Hallett, H. F. (1939). "On Things in Themselves." *Philosophy* 14.54 (April), 155–79.

Hamann, Johann Georg (1759/1998). *Sokratische Denkwürdigkeiten.* Sven-Aage Jørgensen, ed. Vol. 926. Reclam Universal-Bibliothek. Stuttgart: Reclam.

Haraway, Donna Jeanne (1997). *Modest–Witness@Second-Millennium. FemaleMan–Meets–OncoMouse™. Feminism and Technoscience.* New York: Routledge.

Harman, Peter Michael, ed. (1995). *The Scientific Letters and Papers of James Clerk Maxwell.* Vol. 2, 1862–73. Cambridge: Cambridge University Press.

Hars, Florian (2005). "Mechaniker, nicht Diener: Georg Schurr, 1856–1904." In *Auf den Schultern von Zwergen: Essays an den Grenzen von Physik und Biographie.* Beate Ceranski, Florian Hars, and Gerhard Wiesenfeldt, eds. Vol. 31. Berliner Beiträge zur Geschichte der Naturwissenschaften und der Technik. Berlin, Liebenwalde: ERS, 79–93.

Hartcup, Adeline (1980). *Below Stairs in the Great Country Houses.* London: Sidgwick and Jackson.

Haverkamp, Anselm, ed. (1996). *Theorie der Metapher.* 2d enl. ed. Darmstadt: Wissenschaftliche Buchgesellschaft.

Haywood, Eliza Fowler, ed. (1787/1985). *A Present for Servants from Their Ministers, Masters, or Other Friends; And a Present for a Servant-Maid.* Vol. 35. Marriage, Sex, and the Family in England, 1660–1800. New York: Garland.

Hecht, Joseph Jean (1956). *The Domestic Servant Class in Eighteenth-Century England.* London: Routledge and Kegan Paul.

Heckmann, Herbert (1982). *Die andere Schöpfung: Geschichte der frühen Automaten in Wirklichkeit und Dichtung.* Heinz Streicher, ed. Frankfurt am Main: Umschau.

Hegel, Georg Wilhelm Friedrich (1807/1977). *Phenomenology of Spirit.* A. V. Miller, trans. Oxford: Oxford University Press.

———— (1807/1965). "Who Thinks Abstractly?" In *Hegel Texts and Commentary: Hegel's Preface to His System in a New Translation with Commentary and "Who Thinks Abstractly?"* Walter Kaufmann, trans. and ed. Notre Dame: University of Notre Dame Press.

Heidelberger, Michael (2006). "Experiment and Instrument." In *Spektakuläre Experimente: Praktiken der Evidenzproduktion im 17. Jahrhundert.* Helmar Schramm, Ludger Schwarte, and Jan Lazardzig, eds. Vol. 3. Theatrum Scientiarum. Berlin: Walter de Gruyter, 378–97.

Heller, Michael (1991). "Laplace's Demon in the Relativistic Universe." *Astronomy Quarterly* 8, 219–43.

Hellige, Hans Dieter (1994). "Leitbilder in der Genese von Time-Sharing-Systemen: Erklärungswert und Grenzen des Leitbildansatzes in der Computerkommunikation." Bremen: Forschungszentrum Arbeit und Technik artec.

Henderson, W. A. (1791/1800). *The Housekeeper's Instructor; or, Universal Family Cook.* 9th ed. London: Printed and sold by J. Stratford.

Hengerer, Mark (2004). *Kaiserhof und Adel in der Mitte des 17. Jahrhunderts: Eine Kommunikationsgeschichte der Macht in der Vormoderne.* 3. Historische Kulturwissenschaft. Konstanz: UVK Verlags-Gesellschaft.

Hentschel, Klaus (2005). *Gaußens unsichtbare Hand: Der Universitäts-Mechanicus und Maschinen-Inspector Moritz Meyerstein, Ein Instrumentenbauer im 19. Jahrhundert.* Vol. 3, 52. Abhandlungen der Akademie der Wissenschaften zu Göttingen, Mathematisch-Physikalische Klasse. Göttingen: Vandenhoeck and Ruprecht.

———— ed. (2008). *Unsichtbare Hände: Zur Rolle von Laborassistenten, Mechanikern, Zeichnern u. a. Amanuenses in der physikalischen Forschungs-und Entwicklungsarbeit.* Diepholz u.a.: GNT-Verl., Verl. für Geschichte der Naturwiss. und der Technik.

Hepp, Robert (1971). *Selbstherrlichkeit und Selbstbedienung: Zur Dialektik der Emanzipation.* Munich: Beck.

Hertzfeld, Andy (2005). *Revolution in the Valley: The Insanely Great Story of How the Mac Was Made.* Steve Capps, ed. Beijing: O'Reilly.

Heßler, Martina (2001). *"Mrs. Modern Woman": Zur Sozial-und Kulturgeschichte der Haushaltstechnisierung.* Vol. 827. Campus Forschung. Frankfurt: Campus.

Hildreth, Charles R. (1982). *Online Public Access Catalogs: The User Interface.* Dublin, Ohio: OCLC.

———— (1991). "Advancing Toward the E³OPAC: The Imperative and the Path." In *Think Tank on the Present and Future of the Online Catalog: Proceedings.* Chicago: American Library Association, Reference and Adult Services Division, 17–38.

Hilker, Thomas (2006). *Personenschutz, Stalking, Attentate.* Edition Octopus. Münster: Monsenstein und Vannerdat.

Hiltzik, Michael A. (1999/2000). *Dealers of Lightning: Xerox PARC and the Dawn of the Computer Age.* New York: HarperBusiness.

Hochschild, Arlie Russell (2010). "'Mama zu mieten' und andere Dienste." *Das Argument: Zeitschrift für Philosophie und Sozialwissenschaften* 52.285, no. 1, 95–107.

Hoffmann, Daniel (1998). *Stille Lebensmeister: Dienende Menschen bei Hermann Lenz.* Vol. 46. Stauffenburg-Colloquium. Tübingen: Stauffenburg.

———— (2002). "Von der Maske zur Attrappe—Eine Entwicklungslinie der Dienergestalt in der Literatur seit der Aufklärung." *Literatur für Leser* 25.4, 199–216.

Höge, Helmut (2008). *Das Ding an sich und für mich (29)*. blogs.taz.de/hausmeisterblog. URL: blogs.taz.de/hausmeisterblog/2008/10/14/das_ding_an_sich_und_fuer_mich_29.

———— (2010). *Was machen die Geräte eigentlich nachts?* www.taz.de. URL: blogs. taz. de/ hausmeisterblog/2010/03/22/was_machen_die_geraete_ eigentlich_nachts/.

Holden, Edward Singleton (1886). *Photography the Servant of Astronomy*. San Francisco: Self-published.

Holz, Hans Heinz (1968). *Herr und Knecht bei Leibniz und Hegel: Zur Interpretation der Klassengesellschaft*. Soziologische Essays. Neuwied u.a.: Luchterhand.

Homer (730/1998). *The Iliad*. Robert Fagles, trans. London: Penguin.

Horn, Pamela (1975). *The Rise and Fall of the Victorian Servant*. Dublin: Gill and Macmillan.

———— (2001). *Life Below Stairs in the 20th Century*. Thrupp, UK: Sutton.

———— (2004). *Flunkeys and Scullions: Life Below Stairs in Georgian England*. Thrupp, UK: Sutton.

Horst, Georg Conrad (1821). *Zauber-Bibliothek: Oder von Zauberei, Theurgie und Mantik, Zauberern, Hexen und Hexenprocessen, Dämonen, Gespenstern und Geistererscheinungen. Zur Beförderung einer rein-geschichtlichen, von Aberglauben und Unglauben freien Beurtheilung dieser Gegenstände*. Part 1. Mainz: Bei Florian Kupferberg.

Hospitalier, E. (1887). "Un chemin de fer électrique dans une salle à manger." *La Nature: Science progrès* 15 (October 29), 344–46.

Hrabal, Bohumil (1980/2007). *I Served the King of England*. Paul Wilson, trans. New York: New Directions.

———— (1981/2001). *Too Loud a Solitude*. Michael Henry Heim, trans. San Diego: Mariner Books.

Hubig, Christoph, and Peter Koslowski, eds. (2008). *Maschinen, die unsere Brüder werden: Mensch-Maschine-Interaktion in hybriden Systemen*. Vol. 11. Ethische Ökonomie. Paderborn: Wilhelm Fink.

Huggett, Frank E. (1977). *Life Below Stairs: Domestic Servants in England from Victorian Times*. London: Murray.

Hughes, Thomas P. (1983). *Networks of Power*. Baltimore: Johns Hopkins University Press.

Huhtamo, Erkki (1996). "From Cybernation to Interaction: Ein Beitrag zu einer Archäologie der Interaktivität." In *Wunschmaschine Welterfindung: Eine Geschichte der Technikvision seit dem 18. Jahrhundert*. Brigitte Felderer, ed. New York: Springer, 192–207.

Hurter, Friedrich von (1850). *Geschichte Kaiser Ferdinands II. und seiner Eltern, bis zu dessen Krönung in Frankfurt: Personen-Haus-und Landesgeschichte. Mit vielen eigenhändigen Briefen Kaiser Ferdinands und seiner Mutter, der Erzherzogin Maria*. Vol. 11. Schaffhausen: Hurtersche Buchhandlung.

Inwood, Stephen (2002). *The Man Who Knew Too Much: The Strange and Inventive Life of Robert Hooke, 1635–1703*. London: Macmillan.

Irlbeck, Thomas, and Frank Langenau (2002). *Computer-Lexikon: Die umfassende Enzyklopädie*. Beck EDV-Berater. 4th rev. and enl. ed. Munich: Deutscher Taschenbuch-Verlag.

Israel, Jay E., James G. Mitchell, and Howard E. Sturgis (1979). "Separating Data from Function in a Distributed System." In *Operating Systems: Theory and Practice. Proceedings of the*

Second International Symposium on Operating Systems Theory and Practice. D. Lanciaux. ed. Amsterdam: North-Holland Publishing, 17–27.

Jaggard, Geoffrey (1967). *Wooster's World: A companion to the Wooster–Jeeves cycle of P. G. Wodehouse, LL. D.; containing a modicum of honey from the Drones, and reviewing a surging sea of aunts, brief instances, collectors' corner, a pleasing diversity of dumbchummery, racing intelligence, the stately homes of England; together with all that stimulating brouhaha 'The laughing love god has hiccoughs,' with some consideration of what the well-dressed young man is not wearing and a useful now we know department.* London: Macdonald.

Jarzombek, Mark (2006). "From Corridor (Spanish) to Corridor (English); or, What's in Your Corridor?" *Thresholds* 32, 6–11.

Jasper, Willi (2006). *Lessing: Biographie.* Vol. 60.615. List-Taschenbuch. Berlin: List.

Jean Paul (1785/1974). "Menschen sind Maschinen der Engel." In *Sämtliche Werke.* Vol. 1, *Jugendwerke I.* Norbert Miller, ed. Part II. Darmstadt: Wissenschaftliche Buchgesellschaft, 1028–31.

———— (1798/1988). "Palingenesien: Personalien vom Bedienten-und Maschinenmann." In *Sämtliche Werke.* Vol. 4, *Kleinere erzählende Schriften 1796–1801.* Norbert Miller, ed. Part I. 4th ed. Darmstadt: Wissenschaftliche Buchgesellschaft, 901–7.

Jefferson, Thomas, et al. (1776/1979). *The Declaration of Independence of the United States of America, July 4, 1776.* In *Jefferson: Selected Writings.* Harvey C. Mansfield, ed. Malden, MA: Wiley-Blackwell.

Jochum, Uwe (1991). *Bibliotheken und Bibliothekare 1800–1900.* Würzburg: Königshausen und Neumann.

Johnson, Jim (= Bruno Latour) (1988). "Mixing Humans and Non-Humans Together: The Sociology of a Door-Closer." *Social Problems* 35.3. Special Issue: The Sociology of Science and Technology (June 1988), 298–310.

Kafka, Franz (1917/1956). *The Trial.* Willa Muir and Edwin Muir, trans. New York: Modern Library.

———— (1986). *Letters to Milena.* Philipp Boehm, trans. New York: Schocken Books.

Kantorowicz, Ernst H. (1957/1997). *The King's Two Bodies: A Study in Medieval Political Theology.* Princeton: Princeton University Press.

Kapp, Ernst (1877). *Grundlinien einer Philosophie der Technik: Zur Entstehungsgeschichte der Cultur aus neuen Gesichtspunkten.* Braunschweig: Verlag von George Westermann.

Karrass, Theodor (1909). *Geschichte der Telegraphie.* Vol. 4. Telegraphen-und Fernsprechgeschichte in Einzeldarstellungen. Braunschweig: Vieweg.

Kay, Alan (1984). "Computer Software." *Scientific American* 251.3 (September), 52–59.

Kay, William A. (1963). "Recollections of Rutherford: Being the Personal Reminiscences of Lord Rutherford's Laboratory Assistant Here Published for the First Time." *Natural Philosopher* 1, 129–55.

Kedesdy, Erich (1910). "Nichtakademische Hilfskräfte in der chemischen Praxis." *Zeitschrift für angewandte Chemie* 23, 2128–29.

Kehlmann, Daniel (2005). *Wo ist Carlos Montúfar? Über Bücher.* Reinbek bei Hamburg: Rowohlt-Taschenbuch-Verlag.

Kellenbenz, Hermann (1985). "Der Kammerdiener, ein Typus der höfischen Gesellschaft." *Vierteljahrschrift für Sozial-und Wirtschaftsgeschichte* 72.4, 476–507.

Keller, Fritz (2007). "Hallo Dienstmann! Eine sozialhistorische Skizze." *Wiener Geschichts-blätter: Verein für Geschichte der Stadt Wien* 62.4, 1–16.

Kern, Arthur, ed. (1905–7). *Deutsche Hofordnungen des 16. und 17. Jahrhunderts.* Vol. 1, Part II. Denkmäler der deutschen Kulturgeschichte. Georg Steinhausen, ed. Berlin: Weidmannsche Buchhandlung.

Kern, Johannes P. (1977). *Ludwig Tieck: Dichter einer Krise.* Vol. 18. Poesie und Wissenschaft. Heidelberg: Lothar Stiehm.

Kerr, Robert (1865). *The gentleman's house. Or, How to plan English residences, from the parsonage to the palace; with tables of accommodation and cost, and a series of selected plans.* London: J. Murray.

Ketterl, Eugen (1929/1980). *Der alte Kaiser, wie nur Einer ihn sah: Der wahrheitsgetreue Bericht des Leibkammerdieners Kaiser Franz Josephs I.* Vienna: Fritz Molden.

Keyserling, Eduard von (1905/1973). "Zur Psychologie des Komforts." In *Werke.* Rainer Gruenter, ed. Frankfurt am Main: S. Fischer, 551–68.

Kippenberg, Anton, ed. (1921). *Ein Stammbuchblatt des Goethischen Dieners Johann Georg Paul Goetze.* Vol. 2. Schriften der Stadelmann-Gesellschaft. Leipzig: Stadelmann-Gesellschaft.

——— (1922). "Stadelmanns Glück und Ende." *Jahrbuch der Sammlung Kippenberg* 2, 240–84.

——— ed. (1924). *Wie Goethe seine Honorare vertrank.* Weimar: Stadelmann-Gesellschaft.

Kirkness, Alan, et al., eds. (1977). *Deutsches Fremdwörterbuch: Begonnen von Hans Schulz, fortgeführt von Otto Basler, weitergeführt im Institut für deutsche Sprache.* Vol. 3. Q/R. New York: Walter de Gruyter.

Kisch, Bruno (1954). "Forgotten Leaders in Modern Medicine: Valentin, Gruby, Remak, Auerbach." *Transactions of the American Philosophical Society* 44.2, 139–317.

Kitchiner, William (1817/1830). *The cook's oracle; And Housekeeper's manual: Containing receipts for cookery, and directions for carving with a complete system of cookery for Catholic families being the result of actual experiments instituted in the kitchen of William Kitchiner.* New York: J. and J. Harper.

Kittler, Friedrich (1989). *Die Nacht der Substanz.* Reihe um 9. Bern: Benteli Verlag. Kunstmuseum Bern lecture, April 30, 1989.

——— (1993). "Den Riß zwischen Lesen und Schreiben überwinden: Im Computerzeitalter stehen die Geisteswissenschaften unter Reformdruck." *Frankfurter Rundschau* 12 (January 12), 16.

Kleist, Heinrich von (2001). *Sämtliche Werke und Briefe.* Helmut Sembdner, ed. Munich: dtv.

Klemm, Heinrich, ed. (1886). *Das Buch der Livreen: Eine übersichtliche Zusammenstellung der gebräuchlichsten herrschaftlichen Livreen jeder Gattung, mit Rücksicht auf geschmackvolle Wahl und Harmonie der Farben, Decorationen und Abzeichen, zur Auswahl für Herrschaften sowie zur Belehrung für Kleidermacher.* 5th enl. ed. Dresden: H. Klemm.

Klenke, Dorothea (1992). *Herr und Diener in der französischen Komödie des 17. und 18. Jahrhunderts: Eine ideologiekritische Studie.* Vol. 4. Europäische Aufklärung in Literatur und Sprache. Frankfurt am Main: Peter Lang.

Klenz, Heinrich (1909). "Über Dienstbotensprache." *Zeitschrift für Deutsche Wortforschung* 11, 225–35.

Kliegel, Marieluise (1999). *Des Dieners alte Kleider: Livreen und Livreeknöpfe—ausgewählte Beispiele deutscher Adelshöfe des 19. Jahrhunderts.* Vol. 11. Vereinigte Westfälische Adelsarchive e.V. Münster: Vereinigte Westfälische Adelsarchive.

———— (2002). "Die Kleider der Diener." *Textil and Unterricht* 1.1, 34–39.

Kluger, Martin (2006). *Die Gehilfin.* Cologne: DuMont.

Knigge, Adolph Freiherr von (1788/1790). *Ueber den Umgang mit Menschen: In drey Theilen.* 3d enl. ed. Hannover: im Verlage bey Christian Ritscher.

Knoch, Wendelin, ed. (2006). *Engel und Boten.* Vol. 11.2006,1. Das Mittelalter. Berlin: Akademie.

Köhler, Andrea (2007). *Lange Weile: Über das Warten.* Frankfurt am Main: Insel.

Kohler, Robert E. (1996). "Review of *The Private Science of Louis Pasteur* by Gerald L. Geison." *Isis: An International Review Devoted to the History of Science and Its Culture* 87.2 (June), 331–34.

Kojève, Alexandre (1947/1980). *Introduction to the Reading of Hegel: Lectures on the Phenomenology of Spirit.* Assembled by Raymond Queneau. Allan Bloom, ed., James H. Nichols, trans. Ithaca: Cornell University Press.

Konersmann, Ralf (1999). "Vernunftarbeit: Metaphorologie als Quelle der Historischen Semantik." In *Die Kunst des Überlebens: Nachdenken über Hans Blumenberg.* Franz Josef Wetz and Hermann Timm, eds. Vol. 1422. stw. Frankfurt am Main: Suhrkamp, 121–41.

Könnecke, Otto (1912). *Rechtsgeschichte des Gesindes in West-und Süddeutschland.* Marburg: N. G. Elwert.

Konversations-Lexikon, Meyers Großes (1906–19). *Ein Nachschlagewerk des allgemeinen Wissens.* 6th enl. edition. Leipzig: Bibliographisches Institut.

Koselleck, Reinhart (1972–97). "Die Beziehung zwischen 'Herr' und 'Knecht' in ihrer lexikalischen Erfassung." In *Geschichtliche Grundbegriffe: Historisches Lexikon zur politisch-sozialen Sprache in Deutschland.* Otto Brunner, Werner Conze, and Reinhart Koselleck, eds. Vol. 3, H—Me. Stuttgart: Klett-Cotta, 56–63.

Koselleck, Reinhart, et al. (1972–97). "Verwaltung, Amt, Beamter." In *Geschichtliche Grundbegriffe. Historisches Lexikon zur politisch-sozialen Sprache in Deutschland.* Otto Brunner, Werner Conze, and Reinhart Koselleck, eds. Vol. 7, Verw.—Z. Stuttgart: Klett-Cotta, 1–96.

Krajewski, Markus (1997). *Die Rose: Vorstudie zu einer kleinen Geschichte der Rekursion.* www.verzetteln.de. URL: www.verzetteln.de/Rose.pdf.

———— (2002/2011). *Paper Machines: About Cards and Catalogues, 1548–1929.* Peter Krapp, trans. History and Foundations of Information Science. Cambridge: MIT Press.

———— (2007). "Elektra am Herd: Einige medienhistorische Details am Rande einer Technovision." *Neue Rundschau* 118.4, 141–55. Special Issue. "Details."

———— (2010). "'Same procedure as every year': Der virtuose Butler zwischen Regelvollzug und Improvisation." In *Improvisieren: Paradoxien des Unvorhersehbaren: Kunst, Medien, Praxis.* Hans-Friedrich Bormann, Gabriele Brandstetter, and Annemarie Matzke, eds. Kultur-und Medientheorie. Bielefeld: transcript, 107–24.

Krämer, Sybille (2008/2016). *Medium, Messenger, Transmission: An Approach to Media Philosophy.* Anthony Enns, trans. Recursions. Amsterdam: Amsterdam University Press.

Krätz, Otto (1976). "Das Portrait: Peter Griess (1829–1888)." *Chemie in unserer Zeit* 10.2, 42–47.

Krause, Gerhard, and Gerhard Müller, eds. (1981). *Theologische Realenzyklopädie*. Vol. 8, *Chlodwig-Dionysius Areopagita*. Berlin: Walter de Gruyter.

Kreil, Erika, ed. (2000). *Der Gehilfe: Vom Dienstboten zum Service-Design*. Krems / Zürich: Kunsthalle Krems / Museum für Gestaltung Zürich. "Der Gehilfe—vom Dienstboten zum Service-Design" Exhibition Catalogue. February 26–May 7.

Kruse, Laurids (1829). *Denkwürdigkeiten eines jungen Adjutanten Napoleon Bonapartes: Niedergeschrieben von dessen Kammerdiener*. Hamburg: Herold'schen Buchhandlung.

Kudriaffsky, Eufemia von (1880). *Die historische Küche: Ein Culturbild*. Vienna: A. Hartleben's Verlag.

Kuntz, Marion Leathers, and Paul Grimley Kuntz, eds. (1987). *Jacob's Ladder and the Tree of Life: Concepts of Hierarchy and the Great Chain of Being*. Vol. 14. American University Studies. New York: Peter Lang.

Kurdiovsky, Richard, ed. (2008). *Die Österreichische Präsidentschaftskanzlei in der Wiener Hofburg*. Vienna: Christian Brandstätter.

La Mettrie, Julien Offray de (1748/1996). *Machine Man and Other Writings*. Ann Thomson, ed. Cambridge Texts in the History of Philosophy. Cambridge: Cambridge University Press.

Lahnstein, Peter (1989). *Dienstbare Geister: Ein kulturgeschichtliches Lesebuch*. Munich: List.

Lammert, Friedrich (1929). "Strator, der Reitknecht." In *Paulys Real-Encyclopädie der classischen Altertumswissenschaft*. Georg Wissowa, ed. Vol. 3, Silacenis—Stluppi. Second Series [R–Z]. Stuttgart: J. B. Metzlersche Verlagsbuchhandlung, Col. 329–30.

Lamont-Brown, Raymond (2000). *John Brown: Queen Victoria's Highland Servant*. Stroud, UK: Sutton.

Lampson, Butler W. (1979). "Alto Non-programmer's Guide." In *Alto User's Handbook*. Xerox PARC. Palo Alto: PARC, 1–30.

Lange, Anselm (1987). *Elektrische Tischklingeln: Einst riefen sie 'dienstbare Geister.'* Dagmar Grauel-Korn, ed. Kornwestheim: Minner.

Lange, Gertrud (1928). "Der Beruf der technischen Assistentin." In *Das moderne Buch der weiblichen Berufe*. Erich Janke, ed. Minden: Köhler, 171–77.

Laplace, Pierre-Simon de (1773/1776). "Mémoire." In *Mémoires de mathématique et de physique, présentés à l'Académie royale des sciences, par divers savants*. Académie royale des sciences. Vol. 7. Paris: Imprimerie royale, 113.

———— (1814/1902). *A Philosophical Essay on Probabilities*. F. W. Truscott and F. L. Emory, trans. London: Chapman.

Laslett, Peter (1965/2001). *The World We Have Lost Further Explored*. London: Routledge.

Latour, Bruno (1983/2006). "Gebt mir ein Laboratorium, und ich werde die Welt aus den Angeln heben." In *ANThology: Ein einführendes Handbuch zur Akteur-Netzwerk-Theorie*. Andréa Belliger and David J. Krieger, eds. ScienceStudies. Bielefeld: transcript, 103–34.

———— (1986/2006). "Die Macht der Assoziation." In *ANThology: Ein einführendes Handbuch zur Akteur-Netzwerk-Theorie*. Andréa Belliger and David J. Krieger, eds. ScienceStudies. Bielefeld: transcript, 195–212.

———— (1991). "Technology Is Society Made Durable." In *A Sociology of Monsters: Essays on Power, Technology and Domination*. John Law, ed. London: Routledge.

———— (1991/1993). *We Have Never Been Modern*. Catherine Porter, trans. Cambridge: Harvard University Press.

——— (1994). "On Technical Mediation—Philosophy, Sociology, Genealogy." *Common Knowledge* 3.2, 29–64.

——— (1996a). "Der Berliner Schlüssel." In *Der Berliner Schlüssel: Erkundungen eines Liebhabers der Wissenschaften.* Berlin: Akademie Verlag, 37–51.

——— (1996b). "Engel eignen sich nicht als wissenschaftliche Instrumente." In *Der Berliner Schlüssel: Erkundungen eines Liebhabers der Wissenschaften.* Berlin: Akademie Verlag, 249–76.

——— (1999). *Pandora's Hope: Essays on the Reality of Science Studies.* Cambridge, MA: Harvard University.

——— (2001). "Thou shalt not take the Lord's name in vain—being a sort of sermon on the hesitations of religious speech." *RES: Anthropology and Aesthetics,* no. 39, 215–34.

Laube, Heinrich (1837). *Das junge Europa.* Vol. 3, *Die Bürger.* Mannheim: Heinrich Hoff.

Lauffer, Otto (1954). "Der laufende Bote im Nachrichtenwesen der früheren Jahrhunderte: Sein Amt, seine Ausstattung und seine Dienstleistungen." *Beiträge zur deutschen Volks-und Altertumskunde* 1, 19–60.

Laurel, Brenda (1990/1997). "Interface Agents: Metaphors with Character." In *Software Agents.* Jeffrey M. Bradshaw, ed. Menlo Park: AAAI Press, 67–77.

Laver, James (1947). "Homes and Habits." In *The Character of England.* Ernest Barker, ed. Oxford: Clarendon Press, 462–80.

Law, John (1992/2006). "Notizen zur Akteur-Netzwerk-Theorie: Ordnung, Strategie und Heterogenität." In *ANThology: Ein einführendes Handbuch zur Akteur-Netzwerk-Theorie.* Andréa Belliger and David J. Krieger, eds. ScienceStudies. Bielefeld: transcript, 429–46.

Lecheler, Helmut (1981). "Das Laufbahnprinzip: Seine Entwicklung, seine rechtliche Grundlage und Bedeutung für das Berufsbeamtentum." *Verantwortung und Leistung: Arbeitsgemeinschaft höherer Dienst* 3 (February).

Leff, Harvey S., and Andrew F. Rex, eds. (1990). *Maxwell's Demon: Entropy, Information, Computing.* Bristol: Adam Hilger.

——— eds. (2003). *Maxwell's Demon 2: Entropy, Classical and Quantum Information, Computing.* 2d ed. Bristol: Institute of Physics Publications.

Leibniz, Gottfried Wilhelm (1678/1988). *Political Writings.* Patrick Riley, ed. Cambridge: Cambridge University Press.

Lenz, Hermann (1964/1979). *Die Augen eines Dieners: Roman.* Vol. 348. st. Frankfurt am Main: Suhrkamp.

Lesage, Alain René (1715/1997). *Die Geschichte des Gil Blas von Santillana.* Vol. 949. Insel-Taschenbuch. Frankfurt am Main: Insel.

Lessing, Gotthold Ephraim (1755/1878). *Miss Sara Sampson.* In *The Dramatic Works of G. E. Lessing.* Ernest Bell, trans. London: George Bell.

——— (1755/2005). *Miß Sara Sampson: Ein bürgerliches Trauerspiel in fünf Aufzügen. Text und Kommentar.* Vol. 52. Suhrkamp BasisBibliothek. Frankfurt am Main: Suhrkamp.

Lévi-Strauss, Claude (1962). *The Savage Mind:* The Nature of Human Society Series. Chicago: University of Chicago Press.

Lewton, Frederick Lewis (1930). "The Servant in the House: A Brief History of the Sewing Machine." In *Annual Report of the Smithsonian Institution for 1929.* Smithsonian Institution. Washington, DC: Government Printing Office, 559–83.

Leyh, Georg (1961a). "Aufstellung und Signaturen." In *Bibliotheksverwaltung*. Vol. 2. Handbuch der Bibliothekswissenschaft. Founded by Fritz Milkau. 2d enl. ed. Wiesbaden: Otto Harrassowitz, 684–734.

———— ed. (1961b). *Bibliotheksverwaltung*. Vol. 2. Handbuch der Bibliothekswissenschaft. Founded by Fritz Milkau. 2d enl. ed. Wiesbaden: Otto Harrassowitz.

Licklider, Joseph Carl Robnett (1960/1990). "Man–Computer Symbiosis." In *In Memoriam: J. C. R. Licklider 1915–1990*. Robert W. Taylor, ed. Palo Alto: System Research Center, 1–19.

———— (1965). "Man–Computer Partnership." *International Science and Technology* 37.48 (May), 18–26.

Licklider, Joseph Carl Robnett, and Robert W. Taylor (1960/1990). "The Computer as a Communication Device." In *In Memoriam: J. C. R. Licklider 1915–1990*. Robert W. Taylor, ed. Palo Alto: System Research Center, 21–41.

Lietzmann, Hilda (1994). "Die Geschichte zweier Automaten: Ein weiterer Beitrag zum Werk des Valentin Drausch." *Zeitschrift für Kunstgeschichte* 57.3, 390–402.

Lifshey, Earl (1973). *The Housewares Story: A History of the American Housewares Industry*. Chicago: National Housewares Manufacturers Association.

Light, Alison (2007). *Mrs Woolf and the Servants*. London: Penguin/Fig Tree.

Lillo, George (1731/1965). *The London Merchant*. William H. McBurney, ed. Regents Restauration Drama Series. Lincoln: University of Nebraska Press.

Linder, Jutta (2001). *"Falsche Tendenzen": Der Staatsdiener Goethe und der Dichter*. Soveria Mannelli (Catanzaro): Rubbettino Editore.

Linge, Heinz (1980). *Bis zum Untergang: Als Chef des persönlichen Dienstes bei Hitler*. Werner Maser, ed. Munich: F. A. Herbig.

Löbe, William (1852/1855). *Das Dienstbotenwesen unserer Tage: Oder Was hat zu geschehen, um in jeder Beziehung gute Dienstboten heranzuziehen?* 2d ed. Leipzig: Verlag von Otto Wigand.

Locke, John (1689/2003). *Two Treatises of Government and A Letter Concerning Toleration*. Ian Shapiro, ed. Rethinking the Western Tradition. New Haven: Yale University Press.

Loschmidt, Josef (1869). "Der zweite Satz der mechanischen Wärmetheorie." In *Sitzungsberichte*. Akademie der Wissenschaften, ed. Vol. 59. 2. Mathematisch-Naturwissenschaftliche Klasse. Vienna: Akademie der Wissenschaften, 395–418.

Lotz, Albert (1914). *Geschichte des Deutschen Beamtentums*. 2d ed. Berlin: R. V. Decker's Verlag.

Lütt, Isa von der (1892). *Die elegante Hausfrau: Mitteilungen für junge Hauswesen, Mit besonderen Winken für Offiziersfrauen*. 2d ed. Vienna: Deutsche Verlags-Anstalt.

Lutz, Helma (2008). *Vom Weltmarkt in den Privathaushalt: Die neuen Dienstmädchen im Zeitalter der Globalisierung*. Susanne Schwalgin, ed. 2d ed. Opladen, Germany: Verlag Barbara Budrich.

Lyncker, Karl Wilhelm Heinrich von (1912). *Am Weimarischen Hofe unter Amalien und Karl August: Erinnerungen*. Marie Scheller, ed. Mittlers Goethe-Bücherei. Berlin: Ernst Siegfried Mittler und Sohn.

Macho, Thomas (1997). "Himmlisches Geflügel—Beobachtungen zu einer Motivgeschichte der Engel." In *Engel: Legenden der Gegenwart*. Cathrin Pichler, ed. Vienna: Springer, 83–100.

——— (2005). "Die Bäume des Alphabets." *Neue Rundschau* 116.2, 66–80.

Mackensen, Lutz (1962). *Deutsche Etymologie: Ein Leitfaden durch die Geschichte des deutschen Wortes.* Schünemann Leitfaden. Bremen: Schünemann.

Maes, Pattie, Robert H. Guttman, and Alexandros G. Moukas (1999). "Agents That Buy and Sell: Shoppers and sellers alike dispatch them into the digital bazaar to autonomously represent their best interests." *Communications of the ACM* 42.3, 81–83.

Malaparte, Curzio (1931/1988). *Technik des Staatsstreichs.* Berlin: Edition Tiamat.

Mann, Thomas (1901/1994). *Buddenbrooks: The Decline of a Family.* John E. Woods, trans. New York: Random House Vintage.

Mareschal, G. (1887). "Fontaine Lumineuse sur une table de salle à manger." *La Nature: Science Progrès* 17.851 (September 21), 271–72.

Markoff, John (2005). *What the Dormouse Said: How the Sixties Counterculture Shaped the Personal Computer Industry.* New York: Viking Penguin.

——— (2008). *Oliver Selfridge, an Early Innovator in Artificial Intelligence, Dies at 82.* www.nytimes.com. URL: http://www.nytimes.com/2008/12/04/us/04selfridge.html.

Marshall, Dorothy (1929). "The Domestic Servants of the Eighteenth Century." *Economica* 25 (April), 15–40.

——— (1949). *The English Domestic Servant in History.* Vol. G 13. General Series. London: Philip.

Marshall, Kate (2009). "Corridor: Media Architectures in American Fiction." PhD diss., UCLA.

Mason, Ellsworth (1971). "The Great Gas Bubble Prick't; or, Computer Revealed by a Gentleman of Quality." *College and Research Libraries* 32 (May), 183–96.

Mayer, Hans (1971). "Herrschaft und Knechtschaft: Hegels Deutung, ihre literarischen Ursprünge und Folgen." *Jahrbuch der deutschen Schillergesellschaft* 15, 251–79.

Maza, Sarah C. (1983). *Servants and Masters in Eighteenth-Century France: The Uses of Loyalty.* Princeton: Princeton University Press.

Mączak, Antoni, and Elisabeth Müller-Luckner, eds. (1988). *Klientelsysteme im Europa der Frühen Neuzeit.* Vol. 9. Schriften des Historischen Kollegs. Munich: R. Oldenbourg.

McBride, Theresa M. (1976). *The Domestic Revolution: The Modernisation of Household Service in England and France, 1820–1920.* New York: Holmes and Meier.

McClintock, Anne (1993). "Maid to Order: Commercial S/M and Gender Power." In *Dirty Looks: Women, Pornography, Power.* Pamela Gibson and Roma Gibson, eds. London: British Film Institute, 207–31.

McCuskey, Brian (1999). "Fetishizing the Flunkey: Thackeray and the Uses of Deviance." *NOVEL: A Forum on Fiction* 32.3 (Summer), 384–400.

McLuhan, Marshall (1951/2008). *The Mechanical Bride: Folklore of Industrial Man.* Corte Madera, CA: Gingko.

Meier-Oberist, Edmund (1956). *Kulturgeschichte des Wohnens im abendländischen Raum.* Hamburg: F. Holzmann.

Meinel, Christoph (1978). *Die Chemie an der Universität Marburg seit Beginn des 19. Jahrhunderts: Ein Beitrag zu ihrer Entwicklung als Hochschulfach.* Vol. 3. Academia Marburgensis. Marburg: N. G. Elwert.

——— (1997). *Rühmkorff, Röntgen, Regensburg: Historische Instrumente zur Gasentladung.* Regensburg: Lehrstuhl für Wissenschaftsgeschichte.

———— (2006). "Chemische Laboratorien: Funktion und Disposition." *Berichte zur Wissenschaftsgeschichte* 23.3, 287–302.

Meldrum, Tim (2000). *Domestic Service and Gender, 1660–1750: Life and Work in the London Household.* Women and Men in History. Harlow, England: Longman.

Menantes (1716/1730). *Die Manier Höflich und wohl zu Reden und zu Leben So wohl Mit hohen, vornehmen Personen, seines gleichen und Frauenzimmer, Als auch Wie das Frauenzimmer eine geschickte Aufführung gegen uns gebrauchen könne.* Hamburg: Bey Christian Wilhelm Brandt.

Merton, Robert K. (1965). *On the Shoulders of Giants: A Shandean Postscript.* New York: Free Press.

Metcalfe, Robert M. (1994). "How Ethernet Was Invented." *IEEE Annals of the History of Computing* 16, 81–88.

Metcalfe, Robert M., and David R. Boggs (1976). "Ethernet: Distributed Packet Switching for Local Computer Networks." *Communications of the ACM* 19.7 (July), 395–404.

Meyer, Richard M. (1904). "Die Audienz beim Fürsten: Geschichte eines literarischen Motivs." *Modern Philology* 2.2 (October), 151–72.

Meyer, Ulrich (1998). *Soziales Handeln im Zeichen des 'Hauses': Zur Ökonomik in der Spätantike und im frühen Mittelalter.* Vol. 140. Veröffentlichungen des Max-Planck-Instituts für Geschichte. Göttingen: Vandenhoeck and Ruprecht.

Miklautz, Elfie, Herbert Lachmayer, and Reinhard Eisendle, eds. (1999). *Die Küche: Zur Geschichte eines architektonischen, sozialen und imaginativen Raums.* Vienna: Böhlau Verlag.

Milkau, Fritz, ed. (1933). *Handbuch der Bibliothekswissenschaft.* Vol. 2, *Bibliotheksverwaltung.* Leipzig: Otto Harrassowitz.

Mills, David L. (2003). "A Brief History of NTP Time: Memoirs of an Internet Timekeeper." *SIGCOMM Computer Communications Review* 33.2, 9–21.

Misch, Rochus (2008/2010). *Der letzte Zeuge: 'Ich war Hitlers Telefonist, Kurier und Leibwächter.'* Sandra Zarrinbal, Burkhard Nachtigall, and Ralph Giordano, eds. 4th ed. Munich: Piper.

Mitchell, James G. (1982). "File Servers for Local Area Networks." In *Lecture Notes, Course on Local Area Networks.* Canterbury: University of Kent, 83–114.

Mitchell, Jim G. (1970). "Considerations for Future Office Systems: A Summary." Palo Alto: typescript, Xerox PARC. Xerox PARC Archive.

Montaigne, Michel de (1588/1993). *The Complete Essays.* London: Penguin.

Morgenstern, Christian (1918/1986). *Stufen und andere Aphorismen und Sprüche.* Munich: Piper.

Morus, Iwan Rhys (1996). "The Electric Ariel: Telegraphy and Commercial Culture in Early Victorian England." *Victorian Studies* 39.3 (Spring), 339–78.

———— (2004). *Michael Faraday and the Electrical Century.* Cambridge: Icon Books.

Moser, Friedrich Carl (1754–55). *Teutsches Hof= Recht.* Frankfurt: In Commission bey Johann Benjamin Andreä.

———— (1759). *Der Herr und der Diener, geschildert mit patriotischer Freiheit.* Frankfurt: Raspe.

Müller, Friedrich von (1870/1982). *Unterhaltungen mit Goethe.* Ernst Grumach, ed. Munich: C. H. Beck.

Müller, Heidi (1981). *Dienstbare Geister: Leben und Arbeitswelt städtischer Dienstboten.* Berlin: Dietrich Reimer.

Müller-Staats, Dagmar (1987). *Klagen über Dienstboten: Eine Untersuchung über Dienstboten und ihre Herrschaften.* Vol. 683. Insel-Taschenbuch. Frankfurt am Main: Insel.

Mulligan, Lotte (1996). "Self-Scrutiny and the Study of Nature: Robert Hooke's Diary as Natural History." *Journal of British Studies* 35.3 (July), 311–42.

Mullins, Samuel, and Gareth Griffiths, eds. (1986). *"Cap and Apron": An Oral History of Domestic Service in the Shires, 1880–1950.* Vol. 2. Harborough Series. Leicester: Leicestershire Museums, Art Galleries and Record Service.

Munby, Arthur Joseph (1891). *Faithful Servants: Being Epitaphs and Obituaries Recording Their Names and Services.* J. W. Streeten, ed. London: Reeves and Turner.

Münch, Paul (1981). "Haus und Regiment—Überlegungen zum Einfluß der alteuropäischen Ökonomie auf die fürstliche Regierungstheorie und-praxis während der Frühen Neuzeit." In *Europäische Hofkultur im 16. und 17. Jahrhundert: Vorträge und Referate gehalten anläßlich des Kongresses des Wolfenbütteler Arbeitskreises für Renaissanceforschung und des Internationalen Arbeitskreises für Barockliteratur in der Herzog August Bibliothek.* August Buck et al., eds. Vols. 8–10. Wolfenbütteler Arbeiten zur Barockforschung. Hamburg: Hauswedell, 205–10.

——— (1995). "Tiere, Teufel oder Menschen? Zur gesellschaftlichen Einschätzung der 'dienenden Klassen' während der Frühen Neuzeit." In *Gesinde im 18. Jahrhundert.* Gotthardt Frühsorge, Rainer Gruenter, and Beatrix Wolff Metternich, eds. Vol. 12. Studien zum achtzehnten Jahrhundert. Hamburg: Felix Meiner, 83–108.

Musil, Robert (1932/2011). *The Man Without Qualities.* Sophie Wilkins and Burton Pike, trans. London: Picador.

Negroponte, Nicholas (1997). "Agents: From Direct Manipulation to Delegation." In *Software Agents.* Jeffrey M. Bradshaw, ed. Menlo Park: AAAI Press, 57–66.

Nestroy, Johann (1840/1962). "Der Talismann." In *Werke.* Oskar Maurus Fontana, ed. Munich: Winkler, 243–325.

Newton, William Ritchey (2006). *La petite cour: Services et serviteurs à la cour de Versailles au XVIIIe siècle.* Paris: Fayard.

——— (2008). *Derrière la façade: Vivre au château de Versailles au XVIIIe siècle.* Paris: Perrin.

Nichols, Jeffrey, Jacob O. Wobbrock, Darren Gergle, and Jodi Forlizzi (2002). "Mediator and Medium: Doors as Interruption Gateways and Aesthetic Displays." In *DIS '02: Proceedings of the 4th Conference on Designing Interactive Systems.* New York: ACM, 379–86.

Nickisch, Reinhard M. G. (1969). *Die Stilprinzipien in den deutschen Briefstellern des 17. und 18. Jahrhunderts: Mit einer Bibliographie zur Briefschreiblehre (1474–1800).* Vol. 254. Palaestra. Göttingen: Vandenhoeck and Ruprecht.

Nocks, Lisa (2007). *The Robot: The Life Story of a Technology.* Greenwood Technographies. Westport, CT: Greenwood Press.

Norberg, Kathryn (2008). "Women of Versailles, 1682–1789." In *Servants of the Dynasty: Palace Women in World History.* Anne Walthall, ed. Vol. 7. California World History Library. Berkeley: University of California Press, 191–214.

Norton, John D. (2005). "Eaters of the Lotus: Landauer's Principle and the Return of Maxwell's Demon." *Studies in History and Philosophy of Modern Physics* 36, 375–411.

Oppenheim, Janet (1985). *The Other World: Spiritualism and Psychical Research in England, 1850–1914*. Cambridge: Cambridge University Press.

Orland, Barbara (1983). "Effizienz im Heim: Die Rationalisierungsdebatte zur Reform der Hausarbeit in der Weimarer Republik." *Kultur and Technik* 4, 221–27.

——— ed. (1990). *HaushaltsTräume—ein Jahrhundert Technisierung und Rationalisierung im Haushalt: Begleitbuch zur gleichnamigen Ausstellung*. Die blauen Bücher. Königstein im Taunus: Karl Robert Langewiesche Nachfolger, Hans Köster.

——— (1993). "Emanzipation durch Rationalisierung? Der 'rationelle Haushalt' als Konzept institutionalisierter Frauenpolitik in der Weimarer Republik." In *Rationale Beziehungen? Geschlechterverhältnisse im Rationalisierungsprozeß*. Dagmar Reese, Eve Rosenhaft, Carola Sachse, and Tilla Siegel, eds. Vol. 1802. es. Frankfurt am Main: Suhrkamp, 222–50.

——— (1998). "Haushalt, Konsum und Alltagsleben in der Technikgeschichte." *Technikgeschichte* 65, 273–95.

——— (2003). "Dienstmädchenhausse." In *Geschichte in Geschichten: Ein historisches Lesebuch*. Barbara Duden, Karen Hagemann, Regina Schulte, and Ulrike Weckel, eds. Frankfurt am Main: Campus Verlag, 241–50.

Orth, Karin (1993). *"Nur weiblichen Besuch": Dienstbotinnen in Berlin 1890–1914*. Vol. 708. Frankfurt: Campus.

Orwell, George (1965). "Charles Dickens." In *Decline of the English Murder and Other Essays*. Harmondsworth: Penguin Books, 80–141.

Ottillinger, Eva B., and Lieselotte Hanzl (1997). *Kaiserliche Interieurs: Die Wohnkultur des Wiener Hofes im 19. Jahrhundert*. Vienna: Böhlau.

Ottmüller, Uta (1973). *Die Dienstbotenfrage: Zur Sozialgeschichte der doppelten Ausnutzung von Dienstmädchen im deutschen Kaiserreich*. Münster: Verl. Frauenpolitik.

Pangerl, Irmgard (2007a). "'Höfische Öffentlichkeit': Fragen des Kammerzutritts und der räumlichen Repräsentation am Wiener Hof." In *Der Wiener Hof im Spiegel der Zeremonialprotokolle (1652–1800), eine Annäherung*. Irmgard Pangerl, ed. Vol. 47. Forschungen und Beiträge zur Wiener Stadtgeschichte. Innsbruck: Studien-Verlag, 255–85.

——— ed. (2007b). *Der Wiener Hof im Spiegel der Zeremonialprotokolle. (1652–1800), eine Annäherung*. Vol. 47. Forschungen und Beiträge zur Wiener Stadtgeschichte. Innsbruck: Studien-Verlag.

PARC (2007). *Innovation Milestones*. www.parc.com. URL: www.parc.com/about/history/.

Parker, Hershel (1996). *Herman Melville: A Biography*. Vol. 1, *1819–1851*. Baltimore: Johns Hopkins University Press.

Parr, Joy (1999). *Domestic Goods: The Material, the Moral, and the Economic in the Postwar Years*. Toronto: University of Toronto Press.

Pasleau, Suzy, and Isabelle Schopp (2006). *Proceedings of the Servant Project*. Liège: Édition de l'Université de Liège.

Patalong, Frank (2008). *Suchmaschinen vor Google: Am Anfang war die Liste*. www.spiegel.de. URL: www.spiegel.de/netzwelt/web/0,1518,577644,00.html.

Pečar, Andreas (2005). "Das Hofzeremoniell als Herrschaftstechnik? Kritische Einwände und methodische Überlegungen am Beispiel des Kaiserhofes in Wien (1660–1740)." In *Staatsbildung als kultureller Prozeß: Strukturwandel und Legitimation von Herrschaft in der Frühen Neuzeit*. Ronald G. Asch and Dagmar Freist, eds. Vienna: Böhlau, 381–404.

Petersen, Waldemar (1927). "Zukunftsfragen der Elektrizitätswirtschaft." *Wirtschaftshefte der Frankfurter Zeitung* 2, 26.

Pfeifer, Wolfgang, ed. (1995). *Etymologisches Wörterbuch des Deutschen*. Vol. 3358. 2d ed. Munich: dtv.

Pfeilsticker, Walther (1957). *Hof, Regierung, Verwaltung*. Vol. 1. Neues württembergisches Dienerbuch. Stuttgart: Cotta.

Pflüger, Jörg (2004). "Konversation, Manipulation, Delegation: Zur Ideengeschichte der Interaktivität." In *Geschichten der Informatik: Visionen, Paradigmen, Leitmotive*. Hans Dieter Hellige, ed. Berlin, Heidelberg: Springer, 367–410.

Pias, Claus, et al., eds. (2000). *Kursbuch Medienkultur: Die maßgeblichen Theorien von Brecht bis Baudrillard*. 2d ed. Stuttgart: DVA.

Pinter, Harold (1960). *The Caretaker and The Dumb Waiter: Two Plays*. Vol. E-299. Evergreen Original. New York: Grove Press.

Plato (380/2008). *The Symposium*. M. C. Howatson and Frisbee Sheffield, eds. Cambridge: Cambridge University Press.

Polanyi, Michael (1966/2009). *The Tacit Dimension*. Amartya Sen, ed. Chicago: University of Chicago Press.

Polt-Heinzl, Evelyne (1997). "Stationäre Diener der Kommunikation: Motivgeschichtliches Porträt eines literarischen Berufsfeldes." *Sprachkunst: Beiträge zur Literaturwissenschaft* 28.2, 275–90.

Popper, Karl R. (1935/2005). *Logik der Forschung*. Herbert Keuth, ed. 11th rev. and enl. ed. Tübingen: Mohr Siebeck.

——— (1957). "Irreversibility; or, Entropy Since 1905." *British Journal for the Philosophy of Science* 8.30 (May), 151–55.

Porstmann, Walter (1928). "Wilhelm Ostwald wird 75 Jahre alt." *VDI-Nachrichten: Mitteilungen des Vereines Deutscher Ingenieure und des Deutschen Verbandes technisch-wissenschaftlicher Vereine* 8.35 (August 29), 2.

Porter, Roy (1990). *English Society in the Eighteenth Century*. Penguin Social History of Britain. London: Penguin.

Praetorius, Johannes (1669). *Blockes-Berges Verrichtung: Oder Ausführlicher Geographischer Bericht von den hohen trefflich alt-und berühmten Blockes-Berge: ingleichen von der Hexenfahrt und Zauber-Sabbathe so auff solchen Bergen die Unholden aus gantz Teutschland Jährlich den 1. Maii in Sanct Walpurgis Nachte anstellen sollen*. Leipzig: Scheibe, Arnst.

Prause, Karl (1930). *Deutsche Grußformeln in neuhochdeutscher Zeit*. Vol. 19. Wort und Brauch. Volkskundliche Arbeiten namens der Schlesischen Gesellschaft für Volkskunde. Breslau: M. and H. Marcus.

Prendinger, Helmut, and Mitsuru Ishizuka (2004). "Introducing the Cast for Social Computing: Life-Like Characters." In *Life-Like Characters: Tools, Affective Functions and Applications*. Helmut Prendinger and Mitsuru Ishizuka, eds., Cognitive Technologies. Berlin: Springer, 3–16.

Prescott, Henry W. (1936). "Silent Roles in Roman Comedy." *Classical Philology* 31.2 (April), 97–119.

Priestley, Joseph (1772). *Geschichte und gegenwärtiger Zustand der Elektricität: Nebst eigenthümlichen Versuchen*. Übers. von Johann Georg Krünitz. 2d enl. ed. Berlin: Gottlieb August Lange.

Psellus, Michael (1838). *De operatione daemonum: Accedunt inedita opuscula Pselli*. Norimbergae: Apud Fr. Nap. Campe.

Pumfrey, Stephen (1991). "Ideas Above His Station: A Social Study of Hooke's Curatorship of Experiments." *History of Science* 29.83 (March), 1–44.

——— (1995). "Who Did the Work? Experimental Philosophers and Public Demonstrators in Augustan England." *British Journal for the History of Science* 28.2 (June), 131–56.

Purdy, Strother B. (1984). "Technopoetics: Seeing What Literature Has to Do with the Machine." *Critical Inquiry* 11.1 (September), 130–40.

Raabe, Paul (1995). "Der Bibliotheksdiener im 18. Jahrhundert." In *Gesinde im 18. Jahrhundert.* Gotthardt Frühsorge, Rainer Gruenter, and Beatrix Wolff Metternich, eds. Vol. 12. Studien zum achtzehnten Jahrhundert. Hamburg: Felix Meiner, 309–18.

Ramm-Bonwitt, Ingrid (1997). *Commedia dell'arte.* Frankfurt am Main: Nold.

Räuber, Friedrich (1919). "Zur Frage des unteren Bibliotheksdienstes." *Zentralblatt für Bibliothekswesen* 36.7/8, 170–75.

Rees, Remig (1905). *Der stumme Diener (früher 'Moment-Praktikus'): Universal-Schnellrechner.* 7th enl. ed. Wehingen (Württbg.): Merkur.

Reinecke, Paul (1933). "Zur Geschichte des Steigbügels." *Germania: Anzeiger der Römisch-Germanischen Kommission des Deutschen Archäologischen Instituts* 17, 220–22.

Request for Comments (1998). *Hyper Text Coffee Pot Control Protocol (HTCPCP/1.0).* http://www.ietf.org/. URL: tools.ietf.org/html/rfc2324.

Reuß, Heinrich XXVIII Prinz j. L. (1908). *Der korrekte Diener: Handbuch für Herrschaften und deren Diener.* 2d rev. ed. Berlin: Parey.

Rheinberger, Hans-Jörg (2007). *Historische Epistemologie zur Einführung.* Vol. 336. Zur Einführung. Hamburg: Junius.

Richarz, Irmintraut (1991). *Oikos, Haus und Haushalt: Ursprung und Geschichte der Haushaltsökonomik.* Göttingen: Vandenhoeck and Ruprecht.

Ricoeur, Paul (1981). "Mimesis and Representation." *Annals of Scholarship: Metastudies of the Humanities and Social Sciences* 2.3, 15–32.

Riemer, Friedrich Wilhelm (1841/1921). *Mitteilungen über Goethe.* Arthur Pollmer, ed. Leipzig: Insel.

Robbins, Bruce (1986). *The Servant's Hand: English Fiction from Below.* New York: Columbia University Press.

Roberts, Robert (1827/1988). *Roberts' Guide for Butlers and Household Staff.* Chester, CT: Applewood Books.

Rogers, M. A. (1985). "The Servant Problem in Viennese Popular Comedy." In *Viennese Popular Theatre: A Symposium/Das Wiener Volkstheater: Ein Symposion.* W. E. Yates and John R. P. McKenzie, eds. Exeter: University of Exeter Press, 81–92.

Ronell, Avital (2001). *Das Telefonbuch: Technik, Schizophrenie, elektrische Rede.* Berlin: Brinkmann und Bose.

Root, Waverley Lewis, and Richard de Rochemont (1976). *Eating in America: A History.* Richard De Rochemont, ed. New York: William Morrow.

Roseno, Agnes (1933). *Die Entwicklung der Brieftheorie von 1655–1709: Dargestellt an Hand der Briefsteller von Georg Philipp Harsdörfer, Kaspar Stieler, Christian Weise und Benjamin Neukirch.* Würzburg: Konrad Triltsch.

Ross, Lisa (1912). *Weibliche Dienstboten und Dienstbotenhaltung in England.* Tübingen: J. C. B. Mohr (P. Siebeck).

Rothe, Anton (1902). *Ueber den Kanzleistil: Erweiterter und ergänzter Vortrag.* 11th ed. Berlin: Carl Heymanns Verlag.

Rudolph, André (2006). *Figuren der Ähnlichkeit: Johann Georg Hamanns Analogiedenken im Kontext des 18. Jahrhundert.* Vol. 29. Hallesche Beiträge zur europäischen Aufklärung. Tübingen: Max Niemeyer.

Rüss, Hartmut (1994). *Herren und Diener: Die soziale und politische Mentalität des russischen Adels. 9.-17. Jahrhundert.* Vol. 17. Beiträge zur Geschichte Osteuropas. Cologne: Böhlau.

Russell, N. C., E. M. Tansey, and P. V. Lear (2000). "Missing Links in the History and Practice of Science: Teams, Technicians and Technical Work." *History of Science* 38, 237–41.

Rustemeyer, Angela (1996). *Dienstboten in Petersburg und Moskau 1861–1917: Hintergrund, Alltag, soziale Rolle.* Vol. 45. Quellen und Studien zur Geschichte des östlichen Europa. Stuttgart: Steiner.

Sabattier, Jacqueline (1984). *Figaro et son maître: Maîtres et domestiques à Paris au XVIIIe siècle.* Collection pour l'Histoire. Paris: Perrin.

Sachse, Johann Christoph (1822/1977). *Der deutsche Gil Blas: Oder Leben/Wanderungen und Schicksale Johann Christoph Sachses, eines Thüringers.* Berlin: Rütten und Loening.

Sagarra, Eda (1985). "Die Dienstboten im deutschen Roman von Immermann bis Fontane." In *Littérature et culture allemandes: Hommages à Henri Plard.* Roger Goffin, Michel Vanhelleputte, and Henri Plard, eds. Vol. 92. Faculté de Philosophie et Lettres. Brussels: Édition de l'université de Bruxelles, 165–81.

———— (1989). "Barbier, Gärtner und Koch: Poetologische und sozialgeschichtliche Aspekte ihrer Erscheinung in der Biedermeierzeit." In *Viktor Žmegač zum 60. Geburtstag.* Dieter Borchmeyer, ed. Tübingen: Max Niemeyer, 71–86.

Saint-Simon, Louis de Rouvroy, Duc de (1699/1906–19). *Mémoires de duc de Saint-Simon, pub. par MM. Chéruel et Ad. Regnier fils et collationnés de nouveau pour cette éd. sur le manuscrit autographe avec une notice de M. Sainte-Beuve.* Adolphe Chéruel, Adolphe Regnier, Arthur André Gabriel, and Michel de Boislisle, eds. Paris: Hachette.

Sambrook, Pamela (1999). *The Country House Servant.* Stroud: Sutton.

———— (2005). *Keeping Their Place: Domestic Service in the Country House, 1700–1920.* Stroud: Sutton.

Sarti, Raffaella (2001). "Telling Zita's Tale: Holy Servants' Stories and Servants' History." In *Narratives of the Servant.* Regina Schulte and P. Hantzaroula, eds. Vol. HEC no. 2001/1. EUI working paper. Badia Fiesolana, San Domenico (FI): European University Institute, Department of History and Civilization, 1–30.

———— (2002). *Europe at Home: Family and Material Culture, 1500–1800.* Allan Cameron, trans. New Haven: Yale University Press.

———— (2005). "The True Servant: Self-Definition of Male Domestics in an Italian City (Bologna, 17th–19th Centuries)." *History of the Family* 10, 407–33.

———— (2006a). "Freedom and Citizenship? The Legal Status of Servants and Domestic Workers in a Comparative Perspective (16th–20th Centuries)." In *Proceedings of the "Servant Project."* Suzy Pasleau and Isabelle Schopp, eds. Vol. 3. Liège: Éditions de l'Univérsité de Liège, 127–64.

———— (2006b). "Who Are Servants? Defining Domestic Service in Western Europe (16th–21st Centuries)." In *Proceedings of the "Servant Project."* Suzy Pasleau and Isabelle Schopp, eds. Vol. 2. Liège: Éditions de l'Univérsité de Liège, 3–59.

Sayre, Carolyn (2008). "At Your Service." *TIME Magazine* (June 9), 42.

Scarrott, G. G. (1979). "The Clifford Paterson Lecture, 1979: From Computing Slave to

Knowledgeable Servant: The Evolution of Computers." *Proceedings of the Royal Society of London: Series A, Mathematical and Physical Sciences* 369.1736 (December), 1–30.

Schaffer, Simon (1997). "Experimenters' Techniques, Dyers' Hands, and the Electric Planetarium." *Isis. An International Review Devoted to the History of Science and Its Culture* 88, 456–83.

Schalkwyk, David (2008). *Shakespeare, Love and Service.* Cambridge: Cambridge University Press.

Scharf, Armin (2001a). "Alles unter Kontrolle: Der neue Haushalt ist greifbar nah: das vernetzte Heim mit kleinen und großen Helfern, die lautlos zusammenarbeiten." *Design Report: Gestaltung Erleben* 5 (May), 20–28.

———— (2001b). "Universalisten für die Küche: Sie gehört einfach in jeden Haushalt: die Küchenmaschine." *Design Report: Gestaltung Erleben* 5 (May), 32–34.

Schierenberg, Kurt-August (1994). *"In Goethes Haus—in Goethes Hand": Goethe und seine Diener und Helfer, zum 20jährigen Bestehen der Wetzlarer Goethe-Gesellschaft e. V. und als Dankesgruß zum 90. Geburtstag ihres Ehrenvorsitzenden Dr. K. A. Schierenberg am 26. August 1994.* Vol. 1994. Jahresgabe / Wetzlarer Goethe-Gesellschaft, Ortsvereinigung der Goethe-Gesellschaft Weimar. Wetzlar: Wetzlarer Goethe-Gesellschaft.

Schleier, Hans (2003). *Geschichte der deutschen Kulturgeschichtsschreibung.* Vol. 24. Wissen und Kritik. Waltrop, Germany: Hartmut Spenner.

Schleif, Walter (1965). *Goethes Diener.* Vol. 17. Beiträge zur Deutschen Klassik. Berlin: Aufbau-Verlag.

Schlieben, Adolph (1892). "Geschichte der Steigbügel." *Annalen des Vereins für Nassauische Altertumskunde und Geschichtsforschung* 24, 165–219.

Schlözer, August Ludwig von (1776–82). *August Ludwig Schlözer's Briefwechsel: Meist historischen und politischen inhalts, 1776–1782.* Göttingen: im Verlage der Vandenhoeckschen Buchhandlung.

Schmitt, Carl (1954/2008). *Gespräch über die Macht und den Zugang zum Machthaber.* Stuttgart: Klett-Cotta.

Schnitzer, Claudia (1999). *Höfische Maskeraden: Funktion und Ausstattung von Verkleidungsdivertissements an deutschen Höfen der frühen Neuzeit.* Tübingen: Max Niemeyer.

Scholz, Friedrich (1956). "Gruß und Anruf." *Zeitschrift für vergleichende Sprachforschung auf dem Gebiete der indogermanischen Sprachen* 74.3/4. 129–45.

Schoppe, Amalie (1845). "Der alte Diener Goethes." *Neue Pariser Modeblätter* 19.

Schottus, Gasparus (1664). *Technica Curiosa, Sive Mirabilia Artis. Libris XII. Comprehensa; Quibus varia Experimenta, variáque Technasmata Pnevmatica, Hydraulica, Hydrotechnica, Mechanica, Graphica, Cyclometrica, Chronometrica, Automatica, Cabalistica, aliaque Artis arcana ac miracula, rara, curiosa, ingeniosa, magnamque partem nova and antehac inaudita, eruditi rbis utilitati, delectationi, disceptationique proponuntur.* Johannes Philippus, ed. Norimbergae: Endterus.

Schrader, Ernst (1911). *Die Schlussformel in Goethes Briefen.* Greifswald: Buchdruckerei Hans Adler.

Schröder, Rainer (1995). "Gesinderecht im 18. Jahrhundert." In *Gesinde im 18. Jahrhundert.* Gotthardt Frühsorge, Rainer Gruenter, and Beatrix Wolff Metternich, eds. Vol. 12. Studien zum achtzehnten Jahrhundert. Hamburg: Felix Meiner, 13–39.

Schulze, Hans Herbert (1989). *Computer Enzyklopädie: Lexikon und Fachwörterbuch für Datenverarbeitung und Telekommunikation.* Vol. 5. N-R. Reinbek bei Hamburg: Rowohlt.

Schulze-Gattermann, Heinrich (1935). *200 Jahre Georgia-Augusta: Bilder aus der Geschichte der Göttinger Universität.* Göttingen: Verlag der "Göttinger Nachrichten."

Schüttpelz, Erhard (2003). "Frage nach der Frage, auf die das Medium eine Antwort ist." In *Signale der Störung.* Albert Kümmel and Erhard Schüttpelz, eds. Munich: Wilhelm Fink, 15–29.

—— (2006). "Die medienanthropologische Kehre der Kulturtechniken." *Archiv für Mediengeschichte* 6, 87–110.

Schwarz, Leonard (1999). "English Servants and Their Employers During the Eighteenth and Nineteenth Centuries." *Economic History Review* 52.2, 236–56.

Schweizer, Harold (2008). *On Waiting.* Thinking in Action. London: Routledge.

Schwickert, Axel (1995). "Grundlagen des Client-Server-Konzeptes." *Wirtschaftswissenschaftliches Studium* 24.6, 313–16.

Scior, Volker (2006). "Veritas und certitudo oder: Warten auf Wissen. Boten in frühmittelalterlichen Informationsprozessen." *Das Mittelalter* 11.1, 110–31.

Seaton, Thomas (1720/1985). *The Conduct of Servants in Great Families.* Vol. 36. Marriage, Sex, and the Family in England, 1660–1800. New York: Garland.

Seneca, L. Annaeus (2007). *Epistulae morales ad Lucilium. = Briefe an Lucilium.* Gerhard Fink, ed. Tusculum. Düsseldorf: Artemis and Winkler.

Serres, Michel (1968/1982). *Hermes: Literature, Science, Philosophy.* Josue V. Harari and David F. Bell, eds. Baltimore: Johns Hopkins University Press.

—— (1980/2007). *The Parasite.* Lawrence R. Schehr, trans. Minneapolis: University of Minnesota Press.

—— (1995). *Angels, A Modern Myth.* Francis Cowper, trans. Paris: Flammarion.

Shaffer, Richard A. (1994). "Tools of the Trade." *ComputerLetter: Business Issues in Technology* 10.11 (April 11), 1–6.

Shapin, Steven (1989). "The Invisible Technician." *American Scientist* 77 (November/December), 554–63.

—— (1994). *A Social History of Truth: Civility and Science in Seventeenth-Century England.* Science and Its Conceptual Foundations. Chicago: University of Chicago Press.

—— (1998). *Die wissenschaftliche Revolution.* Vol. 14073. Forum Wissenschaft. Frankfurt am Main: Fischer Taschenbuch.

Shapin, Steven, and Simon Schaffer (1985). *Leviathan and the Air-Pump: Hobbes, Boyle, and the Experimental Life.* Princeton: Princeton University Press.

Shenker, Orly R. (1999). "Maxwell's Demon and Baron Munchausen: Free Will as a Perpetuum Mobile." *Studies in History and Philosophy of Modern Physics* 30.3, 347–72.

Sheridan, Richard Brinsley (1775/1997). *The Rivals.* Cambridge: Chadwyck-Healey.

Sherman, Sandra (1995). "Servants and Semiotics: Reversible Signs, Capital Instability, and Defoe's Logic of the Market." *English Literary History* 63.3 (Fall), 551–73.

Shor, Shirley (1998). *Smart House—Version 2.0.* www.heise.de/tp/. URL: www. heise.de/tp /r4/artikel/6/6255/1.html.

Sibum, H. Otto (1995a). "Reworking the Mechanical Value of Heat: Instruments of Precision and Gestures of Accuracy in Early Victorian England." *Studies in History and Philosophy of Science* 26, 73–106.

———— (1995b). "Working Experiments: A History of Gestural Knowledge." *Cambridge Review* 116.2325, 25–37.

———— (1998a). "Die Sprache der Instrumente: Eine Studie zur Praxis und Repräsentation des Experimentierens." In *Experimental Essays—Versuche zum Experiment*. Michael Heidelberger and Friedrich Steinle, eds. Baden-Baden: Nomos, 141–.

———— (1998b). "Les gestes de la mesure: Joule, les pratiques de la brasserie et la science." *Annales: Histoire, Sciences Sociales* 53.4–5, 745–74.

———— (2005). "Wissen aus erster Hand: Mikro-Dynamik wissenschaftlichen Wandels im frühviktorianischen England." *Historische Anthropologie* 13.3, 301–24.

Sieder, Reinhard (2004). "Die Liebe der Ledigen auf dem Land: Intime Beziehungen der Dienstboten um 1800." In *Die Rückkehr des Subjekts in den Kulturwissenschaften*. Vienna: Turia + Kant, 95–125.

Siefkes, Dirk (1998). "Die Rolle von Gruppenprozessen in der Informatikgeschichte." In *Sozialgeschichte der Informatik. Kulturelle Praktiken und Orientierungen*. Dirk Siefkes, Peter Eulenhöfer, and Heike Stach, eds. Studien zur Wissenschafts-und Technikforschung. Wiesbaden: Deutscher Universitäts-Verlag, 85–104.

Siefkes, Dirk, Peter Eulenhöfer, and Heike Stach, eds. (1998). *Sozialgeschichte der Informatik: Kulturelle Praktiken und Orientierungen*. Studien zur Wissenschafts-und Technikforschung. Wiesbaden: Deutscher Universitäts-Verlag.

Siegel, Heinrich (1883). *Die rechtliche Stellung der Dienstmannen in Oesterreich im zwölften und dreizehnten Jahrhundert*. Vienna: In commission bei K. Gerold's Sohn.

Siegert, Bernhard (1990). "Netzwerke der Regimentalität: Harsdörfers Teutscher Scretarius und die Schicklichkeit der Briefe im 17. Jahrhundert." *Modern Language Notes: German Issue* 109 (April), 536–62.

———— (1993/1999). *Relays: Literature as an Epoch of the Postal System*. Kevin Repp, trans. Writing Science. Stanford: Stanford University Press.

———— (1994). "Die Trinität des Gastgebers." In *Cyberspace: Gemeinschaften, virtuelle Kolonien, Öffentlichkeiten*. Manfred Faßler and Wulf R. Halbach, eds. Munich: Wilhelm Fink, 281–94.

———— (1997). "Vögel, Engel und Gesandte: Alteuropas Übertragungsmedien." In *Gespräche —Boten—Briefe: Körpergedächtnis und Schriftgedächtnis im Mittelalter*. Horst Wenzel, ed. Vol. 143. Philologische Studien und Quellen. Berlin: Erich Schmidt, 45–62.

———— (2003a). "Maxwell und Faschoda Pynchons Enden der Geschichte." In *Thomas Pynchon: Archiv, Verschwörung, Geschichte*. Bernhard Siegert and Markus Krajewski, eds. Weimar: VDG, 15–45.

———— (2003b). *Passage des Digitalen: Zeichenpraktiken der neuzeitlichen Wissenschaften 1500– 1900*. Berlin: Brinkmann und Bose.

———— (2005). *Was sind Kulturtechniken?* www.uni-weimar.de. URL: www.uni weimar.de/ medien/kulturtechniken/kultek.html.

Siegert, Paul Ferdinand (2008). *Die Geschichte der E-Mail: Erfolg und Krise eines Massenmediums*. Vol. 1. Technik—Körper—Gesellschaft. Bielefeld: transcript.

Simmel, Georg (1908/1950). *The Sociology of Georg Simmel*. Kurt H. Wolff, ed. and trans. Glencoe: Free Press.

Sinha, Alok (1992). "Client–Server Computing." *Communications of the ACM* 35.7, 77–98.

Skrine, Peter (1985). "Das Bild des Dieners in der deutschen Literatur des 17. Jahrhunderts." In *Literatur und Volk im 17. Jahrhundert: Probleme populärer Kultur in Deutschland*. Wolfgang Brückner, Peter Blickle, and Dieter Breuer, eds. Vol. 13. Wolfenbütteler Arbeiten zur Barockforschung. Wiesbaden: Otto Harrassowitz, 145–257.

Smith, Margaret Bayard (1824). *A Winter in Washington, or, Memoirs of the Seymour Family*. New York: E. Bliss and E. White.

———— (1841/1906). "President's House Forty Years Ago." In *The First Forty Years of Washington Society: Portrayed by the Family Letters of Mrs. Samuel Harrison Smith (Margaret Bayard) from the Collection of Her Grandson, J. Henley Smith*. New York: C. Scribner's Sons, 383–412.

Smoluchowski, Marian von (1914). "Gültigkeitsgrenzen des zweiten Hauptsatzes der Wärmetheorie." In *Vorträge über die kinetische Theorie der Materie und der Elektrizität, gehalten in Göttingen auf Einladung der Kommission der Wolfskehlstiftung*. Max Planck, ed. Leipzig: B. G. Teubner, 361–98.

Society for the Encouragement of Honest and Industrious Servants (1752). *A Proposal for the Amendment and Encouragement of Servants*. Vol. 8755. Goldsmiths'–Kress Library of Economic Literature. London: Printed for J. Shuckburgh.

Sorrenson, Richard (1999). "George Graham: Visible Technician." *British Journal for the History of Science* 32, 203–21.

Spector, A. Z. (1989). "Distributed Transaction Processing Facilities." In *Distributed Systems*. Sape Mullender, ed. New York: ACM Press, 193–214.

Spranger, Peter P. (1984). *Historische Untersuchungen zu den Sklavenfiguren des Plautus und Terenz*. Vol. 17. Forschungen zur antiken Sklaverei. 2d enl. ed. Wiesbaden: Franz Steiner.

Stadelmann, Johann Carl Wilhelm (1815/1846). "Episode aus dem Leben des klassischen Kammerdieners: Mitgetheilt von C. W." *Das Neue Europa: Chronik der gebildeten Welt*. Hg. von August Lewald 1. 18/19. Lieferung, 282–84, 289–99.

———— (1817/1913). *Briefe J. C. W. Stadelmann an Theodor Kräuter. Insel-Almanach auf das Jahr 1913*. Leipzig: Insel Verlag, 110–26.

Stadtlaender, Chris (1966). *'Die kleine Welt' am Frauenplan: Der Alltag Goethes*. Munich: Heimeran.

Steedman, Carolyn (2005). "Poetical Maids and Cooks Who Wrote." *Eighteenth-Century Studies* 39.1, 1–27.

———— (2007). *Master and Servant: Love and Labour in the English Industrial Age*. Vol. 10. Cambridge Social and Cultural Histories. Cambridge: Cambridge University Press.

Stefik, Mark (1996). *Internet Dreams: Archetypes, Myths, and Metaphors*. Cambridge: MIT Press.

———— (2004). *Breakthrough: Stories and Strategies of Radical Innovation*. Barbara Stefik, ed. Cambridge: MIT Press.

Steinberg, Richard (2002). *The Origin of the Word Daemon*. ei.cs.vt.edu/history/. URL: ei.cs.vt.edu/~history/Daemon.html.

Steinfeld, Robert J. (1991). *The Invention of Free Labor: The Employment Relation in English and American Law and Culture, 1350–1870*. Studies in Legal History. Chapel Hill: University of North Carolina Press.

Steinhausen, Georg (1889). *Geschichte des deutschen Briefs*. Berlin: Gaertner.

———— (1899). *Deutsche Privatbriefe des Mittelalters: Mit Unterstützung der K. Preußischen Akademie der Wissenschaften*. Vol. 1, *Fürsten und Magnaten, Edle und Ritter*. Denkmäler der deutschen Kulturgeschichte. Berlin: R. Gaertners Verlagsbuchhandlung.

———— (1907). *Deutsche Privatbriefe des Mittelalters: Mit Unterstützung der K. Preußischen Akademie der Wissenschaften*. Vol. 2, *Geistliche—Bürger I*. Denkmäler der deutschen Kulturgeschichte. Berlin: Weidmannsche Buchhandlung.

Stekl, Hannes (1980). "Das Gesinde." In *Österreichs Sozialstrukturen in historischer Sicht*. Erich Zöllner, ed. Vol. 36. Schriften des Institutes für Österreichkunde. Vienna: Bundesverlag, 107–22.

Stendhal (1830). *The Red and the Black: A Chronicle of the Nineteenth Century*. Horace Samuel, trans. London: Kegan Paul, 1916.

Stieler, Caspar von [Der Spaten] (1673). *Teutsche Sekretariat-Kunst: Was sie sey / worvon sie handele / <th<was darzu gehöre / welcher Gestalt zu derselben glück-und gründlich zugelangen / was Maßen ein Sekretarius beschaffen seyn solle*. Nuremberg: Hofmann.

Stifter, Adalbert (1857/2005). *Indian Summer*. Wendell Frye, trans. Bern: Peter Lang.

Stillich, Oscar (1902). *Die Lage der weiblichen Dienstboten in Berlin*. Berlin: Akademischer Verlag für sociale Wissenschaften.

Stratmann-Döhler, Rosemarie (1995). "Gesinde im Spiegelbild der Architektur." In *Gesinde im 18. Jahrhundert*. Gotthardt Frühsorge, Rainer Gruenter, and Beatrix Wolff Metternich, eds. Vol. 12. Studien zum achtzehnten Jahrhundert. Hamburg: Felix Meiner, 399–405.

Stuart, Dorothy Margaret (1946). *The English Abigail*. London: Macmillan.

Su, Shiao-Feng (1994). "Dialogue with an OPAC: How Visionary Was Swanson in 1964?" *Library Quarterly* 64.2, 130.

Süskind, Patrick (1985/2001). *Perfume: The Story of a Murderer*. New York: Random House.

Svobodova, Liba (1984). "File Servers for Network-Based Distributed Systems." *ACM Computing Surveys* 16.4 (December), 353–98.

Swift, Jonathan (1710/1908). *The Journal to Stella, A.D. 1710–1713*. Vol. 2, *The Prose Works of Jonathan Swift, D.D.* Frederick Ryland, ed. London: George Bell and Sons.

———— (1745/1993). "Regeln für Dienstboten." In *Satiren und Streitschriften*. Manesse-Bibliothek der Weltliteratur. Zurich: Manesse, 369–458.

Swoboda, Helmut (1967). *Der künstliche Mensch*. Munich: Heimeran.

Sydow, Friedrich von (1994). *InformLex: Lexikon für Abkürzungen und Metaphern in Informatik und Umfeld*. Braunschweig: Vieweg.

Szöllösi-Janze, Margit (1998). "Friedrich Kirchenbauer, Diener: Die berufliche Karriere von Fritz Habers Mechaniker an der Technischen Hochschule Karlsruhe." In *Jahrbuch für Universitätsgeschichte*. Rüdiger vom Bruch, ed. Vol. 1. Stuttgart: Franz Steiner, 233–38.

Szondi, Peter (1973/1977). *Die Theorie des bürgerlichen Trauerspiels im 18. Jahrhundert: Der Kaufmann, der Hausvater und der Hofmeister*. Gert Mattenklott, Wolfgang Fietkau, and Jean Bollack., eds. Vol. 1, *The Lectures of Peter Szondi*. Jean Boll, ed. 3d ed. Frankfurt am Main: Suhrkamp.

Tantner, Anton (2007). *Ordnung der Häuser, Beschreibung der Seelen: Hausnummerierung und Seelenkonskription in der Habsburgermonarchie*. Vol. 4. Wiener Schriften zur Geschichte der Neuzeit. Innsbruck: Studien-Verlag.

——— (2008). "Adressbüros in der Habsburgermonarchie und in deutschen Territorien—Eine Vorgeschichte der Suchmaschine?" In *Information in der Frühen Neuzeit: Status, Bestände, Strategien.* Arndt Brendecke, Markus Friedrich, and Susanne Friedrich, eds. Vol. 16. Pluralisierung and Autorität. Münster: LIT, 215–36.

Thacker, C. P., et al. (1979/1982). "Alto: A Personal Computer." In *Computer Structures: Principles and Examples.* Daniel P. Siewiorek, C. Gordon Bell, and Allen Newell, eds. New York: McGraw-Hill, 549–72.

Thackeray, William Makepeace (1845/1856). *The Memoirs of Mr. Charles J. Yellowplush: The Diary of C. Jeames de la Pluche, Esq., with His Letters.* Leipzig: Bernhard Tauchnitz. Originally printed in *Punch* (12 nos.), November 8, 1845–February 7, 1846, as "Jeames's Diary; or Sudden Wealth," by M. A. Titmarsh, Esq.

——— (1848/1986). *History of Pendennis.* Harmondsworth: Penguin.

——— (1898). *Contributions to 'Punch' etc.* Vol. 6, *The Works of William Makepeace Thackeray.* New York: Harper and Brothers.

Theile, Wolfgang, ed. (1997). *Commedia dell'arte: Geschichte, Theorie, Praxis.* Wiesbaden: Otto Harrassowitz.

Thomasius, Christian (1710). *Kurzer Entwurff der Politischen Klugheit, sich selbst und andern in allen Menschlichen Gesellschafften wohl zu rathen und zu einer gescheiden Conduite zu gelangen.* Frankfurt: In Verlag Johann Großens Erben.

Thomson, William (1874). "Kinetic Theory of the Dissipation of Energy." *Nature* 9.

——— (1879/1889). "The Sorting Demon of Maxwell." In *Popular Lectures and Addresses.* Vol. 1, *Constitution of Matter.* London: Macmillan, 137–41.

Thürmann, Ludwig Ferdinand (1839). *Friedrich Joseph Müller, Kaiserlich Königlicher Kammerdiener und Künstler der ergötzenden Physik: Biographie und Charakter-Skizze desselben.* Vienna: Franz Wimmer.

Tieck, Ludwig (1800/1996). *Die verkehrte Welt: Ein historisches Schauspiel in fünf Aufzügen.* Walter Münz, ed. Vol. 2064. Universal-Bibliothek. Stuttgart: Philipp Reclam Jun.

Timm, Arnulf (2005). "Der elektromagnetische Telegraph von Gauß und Weber." In *"Wie der Blitz einschlägt, hat sich das Räthsel gelöst": Carl Friedrich Gauß in Göttingen.* Elmar Mittler, ed. Vol. 30. Göttinger Bibliotheksschriften. Göttingen: Niedersächsische Staats- und Universitäts-Bibliothek, 169–87. "Wie der Blitz einschlägt, hat sich das Räthsel gelöst"—Carl Friedrich Gauss in Göttingen: Exhibition at the Old Townhall February 23–May 15, 2005.

Todes, Daniel P. (1997). "Pavlov's Physiology Factory." *Isis: An International Review Devoted to the History of Science and Its Culture* 88.2 (June), 205–46.

Tolstoy, Leo (1895/2004). "Master and Man." In *The Death of Ivan Ilyich and Master and Man.* Ann Pasternak Slater, trans. New York: Random House.

Toucement, Jean Chrêtien [= Johann Christian Troemer] (1731). *Des Deutsch-Françōs Jean Chrêtien Toucement Sein Lustigk Schrifft. 1. Die curieuse Brief von Lustbarkeit zu Dreß. 2. Das lustigk Suplique an Jupiter. 3. Das Replique an Parthenomus. 4. Das lustigk Adjeu aus kroße Campement. 5. Ehn Brief von Potsdam und Berlin. 6. Der lustigk Leben-Lauff und artigk Avantur. etlick Theile.* Blasius Aeolus, ed. 2d ed. Leipzig: Boetius.

Trappl, Robert, and Paolo Petta, eds. (1997). *Creating Personalities for Synthetic Actors: Towards Autonomous Personality Agents.* Vol. 1195. Lecture Notes in Computer Science. Berlin: Springer.

Treitschke, Heinrich von (1875). *Der Socialismus und seine Gönner: Nebst einem Sendschreiben an Gustav Schmoller.* Gustav von Schmoller, ed. Berlin: Georg Reimer.

Trüby, Stephan (2008). *Exit-Architektur: Design zwischen Krieg und Frieden.* Vienna: Springer.

———— (2010). "Geschichte des Korridors." Staatliche Hochschule für Gestaltung Karlsruhe: Diss. phil.

Turing, Alan M. (2004). *The Essential Turing: Seminal Writings in Computing, Logic, Philosophy, Artificial Intelligence and Artificial Life, Plus the Secrets of Enigma.* B. Jack Copeland, ed. Oxford: Oxford University Press.

Turner, Ernest Sackville (1959). *The Court of St. James's.* London: M. Joseph.

———— (1962). *What the Butler Saw: Two Hundred and Fifty Years of the Servant Problem.* London: Michael Joseph.

Uhlig, Günther (1981). *Kollektivmodell 'Einküchenhaus': Wohnreform und Architekturdebatte zwischen Frauenbewegung und Funktionalismus, 1900–1933.* Giessen: Anabasis.

Ukrow, Rolf (2004). "Nobelpreisträger Eduard Buchner (1860–1917): Ein Leben für die Chemie der Gärungen und—fast vergessen—für die organische Chemie." Berlin: Diss. phil., Technische Universität.

Usborne, Richard (1976). *Wodehouse at Work to the End.* London: Barrie and Jenkins.

Veblen, Thorstein (1899/2007). *The Theory of the Leisure Class.* Martha Banta, ed. Oxford World's Classics. Oxford: Oxford University Press.

Vellusig, Robert (2000). *Schriftliche Gespräche: Briefkultur im 18. Jahrhundert.* Vienna: Böhlau.

Verne, Jules (1872/2003). *Reise um die Erde in achtzig Tagen.* Manfred Kottmann, trans. Frankfurt am Main: Fischer Taschenbuch Verlag.

Vijayan, Jaikumar (2009). *Proxy servers pressed into action to keep Web access in Iran.* www .computerworld.com. URL: www.computerworld.com/s/article/print/9134653/Proxy_ servers_pressed_into_action_to_ keep_Web_access_in_Iran?taxonomyId=17.

Vismann, Cornelia, and Markus Krajewski (2007). "Computer-Juridisms." *Grey Room: Architecture, Art, Media, Politics* 8.29 (Fall), 90–109. Special Issue: "New German Media Theory."

Vogel, Carl (1834). *Goethe in amtlichen Verhältnissen: Aus den Acten, besonders durch Correspondenzen zwischen ihm und dem Großherzoge Carl August, Geh. Rath v. Voigt u.a.* Jena: Frommann.

Voltaire (1784/2007). *Memoirs of the Life of Monsieur de Voltaire.* Andrew Brown, trans. London: Hesperus Press.

Voskuhl, Adelheid (2005). " 'Bewegung' und 'Rührung': Musik spielende Androiden und ihre kulturelle Bedeutung im späten 18. Jahrhundert." In *Artifizielle Körper—lebendige Technik: Technische Modellierungen des Körpers in historischer Perspektive.* Barbara Orland, ed. Vol. 9. Interferenzen: Studien zur Kulturgeschichte der Technik. Zurich: Chronos, 87–103.

———— (2009). "The Mechanics of Sentiment: Automata, Artisans, and Selfhood in Eighteenth-Century Europe." Cambridge, MA: typescript.

Wagener, Silke (1996). *Pedelle, Mägde und Lakaien: Das Dienstpersonal an der Georg-August-Universität Göttingen, 1737–1866.* Vol. 17. Göttinger Universitätsschriften. Göttingen: Vandenhoeck and Ruprecht.

Waldrop, M. Mitchell (2001). *The Dream Machine: J. C. R. Licklider and the Revolution That Made Computing Personal.* New York: Viking.

Walser, Robert (1982). *Selected Stories.* Christopher Middleton et al., trans. FSG Classics. New York: Farrar, Straus and Giroux.

———— (1908/2007). *The Assistant.* Susan Bernofsky, trans. New York: New Directions.

———— (1909/2014). *Jakob von Gunten.* Christopher Middleton, trans. New York: New York Review Books.

Walthall, Anne, ed. (2008). *Servants of the Dynasty: Palace Women in World History.* Vol. 7. California World History Library. Berkeley: University of California Press.

Wang, Jian (1999). *Die Dienerfigur in deutschen und chinesischen Theaterstücken: Zum Phänomen der Komik im theatralischen Kommunikationsmodell.* Vol. 9, *Euro-Sinica.* Berlin: Peter Lang.

Watanabe, Teresa (1990). *House of Controversy—Technology: A new computer standard automates the TRON home with 1,000 microprocessors.* www.latimes.com. URL: articles.latimes.com/1990–07–02/business/fi-598_1_japanese-computer.

Waterfield, Giles, Anne French, and Matthew Craske, eds. (2003). *Below Stairs: 400 Years of Servants' Portraits.* London: National Portrait Gallery. To accompany the exhibition "Below Stairs: 400 Years of Servants' Portraits at the National Portrait Gallery," October 16, 2003–January 11, 2004, Scottish National Portrait Gallery, February 11–May 31, 2004.

Watson, Richard W. (1981). "Distributed System Architecture Model." In *Distributed Systems—Architecture and Implementation: An Advanced Course.* Butler W. Lampson, M. Paul, and H. J. Siegert, eds. Vol. 105. Lecture Notes in Computer Science. Berlin, Heidelberg: Springer, chapter 2, 10–43.

Weber, Heinrich (1893). *Wilhelm Weber: Eine Lebensskizze.* Breslau: Verlag von Eduard Trewendt.

Weigel, Sigrid (2004a). "Das Gedankenexperiment: Nagelprobe auf die facultas fingendi in Wissenschaft und Literatur." In *Science and Fiction: Über Gedankenexperimente in Wissenschaft, Philosophie und Literatur.* Thomas Macho and Annette Wunschel, eds. Vol. 15.838. Frankfurt am Main: Fischer Taschenbuch, 183–205.

———— (2004b). "Zur Rolle von Bildern und Metaphern in der Rhetorik der Biowissenschaften." In *Die andere Intelligenz: Wie wir morgen denken werden; ein Almanach neuer Denkansätze aus Wissenschaft, Gesellschaft und Kultur.* Bernhard von Mutius, ed. Stuttgart: Klett-Cotta, 90–107.

Weil, Judith (2005). *Service and Dependency in Shakespeare's Plays.* Cambridge: Cambridge University Press.

Weinacht, Helmut (1973). "Programmierte Korrespondenz vor 400 Jahren." *Die Korrespondenz: Zeitschrift für überzeugenden Briefstil und Textprogrammierung* 8.6, 12–14.

Weise, Christian (1693/1971). "Der Fall des Französischen Marschalls von Biron." In *Sämtliche Werke: Historische Dramen 3.* John D. Lindberg, ed. Vol. 28. Ausgaben deutscher Literatur des 15. bis 18. Jahrhunderts. Berlin: Walter de Gruyter, 179–411.

Wendel, Carl (1974). "Der antike Bücherschrank." In *Kleine Schriften zum antiken Buch-und Bibliothekswesen.* Cologne: Greven, 64–92.

White, Lynn T. Jr. (1963/1968). *Die mittelalterliche Technik und der Wandel der Gesellschaft.* Munich: Moos.

Wichert, Adalbert (1989). "Herr-Diener-Konstellationen in der deutschen Tragödie zwischen Aufklärung und Restauration." *Jahrbuch der Deutschen Schillergesellschaft* 33, 117–44.

Wierling, Dorothee (1987). *Mädchen für alles: Arbeitsalltag und Lebensgeschichte städtischer Dienstmädchen um die Jahrhundertwende.* Berlin: Dietz.

Wikipedia (2009). *Artikel 'Servent':* en.wikipedia.org. URL: en.wikipedia.org/wiki/Servent.

Williams, James (1847). *The footman's guide: containing plain instructions to the footman and butler, for the proper arrangement and regular performance of their various duties, in large or small families: including the manner of setting-out tables, sideboards, andc., andc., the art of waiting at table, and for superintending large or small breakfast, dinner, and supper parties: directions for cleaning and preserving.* 4th ed. London: T. Dean.

Williams, Nigel (2001). "Mendel's Demon." *Current Biology* 11.3 (February 6), R80–R81.

Wilz, Annemarie, Gisela Framke, and Gisela Marenk, eds. (1989). *Wie belieben? Zur Situation von Dienstboten 1850 bis 1914.* Dortmund: Deutsches Kochbuch Museum.

Wodehouse, Pelham G. (2008). *The World of Jeeves.* London: Random House.

Wolff Metternich, Beatrix Freifrau von (1995). "Über die Bildwürdigkeit von Gesinde." In *Gesinde im 18. Jahrhundert.* Gotthardt Frühsorge, Rainer Gruenter, and Beatrix Wolff Metternich, eds. Vol. 12. Studien zum achtzehnten Jahrhundert. Hamburg: Felix Meiner, 383–97.

Woolf, Virginia (1950). "Mr. Bennett and Mrs. Brown." In *The Captain's Death Bed and Other Essays.* London: Hogarth, 90–111.

Xenophon (1997). *Memorabilia. Oeconomicus. Symposium. Apology.* Cambridge: Harvard University Press.

Young, Michael (1958). *The Rise of the Meritocracy 1870–2033: An Essay on Education and Equality.* London: Thames and Hudson.

Zima, Peter V. (2007). *Theorie des Subjekts: Subjektivität und Identität zwischen Moderne und Postmoderne.* Vol. 2176. UTB für Wissenschaft. 2d rev. edition. Tübingen: A. Francke.

Zimmermann, Rolf Christian (1986). "Über eine bildungsgeschichtlich bedingte Sichtbehinderung bei der Interpretation von Lessing 'Miß Sara Sampson.'" In *Verlorene Klassik? Ein Symposium.* Wolfgang Wittkowski, ed. Tübingen: Max Niemeyer, 255–85.

Zwahr, Hartmut (1990). *Herr und Knecht: Figurenpaare in der Geschichte.* Leipzig: Urania.

Index

absolutism, royal, 5, 238

Actor-Network Theory (ANT), 11, 275, 276, 305, 323; mediation and, 120; "program of action," 251; "punctualization," 287–88; as recursive system, 289

Adelung, Johann Christoph, 31

Agamben, Giorgio, 40

agency, 75, 80, 155, 283, 320; delegation of, 258; demonic, 184, 194; external, 349; human-machine hybrid, 275–79; quasi-objects and, 288; of technical media, 282–83; transfer from human to machine, 5, 292

Akrich, Madeleine, 11

Albaret, Celeste, 150, 151

alchemy, 184, 193

Althusser, Louis, 136

Altman, Robert, 12

Alto computer, 311, 312, 313, 314, 317, 331

amazon.com, 2, 346

American Woman's Home, The (Beecher and Beecher-Stowe, 1869), 274

angelology (Thomas Aquinas), 40

angels, 97–98, 244–45, 273, 347

Anna Amalia, Duchess, 137

Apple computers, 309, 315

apprentices, 25–26, 224

architecture, 3, 60; "active" floor plan, *66;* client–server, 320, *320,* 321, 356; of computer programming, 331; green baize doors, 63, 65, 71–73, 258; hidden corridors, 63, 65, *66,* 67–68, *68,* 81; indirect powers and, 62–73; interior passages, 66–68; secret staircases, 68–71, *68;* of service, 6, 62, 201

aristocrats, as servants, 42, 47

Aristotle, 22, 80, 126, 271, 323

Arlecchino [Harlequin] (fictional character), 126

ARPA (Advanced Research Projects Agency), 310, 336